'This is an excellent tort textbook: well-structured, clear, and con. studied by first-year law undergraduates. In addition, it engages (controversial areas of tort law. It is both accessible and challenging growing number of textbooks in this field.'

Professor Pau.   ...y of Warwick

'This concise introductory textbook is a student-friendly starting point for the study of tort law. It sets out the key areas of law in a clear and accessible way. Students may find the combination of problem question techniques, focus on key cases and brief summaries of academic commentary particularly attractive.'

Dr Philip Bremner, *University of Sussex*

'This helpful textbook provides a clear and concise explanation of key issues in the law of tort. Example problem questions are broken down in a good amount of detail to assist students in learning to apply tort law to practical situations, and flowcharts and diagrams help break down complex issues. The authors offer analyses of academic literature to show different perspectives on topics, helping students develop critical analytical skills.'

Dr Alexandra Bohm, *University of Lincoln*

'This is an excellent text, which does an admirable job of condensing very complex matters into an accessible length, with good pedagogical tools to aid student understanding. It covers all the main issues while posing challenging questions of principle for students too. The best possible revision guide, and many will choose it as their main text.'

Dr Bill O'Brian, *University of Warwick*

'This textbook provides broad and in-depth coverage of the topics covered on most tort law modules, written and presented in a student-friendly style. The layout – with questions followed by diagrams, short answer plans, more detailed guidance and information on how to make answers stand out – is particularly helpful.'

Anil Balan, *University of East London*

'This book is user-friendly for undergraduates because of its strength in topics covered, writing style, and structure. The topics chosen and the depth of content in the book are interestingly and precisely managed. The writing style makes reading and understanding the law of tort easy. The use of features like "key case boxes", "key legislation", "different perspectives" and a summary of each chapter will appeal to today's law students.'

Dr Francis Tansinda, *Manchester Law School, Manchester Metropolitan University*

'Clear and accessible, with key excerpts from leading cases. Visual diagrams and roadmaps help to guide the student through their problem questions. A valuable resource.'

Dr Aislinn O'Connell, *Royal Holloway University of London*

TORT LAW

SARAH GREEN AND JODI GARDNER

First published 2021 by
RED GLOBE PRESS

Red Globe Press in the UK is an imprint of Macmillan Education Limited, registered in England, company number 01755588, of 4 Crinan Street, London, N1 9XW.

Red Globe Press® is a registered trademark in the United States, the United Kingdom, Europe and other countries.

ISBN 978-1-352-01141-8 paperback

This book is printed on paper suitable for recycling and made from fully managed and sustained forest sources. Logging, pulping and manufacturing processes are expected to conform to the environmental regulations of the country of origin.

A catalogue record for this book is available from the British Library.

A catalog record for this book is available from the Library of Congress.

Publisher: Luke Block, Ursula Gavin
Development Editor: Lyndsay Aitken, Milly Weaver
Cover Designer: Sandy Matta
Production Editor: Elizabeth Holmes
Marketing Manager: Helen Jackson, Amy Suratia

Dedication

This book is dedicated to our children:
Alfie, Beatrice, Benjamin, Eleanor, Margaret and Rosalind

BRIEF CONTENTS

1   Introduction   1

PART 1 THE TORT OF NEGLIGENCE   11

2   Duty of Care   13
3   Pure Economic Loss   42
4   Psychiatric Injury   61
5   Breach of Duty   86
6   Causation   105
7   Remoteness   143

PART 2 TORTS RELATING TO LAND AND GOODS   163

8   Occupiers' Liability   164
9   Product Liability   193
10 Nuisance and the Rule in *Rylands v Fletcher*   217

PART 3 INTENTIONAL TORTS   242

11 The Economic Torts   243
12 Intentional Torts against the Person   260

PART 4 DEFAMATION AND PRIVACY   296

13 Defamation   297
14 Privacy   338

PART 5 GENERAL MATTERS   373

15 Vicarious Liability   374
16 Defences   391
17 Damages   421
Index   445

FULL CONTENTS

Table of cases	xvi
Table of legislation	xxvii
About the authors	xxx
Preface	xxxi
Acknowledgements	xxxii
Tour of the book	xxxiv

1 INTRODUCTION — 1

1.1 Introduction	1
1.2 What is a tort and the history of tort law	1
1.3 Aims of tort law	3
1.4 Interests protected by tort law	3
1.5 Limitations of tort law	5
1.6 'Compensation culture'	5
1.7 Tort law and insurance	7
1.8 Alternative systems	8
1.9 Chapter summary	10
Further reading	10

PART 1 THE TORT OF NEGLIGENCE — 11

2 DUTY OF CARE — 13

2.1 Introduction	14
2.2 Foundations of the modern tort of negligence	14
2.3 Establishing a duty of care	16
2.3.1 From *Caparo* to *Robinson*	16
2.3.2 Legally significant features	19
2.4 Acts vs omissions or misfeasance vs nonfeasance	24
2.4.1 The general rule	24
2.4.2 When will liability for omissions arise?	25
2.5 Liability of public bodies	28
2.5.1 General principles	28
2.5.2 Tort and the Human Rights Act 1998	30

2.5.3 Is there a specific application of these principles to the police and emergency services? 37

2.6 Chapter summary 40

Further reading 40

Roadmap 41

3 PURE ECONOMIC LOSS 42

3.1 Introduction 43

3.2 What is pure economic loss? 44

3.3 Relational economic loss 44

3.4 Negligent services 46

3.4.1 The development of *Hedley Byrne* liability 50

3.5 Defective premises 54

3.6 Chapter summary 59

Further reading 59

Roadmap 60

4 PSYCHIATRIC INJURY 61

4.1 Introduction 62

4.2 Abandoning the search for a principle 63

4.3 What is 'psychiatric harm'? 65

4.4 Distinguishing between primary and secondary victims 66

4.4.1 Primary victims 66

4.4.2 Secondary victims 73

4.5 Law in need of reform? 82

4.6 Chapter summary 83

Further reading 84

Roadmap 85

5 BREACH OF DUTY 86

5.1 Introduction 87

5.2 The objective standard of care 87

5.2.1 Specific circumstances 89

5.2.2 The relevance of risk 91

5.3 The standard to be applied to children 93

5.4 The standard to be applied to professionals 96

5.5 Failure to warn patients of risks 100

5.6 Social Action, Responsibility and Heroism (SARAH) Act 2015 101

5.7 *Res ipsa loquitur*   102

5.8 Chapter summary   103

Further reading   103

Roadmap   104

6   CAUSATION   105

6.1 Introduction   106

6.2 Why is the causal inquiry significant and what role does it play?   107

6.3 But for causation   108

    6.3.1 Basic but for causation   108

    6.3.2 Divisible and indivisible injuries   110

    6.3.3 Successive factors   112

    6.3.4 Material contribution to injury   115

    6.3.5 Loss of a chance of avoiding an adverse physical outcome   118

6.4 Exceptions to the but for test   123

    6.4.1 Loss of a chance of achieving a better financial outcome   123

    6.4.2 Overdetermination   125

    6.4.3 Material contribution to risk   126

    6.4.4 Single agent   132

    6.4.5 Failure to warn   138

6.5 Chapter summary   140

Further reading   141

Roadmap   142

7   REMOTENESS   143

7.1 Introduction   144

7.2 Basic form   145

7.3 Eggshell skull rule   148

7.4 Scope of duty   149

7.5 *Novus actus interveniens*   155

    7.5.1 Act of a third party   155

    7.5.2 Act of the claimant   156

7.6 Intentional torts   158

7.7 Chapter summary   161

Further reading   161

Roadmap   162

PART 2   TORTS RELATING TO LAND AND GOODS   163

8   OCCUPIERS' LIABILITY   164

8.1 Introduction   165
8.2 Who is an occupier?   165
8.3 The Occupiers' Liability Act 1957 – liability to 'visitors' 167
    8.3.1 Who is a visitor?   167
    8.3.2 What are premises?   169
    8.3.3 What is the content of the occupier's duty? 170
    8.3.4 How can that duty be discharged?   176
8.4 The Occupiers' Liability Act 1984 – liability to those not classed as 'visitors'   183
    8.4.1 Who is classed as a non-visitor?   186
    8.4.2 In what circumstances will non-visitors be owed a duty?   187
    8.4.3 What is the content of that duty?   188
    8.4.4 How can that duty be discharged?   189
8.5 Chapter summary   191
Further reading   191
Roadmap   192

9   PRODUCT LIABILITY   193

9.1 Introduction   194
9.2 Contractual remedies   195
9.3 Common law negligence   197
9.4 Consumer Protection Act 1987   198
    9.4.1 Product   199
    9.4.2 Damage   200
    9.4.3 Producer   202
    9.4.4 Defect   203
    9.4.5 Defences   209
9.5 Limitation   212
9.6 Chapter summary   215
Further reading   216

10   NUISANCE AND THE RULE IN *RYLANDS V FLETCHER*   217

10.1 Introduction   218
10.2 What is private nuisance?   219
    10.2.1 Title to sue and nature of damage suffered   219
    10.2.2 What amounts to an unreasonable interference   221

10.3 Remedies 226

    10.3.1 Injunction v damages 226

    10.3.2 Abatement 229

10.4 Defences in private nuisance 229

    10.4.1 Prescription 229

    10.4.2 Act of a stranger 230

    10.4.3 Statutory authority 230

10.5 The rule in *Rylands v Fletcher* 231

    10.5.1 Defences to the rule in *Rylands v Fletcher* 234

10.6 Public nuisance: a very different thing 237

10.7 Trespass to land 239

10.8 Chapter summary 240

Further reading 240

Roadmap 241

PART 3 INTENTIONAL TORTS

PART 3 INTENTIONAL TORTS 242

11 THE ECONOMIC TORTS

11 THE ECONOMIC TORTS 243

11.1 Introduction 244

11.2 The distinction made by the House of Lords in *OBG* 245

    11.2.1 Inducing breach of contract 247

    11.2.2 Causing loss by unlawful means 249

11.3 (The former tort of) intimidation – now covered by causing loss by
unlawful means 251

11.4 Conspiracy 252

    11.4.1 Lawful means conspiracy (or simple conspiracy) 252

    11.4.2 Unlawful means conspiracy 253

11.5 Chapter summary 257

Further reading 257

Roadmaps 258

12 INTENTIONAL TORTS AGAINST THE PERSON

12 INTENTIONAL TORTS AGAINST THE PERSON 260

12.1 Introduction 261

12.2 Comparing the torts 262

12.3 Assault 265

    12.3.1 Intentional threat 265

    12.3.2 Immediate and direct violence 266

    12.3.3 Reasonable expectation by claimant 267

12.4 Battery   268

    12.4.1 Intention   268

    12.4.2 Direct and immediate force   268

    12.4.3 Without consent   270

    12.4.4 Hostility?   270

12.5 False Imprisonment   272

    12.5.1 Confinement   272

    12.5.2 Awareness   274

    12.5.3 False imprisonment within the prison system   275

12.6 Defences   278

    12.6.1 Consent   278

    12.6.2 Necessity   279

    12.6.3 Self-defence (including defence of others)   281

    12.6.4 Contributory negligence   282

    12.6.5 Lawful arrest and detention/lawful authority   282

12.7 Additional intentional torts against the person   283

    12.7.1 The tort in *Wilkinson v Downton*   284

    12.7.2 Protection from Harassment Act 1997   287

    12.7.3 Malicious prosecution   292

12.8 Chapter summary   294

Further reading   294

Roadmap   295

PART 4 DEFAMATION AND PRIVACY   296

13 DEFAMATION   297

13.1 Introduction   298

13.2 Defamation structure   299

    13.2.1 Was the publication *defamatory*?   300

    13.2.2 Is the publication *defensible*?   300

    13.2.3 What *damages* should be awarded?   300

13.3 Initial issues to consider   300

    13.3.1 Legislative reform   301

    13.3.2 Libel and slander   302

    13.3.3 Who can sue?   304

13.4 Elements of defamation   309

    13.4.1 Was the publication defamatory?   309

    13.4.2 The statement referred to the claimant   316

    13.4.3 The statement was published to a third party   317

13.5 Defences   319

    13.5.1 Truth   320

    13.5.2 Honest opinion   321

    13.5.3 Privilege and public interest   323

    13.5.4 Operators of websites   327

    13.5.5 Consent   328

13.6 Remedies   329

    13.6.1 Damages   329

    13.6.2 Other remedies   330

13.7 Challenges   330

    13.7.1 Human rights and defamation   331

    13.7.2 Defamation and social media   332

    13.7.3 Society's views and defamation   333

13.8 Chapter summary   335

Further reading   335

Roadmap   336

14 PRIVACY   338

14.1 Introduction   339

14.2 Current protection of privacy   340

    14.2.1 Common law protection of privacy   340

    14.2.2 Government regulation of privacy rights   344

14.3 Breach of confidence   348

    14.3.1 Breach of confidence or 'misuse of private information'? 350

    14.3.2 Reasonable expectation of privacy   351

    14.3.3 Unauthorised use   357

    14.3.4 Remedies   360

    14.3.5 Breach of confidence: concluding remarks   362

14.4 A freestanding privacy tort?   363

14.5 Privacy protection in the 21st century   369

14.6 Chapter summary   370

Further reading   371

Roadmap   372

PART 5 GENERAL MATTERS   373

15 VICARIOUS LIABILITY   374

15.1 Introduction   375

15.2 The development of the principle   375

15.3 Relationships of employment 376

    15.3.1 The relationship 377

    15.3.2 The connection 381

15.4 Non-delegable duties 385

15.5 Chapter summary 388

Further reading 389

Roadmap 390

16 DEFENCES 391

16.1 Introduction 392

16.2 What is a defence? 393

16.3 Contributory negligence 394

    16.3.1 Historical approach to contributory negligence 394

    16.3.2 Elements of contributory negligence 397

    16.3.3 Contributory negligence: concluding remarks 401

16.4 *Volenti non fit injuria* 402

    16.4.1 *Volenti* and consent 403

    16.4.2 Elements of *volenti* 403

    16.4.3 *Volenti*: concluding remarks 408

16.5 Illegality 409

    16.5.1 Rationale of illegality 409

    16.5.2 Elements of illegality 410

    16.5.3 Illegality: concluding remarks 418

16.6 Chapter summary 418

Further reading 419

Roadmap 420

17 DAMAGES 421

17.1 Introduction 422

17.2 Purpose of damages in tort law 423

17.3 Property damage 426

17.4 Personal injury 427

    17.4.1 Pecuniary losses 427

    17.4.2 Non-pecuniary losses 430

17.5 Compensating benefits 430

17.6 Actions after death 432

    17.6.1 Law Reform (Miscellaneous Provisions) Act 1934 432

    17.6.2 Fatal Accidents Act 1976 433

17.7 Time limitations on tort law claims   435

17.8 How damages can be awarded   439

17.9 Contribution and apportionment   442

17.10 Chapter summary   443

Further reading   444

Index   445

TABLE OF CASES

Note: Cases in **bold** feature in 'Key Case' boxes and page numbers with "n" denotes Footnotes

A

A (Children) (Conjoined Twins: Surgical Separa-tion), Re [2001] Fam 147, 279n81

A & B v Person Unknown [2016] EWHC 3295 (Ch), 356

A v B Plc [2002] EWCA Civ 337, [2003] QB 195, 353

A v Hoare; X and another v Wandsworth London Borough Council; C v Middlesbrough Coun-cil; H v Suffolk County Council; Young v Catho-lic Care (Diocese of Leeds) and others [2008] UKHL 6, [2008] 1 AC 844, 438–439

A v National Blood Authority [2001] EWHC QB 446, [2001] 3 All ER 289, 205–206

AAA v Associated Newspapers Ltd [2013] EWCA Civ 554, 355n61

AB v Ministry of Defence [2012] 1 AC 78, 134n81

ABC v St George's Hospital NHS Trust [2017] EWCA Civ 336, 28

ABC v Telegraph Media Group Ltd [2018] EWCA Civ 2329, [2019] 2 All ER 684, 351

ABK v KDT [2013] EWHC 1192 (QB), 351n41, 370

Abouzaid v Mothercare (UK) Ltd [2000] All ER (D) 2436, 206–207

Achilleas, The [2008] UKHL 48, 160n34, 161

Airedale NHS Trust v Bland [1993] 1 All ER 821, 280n84

Al-Amoudi v Brisard [2006] EWHC 1062 (QB), 317n69

Alcock v Chief Constable of South Yorkshire Police [1992] 1 AC 310, 67n8, 80

Allen v Flood [1898] AC 1, 245

Allied Maples v Simmons & Simmons [1995] 1 WLR 1602, 123

Andreae v Selfridge & Co Ltd [1938] Ch 1, 222

Anns v Merton LBC [1978] AC 728, 55

Appleton v Garrett (1995) 34 BMLR 23, [1996] PIQR P1, 278

Armes v Nottinghamshire CC [2017] UKSC 60, [2018] AC 355, 378

Ashley v Chief Constable of Sussex Police [2007] 1 WLR 398; [2008] 1 AC 962, [2008] 2 WLR 975, 278n73

Ashton v Turner [1981] QB 137, 409n63

Attorney General v PYA Quarries [1957] 2 QB 169, 237n30

Austin v Metropolitan Police Commissioner [2009] UKHL 5, 275, 283

B

B (Adult: Refusal of Treatment), Re [2002] 1 All ER 449, 281n87

Badger v Ministry of Defence [2006] 3 All ER 173, 400n29

Baker v TE Hopkins & Son Ltd [1959] 1 WLR 966, 406n49

Baker v Willoughby [1970] AC 467, 112–113

Banca Nazionale del Lavoro SPA v Playboy Club London Ltd and others [2018] UKSC 43, [2019] 2 All ER 478, 50

Barber v Somerset County Council [2004] UKHL 13, [2004] 1 WLR 1089, 71–73

Barclays Bank Plc v Various Claimants [2020] UKSC 13, [2020] 2 WLR 960, 379

Barker v Corus [2006] UKHL 20, [2006] 2 AC 572, 128–129

Barnett v Chelsea and Kensington Hospital Man-agement Committee [1969] 1 QB 428, 21, 109

Barrett v Ministry of Defence [1995] 1 WLR 1217, 26n26

Barretts & Baird (Wholesale) Ltd v IPCS [1987] IRLR 3, 251

Bazley v Curry [1999] 2 SCR 534, 382

Bell v Great Northern Railway Co of Ireland (1890) 26 LR Ir 428, 284n109

Bici v Ministry of Defence [2004] EWHC 786 (QB), 265n18, 268n27

Bilta (UK) Ltd v Nazir (No 2) [2016] AC 1, 413

Bird v Jones (1845) 7 QB 742, 272, 277

Blake v Galloway [2004] EWCA Civ 814, 90

Bloodworth v Gray (1844) 7 Man & Gr 334, 303n15

Bogle & Others v McDonald's Restaurants Ltd [2002] EWHC 490 (QB), 206n26

Bognor Regis UDC v Campion [1972] 2 QB 169, 306–308

Bolam v Friern Hospital Management Committee [1957] 1 WLR 583, 96, 96n18, 96n19

Bolitho v City of Hackney Health Authority [1998] AC 232, 97–98

Bolton v Stone [1951] AC 850, 91–92

Bonnard v Perryman [1891] 2 Ch 269, 330n127

Bonnington Castings Ltd v Wardlaw [1956] AC 613, 115–116

Bowater v Rowley Regis BC [1944] KB 476, 400n41

Bradburn v Great Western Rail Co (1874) LR 10 Ex 1, 431

Bradford Corp v Pickles [1895] AC 587, 225

Breslin v McKevitt [2011] NICA 33, 264n10, 269

Brett Wilson LLP v Persons Unknown [2015] EWHC 2628 (QB), 306

British Chiropractic Association v Singh [2010] EWCA Civ 350, [2011] WLR 133, 322

British Railways Board v Herrington [1972] AC 877, 184

British Transport Commission v Gourley [1956] AC 185, 428n12

Brooks v Commissioner of Police for the Metropolis [2005] UKHL 24, 33n45, 37n53

Bunker v Charles Brand & Son Ltd [1969] 2 QB 480, 177

Butterfield v Forrester (1809) 103 ER 926, 394, 395

Byrne v Deane [1937] 1 KB 818, 311, 312, 317, 333

C

C v D [2006] EWHC 166 (QB), 285n113

Calgarth, The [1927] P 93, 168n3

Cambridge Water v Eastern Counties Leather plc [1994] 2 AC 264, 230

Campbell v MGN Ltd [2004] UKHL 22, [2004] 2 WLR 1232, 341, 349, 350, 352, 358, 360, 361, 425

Caparo Industries v Dickman [1990] 2 AC 605, 16

Capital & Counties plc v Hampshire County Council [1997] QB 1004, 38

Cassell v Broome [1972] AC 1027, 425

Cassidy v Daily Mirror Newspapers Ltd [1929] 2 KB 331, 310n43, 312, 316n64, 334, 342

Catholic Child Welfare Society v Various Claimants [2012] UKSC 56, [2013] 1 All ER 670, 376–377

CDE v MGN Ltd [2010] EWHC 3309 (QB), 353

CG v Facebook Ireland Ltd [2015] NIQB 28, 288n134

Chadwick v British Railways Board [1967] 1 WLR 912, 78, 81, 85

Chancellor, Masters and Scholars of the University of Oxford v Broughton [2006] All ER (D) 78 (Aug), 288n133

Chaplin v Hicks [1911] 2 KB 786, 123, 124

Chapman v Lord Ellesmere [1932] 2 KB 431, 328n120, 329n120

Charing Cross Electricity Supply Co v Hydraulic Power Co [1914] 3 KB 772, 235n31

Chatterton v Gerson (1980) 1 BMLR 80, 278n75, 278n76

Chatterton v Secretary of State for India [1895] 2 QB 189, 324n95

Chester v Afshar [2004] UKHL 41, [2005] 1 AC 134, 138–139

Christie v Davey [1893] 1 Ch 316, 224

Clark v Chief Constable of Cleveland [2000] CP Rep 22, 293n155

Clunis v Camden and Islington Health Authority [1998] QB 978, 411

Coco v AN Clark (Engineers) Ltd [1969] RPC 41, 348n26, 361n80

Cole v Turner (1704) 6 Mod Rep 149, 270, 271

Collins v Wilcock [1984] 1 WLR 1172, 265, 270, 282n100

Commission v United Kingdom [1997] All ER (EC) 481, 210n30

Condon v Basi [1985] 1 WLR 866, [1985] 2 All ER 453, 90, 406n50

Co-operative Group (CWS) Ltd v Pritchard [2012] 1 All ER 205, 282n95, 397n18

Corr v IBC [2008] UKHL 13, [2008] 1 AC 884, 147

Council of the Shire of Sutherland v Heyman (1985) 157 CLR 424, 55, 57n28

Coventry v Lawrence [2014] UKSC 13, [2014] 2 WLR 433, 223, 228

Cox v Ergo Versicherung AG (formerly known as Victoria) [2014] UKSC 22, 434n37

Cox v Ministry of Justice [2016] UKSC 10, [2016] 2 WLR 806, 7n26, 377, 378

Crofter Hand Woven Harris Tweed Co Ltd v Veitch [1942] AC 435, 253

Cross v Kikby (2000) The Times, 5 April, 281n92

Customs and Excise Comrs v Barclays Bank plc [2007] 1 AC 181, 18n11

D

D v East Berkshire Community NHS Trust [2005] UKHL 23, 32

Daiichi UK Ltd and others v Stop Huntingdon Animal Cruelty and others and other cases [2003] All ER (D) 194 (Oct), 288n133

Dann v Hamilton [1939] 1 KB 509, 407

Darby v National Trust [2001] EWCA Civ 189, [2001] PIQR 372, 177

Darnley v Croydon NHS Trust [2018] UKSC 50, [2018] 3 WLR 1153, 21

Davidson v Chief Constable of North Wales [1994] 2 All ER 597, 293

Davies v Mann (1842) 10 M & W 546, 395

Davies v Solomon (1871) LR 7 QB 112, 303n12

Davies v Swan Motor Co (Swansea) Ltd [1949] 1 All ER 620, 399

De Keyser's Royal Hotel v Spicer Bros Ltd (1914) 30 TLR 257, 222

Delaney v Pickett [2011] EWCA Civ 1532, 411

Dennis v Ministry of Defence [2003] EWHC 793 (QB, 227

Derbyshire County Council v Times Newspapers Ltd [1993] AC 534, 306, 308, 309

Derry v Peek [1889] UKHL 1, 48n6, 49n10, 159

Dingle v Associated Newspapers [1961] 2 QB 162, 111–112, 112n12

Dobson v Thames Water Utilities [2009] EWCA Civ 28, 227n11

Dodd Properties v Canterbury City Council [1980] 1 WLR 433, 428

Donnelly v Joyce [1974] QB 454, 428

Donoghue v Stevenson [1932] AC 562, 14, 15, 194, 196, 197

Dorset Yacht Co Ltd v Home Office [1970] AC 1004, 26

Douglas v Hello! (No 3) [2006] QB 125, [2005] 3 WLR 881, 246, 350, 354n59

Doyle v Olby (Ironmongers) Ltd [1969] 2 QB 158, 158

DPP v K [1990] 1 All ER 331, 270

Dubai Aluminium Co Ltd v Salaam [2002] UKHL 48, 382n13, 383

Duke of Brunswick v Harmer (1849) 14 QB 185, 318n70

Dunne v North Western Gas Board [1964] 2 QB 806, 235n30

Durham v BAI (Run-off) Ltd [2012] UKSC 14, 135

E

E v English Province of Our Lady of Charity [2012] EWCA Civ 938, 379n6

Eeles v Cobham Hire Services Ltd [2009] EWCA Civ 204, [2010] 1 WLR 409, 440–442

Esso Petroleum v Southport Corporation [1956] AC 218, 240n38

Ex parte British Broadcasting Corporation: R v F [2016] EWCA Crim 12, 356n65

F

F (sterilisation), Re [1990] 2 AC 1, [1989] 2 WLR 1025, 279–280

Fagan v Metropolitan Police Commissioner [1969] 1 QB 439, 268

Fairchild v Glenhaven Funeral Services [2002] UKHL 22, [2003] 1 AC 32, 115n24, 126–128

Fearn and others v Board of Trustees of the Tate Gallery [2020] EWCA Civ 104, [2020] 2 WLR 1081, 220, 343–344

Ferdinand v MGN Ltd [2011] EWHC 2454 (QB), 352n45

Ferguson v British Gas Trading Ltd [2009] 3 All ER 304, 288n135

Ferguson v Welsh [1987] 3 All ER 777, 170

Fish & Fish Ltd v Sea Shephard UK [2015] AC 1229, 247n8

Fowler v Lanning [1959] 1 All ER 290, 262, 263

Freeman v Home Office (No 2) [1983] 3 All ER 589; [1984] QB 524, 270n40, 278n73

Froom v Butcher [1976] 1 QB 286, 398–400

G

Gillingham BC v Medway (Chatham) Dock Ltd [1993] QB 343, 223

Glasgow Corporation v Taylor [1922] 1 AC 44, 172, 173

Godfred v Demon Internet [1999] 4 All ER 342, 327n113

Goldman v Hargrave [1967] 1 AC 645, 27, 30

Goldsmith v Bhoyrul [1996] QB 459, 309

Goodwin v NGN Ltd [2011] EWHC 1437 (QB), 352n44

Gorringe v Calderdale [2004] UKHL 15, [2004] 1 WLR 1057, 29–30

Gray v Thames Trains Ltd [2009] 1 AC 1339, [2009] UKHL 33, 414

Gregg v Scott [2005] UKHL 2, [2005] 2 AC 176, 119–120

Guluti v MGN Ltd [2015] EWHC 1482 (Ch), 361n90

Gwilliam v West Hertfordshire Hospitals NHS Trust [2002] EWCA Civ 1041, [2003] QB 443, 182

H

Hadley v Baxendale (1854) 9 Exch 341, 160n34, 161

Hall v Herbert [1993] 2 SCR 159, 410

Halsey v Esso Petroleum [1961] 2 All ER 145, 222n5

Harbutt's 'Plasticine' Ltd v Wayne Tank and Pump Co Ltd [1970] 1 QB 447, 427

Harnett v Bond [1925] All ER Rep 110, 293n156

Haynes v Harwood [1935] 1 KB 146, 27, 406

Haystead v Chief Constable of Derbyshire [2000] 3 All ER 890, 264n10, 268

Hayward v Thompson [1982] QB 47, 316n60

Hedley Byrne v Heller [1964] AC 465, 46–47

Heil v Rankin [2001] QB 272, 430

Henderson v Dorset Healthcare University NHS Foundation Trust [2018] EWCA Civ 1841, [2018] 3 WLR 1651, 412n78, 414–416

Henderson v Merrett Syndicates [1995] 2 AC 145, 50–51, 57

Herd v Weardale Steel, Coal and Coke Co Ltd [1915] AC 67, 272

Heron II, The [1969] 1 AC 350, 161n36

Herring v Boyle (1834) 1 CM & R 377, 275

Hill v Chief Constable of South Yorkshire Police [1989] 1 AC 53, 30–31

Hinz v Berry [1970] 2 QB 40, 77

HL v United Kingdom (2004) 81 BMLR 131, 274

Hollywood Silver Fox Farm v Emmet [1936] 2 KB 468, 224

Holman v Johnson (1775) 1 Cowp 341, 409

Holtby v Brigham Cowan (Hull) Ltd [2000] 3 All ER 421, 443n64, 445n64

Horrock v Lowe [1975] AC 135, 324n100

Hotson v East Berkshire Area Health Authority [1987] AC 750, 119

Hounga v Allen [2014] UKSC 47, [2014] 1 WLR 2889, 409n68, 413, 414

Hughes v Lord Advocate [1963] AC 837, 146

Hughes-Holland v BPE Solicitors [2017] UKSC 21, [2018] AC 599, 150–151

Hunt v Severs [1994] 2 AC 350, 428n17, 429

Hunter v British Coal Corpn [1999] QB 140, 69n10

Hunter v Canary Wharf Ltd [1997] AC 655, 219–220, 230n20, 238, 341, 344

Hussain v Lancaster City Council [2000] QB 1, 230n20

Hussain v New Taplow Paper Mills Ltd [1988] AC 514, 431

I

ICI Ltd v Shatwell [1965] AC 656, 404–405, 406–407

Imerman v Tchenguiz [2010] EWCA Civ 908, 351n35

Innes v Wylie (1844) 1 C & K 257, 266n20

Intruder Detection & Surveillance Ltd v Fulton [2008] EWCA Civ 1009, 176

Invercargill City Council v Hamlin [1996] AC 624, 57

Iqbal v Prison Officers Association [2009] EWCA Civ 1312, [2010] QB 732, 276

J

Jackson v Murray [2015] UKSC 5, 400

Jagger v Darling [2005] EWHC 683 (Ch), 354

Jameel v Down Jones & Co Ltd [2005] QB 946, 302n10, 303n10

James v Campbell (1832) 5 C & P 372, 268n27, 268n22

James v Crown Prosecution Service [2009] EWHC 2925 (Admin), 289n140

James-Bowen v Commissioner of Police for the
Metropolis [2018] UKSC 40, [2018] 1 WLR
3945, 20–21

Janvier v Sweeney [1919] 2 KB 316, 285n113,
286n113

Jeynes v News Magazines Ltd [2008] EWCA Civ
130, 315

Jobling v Associated Dairies Ltd [1982] AC 794,
112, 113

John v MGN Ltd [1996] 2 All ER 35, 330

Jolley v Sutton LBC [2000] 1 WLR 1082, 147

Jones v Jones [1916] 2 AC 481, 303n14

Jones v Kaney [2011] UKSC 13, 323n93

Jones v Livox Quarries Ltd [1952] 2 QB 608,
397n20

Jones v Ruth [2012] 1 All ER 490, 288n132

Jones v Secretary of State for Energy & Climate
Change [2012] EWHC 2936 (QB), 131n66

Jones v Stroud District Council [1988] 1 All ER 5, 431

JSC BTA Bank v Ablyazov [2018] UKSC 19, 255

Juman v Attorney General [2017] 2 LRC 610,
264n13

K

Kaye v Robertson [1991] FSR 62, 343, 366, 367

Kent v Griffiths [2001] QB 36, 38

Keown v Coventry Healthcare NHS Trust [2006]
EWCA Civ 39, [2006] 1 WLR 653, 188–189

Khorasandjian v Bush [1993] QB 727, 219,
285n113, 341, 342, 286n113, 342, 343

Kiam v MGN Ltd [2003] QB 281, 330n126

King v Lake (1667) 1 Hardres 470, 302n6

Kirkham v Chief Constable of Greater Manchester
[1990] 2 QB 283, 406n52

Knightley v Johns [1982] 1 WLR 349, 155

Kotke v Saffarini [2005] EWCA Civ 221, 424

Kuddus v Chief Constable of Leicestershire
[2001] UKHL 29, 425

L

Lachaux v Independent Print Ltd [2019] UKSC
27, 301, 302, 310, 311, 313, 314, 332, 333

Lagden v O'Connor [2004] 1 AC 1067, 149

Lane v Holloway [1968] 1 QB 379, 278n72,
281n91

Law Society v Kordowski [2011] All ER (D) 46
(Dec), 288n128, 289, 342

Les Laboratoires Servier v Apotex Inc [2015] AC
430, 412n81, 413, 414n81, 415, 417n91

Letang v Cooper [1965] 1 QB 232, 262

Letang v Ottawa Electric Railway Co [1926] AC
725, 402–403

Levi v Bates [2015] EWCA Civ 206, [2016] 1 All
ER 625, 288n128, 290n48

Lewis v Daily Telegraph [1964] AC 234, 311n46,
312, 314n53, 315

Liesboch, The [1933] AC 449, 148, 149

Lim Poh Choo v Camden and Islington Area Health
Authority [1980] AC 174, 428n11, 439n58

Linklaters LLP v Mellish [2019] EWHC 177 (QB),
370

Lippiatt v South Gloucestershire CC [2000] QB
51, 230

Lister v Hesley Hall Ltd [2001] UKHL 22,
[2002] 1 AC 215, 381

Lister v Romford Cold Storage [1957] AC 555,
375n3

Livingstone v Rawyards Coal Co (1880) 5 App
Cas 25, 3, 424

Logdon v DPP [1976] Crim LR 121, 267n26

London Artists Ltd v Littler [1969] 2 QB 375, 322

Lonrho Ltd v Shell Petroleum Co Ltd [1983] AC
173, 252n28

Lonrho Plc v Fayed [1992] 1 AC 448, 255

Loutchansky v Times Newspapers [2001] EMLR
876, 317n69

Lumley v Gye (1853) 2 E&B 216, 245

Lykiardopulo v Lykiardopulo [2010] EWCA Civ
1315, 351n43, 352n43

M

Maguire v Sefton MBC [2006] EWCA Civ 316,
[2006] 1 WLR 2550, 182

Majrowski v Guy's and St Thomas's NHS Trust
[2007] 1 AC 224, [2006] 4 All ER 395, 5,
288n136, 290, 289n136, 291

Malone v Laskey [1907] 2 KB 141, 219

Malone v Metropolitan Police Commissioner (No
2) [1979] Ch 344, 340, 365

Manchester Corporation v Williams [1891] 1 QB
94, 306

Mansfield v Weetabix [1997] EWCA Civ 1352, 5

Marcic v Thames Water Utilities [2003] UKHL
66, 227n11

Market Investigations v Minister of Social Security [1969] 2 QB 173, 376

Martin v Watson [1995] 3 All ER 559, 293

Mattis v Pollock (t/a Flamingo's Nightclub) [2003] EWCA Civ 887, 382n15

MB (Caesarean Section), Re [1997] 2 FLR 426, 281n88

Mbasogo v Logo Ltd (No 1) [2007] QB 846, 267n25

McAlpine v Bercow [2013] EWHC 1342 (QB), 332n134

McGeown v Northern Ireland Housing Executive [1995] 1 AC 233, 167

McGhee v National Coal Board [1973] 1 WLR 1, 126–127

McKennitt v Ash [2006] EWCA Civ 1714, 351n40, 353, 359, 361, 352n40, 354, 360, 362

McKew v Holland & Hannen & Cubitts (Scotland) Ltd [1969] 3 All ER 1621, 156, 157

McKinnon Industries v Walker (1951) 3 DLR 577, 225

McLoughlin v O'Brian [1983] 1 AC 410, 65, 74, 75, 79

McManus v Beckham [2002] 1 WLR 2982, 303n12, 319n76

Meade's & Belt's Case (1823) 1 Lew CC 184, 266n21

Meering v Grahame-White Aviation Co Ltd (1920) 122 LT 44, 274n60

Mersey Docks and Harbour Board v Coggins and Griffith (Liverpool) Ltd [1947] AC 1, 380n8

Michael v Chief Constable of South Wales [2015] UKSC 2, [2015] 2 WLR 343, 16–17

Middleton v Persons Unknown [2016] EWHC 2354 (QB), 354, 369

Millar v Bassey [1994] EMLR 44, 248n13

Miller v Jackson [1977] QB 966, 227, 230n21

Minter v Priest [1930] AC 558, 324n98, 325n98

Mitchell v Glasgow City Council [2009] UKHL 11, 37n54

Mohamud v WM Morrison Supermarkets Plc [2016] UKSC 11, [2016] ICR 485, 382

Monroe v Hopkins [2017] 4 WLR 68, 313, 332

Monson v Tussauds Ltd [1894] 1 QB 67, 302, 312

Montgomery v Lanarkshire Health Board [2015] UKSC 11, [2015] AC 1430, 97n22, 100

Moore v Meagher (1807) 1 Taunt 39, 303n12

Morgan v Odhams Press [1971] 1 WLR 1239, 316

Morris v Murray [1991] 2 QB 6, 403n37, 406, 407, 408n58

Morris v Network Rail [2004] EWCA Civ 172, 226

Mosley v News Group Newspapers Ltd [2008] EMLR 20, 354n59, 355, 361

Mullin v Richards [1998] 1 WLR 1304, 93, 94

Murphy v Brentwood DC [1991] AC 398, 55, 57n28

Murphy v Culhane [1977] 1 QB 94, [1976] 3 All ER 533, 278n72, 282

Murray v Express Newspapers Plc [2008] EWCA Civ 446, 354, 355

Murray v Ministry of Defence [1988] 1 WLR 692, 275n61

N

National Coal Board v England [1954] AC 403, 411

National Union of General and Municipal Workers v Gillian [1945] 2 All ER 593; [1946] KB 81, 307

Nettleship v Weston [1971] 2 QB 691, 7n25, 19, 88, 403n38

Newstead v London Express Newspapers Ltd [1940] 1 KB 377, 316

Nichols v Marsland (1876) 2 Ex D 1, 235

O

O2 v Dickins plc [2008] EWCA Civ 1144, 117n28

OBG Ltd v Allan; Douglas v Hello! Ltd; Mainstream Properties Ltd v Young [2007] UKHL 21, [2008] 1 AC 1, 246

O'Byrne v Aventis Pasteur MSD Ltd [2010] UKSC 23, 213

One Money Mail Ltd v Ria Financial Services [2015] EWCA Civ 1084, 247n10

OPO v Rhodes [2016] AC 219, [2015] 4 All ER 1, 4n11

O'Shea v MGN Ltd [2001] EMLR 40, 316

Osman v UK [1999] 1 FLR 193, 31, 33

Overseas Tankship v Morts Dock & Engineering Co Ltd (The Wagon Mound No 1) [1961] AC 388, 145

P

Page v Smith [1996] AC 155, 65–67, 70, 71, 79, 82–83

Paris v Stepney Borough Council [1951] AC 367, 92–93

Parmiter v Coupland (1840) 6 M&W 105, 310n44

Parry v Cleaver [1970] AC 1, 431n25

Parsons v Uttley Ingham & Co Ltd [1978] QB 791, 161n36

Patel v Mirza [2016] UKSC 42, [2017] AC 467, 409n65, 409n67, 412n80, 413

Performance Cars Ltd v Abraham [1962] 1 QB 33, 111

Peters v Prince of Wales Theatre [1943] KB 73, 234

PG and JH v United Kingdom, Application No 44787/98, 351n42

Phipps v Rochester Corporation [1955] 1 QB 450, 168, 173

Pickett v British Rail Engineering Ltd [1980] AC 136, 429

Piepenbrock v London School of Economics and Political Science [2018] ELR 596, 288n129, 289n129

Pitts v Hunt [1991] 1 QB 24, 19, 407n56, 411

PJS v News Group Newspapers Ltd [2016] UKSC 26, 351, 355, 361, 363

Polemis and Furness Withy & Co, Re [1921] 3 KB 560, 145

Ponting v Noakes [1894] 2 QB 281, 235

Poole BC v GN [2019] UKSC 25, [2019] 2 WLR 1478, 34

Portsmouth Youth Activities Committee v Poppleton [2008] EWCA Civ 646, 171

Prendergast v Sam and Dee Ltd [1989] 1 Med LR 36, 443n65

Prichard v Co-operative Group Ltd [2012] QB 320, 264n10

Pugh v The London, Brighton and South Coast Railway Co [1896] 2 QB 248, 284n108

Q

Quinn v Leathem [1901] AC 495, 158, 253

R

R v Bishop [1975] QB 275, 311, 311n49, 312, 334

R v Bournewood Community and Mental Health NHS Trust, ex parte L [1998] UKHL 24, [1998] 1 All ER 634, 4n10, 273–274

R v Brown [1994] 1 AC 212, 279

R v Central Independent Television plc [1995] 1 FCR 521, 358n68

R v Chief Constable of Devon and Cornwall, ex parte Central Electricity Generating Board [1982] QB 458, 272n47

R v Deputy Governor of Parkhurst Prison, ex p Hague [1991] 3 All ER 733, 276

R v Governor of Brockhill Prison; ex p Exans [2001] 1 AC 19, 275

R v Ireland [1998] AC 147, 266, 267

R v Lydsey [1995] 3 All ER 654, 270

R v Miller [1983] 2 AC 161, 27

R v Norden (1755) Fost 129, 265n19

R (on the application of Jalloh) v Secretary of State for the Home Department [2020] UKSC 4, 276, 277, 283

R (Lumba) v Secretary of State for the Home Department [2011] UKSC 12, [2012] 1 AC 245, 263n8, 274, 276, 424

R v St George (1840) 9 C & P 483, 493, 267n69

R v Venna [1976] QB 421, 265n18

R v Williams [1923] 1 KB 340, 278n75

Rabone v Pennine Care NHS Trust [2012] UKSC 2, [2012] 2 WLR 381, 33–34

Rahman v Arearose [2001] QB 351, 113n17

Ratcliffe v McConnell [1999] 1 WLR 670, 189–190

RCA Corp v Pollard [1983] Ch 135, 250n18

Ready Mixed Concrete v Minister of Pensions and National Insurance [1968] 2 QB 497, 376

Rees v Darlington Memorial Hospital NHS Trust [2003] UKHL 52, 139n89

Reeves v Commissioner of Police for Metropolis [2000] 1 AC 360, 156

Reynolds v Clarke (1725) 1 Stra 634, 270n39

Reynolds v Times Newspapers Ltd [2001] 2 AC 127, 301, 324–325

Rhodes v OPO [2015] UKSC 32, [2016] AC 219, [2015] 4 All ER 1, 263n9, 285, 286, 288

Ribee v Norrie [2001] PIQR P8, 235

Richard v BBC [2018] EWHC 1837 (Ch), [2018] 3 WLR 1715, 361–362

Richardson v LRC Products Ltd [2000] Lloyd's Rep Med 280, 205

Rickards v Lothian [1913] AC 263, 235

Robert Addie & Sons (Collieries) Ltd v Dumbreck [1929] AC 358, 183n13

Roberts v Bank of Scotland plc [2013] All ER (D) 88 (Jun), 288n131

Robinson v Balmain New Ferry Co [1910] AC 295, 273n49

Robinson v Chief Constable of West Yorkshire Police [2018] UKSC 4, [2018] 2 WLR 595, 16, 18–19

Robinson v Kilvert (1889) 41 Ch D 88, 225

Robinson v Post Office [1974] 1 WLR 1176, 155

RocknRoll v News Group Newspapers [2013] EWHC 24, 364

Roles v Nathan [1963] 1 WLR 1117, 174–175

Rookes v Barnard [1964] AC 1129, 251, 425

Rothwell v Chemical and Insulating Co Ltd [2007] UKHL 39, [2007] ICR 1745, 70

Rowlands v Chief Constable of Merseyside Police [2006] EWCA Civ 1773, 425

Royscott Trust v Rogerson [1991] 2 QB 297, 49n12

Rylands v Fletcher (1868) LR 3 HL 330, 2, 4, 145n3, 218–221, 231–238

S

S (A child), Re [2004] UKHL 47, 358

S v W (Child abuse: damages) [1995] 1 FLR 862, 437

Salmon v Seafarer Restaurants Ltd [1983] 1 WLR 1264, 175

Saunders v Edwards [1987] 1 WLR 1116, 410n71

Scott v Shepherd [1558-1774] All ER Rep 295, 158n25, 269

Scott v The London and St Katherine Docks Company [1865] H & C 596, 102

Secretary of State for the Home Department v JJ [2007] UKHL 45, [2008] AC 385, 277, 283

Secretary of State for the Home Office v British Union for the Abolition of Vivisection [2008] EWHC 892 (QB), 351n35

Sedleigh-Denfield v O'Callaghan [1940] AC 880, 230

Serafin v Malkiewicz [2020] UKSC 23, 327n111

Sheffield City Council v Shaw [2007] HLR 374, 288n130

Shelfer v City of London Electric Lighting Co (No 1) [1895] 1 Ch 287, 228, 229

Shell UK Ltd v Total UK Ltd [2010] EWCA Civ 180, 46

Shepherd v Post Office [1995] 6 WLUK 107, 434n34

Sherratt v Chief Constable of Greater Manchester Police [2018] EWHC 1746 (QB), 39

Sidaway v Bethlem Royal Hospital [1985] AC 871, 97

Sienkiewicz v Grief (UK) Ltd [2011] UKSC 10, [2011] 2 AC 229, 130–131

Sim v Stretch [1936] 2 All ER 1237, 310n44

Simmons & Simmons [1995] 1 WLR 1602, 123, 124

Slipper v BBC [1991] 1 QB 283, 319n75

Smith New Court Securities v Citibank NA [1997] AC 254, 158

Smith v Baker [1891] AC 325, 404

Smith v Chief Constable of Sussex Police [2009] AC 225, 31n37

Smith v Eric S. Bush; Harris v Wyre Forest District Council [1990] 1 AC 831, 49

Smith v Finch [2009] EWHC 53 (QB), 400n27

Smith v Leech Brain and Co Ltd [1962] 2 QB 405, 148

Smith v Littlewoods Organisation Ltd [1987] AC 241, 25

Smith v Manchester City Council (1974) 17 KIR 1, 428n14

South Australia Asset Management Corporation v York Montague Ltd [1997] AC 191, 149

Southampton Container Terminals Ltd v Hansa Schiffahrtsgesellscaft mbH (MV 'Maersk Colombo') [1999] All ER (D) 960, 426

Southwark LBC v Mills [1999] UKHL 40, [2001] 1 AC 1, 224

Spartan Steel & Alloys v Martin & Co [1973] QB 27, 44

Speight v Gosnay (1819) 60 LJQB 231, 319n74

Spring v Guardian Assurance [1995] 2 AC 296, 52

St George v Home Office [2008] EWCA Civ 1068, [2009] 1 WLR 1670, 398–399

St Helen's Smelting Co v Tipping (1865) 11 HL Cas 642, 223

Standard Chartered Bank v Pakistan [2003] 1 AC 959, 282n95

Stansbie v Troman [1948] 2 KB 48, 26

Stanton v Callaghan [1998] 4 All ER 96, 323n93

Stapley v Gypsum Mines Ltd [1953] 2 All ER 478, 398n23

Starr v Ward [2015] EWHC 1987 (QB), 332

Stephens v Myers (1830) 4 Car & P 349, 265

Stocker v Stocker [2019] UKSC 27, 313, 318n73

Stovin v Wise [1996] AC 923, 24, 27n33, 29

Stringman (A Minor) v McArdle [1994] 1 WLR 1653, 439n59, 441

Stubbings v Webb [1993] AC 498, 437, 439

Sturges v Bridgman (1879) 11 Ch D 852, 223n6, 230

Sullivan v Boylan [2013] IEHC 104, 285n113

Sunderland CC v Conn [2007] EWCA Civ 1492, 290n146

Sutherland v Her Majesty's Advocate [2020] UKSC 32, 369

Sutradhar v National Environmental Research Council [2006] UKHL 33, 25

Syed Mahamad Yusuf-ud-Din v Secretary of State for India in Council (1903) 19 TLR 496, 273

T

T v North Yorkshire CC [1999] IRLR 98, 381

Taberna Europe CDO II Plc v Selskabet (Fomerly Roskild Bank A/S) (In Bankruptcy) [2016] EWCA Civ 1262, 159n32

Tamiz v Google [2013] EWCA Civ 68, 327

Tate & Lyle Industries Ltd v GLC [1983] 2 AC 509, 237

Tesco Stores Ltd v Pollard [2006] EWCA Civ 393, 206, 207

Theaker v Richardson [1962] 1 WLR 151, 317n68

Thomas v Bradbury, Agnew & Co Ltd [1906] 2 KB 627, 322n90

Thomas v National Union of Miners (South Wales Area) [1986] Ch 20, 267

Thomas v News Groups Newspapers [2001] EWCA Civ 1233, [2002] EMLR 78, 4n11, 288

Thomas v Quartermaine (1887) 18 QBD 685, 403, 404

Thompson v Smiths Shiprepairers (North Shields) Ltd [1984] QB 405, 110, 112

Thrussell v Handyside (1888) 20 QBD 359, 404

Tinsley v Milligan [1994] 1 AC 340, 417n94

Tolley v JS Fry & Sons Ltd [1931] AC 333, 312, 314n52

Tomlinson v Congleton BC [2003] UKHL 47, [2003] 3 WLR 705, 168, 185–186

Total Network SL v Customs & Excise Commissioners [2008] UKHL 19, [2008] AC 1174, 252, 254

Transco plc v Stockport MBC [2003] UKHL 61, [2004] 2 AC 1, 233

Triad Group plc v Makar [2019] EWHC 423 (QB), 288n128

Trimingham v Associated Newspapers Ltd [2012] EWHC 1296 (QB), 352n44

Tuberville v Savage (1669) 2 Keb 545, 267

V

Vacwell Engineering Co Ltd v BDH Chemicals Ltd [1971] 1 QB 111, 146n9

Van Colle v Chief Constable of Hertfordshire; Smith v Chief Constable of Sussex [2008] UKHL 50, [2008] 3 All ER 977, 32–33

Vellino v Chief Constable of Greater Manchester [2002] 1 WLR 218, [2002] 3 All ER 78, 409, 410

Venables & Thompson v News Group Newspapers Ltd [2001] EWHC 32 (QB), [2001] Fam 430, [2001] 1 All ER 908, 359–359, 364

Viasystems Ltd v Thermal Transfer Ltd [2005] EWCA Civ 1151, [2005] IRLR 983, 380

Victorian Railways Comrs v Coultas (1888) PC 21, 284

Vidal-Hall v Google Inc [2014] EWHC 13 (QB); [2015] 3 WLR 409, 351

Voaden v Champion [2002] EWCA Civ 89, 426

Von Hannover v Germany (No 2) (2012) 55 EHRR 15, 354, 359, 360n78

Vowles v Evans [2002] EWHC 2612 (QB); [2003] EWCA Civ 318, 8

W

W v Essex CC [2000] UKHL 17, [2001] 2 AC 592, 68–69

Wainwright v Home Office [2003] UKHL 53, [2004] 2 AC 406, [2003] 3 WLR 1137, 271, 285, 286, 291, 340–342, 363, 365

Walker v Commissioner of Police of the Metropolis [2015] 1 WLR 312, 263n8, 274

Walsh v Shanahan [2013] EWCA Civ 411, 351n35

Wason v Walter (1868) LR 4 QB 73, 324n97

Watt v Hertfordshire CC [1954] 1 WLR 835, 90

Watt v Longsdon [1930] 1 KB 130, 324n96

Webb v Beavan (1883) 11 QBD 609, 303n13

Weldon v Home Office [1990] 3 All ER 672, 275

Weller v Associated Newspapers Ltd [2014] EWHC 1163 (QB), 355n63

Wellesley Partners LLP v Withers LLP [2015] EWCA Civ 1146, 161

West Sussex CC v Pierce [2013] EWCA Civ 1230, 173

Wheat v Lacon [1966] AC 552, 166, 167

Wheeler v Copas [1981] 3 All ER 405, 169

Whipps Cross University NHS Trust v Iqbal (by his mother & litigation friend Iqbal) [2007] EWCA Civ 1190, 429n20

White v Blackmore [1972] 2 QB 651, 180–181

White v Chief Constable of South Yorkshire Police [1999] 2 AC 455, 63n1, 78–80

White v Jones [1995] 2 AC 207, 52–54, 57

Whittington Hospital NHS Trust v XX [2020] UKSC 14, [2020] 2 WLR 972, 423–424

Wieland v Cyril Lord Carpets [1969] 3 All ER 1006, 156, 157

Wilkes v DePuy International Ltd [2016] EWHC 3096 (QB), [2018] 2 WLR 531, 207

Wilkinson v Downton [1897] 2 QB 57, 4, 242, 261–264, 284–287, 291, 292, 294, 340

Williams v Bermuda Hospitals Board [2016] UKPC 4, [2016] AC 888, 117

Williams v BOC Gases Ltd [2000] ICR 1181, 431

Williams v Humphrey (1975) The Times, 20 February, 268

Wilsher v Essex Area Health Authority [1987] QB 730; [1988] AC 1074, 89, 133–134

Wilson v Pringle [1986] 2 All ER 440, [1986] 3 WLR 1, 270–272

Wise v Kaye [1962] 2 WLR 96, 429n20

WM Morrison Supermarkets Plc v Various Claimants [2020] UKSC 12, [2020] 2 WLR 941, 382–384

Wong v Parkside Health NHS Trust [2001] EWCA Civ 1721, 285n113, 291

Woodland v Essex CC [2013] UKSC 66, [2013] 3 WLR 1227, 385–386

Wooldridge v Sumner [1963] 2 QB 43, 89, 406n50

Worsley v Tambrands Ltd [2000] PIQR P95, 205

Worthington v Metropolitan Housing Trust Ltd [2018] EWCA Civ 1125, 288n130

X

X (formerly known as Mary Bell) & Y v News Group Newspapers Ltd [2003] EWHC 1101 (QB), 356

X (Minors) v Bedfordshire CC [1995] 2 AC 633, 31

Y

Youssoupoff v MGM Ltd (1934) 50 TLR 581, 302n7

ECTHR

Austin v United Kingdom (Application No 39692/09), 283n102

Axel Springer AG v Germany (2012) 55 EHRR 6, 353n46

Craxi v Italy (No 2) (2004) 38 EHRR 47, 353n47

PG and JH v United Kingdom, Application No 44787/98, 351n42

Spencer v United Kingdom (1998) 25 EHRR CD 105, 368n106

Tammer v Estonia (2003) 37 EHRR 43, 353n47

Tolstoy Miloslavsky v United Kingdom (1995) 20 EHRR 442, 301n3, 330, 331

Von Hannover v Germany (No 2) (2012) 55 EHRR 15, 354, 359, 360n78

Z v UK [2001] ECHR 333, [2001] 2 FLR 612, 31–32

AUSTRALIA

Amaca Pty Ltd v Booth [2011] HCA 53, 130n64

Binsaris v Northern Territory; Webster v Northern Territory; O'Shea v Northern Territory; Austral v Northern Territory [2020] HCA 22, 268n30

Brookfield Multiplex [2014] HCA 36, 57n28

Burnie Port Authority v General Jones Pty Ltd (1994) 179 CLR 520, 233

Council of the Shire of Sutherland v Heyman (1985) 157 CLR 424, 55, 57n28

Gardiner v John Fairfax & Sons Pty Ltd (1942) 42 SR (NSW) 171, 311n47

Rootes v Shelton [1968] ALR 33, 90

CANADA

Cook v Lewis [1951] SCR 830, 125

Winnipeg [1995] 1 SCR 85, 57n26

NEW ZEALAND

Bowen v Paramount Builders (Hamilton) Ltd [1975] 2 NZLR 546, 57n30

US

New York Times Co v Sullivan (1964) 376 US 254, 308

Oliver v Miles [1926] 144 Miss. 852, 110 So. 666, 125, 126

Summers v Tice [1948] 33 Cal.2d 80, 125, 126n48

Ultramares Corp v Touche 174 NE 441 (1932), 56n25

United States v Carroll Towing Co, 159 F.2d 169, 93n16

TABLE OF LEGISLATION

Note: Legislation in **bold** features in 'Key Legislation' boxes and page numbers with "n" denotes Footnotes

A

Administration of Justice Act 1982
  s 1(1)(a), 429n20
  s 1(1)(b), 429n20

B

Bill of Rights 1689
  Article 9, 323n91
Broadcasting Act 1990
  s 166, 302

C

Civil Liability (Contribution) Act 1978
  s 2(1), 443n65
Compensation Act 2006
  s 3, 128n59, 129, 131
Consumer Protection Act 1987
  s 1(2), 203
  s 2, 203
  s 2(1)–(3), 177, 179, 190, 202
  s 2(5), 199n13, 203
  s 3(1), 204
  s 3(2), 204
  s 3(2)(a), 204
  s 3(2)(b), 204
  s 4(1)(a)–(d), 209–210
  s 4(1)(e), 210
  s 4(1)(f), 199
  s 5(1), 200
  s 5(2), 200
  s 5(3), 202
  s 5(3)(a), 201
  s 5(3)(b), 201
  s 5(4), 201
  s 5(5)–(7), 200
  s 6(4), 213n36
  s 45, 199
Consumer Protection Act 1987 (Product Liability) (Modification) Order 2000, 199n11
Consumer Rights Act 2015
  s 2(2), 179
  s 9, 196n7
  s 10, 196n7
  s 20, 196n8
  s 22, 196n8
  s 24, 196n8
  s 62, 180n11, 192
  s 65, 179
  s 65(1)–(5), 179–180
Contracts (Rights of Third Parties) Act 1999, 54, 196n9
Countryside and Rights of Way Act 2000, 186, 192
Courts Act 2003
  s 100, 440
Courts and Legal Services Act 1990, 330

D

Damages Act 1996
  s 2, 440
Data Protection Act 2018, 341, 344, 366, 383
Defamation Act 1952
  s 5, 320
  s 6, 321, 322
Defamation Act 1996
  s 1, 327
  s 1(3)(a)–(e), 327n115–118
  s 2(2), 301
Defamation Act 2013
  s 1, 303n20
  s 1(1), 302n10, 310
  s 1(2), 306
  s 2, 314
  s 2(1)–(4), 320

s 3, 321
s 3(1)–(4), 321
s 3(5), 321
s 3(6), 321
s 3(8), 321
s 4, 324
s 4(1)–(6), 326
s 5, 328
s 5(1)–(4), 328
s 5(11), (12), 328
s 8, 318
s 8(1)–(3), 318
s 8(4), 318
s 8(5), 318
s 8(6)(a), 318n72
s 9(1), 304
s 9(2), 304
s 10, 328
s 10(1), 328
s 11, 330
s 12, 330
s 14, 303n16
Defective Premises Act 1972, 56, 58

E

EU Council Directive 85/374/EEC (Product Liability)
Article 6, 206
Article 7(e), 206n24, 210
European Convention on Human Rights
Article 2, 32
Article 3, 32
Article 5(1), 272
Article 6, 32
Article 8, 32, 220, 227, 299, 364
Article 10, 296, 299, 305, 317, 330
Article 11, 288
Article 13, 32
Protocol 1, Article 1, 227

F

Fatal Accidents Act 1976
s 1(1), 433
s 1(2), 433
s 1(3), 433
s 1(3)(b), 434

s 1A, 80, 432
s 1A(3), 435n40
s 3(3), 434n37
s 4, 434n36

H

Human Rights Act 1998
s 6, 220
s 12, 331n130, 339, 357–358
Sch 1 (see Articles of the European Convention on Human Rights)

L

Law Reform (Contributory Negligence) Act 1945
s 1(1), 396
s 1(2), 396
s 1(5), 396
s 1(6), 396
s 4, 282n96, 396
Law Reform (Miscellaneous Provisions) Act 1934
s 1(1), 305n23, 432
s 1(1A), 432
s 1(2), 432
Law Reform (Personal Injuries) Act 1948
s 2(4), 427
Limitation Act 1980
s 2, 436
s 4A, 436
s 11, 212, 436
s 11(1)–(3), 212, 436
s 11(4), 212, 436
s 11A, 212, 436
s 11A(3), 212, 436
s 14, 213n34
s 28, 436n47
s 33(1), 436n48
s 33(2), 437n49
s 38(2), 436

M

Mental Capacity Act 2005
s 1(1)–(6), 280
s 2(1), 280
s 3(1), 281n85
Misrepresentation Act 1967
s 2(1), 159

O

Occupiers' Liability Act 1957
s 1(1), 169
s 1(2), 166
s 1(3), 169
s 2(1), 171
s 2(2), 172
s 2(3), 172, 174
s 2(3)(b), 169
s 2(4), 176
s 2(4)(b), 181
s 2(5), 176, 177
Occupiers' Liability Act 1984
s 1, 166
s 1(1)(a), 187
s 1(2), 166
s 1(3), 184
s 1(3)(a), 184, 187
s 1(3)(b), 184, 187
s 1(3)(c), 184, 187
s 1(4), 188
s 1(6), 189
s 1(7), 187
s 1(8), 187

P

Parliamentary Papers Act 1840
s 1, 323n92
Protection from Harassment Act 1997
s 1(1), 288
s 1(1)(a), 288
s 1(1)(b), 264n12
s 3(1), 288
s 3(2), 288
s 7(2), 290n144
s 7(3), 290

R

Road Traffic Act 1988
s 149, 407
s 149(3), 408n60

S

Sale of Goods Act 1979
s 13, 195n4
s 14, 195n4
s 15, 195n4
Social Action, Responsibility and Heroism Act 2015
s 1, 102
s 2, 102
s 3, 102
s 4, 102

T

Theatres Act 1968
s 4(1), 302
Trade Union and Labour Relations (Consolidation) Act 1992
s 219(1), 248
s 219(2), 248

U

Unfair Contract Terms Act 1977
s 1(1)(c), 178n8
s 1(3), 178, 179
s 2(1), 179
s 2(2), 179
s 2(3), 179
s 11, 180n10
Sch 2, 180n10

ABOUT THE AUTHORS

Sarah Green is the Law Commissioner for Commercial and Common Law at the Law Commission of England and Wales. Prior to that, she was Professor of Private Law at the University of Bristol, Professor of the Law of Obligations at the University of Oxford and a lecturer at the University of Birmingham. She has written two books about specific elements of tort law, and has also published on a variety of other topics including virtual currencies, blockchain issues surrounding intermediated securities, smart contracts, sale of goods law as applicable to digitised assets, and wage theft.

Jodi Gardner is a University Lecturer in Private Law at the University of Cambridge, and a Fellow of St John's College. She is also a Senior Adjunct Research Fellow at the Centre for Banking & Finance Law, National University of Singapore. Jodi's research is primarily focused on the intersection between private law and social policy. She has written on a variety of different topics in this area including the regulation of high-cost credit contracts, the impact of austerity measures, the effect of open banking on financial exclusion, online auctions, and concurrent liability in tort and contract.

PREFACE

Tort law has an unfortunate, and we believe, very unfair reputation for being one of the most difficult and least interesting law subjects. We have therefore attempted to create a tort law textbook that is *accessible* and *engaging* for students encountering this area of law for the first time. We want to make the study of tort law *accessible*; breaking down some complicated legal tests into concise and manageable principles that can be understood by students and applied easily in assessment tasks. More importantly, we wanted to make the study of tort law *engaging*; highlighting that amongst all of the complex legal principles and statutes, there is a fascinating array of questions about individual responsibility, socio-legal issues, moral blameworthiness, law in practice versus law in theory, and general philosophical challenges. The discussion of our pedagogical features in the next section will highlight how we have approached these aims.

The book is divided into five main sections, generally aimed at following the tort syllabus at most UK law schools:

I. The Tort of Negligence covers the different elements of the most common tort law action: negligence. There are chapters on duty of care, breach of duty, causation, remoteness, pure economic loss, and psychiatric injury.

II. Torts Relating to Land and Goods focuses on several different causes of action in tort, including occupiers' liability, product liability, nuisance, trespass to land and *Rylands v Fletcher*.

III. Intentional Torts deals with the economic torts (i.e. inducing breach of contract, causing loss by unlawful means and conspiracy) and intentional torts against the person (including assault, battery and trespass to the person).

IV. Defamation and Privacy addresses torts based on the dissemination of information, with defamation protecting people from untrue representations and privacy focusing on the publication of correct but private information.

V. General Matters covers a range of topics relevant to all of the previous chapters, including vicarious liability, defences and damages.

A book of this nature must be divided in some manner. Sarah has written the chapters on negligence, torts related to land and goods, economic torts and vicarious liability. Jodi has taken responsibility for intentional torts to the person, defamation, privacy, defences and damages. Despite this division, the authors have benefited immensely from working together, and very much consider this to be a joint project.

A few notes on terminology when reading through the book. We have used masculine and feminine pronouns interchangeably but, unless the specific context requires otherwise, readers should take a reference to one to be a reference to people more generally. Throughout the text of the book, we refer to the party commencing the claim as the 'claimant'. It is, however, recognised that this party is the 'plaintiff' in some other jurisdictions and in England until 1999. The term 'plaintiff' may therefore be used in some of the case quotations. Finally, a reference to English laws should be taken to include the laws of Wales, unless it explicitly states otherwise.

The authors have strived to reflect the law as it stood on 1 June 2020.

Sarah Green, Bristol & London
Jodi Gardner, Cambridge

ACKNOWLEDGEMENTS

During the writing of this book, the authors received significant support from friends, family and colleagues. We would specifically like to thank Justice Peter Applegarth AM, Paul S. Davies, James Lee, Kate Kelly, John Murphy, Nicholas McBride and Stelios Tofaris for their help and encouragement. Any errors remain our own. The authors have been fortunate enough to work on this project with a range of excellent people at Macmillan International Higher Education. The original idea for this textbook arose from discussions with Luke Block, who was highly enthusiastic about the project and played a crucial part in its formative stages. Since that time, we have benefited from the supportive and efficient assistance of Lyndsay Aitken, Ursula Gavin and Milly Weaver. The book was finalised during the 2020 and 2021 COVID-19 lockdowns, so we are particularly grateful for the professional and effective editorial assistance of the publishing team, especially the exceptional copyediting work by David Stott. It would not have been possible for us to complete the book on time without the brilliant research assistance of Devon-Jane Airey. We would also like to thank our husbands, Alan and Sebastian, for their support balancing the childcare, home-schooling and general domestic challenges arising from the pandemic.

Jodi's fourth daughter was born during this period, so she is especially grateful for her parents' invaluable assistance – it was the only way she could balance writing with the demands of a new-born. During the writing of the book, but before the lockdown, Sarah made the professional move from academia to the Law Commission of England and Wales, becoming Law Commissioner for Commercial and Common Law in January 2020. Thanks to the wonderful working environment and transitional assistance offered by the Commission, this was in no way as demanding a life-change as that presented by the arrival of a new baby.

Finally, we would like to thank our past and present students. The authors have had the privilege of teaching tort law to so many bright and enthusiastic young minds over the years. This opportunity has improved and deepened our understanding of – and passion for – the subject, and we are grateful to you all.

TOUR OF THE BOOK

Tort law is a complex and fascinating subject. We recognise that it can be challenging for you to get to grips with the technical detail and philosophical debates associated with the law of torts. This book is therefore specifically designed to make tort law studies as *accessible* and *engaging* as possible. We have done this through a range of pedagogical features designed for the benefit of law students:

At the beginning of each chapter

Learning objectives provide a brief overview of what you should get out of each topic. Keep these in mind while reading the chapter. You can also use these during revision, as they act as a 'checklist' of the chapter's main points.

LEARNING OBJECTIVES

- Explain the role played by the negligence inquiry
- Understand the different leg for established and novel d
- aw a distinction b

The **Introduction** provides a summary of what will be discussed in each chapter, giving you an overview of the topic and explaining any key developments in the specific area of tort law that the chapter covers.

1.1 Introduction

This chapter provides at specific causes of act taught as a single und of different torts th ilst the law of

PROBLEM QUESTION

One day in July, four officers fro of a drug-dealing gang whom they know the gang is likely to resist ar pull out knives and guns, causing to what he does or where he g reams. Startled, a member hris's mother, Dio

One of the most difficult aspects of tort law is answering problem questions, as it is so different from most other forms of assessment. Each chapter starts with a sample problem question, designed to be similar to those you will encounter in assignments or exam questions. Keep the **Problem Question** in mind as you read the chapter.

Problem Question Technique boxes feature in relevant sections throughout each chapter, guiding you through how to answer the opening problem question using what you have learned. By the end of the chapter, you should feel confident in tackling the problem question.

ae question. patients not to cause phy n *Darnley* as being analogous to t to cause reasonably foreseeable harm blished category. Another significant poin e next chapter, is the crucial importance of a reach. The question of whether a duty of care question of whether that duty has been breached

PROBLEM QUESTION TECHNIQUE

ne day in July, four officers from Ambledon P drug-dealing gang whom they know meet the gang is likely to resist arrest. Whe ives and guns, causing a stand or where he g

All law students understand the importance of cases and legislation to their legal studies; however, it can be difficult to pick which are the most important. **Key Case** boxes allow you to focus on the most significant aspects of important cases, helping you to understand their relevance.

KEY CASE

Sutradhar v Nationa

The claimant suffered a result of drinking wa the British Geologic for a nu

ensation Act

KEY LEGISLATION

Compensation Act 200

3   Mesothelioma: dam
(1) This section applie
   (a) a person '

Sometimes the sheer volume of cases and statutes can be daunting, and it can be difficult for you to pick which are the most important. **Key Legislation** boxes offer quotations and summaries of key sections, allowing you to focus on the most relevant parts.

Tort law raises a number of interesting theoretical and philosophical challenges, which in assessment often form the basis of essay questions. These **Viewpoint** boxes engage in these debates and challenges, providing a range of questions – similar to those you might encounter in assessments – for you to consider.

...re is current...
...ems in the UK have i...

■ VIEWPOINT

What are the benefits and de...

Insurance can also be conside...
Damages Lottery argues that t'...
...nsurance. He argues that...
...tort law is not nece...
...iinjury[31] in...

...ine time peri...
...uses Act 1972 inapplicab...

Tort law does not exist in a vacuum and many of the topics overlap and engage with other areas of the law, including contract, crime and equity. **Making Connections** highlight and briefly discuss these overlaps, giving you an understanding of how tort law principles fit into the legal system as a whole.

TORT OF NEGLIGEN...

MAKING CONNECTIONS

The distinction between negligence an...
both because of the remoteness issue...
negligence and deceit.[29] It is also, how...
...concerned with misrepresentation, a...
...ntexts. If a party to a contract is...
...an lead to a claim in either...
...rporated into the...

...g deterren...
...pensatory damages c...
...mages, aggravated damage...

Table 17.1 Summary of damage

Type of Damage	Explanation
Nominal Damages	Tokenistic dam...
	highlight tha'
	been comr
	substan'
	h...

DIFFERENT PERSPECTIVES

P.S. Davies and S. Green, '"Pure Eco and M. Tilbury (eds), Convergence a
This piece argues that the English comr...
...s 'purely economic' is less coherent a...
...a common law world, which takes...
...laimant is in a relatively vuln...
...lv economic in th...

There is a wonderful, detailed range of academic literature on all aspects of tort law. Many of the writings conflict with, and at least appear to contradict, other work, and this is because there is no right or wrong answer to many of the issues considered. This can sometimes be overwhelming. **Different Perspectives** boxes summarise the diverse views of key academics in an easy to understand manner.

Tables and **figures** explain key concepts, helping you to break down issues into different and more manageable elements, and providing visual summaries of some of the more complex issues.

At the end of each chapter

Chapter summaries give a recap of the key points covered in each chapter. They help you to check your understanding of what you have learned and revise the key points. They also offer some suggestions of ongoing issues to explore further.

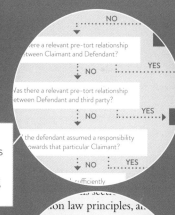

...NO...
...here a relevant pre-tort relationship
...etween Claimant and Defendant?
...NO...YES...
...Vas there a relevant pre-tort relationship
...etween Defendant and third party?
...NO...YES...
...'the defendant assumed a responsibility
...owards that particular Claimant?
...NO...YES...
...sufficiently...

CHAPTER SUMMARY

...tort of defamation concerns the
...ed reputation and the public inter...
...h can include information that m...
...he centuries, with judge-made...
...nodern conditions in a de...
...d common law rul...

These **roadmaps** are a tool for navigating complex areas of law, and provide a step-by-step guide for answering problem questions.

...s sec...
...on law principles, a...

FURTHER READING

W. Buckland, 'The Duty To Take Care...
J. Goudkamp, 'A Revolution in Duty...
N. McBride, '*Michael* and the Future...
J. Morgan, 'Parallel lines that neve...
...Robertston, 'Policy-Based R...
...'Rationalising Or...

It is impossible to cover the breadth of tort law topics in a single textbook chapter. The **Further Reading** section at the end of each provides a number of academic pieces for students who have a particular interest in a topic. In light of the importance of decolonising the curriculum, we have tried to go beyond the 'standard' articles and chapters, engaging with a wider range of further readings, including critical legal theory, feminist perspectives and interdisciplinary work.

We hope that these features assist you not only to survive – but hopefully enjoy – your tort law studies.

ONLINE RESOURCES

The companion website for this book contains further learning and teaching tools to aid students in their tort law studies and to support lecturers in the delivery of their courses.

Visit **http://www.macmillanihe.com/green-tort** to find a wealth of further resources, including:

- **Exam-style essay questions** to help students prepare for exams
- **Practical guidance for answering exam and essay questions** to help students perform at their best
- **Useful web links** for further reading and research
- **Commentaries on recently-decided cases** to keep the discussion up-to-date
- **Multiple choice questions** for use in exams and assessments

INTRODUCTION

CHAPTER CONTENTS

1.1 Introduction	1
1.2 What is a tort and the history of tort law	1
1.3 Aims of tort law	3
1.4 Interests protected by tort law	3
1.5 Limitations of tort law	5
1.6 'Compensation culture'	5
1.7 Tort law and insurance	7
1.8 Alternative systems	8
1.9 Chapter summary	10
Further reading	10

1.1 Introduction

This chapter provides a general introduction to the law of torts before the subsequent chapters look at specific causes of action. It will show that, despite often being considered a discrete area of law and taught as a single undergraduate subject, the law of torts is anything but unified: there are a number of different torts that protect a diverse range of different interests. This chapter will consider how, whilst the law of torts is often focused primarily on ensuring compensation for the injured party, there are several other principles and potential aims associated with it, and this often adds to the complexities of the subject. Tort law has developed to protect numerous interests, including physical and mental integrity, financial interests, property rights and personal rights of autonomy, privacy and reputation. The development of human rights law, particularly in the form of the Human Rights Act 1998, has also had a marked impact on this area of the law. Whilst tort law gives rise to considerable powers to protect individuals and interests, it is also subject to significant practical limitations, and these too are discussed in the chapter, alongside the question of whether a 'compensation culture' has developed in the UK. This introduction also considers the increasingly important role played by insurance in the law of torts, including the degree to which it affects both liability and, most controversially, the development of substantive legal principles. In light of these challenges, the chapter's conclusion discusses briefly the various alternatives to the current tort system.

1.2 What is a tort and the history of tort law

A tort is a 'civil wrong', meaning that the wronged party can claim monetary damages[1] from the wrongdoer (also referred to as the 'tortfeasor'). This can be contrasted with criminal law, where the wrong results in prosecution by the state. Whilst it is common to hear the phrase 'tort law',

---

1   Or, in certain circumstances, injunctive relief.

there is not one single tort, nor a single law of tort. This area is, in fact, made up of a wide variety of different separate causes of action – ranging from a duty of care not to cause someone physical harm, to a duty not to injure someone's reputation, to a duty not to cause unreasonable interference with property interests. It is therefore more accurately thought of as 'the law of torts'. As outlined by Baker,

> The law of torts, or civil wrongs, is extensive and its boundaries are not fixed by any unifying general principle. The very word 'tort', which has long been appropriated by lawyers, was far from technical in origin. The nearest medieval equivalent was 'trespass', whereas the old French word *tort* (*injuria* in Latin) denoted any kind of legal injury and is best translated as 'wrong'.[2]

A more modern definition is provided by Birks, that a tort is the 'breach of a legal duty which affects the interests of an individual to complain on his or her own account rather than as a representative of society as a whole'.[3]

Whilst tort law is the law of civil wrongs, the concept of 'wrongfulness' or 'fault' varies dramatically between different torts. Some torts, such as negligence, require the defendant to be at fault in order to be held liable, whereas others, including statutory product liability and the rule in *Rylands v Fletcher*, have a stricter basis of liability, which means that a defendant can be held liable without necessarily having behaved in a culpable way. The only truly 'strict' liability in tort law is found in vicarious liability, which is discussed in more detail in Chapter 15.

Tort law has a strong pedigree; it may even be older than criminal law. When writing about 'ancient law', Sir Henry Maine stated that

> the penal law of ancient communities is not the law of Crimes; it is the law of Wrongs, or, to use the English technical word, of Torts. The person injured proceeds against the wrong-doer by an ordinary civil action, and recovers compensation in the shape of money-damages if he succeeds ... it will be seen that at the head of the civil wrongs recognised by the Roman law stood Furtum or Theft. Offences which we are accustomed to regard exclusively as crimes are exclusively treated as torts, and not theft only, but assault and violent robbery, are associated by the jurisconsult with trespass, libel and slander. All alike gave rise to an Obligation or *vinculum juris*, and were all requited by a payment of money.[4]

The first recognised torts were the writs of trespass, which became common after 1250, and were based on a wrong that had been committed for which the claimant requested damages. There were a number of potential writs, including trespass to land, trespass to goods and trespass to the person. Negligence, the current 'predominant' tort, was actually rarely imposed by the court until after 1700, and was not recognised as a separate tort until the 20th century. Baker highlights that the practitioner text *Clerk and Lindsell on Torts* did not have a separate chapter on negligence until 1947.[5] Negligence now tends to dominate, and could be said to be the principal English tort. As an example, five chapters of this textbook are devoted solely to common law negligence.

---

2   J.H. Baker, *Introduction to English Legal History*, 5th edn (Butterworths, 2019), 427.
3   P. Birks, 'The Concept of a Civil Wrong' in D. Owen (ed.), *Philosophical Foundations of Tort Law* (Clarendon Press 1995), 51.
4   Sir Henry Maine, *Ancient Law* (J.M. Dent & Sons Ltd, 1917), 218.
5   See discussion in J.H. Baker, *Introduction to English Legal History*, 5th edn (Butterworths, 2019), 428.

1.3 Aims of tort law

The overriding purpose of tort law is generally considered to be compensation for losses caused by the tortfeasor's actions. Whilst this is one key aim, it is not the only one. For example, the application of the different defences in Chapter 16 challenges the importance of compensation – why should a victim of a tort not be compensated because there is a link between the tort and the commission of a criminal offence? Or because she consented to the risk of the tort? It would seem that there are also aspects of deterrence and behavioural incentives at play, suggesting that compensation is not the sole objective of tort law.

Tort law aims – as far as money can do so – to put claimants in the position in which they would have been had the tort not been committed against them. The main reason a claimant will bring an action in tort is to be compensated for the harm that they have suffered, either in the form of financial loss or of non-financial loss (such as pain and suffering). This was outlined by Lord Blackburn in *Livingstone v Rawyards Coal Co*, who stated that tort law should award 'that sum of money which will put the party who has been injured, or who has suffered, in the same position as he would have been in if he had not sustained the wrong for which he is now getting his compensation or reparation'.[6] This is often not straightforward. The wrongful death of a loved one, the loss of someone's reputation, the development of a serious psychiatric illness or the loss of the ability to walk are all consequences of tortious actions that the law struggles adequately to 'compensate' with financial damages. As a response, both the common law and statute have developed a wide range of principles for determining how much compensation a claimant should be awarded in different circumstances, as will be explored further in Chapter 17.

Tort law can also be seen as having an important role in fostering deterrence and accountability. By holding individuals and institutions liable for their actions, and requiring them to compensate those they harm, tortfeasors are held accountable for their actions and future behaviour of the same type is disincentivised. This deterrent impact can be further strengthened by the court's ability to award 'exemplary' or 'punitive' damages for particularly egregious breaches of duties. Whilst there is some theoretical importance to deterrence and accountability as aims of tort law, it is not so clear that they are always pursued in practice. As will be discussed below, an overwhelming majority of tort law defendants have insurance, meaning that the tortfeasor is rarely the party that suffers financially from a finding of liability. The deterrence effect could also be said to be undermined to some extent by the concept of vicarious liability. This is liability imposed on one party as a result of a tort committed by another, and is covered in Chapter 15. It is most often applied in the employment context, where an employer may be held liable for loss caused by the wrong of an employee. The practical limitations of tort law (also discussed below) can further undermine the deterrent impact of tort law, in that only a very small percentage of accident victims successfully receive damages under the current system.

This section has only provided a general outline of some of the key aims of tort law. The various aims can also be emphasised in different torts or elements of torts, and these aspects will be discussed in more detail where relevant in the subsequent chapters.

1.4 Interests protected by tort law

The diverse range of interests protected by the law of tort is reflected in the table below.[7] The table, however, reflects only the 'main' torts protecting the relevant interest. The reality is often significantly more complicated. A single tort can protect more than one interest: once a particular

---

6   (1880) 5 App Cas 25, 39.
7   Note that the table lists only those torts covered in this book.

type of injury has been caused (for example physical harm), this often allows the claimant to sue for other types of harm, such as consequential mental harm or financial loss.

It is also worth noting the impact that the development of human rights has had on modern tort law. This arguably increased after the enactment of the Human Rights Act 1998, which has to some extent influenced the development of the common law, particularly in relation to the obligations of public authorities. The specific impact of human rights jurisprudence will be discussed in the relevant chapters, but, in brief, its influence has been notable in the following areas:

- when a duty of care is owed, particularly by a public authority;[8]

- nuisance claims, particularly interference with the claimant's human rights under Article 1, Protocol 1 and Article 8 of Schedule 1 to the Human Rights Act 1998;[9]

- false imprisonment;[10]

- interpretation of the Protection from Harassment Act 1997;[11]

- privacy, particularly relating to the balancing of rights under Articles 8 and 10 of Schedule 1 to the Human Rights Act 1998 for a breach of confidence claim;[12] and

- defamation, again specifically focused on the balancing of rights under Articles 8 and 10 of Schedule 1 to the Human Rights Act 1998.[13]

Table 1.1: Summary of interests protected by tort law

Interest Protected	Main Torts and Remedies
Physical integrity	Negligence (duty of care for physical injury); battery; product liability; occupiers' liability; non-pecuniary damages
Mental integrity	Negligence (duty of care for psychiatric harm); assault; the tort in *Wilkinson v Downton*; Protection from Harassment Act 1997
Financial interests	Negligence (duty of care for pure economic loss); economic torts; pecuniary damages
Rights and enjoyment of property	Nuisance; occupiers' liability; product liability; trespass to land; *Rylands v Fletcher*; compensation for damage for property
Autonomy/preventing restrictions of movement	False imprisonment
Privacy	Breach of confidence; Protection from Harassment Act 1997
Reputation	Defamation; breach of confidence; malicious prosecution
Human rights	The impact of the Human Rights Act 1998 on numerous torts (see above discussion)

8   See 2.5. Although, as noted at 2.5.2, the courts seem more willing to allow the development of common law negligence outside and alongside the human rights regime, as opposed to trying to accommodate the one within the other.
9   See footnote 11 on page 227 and 10.3.1.
10   R *v Bournewood Community and Mental Health NHS Trust, ex parte L* [1998] UKHL 24, [1998] 1 All ER 634 and *HL v United Kingdom* (2004) 81 BMLR 131 discussed in section 12.5.
11   As discussed in *Thomas v News Groups Newspapers* [2002] EMLR 78 and *OPO v Rhodes* [2016] AC 219 discussed at 12.7.2.
12   See 13.7.1.
13   See 14.3.3 and 14.4.

1.5 Limitations of tort law

There are some significant limitations on the ability of the tort system to provide recourse for civil wrongs. The main shortcoming is just how few people ultimately benefit from its protection. Whilst different reviews have found different figures, it is clear that only a very small percentage of accident victims receive damages from the current tort law system.[14] As famously shown in Atiyah's *The Damages Lottery*, whether or not someone will successfully receive damages for injuries they have suffered is more often a matter of luck than whether or not they are deserving.[15] This raises concerns of equality between different victims; some are able to obtain large damages whilst many get nothing. The difference is often down to little more than moral luck. For example, in both *Roberts v Ramsbottom* and *Mansfield v Weetabix*, the claimants were injured by defendant drivers suffering from medical conditions that affected their ability to drive safely. The specific nature of the different illnesses in each case, however, meant that one claimant had a successful cause of action and the other did not.

In addition, tort rights which are available in theory have also to be enforced in practice. Proceeding to litigation is expensive, time consuming, emotionally draining and often risky. There is also a considerable and sometimes intolerable delay between the commission of the tort and the award of damages. Even with the increased use of 'no win, no fee' lawyers, there is still often considerable personal and financial risk associated with commencing a tort action. The related costs are often prohibitive for claimants with limited means, or for people suing for smaller amounts of money. There is always the option of litigants representing themselves, but that creates another set of problems. There are still filing fees associated with all levels of court cases. The complexity of both the substantive law of torts, not to mention the procedural difficulties, means that self-represented litigants are likely to struggle if they come up against defendants represented by lawyers. These limitations highlight the significant and potentially unfair distinction between 'tort law in theory' and 'tort law in practice'.[16]

1.6 'Compensation culture'

It is sometimes argued that a 'compensation culture' is developing in the UK. This describes a situation in which people too frequently sue others for their misfortune instead of either taking personal responsibility for their losses, or accepting that accidents sometimes happen which cannot be attributed to anyone's fault. Concerns about the impact of tort liability and an increasing compensation culture have been outlined in a range of cases, including *CBS Songs Ltd v Amstrad Consumer Electronics plc*, *Gorringe v Calderdale Metropolitan Borough Council*, *Tomlinson v Congleton Borough Council* and *Majrowski v Guy's and St Thomas's NHS Trust*. The judges in these cases highlighted concerns about decreasing individual responsibility and the potential for tort liability to result in institutions reducing access to services because they are fearful of being sued.

In a 2017 speech, Lord Sumption pointed out that

the mounting concern about compensation culture is powered by a number of factors. The main ones are the upward pressure on motor insurance premiums arising from an increase in

---

14 For example, the Royal Commission on Civil Liability and Compensation for Personal Injury (Cmnd 7054) estimated it was around 6.5% of victims: Vol 1, Table 5(i). Discussion of different statistical information is available in R. Lewis, A. Morris and K. Oliphant, 'Tort personal injury claims statistics: is there a compensation culture in the United Kingdom?' (2006) 14(2) *Torts Law Journal* 158.

15 P. Atiyah, *The Damages Lottery* (Hart Publishing, 1997).

16 For a, slightly dated, analysis of these issues, see E. Allan Lind, R.J. Maccoun, P.A. Ebener, W.L.F. Felstiner, D.R. Hensler, J. Resnik and T.R. Tyler, 'In the Eye of the Beholder: Tort Litigants' Evaluations of Their Experiences in the Civil Justice System' (1990) 24(4) *Law & Society Review* 953.

the number and value of claims, governmental concern about the cost of claims against the National Health Service, and persistent stories in the press (not always strictly accurate) about unmeritorious claims.

He further outlined the nature of the compensation culture debate as turning on

complex cultural issues about moral responsibility and blame which have very little to do with economic efficiency. The public's view is based on two simple moral judgments. One is that he who causes physical injury must make it good financially. The other is that it is a proper function of the courts to find facts and distribute blame, simply as a satisfaction for victims or their relatives.[17]

Claims that a compensation culture exists have arisen both from the courts[18] and from political rhetoric. For example, the former Prime Minister, David Cameron, in the foreword to the Young Report argued that a 'damaging compensation culture has arisen, as if people can absolve themselves from any personal responsibility for their own actions'.[19]

Whilst there have been repeated claims of a compensation culture arising in the UK, these are rarely supported by evidence. In contrast, academic and empirical analysis of the situation contends that there is very little justification for the compensation culture concerns, and these accusations unfairly perpetuate a myth of an over-litigious society. For example, Morris undertook a detailed analysis of tort law litigation and found that, whilst there had been an increase in litigation since the 1970s, this has been relatively stable since the late 1990s. She found little evidence of a compensation culture and instead stated that the situation had been distorted by the media. Morris further argued that

the phenomenon of the 'compensation culture' provides a fascinating case study in how our legal consciousness develops. Our knowledge and understanding of trends in our propensity to claim have not developed on the basis of representative and impartial evidence but through a number of inter-related, subtle processes.[20]

This finding was supported by the Young Report, despite the fearful tone of the Prime Minister in its introduction. When reviewing the evidence related to the supposed compensation culture, the Young Report stated that

Britain's 'compensation culture' is fuelled by media stories about individuals receiving large compensation payouts for personal injury claims and by constant adverts in the media offering people non-refundable inducements and the promise of a handsome settlement if they claim. It places an unnecessary strain on businesses of all sizes, who fear litigation and are subjected to increasingly expensive insurance premiums. The problem of the *compensation culture prevalent in society today is, however, one of perception rather than reality*.[21]

Whilst being aware of the theoretical concerns of tort liability creating an undesirable compensation culture in the UK, tort law students must understand that the reality of the situation is far less dramatic than is often portrayed in the media and by certain interest groups.

17 Lord Sumption, 'Abolishing Personal Injuries Law – A project', a speech at the Personal Injuries Bar Association Annual Lecture, London, 16 November 2017, p 10.
18 Lord Hobhouse in *Tomlinson v Congleton Borough Council* commented that 'the pursuit of an unrestrained culture of blame and compensation has many evil consequences and one is certainly the interference with the liberty of the citizen': [2004] 1 AC 46, 96.
19 'Foreword by the Prime Minster' in Lord Young, *Common Sense, Common Safety* (Cabinet Office, 2010), p 5.
20 A. Morris, 'Spiralling or Stabilising? The Compensation Culture and our Propensity to Claim Damages for Personal Injury' (2007) 70 MLR 349, 378.
21 Lord Young, *Common Sense, Common Safety* (Cabinet Office, 2010), p 19.

1.7 Tort law and insurance

Insurance has an increasingly important role to play in the practicalities of everyday life, as evidenced by the legal requirement to have insurance to drive a car, to hire employees, to provide many professional services, and often to obtain a mortgage. There is, however, a more complicated question as to what role insurance plays in the development of procedural or substantive tort law principles. From a historical perspective, Baker commented that

> after the introduction of liability-insurance in the last quarter of the nineteenth century, most negligence actions were in reality defended by insurance companies, and the assumption that a prudent business should be fully insured may well have influenced courts tacitly in extending business liability. The use of insurance also explains the tendency to escalate the sums recoverable in personal injury cases far beyond anything which an uninsured individual could hope to pay.[22]

As discussed above, insurance could be said to undermine the deterrent effect of the law of torts, as the party who pays the damages is not the party who commits the tort. Insurance also results in loss distribution. It has the benefit of spreading the cost of the damages across a pool of insurance premium payers, as opposed to letting it all fall on one party (or leaving a claimant without access to compensation). In 2005, Lewis reported that insurers pay out 94% of tort compensation, and nine times out of ten, the real defendants to tort claims are insurance companies.[23] He further contended that 'without insurance, it is probable that tort liability itself could not survive'.[24]

Some cases have quite explicitly highlighted the impact of insurance on the decision-making process. For example, in *Nettleship v Weston*, the Court of Appeal imposed an objective standard of care on the learner driver defendant, and in doing so made reference to the requirement for all drivers to have motor insurance. As stated by Lord Denning MR;

> The high standard thus imposed by the judges is, I believe, largely the result of the policy of the Road Traffic Acts. Parliament requires every driver to be insured against third party risks. The reason is so that a person injured by a motor car should not be left to bear the loss on his own, but should be compensated out of the insurance fund …. Thus we are, in this branch of the law, moving away from the concept: 'No liability without fault', We are beginning to apply the test: 'On whom should the risk fall?' Morally the learner driver is not at fault; but legally she is liable to be because she is insured and the risk should fall on her.[25]

The availability of insurance has been considered by courts in a range of cases.[26] There is also a significant thread of academic commentary on the role of insurance in the development of common law tort principles. Both Stapleton and Morgan, for instance, argue that the role of insurance has the potential to undermine the important purposes of tort law, but have different views on whether access to insurance actually impacts substantive tort law principles.

---

22 J.H. Baker, *Introduction to English Legal History*, 5th edn (Butterworths, 2019), 448. See also D. Ibbetson, 'The Tort of Negligence in the Common Law in the Nineteenth and Twentieth Centuries' in E. Schrange (ed.), *Negligence: The Comparative Legal History of the Law of Torts* (Duncker & Humblot, 2001).
23 R. Lewis, 'Insurance and the Tort System' (2005) 25 LS 85.
24 R. Lewis, 'Insurance and the Tort System' (2005) 25 LS 85, 92.
25 *Nettleship v Weston* [1971] 2 QB 691, 699–700.
26 See, for example, *Cox v Ministry of Justice* [2016] AC 660; *Armes v Nottinghamshire County Council* [2017] UKSC 60; *Post Office v Norwich Union Fire Insurance Society Ltd* [1967] 2 QB 363.

DIFFERENT PERSPECTIVES

J. Stapleton, 'Tort, Insurance and Ideology' (1995) 58 MLR 820

In this article, Stapleton downplays the role played by insurance in the development of tort law. She argues that whilst the availability of insurance will clearly impact some aspects, particularly whether or not a victim will litigate a potential claim, 'neither actual insurance nor insurability are or should be relevant to the reach and shape of tort liability'. Stapleton starts her analysis with Viscount Simond's decision in *Lister v Romford Ice and Cold Storage Co Ltd*, where he states that 'as a general proposition it has not, I think, been questioned for nearly 200 years that in determining the rights *inter se* of A and B the fact that one or other of them is insured is to be disregarded'.[27] She contends that courts ignore the availability of insurance because they reject that it has any relevance to the issue of whether liability should be imposed on the defendant. Stapleton is particularly concerned that focusing on the insurance status of the defendant may lead to the suppression of the corrective justice or deterrence goals of tort law, and instead risks the tort becoming a surrogate for first party insurance.

J. Morgan, 'Tort, Insurance and Incoherence' (2004) 67 MLR 384

Morgan, writing nine years after Stapleton, contends that insurance has a significant role to play in the development of tort law. He specifically utilises two cases, *Vowles v Evans*[28] and *Gwilliam v West Hertfordshire NHS Trust*[29] (both decided after Stapleton's article) in support of this argument. The first case involved an amateur rugby match, and held that the referee owed the players a duty of care to enforce the rules of the game to ensure the safety of everyone involved. In the first instance decision, Lord Phillips stated:

> We accept that the availability of insurance, both to players against the risk of injury and to referees against the risk of third party liability could bear on the policy question of whether it is fair, just and reasonable to impose a duty of care on referees.

The trial judge's decision was approved by the Court of Appeal. Morgan argues that this type of approach highlights judicial acceptance 'for loss-spreading, via insurance, as a positive reason for imposing liability in negligence'. Despite finding that the courts are increasingly considering insurance as a basis for substantive decision-making, he argues – along similar lines to Stapleton – that this is a negative development and undermines the personal responsibility role of tort law.

■ VIEWPOINT

What role do you think access to insurance should have on the development of tort law principles?

1.8 Alternative systems

In light of the significant criticisms levelled at the current tort law system, it is important to consider whether an alternative compensation scheme would be preferable. It is too often assumed that tort law is the only way in which victims can be compensated, but in reality there are alternatives to a system of litigation based on the principle that loss should be corrected by the party who caused it. There are other ways to address victims' losses, including personal insurance policies[30]

---

27 [1957] AC 555, 576–7.
28 [2002] EWHC 2612 (QB); on appeal [2003] EWCA Civ 318; [2003] 1 WLR 1607.
29 [2002] EWCA Civ 1041.
30 See discussion above about the role of insurance in tort law damages.

and social security payments. There are also different government-run compensation schemes, including the Criminal Injuries Compensation Scheme, the Police Pension Scheme and Diffuse Mesothelioma Payment Scheme. It is highly doubtful that any of these different options provide adequate compensation since the amount that they pay out is limited, but they do at least produce some sort of social safety net for victims of torts.

It was these limitations, amongst others, that led New Zealand to institute a no-fault accident compensation scheme in 1974. This scheme involved the abolition of tort actions for personal injury in favour of government compensation for accidents causing personal injury or death. This was later extended to include medical complications and intentional torts (such as physical and sexual assaults). The scheme is funded through the payments of premiums by those who generate the risk of accidents, such as road users and medical practitioners, as well as being covered by general taxation costs, and is administered by the Accident Compensation Commission. There are clearly a number of positive and negative aspects to the implementation of no-fault schemes. Compensation is much easier to access in this context because a claimant only needs to show that her loss was caused in one of the ways covered by the scheme. There is no need to prove that anyone in particular was at fault for the loss. The amount awarded, however, is likely to be much lower than the individual would receive through the tort law system, and is not designed to put the victim 'in the same position as she would have been in if she had not sustained the wrong'. It can be seen as providing fair compensation for the many, as opposed to full compensation for the few. It would seem, however, that there is currently no political appetite for this type of drastic reform, and proposals for similar systems in the UK have not been embraced.

■ VIEWPOINT

What are the benefits and detriments of instituting a no-fault accident compensation scheme?

Insurance can also be considered as an alternative to a fault-based tort law system. Atiyah in *The Damages Lottery* argues that the tort system should be entirely replaced with a system of first-party insurance. He highlights that requiring everyone to purchase insurance for themselves would mean that tort law is not necessary because everyone would be protected by their own insurance in the event of injury.[31] Whilst this would have the effect of replacing the flawed and expensive tort law system with a clear and more efficient alternative, it would also mean replacing, to some extent, individual responsibility with market-based incentives. Critics of this approach have highlighted that putting the burden on victims to obtain insurance to protect themselves dilutes the aim of deterring wrongdoing and holding tortfeasors accountable for their actions. Whilst there is some merit in this concern, we have explained above how third-party insurance and vicarious liability could already be said to dilute tort law's deterrence effects. One further criticism of first-party insurance is the potential for it to exacerbate pre-existing disadvantages; people on lower incomes are unlikely to afford insurance (or to afford cover as comprehensive as others), and therefore will be further disadvantaged when they are victims of torts.[32]

---

31 P. Atiyah, *The Damages Lottery* (Hart Publishing, 1997).
32 For further discussion and analysis of Atiyah's arguments, see J. Conaghan and W. Mansell, 'From the Permissive to the Dismissive Society: Patrick Atiyah's Accidents, Compensation and the Market' (1998) 25 JLS 284.

1.9 CHAPTER SUMMARY

This chapter has provided a framework for the remaining substantive chapters. It has addressed the fundamental question of 'what is a tort?', as well as highlighting a number of themes and challenges associated with the law of torts. The legal grounding of tort is important; the historical development of this area illustrates the fact that there exists a wide range of different torts as opposed to a single unified 'law of tort'. These different torts also have diverse aims, the first and foremost of which is compensation, but deterrence, accountability and loss distribution also have a role to play. Tort law protects a number of different interests including physical and mental integrity, financial security, property rights, and personal rights of autonomy, privacy and reputation. Whilst it is a powerful tool, it is subject to a number of practical limitations – often associated with the challenge of enforcing tort law rights in court – that potentially undermine what it can do in practice. Recently there has been increased concern that liability in tort law is leading to the development of an undesirable 'compensation culture'. This does, however, seem to be more of a problem of perception than reality, as levels of tort law actions have remained relatively stable.

As you read through the different tort causes of actions covered in the rest of the book, it is important to keep these debates and challenges in mind. The legal and moral questions raised by potential tort liability are often deeper and more complicated than the application of the relevant principles and tests. There is a considerable range of insightful, engaging and challenging reading material on the topics covered in this chapter, some of which is set out in the Further Reading section below. We encourage you to delve into this material to consider the issues in further depth – as it will add to and enrich your study of the law of torts.

FURTHER READING

P. Atiyah, *The Damages Lottery* (Hart, 1997)

L. Bender, 'A Lawyer's Primer on Feminist Theory and Tort' (1988) 38(1/2) *Journal of Legal Education* 3

P. Birks, 'The Concept of a Civil Wrong' in D. Owen (ed.), *Philosophical Foundations of Tort Law* (1995), ch 1

P. Cane, 'Justice and Justifications for Tort Liability' (1982) 2 *OJLS* 30

P. Cane, *The Anatomy of Tort Law* (Hart, 1997)

Lord Dyson, 'Compensation Culture: Fact or Fantasy?', Holdsworth Club Lecture, 15 March 2013

J. Goldberg, 'Ten Half-Truths about Tort Law' (2008) 42 *Valparaiso University LR* 1221

J. Goudkamp and J. Murphy, 'The Failure of Universal Theories of Tort Law' (2016) 22 *Legal Studies* 1

C. Harlow, *Understanding Tort Law* (Sweet & Maxwell, 2005)

N. McBride, *The Humanity of Private Law: Part 1: Explanation* (Hart, 2018)

R. Merkin, 'Tort, Insurance and Ideology: Further Thoughts' (2012) 75 *MLR* 301

G. Williams, 'The Aims of the Law of Tort' (1951) 4 *CLP* 137

THE TORT OF NEGLIGENCE

PART 1

2.	Duty of Care	13
3.	Pure Economic Loss	42
4.	Psychiatric Injury	61
5.	Breach of Duty	86
6.	Causation	105
7.	Remoteness	143

This is the tort on which most undergraduate courses focus, and is also the basis of much modern civil litigation. Its principal aim is to compensate those who have suffered loss as the result of another's breach of duty. There are, however, limitations to the way in which the law of tort pursues this aim. First, the damage suffered by the claimant has to be of a certain type in order to be actionable. Even then, that damage or loss will only be recoverable if it is deemed not to be too remote from the defendant's breach of duty. The duty of care itself is one of the most significant limiting factors to negligence liability. It is simply not the case that the law mandates all of those who have caused harm to make good that harm in monetary terms. The tort of negligence holds us responsible for the consequences of our actions only to those within a certain sphere of influence. The shape and extent of this sphere are determined by the duty of care inquiry; an inquiry which employs the essential but often difficult concepts of reasonable foreseeability, proximity and fairness, justice and reasonableness. Note, however, that the court will not need to conduct this complicated inquiry in every case: often, it will proceed on the basis that the set of facts before it will be analogous to an established duty situation.

The question of breach is a fascinating one. In one sense, a defendant will only be held to be in breach of her duty of care if she is at fault. But this 'fault' is objectively, rather than subjectively, ascertained, so if the defendant in question was simply not capable of doing what the reasonable person in her situation would have done, she is nonetheless found to be in breach. One of the clearest illustrations of this, as you will see, is the learner driver who was held to be in breach of her duty of care for losing control of the car, even though she was a mere beginner. This might seem unfair, but is it any fairer to deny recovery to an injured claimant on the basis only that he had the misfortune to be hit by a novice driver?

Even where a duty of care has been established, and it has been breached by the defendant, and a claimant has suffered damage of an actionable type, there will still be no liability if the claimant cannot prove on the balance of probabilities that the breach was the factual cause of his harm. This part of the inquiry gives rise to some of the thorniest problems in the whole negligence inquiry, particularly in the medical negligence context, in which claimants are suffering from some form of physical problem even before they encounter the defendant. Where physical injury is concerned, our inability to know precisely how each individual's physiology reacts and responds to external factors means that causal questions are often very difficult to answer.

2 DUTY OF CARE

LEARNING OBJECTIVES

By the end of this chapter, you should be able to:

- Explain the role played by the duty of care in the negligence inquiry
- Understand the different legal treatment required for established and novel duty of care situations
- Draw a distinction between misfeasance and nonfeasance and summarise what the implications are for the negligence inquiry
- Outline why the duty of care inquiry is particularly difficult in relation to public bodies
- Describe how the common law of negligence interacts with human rights law
- Navigate the case law on duty of care and be able to apply the most appropriate rule to a given set of facts

CHAPTER CONTENTS

2.1	Introduction	14
2.2	Foundations of the modern tort of negligence	14
2.3	Establishing a duty of care	16
	2.3.1 From *Caparo* to *Robinson*	16
	2.3.2 Legally significant features	19
2.4	Acts vs omissions or misfeasance vs nonfeasance	24
	2.4.1 The general rule	24
	2.4.2 When will liability for omissions arise?	25
2.5	Liability of public bodies	28
	2.5.1 General principles	28
	2.5.2 Tort and the Human Rights Act 1998	30
	2.5.3 Is there a specific application of these principles to the police and emergency services?	37
2.6	Chapter summary	40
	Further reading	40
	Roadmap	41

PROBLEM QUESTION

One day in July, four officers from Ambledon Police go to the local park, intending to arrest members of a drug-dealing gang whom they know meet there in the evenings. They enter the park at 11pm. They know the gang is likely to resist arrest. When the gang notices the arrival of the Ambledon officers, they pull out knives and guns, causing a stand-off. Chris, a 9-year-old boy whose parents pay little attention to what he does or where he goes, is in the park at the time and, seeing the events unfold, panics and screams. Startled, a member of the gang shoots Chris, and he falls to the ground, injured.

Chris's mother, Dionne, is walking past the park on her way home from the pub. She sees, and recognises Chris, but she is heavily under the influence of several substances, and thinks he is probably just having a nap. She does not bother to check on him and walks home. Meanwhile, the Ambledon officers are so focused on preventing the gang from escaping that nobody pays any attention to Chris for nearly ten minutes. By the time one of the officers reaches him, he has lost a huge amount of blood and, as a result, later suffers from brain damage.

Eventually, the officers get the gang into their riot van. As they are escorting them in, they hear several members of the gang blaming the youngest member, Ed, for the arrest, calling him a 'snitch' and threatening to hurt him. On reaching the police station, one of the officers, Fern, opens the door to find Ed bleeding from several stab wounds to the chest. Fern calls an ambulance. The call handler informs Fern that there has been a terrorist incident in the city and, as a result, all of the ambulances are currently occupied with that. She tells her that she will get an ambulance to the police station as soon as possible but does not know when that will be. It is nearly three hours until an ambulance arrives, by which time Ed has died.

As a result of the incident with Chris, Gatesby County Council is notified that Dionne's younger son, Hans, is likely to be in danger of neglect and mistreatment. Consequently, it takes Hans into care. In fact, Hans is a very talented footballer and has already been signed by Manchester United Youth. Since Dionne is an avid football fan, she treats Hans very well indeed, and always ensures that he is with his (doting) grandmother during her frequent pub visits and absences. As a result of being removed from his supportive family environment, Hans develops an anxiety disorder, can no longer play football and loses his contract with Manchester United. Dionne cannot cope with this development and commits suicide.

2.1 Introduction

The duty of care is the primary means of discriminating between those instances of damage which attract compensation in negligence and those which do not. It is sometimes thus referred to as a control mechanism. Its essence lies in identifying a defendant's sphere of legal influence: which people, property and interests are those to whom the defendant has some potential responsibility. It is always worth remembering that negligence is not an intentional tort: this means that none of us knows whether we are going to be a defendant or a claimant in a negligence action in the future. This is why it makes sense to limit the potential liability of defendants to some extent, in a way which is less appropriate where the defendant has acted with the *intention* of causing harm to another. If someone makes a conscious choice to harm another, it is more intuitively acceptable to leave them to bear the full consequences of that choice. Whilst it is true that, in negligence, a defendant might to some extent have made a choice not to act reasonably, there is an intuitive moral distinction between this and the intention deliberately to cause harm.

2.2 Foundations of the modern tort of negligence

The tort of negligence, as we know it today, can be traced back to what is probably one of the most well-known cases of all, *Donoghue v Stevenson* [1932].[1] Prior to this, any judicial recognition of negligence that there was occurred in specific instances only, the most well known being that of innkeepers or medics who did not behave at a level that could be expected from their profession.[2] In *Donoghue*, however, the common law first recognised that harm caused by anyone's negligent actions

1   [1932] AC 562.
2   For an engaging and detailed account of the history of this tort, see P.H. Winfield, 'The history of negligence in the law of torts' (1926) 42 LQR 184.

could be compensated under certain conditions. It is difficult to understand, from a 21st-century perspective, just what a sea-change *Donoghue* represented, particularly since negligence can now be said to be the dominant tort in terms of both notoriety and volume of litigation. Prior to 1932, however, most people injured by another's negligent behaviour had no means of recovery unless they were in a contractual relationship with their injurer. Happily for those who need to learn about this area of law, *Donoghue* itself is a highly memorable case.

KEY CASE

Donoghue v Stevenson [1932] AC 562

The claimant's friend bought her a ginger beer float[3] at a café in Paisley. The café owner poured out some of the ginger beer and the claimant consumed part of the float before her friend dispensed the remainder of the bottle's contents into her glass. It was at this point, the claimant alleged, that the remains of a decomposed snail came out of the bottle.[4] The claimant sued the manufacturer of the ginger beer for the shock and gastroenteritis which she developed as a result of seeing the snail's presence in her half-consumed drink, and this was deemed by the House of Lords to disclose a valid cause of action.

Since the claimant herself had not bought the ginger beer, she was not privy to any contract under which she could have recovered.[5] There was, therefore, no remedy available in the common law as it then stood to assist her, or indeed to assist any individual in her position. This was the state of affairs which gave rise to one of the most famous judgments in English law: Lord Atkins' enunciation of the 'neighbour principle':

> At present I content myself with pointing out that in English law there must be, and is, some general conception of relations giving rise to a

duty of care, of which the particular cases found in the books are but instances. The liability for negligence, whether you style it such or treat it as in other systems as a species of 'culpa', is no doubt based upon a general public sentiment of moral wrongdoing for which the offender must pay. But acts or omissions which any moral code would censure cannot in a practical world be treated so as to give a right to every person injured by them to demand relief. In this way rules of law arise which limit the range of complainants and the extent of their remedy. The rule that you are to love your neighbour becomes in law, you must not injure your neighbour; and the lawyer's question, Who is my neighbour? receives a restricted reply. You must take reasonable care to avoid acts or omissions which you can reasonably foresee would be likely to injure your neighbour. Who, then, in law is my neighbour? The answer seems to be – persons who are so closely and directly affected by my act that I ought reasonably to have them in contemplation as being so affected when I am directing my mind to the acts or omissions which are called in question.[6]

In 236 words, Lord Atkin thereby launched the tort of negligence as we know it today.

Lord Atkin's concise framing of the neighbour principle forms the basis of the duty of care in the modern tort, and, whilst it is not sufficient in its own right to tell us all we need to know about duty in the 21st century, it remains a crucial bedrock of principle on which subsequent developments have been based. It is, therefore, very valuable as a first principle from which to build an understanding

---

3 Ginger beer poured over ice cream.
4 The facts of this were never actually proved, since the House of Lords dealt only with the purely legal question of whether the assumed facts disclosed a valid cause of action.
5 Which would have been straightforward.
6 At 580–1.

of the duty of care concept: we have a duty to prevent injury to those and to that which we foresee we might injure if we act negligently. Since 1932, the tort of negligence has developed extensively, and, whilst *Donoghue* remains highly significant in terms of the tort's basic principle, there are now (unsurprisingly) a wide range of more recent authorities with which you need to be familiar.

2.3 Establishing a duty of care

2.3.1   From *Caparo* to *Robinson*

There is no single test for establishing whether a duty of care exists in the tort of negligence. Lord Bridge made this clear in *Caparo Industries v Dickman* [1990].

KEY CASE

Caparo Industries v Dickman [1990] 2 AC 605

The defendants were auditors, who had prepared an annual report in respect of a company, F plc, in accordance with ss 236 and 237 of the Companies Act 1985. The claimants, who were existing shareholders in F plc, bought some shares before the publication of the defendant's report and, after it was published, purchased more shares in order to take over the company. They claimed that the defendants had been negligent in their preparation of the accounts and that, since it was foreseeable that potential investors would rely on such a report in making investment decisions, a duty of care was owed by those defendants to such investors and to shareholders. The House of Lords held that no such duty was owed. Reasonable foreseeability, it said, was not sufficient in the circumstances, and there had to be more to the relationship between the parties.[7] In these situations, reports were created in order to allow shareholders to exercise their rights in general meetings, and were not generated in order to inform investment decisions.

Ironically, the judgment in which Lord Bridge made this assertion went on to be used as just such a test for nearly a quarter of a century, until the Supreme Court gave renewed emphasis to his point in *Michael v Chief Constable of South Wales* [2015] and *Robinson v Chief Constable of West Yorkshire Police* [2018].

KEY CASE

Michael v Chief Constable of South Wales [2015] UKSC 2

The victim had called the police from her mobile phone in the early of hours of one morning. The call was picked up across the county border by a neighbouring police force. During the call, the victim told the call handler that her ex-partner had come to her house, assaulted her and threatened to come back to kill her. The call handler apparently failed to hear the victim's recounting of the death threat, and reported hearing her say only that her ex-partner had threatened to hit her. Consequently, when the call was passed on to the local police force, it was downgraded from an issue requiring a response within five minutes to one requiring a response within 60 minutes. The handler told the victim to keep her phone free because local police would need to contact her. Fifteen minutes after the emergency call was made, and before any police had attended

---

7   We will return to what is required for this relationship in Chapter 3 (Pure Economic Loss).

the scene, the victim made another call to the police, in which she was heard to scream. On attending the house, the police found that she had been stabbed to death by her former partner. He was subsequently convicted of murder, and the victim's estate and dependants sued the police for negligence and for breach of Article 2 of the Convention for the Protection of Human Rights and Fundamental Freedoms. The Supreme Court held that the police owed no duty of care in negligence, but allowed the Article 2 claim to proceed to trial. In the view of the Supreme Court, there was insufficient proximity between the police force and the victim on the facts of this case, since the duty of care of the police force was owed to the public at large.[8]

■ VIEWPOINT

Does it surprise you that there is insufficient proximity between the police force and victims of crime on facts such as these? Do you think the current common law approach is defensible?

In *Michael*, Lord Toulson said:

> In *Caparo Industries plc v Dickman* [1990] 2 AC 605 Lord Bridge (with whom Lords Roskill, Ackner and Oliver of Aylmerton agreed) emphasised the inability of any single general principle to provide a practical test which could be applied to every situation to determine whether a duty of care is owed and, if so, what is its scope. He said, at pp 617–618, that there must be not only foreseeability of damage, but there must also exist between the party owing the duty and the party to whom it is owed a relationship characterised by the law as one of 'proximity' or 'neighbourhood', and the situation should be one in which the court considers it fair, just and reasonable that the court should impose a duty of a given scope on one party for the benefit of the other. He added that the concepts both of 'proximity' and 'fairness' were not susceptible of any definition which would make them useful as practical tests, but were little more than labels to attach to features of situations which the law recognised as giving rise to a duty of care. Paradoxically, this passage in Lord Bridge's speech has sometimes come to be treated as a blueprint for deciding cases, despite the pains which the author took to make clear that it was not intended to be any such thing.[9]

What Lord Bridge actually said in *Caparo* was:

> [I]n addition to the foreseeability of damage, necessary ingredients in any situation giving rise to a duty of care are that there should exist between the party owing the duty and the party to whom it is owed a relationship characterised by the law as one of 'proximity' or 'neighbourhood' and that the situation should be one in which the court considers it fair, just and reasonable that the law should impose a duty of a given scope upon the one party for the benefit of the other. But it is implicit in the passages referred to that the concepts of proximity and fairness embodied in these additional ingredients are not susceptible of any such precise definition as would be necessary to give them utility as practical tests, but amount in effect to little more than convenient labels to attach to the features of different specific situations which, on a detailed examination of all the circumstances, the law recognises pragmatically as giving rise to a duty of care of a given scope. Whilst recognising, of course, the importance of the underlying general principles common to the whole field of

---

8   We will return to this issue at 2.5 below (Liability of Public Bodies).
9   At [106].

negligence, I think the law has now moved in the direction of attaching greater significance to the more traditional categorisation of distinct and recognisable situations as guides to the existence, the scope and the limits of the varied duties of care which the law imposes. We must now, I think, recognise the wisdom of the words of Brennan J. in the High Court of Australia in *Sutherland Shire Council v Heyman* (1985) 60 A.L.R. 1, 43–44, where he said:

> 'It is preferable, in my view, that the law should develop novel categories of negligence incrementally and by analogy with established categories, rather than by a massive extension of a prima facie duty of care restrained only by indefinable considerations which ought to negative, or to reduce or limit the scope of the duty or the class of person to whom it is owed.'[10]

You will often see, therefore, references made to a '*Caparo* test', which is said to have three stages:

- Was the damage reasonably foreseeable?
- Was there a sufficiently proximate relationship between the parties?
- Would it be 'fair, just and reasonable' for the court to impose a duty of care, having regard to policy concerns?

In *Robinson*, the most recent Supreme Court consideration of the issue, Lord Reed said:

> Where the existence or non-existence of a duty of care has been established, a consideration of justice and reasonableness forms part of the basis on which the law has arrived at the relevant principles. It is therefore unnecessary and inappropriate to reconsider whether the existence of the duty is fair, just and reasonable (subject to the possibility that this court may be invited to depart from an established line of authority) …
>
> It is normally only in a novel type of case, where established principles do not provide an answer, that the courts need to go beyond those principles in order to decide whether a duty of care should be recognised. Following the *Caparo* case, the characteristic approach of the common law in such situations is to develop incrementally and by analogy with established authority. The drawing of an analogy depends on identifying the legally significant features of the situations with which the earlier authorities were concerned. The courts also have to exercise judgement when deciding whether a duty of care should be recognised in a novel type of case. It is the exercise of judgement in those circumstances that involves consideration of what is 'fair, just and reasonable'. As Lord Millett observed in *McFarlane v Tayside Health Board* [2000] 2 AC 59, 108, the court is concerned to maintain the coherence of the law and the avoidance of inappropriate distinctions if injustice is to be avoided in other cases. But it is also 'engaged in a search for justice, and this demands that the dispute be resolved in a way which is fair and reasonable and accords with ordinary notions of what is fit and proper'.[11]

KEY CASE

Robinson v Chief Constable of West Yorkshire Police [2018] UKSC 4

The claimant was a 76-year-old pedestrian when she was injured during an attempted arrest carried out by the police. The arrest had taken place in a busy shopping street in a city centre, and those officers involved had recognised that the suspect was likely to resist arrest. The Supreme Court held

---

10 At 617–8.
11 At [26]–[27]. See also Lord Bingham in *Customs and Excise Comrs v Barclays Bank plc* [2007] 1 AC 181 at [7].

that the police in this case did owe the claimant a duty of care because they had actively created a risk of harm to passers-by and they had foreseen that such harm might well result from their actions.

The Court made it clear that it was applying normal common law principles of negligence in reaching this result, from which the police were not immune.[12]

2.3.2 Legally significant features

Where does this leave us? It might seem as if the combination of these three decisions provides less than helpful guidance for those trying to establish, on any given set of facts, whether a duty of care in negligence should be imposed or not. Since, as students, you are in the happy position of not having to consider the real-life implications of any conclusions you might reach about the existence or otherwise of a duty of care, your principal objective is to make it clear that you know what the relevant cases say, and to apply them in a reasonable way to the facts of any problem question you may encounter. There is no escaping the fact that establishing the existence of a duty of care in negligence is fraught with difficulty. Indeed, as the judgments of Lords Toulson and Reed in *Michael* and *Robinson* both suggest, common law courts, even at the highest level, have been doing it wrong for years. Try, therefore, not to be intimidated by what is a very difficult task: taking concepts that appear to be both nebulous and overlapping, and attempting to explain how you have used them. In truth, judges have long felt the same, and we have it on excellent authority that not only the labels, but the substantive ideas themselves, are not always easily separable:

> It is difficult to resist the conclusion that what have been treated as three separate requirements are, at least in most cases, in fact merely facets of the same thing, for in some cases the degree of foreseeability is such that it is from that alone the requisite proximity can be deduced, whilst in others the absence of the essential relationship can most rationally be attributed simply to the court's view that it would not be fair and reasonable to hold the defendant responsible.[13]

Following both *Michael* and *Robinson*, therefore, employing the three considerations set out by Lord Bridge in *Caparo* as a standalone test for the existence of a duty of care in negligence would be inadvisable. In both recent cases, the Supreme Court put far more emphasis on the importance of developing the law 'incrementally and by analogy with established authority'. The starting point of any duty inquiry was always to ask whether the defendant was in a relationship with the claimant which the law already recognises as giving rise to a duty of care. Obvious examples of such relationships are doctor and patient, lawyer and client, teacher and pupil, parent and child, and driver and passenger. Presented with such a relationship, there is no need to ask questions about fairness, justice or reasonableness. It is enough to explain that the relationship in question is an established duty situation, and to cite any of the authorities in which such a duty has been recognised or assumed. For example, if the defendant is a doctor and the claimant a patient of hers, cite *Bolam v Friern HMC*, *Wilsher v Essex Health Authority* [1957] or *Barnett v Kensington and Chelsea HMC*, [1968] for example. If the defendant is a driver and the claimant a passenger, cite *Nettleship v Weston* [1971], *Pitts v Hunt* [1990] [1990] or *Owens v Brimmell* [1977], and so on. Do not, therefore, embark on an analysis of the situation according to *Caparo* [1990] considerations. This is unnecessary and incorrect as a matter of law.

Situations such as those referred to above, where the relationship is clearly one for which numerous examples could straightforwardly be given, are the easy ones. Matters become a little

---

12 Again, for more detail on the application of common law principles of negligence to the police and similar bodies, see below at 2.5.
13 Lord Oliver in *Caparo* [1990] 2 AC 605 at 633.

more challenging when the relationship in question does not map exactly on to an existing duty situation. This is where Lord Reed's words in *Robinson* are helpful. Recall:

> The drawing of an analogy depends on identifying *the legally significant features* of the situations with which the earlier authorities were concerned. The courts also have to exercise judgement when deciding whether a duty of care should be recognised in a novel type of case. It is the exercise of judgement in those circumstances that involves consideration of what is 'fair, just and reasonable'.

This is precisely what the Supreme Court had to do in *James-Bowen v Commissioner of Police for the Metropolis* [2018].

KEY CASE

James-Bowen v Commissioner of Police for the Metropolis [2018] UKSC 40

The claimants were police officers who alleged that the Commissioner had been negligent in defending proceedings brought against her by a suspected terrorist. In those proceedings, the suspect claimed that the Commissioner's officers (the claimants) had subjected him to gratuitous violence during his arrest, and that she was vicariously liable for his damage. In not conducting her defence reasonably, the officers claimed that the Commissioner had thereby caused them reputational and economic harm, and that she owed them a duty of care in relation to these interests. In the Supreme Court, the claimants' case was based on there being an implied duty of trust and confidence between them and the Commissioner; such a term being one implied into all contracts of employment. Whilst police officers do not have contracts of employment,[14] their argument was that their relationship with the Commissioner was sufficiently analogous to an employment relationship that the same term could be implied. The Supreme Court did not agree that the implied duty of trust and confidence could be extended to generate a general duty to protect employees (or quasi-employees) from reputational and economic harm, and further found that no duty arose using the principles derived from *Caparo* and *Robinson*. Lord Lloyd-Jones was very clear about the fact that:

the present case is very clearly one in which it is sought to extend a duty of care to a new situation. As Lord Reed explained in *Robinson*, in determining whether such a duty should be recognised the law will proceed incrementally and by analogy with previous decisions ... In addition, the proposed duty will be tested against considerations of legal policy and judgement will have to be exercised with particular regard to both the achievement of justice in the particular case and the coherent development of the law.[15]

The judgment goes on to consider the legally significant features of several cases which could be said to have certain similarities to the facts of *James-Bowen*, before concluding that an analogy could not be made with those on which a duty of care had been found to exist. Lord Lloyd-Jones then went on to exercise 'legal judgement' to decide whether this new situation should nevertheless be one in which a duty of care should be recognised. It is worth setting out the 'considerations of legal policy' which were employed in this reasoning:

> The interests of an employer who is sued on the basis that he is vicariously liable for the tortious conduct of his employees differ fundamentally from the interests of those employees. The financial, commercial and reputational standing of the employer may be at stake. It is the employer who will incur the cost of defending

---

14   Rather, the terms on which they hold their office are governed by the Police Regulations 2003 (SI 2003/527).
15   At [23].

the proceedings which, however successful the defence may be, is most unlikely to be recovered in full, and who, if unsuccessful, will bear the liability to the claimant. The employer must be able to make his own investigation into the claim and to assess its strength based on the conduct of his employee and the prospects of a successful defence. In this regard, he will need to form his own view as to the reliability and veracity of his employee and as to how the employee is likely to perform as a witness. The interests of insurers may have to be taken into account ...

These stark differences between the interests of employer and employee strongly suggest that it would not be fair, just or reasonable to impose on an employer a duty of care to defend legal proceedings so as to protect the economic or reputational interests of his employee.

In the present case, moreover, the Commissioner is not merely in a position analogous to that of an employer. She also holds public office and has responsibility for the Metropolitan Police Service. This adds a further dimension to this appeal because in the conduct of the proceedings against her she must be free to act as she considers appropriate in accordance with her public duty. This duty is, to my mind, totally inconsistent with her owing a duty of care to protect the reputational interests of her employees when defending litigation based on vicarious liability for their alleged misconduct.[16]

In concluding his judgment with the words, 'For these reasons I would allow the appeal. The imposition of the claimed duty would not be fair, just or reasonable',[17] Lord Lloyd-Jones demonstrates that the *Caparo* considerations, whilst not to be regarded as a standalone test, are clearly still highly influential in the duty of care inquiry. Lord Lloyd-Jones returned to that inquiry some months later in *Darnley v Croydon NHS Trust* [2018] UKSC 50.

KEY CASE

Darnley v Croydon NHS Trust [2018] UKSC 50

The claimant attended the defendant's Accident and Emergency Department with his friend, having incurred a head injury during an unprovoked attack. The administrative receptionist on duty informed him that he would have to wait up to four or five hours before being seen by a medical practitioner. In fact, the standard procedure at the hospital was for head injury patients to be seen within 30 minutes by a triage nurse. As a result of being giving misleading information about the likely length of his wait, the claimant decided that he felt too ill to stay in the waiting room, and went home to bed. Had he known that he was likely to be seen within 30 minutes, he would have stayed and been examined. He was later returned to hospital by ambulance and had to undergo emergency neurosurgery. Ultimately, however, he was left with permanent brain damage as a result of his injuries. Both the trial judge and the Court of Appeal found in favour of the NHS Trust, the latter by majority on the basis that the hospital owed no duty of care to advise patients about waiting times. The Supreme Court allowed the claimant's appeal, finding that the case fell within an established duty of care situation for NHS Trusts. At [16], Lord Lloyd-Jones, with whom the other members of the Panel agreed, said:

To my mind ... the present case falls squarely within an established category of duty of care. It has long been established that such a duty is owed by those who provide and run a casualty department to persons presenting themselves complaining of illness or injury and before they are treated or received into care in the hospital's wards. The duty is one to take reasonable care not to cause physical injury to the patient (*Barnett v Chelsea and Kensington Hospital Management Committee* [1969] 1 QB 428, per Nield J at pp 435-

---

16   At [30] – [33].
17   At [47].

436). In the present case, as soon as the appellant had attended at the respondent's A & E department seeking medical attention for the injury he had sustained, had provided the information requested by the receptionist and had been 'booked in', he was accepted into the system and entered into a relationship with the respondent of patient and health care provider ... This is a distinct and recognisable situation in which the law imposes a duty of care. Moreover, the scope of the duty to take reasonable care not to act in such a way as foreseeably to cause such a patient to sustain physical injury clearly extends to a duty to take reasonable care not to provide misleading information which may foreseeably cause physical injury. While it is correct that no authority has been cited in these proceedings which deals specifically with misleading information provided by a receptionist in an A & E department causing physical injury, it is not necessary to address, in every instance where the precise factual situation has not previously been the subject of a reported judicial decision, whether it would be fair, just and reasonable to impose a duty of care. It is sufficient that the case falls within an established category in which the law imposes a duty of care.

Darnley stands as something of an admonitory reminder not to complicate the duty of care question by failing to apply the established categories approach properly. The Supreme Court's judgment makes it clear that the question in this case was a very simple one: namely, 'do hospitals owe a duty of care to patients not to cause physical injury by providing misleading information?' This was treated in *Darnley* as being analogous to asking whether hospitals have a duty to act in such a way as not to cause reasonably foreseeable harm to their patients; a duty which clearly falls within an established category. Another significant point made in *Darnley*, and to which we will return in the next chapter, is the crucial importance of distinguishing between the questions of duty and of breach. The question of whether a duty of care exists is both anterior to, and independent of, the question of whether that duty has been breached.[18]

PROBLEM QUESTION TECHNIQUE

One day in July, four officers from Ambledon Police go to the local park, intending to arrest members of a drug-dealing gang whom they know meet there in the evenings. They enter the park at 11pm. They know the gang is likely to resist arrest. When the gang notices the arrival of the Ambledon officers, they pull out knives and guns, causing a stand-off. Chris, a 9-year-old boy whose parents pay little attention to what he does or where he goes, is in the park at the time and, seeing the events unfold, panics and screams. Startled, a member of the gang shoots Chris, and he falls to the ground, injured.

▸ In order to apply the incremental approach, it is necessary to have a clear idea of what 'legally significant features' are, so that the relevant analogies can be made in identifying new duty of care situations. Of course, the common law being what it is, there exists no definitive list of what these features might be. It is possible, however, to glean from the reasoning employed in existing cases what they are, particularly when we combine this with what we know the purpose of the exercise to be: a coherent development of the law.

▸ This is the point at which the *Caparo* considerations come into play, so that, in comparing factual situations, we are comparing the degree of reasonable foreseeability of damage, the proximity of the relationship and the fairness, justice and reasonableness of there being a duty imposed. The tenor

---

18   See Chapter 5 (Breach of Duty).

of the judgments in both *Michael* and *Robinson*, however, suggest that these are all parts of a holistic exercise, and not a series of discrete stages.

▸ It would be worthwhile to ask to what degree the injury to Chris was reasonably foreseeable when compared to the injury to Mrs Robinson. The answer to this will give us some indication of how proximate the relationship between the police and Chris was, in comparison to that in the *Robinson* case.

▸ Finally, the answer to both of the previous questions will provide input into the assessment of how fair, just and reasonable it would be to impose a duty of care on the police in such circumstances. Making it clear that this is the process with which you are engaging, on the basis of the recent Supreme Court decisions, should be your aim. Try not to be put off by the fact that it might not be clear to you whether this should generate an outcome of duty or an outcome of no duty. Remember, it is the quality of your case law application that counts.

DIFFERENT PERSPECTIVES on duty of care

D. Nolan, 'Deconstructing the Duty of Care' (2013) 129 LQR 559

Nolan makes the case for moving away from the duty of care as a standalone analytical stage of the negligence inquiry, and explains how, strictly speaking, the duty of care is not a duty in the true sense of the term. Were it to be a duty, conventionally conceived, a breach of it would be actionable without proof of damage, and yet damage, Nolan points out, is the gist of negligence. Nolan goes on to argue that what is referred to as the 'duty of care' is really just an umbrella term to cover several issues, and that negligence law would be far more coherent and effective were these issues to be examined under separate categories such as, for example, remoteness. In other words, rather than asking whether a claimant was foreseeable from the defendant's point of view as a question of duty, the same aim could be achieved through the remoteness inquiry. Were the duty of care to be deconstructed in this way, Nolan argues that the negligence inquiry would be more focused and structured, that significant issues would be better scrutinised, that law and fact would no longer be confused and that much confusion and incoherence could be avoided.

N. McBride, 'Duties of Care in Negligence – Do They Really Exist?' (2004) 3 OJLS 417–41

McBride here argues that the duties of care in negligence really do exist. His analysis separates perspectives on this issue into two: cynics and idealists. Cynics are those who believe that individual A has no duty to be careful towards B, but just a duty to pay damages to B, should B suffer a loss caused by A's fault. Idealists, on the other hand, regard the duty of care in negligence as requiring A to act carefully towards B and that any subsequent obligation to pay damages is only secondary to that. It is the latter, idealist view that McBride considers to be the correct one. The principal justifications for his position are that, under the cynical view, the law would only take an interest in claimants once they have been injured (rather than taking an interest in preventing their being injured); that the cynical view cannot explain the potential to award exemplary damages (because cynics do not regard those who breach duties of care as doing anything wrong), or courts' willingness to award injunctions (because cynics would say that the courts have no reason to intervene before harm occurs); and neither can it explain the law's willingness to expand causal tests to ensure that certain claimants receive compensation, as in *Reeves*[19] and *Fairchild*,[20] for example (because cynics would say that defendants have an option whether to be careful towards claimants, which is the opposite of what these cases imply).

---

19   See 7.5.2.
20   See 6.4.3.

2.4 Acts vs omissions or misfeasance vs nonfeasance

2.4.1 The general rule

Generally, and despite the suggestion to the contrary made by Lord Atkin in *Donoghue*,[21] there is no liability in negligence for failing to act. Outside of certain situations, we have no duty to intervene in others' lives to make them better. There is, for example, no general duty in English law to rescue a fellow human being from danger, even if no harm to oneself is likely to occur. Nor, as we saw in *Michael*, is there any general duty to prevent any individual from harming another.[22] There are two principal reasons for this. First, there is the 'Why pick on me?' argument, outlined by Lord Hoffmann in *Stovin v Wise* [1996]:[23]

> There are sound reasons why omissions require different treatment from positive conduct. It is one thing for the law to say that a person who undertakes some activity shall take reasonable care not to cause damage to others. It is another thing for the law to require that a person who is doing nothing in particular shall take steps to prevent another from suffering harm from the acts of third parties … or natural causes. One can put the matter in political, moral or economic terms. In political terms it is less of an invasion of an individual's freedom for the law to require him to consider the safety of others in his actions than to impose upon him a duty to rescue or protect. A moral version of this point may be called the 'why pick on me?' argument. A duty to prevent harm to others or to render assistance to a person in danger or distress may apply to a large and indeterminate class of people who happen to be able to do something. Why should one be held liable rather than another? In economic terms, the efficient allocation of resources usually requires an activity should bear its own costs. If it benefits from being able to impose some of its costs on other people (what economists call 'externalities') the market is distorted because the activity appears cheaper than it really is. So liability to pay compensation for loss caused by negligent conduct acts as a deterrent against increasing the cost of the activity to the community and reduces externalities. But there is no similar justification for requiring a person who is not doing anything to spend money on behalf of someone else. Except in special cases (such as marine salvage) English law does not reward someone who voluntarily confers a benefit on another. So there must be some special reason why he should have to put his hand in his pocket.

The second reason for the law's reluctance to treat omissions in the same way as acts is that there are only so many ways in which one can perform a certain act, but potentially countless ways in which one can omit to do something. A law which prevented omissions would often have the effect of compelling individuals to act in certain ways; something which English law is, outside of very specific circumstances, loath to do.[24] To do so would be regarded as too great an infringement of personal autonomy.

---

21 [1932] AC 562 at 580–1 and see above at 2.2.

22 This was one of the 'ordinary principles of common law negligence' the Supreme Court said it was applying in that case. See, e.g., Baroness Hale at [190].

23 [1996] AC 923 at 943.

24 In terms of remedies, for example, English law is far more likely to issue a prohibitory injunction, preventing someone from acting in a certain way, than it is to award a mandatory injunction, *compelling* someone to act in a certain way. See A. Burrows, *Remedies for Torts, Breach of Contract and Equitable Wrongs*, 4th edn (Oxford University Press, 2019), p 442 and p 538.

KEY CASE

Sutradhar v National Environmental Research Council [2006] UKHL 33

The claimant suffered from arsenic poisoning as a result of drinking water that had been tested by the British Geological Society (BGS). BGS had tested the water for a number of toxins, and had certified it safe as far as those substances were concerned, but arsenic was not one of those for which it tested. It had not, therefore, executed its activities poorly; it had simply not engaged in a particular activity. The House of Lords held that there could be no liability on such facts for what BGS had not done.

Often, the question of omissions liability arises in relation to the actions of third parties, where the claimant alleges that the defendant failed to act to prevent damage being caused by another.

KEY CASE

Smith v Littlewoods Organisation Ltd [1987] AC 241

The defendants acquired a disused cinema with the intention of developing it. Vagrants moved into the site and, having lit a couple of small fires before, of which the defendants and police were unaware, ultimately set fire to the building. This fire spread and caused damage to the claimants' neighbouring property, for which they sued the defendants in negligence. The House of Lords held that there was no liability on the facts, and that the defendants were not therefore responsible in law for the behaviour of the third party vagrants. Lord Goff's reasoning emphasised the absence of a duty of care in this situation, owing primarily to the lack of foreseeability of the damage occurring, and it is his judgment which has endured, and been referred to with approval most recently by the Supreme Court in *Michael*.[25]

It is common for this also to involve public authorities, where the claimant alleges that the authority should have acted to prevent a certain injurious course of action from happening; caused either by a third party or by a natural event. We saw this in the case of *Michael*, above, and will return to it in greater detail at 2.5 below (Liability of Public Bodies).

2.4.2   When will liability for omissions arise?

Despite the existence of this significant general rule, there are situations in which liability will be imposed on a defendant for omitting to act. These, however, all require there to be some preexisting reason for the defendant to be expected to act positively to protect the claimant from harm.

In these situations, the nature of the relationship between the claimant and the defendant, or between the defendant and a third party, is such that the law *does* expect that defendant to take active steps to prevent foreseeable harm coming to the claimant. In such situations, the problems that arise in relation to the open-ended nature of omissions liability are diluted, if not dispelled, by the fact that the defendant generally exercises some form of control over factors which affect the claimant's

---

25   See, e.g., Lord Toulson at [97].

situation. These situations could be described, therefore, as being not so much about omitting to act, but about omitting to direct that control appropriately.

One of the most well-known examples of this, in which the defendant exercised control over third parties, is *Dorset Yacht Co Ltd v Home Office* [1970].

KEY CASE

Dorset Yacht Co Ltd v Home Office [1970] AC 1004

The claimant's yacht was damaged by seven boys who were, at the relevant time, detainees of a borstal (a detention institution for young offenders), and so were under the supervision of the Home Office's employees. The boys had evaded the supervision of the borstal officers, and had a history of behaving in a similar way, a fact that was known to the officers. The House of Lords did not agree with the Home Office's argument that liability cannot be imposed for wrongs done by another who is of full age and capacity, unless that other was acting as a servant or agent of the defendant. It held that where the defendant's duty was to guard against the very risk that eventuated in the harm of which the claimant complains, an omission to prevent that risk from materialising could ground liability in negligence.

A similar point to *Dorset Yacht Co Ltd* was made by the House of Lords in *Reeves v Commissioner of Metropolitan Police* [2000], where the defendant's control was exercised over the victim of the wrong, as opposed to the perpetrator of it.

KEY CASE

Reeves v Commissioner of Metropolitan Police [2000] 1 AC 360

The victim committed suicide whilst in police custody. He had been a known suicide risk and the police had not taken all reasonable precautions to prevent his suicide in the circumstances. The House of Lords once more had to respond to an argument that an individual of sound mind had committed the act which caused the damage, and that liability should not attach to a failure to prevent this. It took a similar line in this case, and rejected the argument, imposing liability because of the degree of control the defendant exercised over individuals in custody. Were the suicide of a prisoner to be held to negate the police's duty of care in such circumstances (where the duty required the police to guard against such an eventuality), that duty would be redundant.[26]

The control exercised by the defendant can also be exercised over the property of the claimant, as in *Stansbie v Troman*,[27] in which the defendant decorator, whilst working on the claimant's house, left it unlocked, despite having received explicit instructions not to do so. When the claimant's house was burgled as a result, the defendant was held liable for the loss: another illustration of control requiring a defendant to do more than passively to allow risks to eventuate.

---

26 This case overlaps with discussions of remoteness (Chapter 7), *novus actus interveniens* (7.5) and defences (Chapter 16). For the exercise of control over the victim, see also *Barrett v Ministry of Defence* [1995] 1 WLR 1217, CA.

27 [1948] 2 KB 48.

Omissions are also actionable in general terms under the Occupiers' Liability Acts 1957 and 1984.[28] These will be dealt with in detail in Chapter 8. Occupiers' liability is, however, another illustration of the law imposing liability for not acting where to do so would be appropriate, given the control exercised by the defendant in relation to the claimant: in this case, having control over premises which could injure the claimant or her property.

This is another well-established category in which liability will attach to an omission. In this context, the omission must be one which allows a risk created by the defendant to eventuate. The same principle applies in the criminal law, and prevents individuals from effectively externalising their risks: in other words, it prevents individuals from creating those risks and imposing their costs on others by not acting to abate their effects.

MAKING CONNECTIONS

In the criminal law, the case of *R v Miller*[29] illustrates this point. The defendant in that case was a vagrant who had allowed his cigarette to set fire to his mattress. Having been asleep when the chain of events began, he awoke to find the mattress smouldering. Rather than taking any steps to ameliorate the situation, he simply moved into another room and resumed his sleep. The House of Lords upheld his conviction for arson on the specific basis that Miller's (albeit unintentional) starting of the fire was what created the duty to abate it. Lord Diplock described the duty as being 'to take measures that lie within one's power to counteract a danger that one has oneself created'.[30]

The most well-known illustration of this principle in tort is *Haynes v Harwood*,[31] in which the defendants were deemed to have created a risk by keeping horses tethered in the street. When the horses bolted after being hit with a stone thrown by a boy, and the claimant was injured in the ensuing chaos, the defendants were held liable for not preventing the injuries which were an eventuation of the risk they had initially created. The notion of risk creation has a further reach. A defendant does not, however, have to be the initial source of a risk in order to be liable for omitting to abate it. In *Goldman v Hargrave*,[32] the defendant landowner was found liable for the damage done to a neighbouring property by a fire which spread from a burning tree on his land. Whilst the tree had been set on fire by lightning, the defendant was deemed to have adopted the risk because he cut the tree down, but did no more than that to prevent the fire from spreading. This reasoning fits well with the control analysis explored above, and is certainly consistent with the law of torts' general willingness to hold occupiers of land liable for omitting to take active steps to mitigate risks arising on their premises. The presence of control in all of these situations could of course be said to mean that they are not really cases of 'pure' omission at all, in the same way that failing to apply car brakes when driving towards a pedestrian is not a true omission. Once one has assumed control of something, be that property, another's welfare, or another's behaviour, then failing to exercise that control in an effective way becomes an omission to deal with the consequences of an earlier act, rather than a standalone omission to intervene in the world. It is only in relation to the latter that the policy concerns outlined by Lord Hoffmann, for example,[33] are relevant.

---

28 See Chapter 8 (Occupiers' Liability).
29 [1983] 2 AC 161.
30 At 176.
31 [1935] 1 KB 146.
32 [1967] 1 AC 645.
33 *Stovin v Wise* [1996] AC 923 at 943.

It is not, however, only in relation to the *creation* of a risk that liability for omissions can arise. In *ABC v St George's Hospital NHS Trust* [2017],[34] the Court of Appeal found that a duty of care could exist where, even in the absence of an express assumption of responsibility, the defendant has the knowledge and resources to mitigate a risk to which the claimant is exposed, and from which that claimant is unable to protect herself.

PROBLEM QUESTION TECHNIQUE

Chris's mother, Dionne, is walking past the park on her way home from the pub. She sees, and recognises Chris, but she is heavily under the influence of several substances, and thinks he is probably just having a nap. She does not bother to check on him and walks home. Meanwhile, the Ambledon officers are so focused on preventing the gang from escaping that nobody pays any attention to Chris for nearly ten minutes. By the time one of the officers reaches him, he has lost a huge amount of blood and, as a result, later suffers from brain damage.

Eventually, the officers get the gang into their riot van. As they are escorting them in, they hear several members of the gang blaming the youngest member, Ed, for the arrest, calling him a 'snitch' and threatening to hurt him. On reaching the police station, one of the officers, Fern, opens the door to find Ed bleeding from several stab wounds to the chest.

▸ Here, there are three omissions – by Chris's mother, by the Ambledon police officers in the park, and by the police officers in the van.

▸ You need to consider which, if any, of these are actionable omissions. Is there, for example, a pre-existing relationship or an element of control over third parties? If so, a duty of care for the defendant to take positive steps may arise.

2.5 Liability of public bodies

2.5.1 General principles

Historically, this has been an area of some difficulty, owing in large part to some complicated, and apparently conflicting, judicial reasoning. There also arise, in relation to public bodies, policy considerations which do not apply to private individuals. For instance, there is a concern that exposing bodies to potential negligence liability will cause them to alter their means of functioning, so as to focus on being defensive, rather than on reaching their objectives. Then, there is the financial issue: every successful negligence action against a public body will divert funds away from what can be spent in the public interest (perhaps guarding against future injury or damage). Both of these points are part of a broader argument, which is that regulating the behaviour and conduct of public bodies is properly the concern of public, rather than private, law. Thankfully, some recent Supreme Court guidance has made the area quite a lot clearer and there is a sense that the case law has become more coherent. The crucial and overriding point to remember is that:

> Any liability of public bodies in the common law of negligence arises in the same way as it does for private individuals. Public bodies will, therefore, be subject to the same incremental, analogical approach, derived from *Caparo*, *Michael* and *Robinson*, as private individuals. The fact

---

34   [2017] EWCA Civ 336.

that such bodies have a public function to perform, and are authorised in this by statute, is never a standalone reason for imposing a duty of care at common law.

■ VIEWPOINT

Do you think the common law's way of dealing with public authorities in negligence is justifiable? Is it easy to explain why such authorities are treated for these purposes in the same way as individuals when they do, in many cases, have the power to affect many lives?

For common law purposes, therefore, the fact that such bodies also have a common law function is a red herring in terms of their potential liability in negligence at common law. Their public law function is regulated by public law, which means for instance that their actions and decisions can be subject to judicial review or governmental inquiry, but the case law now makes clear that these avenues exist independently of any liability to private individuals in negligence. The following two decisions made this principle clear.

KEY CASE

Stovin v Wise [1996] AC 293[35]

The defendant local authority had a power under s 79 of the Highways Act 1980 to remove highway obstructions. Despite having resolved to do so in relation to a particular bank of land, the proposed work had not been carried out when the claimant was injured in a collision caused by its presence. The claimant sued the local authority, alleging that it had a common law duty to take positive steps to remove the obstruction. The principal conclusion reached by the House of Lords was that the power afforded to the Council by s 79 did not of itself give rise to a common law duty of care in negligence. Were there to be such a duty of care (which in this case there was not), it would arise independently, and on the basis of standard common law principles.

KEY CASE

Gorringe v Calderdale [2004] UKHL 15

The claimant was driving at the speed limit over the brow of a hill when she saw a bus coming the other way. Despite the fact that the bus was in the correct lane, the claimant panicked, crashed her car and was injured. She claimed that the local authority was in breach of its duty of care by not providing warning signs at that stretch of road. The word 'Slow' had previously been painted on the road approaching the hill, but was no longer visible by the time the claimant's accident occurred. The House of Lords dismissed the claimant's appeal, finding that the authority did not owe a common law duty of care to individual road users. Although it was accepted that the defendant authority had a broad statutory duty under s 39 of the Road Safety Act 1988 to promote road safety, this did not give rise to a duty of care at common law to confer a benefit on private individuals. This decision built on *Stovin*, emphasising the point that common law duties, if they arise at all in relation to bodies carrying out statutory activities, will only do so if justified by independent common law principles, and will not be justified by the existence of a statutory duty.

---

35   We have already encountered this decision above, in terms of Lord Hoffmann's explanation of why the law treats omissions differently to positive acts; another significant aspect of the case.

Lord Hoffmann stated (at [17]):

> It is not sufficient that it might reasonably have foreseen that in the absence of such warnings, some road users might injure themselves or others. Reasonable foreseeability of physical injury is the standard criterion for determining the duty of care owed by people who undertake an activity which carries a risk of injury to others. But it is insufficient to justify the imposition of liability upon someone who simply does nothing: who neither creates the risk nor undertakes to do anything to avert it. The law does recognise such duties in special circumstances: see, for example, *Goldman v Hargrave* [1967] 1 AC 645 on the positive duties of adjoining landowners to prevent fire or harmful matter from crossing the boundary. But the imposition of such a liability upon a highway authority through the law of negligence would be inconsistent with the well established rules which have always limited its liability at common law.

Lord Hoffmann further stated (at [35]):

> Of course it is in the public interest that local authorities should take steps to promote road safety. And it would also be unwise for them to assume that all drivers will take reasonable care for their own safety or that of others. If a driver kills or injures someone else by ignoring an obvious danger, it is little consolation to the victim or his family that the other driver was wholly to blame. And even if the careless driver kills or injures only himself, the accident may have a wider impact upon his family, his economic relationships and the burden on the public services. That is why section 39 of the 1988 Act is framed as a broad public duty. ... But the public interest in promoting road safety by taking steps to reduce the likelihood that even careless drivers will have accidents does not require a private law duty to a careless driver or any other road user.

2.5.2 Tort and the Human Rights Act 1998

An extra complicating factor in the context of claims made against public bodies is the existence of the Human Rights Act (HRA) 1998, and the corresponding ability of claimants to take their cases to the European Court of Human Rights (ECtHR) if they feel that any of their rights under the European Convention on Human Rights (ECHR) has been violated. Over the past 20 years, there has been some shifting in the courts' approach to this issue. For a while, for instance, it appeared as if the tort of negligence might be adapted in order to accommodate the requirements of human rights legislation. More recently, however, the trend seems to be to allow the two avenues (claims under the HRA 1998 and claims in common law negligence) to develop independently of one another.

In order to understand how this has come about, it is worth starting with another case dealing with a claim in negligence against the police: *Hill v Chief Constable of South Yorkshire Police* [1989].

KEY CASE

Hill v Chief Constable of South Yorkshire Police [1989] 1 AC 53

The claimant's daughter was the last person to be killed by Peter Sutcliffe, the serial killer known as the Yorkshire Ripper. The claim in negligence was based on the argument that the police had breached their duty of care in carrying out their investigation and that, had they not done so, Sutcliffe would have been caught before he killed his final victim. The House of Lords held, in agreement with the first instance judge, that the police owed no duty of care to the public to apprehend criminals, and the claim was accordingly struck out. Lord Keith's judgment was highly significant for two reasons: first, for its account of why there was insufficient proximity on the facts of this case for a duty of care to arise. The second reason was his infamous use of the word 'immunity' when referring to the police and their relationship to the tort of negligence. Whilst it has now been made clear that there is no such immunity (if indeed there ever really was),[36] the

reference to this concept in *Hill* was enough to give rise to interesting developments in terms of the ECtHR's attitude towards the UK's means of dealing with such cases.

KEY CASE

Osman v UK [1999] 1 FLR 193

This was a claim made to the ECtHR by a mother and son, whose claim in negligence had been struck out by the House of Lords on the basis of the policy arguments outlined in *Hill* as to why the police did not owe a duty of care in relation to their 'investigation and suppression of crime'.[37] The original claim (*Osman v Ferguson*[38]) related to the activities of the son's teacher who, having harassed the family for a prolonged period, eventually shot

both the son and his father, killing the latter. The claimants alleged that the police had breached their duty of care in not apprehending the teacher on the basis of what he had previously done, thereby failing to prevent the ultimate shooting. The ECtHR agreed with the claimants that, in striking out their claim on the strength of *Hill* and without considering the individual merits of their case, the UK had infringed their Article 6 right to a fair trial.

Osman represents something of a nadir in terms of a constructive interaction between English courts and the ECtHR, and it received, unsurprisingly, a frosty reception from some quarters.[39] In the following case, however, the ECtHR modified its approach to the UK's use of its striking out procedure, perhaps because it was made clearer by the UK's defence team, knowing what it knew about *Osman*, that the tort of negligence does not accommodate an 'immunity' for public bodies, but instead sets out legitimate policy reasons for why, in any given case, a claim should not be allowed to proceed.

KEY CASE

Z v UK [2001] 2 FLR 612

These appeals to the ECtHR were from the conjoined appeals to the House of Lords, known as *X (Minors) v Bedfordshire CC* [1995].[40] In the first group of cases, the claim was that a local authority had failed to take into care several children who had suffered extensive abuse and neglect in their home environment. Another case concerned the local authority's removal of a child from her mother as a result of mistakenly believing that the mother's

partner had been abusing the daughter. The House of Lords had rejected the appeals, holding that none of the authorities owed a common law duty of care on such facts, because the statutory scheme in place for dealing with child abuse was incompatible with the imposition of a duty of care at common law. It was a multiple-agency system, which meant that it would not be possible justly to impose liability for failings on any one part of

36 See, e.g., *Michael and Robinson*, below, at 2.3.2.
37 This has been referred to in subsequent case law as the 'core *Hill* principle'. See, e.g., Lord Hope of Craighead in *Smith v Chief Constable of Sussex Police* [2009] AC 225 at [75].
38 [1993] 4 All ER 344.
39 See, e.g., Rt Hon Lord Hoffmann, 'Human Rights and the House of Lords' (1999) 62 MLR 159.
40 [1995] 2 AC 633.

it as opposed to another. In recognising that the claimants' human rights had indeed been infringed (the right to be free from inhumane and degrading treatment contrary to Article 3 where the first group of children were concerned, the right to private, home and family life contrary to Article 8 where the daughter in the second claim was concerned, and the right to a remedy contrary to Article 13 in both cases), the ECtHR nonetheless retreated from its previous view, taken in *Osman*, that the UK's striking out action was in principle an infringement of a claimant's right to a fair trial under Article 6. It recognised (although not unanimously) that the striking out process did not present a procedural bar to certain claimants, but was instead a forum for considering competing and legitimate policy concerns that might or might not lead to the denial of a substantive claim.

Z v UK signalled the beginning of what is likely to be viewed, particularly from the point of view of English law, as a more positive and facilitative relationship between the English courts and the ECtHR. The course of litigation in *X v Bedfordshire* to *Z v UK* provides a good illustration of why the courts seem more willing to allow the development of common law negligence to occur outside and alongside the human rights regime, as opposed to trying to accommodate the one within the other. The public law framework within which such bodies function is not conducive to the sort of bilateral private claim which is the essence of the tort of negligence. Allowing a human rights claim notwithstanding the denial of a claim in negligence on the same facts thus allows a vindication of the claimant's rights (as well as an observance of the UK's convention obligations) without unduly distorting the established form of the tort of negligence. Most of the case law since *Z v UK* with which you need to be familiar has followed this general pattern, and has maintained a conceptual and a practical separation of the two spheres.[41] There could be said to one exception to this, in *D v East Berkshire Community NHS Trust* [2005],[42] in which, faced with claims based on the wrongful removal of children from their parents, the Court of Appeal found that the public bodies concerned did owe a duty of care to the children (but not to their parents), thereby not following the House of Lords' earlier decision in *X v Bedfordshire*. On appeal by the parents, the House of Lords did not disturb the Court of Appeal's conclusions. This particular case could, however, well be explained by its timing: denying a claim in negligence but allowing a claim under the HRA 1998 to proceed, which has been the dominant approach since *Z v UK*, was not an option on these facts because the relevant infringements predated the Act.

What follows is one of the first cases to mark the division between the two remedial spheres, and it is particularly illuminating in this respect because one of the conjoined claims was considered under Article 2 of the ECHR (the right to life),[43] whilst the other was brought at common law. The House of Lords' reasoning is clearly tailored to each as a discrete issue, with independent considerations.

KEY CASE

Van Colle v Chief Constable of Hertfordshire; Smith v Chief Constable of Sussex [2008] UKHL 50

The first set of claimants were the parents of G, who was killed by a man against whom he was due to act as a prosecution witness. The second claimant was a man who had been attacked and injured by his former partner. In both cases, the victims had received several threats in advance of

---

41   See F. du Bois, 'Human rights and the tort liability of public authorities' (2011) 127 LQR 589.

42   [2005] UKHL 23.

43   A simultaneous common law claim had initially been brought in relation to the same facts, but was rejected by the Court of Appeal on the basis of the *Hill* principle, as then understood.

the attacks, and the police were aware of these.[44] The Court of Appeal had found in favour of both claimants, but the House of Lords thought that it had been wrong to do so. Its analysis of the two claims was, however, clearly distinct. In relation to the Article 2 claim, it applied the test in *Osman v UK* that, in order to be in breach of a positive obligation, the relevant authority had to know or ought to have known 'at the time' of the existence of 'a real and immediate risk to the life' of an identified individual from the acts of a third party. Since the killer of G (who had since been convicted of his murder) was unpredictable and had no history of such violence, the test on these facts had not been met. As a *separate issue*, the House of Lords (with a powerful dissent from Lord Bingham) applied the principle in *Hill* that, in the absence of special circumstances, the police owed no duty of care to individuals injured by the acts of criminals.[45]

A more recent consideration of the issue, which arguably distinguishes common law claims even more starkly from those made under the HRA 1998 is *Rabone v Pennine Care NHS Trust* [2012],[46] partly because the claimants had already settled a negligence claim on the same facts,[47] and partly because the damage for which they sought compensation (bereavement and mental anguish) was not of a type generally recognised as actionable in the tort of negligence. The claim concerned the same Article 2 issue as in *Van Colle*; that is, when will a public body owe a positive duty to protect the life of individuals? The test formulated in *Osman* and used in *Van Colle*, above, is that

> the authorities knew or ought to have known at the time of the existence of a real and immediate risk to the life of an identified individual or individuals from the criminal acts of a third party and … failed to take measures within the scope of their powers which, judged reasonably, might have been expected to avoid that risk.[48]

This test is only really useful to you, however, if you have a clear idea of how English courts have applied it, as in *Rabone*.

KEY CASE

Rabone v Pennine Care NHS Trust [2012] UKSC 2

The claimants' daughter had been admitted to the defendant hospital following a suicide attempt. In contravention of her parents' wishes, she was subsequently allowed a home visit for two days, during which she committed suicide. The Supreme Court interpreted the Strasbourg jurisprudence as holding that a duty existed to protect individuals who were under a

---

44 In *Van Colle*, the officer responsible for dealing with these threats was found by an internal disciplinary inquiry not to have done so.

45 See also *Brooks v Commissioner of Police for the Metropolis* [2005] UKHL 24, in which the House of Lords considered whether *Hill* is compatible with Article 6. Its conclusion was in the affirmative, finding that *Hill* does not confer an immunity because in 'exceptional circumstances' a duty will be held to exist by the police to individuals. The facts of *Brooks* were not deemed to be sufficiently exceptional and so Duwayne Brooks (who had been the friend present when Stephen Lawrence was murdered in a racist attack) would have to be restricted to his rights under Police Complaints Procedure in relation to his claim that he was given insufficient support and credibility following his friend's murder.

46 [2012] UKSC 2.

47 Although this was a claim under the Law Reform (Miscellaneous Provisions) Act 1934 for the benefit of the deceased's estate and not for their bereavement. See A. Tettenborn, 'Wrongful Death, Human Rights, and the Fatal Accidents Act' (2012) 128 LQR 327.

48 (1998) 29 EHRR 245 at [116].

state's control from a real and immediate risk of suicide. It found on the facts of *Rabone* that the deceased was highly vulnerable, that the defendant had assumed responsibility for her, and that she was under its control. The parents' Article 2 claim therefore succeeded.

This is an interesting case in terms of what it tells us about the way in which English courts have responded to the challenges of dealing with Strasbourg jurisprudence alongside long-established principles of negligence. On the one hand, the Supreme Court in *Rabone* was very clear

that the Article 2 claim was completely independent of common law negligence (and in fact that allowing the Article 2 claim effectively enabled the claimants to sidestep the restrictions of a common law claim). On the other hand, the language and the concepts employed in deciding whether the claimants fitted the category of 'victim' for the purposes of the HRA 1998 claim look very familiar to those used in establishing the existence of a duty of care in common law negligence; particularly in relation to the defendant's assumption of responsibility and control.

The Supreme Court considered the issue in *Rabone* once more in *Poole BC v GN* [2019], and Lord Reed took the opportunity to restate the principles governing the liability of public authorities.

KEY CASE

Poole BC v GN [2019] UKSC 25

The claimants in this case were brothers, aged nine and seven at the relevant time, who were housed with their mother by the defendant council next door to a household known for its anti-social behaviour. The family was subjected to prolonged abuse and harassment by its neighbours, and, although attempts were made by the local authority to address the situation, these were not successful. As a result, the claimants and their mother suffered from threats, damage to their house and car, and physical assault, resulting in physical and psychological damage. Both children were assessed as being in need under the Children Act 1989; one was physically and mentally disabled and the other became mentally unwell as a result of the events giving rise to the claim. They were not rehoused for five years. The claimants' case was that the local

authority owed them a duty of care at common law when exercising its functions under s 17 and s 47 of the Children Act 1989.

Lord Reed clarified the position of public authorities with respect to the existence of a common law duty of care. The message fits with the recent Supreme Court decisions discussed above: public bodies are not treated differently to private parties for this purpose. They are not therefore generally liable for failing to confer a benefit, or for harms caused by third parties. Lord Reed reiterated the point made by the Supreme Court in *Robinson v Chief Constable of West Yorkshire* – a public authority will only be liable where it foreseeably causes physical harm to another through a positive act amounting to negligence. The test in *Caparo Industries plc v Dickman* does not apply to such a case.

In a case note in the *Cambridge Law Journal*,[49] Simon Deakin questions the extent to which this result is reconcilable with the reasoning in *ABC v St George's Healthcare*, above,[50] on the grounds that the defendant local authority in *Poole* could be said to have been in a position to address the

---

49   S. Deakin, 'Liability in negligence in providing a public good: really not so different?' (2019) 78(3) CLJ 513, 515.
50   Above, fn 34.

risks to which the claimants were subject. He also makes the point, however, that *Poole* is not a pure omissions case in the way that *ABC* was.

■ VIEWPOINT

Do you think the two cases referred to here are reconcilable?[51]

PROBLEM QUESTION TECHNIQUE

As a result of the incident with Chris, Gatesby County Council is notified that Dionne's younger son, Hans, is likely to be in danger of neglect and mistreatment. Consequently, it takes Hans into care. In fact, Hans is a very talented footballer and has already been signed by Manchester United Youth. Since Dionne is an avid football fan, she treats Hans very well indeed, and always ensures that he is with his (doting) grandmother during her frequent pub visits and absences. As a result of being removed from his supportive family environment, Hans develops an anxiety disorder, can no longer play football and loses his contract with Manchester United. Dionne cannot cope with this development and commits suicide.

▶ This is clearly a question of public authority liability. Remember that a correct application of the relevant cases will require you to consider the same incremental approach as you would use in relation to a private individual (as per **Robinson** and **Michael**). Be clear that there will be no duty which arises simply by virtue of a body having public powers.

▶ You will also need to consider any potential HRA 1998 claims independent of any action in negligence.

DIFFERENT PERSPECTIVES on the liability of public bodies

A. Ripstein, 'Using What You Have: Misfeasance and Nonfeasance', Private Wrongs (Harvard, 2016), ch 3

Ripstein argues that the reason that the law distinguishes between misfeasance and nonfeasance is that no individual has the right, outside of a contractual arrangement, to determine how another individual uses her person or property. No one has a general right, therefore, that anyone else provide her with a 'favourable context' in which to conduct her life: in other words, to be made better off. This applies both to situations of provision, e.g. you have no obligation to provide me with sunlight, and to situations of rescue, e.g. you have no duty to save my life, even if to do so would pose no risk to you. Ripstein's basic point is to defend the extent to which the common law refrains from holding individuals liable for omissions by means of a rights analysis: the law of torts protects what you already have, and what you have is the right to use your body and property as you choose. It is an integral part of that right that others do not get to choose how you use those things.

D. Nolan, 'The Liability of Public Authorities for Failing to Confer Benefits' (2011) 127 LQR 260

Nolan here considers the specific question which, as he points out had received limited attention elsewhere, whether and to what extent public authorities should be liable for failing to confer benefits on private individuals. (Note that he specifically limits his analysis to negligence law, rather than including considerations of the HRA 1998.) One of his principal conclusions, in evaluating *Gorringe* and its

---

51   See also the article on omissions liability by Sandy Steel in the Further Reading section, below.

implications, is that the duty of a public body to confer a benefit can never be grounded simply on the existence of a statutory power or duty. He goes on to conclude that, whilst *Gorringe* is undoubtedly a restrictive decision, it represents a 'welcome rationalisation of the law' because there are no justifiable reasons for failing to distinguish between private parties and public authorities when it comes to a failure to confer benefits. Nolan makes clear the importance of distinguishing between making things worse and failing to make things better: here, he refers to Tony Honoré's well-known argument that harmful abstentions are less culpable than wrongful acts, because acts infringe on security, but omissions only affect the expectation of improvement, which is an independent and secondary value.

S. Tofaris and S. Steel, 'Negligence Liability for Omissions and the Police' [2016] CLJ 128

In this article, Tofaris and Steel criticise the law's non-imposition of duties of care on the police, and make the case for liability to be imposed where there is a sufficiently proximate relationship between claimant and defendant. The authors further argue that the omissions principle should not apply to public authorities, and particularly to the police, in the same way that it does to private individuals, and that there are ways in which the imposition of such a duty can be limited in a coherent way. Their argument is rooted on the basic premises that wrongs should be remedied, that the police have a special status in society by virtue of their power to use force to intervene, that individuals are therefore in certain circumstances going to be dependent on the police, and that the police have to be accountable for their position. According to Tofaris and Steel, a duty of care in this context could be coherently delimited by imposing it where the claimant is at a special risk of personal harm, where the police know or reasonably should have known of that risk, where the police have the power to protect such an individual, and where the claimant in question is dependent on the police.

F. du Bois, 'Human Rights and the Tort liability of Public Authorities' (2011) 127 LQR 589

Du Bois here examines the way in which the common law has separated public authority liability in tort from claims made under the HRA 1998. His argument is that this is the correct way to proceed, and is certainly preferable to an approach which tries to funnel both types of claim through the requirements of common law negligence; an avenue which was created for, and still exists to accommodate, claims between private individuals. Claims against public authorities have too many characteristics distinct from private claims to benefit from being subject to the same forensic criteria. One significant distinction is that made between positive acts and omissions: human rights legislation and jurisprudence both support the imposition of positive duties in a way which is not appropriate to private law claims. As Du Bois points out, such recognition of 'negative rights' is not easily accommodated within the bilateral structure of common law negligence. Whilst the latter is concerned principally with corrective justice, the structure of human rights law facilitates consideration of distributive justice concerns; something far more fitting to questions of public law liability. In focusing on the vindication of rights over the provision of compensation, Du Bois argues that the human rights sphere is moving towards something which would not have been possible on a common law basis – a specifically public law of liability.

■ VIEWPOINT

What do you think of the argument that the existence of these common law principles can be explained on the basis that nobody has a basic right to be made better off?[52]

---

52   Although such a right can of course be acquired through, for instance, the making of a contract.

2.5.3 Is there a specific application of these principles to the police and emergency services?

We have already encountered a number of cases which involve the police force. Given its function, and its everyday contact with harm-causing activities, this is perhaps unsurprising. The reach of the case of *Hill v Chief Constable of South Yorkshire Police*, however, and the enduring principle derived from it, continue to be tested in the highest courts. That core principle is:

> Absent exceptional circumstances,[53] the police will not owe individual members of the public a common law duty of care in undertaking their operational duties of investigating, detecting, suppressing and prosecuting crime.

On one view, the current relevant authorities could be said merely to affirm the principle we encountered above in relation to public bodies in general that no duty of care will be imposed on them by virtue of their public nature or statutory basis. Rather, as far as negligence is concerned, the police will be treated in exactly the same way as private individuals, so that a duty of care will arise only where it would do so on conventional common law principles. Where, therefore, the police are being sued for harm caused to the claimant by a third party criminal, as in *Michael*, a duty will not arise in the absence of an express assumption of responsibility.[54] This is the same as the rule applied to private individuals, and the Supreme Court has seen no reason to depart from it in relation to public bodies:

> It does not follow from the setting up of a protective system from public resources that if it fails to achieve its purpose, through organisational defects or fault on the part of an individual, the public at large should bear the additional burden of compensating a victim for harm caused by the actions of a third party for whose behaviour the state is not responsible. To impose such a burden would be contrary to the ordinary principles of the common law. The refusal of the courts to impose a private law duty on the police to exercise reasonable care to safeguard victims or potential victims of crime, except in cases where there has been a representation and reliance, does not involve giving special treatment to the police. It is consistent with the way in which the common law has been applied to other authorities vested with powers or duties as a matter of public law for the protection of the public.[55]

This excerpt makes an important point: were the state not to provide these services in the first place, there would not even be an attempt made at making the situation better. The fact, therefore, that the state has expended resources in ameliorating the situation for society in general should not, in itself, expose it to potential liability if it fails to do so in every instance.[56]

Similarly, as *Robinson* illustrates, where the police themselves actively intervene in another's life and cause foreseeable damage by behaving unreasonably, they will be liable in the same way as would a private individual:[57]

> Equally, concerns about public policy cannot in themselves override a liability which would arise at common law for a positive act carried out in the course of performing a statutory

---

53 *Brooks v Commissioner of Police for the Metropolis* [2005] UKHL 24.
54 See also *Mitchell v Glasgow City Council* [2009] UKHL 11.
55 Lord Toulson in *Michael* at [114]–[115].
56 See N.J. McBride, 'Michael and the Future of Tort Law' (2016) 32 *Journal of Professional Negligence* 14.
57 See Lord Hughes in *Robinson* at [120].

function: the true question is whether, properly construed, the statute excludes the liability which would otherwise arise.[58]

The principles to be derived from these cases have helpfully been summarised by Tofaris and Steel:

> In the tort of negligence, a person A is not under a duty to take care to prevent harm occurring to person B through a source of danger not created by A unless (i) A has assumed a responsibility to protect B from that danger, (ii) A has done something which prevents another from protecting B from that danger, (iii) A has a special level of control over that source of danger, or (iv) A's status creates an obligation to protect B from that danger.[59]

Added to this could be the principle, explained above, that A is also under a duty in these circumstances where it has acted so as to make the danger worse. This is the well-known principle derived from *Capital & Counties plc v Hampshire County Council*,[60] in which it was held by the Court of Appeal that, although the fire service owes no duty of care to the public to respond to emergency calls, where it actively intervenes, it does owe a duty of care not to make the situation worse.

The ambulance service has been distinguished, however, from both the police and the fire brigade in terms of its duty of care to respond.

KEY CASE

Kent v Griffiths [2001] QB 36

A GP, who was at the home of a pregnant woman suffering from an asthma attack, called an ambulance on her patient's behalf. Despite her having made two follow-up calls, the ambulance took 38 minutes to arrive with the consequence that the woman lost her baby, and suffered from mental impairments including memory loss and personality change. The defendants argued that, on the basis of *Capital & Counties*, they had no duty to respond, but the Court of Appeal took a different view. It was found that the ambulance service, as part of the NHS, did owe a duty of care to individual patients and that, once a call had been accepted, there was only one individual who would be affected by any failure to respond.

The outcome in *Kent v Griffiths* has been explained on the basis of the 'misleading assurances'[61] given and the consequent reliance by the parties on those assurances. The doctor in *Kent*, for instance, gave evidence to the effect that, had she known the ambulance was not going to arrive promptly, she would have advised the claimant's husband to drive her to hospital himself. This element of reliance on a misleading assurance was also referred to by the Lord Lloyd-Jones in *Darnley*, above,[62] and fortified his decision in the claimant's favour in that case. The NHS aspect of the case might also be seen as the courts wanting to align the remedies available to those who use private healthcare, who would have a claim in contract, and those who use the NHS who, absent a duty of care in negligence, would have no comparably remedy. The same cannot be said, after all, for the police and fire services, for which general private provision is not available. *Sherratt v Chief Constable of*

58 Lord Reed in Robinson at [41].
59 S. Tofaris and S. Steel, 'Negligence Liability for Omissions and the Police' (2016) 75 CLJ 128.
60 [1997] QB 1004.
61 Lord Toulson in *Michael* at [138].
62 At [20].

Greater Manchester Police [2018], however, suggests that the distinction between the police and the ambulance service will not always be determinative.

KEY CASE

Sherratt v Chief Constable of Greater Manchester Police [2018] EWHC 1746 (QB)

The claimant was the partner of a woman who had committed suicide after her mother had sought the help of the defendant police force. He alleged that, in taking the mother's call and assuring her that it would attend the deceased's house, the police force had assumed a duty of care which it had then breached by not responding within a reasonable time. King J in the High Court regarded it as crucial that:

> the police, on the facts found by the Recorder, in giving the assurances they did, were focused on a particular individual and a particular individual's welfare. They were not purporting to be performing their public duty directed at investigation or prevention of crime (albeit it might be said they were in relation to the protection of life). There is force in my judgment that, properly analysed, on the facts as found by the Recorder, the Appellant was in effect agreeing to perform the same function as the ambulance service in coming to the aid of someone reported to be in extremis – in need of welfare assistance – specifically in agreeing to go around to check on that individual and to arrange for her transfer to hospital if necessary. In these circumstances the fact it was the police who agreed to perform this function rather than some other emergency service should not in my judgment deprive the person in need of a private law remedy in tort, if the facts otherwise support a finding of an assumption of responsibility towards her... these facts are not covered by the core *Hill* principle protecting the police in their carrying out their public duty in the investigation and prevention of crime.

As with private individuals, therefore, it would seem as if the emergency services will only owe a duty of care to protect individuals from an external source of harm[63] where they have assumed a responsibility to a specific individual to do so, and where that individual has relied on the assurances given. In *Sherratt*, King J made it explicit that the facts of that case were, in his opinion, different from *Michael*, and more analogous to *Kent*:

> These were clearly different from the assurances or lack assurances given in *Michael* and I agree they were broadly in line with the assurances given in *Kent* and broadly to like effect.[64]

Whilst it may be that an assumption of responsibility will more easily be found in the case of the ambulance service than in relation to the police, it appears from the case law that the presence of that assumption of responsibility is essential for a duty to apply in these circumstances. As *Sherratt* shows, where that assumption exists in a police situation, a duty of care may arise just as it does in the context of other emergency services.

---

63   That is, either from a third party or from natural causes: any source other than the defendant.
64   At [74].

PROBLEM QUESTION TECHNIQUE

Fern calls an ambulance. The call handler informs Fern that there has been a terrorist incident in the city and, as a result, all of the ambulances are currently occupied with that. She tells her that she will get an ambulance to the police station as soon as possible but does not know when that will be. It is nearly three hours until an ambulance arrives, by which time Ed has died.

▸ On these facts, you need to consider the nature of the assurances, and the qualifications to them, given by the defendant.

▸ You will need to decide which of the above cases has the most analogous facts to the problem question, and apply the analysis therein – has there been an assumption of responsibility by the defendant and has the claimant relied on it?

2.6 CHAPTER SUMMARY

The aim of this chapter has been to explain how the duty of care concept in negligence has been developed in a practical sense, and also how it has been interpreted and analysed by commentators. We have seen how it operates as a control device, limiting the liability of those whose actions cause harm to others. The main difficulties that we have encountered so far have arisen in the context of public authority liability, particularly in relation to the misfeasance v nonfeasance distinction, and to the interaction of the common law with human rights jurisprudence. This last part has been complicated, somewhat inevitably, by the fact that the potential liability of public authorities falls at the interface of public and private law: two spheres with highly distinct objectives, functions and methods. This should make more sense to you when you consider it alongside your public law knowledge. As the following roadmap makes clear, one of the most important points to take away from this section is that any negligence liability of public bodies will be grounded on standard common law principles, and will remain independent from the statutory basis of their authority.

FURTHER READING

W. Buckland, 'The Duty To Take Care' (1935) 51 *LQR* 637

J. Goudkamp, 'A Revolution in Duty of Care?' (2015) 131 *LQR* 519

N. McBride, '*Michael* and the Future of Tort Law' (2016) 32(1) *Professional Negligence* 14

J. Morgan, 'Parallel Lines that Never Meet: Tort and the ECHR Again' (2018) 77(2) *CLJ* 244

A. Robertston, 'Policy-Based Reasoning in Negligence' (2013) 33 *Legal Studies* 119

S. Steel, 'Rationalising Omissions Liability in Negligence' (2019) 135 *LQR* 484

T. Weir, 'The Staggering March of Negligence' in P. Cane and J. Stapleton (eds), *The Law of Obligations: Essays in Honour of John Fleming* (OUP, 1998), 97

Roadmap: Will there be a duty of care in negligence?

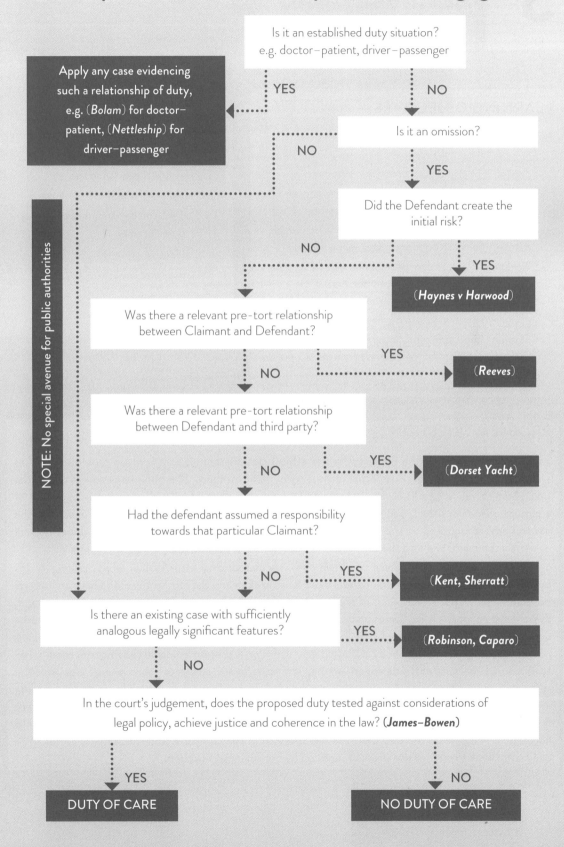

3 PURE ECONOMIC LOSS

LEARNING OBJECTIVES

By the end of this chapter, you should be able to:

- Explain the important distinction between consequential and pure economic loss
- Understand why the recovery of pure economic loss is so restricted in the tort of negligence
- Recognise and explain the situations in which recovery for pure economic loss will be allowed
- Navigate the case law developments in this area since *Hedley Byrne v Heller* was decided
- Engage with policy arguments about the recovery of pure economic loss in negligence
- Discuss the different arguments surrounding the classification of defective premises as pure economic loss

CHAPTER CONTENTS

3.1 Introduction	43
3.2 What is pure economic loss?	44
3.3 Relational economic loss	44
3.4 Negligent services	46
3.4.1 The development of *Hedley Byrne* liability	50
3.5 Defective premises	54
3.6 Chapter summary	59
Further reading	59
Roadmap	60

PROBLEM QUESTION

Fallon wants to increase the publicity for her ethical clothing brand, EthiX, which promotes itself as a company that would never use exploitative employment methods. She has a large advert made, the text of which reads 'EthiX: always fighting against the use of child labour!' against the backdrop of a picture of malnourished, young children working in a cramped factory. On Monday morning, she has this advert mounted on the side wall of Axville City Council's Community Centre, since this wall overlooks the main road into the city, meaning that her advert will reach the biggest audience.

On Monday lunchtime, Tanvir is driving an articulated lorry into Axville, whilst talking to his boyfriend on his mobile phone (his hands-free kit has broken and the lorry is too old to have an integral Bluetooth connection). As a result of trying to manoeuvre the lorry round a corner with only one hand, Tanvir crashes into Axville Community Centre, causing severe damage to its side wall. Fortunately, nobody is hurt, but Axville City Council cannot afford to fix the wall for several weeks. Since the wall is now dangerously unstable, nobody is allowed near it. Fallon is therefore unable to remove or modify her advert, which, because of the damaged surface, now reads 'EthiX: always use child labour!' alongside the still clearly visible picture of the miserable, exploited children. Thousands of people see this misleading image, and Fallon's clothing brand is shunned by the loyal customer base it once had, and attracts very few of the new customers to which the advert was supposed to appeal. Consequently, EthiX goes into liquidation, Fallon loses the £50,000 she had invested in the company, and she starts to suffer from panic attacks as a result of the stress brought on by her financial situation.

Her financial problems are also an issue for James, who is the landlord of EthiX's business premises. James usually only lets his units to already-established businesses, rather than young start-ups like EthiX, but James' dad, Ed, regularly plays golf with Fallon's brother, Dapo. One day, during a game, they had been talking about their families when Dapo told Ed all about his sister's 'fantastic, fast-growing business, EthiX, which is certain to be very successful'. Dapo works as a mortgage adviser, so Ed presumed he would know what he was talking about when it came to people's finances. Dapo knows full well that Ed is James' dad and that Fallon will soon be applying for a lease of one of James' highly desirable business units. Ed happens to be in James' office when EthiX's application for a tenancy is being considered, and recognises the name. He tells James what Dapo had told him, and emphasised what a great, reliable guy Dapo is. When EthiX goes into liquidation, James loses 6 months' rental payments, which amounts to £18,000.

Enya lives next door to Axville Community Centre, in a house that was built eight years ago. A few weeks before Tanvir's lorry crashed into the neighbouring building, the plaster on Enya's walls had begun to crack, the mirrors and pictures mounted on her walls started to fall off, and her wall shelves collapsed. The surveyor sent by her insurance company to inspect the damage discovered that the house's walls had been built with defective materials, in contravention of the applicable building regulations. Had they been built properly, and in accordance with those regulations, the damage would not have occurred. The builder of Enya's house, Julius, did seek approval from Axville City Council for both his plans and for the build itself. Axville sent an inspector out three times during the building process, and no objection was raised. As a result of these severe structural issues, Enya's house, which would otherwise be worth £400,000, is now worth only £75,000.

3.1 Introduction

A claimant suffers pure economic loss where the damage she suffers is not damage to, or consequent upon damage to, a physical thing, such as her body or her property. This should be contrasted with economic losses that are consequent upon physical damage which are known as consequential economic losses, and are recoverable in the orthodox way.[1] For example, loss of earnings as a consequence of having one's leg broken as a result of a defendant's negligence is an example of consequential economic loss, whereas loss of money invested as a result of negligent financial advice is an example of pure economic loss. As outlined in the introduction to Chapter 4 (Psychiatric Injury), the nature of pure economic loss is such that indeterminate liability is potentially a problem. A common argument levelled against the recovery of pure economic loss in the tort of negligence is that the claimant should have protected himself against such losses through contractual means. Therefore, much of the case law in this area is concerned with avoiding that outcome, as well as with achieving the right balance between the protective spheres of tort and contract. A common objective of the case law on pure economic loss is to establish proximity rules specific to this type of damage: these are often based on the identification of an assumption of responsibility by the defendant towards the claimant. This chapter will look at the range of different ways in which pure economic loss can be caused, and the approaches that the courts have taken in dealing with this. In essence, where recovery is allowed for this type of loss, the courts have managed to identify a particular relationship of proximity between the claimant and the defendant on the facts of the case.

---

1   See Chapter 17 (Damages).

3.2 What is pure economic loss?

It is vital that you are able to distinguish correctly between pure and consequential economic loss in the tort of negligence. You should also ensure that you always use accurate terminology when discussing each one; *consequential* economic loss (which results from damage to a tangible thing, either person or property) is not only an entirely orthodox head of recovery in negligence, but actually forms the basis of most claims in negligence. Pure economic loss, which is not consequent upon damage to a tangible thing, is on the other hand recoverable only in very limited circumstances, as we will see.

In order to distinguish between pure and consequential economic loss, there are three principal factual situations of which you need to be aware. They are not all situations in which claimants have been able to recover. The first is often referred to as *relational* economic loss, which really just means that the loss has been caused as a result of damage belonging to someone other than the claimant. The second situation arises where the claimant's pure economic loss is a consequence of a negligently performed service: where there has been no tangible damage to person or property, but where the claimant has lost money, or suffered a setback to her pecuniary interest. The third and final type of situation in which pure economic loss has been deemed by English courts to have occurred is one in which the claimant has acquired a tangible item of property which then turns out always to have been defective in some way, and therefore worth less than was originally thought (and so usually worth less than the claimant paid for it). As we will see, whilst there are some narrow parameters within which recovery might be granted within the first category, it is generally only in the second category that pure economic loss has been found by the courts to be recoverable and, even then, only in very restricted circumstances. The third category has become one in which English courts deny recovery. This chapter will consider these three categories in turn.

3.3 Relational economic loss

This situation, in which economic loss results from damage to property belonging to a third party, is best illustrated by the well-known case of *Spartan Steel & Alloys v Martin & Co* [1973].

KEY CASE

Spartan Steel & Alloys v Martin & Co [1973] QB 27

Employees of the defendants damaged an electricity cable, which belonged to the electricity board, but which supplied the claimants' factory. As a consequence, the claimants' factory was without power until the electricity board managed to repair the damaged cable. When the power supply was first interrupted, the claimants had to remove molten metal from their furnace, and this 'melt' was therefore ruined. In their actions against the defendants in negligence, the claimants claimed for the value of the ruined melt and for the profit they would have made had they been able to sell it. Crucially, they also claimed for the profits they would have made on the melts that they would have produced had the

power supply not been cut off. These latter profits were, of course, not consequential upon physical injury to any tangible thing, since they were purely hypothetical and based on melts that did not actually exist. Whilst the trial judge allowed the full claim, the Court of Appeal took a different view: it allowed the claimants to recover for the ruined melt and the lost profit consequential upon damage to that physical asset, but was not prepared to allow recovery for lost profits relating to future, as yet non-existent, melts. These future profits were deemed to be pure economic loss (consequent upon damage caused to the power company's cable, and not any property belonging to the claimant).

The judgment of Lord Denning MR in *Spartan Steel* is often referred to. He gives several reasons of policy for restricting recovery in negligence for pure economic loss. One of these is that the risk of temporarily losing a power supply is one which is common to most members of society, and causes relatively modest losses when it does. It is also a risk against which individuals can guard either by putting in place a backup source, or by taking out insurance against such losses. Failing that, it is a hazard that people, in Lord Denning's opinion, should just put up with. He goes on to make the point that allowing recovery for loss of this kind would potentially expose defendants to many small-value claims, some of which might be artificially inflated. Finally, Lord Denning suggests that losses such as those suffered in this case should be borne by the community, many of whom might suffer relatively small losses, as opposed to heaping the cost of all those combined losses on to the shoulders of a single defendant.

■ VIEWPOINT

Do you agree with Lord Denning? Do you think that the claimants' lost future profits should have been recoverable? Note that Edmund-Davies LJ dissented in the Court of Appeal, and would have awarded the claimants their full loss, including the lost profits from the sale of future melts. He said (at 45):

> I should perhaps again stress that we are here dealing with economic loss which was both reasonably foreseeable and a direct consequence of the defendants' negligent act.

PROBLEM QUESTION TECHNIQUE

Fallon wants to increase the publicity for her ethical clothing brand, Ethix, which promotes itself as a company which would never use exploitative employment methods. She has a large advert made, the text of which reads 'EthiX: always fighting against the use of child labour!' against the backdrop of a picture of malnourished, young children working in a cramped factory. On Monday morning, she has this advert mounted on the side wall of Axville City Council's Community Centre, since this wall overlooks the main road into the city, meaning that her advert will reach the biggest audience.

On Monday lunchtime, Tanvir is driving an articulated lorry into Axville, whilst talking to his boyfriend on his mobile phone (his hands-free kit has broken and the lorry is too old to have an integral Bluetooth connection). As a result of trying to manoeuvre the lorry round a corner with only one hand, Tanvir crashes into Axville Community Centre, causing severe damage to its side wall. Fortunately, nobody is hurt, but Axville City Council cannot afford to fix the wall for several weeks. Since the wall is now dangerously unstable, nobody is allowed near it. Fallon is therefore unable to remove or modify her advert, which, because of the damaged surface, now reads 'EthiX: always use child labour!' alongside the still clearly visible picture of the miserable, exploited children. Thousands of people see this misleading image, and Fallon's clothing brand is shunned by the loyal customer base it once had, and attracts very few of the new customers to which the advert was supposed to appeal. Consequently, EthiX goes into liquidation, Fallon loses the £50,000 she had invested in the company, and she starts to suffer from panic attacks as a result of the stress brought on by her financial situation.

Don't forget the basics. You need to establish whether there exists a duty of care on these facts, whether it has been breached, and whether it has caused the claimant to suffer any legally recognised actionable damage which is not too remote from the breach:

- There is a duty of care because the relationship of a driver to those with property physically proximate to the highway is an established duty situation – see, e.g., *Mansfield v Weetabix*.[2]

- The question of breach is addressed by asking whether Tanvir's driving fell below the standard to be expected of a reasonable driver – see, e.g., *Nettleship v Weston*.

- In applying *Spartan Steel* principles to this part of the problem question, consider:

- The fact that the lorry damaged property belonging to someone other than the claimant (here, Axville City Council rather than Fallon).

- Fallon's loss of custom and profits is, therefore, analogous to the profits from the future melts in *Spartan Steel*.

- The damage caused to her poster is, however, property damage analogous to the current melt in the furnace in *Spartan Steel*, and so needs to be distinguished from her future losses.

- The question of whether she can recover for her panic attacks is one of remoteness: is such mental distress damage of a reasonably foreseeable type to a defendant who is driving carelessly? See, e.g., *Wagon Mound* and *Reeves v Commissioner of Police for Metropolis* in Chapter 7.

In a recent development on this point, the Court of Appeal in *Shell UK Ltd v Total UK Ltd* [2010][3] considered the question of whether a party who had a beneficial, rather than a legal, interest in property could sue for loss consequent upon its damage. This situation will arise, as it did in *Shell*, where one party holds the property on trust for another. On such facts, the party which holds the property on trust is the legal owner and the party for whom it holds the property on trust is the beneficial owner. In this case, the defendant argued that the beneficial owner did not have a sufficient proprietary interest in the damaged property (mainly pipework and tanks used to store and transport Shell's oil). The Court of Appeal found, however, that a beneficial owner can recover on such facts as long as it joins the legal owner to the action. It also found that a duty of care was owed to a beneficial owner of property just as much as to a legal owner of property by a defendant, as long as that defendant could reasonably foresee that its negligent actions would damage the property concerned. Recovery would therefore be available on these facts in respect of physical loss of property, and also for the foreseeable consequences of that loss, such as the loss of profit incurred as a result of the damage.

3.4 Negligent services

The second category, negligent services, represents the only set of circumstances in which it is possible to recover for pure economic loss in the tort of negligence. The principal authority with which you need to be familiar is *Hedley Byrne v Heller*.

KEY CASE

Hedley Byrne v Heller [1964] AC 465

The claimants, Hedley Byrne, were advertising agents who consulted the defendant bankers as to the financial health of a client, on whose behalf the claimants were about to place several orders. The bank gave favourable references for the client company, gratuitously, and with the

---

2   [1997] EWCA Civ 1352.
3   [2010] EWCA Civ 180.

express disclaimer that they were given 'without responsibility'. When the claimant agents lost £17,000 on the orders as a result of the client's liquidation, they sued the defendant bankers on the basis that they had been negligent in giving a favourable reference.

A strong House of Lords (with notable judgments handed down by Lords Reid, Morris and Devlin in particular) found that, although such liability would not attach to the defendant in this particular case because it gave its statement subject to a disclaimer, such facts could in principle give rise to liability in negligence. Liability will attach to the negligent provision of a statement where there is a 'special relationship' between the claimant and the defendant on the following terms:

the party seeking the information and advice was trusting the other to exercise such a degree of care as the circumstances required, where it was reasonable for him to do that and where the other gave the information or advice when he knew or ought to have known that the inquirer was relying on him.[4]

Much has been made of the special 'criteria' that *Hedley Byrne v Heller* supposedly set out as being necessary for negligence liability to attach to a negligent misstatement which causes loss. A full reading of the judgment in context, however, shows that the House of Lords was really just identifying the considerations that will be relevant in order to establish whether there is sufficient proximity between the claimant and the defendant in a case of this kind. Particularly now that *Robinson* (see Chapter 2 (Duty of Care)) reaffirms the need for courts to engage in incremental development when deciding whether a duty of care exists, the *Hedley Byrne* factors should really be seen as indicators of proximity, rather than as an exhaustive list of criteria necessary in their own right. In his judgment in *Hedley Byrne*, Lord Devlin articulated this in the following way:

> The categories of special relationships which may give rise to a duty to take care in word as well as in deed are not limited to contractual relationships or to relationships of fiduciary duty, but include also relationships which in the words of Lord Shaw in *Nocton v Lord Ashburton* are 'equivalent to contract', that is, where there is an assumption of responsibility in circumstances in which, but for the absence of consideration, there would be a contract. Where there is an express undertaking, … there can be little difficulty. The difficulty arises in discerning those cases in which the undertaking is to be implied. In this respect the absence of consideration is not irrelevant. Payment for information or advice is very good evidence that it is being relied upon and that the informer or adviser knows that it is. Where there is no consideration, it will be necessary to exercise greater care in distinguishing between social and professional relationships and between those which are of a contractual character and those which are not. It may often be material to consider whether the adviser is acting purely out of good nature or whether he is getting his reward in some indirect form. The service that a bank performs in giving a reference is not done simply out of a desire to assist commerce. It would discourage the customers of the bank if their deals fell through because the bank had refused to testify to their credit when it was good.
>
> I have had the advantage of reading all the opinions prepared by your Lordships and of studying the terms which your Lordships have framed by way of definition of the sort of relationship which gives rise to a responsibility towards those who act upon information or advice and so creates a duty of care towards them. I do not understand any of your Lordships to hold that it is a responsibility imposed by law upon certain types of persons or in certain sorts of situations. It is a responsibility that is voluntarily accepted or undertaken, either generally where a general relationship, such as that of solicitor and client or banker and customer, is created, or

---

4   Lord Reid at 534.

specifically in relation to a particular transaction … Responsibility can attach only to the single act, that is, the giving of the reference, and only if the doing of that act implied a voluntary undertaking to assume responsibility … I do not think it possible to formulate with exactitude all the conditions under which the law will in a specific case imply a voluntary undertaking any more than it is possible to formulate those in which the law will imply a contract.[5]

Before *Hedley Byrne* was decided, tortious liability attached only to statements made fraudulently,[6] and so the question for the court was whether such liability should be extended to statements made innocently but negligently. This, rather than the nature of the loss thereby caused, was the real focus of the judgments. There is no question that *Hedley Byrne* is a landmark case in the law of tort, although some think it represents a wrong turning in the law.[7] In the following excerpt, Lord Devlin explains why, in his view, this development was necessary in order to avoid arbitrary distinctions between those situations in which recovery for economic loss is available and those where it is not:

This is why the distinction is now said to depend on whether financial loss is caused through physical injury or whether it is caused directly. The interposition of the physical injury is said to make a difference of principle. I can find neither logic nor common sense in this. If irrespective of contract, a doctor negligently advises a patient that he can safely pursue his occupation and he cannot and the patient's health suffers and he loses his livelihood, the patient has a remedy. But if the doctor negligently advises him that he cannot safely pursue his occupation when in fact he can and he loses his livelihood, there is said to be no remedy. Unless, of course, the patient was a private patient and the doctor accepted half a guinea for his trouble: then the patient can recover all. I am bound to say, my Lords, that I think this to be nonsense. It is not the sort of nonsense that can arise even in the best system of law out of the need to draw nice distinctions between borderline cases. It arises, if it is the law, simply out of a refusal to make sense. The line is not drawn on any intelligible principle. It just happens to be the line which those who have been driven from the extreme assertion that negligent statements in the absence of contractual or fiduciary duty give no cause of action have in the course of their retreat so far reached.[8]

■ VIEWPOINT

Do you agree that the development in *Hedley Byrne* was a necessary one?

Consider: Over the last century, the financial services industry has grown dramatically. Without the *Hedley Byrne* exception, therefore, vast numbers of professionals would be effectively immune from negligence actions simply because of the type of loss they are likely to cause if they act without reasonable care.

But: Should the tort of negligence be the means by which this is addressed? Parties in situations involving financial dependence on professional services could, in most cases at least, protect themselves fairly easily by making their relationship a contractual one (that is, by insisting on some form of consideration, albeit minimal).[9]

---

5   At 528–9.
6   *Derry v Peek* [1889] UKHL 1.
7   See, e.g., D. Campbell, 'The Curious Incident of the Dog that Did Bark in the Night-time: What Mischief Does *Hedley Byrne v Heller Correct?*' in K. Barker et al (eds), *The Law of Misstatements* (Hart Publishing, 2015) and T. Weir, 'Liability for Syntax' (1963) CLJ 216.
8   At 517.
9   See N.J. McBride, *The Humanity of Private Law* (Hart Publishing, 2019), 235–7.

MAKING CONNECTIONS

Hedley Byrne v Heller is also a significant case in the law of contract, although less than it was before the Misrepresentation Act 1967 was enacted. It allows claimants to recover if they have entered into a contract as a result of relying on a misrepresentation made negligently to them. Prior to this, as we saw above,[10] misrepresentations (or misstatements) had to be made fraudulently if they were to be actionable. Fraud is far more difficult for claimants to prove than negligence, since it requires the defendant either to have known the statement to be false, or to not believe the statement, or to be reckless as to its truth. *Hedley Byrne* made it possible for far more claimants to obtain a remedy for having entered into contracts that they would not have made, but for the defendant's inducement. Since the Misrepresentation Act 1967, claimants who have entered into a contract on the basis of an actionable misrepresentation made to them by the other party to the contract should bring their claims under the Act, rather than at common law. Not only does the statute require them to prove less in order to succeed,[11] the common law interpretation of it means that damages are likely to be awarded on the basis of the fraudulent measure, which is potentially higher than the non-intentional tort measure.[12] *Hedley Byrne* remains relevant, however, to those situations in which the representation was made to the claimant by someone other than the other contracting party. On such facts as these, claimants will need to bring a common law claim.

KEY CASE

Smith v Eric S. Bush; Harris v Wyre Forest District Council [1990] 1 AC 831

The claimants in this case were the purchasers of modest residential property. The defendants were surveyors who produced a valuation assessment of the house for the claimants' mortgage company. Although the claimants paid for the report, it was the mortgage company who commissioned and relied on it in their provision of a mortgage to the claimants. When it transpired that the report had been produced negligently, and contained inaccurate information, the claimants sued the defendants for the pure economic loss they suffered as a result. Despite the fact that the report stated expressly that only the mortgage company should rely on the report, the House of Lords found that a surveyor in such a situation does owe a duty of care to the purchasers of the property concerned. In order to reach this conclusion, it was necessary to make the requisite 'assumption of responsibility' survive the existence of the express disclaimer. One of the ways in which the House did this was to deem the disclaimer 'unreasonable' and therefore unenforceable under the Unfair Contract Terms Act 1977.[13]

---

10 *Derry v Peek* [1889] UKHL 1.

11 That is, that they entered into the contract as a result of a misrepresentation having been made to them. The defendant then has to prove that she acted reasonably in making the representation.

12 *Royscott Trust v Rogerson* [1991] 2 QB 297, CA. As we will see in the chapters on causation and remoteness, non-intentional torts, such as negligence, are subject to the test of remoteness in *The Wagon Mound*, which limits them to damage of a reasonably foreseeable type. Intentional torts such as deceit (fraud), on the other hand, remain subject to the *Re Polemis* test, under which all damage which flows from the breach is recoverable, regardless of type. Imagine, for instance, that I enter into a contract with you to buy your burger business because you tell me it has a certain turnover, but it turns out that its turnover is in fact much lower than you represented it to be, and your representation was made recklessly as to its truth. I will be able to recover the financial losses I have suffered as a result of your misrepresentation, but I will also be able to recover for any illness from which I suffer as a result of my disastrous purchase. The latter is very unlikely to be recoverable in a situation in which your representation was made negligently, rather than intentionally. The difference in practice can be considerable.

13 Lord Griffiths, on the other hand, retreated from the 'voluntary assumption of responsibility' as being the principal consideration, preferring instead a more generic analysis of proximity. Subsequent case law has, however, as we will see below, continued to develop the assumption of responsibility analysis in this area.

■ VIEWPOINT

Do you think this is enough to establish a 'voluntary assumption of responsibility', given that the very existence of a disclaimer, whether reasonable or not, indicates a lack of intention to assume responsibility on the part of the defendants?

On the other hand, the existence of the disclaimer also shows that surveyors in such circumstances are clearly aware of who will rely on their reports in practice.

A defendant's knowledge as to the identity of the party who will rely on its information was a significant factor in the most recent appellate consideration of *Hedley Byrne* proximity in *Banca Nazionale del Lavoro SPA v Playboy Club London Ltd and others.*

KEY CASE

Banca Nazionale del Lavoro SPA v Playboy Club London Ltd and others [2018] UKSC 43

Here, the claimant was the Playboy Club in London which had, in accordance with its usual practice, sought assurances of creditworthiness from a client's bank before advancing gambling credit to the client. Given the name and reputation of the club, it used a different entity, Burlington, in order to approach clients' banks. It was, therefore, to Burlington that BNL gave its assurances in this case. When, despite those assurances (which were, in any event, given when the client was not even a customer of BNL) the client defaulted on the credit agreement, the claimant sought to recover its £800,000 loss from BNL on the basis of *Hedley Byrne*.

The Supreme Court held that there was insufficient proximity in this case between BNL and the Playboy Club, since BNL gave the information to Burlington and not to the claimant. This is known as a situation of undisclosed agency, in which one party can enter into contractual relations on behalf of another under certain circumstances. The undisclosed agency relationship, however, within which a party can contract with another party whose identity is not known to it, was deemed by the Supreme Court not to be 'akin to contract' in the way that *Hedley Byrne* liability requires. BNL was not therefore liable to the Playboy Club. It would seem, then, that a defendant must know *to whom* its statement is directed if the facts are to give rise to the requisite special relationship under *Hedley Byrne*.

3.4.1 The development of *Hedley Byrne* liability

Whilst the focus of *Hedley Byrne* itself was on liability for words, as opposed to deeds, the reach of the decision has been increased by the following notable subsequent cases, all of which, bizarrely, appeared in the law reports in 1995: *Henderson v Merrett Syndicates, Spring v Guardian Assurance* and *White v Jones.* The following Key Case boxes consider each in turn.

KEY CASE

Henderson v Merrett Syndicates [1995] 2 AC 145

The claimants in this case were investors who lost significant amounts of money as a result of massive insurance claims made against Lloyds in the 1980s.

They sued the defendants for negligently managing the syndicates (this is the insurance market term for groups of investors who pool funds in order to insure high value risks) in which they had invested. The facts of this case gave rise to two principal issues in the wake of *Hedley Byrne*: first, whether such liability for pure economic loss should attach to the performance of services, as opposed to the narrower action of giving a particular statement and, second, whether the existence of a contract between claimant and defendant[14] precluded the finding of liability in tort. The House of Lords decided that liability could arise in relation to the provision of a service where the professional, or quasi-professional, skills of the defendant had been relied upon and that, unless the terms of a contract between the parties excluded liability in tort, the existence of the contract itself did not preclude the existence of a duty of care in tort. In such a case, where there was both a contractual and a tortious duty, the claimant could elect which action to pursue.

In *Henderson*, Lord Goff gave the following account of the position as he saw it:

> Since it has been submitted on behalf of the managing agents that no liability should attach to them in negligence in the present case because the only damage suffered by the Names consists of pure economic loss, the question arises whether the principle in *Hedley Byrne* is capable of applying in the case of underwriting agents at Lloyd's who are managing agents ... I have no difficulty in concluding that the principle is indeed capable of such application. The principle has been expressly applied to a number of different categories of person who perform services of a professional or quasi-professional nature ... For my part I can see no reason why a duty of care should not ... be owed by managing agents at Lloyd's to a Name who is a member of a syndicate under the management of the agents ... the relationship between Name and managing agent appears to provide a classic example of the type of relationship to which the principle in *Hedley Byrne* applies ... there is in my opinion plainly an assumption of responsibility in the relevant sense by the managing agents towards the Names in their syndicates. The managing agents have accepted the Names as members of a syndicate under their management. They obviously hold themselves out as possessing a special expertise to advise the Names on the suitability of risks to be underwritten; and on the circumstances in which, and the extent to which, reinsurance should be taken out and claims should be settled. The Names, as the managing agents well knew, placed implicit reliance on that expertise, in that they gave authority to the managing agents to bind them to contracts of insurance and reinsurance and to the settlement of claims. I can see no escape from the conclusion that, in these circumstances, prima facie a duty of care is owed in tort by the managing agents to such Names. To me, it does not matter if one proceeds by way of analogy from the categories of relationship already recognised as falling within the principle in *Hedley Byrne* [1964] A.C. 465 or by a straight application of the principle stated in the *Hedley Byrne* case itself. On either basis the conclusion is, in my opinion, clear. Furthermore, since the duty rests on the principle in *Hedley Byrne*, no problem arises from the fact that the loss suffered by the Names is pure economic loss.[15]

The decision in *Henderson* not only establishes the potential for concurrent liability in contract and tort for the same action of the defendant, but also emphasises the significance of both the relationship between the parties and the claimant's reliance. These two aspects are clearly more relevant than the nature of the defendant's action and the nature of the claimant's loss.

14 Some of the claimants in *Henderson* had a direct contract with the defendants, whilst others did not. In the case, these are referred to as 'direct names' and 'indirect names' – see Lord Goff at 170.
15 At 181.

KEY CASE

Spring v Guardian Assurance [1995] 2 AC 296

This case concerned the negligent provision of a reference by a former employer; the question being whether a duty of care was owed to the employee in formulating such a reference. These facts are not completely analogous to *Hedley Byrne* since the statements in the reference were neither directed to, nor relied upon by, the claimant. This case also gave rise to the question of whether a negligence action should lie on facts which might be thought more naturally to come within the remit of the tort of defamation, which is a tort expressly concerned with protecting a claimant's reputation. The problem with a defamation action, as far as the claimant was concerned, was that the giving of a reference is protected by qualified privilege, and therefore actionable only where the giving of the relevant statement was motivated by malice, which was not the case here. The House of Lords decided, although not unanimously, in the claimant's favour, thereby extending *Hedley Byrne* further still. As McBride points out, this is not an inconsiderable extension of the principle because:

(i)   the defendant's references for Spring were supplied over Spring's head and were not solicited by Spring in the expectation that the defendant would take care in providing those references; and

(ii) there never existed any relationship between the defendant and Spring that would have allowed Spring to argue that the defendant 'assumed a responsibility' to Spring that it would use care in providing references for him.[16]

A majority of the House of Lords felt, however, that there was sufficient 'general' reliance on such facts, coupled with a similarly general 'assumption of responsibility', to found a duty of care.

■ VIEWPOINT

What do you think? Does *Spring* take *Hedley Byrne* too far? Does it undermine the existence of the qualified privilege defence in defamation?[17] Or are there sufficient policy reasons for holding employers liable when, in not taking care in providing a reference, they risk destroying their former employees' ability to earn a decent living?

KEY CASE

White v Jones [1995] 2 AC 207

This is a very tricky case owing to its particular facts. As such, it is probably better regarded as being explicable as a problematic and specific situation requiring a remedy, rather than a helpful application of any general point. The defendant here was a solicitor, who had been instructed by a testator to alter the latter's will. Having previously removed his daughters from his will as a result of a family feud, the testator wanted to reinstate them as named beneficiaries in that will. The solicitor failed to do so, meaning that the daughters inherited nothing under the will. They, therefore, had suffered pure economic loss. The difficulty lies in the fact that, whilst the defendant clearly owed a duty of care to the testator, the testator/his estate had suffered no loss. The crux of the difficulty on these facts is that the defendant solicitor could not really be said to have assumed a responsibility towards the claimants. Nevertheless, the House of Lords held the solicitor liable for the claimants' loss on the basis that its 'voluntary assumption of responsibility' extended from the testator to the claimant beneficiaries. Lord Goff's analysis of the situation tends towards an admission that this extension is

---

16   N.J. McBride, *The Humanity of Private Law* (Hart Publishing, 2018), 135.
17   See Chapter 13 (Defamation).

a somewhat artificial device, necessary in order to achieve practical justice.[18] Lord Browne-Wilkinson, on the other hand, took a more conceptual route to the same result, preferring to emphasise the solicitor's role as a fiduciary (a legal construct which imposes on one party a duty to safeguard the interests of another). As such, the defendant solicitor knew that the claimants' 'economic well-being is dependent upon the proper discharge ... of his duty'.[19]

■ VIEWPOINT

Was the need for practical justice sufficient in *White v Jones* for the artificiality of (at least some of) the judicial approaches to 'voluntary assumption of responsibility'?

It might have seemed, in 1995, as if *Hedley Byrne* was set for unchecked expansion. This has not, however, been the case, and the principle has remained fairly well-contained within the parameters outlined in the above cases. The view taken of them might, therefore, be more sympathetic with hindsight than it would have been at the time they were decided. It is worth forming a view of the overall effect of these cases and what you make of their role within the law, either separately or combined. Given the contentious nature of several of these cases, and the fact they are all exceptions to the general rule that pure economic loss is not recoverable in the tort of negligence, this area is a fertile source of essay questions.

PROBLEM QUESTION TECHNIQUE

Her financial problems are also an issue for James, who is the landlord of EthiX's business premises. James usually only lets his units to already-established businesses, rather than young start-ups like EthiX, but James' dad, Ed, regularly plays golf with Fallon's brother, Dapo. One day, during a game, they had been talking about their families when Dapo told Ed all about his sister's 'fantastic, fast-growing business, EthiX, which is certain to be very successful'. Dapo works as a mortgage adviser, so Ed presumed he would know what he was talking about when it came to people's finances. Dapo knows full well that Ed is James' dad and that Fallon will soon be applying for a lease of one of James' highly desirable business units. Ed happens to be in James' office when EthiX's application for a tenancy is being considered, and recognises the name. He tells James what Dapo had told him, and emphasised what a great, reliable guy Dapo is. When EthiX goes into liquidation, James loses 6 months' rental payments, which amounts to £18,000.

In order to answer this part of the problem question, you need to consider the following:

▸ Had Ed assumed a responsibility towards James in the way that *Hedley Bryne* requires? Was there a relationship akin to contract? Was James trusting Ed to exercise a degree of care, was it reasonable for him to do so, and did Ed know that James was relying on him to take such care in supplying the information?

▸ Is there any possibility of Dapo being liable? It might be worthwhile here to consider *Banca Nazionale del Lavoro SPA* and ask whether, since Dapo knew that Ed was James' father and that Fallon would soon be applying to James, he could be held to have assumed a duty of care to the intended recipient of the information he passed on (these facts would, of course, need to be distinguished from those in *Banca Nazionale del Lavoro SPA*, in which there was no liability because such knowledge did not exist in that case).

---

18   At 265–8.
19   At 275.

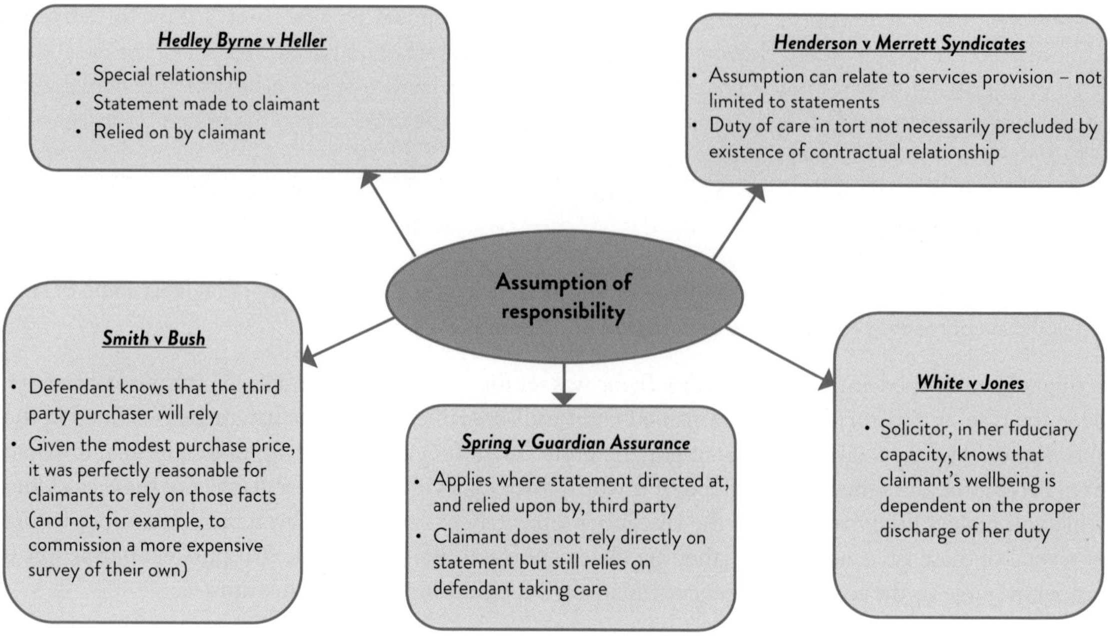

Figure 3.1: Assumption of responsibility

DIFFERENT PERSPECTIVES on *Hedley Byrne* liability

K. Barker, 'Are We Up to Expectations? Solicitors, Beneficiaries, and the Tort/Contract Divide' (1994) 14 Oxford Journal of Legal Studies 137

Barker argues that the approach to the problem in *White v Jones*, based on a tortious route to a remedy, is both defensible and preferable to using the law of contract to compensate the claimant. In the days before the Contracts (Rights of Third Parties) Act 1999, when this piece was written, there was growing support for giving third parties certain rights under contracts. Barker here argues that giving beneficiaries rights to the contracts made between testators and their solicitors would not be the most appropriate way of dealing with the situation because it would require too much violence to be done to established contractual rules. A similar position was taken by the Law Commission, and it remains the position that beneficiaries are unable to claim in contract under the 1999 Act.

R. Stevens, Torts and Rights (OUP, 2007), pp 34–7

Stevens advocates a broader interpretation of *Hedley Byrne* liability. His point is not that the principle carved out a particular novel kind of liability for words, as opposed to acts, or even that *Hedley Byrne* liability is specific to the negligent provision of services. He explains that the liability deriving from that case is both simpler and wider than that: that it is possible to claim for pure economic loss that results from the failure to comply with a gratuitous assumption of responsibility, whatever that responsibility is for.

3.5 Defective premises

Imagine that you buy a house for £300,000, basing your decision to pay that price on a survey which states that the property is structurally sound, but that property turns out not to be structurally sound and your house is then worth significantly less than you paid for it. If the surveyor was negligent in producing her report, you are bound to feel as if you can recover the difference between what you paid for the property, and what it is now worth, from her. The classification of your loss in these circumstances affects your ability to recover. In relatively recent times, the law has changed its mind on the issue of how loss should be classified in relation to defective premises. This can be seen most clearly in the shift in judicial analysis from *Anns v Merton LBC* [1978][20] to *Murphy v Brentwood DC* [1991].[21] These cases show how the law deals with property which, after the claimant has acquired it, and unbeknownst to the claimant, turns out to be defective. In *Anns*, a very strong House of Lords (Lords Diplock, Salmon, Russell, Wilberforce and Simon) regarded this loss as being a form of property damage. In the subsequent case of *Murphy*, however, another strong House of Lords (Lords McKay, Keith, Bridge, Brandon, Ackner, Oliver and Jauncey) reached a different conclusion.

In explaining the House's departure from its previous decision in *Anns*, Lord Keith of Kinkel said:[22]

> In my opinion it must now be recognised that, although the damage in *Anns* was characterised as physical damage by Lord Wilberforce, it was purely economic loss. In *Council of the Shire of Sutherland v Heyman*, 157 C.L.R. 424 where … the High Court of Australia declined to follow *Anns* when dealing with a claim against a local authority in respect of a defectively constructed house, Deane J. said, at pp. 503-505:
>
>> 'Nor is the respondents' claim in the present case for ordinary physical damage to themselves or their property. Their claim, as now crystallized, is not in respect of damage to the fabric of the house or to other property caused by collapse or subsidence of the house as a result of the inadequate foundations. It is for the loss or damage represented by the actual inadequacy of the foundations, that is to say, it is for the cost of remedying a structural defect in their property which already existed at the time when they acquired it. In *Anns v Merton London Borough Council* [1978] A.C. 728, it was held by the House of Lords that a local government authority owed a relevant duty of care, in respect of inspection of the foundations of a building, to persons who subsequently became long term lessees (either as original lessees or as assignees) of parts of the building. Lord Wilberforce, at p. 759, in a speech with which three of the other four members of the House of Lords agreed, expressed the conclusion that the appropriate classification of damage sustained by the lessees by reason of the inadequacy of the foundations of the completed building was "material, physical damage, and what is recoverable is the amount of expenditure necessary to restore the dwelling to a condition in which it is no longer a danger to the health or safety of persons occupying and possibly (depending on the circumstances) expenses arising from necessary displacement." … I respectfully disagree with the classification of the loss sustained in such circumstances as "material, physical damage". Whatever may be the position with respect to consequential damage to the fabric of the building or to other property caused by subsequent collapse or subsidence, the loss or injury involved in the actual inadequacy of the foundations cannot, in the case of a person who purchased or leased the property after the inadequacy existed but before it was known or manifest, properly be seen as ordinary physical or material damage. The only property which could be said to have been damaged in such a case is the building. The building itself could not be said to have been subjected to "material, physical damage"

20   [1978] AC 728.
21   [1991] AC 398.
22   At 466–8.

by reason merely of the inadequacy of its foundations since the building never existed otherwise than with its foundations in that state. Moreover, even if the inadequacy of the foundations could be seen as material, physical damage to the building, it would be damage to property in which a future purchaser or tenant had no interest at all at the time when it occurred. Loss or injury could only be sustained by such a purchaser or tenant on or after the acquisition of the freehold or leasehold estate without knowledge of the faulty foundations. It is arguable that any such loss or injury should be seen as being sustained at the time of acquisition when, because of ignorance of the inadequacy of the foundations, a higher price is paid (or a higher rent is agreed to be paid) than is warranted by the intrinsic worth of the freehold or leasehold estate that is being acquired. Militating against that approach is the consideration that, for so long as the inadequacy of the foundations is neither known nor manifest, no identifiable loss has come home: if the purchaser or tenant sells the freehold or leasehold estate within that time, he or she will sustain no loss by reason of the inadequacy of the foundations. The alternative, and in my view preferable, approach is that any loss or injury involved in the actual inadequacy of the foundations is sustained only at the time when that inadequacy is first known or manifest. It is only then that the actual diminution in the market value of the premises occurs. On either approach, however, any loss involved in the actual inadequacy of the foundations by a person who acquires an interest in the premises after the building has been completed is merely economic in its nature.'

I find myself in respectful agreement with the reasoning contained in this passage, which seems to me to be incontrovertible.

Another significant reason given by the House of Lords for its change of direction between *Anns* and *Murphy* was the existence of the Defective Premises Act 1972:

By section 1 of the Defective Premises Act 1972 Parliament has in fact imposed on builders and others undertaking work in the provision of dwellings the obligations of a transmissible warranty of the quality of their work and of the fitness for habitation of the completed dwelling. But besides being limited to dwellings, liability under the Act is subject to a limitation period of six years from the completion of the work and to the exclusion provided for by section 2. It would be remarkable to find that similar obligations in the nature of a transmissible warranty of quality, applicable to buildings of every kind and subject to no such limitations or exclusions as are imposed by the Act of 1972, could be derived from the builder's common law duty of care or from the duty imposed by building byelaws or regulations.[23]

The primary problem with the Act, however, is that it limits liability to defects arising within six years of the completion of the work. Whilst this prevents defendants from being subject to indeterminate liability, it also blunts the statute's teeth. Given that the average UK house price is now £224,000,[24] it is reasonable for purchasers to expect a longer useful life than half a dozen years. What is more, there was no need to put an arbitrary time limit on such claims in order to prevent liability of an indeterminate amount for an indeterminate time to an indeterminate class[25] because

---

23   At 480–1 per Lord Bridge.
24   https://www.theguardian.com/money/2019/feb/07/uk-house-prices-fall-in-january-as-brexit-puts-off-buyers: last accessed 20 March 2019.
25   Cardozo J's famous articulation, in *Ultramares Corp v Touche* 174 NE 441 (1932), of the prospect against which the tort of negligence is always vigilant.

there is no danger of a floodgates problem arising where loss is related (howsoever it is classified) to physical property. As has been recognised elsewhere in the common law world,[26] liability will naturally be limited to the cost of remedying the defects, during the useful life of the building, and in relation to those with sufficient title to that property when the defects 'occur'.[27] These intrinsic limits to such a claim could be said to exist because the loss is not really purely economic, but is instead parasitic upon the state of the subject matter of property rights.

Regardless of how satisfactory it is to see this type of loss as being purely economic, it remains the case that, following *Murphy*, in English law the diminution in value of property (whether real or personal) which results from a defect is deemed to be irrecoverable. And yet, elsewhere in the common law world, with the exception of Malaysia, appellate courts have refused to follow *Murphy* and have tended to favour recovery in such situations, particularly where the claimant is not a commercial entity. This has either been through a refusal to classify such loss as being purely economic (and adopting an approach closer to that taken by the House of Lords in *Anns*), or by focusing on the relative vulnerability of the claimant in the marketplace.

In the High Court of Australia, for instance, Brennan J declared that:

> it is artificial to classify defects in a building as pure economic loss. Defects in a building are physical defects and the cost of their rectification is consequential on their existence.[28]

In *Invercargill City Council v Hamlin* [1996],[29] Lord Lloyd made explicit reference to the divergent interpretations of 'pure economic loss' within common law systems, when, after referring to a series of New Zealand cases in which recovery had been granted for reduction in value alone, he said:

> These cases … are important because they extended the principle[30] to cases where there was no physical damage as such, nor any certainty that there would be. It was enough that the value of the premises had been reduced. Whether it is right to describe such cases as 'pure' economic loss may not matter very much. They do not depend on pure economic loss in the sense of *White v Jones* [1995] 2 AC 207 or *Henderson v Merrett Syndicates Ltd* [1995] 2 AC 145. For in the building cases the economic loss is suffered by reason of a defect on a physical object.[31]

■ VIEWPOINT

What do you think? Is the type of loss suffered in *Anns* and in *Murphy* really purely economic? Or is it something different? Is it exactly the same thing as conventional property damage? Your answers to these questions will tell you whether your thinking is more in line with English law, or with other Commonwealth approaches.

---

26 e.g. La Forest J in *Winnipeg* [1995] 1 SCR 85 at [48]–[50].

27 For more on this point, see next section.

28 [1995] HCA 17 at [23]. This is particularly notable since the judgment of Brennan J in *Council of the Shire of Sutherland v Heyman* (1985) 157 CLR 424 was influential in the House of Lords' about-turn in *Murphy v Brentwood DC* [1991] AC 398. See also *Brookfield Multiplex v Owners Corporation Strata Plan 61288* [2014] HCA 36 at [30], [58] and [185]. The judgments in the latter case provide an excellent example of the way in which Australian courts deal with the question as one of duty (which is determinable by the facts of a particular case) as opposed to damage (which is determined absolutely and in an *a priori* sense as irrecoverable).

29 [1996] AC 624.

30 The principle of recovery for pure economic loss, derived from *Bowen v Paramount Builders (Hamilton) Ltd* [1975] 2 NZLR 546.

31 [1996] AC 624 at 636.

PROBLEM QUESTION TECHNIQUE

Enya lives next door to Axville Community Centre, in a house that was built eight years ago. A few weeks before Tanvir's lorry crashed into the neighbouring building, the plaster on Enya's walls had begun to crack, the mirrors and pictures mounted on her walls started to fall off, and her wall shelves collapsed. The surveyor sent by her insurance company to inspect the damage discovered that the house's walls had been built with defective materials, in contravention of the applicable building regulations. Had they been built properly, and in accordance with those regulations, the damage would not have occurred. The builder of Enya's house, Julius, did seek approval from Axville City Council for both his plans and for the build itself. Axville sent an inspector out three times during the building process, and no objection was raised. As a result of these severe structural issues, Enya's house, which would otherwise be worth £400,000, is now worth only £75,000.

▸ Note here the causation point – the damage to E's house occurred before T's breach, and so is not property damage as a result of the crash.

▸ Following *Murphy v Brentwood*, E's loss would fall within the category of pure economic loss and so make it very hard to recover.

▸ Recovery was possible in *Smith v Bush*, but you would need to consider whether the facts of this question are sufficiently analogous to that case.

▸ Consider the time period here – eight years after construction – which makes the Defective Premises Act 1972 inapplicable.

DIFFERENT PERSPECTIVES on loss as a result of defective premises

P.S. Davies and S. Green, '"Pure Economic Loss" and Defective Buildings' in A. Robertson and M. Tilbury (eds), Convergence and Divergence in the Common Law (Hart, 2015)

This piece argues that the English common law's classification of the loss caused by defective premises as 'purely economic' is less coherent and effective than the approach commonly adopted elsewhere in the common law world, which takes a less restrictive view, and often allows recovery, particularly where the claimant is in a relatively vulnerable position. It also makes the point that the loss in these situations is not purely economic in the way that *Hedley Byrne*-type loss is because it is connected to a physical entity. Consequently, the problem of indeterminacy does not arise, meaning that the law does not need to impose tight limits on recovery.

P. Benson, 'The Basis for Excluding Economic Loss in Tort Law' in D. Owen (ed.), Philosophical Foundations of Tort Law (OUP, 1995)

This chapter sets out a justification for the exclusionary rule, defending the limits placed by the law of tort on recovery for pure economic loss in all of the situations dealt with in this chapter. The basic distinction Benson makes is between misfeasance and nonfeasance. In the case of defective premises situations, the claimant is pointing to a right she does not have in law: the defendant has no active duty to make her property safe in order that she might use it without risk. This is an issue of nonfeasance, as opposed to misfeasance, and the law of tort makes a general and clear distinction between the two.

3.6 CHAPTER SUMMARY

This chapter has dealt with one of the two areas of negligence in which the potential for indeterminacy can be acute. Since pure economic loss, unconnected with any tangible entity in the world, can be caused remotely, and passed on indefinitely, the tort of negligence needs to impose some sort of limit on recovery if defendants' liability is not going to be out of all proportion to their wrongdoing and/or unpredictable, and therefore uninsurable in advance. This section has shown, however, how and why it is important to distinguish between the different ways in which pure economic loss can be caused, how it is classified in England and Wales and elsewhere in the common law world, and under which conditions its recovery will be permitted. Whilst some of the judicial reasoning in this area is notoriously difficult to reconcile, looking at the bigger picture demonstrates that there is a unifying theme: identifying sufficient proximity between the parties. The reasoning and techniques from Chapter 2 (Duty of Care), particularly in the judgments of *Caparo* and *Robinson*, will prove very useful in complementing those covered in this chapter.

FURTHER READING

K. Barker, 'Economic Loss and the Duty of Care: A Study in the Exercise of Legal Justification' in C. Rickett (ed.), *Justifying Private Law Remedies* (Hart, 2008)

A. Burrows, 'Solving the Problem of Concurrent Liability' (1995) *Current Legal Problems* 103

J. Hartshorne, 'Contemporary Approaches Towards Pure Economic Loss in the Law of Negligence' (2014) 5 *JBL* 425–42.

P. Mitchell and C. Mitchell, 'Negligence Liability for Pure Economic Loss' (2005) 121 *LQR* 194

D. Nolan, 'Preventive Damages' (2016) 132 (Jan) *LQR* 68–95

J. Stapleton, 'Duty of Care and Economic Loss: A Wider Agenda' (1991) 107 *LQR* 249

Roadmap: Is the financial cost recoverable?

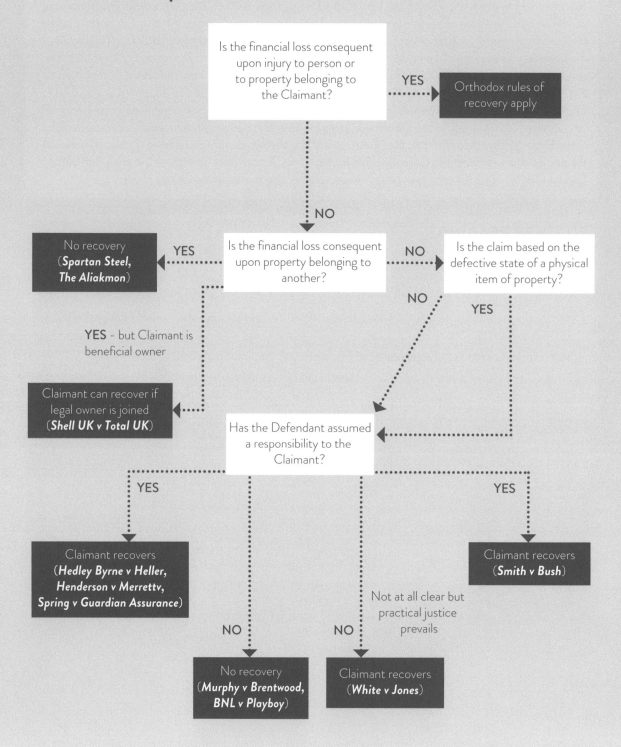

4 PSYCHIATRIC INJURY

LEARNING OBJECTIVES

By the end of this chapter, you should be able to:

- Apply the common law distinction between primary and secondary victims in psychiatric injury cases
- Apply the 'control mechanisms' fashioned by the common law to secondary victims in psychiatric injury cases
- Navigate the case law in this area
- Engage with the policy arguments surrounding this controversial area of the law, and make a coherent argument about their relative merits and demerits
- Recognise the influence that the particular effects of the Hillsborough disaster have had on the rules (and exceptions) in this field
- Consolidate your understanding of the indeterminacy issue, and the potential problems it creates for the tort of negligence

CHAPTER CONTENTS

4.1 Introduction 62

4.2 Abandoning the search for a principle 63

4.3 What is psychiatric harm? 65

4.4 Distinguishing between primary and secondary victims 66

    4.4.1 Primary victims 66

    4.4.2 Secondary victims 73

4.5 Law in need of reform? 82

4.6 Chapter summary 83

Further reading 84

Roadmap 85

PROBLEM QUESTION

Mej owns a mobile vegan food business, and attends events all over the country, selling products from her VegVan. Nina, her best friend, is the company's head chef, and Mej has also paid for her to be trained as a first aider. In their VegVan, they attend the Hot Air Balloon Carnival in Clafton, which is a very popular annual fair. Nina had originally booked that time off six months previously, but Mej begged her to postpone her holiday and come along, since it promised to be a lucrative event. Nina eventually agreed because Mej is such a good friend and has recently been struggling to make her business profitable. On arrival, they park in the dedicated catering section and attach their van to the electricity and water supplies provided by Overall Productions, the company organising the Carnival.

Piet is the events manager for Overall, and he is busy supervising preparations for the first hot air balloon flight of the day, which is a trip in the Paw Patrol balloon for three children from the local primary school, along with their class teacher. As the balloon takes off, its guide rope fails to detach. As the balloon rises, this rope coils around Piet's leg and he is lifted into the air, helpless to resist. In response to Piet's screams of pain and fear, several people rush to his aid, and try to grab the rope to prevent the balloon's further ascent. One of these is Quinn, an off-duty paramedic. Quinn was the first to reach the rope and holds it as tight as he can. The rope creates a huge amount of friction as it runs through his grip, which would have burnt the skin off unprotected hands. Fortunately, Quinn cycled to the carnival and he is still wearing his high-performance sports gloves, which prevent any injury to his palms. Eventually, Quinn and the other bystanders who have come to help manage to stop the balloon's ascent and, with the help of the pilot, it returns to the ground. As it lands, however, Piet falls awkwardly and breaks his neck with an audible snap. Quinn and three of the other people holding the rope suffer post-traumatic stress disorder (PTSD) as a result of seeing these events. Five members of the crowd suffer from sleep problems in the months following the accident, one develops an eating disorder and another suffers from a relapse of her longstanding anxiety disorder. Several of the onlookers record footage of the entire incident at close quarters on their mobile phones, and upload it to various websites, such as Facebook and YouTube. Moderators of both sites remove the footage as soon as they are aware of its presence but it has by then already had over 500,000 views. The video includes full details of the accident, in which Piet is fully identifiable and in which the sounds of his neck snapping can be heard. Within six months of the incident, over 5,000 people have complained of developing substance dependency as a result of watching the footage online.

Nina, who had been busy grilling vegan burgers, looks up to admire the view and sees people gathered around Piet, lying on the ground with his neck broken. Instinctively, she runs over to assist, forgetting to turn off the grill. Nobody is supposed to be left on their own in the VegVan, but Mej went off for a walk to phone her new girlfriend, thinking that Nina wouldn't mind. When Nina reaches the scene of the accident, she explains to the crowd that she is a qualified first aider and kneels on the ground next to Piet. She quickly realises there is nothing she can do, and Piet dies in her arms. At that moment, she hears a loud explosion and looks over to the VegVan. It is a ball of flames, and Renata, a customer who had been waiting to be served, runs away from the fire, choking and spluttering on the black smoke. Seamus, the Health and Safety Director of Overall Productions, emerges from the administration offices to see what all the noise is about. He should have been overseeing the balloon flights and supervising his team to check the catering vans, but he has just returned from three months' sick leave owing to stress caused by overwork, and has returned to find that the extra employees he was promised have not been hired. Whilst the drama was unfolding, he was lying down in a darkened office to stave off a panic attack. On seeing what has happened in his absence, he suffers a breakdown. Seamus never recovers sufficiently to work again. Renata is examined at the local hospital and found to be physically fine, but she is permanently anxious about developing a respiratory illness as a result of the smoke she inhaled. Nina, who has always been a very cheerful and positive individual, becomes morose, unsociable and develops a dependency on prescription painkillers. Mej finds it intolerable to see her friend's life deteriorate in this way, especially as she feels that it is her fault for persuading Nina to come, and then leaving her alone in the van. Mej suffers from chronic insomnia as a consequence.

4.1 Introduction

Psychiatric injury used to be referred to in a forensic context as 'nervous shock', and this term betrays the historical attitude towards this type of damage. Although the legal perception of psychiatric injury is slowly developing along with the more enlightened social and medical treatment today, it is still clear from the case law that injury to the person and injury to the mind are regarded as very different things. There is still, however, a clear distinction to be made when it comes to the question of a defendant's duty of care. As outlined in the general introduction to this chapter and Chapter 11 (Economic Torts), this is, in recent times at least, more a result of courts' concerns about indeterminate liability than it is a refusal to recognise psychiatric injury as a legitimate ground for complaint.

To complicate matters further, the law in this area has been significantly affected by the catastrophic effects of the Hillsborough disaster, which gave rise to claims for psychiatric injury on an unprecedented scale. This in itself might well have affected the extent to which the law imposed limits on recovery for psychiatric injury by those who were not themselves physically endangered by the perilous events concerned.

This chapter will examine the different ways in which the law classifies victims of psychiatric injury, and the implications this classification has for the ability of each to recover. It will set out the different criteria which need to be met by each type of victim, and analyse the extent to which the considerable variation is fair and effective, given the objectives of tort law and the inevitable restraints upon recovery in the context of large-scale disasters. This is a very contentious area of the law, and this chapter will provide an opportunity to evaluate its inherent policy considerations.

4.2 Abandoning the search for a principle

This area of the law is riddled with outdated concepts and the baggage of old-fashioned attitudes to psychiatric illness. This, in combination with the potential for indeterminate claims, and the intervention of a particularly catastrophic event in the form of the Hillsborough disaster, all make for a contentious and sometimes incoherent field of legal reasoning. In fact, Lord Hoffmann was moved to say that 'the search for principle' has been 'called off'.[1] Your aim in mastering it must therefore be to gain a sound grasp of the case law and of the potential difficulties in reconciling the different judgments. This will help you both in terms of dealing with ambiguities in problem questions, and in formulating persuasive arguments in answers to essay questions.

As outlined in the introduction to this section, the potential for indeterminacy in situations involving psychiatric injury arises because it is a type of loss that does not necessarily depend on any physical damage. The natural limits generated by the need for physical proximity are therefore absent and need to be imposed by the law. What is more, even though the significant cases in this area attempted to deal with the mass transmission of distressing images, they were decided before the age of 24-hour news coverage and commercial internet platforms. Today, with relatively unregulated internet hosting sites such as YouTube, Facebook and Instagram, the problem is far more acute. In March 2019, for instance, footage of a terrorist attack in New Zealand, in which 50 people were shot by a gunman in a mosque, was uploaded to Facebook and viewed 4,000 times before it was removed.[2] It is incredibly difficult to imagine how anyone, in current conditions, can have a clear-cut idea of the likely reach that any distressing images resulting from their negligent act will have: the transmission of such images over the internet would seem to constitute a classic example of 'liability in an indeterminate amount for an indeterminate time to an indeterminate class'.[3] It is important to note, therefore, that the limits imposed by the law in this area are expressly artificial; they do not attempt to trace the lines of where psychiatric injury does or should occur. On the contrary, there is a clear recognition in the case law that much negligently caused psychiatric injury will go uncompensated. Lord Steyn recognised this in *White v Chief Constable of South Yorkshire Police* [1999]:[4]

> In an ideal world all those who have suffered as a result of the negligence ought to be compensated. But we do not live in Utopia: we live in a practical world where the tort system imposes limits to the classes of claims that rank for consideration as well as to the heads of

---

1   In *White v Chief Constable of South Yorkshire Police* [1999] 2 AC 455 at 511.
2   https://www.bbc.co.uk/news/technology-47758455: last accessed 3 April 2019.
3   Cardozo J in *Ultramares Corporation v Touche*, 174 NE 441 (1932).
4   [1999] 2 AC 455.

recoverable damages. This results, of course, in imperfect justice but it is by and large the best that the common law can do. The application of the requirement of reasonable foreseeability was sufficient for the disposal of the resulting claims for death and physical injury. But the common law regards reasonable foreseeability as an inadequate tool for the disposal of claims in respect of emotional injury … Courts of law must act on the best medical insight of the day. Nowadays courts accept that there is no rigid distinction between body and mind. Courts accept that a recognisable psychiatric illness results from an impact on the central nervous system. In this sense therefore there is no qualitative difference between physical harm and psychiatric harm. And psychiatric harm may be far more debilitating than physical harm.

It would, however, be an altogether different proposition to say that no distinction is made or ought to be made between principles governing the recovery of damages in tort for physical injury and psychiatric harm. The contours of tort law are profoundly affected by distinctions between different kinds of damage or harm … Policy considerations have undoubtedly played a role in shaping the law governing recovery for pure psychiatric harm. The common law imposes different rules for the recovery of compensation for physical injury and psychiatric harm … It seems to me useful to ask why such different rules have been created for the recovery of the two kinds of damage …

Lord Steyn then goes on to set out precisely why he thinks that a distinction exists between the two types of harm:

My impression is that there are at least four distinctive features of claims for psychiatric harm which in combination may account for the differential treatment. Firstly, there is the complexity of drawing the line between acute grief and psychiatric harm: see Steve Hedley, 'Nervous Shock: Wider Still and Wider?' [1997] C.L.J. 254. The symptoms may be the same. But there is greater diagnostic uncertainty in psychiatric injury cases than in physical injury cases. The classification of emotional injury is often controversial. In order to establish psychiatric harm expert evidence is required. That involves the calling of consultant psychiatrists on both sides. It is a costly and time-consuming exercise. If claims for psychiatric harm were to be treated as generally on a par with physical injury it would have implications for the administration of justice. On its own this factor may not be entitled to great weight and may not outweigh the considerations of justice supporting genuine claims in respect of pure psychiatric injury.

It could be argued that the initial view espoused here by Lord Steyn is somewhat outdated. Modern attitudes to psychiatric and emotional injury are more likely to be in line with his final point; that the expense of calling expert witnesses to attest to psychiatric injury is indeed outweighed by the need for redress in such cases.

Secondly, there is the effect of the expansion of the availability of compensation on potential claimants who have witnessed gruesome events. I do not have in mind fraudulent or bogus claims. In general it ought to be possible for the administration of justice to expose such claims. But I do have in mind the unconscious effect of the prospect of compensation on potential claimants. Where there is generally no prospect of recovery, such as in the case of injuries sustained in sport, psychiatric harm appears not to obtrude often. On the other hand, in the case of industrial accidents, where there is often a prospect of recovery of compensation, psychiatric harm is repeatedly encountered and often endures until the process of claiming compensation comes to an end … The litigation is sometimes an unconscious disincentive to rehabilitation. It is true that this factor is already present in cases of physical injuries with concomitant mental suffering. But it may play a larger role in cases of pure psychiatric harm, particularly if the categories of potential recovery are enlarged. For my part this factor cannot be dismissed.

This point is less a reflection of a particular attitude toward mental health, and is instead more of a practical consideration. There can be little doubt that litigation is a very mentally and emotionally challenging process, and it may well serve to perpetuate the adverse effects of a psychiatric problem.

> The third factor is important. The abolition or a relaxation of the special rules governing the recovery of damages for psychiatric harm would greatly increase the class of persons who can recover damages in tort. It is true that compensation is routinely awarded for psychiatric harm where the plaintiff has suffered some physical harm. It is also well established that psychiatric harm resulting from the apprehension of physical harm is enough: *Page v Smith* [1996] A.C. 155. These two principles are not surprising. In built in such situations are restrictions on the classes of plaintiff who can sue: the requirement of the infliction of some physical injury or apprehension of it introduces an element of immediacy which restricts the category of potential plaintiffs. But in cases of pure psychiatric harm there is potentially a wide class of plaintiffs involved.

This too is undoubtedly a practical consideration, making the point that, where pure psychiatric injury is concerned, unconnected to any tangible harm, the potential for indeterminate claims is a concern.

> Fourthly, the imposition of liability for pure psychiatric harm in a wide range of situations may result in a burden of liability on defendants which may be disproportionate to tortious conduct involving perhaps momentary lapses of concentration, e.g. in a motor car accident.[5]

This is perhaps one of Lord Steyn's strongest arguments on this point. Always bear in mind that negligence is a non-intentional tort, and we are all as much potential defendants as we are claimants. It makes sense, therefore, to balance the interests of defendants and claimants, and to ensure that neither class carries a disproportionate burden either of liability or of loss.

These, then, are some of the policy factors that have contributed to the development of the law in this area. We now need to consider what psychiatric harm means in the context of negligence.

4.3 What is 'psychiatric harm'?

For the purposes of the tort of negligence, 'psychiatric harm' has a specific definition. Significantly, in order to be recoverable, damage has to be of a medically recognisable type. It cannot, for instance, be emotional upset, grief or distress which falls short of formal medical recognition. Obviously, this is a distinction which is by no means always easy to make and is also one which has changed over time as medical and social parameters have shifted. Famously, in *McLoughlin v O'Brian* [1983],[6] Lord Bridge said:

> The common law gives no damages for the emotional distress which any normal person experiences when someone he loves is killed or injured. Anxiety and depression are normal human emotions … the first hurdle which a plaintiff claiming damages of the kind in question must surmount is to establish that he is suffering, not merely grief, distress or any other normal human emotion, but a positive psychiatric illness.

---

5   Lord Steyn in *White* at 491–3.
6   [1983] 1 AC 410 at 431.

The language used here, particularly the frequent references to 'normal' as being something distinct from the suffering of psychiatric harm, would probably be avoided in the modern judicial context. It shows how, in the intervening 40 years since *McLoughlin* was decided, attitudes to afflictions associated with the mind have altered. Howsoever it is phrased, the point remains in law: the first thing that a claimant must establish if she is going to succeed in her claim for psychiatric injury is that she is suffering from a medically recognised condition.

Next, it is important to be able to make the distinction between primary and secondary victims because it determines what legal analysis applies and, consequently, affects a claimant's prospects of a successful action.

4.4 Distinguishing between primary and secondary victims

In short, it is a lot more straightforward for a primary victim to recover for psychiatric injury than it is for a secondary victim to do so. Primary victims are those who are directly involved in the incident concerned, to the extent that they are exposed to the risk of physical harm (although they need not actually suffer it). Secondary victims, on the other hand, are (generally) those who see the disturbing event remotely, or come across the scene of the incident at a later stage, meaning that they are not within the zone of physical danger. The absence of an immediate and physical connection between the effects of the defendant's breach and the claimant's injury in secondary victim cases, therefore, means that the potential for indeterminate liability is a factor in secondary victim situations in a way that it is not in cases involving primary victims.

4.4.1 Primary victims

KEY CASE

Page v Smith [1996] AC 155

The defendant in this case caused, through his negligence, a minor vehicle collision. The claimant who was involved in the incident had a history of suffering from myalgic encephalomyelitis (M.E.), a condition characterised by long-term fatigue among other symptoms. His condition became chronic and permanent as a result of the accident, making it unlikely that he would be able to find full-time employment in the future. Whilst the claimant succeeded at first instance, the Court of Appeal allowed the defendant's appeal on the basis that the claimant's injury was not foreseeable. The House of Lords disagreed, and restored the finding in favour of the claimant. The most well-known analysis of the foreseeability point can be found in Lord Lloyd's judgment:

> The test in every case ought to be whether the defendant can reasonably foresee that his conduct will expose the plaintiff to risk of

personal injury. If so, then he comes under a duty of care to that plaintiff. If a working definition of "personal injury" is needed, it can be found in section 38(1) of the Limitation Act 1980: "Personal injuries" includes any disease and any impairment of a person's physical or mental condition' ... In the case of a secondary victim, the question will usually turn on whether the foreseeable injury is psychiatric, for the reasons already explained. In the case of a primary victim the question will almost always turn on whether the foreseeable injury is physical. But it is the same test in both cases, with different applications. There is no justification for regarding physical and psychiatric injury as different 'kinds' of injury. Once it is established that the defendant is under a duty of care to avoid causing personal injury to the plaintiff, it matters not whether the injury in fact sustained is physical, psychiatric or both. ... in the present case, it was enough to ask whether the defendant should have reasonably foreseen that the plaintiff might suffer physical injury as a result of the defendant's negligence, so as to bring him within the range of the defendant's duty of care. It was unnecessary to ask, as a separate question, whether the defendant should reasonably have foreseen injury by shock; and it is irrelevant that the plaintiff did not, in fact, suffer any external physical injury.[7]

In the circumstances, the claimant in *Page* was deemed to fall squarely within the category of primary victim.

In essence, *Page* tells us that, where a claimant is a primary victim, only physical injury must be reasonably foreseeable in order for psychiatric injury to be recoverable. This is the case, even where physical injury does not actually occur but psychiatric injury does, as was the case in *Page*:

> Although the plaintiff was, as I have said, the primary victim, the peculiarity of the present case is that, by good fortune, he suffered no broken bones and no bruising; indeed he had no external physical injury of any kind. But as a direct result of the accident he suffered a recrudescence of an illness or condition known variously as M.E., C.F.S. or P.V.F.S., from which he had previously suffered in a mild form on sporadic occasions, but which, since the accident, has become an illness of 'chronic intensity and permanency.'

The distinction is also important when considering whether or not the claimant responded to the event as a 'person of normal fortitude':

> In claims by secondary victims the law insists on certain control mechanisms, in order as a matter of policy to limit the number of potential claimants. Thus, the defendant will not be liable unless psychiatric injury is foreseeable in a person of normal fortitude. These control mechanisms have no place where the plaintiff is the primary victim.

This control mechanism constitutes a departure from the orthodox tort law position that a defendant takes her victim as she finds him, and so widens the gap even further between primary and secondary victims in terms of their ability to recover for psychiatric injury. It is another reason why the distinction is such a significant one to make.

The means used to make the distinction has, however, changed over time. In *Page*, Lord Lloyd referred to the distinction made by Lord Keith in *Alcock*,[8] a case to which we will return below:

> Broadly they divide into two categories, that is to say, those cases in which the injured plaintiff was involved, either mediately, or immediately, as a participant, and those in which the plaintiff was no more than the passive and unwilling witness of injury caused to others.

PROBLEM QUESTION TECHNIQUE

In response to Piet's screams of pain and fear, several people rush to his aid, and try to grab the rope to prevent the balloon's further ascent. One of these is Quinn, an off-duty paramedic. Quinn was the first to reach the rope and holds it as tight as he can. The rope creates a huge amount of friction as it runs through his grip, which would have burnt the skin off unprotected hands. Fortunately, Quinn had cycled to the carnival and was still wearing his high-performance sports gloves, which prevent any injury to his palms. Eventually, Quinn and the other bystanders who have come to help manage to arrest the

---

7   Lord Lloyd at 190.
8   *Alcock v Chief Constable of South Yorkshire Police* [1992] 1 AC 310 at 407.

balloon's ascent and, with the help of the pilot, it returns to the ground. As it lands, however, Piet falls awkwardly and breaks his neck with an audible snap. Quinn and three of the other people holding the rope suffer post-traumatic stress disorder (PTSD) as a result of seeing these events. Five members of the crowd suffer from sleep problems in the months following the accident, one develops an eating disorder and another suffers from a relapse of her longstanding anxiety disorder.

▸ It is important here to distinguish between primary and secondary victims, so that you can apply the correct legal test (to which we will return below).

▸ It is material that Quinn, and others holding the rope, all face the risk of physical injury, and so are within the zone of danger necessary to make them primary victims.

▸ It is not so obvious, however, that the other members of the crowd are at risk of physical injury, and so are more likely to be regarded in legal terms as secondary victims.

▸ It is possible, however, that members of the crowd could be regarded as primary victims if they were near enough to the descending balloon to be at risk of physical injury.

▸ It is hard to come to any concrete answers in terms of the classification of victims, but what is important is that you know what the criteria for each category are and which cases those principles come from. You can then apply the criteria appropriately to the facts of any problem question with which you are presented.

The reasoning of the House of Lords in the following case, *W v Essex CC* [2001], however, makes it clear that the categories of primary and secondary victims are not closed.

KEY CASE

W v Essex CC [2001] 2 AC 592

The claimants were parents whose children had been sexually abused by a foster child, placed with them by the local council in breach of its duty of care after the parents had explicitly specified that they were not prepared to foster a child with a history of sexually abusing others. In deciding whether to allow the parents to recover for their psychiatric injury, the question for the court was whether their claim should be struck out. This judgment, therefore, makes no finding one way or another on whether the claimants were actually classed as primary or secondary victims, but it does show that the House unanimously felt that their case for being primary victims was arguable and had, therefore, a chance of succeeding.

Is it clear beyond reasonable doubt that the parents cannot satisfy the necessary criteria as 'primary' or 'secondary' victims? As to being primary victims it is beyond doubt that

they were not physically injured by the abuse and on the present allegations it does not seem reasonably foreseeable that there was risk of sexual abuse of the parents. But the categorisation of those claiming to be included as primary or secondary victims is not as I read the cases finally closed. It is a concept still to be developed in different factual situations. Lord Goff of Chieveley (dissenting) in *Frost* [1999] 2 AC 455, 472G said that Lord Oliver 'did not attempt any definition of this category [i.e. of primary victims] but simply referred to a number of examples.' In *Robertson v Forth Road Bridge Joint Board* 1995 SCLR 466 at 475D the Lord President (Hope) said 'Nor is there any basis in the evidence for attributing their illnesses to a belief that they had been the unwitting cause of Smith's death.' That seems to recognise that if there had been such a basis a claim might have been arguable ... I do not consider that any of the cases to which your Lordships have been referred conclusively shows that, if the psychiatric injury suffered by the parents flows from a feeling that they brought the abuser and the abused together or that they have a feeling of responsibility that they did not detect earlier what was happening, they are prevented from being primary victims ... Whilst I accept that there has to be some temporal and spatial limitation on the persons who can claim to be secondary victims, very much for the reasons given by Lord Steyn in the *Frost* case, it seems to me that the concept of 'the immediate aftermath' of the incident has to be assessed in the particular factual situation. I am not persuaded that in a situation like the present the parents must come across the abuser or the abused 'immediately' after the sexual incident has terminated. All the incidents here happened in the period of four weeks before the parents learned of them. It might well be that if the matter were investigated in depth a judge would think that the temporal and spatial limitations were not satisfied. On the other hand he might find that the flexibility to which Lord Scarman referred indicated that they were ... If this were, on the authorities, a clear cut case, I would not hesitate to strike it out. However I ... have come to the conclusion that the parents' claim cannot be said to be so certainly or clearly bad that they should be barred from pursuing it to trial.'[9]

It might be that *W v Essex* appears to hinder, rather than help, the process of distinguishing between primary and secondary victims, but it is useful to show how the categories remain to some extent fluid. If you are faced with a problem question, for instance, with similar facts in that the claimant feels in some way instrumental in bringing about the harm to a third party, and there is a strong emotional nexus between the victim and the claimant, the reasoning in *W v Essex* will be relevant.[10]

PROBLEM QUESTION TECHNIQUE

Nina, who has always been a very cheerful and positive individual, becomes morose, unsociable and develops a dependency on prescription painkillers. Mej finds it intolerable to see her friend's life deteriorate in this way, especially as she feels that it is her fault for persuading Nina to come, and then leaving her alone in the van. Mej suffers from chronic insomnia as a consequence.

▶ We will return to Nina below, when discussing rescuers.

▶ Mej is not necessarily straightforward to classify. In her case, consider whether the reasoning in *W v Essex* might be applied: she is best friends with Nina, and feels responsible for persuading her to come to the event, having trained her as a first aider, and for leaving her alone in the van, and thereby probably causing the explosion. If this is deemed sufficiently analogous to the facts of *W v Essex*, Mej could qualify as a primary victim.

The primary/secondary victim distinction will often be difficult to make in practice. For academic purposes, though, you can deal with it by having a good knowledge of just a handful of key cases (those dealt with here), and applying those that are most analogous to the facts in front of you. It is also perfectly legitimate to point out, in both essays and problem questions, that the law in this area is

---

9   Lord Slynn at 600–2.

10   It is worth noting that Lord Slynn felt that the earlier Court of Appeal decision in *Hunter v British Coal Corporation* [1999] QB 140, in which the claimant suffered psychiatric injury as a result of feeling responsible for an accident which caused the death of a fellow employee, and was deemed to be a secondary victim and therefore not able to recover, was not sufficient to deem the parents' case in *W v Essex* to be unarguable.

not straightforward, with outcomes therefore being hard to predict. Not being able to predict with certainty what classification would be made, however, is not a problem for assessment purposes (since nobody can do this): what is important is to demonstrate your knowledge of the principles that will be considered, which cases they originate from, and therefore what reasoning to apply to a given situation. The good news is that the distinction between primary and secondary will not always be a difficult one to make. There is a group of cases dealing with psychiatric injury in which the question of whether or not the claimant is a primary or secondary victim is more straightforward. These are the cases dealing with psychiatric injury caused to employees by the actions (or omissions) of an employer, as in *Rothwell v Chemical and Insulation Co Ltd* [2007].

KEY CASE

Rothwell v Chemical and Insulating Co Ltd [2007] UKHL 39

The claimants in these cases were employees who had been exposed to asbestos in the workplace through the defendant employers' breaches of duty. As a result, they had developed pleural plaques (patches of scar tissue) on their lungs. The existence of such pleural plaques is not deemed to amount to physical injury for the purposes of grounding a negligence action in its own right: first, the plaques are symptomless; second, although the plaques signify that exposure to asbestos dust has occurred, they do not in themselves mean that those who have them are any more likely to develop an asbestos-related disease than those who have been exposed to asbestos but have not developed pleural plaques. The claimants conceded this, but tried to aggregate the existence of their pleural plaques with the fact that, as a result of becoming aware of the plaques, they had also developed anxiety about their risk of sustaining an asbestos-related disease in the future. Agreeing with the Court of Appeal, the House of Lords found that the defendant employers were not liable because the claimants had only suffered an increased risk of developing a disease in the future. Unless and until such injury actually occurred, there was nothing recognised by the tort of negligence for which the claimants could recover: mere anxiety about an increased risk was not sufficient to ground a claim. Whilst one of the claimants, Grieves, had suffered more than anxiety, in that he had been diagnosed with a recognised psychiatric illness, this was still found to be insufficient to ground a successful claim since it was based not on an actual physical injury, but upon the risk of a future injury.[11]

The claimants in *Rothwell* are classified as primary victims because they were the ones physically exposed to asbestos by their employers. And yet, in *Rothwell*, Lord Hoffmann, with no disagreement from the rest of the court, said:

> The general rule still requires one to decide whether it was reasonably foreseeable that the event which actually happened (in this case, the creation of a risk of an asbestos-related disease) would cause psychiatric illness to a person of reasonable fortitude.[12]

Since there was no basis on the facts of *Rothwell* for finding that a person of reasonable fortitude would have suffered in the way that Mr Grieves did, this was another reason for denying his claim. The obvious question to which this gives rise, and the point made by counsel for Mr Grieves, is that this approach appears to be inconsistent with that of the House of Lords to the foreseeability issue in *Page v Smith*. In response to this, Lord Hoffmann went on to say:

---

11 See Lord Hope at [55].
12 At [30].

I do not think that it would be right to depart from *Page v Smith*. It does not appear to have caused any practical difficulties and is not, I think, likely to do so if confined to the kind of situation which the majority in that case had in mind. That was a foreseeable event (a collision) which, viewed in prospect, was such as might cause physical injury or psychiatric injury or both. Where such an event has in fact happened and caused psychiatric injury, the House decided that it is unnecessary to ask whether it was foreseeable that what actually happened would have that consequence. Either form of injury is recoverable ... In the present case, the foreseeable event was that the claimant would contract an asbestos-related disease. If that event occurred, it could no doubt cause psychiatric as well as physical injury. But the event has not occurred. The psychiatric illness has been caused by apprehension that the event may occur. The creation of such a risk is, as I have said, not in itself actionable. I think it would be an unwarranted extension of the principle in *Page v Smith* to apply it to psychiatric illness caused by apprehension of the possibility of an unfavourable event which had not actually happened.[13]

The most straightforward way of processing this is to see *Rothwell* as being a case involving potential primary victims, as opposed to actual primary victims. *Page v Smith* continues to apply to those situations where a claimant has been within the physical vicinity of an event which has actually occurred. Here, such a claimant can recover for psychiatric injury even where a person of reasonable fortitude would not have suffered the same way. In cases like *Rothwell*, however, in which the claimants are not in the physical vicinity of an event which actually occurred but are, rather, in a physical vicinity which has increased the risk of an event happening in the future (on these facts the development of an asbestos-related disease), the consideration of how a person of reasonable fortitude would have responded remains material.

PROBLEM QUESTION TECHNIQUE

Renata, a customer who had been waiting to be served, runs away from the fire, choking and spluttering on the black smoke ... Renata is examined at the local hospital and found to be physically fine, but she is permanently anxious about developing a respiratory illness as a result of the smoke she inhaled.

▶ This is a situation to which you need to apply *Rothwell* because Renata's anxiety is not consequent upon any actual physical harm.

Rothwell currently stands on its own facts, distinguishable on the basis that the claimants' case was premised on exposure to increased *risk* of harm, rather than on any established harm. This sets it apart from *Page v Smith*, as we have seen in the judgment of Lord Hoffmann, but it also sets it apart from those cases in which employees have been exposed by their employers to stress, as opposed to risk, at work. We will now look at the case of *Barber v Somerset County Council* [2004] on this subject.

KEY CASE

Barber v Somerset County Council [2004] UKHL 13

The claimant was a teacher who, overwhelmed by work, had been signed off for three weeks by his doctor as a result of stress and depression. On his return to work, he met with his managers to discuss his situation, and was promised a greater level of support. When this was not forthcoming, and the

---

13 At [32]–[33].

situation did not improve, he suffered a mental breakdown and sued his employers in negligence. The House of Lords allowed the claimant's appeal, finding that the defendant, his employer, had been in breach of its duty of care to him once it knew (or ought reasonably to have known) that he had a particular problem or vulnerability. Although it came to a different conclusion to the Court of Appeal on the facts, the House of Lords endorsed the 'practical propositions' formulated by Hale LJ in the lower court:[14]

(1) There are no special control mechanisms applying to claims for psychiatric (or physical) illness or injury arising from the stress of doing the work the employee is required to do. The ordinary principles of employer's liability apply.

(2) The threshold question is whether this kind of harm to this particular employee was reasonably foreseeable: this has two components (a) an injury to health (as distinct from occupational stress) which (b) is attributable to stress at work (as distinct from other factors).

(3) Foreseeability depends upon what the employer knows (or ought reasonably to know) about the individual employee. Because of the nature of mental disorder, it is harder to foresee than physical injury, but may be easier to foresee in a known individual than in the population at large. An employer is usually entitled to assume that the employee can withstand the normal pressures of the job unless he knows of some particular problem or vulnerability.

(4) The test is the same whatever the employment: there are no occupations which should be regarded as intrinsically dangerous to mental health.

(5) Factors likely to be relevant in answering the threshold question include: (a) The nature and extent of the work done by the employee. Is the workload much more than is normal for the particular job? Is the work particularly intellectually or emotionally demanding for this employee? Are demands being made of this employee unreasonable when compared with the demands made of others in the same or comparable jobs? Or are there signs that others doing this job are suffering harmful levels of stress? Is there an abnormal level of sickness or absenteeism in the same job or the same department? (b) Signs from the employee of impending harm to health. Has he a particular problem or vulnerability? Has he already suffered from illness attributable to stress at work? Have there recently been frequent or prolonged absences which are uncharacteristic of him? Is there reason to think that these are attributable to stress at work, for example because of complaints or warnings from him or others?

(6) The employer is generally entitled to take what he is told by his employee at face value, unless he has good reason to think to the contrary. He does not generally have to make searching inquiries of the employee or seek permission to make further inquiries of his medical advisers.

(7) To trigger a duty to take steps, the indications of impending harm to health arising from stress at work must be plain enough for any reasonable employer to realise that he should do something about it.

(8) The employer is only in breach of duty if he has failed to take the steps which are reasonable in the circumstances, bearing in mind the magnitude of the risk of harm occurring, the gravity of the harm which may occur, the costs and practicability of preventing it, and the justifications for running the risk.

(9) The size and scope of the employer's operation, its resources and the demands it faces are relevant in deciding what is reasonable; these include the interests of other employees and the need to treat them fairly, for example, in any redistribution of duties.

(10) An employer can only reasonably be expected to take steps which are likely to do some good: the court is likely to need expert evidence on this.

(11) An employer who offers a confidential advice service, with referral to appropriate

---

14   See in particular Lord Scott at [7].

counselling or treatment services, is unlikely to be found in breach of duty.

(12) If the only reasonable and effective step would have been to dismiss or demote the employee, the employer will not be in breach of duty in allowing a willing employee to continue in the job.

(13) In all cases, therefore, it is necessary to identify the steps which the employer both could and should have taken before finding him in breach of his duty of care.

(14) The claimant must show that that breach of duty has caused or materially contributed to the harm suffered. It is not enough to show that occupational stress has caused the harm.

(15) Where the harm suffered has more than one cause, the employer should only pay for that proportion of the harm suffered which is attributable to his wrongdoing, unless the harm is truly indivisible. It is for the defendant to raise the question of apportionment.

(16) The assessment of damages will take account of any pre-existing disorder or vulnerability and of the chance that the claimant would have succumbed to a stress related disorder in any event.[15]

PROBLEM QUESTION TECHNIQUE

Seamus, the Health and Safety Director of Overall Productions, emerges from the administration offices to see what all the noise is about. He should have been overseeing the balloon flights and supervising his team to check the catering vans, but he has just returned from a three months' sick leave owing to stress caused by overwork, and has returned to find that the extra employees he was promised have not been hired. Whilst the drama was unfolding, therefore, he was lying down in a darkened office to stave off a panic attack. On seeing what has happened in his absence, he suffers a breakdown. Seamus never recovers sufficiently to work again.

▸ The situation of employees who suffer from psychiatric injury as a result of being exposed to unreasonable stress at work is different from that involving a sudden incident or event because it does not require the psychiatric damage to have resulted from a sudden, acute and shocking event. Rather, it is characterised by ongoing, chronic mental pressure.

▸ Remember, as *Barber* tells us, it is not the nature of the job or profession which is important in establishing liability, but this particular employee's factual situation, and this particular employer's knowledge of it.

4.4.2 Secondary victims

Broadly, secondary victims are those who suffer from psychiatric harm as a result of injury occurring to someone else, rather than to themselves. In order to understand fully the way in which the law deals with the psychiatric injury caused to secondary victims, you will need to be familiar with the cases arising as a result of the Hillsborough disaster. On 15 April 1989, 96 people died as a result of the Hillsborough Football Stadium disaster. The catastrophic events occurred because the South Yorkshire Police, in breach of duty, allowed too many people into the stadium, leading to overcrowding which in turn crushed many of those spectators, killing some and injuring others. Arguably, the cases that followed (particularly the second one, *White*, below) distorted the way in which the law on psychiatric injury would otherwise have developed, and are widely regarded as being less than satisfactory. Nonetheless, they represent the positive law in this area and therefore need to be understood and applied.

We will first consider the case of *Alcock v Chief Constable of South Yorkshire* [1992].

---

15 *Hatton v Sutherland* [2002] EWCA Civ 76 at [43].

KEY CASE

Alcock v Chief Constable of South Yorkshire [1992] 1 AC 310

Alcock was made up of a group of actions brought by people who were not physically involved in the crush at the Hillsborough football stadium, but were connected in some way to people who were, some of whom had died or been injured.[16] The claimants were not therefore primary victims. The highly distressing nature of these events, the images of which were to some extent broadcast on television, both live at the time and several times afterwards, makes the cases very difficult to read, and the legal analysis difficult to assess dispassionately. It might also be argued that the scale of the disaster contributed in some way to the very restrictive nature of the approach adopted by a House of Lords keenly aware of the potential for indeterminate liability on such facts.

The judgment produced three criteria which those classed as secondary victims must satisfy in order to recover for psychiatric injury:

The three elements
Because 'shock' in its nature is capable of affecting such a wide range of persons, Lord Wilberforce in *McLoughlin v O'Brian* [1983] 1 A.C. 410, 422, concluded that there was a real need for the law to place some limitation upon the extent of admissible claims and in this context he considered that there were three elements inherent in any claim. It is common ground that such elements do exist and are required to be considered in connection with all these claims. ....
The three elements are
(1) The class of persons whose claims should be recognised.
(2) The proximity of such persons to the accident – in time and space.
(3) The means by which the shock has been caused.

(1) The class of persons whose claim should be recognised

When dealing with the possible range of the class of persons who might sue, Lord Wilberforce in *McLoughlin v O'Brian* [1983] 1 A.C. 410 contrasted the closest of family ties – parent and child and husband and wife – with that of the ordinary bystander. He said that while existing law recognises the claims of the first, it denied that of the second, either on the basis that such persons must be assumed to be possessed with fortitude sufficient to enable them to endure the calamities of modern life, or that defendants cannot be expected to compensate the world at large. He considered that these positions were justified, that other cases involving less close relationships must be very carefully considered, adding, at p. 422:

> 'The closer the tie (not merely in relationship, but in care) the greater the claim for consideration. The claim, in any case, has to be judged in the light of the other factors, such as proximity to the scene in time and place, and the nature of the accident.'

Whether the degree of love and affection in any given relationship, be it that of relative or friend, is such that the defendant, in the light of the plaintiff's proximity to the scene of the accident in time and space and its nature, should reasonably have foreseen the shock-induced psychiatric illness, has to be decided on a case by case basis.

(2) The proximity of the plaintiff to the accident

It is accepted that the proximity to the accident must be close both in time and space. Direct and immediate sight or hearing of the accident is not required. It is reasonably foreseeable that injury by shock can be caused to a plaintiff, not only through the sight or hearing of the event, but of its immediate aftermath.

Only two of the plaintiffs before us were at the ground. However, it is clear from *McLoughlin v O'Brian* [1983] 1 A.C. 410 that there may be

---

16   Although, in one case, the person about whom the claimant was concerned turned out not to have been injured.

liability where subsequent identification can be regarded as part of the 'immediate aftermath' of the accident. Mr. Alcock identified his brother-in-law in a bad condition in the mortuary at about midnight, that is some eight hours after the accident. This was the earliest of the identification cases. Even if this identification could be described as part of the 'aftermath', it could not in my judgment be described as part of the immediate aftermath. McLoughlin's case was described by Lord Wilberforce as being upon the margin of what the process of logical progression from case to case would allow. Mrs. McLoughlin had arrived at the hospital within an hour or so after the accident. Accordingly in the post-accident identification cases before your Lordships there was not sufficient proximity in time and space to the accident.

(3) The means by which the shock is caused
Lord Wilberforce concluded that the shock must come through sight or hearing of the event or its immediate aftermath but specifically left for later consideration whether some equivalent of sight or hearing, e.g. through simultaneous television, would suffice ... Of course it is common ground that it was clearly foreseeable by the defendant that the scenes at Hillsborough would be broadcast live and that amongst those who would be watching would be parents and spouses and other relatives and friends of those in the pens behind the goal at the Leppings Lane end. However he would also

know of the code of ethics which the television authorities televising this event could be expected to follow, namely that they would not show pictures of suffering by recognisable individuals. Had they done so ... this would have been a 'novus actus' breaking the chain of causation between the defendant's alleged breach of duty and the psychiatric illness. As the defendant was reasonably entitled to expect to be the case, there were no such pictures. Although the television pictures certainly gave rise to feelings of the deepest anxiety and distress, in the circumstances of this case the simultaneous television broadcasts of what occurred cannot be equated with the 'sight or hearing of the event or its immediate aftermath'. Accordingly shocks sustained by reason of these broadcasts cannot found a claim ... simultaneous broadcasts of a disaster cannot in all cases be ruled out as providing the equivalent of the actual sight or hearing of the event or its immediate aftermath. Nolan L.J. gave ... an example of a situation where it was reasonable to anticipate that the television cameras, whilst filming and transmitting pictures of a special event of children travelling in a balloon, in which there was media interest, particularly amongst the parents, showed the balloon suddenly bursting into flames. Many other such situations could be imagined where the impact of the simultaneous television pictures would be as great, if not greater, than the actual sight of the accident.[17]

In summary, in order to recover, secondary victims need to be able to prove:
(1) First, that they are in a close and loving relationship with the victim. This will be presumed where the relationship is one of spouse, parent or child but not, perhaps inexplicably, where the victim and the observer are siblings. The presumption can in any case be rebutted by any defendant who is able to show that the relationship was not one of a close and loving nature.
(2) Second, that they are sufficiently close to the shocking event in time and space. This can include proximity to the aftermath of the event, but it must be the *immediate* aftermath. Although there is no concrete guidance provided as to what amounts to 'immediate' for these purposes, we know that Alcock himself saw his brother-in-law in the mortuary eight hours after the disaster, and that this was deemed by the House of Lords *not* to be sufficient in proximity terms. We also know that, in the earlier case of *McLoughlin v O'Brian*, the claimant saw her

17   Lord Ackner at 402–6.

family in the hospital within an hour of their injuries occurring, and this was deemed by Lord Wilberforce to be 'on the margin' of what could count as proximate. Significantly, Lord Wilberforce also suggested that the passage of time was not the only relevant consideration, and that the condition of the victims at the time the claimant saw them can also affect what amounts to 'immediate aftermath':

> She was not present at the accident, but she came very soon after upon its aftermath. If, from a distance of some 100 yards (cf. *Benson v Lee*), she had found her family by the roadside, she would have come within principle 4 above. Can it make any difference that she comes upon them in an ambulance or, as here, in a nearby hospital, when, as the evidence shows, they were in the same condition, covered with oil and mud, and distraught with pain?[18]

(3)   Finally, that their psychiatric damage was caused either by direct perception of a shocking event, or by something very similar to that. The discussion at the time revolved around broadcasts made by regulated television platforms since that was, in 1989, the only significant way in which images could be widely transmitted. Such broadcasters were (and still are) subject to the *Broadcasting Code of Ethics*, and they would be in contravention of this were they to show footage of any identifiable individual's pain and suffering. This was the reason why the House of Lords in *Alcock* concluded that viewing such regulated images would not on the facts of that case amount to the sort of direct perception necessary to recover. The further point was made that, should a broadcaster fail to follow the Code in this way, it might itself incur liability for the psychiatric injury as a *novus actus interveniens*. The judgment does not, however, go so far as to rule out recovery *in principle* for anyone who has watched broadcast images of a shocking and distressing event, meaning that each case can be considered on its own facts. It may well be that reasoning has in any event been superseded by the almost ubiquitous presence of the internet and its image-hosting sites. Such platforms are not subject to the same practical limitations as mainstream broadcasters because any individual can upload pictures or footage to many sites, with the likely result that they will be distributed widely before any regulated entity can remove them. In technological terms, the world in which we live now would have been unimaginable to the House of Lords in 1992, and the broadcasting landscape is now unrecognisable when compared to the one that existed when these criteria were formulated. It is hard to imagine that people watching unedited mobile phone footage of a disaster similar in scale and horror to that of Hillsborough on YouTube, for instance, could be considered to have the same indirectness of perception as those watching regulated footage on the BBC evening news. This poses several challenges for the common law in this area: not only do the *Alcock* rules seem dated, particularly in terms of the ability directly to perceive events through modern broadcast media, but the potential for indeterminate liability, considerable even in the pre-internet era, is now far greater than ever before. The internet makes the likelihood of widespread detailed perception of distressing events, and therefore psychiatric harm, far more likely, but the *Alcock* mechanisms were designed to *limit* defendants' liability, so loosening them would be counter-productive to guarding against indeterminate liability. Perhaps the answer is to distribute liability more widely: allow claimants to recover for psychiatric injury caused by broadcast images, but, in certain situations, hold internet service providers or platform hosts liable instead of the defendant responsible for causing

---

18   At 418.

the initial shocking event. In other words, extend the *novus actus interveniens* reasoning suggested in *Alcock*.

■ VIEWPOINT

- What do you think, if anything, should happen to the *Alcock* criteria in the digital age? Do they, in your view, remain fit for purpose?
- Does the fact that there is now enormous potential for causing psychiatric harm through the transmission of digital images mean that the rules governing recovery for such damage should be more or less restrictive than those formulated in 1992?

PROBLEM QUESTION TECHNIQUE

Five members of the crowd suffer from sleep problems in the months following the accident, one develops an eating disorder and another suffers from a relapse of her longstanding anxiety disorder. Several of the onlookers record footage of the entire incident at close quarters on their mobile phones, and upload it to various websites, such as Facebook and YouTube. Moderators of both sites remove the footage as soon as they are aware of its presence but it has by then already had over 500,000 views. The video includes full details of the accident, in which Piet is fully identifiable and in which the sounds of his neck snapping can be heard. Within six months of the incident, over 5,000 people have complained of developing substance dependency as a result of watching the footage online.

▶ If the members of the crowd were not at risk of physical harm, they will be secondary victims and, as such, will only be able to recover if they satisfy the criteria set out in *Alcock*. Here, they perceive the shocking event immediately and with their unaided senses, and are physically proximate to what happened.

▶ They are unlikely to be able to recover, however, unless they can establish that they had a close tie of love and affection to any of those injured in the incident.

▶ It will also be necessary to distinguish between those who have suffered from a recognised psychiatric injury, and those whose sleep problems might not amount to that (*Hinz v Berry* [1970][19]).

▶ Those who view the footage online are clearly secondary victims, and it is material in their case that they have not witnessed the incident with their unaided senses.

▶ Although internet technology was not in use at the time *Alcock* was decided, it is worth suggesting that the hosts of the platforms on which the content was posted might be liable in negligence.

The next case, *White v Chief Constable of South Yorkshire Police,* is one of the trickiest cases in English tort law, with reasoning to match. There are several reasons for this. First, the claimants were rescuers, who had been trying to assist the victims of the Hillsborough disaster. Secondly, and more problematically, those rescuers were police officers who were, in technical terms at least, working under the auspices of the Chief Constable, the very office against which the original negligence

---

19   [1970] 2 QB 40.

action was brought. In principle, therefore, although not in practice,[20] the claimants in *White* were those who were responsible for the occurrence of the disaster in the first place.

KEY CASE

White v Chief Constable of South Yorkshire Police [1999] 2 AC 455

This case related to the same incident, the Hillsborough disaster; however, the claimants were police officers who had been working at the ground when the disaster occurred. Whilst none of the claimants had been working in the immediate area where the crush had occurred (liability to those officers had been admitted), four had been working at the stadium at the time, and a fifth dealt with the bodies and paperwork at the hospital to which they were taken. The claims for psychiatric harm were dismissed at first instance, but allowed by the Court of Appeal. By a majority, the House of Lords found in favour of the defendant and, in doing so, it made two principal points:

(1) Although the Chief Constable owed the claimants a duty of care analogous to that owed by an employer to its employees[21] not to cause them physical injury, this does not extend to a duty not to cause them psychiatric harm where there has been no breach of the duty not to cause physical harm. The claimants were, therefore, secondary victims in the ordinary sense and, as such, had to satisfy the criteria outlined in *Alcock* in order to recover for their psychiatric injury.

(2) The claimants were rescuers and, as they were not part of the group to whom physical injury was reasonably foreseeable, they were, like other bystanders and spectators, secondary victims who are required to meet the *Alcock* criteria.

Since none of the claimants in *White* had any pre-existing emotional ties to any of the victims of the disaster, they could not fulfil the *Alcock* criteria and were all unable to recover for their psychiatric injury.

Lord Hoffmann's judgment is probably most notable for its apparent impatience with the way in which the law in this area has developed thus far:

The cases on rescuers are therefore quite simple illustrations of the application of general principles of foreseeability and causation to particular facts. There is no authority which decides that a rescuer is in any special position in relation to liability for psychiatric injury. And it is no criticism of the excellent judgment of Waller J. in *Chadwick v British Railways Board* [1967] 1 W.L.R. 912 to say that such a question obviously never entered his head. Questions of such nicety did not arise until the *Alcock* control mechanisms had been enunciated.

There does not seem to me to be any logical reason why the normal treatment of rescuers on the issues of foreseeability and causation should lead to the conclusion that, for the purpose of liability for psychiatric injury, they should be given special treatment as primary victims when they were not within the range of foreseeable physical injury and their psychiatric injury was caused by witnessing or participating in the aftermath of accidents which caused death or injury to others. It would of course be possible to create such a rule by an ex post facto rationalisation of *Chadwick v British Railways*

---

20 Those officers who were working on the ground were not responsible for the strategic decisions which formed the basis of the negligence action in *Alcock*.

21 Police officers are not technically employees of the chief constable. See *James-Bowen v Commissioner of Police of the Metropolis* [2018] UKSC 40 at [15]: 'Police officers hold the public office of constable and are not employees. They have no contract of employment and the terms on which they hold their office are governed principally by the Police Regulations 2003 (SI 2003/527).'

Board [1967] 1 W.L.R. 912. In both *McLoughlin v O'Brian* [1983] 1 A.C. 410 and in *Alcock v Chief Constable of South Yorkshire* [1992] 1 A.C. 310, members of the House referred to Chadwick's case [1967] 1 W.L.R. 912 with approval. But I do not think that too much should be read into these remarks. In neither case was it argued that the plaintiffs were entitled to succeed as rescuers and anything said about the duty to rescuers was therefore necessarily obiter. If one is looking for an ex post facto rationalisation of Chadwick's case, I think that the most satisfactory is that offered in the Court of Appeal in *McLoughlin v O'Brian* [1981] Q.B. 599, 622 by my noble and learned friend, Lord Griffiths, who had been the successful counsel for Mr. Chadwick. He said:

'Mr. Chadwick might have been injured by a wrecked carriage collapsing on him as he worked among the injured. A duty of care is owed to a rescuer in such circumstances ...'

If Mr. Chadwick was, as Lord Griffiths said, within the range of foreseeable physical injury, then the case is no more than an illustration of the principle applied by the House in *Page v Smith* [1996] A.C. 155, namely that such a person can recover even if the injury he actually suffers is not physical but psychiatric. And in addition (unlike *Page v Smith* [1996] A.C. 155) Waller J. made a finding that psychiatric injury was also foreseeable.

Should then your Lordships take the incremental step of extending liability for psychiatric injury to 'rescuers' (a class which would now require definition) who give assistance at or after some disaster without coming within the range of foreseeable physical injury? It may be said that this would encourage people to offer assistance. The category of secondary victims would be confined to 'spectators and bystanders' who take no part in dealing with the incident or its aftermath. On the authorities, as it seems to me, your Lordships are free to take such a step.

In my opinion there are two reasons why your Lordships should not do so. The less

important reason is the definitional problem to which I have alluded. The concept of a rescuer as someone who puts himself in danger of physical injury is easy to understand.

But once this notion is extended to include others who give assistance, the line between them and bystanders becomes difficult to draw with any precision. For example, one of the plaintiffs in the *Alcock* case [1992] 1 A.C. 310, a Mr. O'Dell, went to look for his nephew. 'He searched among the bodies ... and assisted those who staggered out from the terraces:' p. 354. He did not contend that his case was different from those of the other relatives and it was also dismissed. Should he have put himself forward as a rescuer?

But the more important reason for not extending the law is that in my opinion the result would be quite unacceptable. I have used this word on a number of occasions and the time has come to explain what I mean. I do not mean that the burden of claims would be too great for the insurance market or the public funds, the two main sources for the payment of damages in tort. The Law Commission may have had this in mind when they said that removal of all the control mechanism would lead to an 'unacceptable' increase in claims, since they described it as a 'floodgates' argument. These are questions on which it is difficult to offer any concrete evidence and I am simply not in a position to form a view one way or the other. I am therefore willing to accept that, viewed against the total sums paid as damages for personal injury, the increase resulting from an extension of liability to helpers would be modest. But I think that such an extension would be unacceptable to the ordinary person because (though he might not put it this way) it would offend against his notions of distributive justice. He would think it unfair between one class of claimants and another, at best not treating like cases alike and, at worst, favouring the less deserving against the more deserving. He would think it wrong that policemen, even as part of a general class of persons who rendered assistance, should have the right to compensation for psychiatric injury out of public funds while the bereaved relatives are sent away with nothing.

To some extent this opinion would be based upon notions which the law would not accept. Many people feel that the statutory £7,500 (see section 1A of the Fatal Accidents Act 1976) is an inadequate payment to someone like Mr. Hicks, who lost his two daughters in such horrifying circumstances. And on the other side of the comparison, there is the view that policemen must expect to encounter harrowing experiences in the course of their duties and that their conditions of employment provide for ill-health pensions and injury pensions if they suffer injuries, physical or psychiatric, which result in their having to leave the force before normal retirement age. There may be other reasons also, from which I do not exclude ignorance about the nature of mental illness, but, all in all, I have no doubt that most people would regard it as wrong to award compensation for psychiatric injury to the professionals and deny compensation for similar injury to the relatives.

It may be said that the common law should not pay attention to these feelings about the relative merits of different classes of claimants. It should stick to principle and not concern itself with distributive justice. An extension of liability to rescuers and helpers would be a modest incremental development in the common law tradition and, as between these plaintiffs and these defendants, produce a just result. My Lords, I disagree. It seems to me that in this area of the law, the search for principle was called off in *Alcock v Chief Constable of South Yorkshire Police* [1992] 1 A.C. 310. No one can pretend that the existing law, which your Lordships have to accept, is founded upon principle. I agree with Jane Stapleton's remark that 'once the law has taken a wrong turning or otherwise fallen into an unsatisfactory internal state in relation to a particular cause of action, incrementalism cannot provide the answer': see The Frontiers of Liability, vol. 2, p. 87.

Consequently your Lordships are now engaged, not in the bold development of principle, but in a practical attempt, under adverse conditions, to preserve the general perception of the law as a system of rules which is fair between one citizen and another.[22]

The judgment in *White v Chief Constable of South Yorkshire Police* highlights in fairly explicit terms the thorny problems with this case. First, there is the very pressing concern, which was obvious to the court from the beginning, that it would have been incredibly difficult to justify allowing the police officers to recover where the relatives of the victims had been unsuccessful. This issue was exacerbated by the fact that it was the police who were (in broad terms) to blame for the incident in the first place. Of course, in practice, the police officers on the ground on the day were not morally to blame for the negligent operational decisions taken by their superior officers, but the fact that they are all technically part of the same organisation would have made a decision in their favour hard to justify in the light of the decision in *Alcock*. Then, there is the problem of the law's treatment of rescuers. Until *White*, tort had arguably been accommodating of rescuers, and for good reason; if someone puts themselves out to help others and, as a result, suffers from psychiatric injury, it seems reasonable to allow them to recover from whomever made the rescue necessary in the first place (not least because the need for such rescue is often going to be as reasonably foreseeable as the damaging event). The result that the House of Lords felt that it had to reach in *White*, however, could be seen to go against this reasoning, and to provide a perverse disincentive to rescuers. In this respect, the

---

22 At 508–11.

House of Lords' treatment of *Chadwick v British Railways Board* [1967][23] is an interesting one: the case is mentioned numerous times, and it is made very clear that, in deciding against recovery for the rescuers in *White*, the House, is at the same time expressly approving of the decision of Waller J in *Chadwick*. As we can see in the excerpt from Lord Hoffmann's judgment above, a formal distinction was made on the basis that the rescuer in *Chadwick* was within the zone of physical danger because the wreckage could have fallen on him at any time.[24] This was not analogous, according to the Court, to the situation faced by the police officers in *White*, who were involved with carrying the dead and the dying, and with resuscitation attempts. It may well be that the express preservation of the authority of *Chadwick* was a deliberate attempt by the Court to prevent the particular and unusual political difficulties of *White* from distorting the law on psychiatric injury to too great an extent. Had the House of Lords not done this, its decision in *White* would have made it very difficult for many rescuers to recover for psychiatric injury in subsequent cases.

■ VIEWPOINT

- What do you think about the result in *White*? Do you think the police officers who were working on the day, in the ground, should have been denied recovery?
- Do you think there is a legitimate distinction to be made between the police officers in *White* and the rescuer in the rail crash in *Chadwick*?

PROBLEM QUESTION TECHNIQUE

Nina, who had been busy grilling vegan burgers, looks up to admire the view and sees people gathered around Piet, lying on the ground with his neck broken. Instinctively, she runs over to assist, forgetting to turn off the grill. Nobody is supposed to be left on their own in the VegVan, but Mej went off for a walk to phone her new girlfriend, thinking that Nina wouldn't mind. When Nina reaches the scene of the accident, she explains to the crowd that she is a qualified first aider and kneels on the ground next to Piet. She quickly realises there is nothing she can do, and Piet dies in her arms ...

Nina, who has always been a very cheerful and positive individual, becomes morose, unsociable and develops a dependency on prescription painkillers.

▸ Nina does not at any point appear to be at risk of any physical harm, and so looks like a secondary victim, to which the *Alcock* criteria will need to be applied.

▸ Since she could be regarded as a rescuer, however, it is worth considering whether her situation is more analogous to *White* or to *Chadwick*. If the latter, she is likely to be able to recover.

▸ Remember also to consider whether she is suffering from a medically recognised condition.

---

23 [1967] 1 WLR 912.

24 Although the trial judge in that case, Waller J, dismissed that fact as irrelevant, focusing instead on the full horror of the entire situation and its effects on the rescuer. It must be remembered, however, that *Chadwick* was decided before *Alcock*, and so the significance and form of the primary/secondary distinction was of a different order when Waller J was analysing the case in front of him.

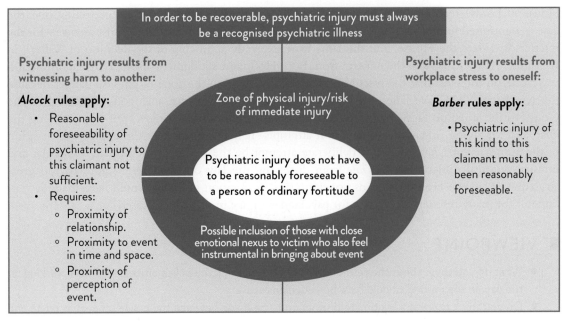

Figure 4.1: Psychiatric injury

4.5 Law in need of reform?

In *White*, Lord Hoffmann alluded to the need for legislative change in this area;[25] something also recommended by the Law Commission in its *Report on Liability for Psychiatric Illness*,[26] but not yet implemented.[27] In essence, the Law Commission recommended that, of the *Alcock* control mechanisms, only the need for a close tie of love and affection between victim and claimant should be retained, but that the presumptive category of those having such a relationship should be extended to include siblings and co-habitants. Significantly, the Law Commission recommended that the requirements for psychiatric injury to have been brought about by a sudden shock, or by witnessing or being physically present (or proximate) to the distressing event, should be discarded, but that it should remain necessary for the defendant's psychiatric injury to have been reasonably foreseeable.

■ VIEWPOINT

- Do you think the criteria proposed by the Law Commission will be sufficient to guard against the spectre of indeterminate liability?
- Are they, in your view, better than the common law mechanisms that are currently in place?

DIFFERENT PERSPECTIVES on how the law should approach psychiatric injury

S. Bailey and D. Nolan, 'The Page v Smith Saga: A Tale of Inauspicious Origins and Unintended Consequences' (2010) 69 Cambridge Law Journal 495

This article takes the position that *Page v Smith* was based on poor conceptual reasoning and that its future impact on the common law principles approach to recovery for psychiatric injury should be limited. Specifically, the authors argue that a claimant's proximity to risk of physical injury should no longer

---

25   At 504.
26   Law Com Report No 249, 1998.
27   Nor are there any signs of likely future implementation.

ensure that she is classed as a primary victim. Instead, the primary victim category should be limited to all those who suffer psychiatric injury other than as the result of another's death, injury or hazard. An argument is also made that the law in this area would be made much more coherent if physical and psychiatric injury were always recognised as being distinct for the purposes of assessing foreseeability: for all primary victims to recover, they must establish that psychiatric injury was foreseeable in a person of ordinary fortitude (unless, as in the stress at work cases, the defendant had reason to know about a particular vulnerability of the claimant).

H. Teff, 'Liability for Psychiatric Illness: Advancing Cautiously' (1998) 61 Modern Law Review 849

Whilst this article also argues for a revision of the principles used to determine when claimants can recover for psychiatric injury, it suggests a step which is, at least in formal terms, more dramatic. Teff takes the view that the making of a primary/secondary distinction is in itself unhelpful, and that a far more effective and authentic analysis of deserving recovery could be achieved through a more holistic exploration of all the circumstances of each case on its facts. The application of 'bare labels' is, he maintains, bound to cause problems at the boundaries of each category, and to contribute therefore to further incoherence in this area of law. Throughout the article, Teff also urges the common law to pay greater attention to advancements in the medical understanding of psychiatric injury.

R. Stevens, Torts and Rights (OUP, 2007), pp 202–3

Stevens makes the point here that the facts of *White* are not properly analogous to those of *Alcock* because, in the former case, there are two different rights of the claimant at issue. First, there is the right to bodily integrity, which was also the right underpinning the claims in *Alcock*. Second, however, there is the right of the claimants that their employer provide them with a safe system of work, and this is analytically separable from the former. In fact, since it is a non-delegable duty, meaning that the employer cannot discharge it simply by taking due care, Stevens argues that as a matter of principle, it is hard to justify the denial of liability on this point. He concludes, therefore, that the result in *White* was made inevitable by the political sensitivities of the situation, generated by the earlier decision in *Alcock* (i.e. that allowing the police officers to recover where the relatives could not would not be a generally acceptable result to ordinary people).

4.6 CHAPTER SUMMARY

This chapter has dealt with an area which is widely regarded as containing some of the silliest and least coherent rules in the common law. The fact that psychiatric injury can be caused remotely removes it from the natural limits created by physical or relational proximity, exposing it to the same risk of potential indeterminacy as recovery for pure economic loss. Given the nature of psychiatric injury, however, the case law is far more emotive, and the underlying political issues more sensitive. This may well explain why there have been calls for legislative reform of the common law principles, in a way which has not been seen in relation to recovery for pure economic loss. This chapter has also shown that the rules to be applied to situations involving psychiatric injury, particularly to secondary victims, are in some ways harder to justify than those applied to cases concerning pure economic loss. Hopefully, this section has also made clear that it is not really possible to make complete sense of the case law in this area, and that the best way to deal with it is to be aware of the reasoning employed in each situation, and also to have a sound sense of where the inconsistencies and ambiguities lie. This will then enable you to analyse them in an essay, or to apply them as analogously as possible to the facts of a problem question.

FURTHER READING

A. Beever, *Rediscovering the Law of Negligence* (Hart, 2007) at 406

C. Hilson, 'Nervous Shock and the Categorisation of Victims' (1998) 6 *Tort L Rev* 37

M. Jones, 'Liability for Psychiatric Damage: Searching for a Path Between Pragmatism and Principle' in Jason Neyers et al (eds), *Emerging Issues in Tort Law* (Hart, 2007) at 119

Dr. T. Keng Feng, 'Nervous Shock to Primary Victims' [1995] *Singapore JLS* 649

J. Lee, 'The Fertile Imagination of the Common Law' (2009) 17 *Torts Law Journal* 130

N. Mullany and P. Handford, 'Hillsborough Replayed' (1997) 113 *LQR* 410

J. Stapleton, 'In Restraint of Tort' in P Birks (ed.), *The Frontiers of Liability*, vol 2 (OUP, 1994)

T. Weir, *An Introduction to Tort Law*, 2nd edn (OUP, 2006) at 50

Roadmap: Was the Claimant suffering from 'recognised psychiatric injury'?

In order for Claimant to recover, he must be suffering from 'recognised psychiatric injury'. – (*McLoughlin v O'Brian*)

Claimant does not recover where risk has not eventuated (*Rothwell v CIC*)

Claimant will recover if this kind of harm to this particular employee was reasonably foreseeable (*Barber v Somerset CC*)

(*Page v Smith*)
- Physical injury must have been reasonably foreseeable but does not need to have eventuated
- Psychiatric injury itself does not have to have been reasonably foreseeable

YES

Risk   **Stress**

Has the Claimant been exposed to the risk of stress in the workplace?

NO

Was the Claimant physically injured, or at risk of being physically injured, as a direct and immediate result of the Defendant's negligence?

YES

Claimant can recover as rescuer (*Chadwick v British Railways Board*)

Did the Claimant feel instrumental in bringing about the harm of another?

NO

YES   NO

Might be classed as primary victim (*W v Essex*)

Claimant is secondary victim – (*Alcock*) rules must be applied even if Claimant is claiming as rescuer and/or employee (*White v CC of South Yorkshire*)

Claimant must answer yes to all three criteria in order to recover:
- Does Claimant have sufficiently loving relationship with victim?
- Was Claimant sufficiently proximate in time and space?
- Was psychiatric injury caused by direct perception or something very close to it?

5 BREACH OF DUTY

LEARNING OBJECTIVES

By the end of this chapter, you should be able to:
- Explain the role played by the breach of duty inquiry in the tort of negligence
- Distinguish effectively between the questions of where a duty of care exists and where it has been breached
- Recognise the distinction between the duty of care and the standard of care
- Understand how and why the standard of care in negligence is objective, and the implications of this
- Outline how the courts determine what is reasonable and what is not in both general situations and those requiring specific professional judgement
- Navigate the case law on breach of duty and apply the most appropriate rule to a given set of facts

CHAPTER CONTENTS

5.1 Introduction	87
5.2 The objective standard of care	87
5.2.1 Specific circumstances	89
5.2.2 The relevance of risk	91
5.3 The standard to be applied to children	93
5.4 The standard to be applied to professionals	96
5.5 Failure to warn patients of risks	100
5.6 Social Action, Responsibility and Heroism (SARAH) Act 2015	101
5.7 *Res ipsa loquitur*	102
5.8 Chapter summary	103
Further reading	103
Roadmap	104

PROBLEM QUESTION

Gina writes computer programs, which she makes freely available online for interested parties to download and use. She and a group of her friends, who all studied computer science together at the University of Westbury, have built up a library of code and coding protocols, which they share amongst themselves. One of the programs Gina writes allows users to operate their kitchen appliances remotely, using their handheld devices. Harj downloads this particular app onto his phone, since he likes the idea of having his evening meal already cooked by the time he gets in from work. One morning, he puts a raw chicken in the oven, and uses Gina's app to set a time of 5pm for the appliance to come on, an hour and a half before he is due to arrive home. The app, however, turns his oven on at midday because its default internal clock is set to Toronto time. This happens because Gina had followed one of the coding protocols from her group's library, which suggested that, once downloaded, the app would update its clock based on the time zone in which the phone was operating. This did not work in Harj's case, and, by the time he gets home, his kitchen has caught fire, causing serious damage to his home. Gina could have tested the operation of the code rigorously across all makes of phone, but it would have cost her £2,000, and taken her an extra six months, to have done so.

On arriving home and encountering the fire, Harj pulls onto his drive and, in his rush to get out of the car, forgets to put on the handbrake. Consequently, a minute later, the car rolls down the sloping driveway and into the road, where it hits Ian, a passing cyclist. Ian dies as a result of his injuries.

5.1 Introduction

Remember that, in order to establish a successful claim in negligence, a claimant has to establish several elements. First, the claimant needs to show that the defendant owed her a duty of care not to cause the damage from which she is suffering. Only then does the question arise whether this duty of care has been breached, and it is this inquiry which is the focus of this chapter. After that, the claimant must also show that this breach caused the claimant's damage and that it was not too remote from the breach of duty.

It cannot be emphasised enough that the question of whether a duty of care has been breached is separate from the question of whether such a duty exists in the first place. This might seem like an obvious point to make in the abstract, but it is one of the most common mistakes that students make when answering problem questions on the tort of negligence. *First*, you must establish whether the defendant owed the claimant a duty of care, using the approach explained in Chapter 2. *Then*, if a duty of care has been established, you must move on to asking whether that duty has been breached on the facts presented to you. For this latter step, you will need to employ the methods and reasoning set out in this chapter. Do not fall into the (common) trap of presuming that, because a duty of care exists, you can move on to the question of causation: duties of care abound, but that does not mean that there is necessarily any fault or culpability, as there is with breach. All doctors, for instance, owe their patients a duty of care, but it is only if and when that duty is breached that the tort of negligence is potentially engaged.

A defendant has breached its duty of care where it has fallen below the legally established standard. In situations in which the defendant is acting in a way which does not require specialist or professional knowledge, this standard is broadly that of a reasonable person in the same situation. In other words, defendants will be held to have fallen below that standard of care, and so breached their duty, where they have not behaved as a reasonable person in their situation would have done. Where the defendant is acting in a capacity which calls for specialised professional judgement or knowledge, the standard to which he or she will be held is that of the reasonable person with that specialist training or knowledge. Significantly, this is an *objective* test, meaning that, as we shall see, the inexperience or subjective lack of capacity of a particular defendant is irrelevant to the standard expected of them. This has to be right: if an individual holds herself out as having a particular skill, and purports to exercise that skill, those affected by her actions would not expect the standard of care owed to them to vary according to whether or not the defendant is newly qualified or highly experienced. This is particularly true with road-users: if I am severely injured in a car accident, I would not expect to be told by a court that I had to bear my own loss because I had the misfortune to collide with someone who was either newly qualified or simply not very capable.

5.2 The objective standard of care

As outlined above, a defendant breaches her duty of care if her conduct falls below the standard established by the law, and that standard is an objective one, meaning that the defendant will be judged against what would have been a reasonable way to act in the circumstances, regardless of whether that particular defendant was capable of doing so. In other words, in making this inquiry, courts do not ask 'Was this defendant doing as well as *she* could?' Rather, they ask 'Was the defendant doing what *a reasonable person* in those circumstances would have done?' No concessions are therefore made for individual abilities or idiosyncrasies.[1] As we will see, however, defendants are imbued with

---

1 Although, as we shall see, children are evaluated against children of a similar age, rather than against adults in the same circumstances.

the skills which they hold themselves as having by acting in a given way: anyone performing brain surgery will be judged against the reasonable brain surgeon; anyone doing plumbing work will be judged against the reasonable plumber, and so on.

KEY CASE

Nettleship v Weston [1971] 2 QB 691

The defendant was a learner driver and the claimant was a family friend, who was teaching her to drive. On the third lesson, both were in joint control of the car, in that the defendant was steering and operating the pedals, whilst the claimant was changing gear and using the handbrake. The defendant 'froze' after making a left turn, with the consequence that the car hit a tree and the claimant suffered injuries, including a broken kneecap. After Thesiger J at first instance found that the defendant's only duty was to do her best, given the special relationship between a learner driver and her instructor,[2] the claimant appealed to the Court of Appeal. The Court of Appeal took a different approach, finding that the standard of a reasonably competent driver was to be applied to all drivers, regardless of experience or stage of development. The defendant had, therefore, breached this duty and so was liable to the claimant for the injuries she had caused. However, there was also a reduction of the damages he received as a result of his contributory negligence (see Chapter 16 (Defences)) in not, for instance, using the handbrake to stop the car hitting the tree.

One of the justifications given by the Court of Appeal for imposing an objective standard to such facts, in which the claimant by definition knew that the defendant driver was very inexperienced, was that:

> ... if the driver were to be excused according to the knowledge of the passenger, it would result in endless confusion and injustice. One of the passengers may know that the driver is a mere novice. Another passenger may believe him to be entirely competent. One of the passengers may believe the driver to have had only two drinks. Another passenger may know that he has had a dozen. Is the one passenger to recover and the other not?[3]

Often, when people encounter *Nettleship* for the first time, their instinctive response is to think that its result is unfair. Considering the facts in isolation, it is easy to appreciate why it might seem 'unfair' to hold the defendant to a standard of a reasonably competent driver, and not to take into account the fact that she is a learner and therefore very inexperienced. The interests of defendants, however, are not the sole concern of the tort of negligence. As Lord Denning points out above, not only would it be confusing to tailor the standard of care to the individual defendant, but the effects would also run counter to the corrective justice endeavours of the tort. Take, for instance, the example of a hypothetical claimant who has been seriously injured in a car accident caused by the inexperience of a learner driver. On those facts, it is certainly not clear why the claimant should bear the costs of that accident, and not be able to recover compensatory damages simply because she had the misfortune to be hit by a learner and not by a more experienced individual. This, a situation in which the unsuspecting victim bears the loss rather than the defendant who has engaged in the risk-generating behaviour, would seem to be even less intuitively acceptable than the result in *Nettleship*.

The same argument applies where the defendant professes to have a specialist skill; anyone who holds herself out as having such a skill will be held by the law to the standard of a reasonable individual with that specialist skill. This applies from the first day of qualification, regardless of the absence of

---

2   It also found that the claimant had voluntarily assumed the risk of the injury from which he ultimately suffered, another point on which the Court of Appeal disagreed. See Chapter 16 (Defences) at 16.4.2.1.

3   per Lord Denning MR.

experience. Junior doctors, for instance, will be held to the same objective standard of care as those who have held their medical qualifications for much longer. This topic will be covered in more detail later in the chapter. We will return to the case of *Wilsher v Essex Area Health Authority* [1987][4] in more detail when we look at causation, and its facts are set out in full in Chapter 6.[5] For the purposes of the current chapter, however, the judgment of Mustill LJ in the Court of Appeal is relevant:[6]

> To my mind, this notion of a duty tailored to the actor, rather than to the act which he elects to perform, has no place in the law of tort … [we must relate] the duty of care not to the individual, but to the post which he occupies. I would differentiate 'post' from 'rank' or 'status.' In a case such as the present, the standard is not just that of the averagely competent and well-informed junior houseman (or whatever the position of the doctor) but of such a person who fills a post in a unit offering a highly specialised service. But, even so, it must be recognised that different posts make different demands.

It is clear from this, therefore, that the 'latitudinal' circumstances of the situation, i.e. those that set the scene, are relevant to establishing the standard of care, but that the 'longitudinal' circumstances, i.e. those that relate to the specific characteristics of the defendant agent, are not relevant. Consider an analogy with a play: anything that tells the story, or illustrates the state of the world at the relevant time, such as the set or the music, will be taken into account by the court, as will anything about the roles played by the actors, such as costumes and make-up. Any facts which relate to the actors playing those parts, however, such as whether they are tall or short, majestic or mousy, for example, will have no effect on the setting of the standard of care.

PROBLEM QUESTION TECHNIQUE

Gina writes computer programs, which she makes freely available online for interested parties to download and use. She and a group of her friends, who all studied computer science together at the University of Westbury, have built up a library of code and coding protocols, which they share amongst themselves …

▸ Consider what standard Gina would be held to. She is a computer science graduate, and, by writing programs and making them available online, she is holding herself out as having the ability to produce such material.

5.2.1 Specific circumstances

Specialist skills are not the only elements which will determine how the court sets a standard of care for defendants. Sometimes, the specific circumstances in which the defendant was acting will be taken into account when establishing what would have been reasonable in the circumstances. Both sporting environments and emergency circumstances can lead to an individual having to make a decision or act quickly and without much time for reflection. What is reasonable conduct in such circumstances might look different to what would be deemed reasonable in a less hurried context.

In *Wooldridge v Sumner* [1963],[7] the claimant was a photographer, who suffered serious injuries as a result of the defendant's horse charging into the area in which he was standing. Ridden by one of the defendant's employees, the defendant's horse was taking part in a competitive horse show at

4   [1987] QB 730, CA.
5   See 6.4.4.
6   N.B. the question of causation was taken to the House of Lords.
7   [1963] 2 QB 43.

the time. Whilst it was accepted by the court that the defendant's employee had made an error of judgement in approaching a corner of the track too fast, this was deemed not to be a breach of duty in the circumstances. Diplock LJ pointed out that participants in sporting activities are bound to focus their concentration on winning the competition, and that this is bound to affect the exercise of their judgement. He went on to note of the defendant in such an action that 'the duty which he owes is a duty of care, not a duty of skill': meaning that a lapse in skill is not to be equated necessarily with a breach of the duty of care.

There were really two dimensions to Diplock LJ's approach to this issue: first, the variation of the standard of care in competitive situations and, second, an element of consent on the part of those who willingly expose themselves to the risk of injury by being in physical proximity to sporting events. If the latter consideration applies to spectators of such events, then it applies a fortiori to participants. This is borne out by cases such as *Blake v Galloway* [2004],[8] in which all of those participating in a game involving the throwing of bark and twigs were held tacitly to have consented to the risk of being injured by such a missile in the event of a lapse of skill by another player. Games and sports, by virtue of their physical nature and fast-moving pace, inevitably involve an increased risk of physical harm. This is one of the reasons why those participating are deemed to consent to such an increased risk. This does not mean, however, that participants consent to *all* risks: just those that arise as a result of reasonable conduct in the context of a particular activity. In *Condon v Basi* [1985],[9] for instance, the defendant broke the claimant's leg as a result of performing a late and dangerous tackle during a football match. In finding that this had amounted to a breach of duty, the Court of Appeal referred to the words of Chief Justice Barwick in the Australian High court decision of *Rootes v Shelton* [1968]:[10]

> By engaging in a sport or pastime the participants may be held to have accepted risks which are inherent in that sport or pastime: the tribunal of fact can make its own assessment of what the accepted risks are: but this does not eliminate all duty of care of the one participant to the other. Whether or not such a duty arises, and, if it does, its extent must necessarily depend in each case upon its own circumstances. In this connexion, the rules of the sport or game may constitute one of those circumstances: but, in my opinion, they are neither definitive of the existence nor of the extent of the duty; nor does their breach or non-observance necessarily constitute a breach of any duty found to exist.

The question always reverts to a consideration of what is reasonable in the circumstances of the case. In emergency situations, for instance, a defendant who acts in a way which might independently be considered dangerous will not necessarily be deemed to have breached his duty of care if he did so in order to try and avert another grave risk. In *Watt v Hertfordshire CC* [1954],[11] for example, Denning LJ famously said:[12]

> It is well settled that in measuring due care you must balance the risk against the measures necessary to eliminate the risk. To that proposition there ought to be added this: you must balance the risk against the end to be achieved.

In that case, the fire service were not liable for injury caused to the claimant, its employee, by equipment which had not been secured in an emergency vehicle attending a fire. In the circumstances, given

8   [2004] EWCA Civ 814.
9   [1985] 1 WLR 866.
10   [1968] ALR 33.
11   [1954] 1 WLR 835.
12   [1954] EWCA Civ 6.

that the firemen were trying to save lives, it was reasonable for them not to have attempted to secure the equipment concerned.

5.2.2 The relevance of risk

One of the implications of the standard of care in negligence being an objective one is that defendants who are simply not capable of attaining an objectively reasonable standard of care will always be liable for any harm which results from their breach, regardless of how hard they try to reach that standard. In this way, the tort of negligence creates an incentive: individuals knowing that they are unable to reach an objective standard of reasonableness in a given activity either accept their potential liability or choose not to engage in that particular conduct at all.

This means that any loss caused will be compensated or that the loss will not be caused in the first place. By providing some form of deterrence to those who are not able to conduct certain activities in a reasonably safe way, the tort of negligence aims to keep the generation of risk within society at a reasonable level. The aim is not to eradicate risk; this would be both impossible and undesirable, since a society cannot function or progress without creating risks. Rather, the objective is to balance risks with the benefits, thereby achieving a situation in which the only risks generated are those which are reasonable, and whose costs are worth paying.

One of the sharpest illustrations of the relevance of risk to the question of breach can be found in *Bolton v Stone* [1951].

KEY CASE

Bolton v Stone [1951] AC 850

The claimant in this case was injured by a cricket ball which had been hit out of a cricket ground and into the residential street in which she was standing. There was evidence that cricket balls had been hit out of the ground in a similar fashion 'five or six times' before, but not that they had previously caused any injury. The question for the House of Lords was whether the club had been in breach of its duty in conducting cricket matches too close to the road, in failing to erect a fence of sufficient height, and thereby creating the risk of injury to those in the vicinity. The House restored the first instance decision of Oliver J in favour of the defendant, finding that the club had not been in breach of its duty of care. In so doing, Lord Porter said of the defendant:

> What degree of care must they exercise to escape liability for anything which may occur as a result of this intended use of the field? Undoubtedly they knew that the hitting of a cricket ball out of the ground was an event

which might occur and, therefore, that there was a conceivable possibility that someone would be hit by it. But so extreme an obligation of care cannot be imposed in all cases. If it were, no one could safely drive a motor car since the possibility of an accident could not be overlooked and if it occurred some stranger might well be injured however careful the driver might be. It is true that the driver desires to do everything possible to avoid an accident, whereas the hitting of a ball out of the ground is an incident in the game and, indeed, one which the batsman would wish to bring about; but in order that the act may be negligent there must not only be a reasonable possibility of its happening but also of injury being caused.[13]

To which Lord Oaksey added:

> The standard of care in the law of negligence is the standard of an ordinarily careful man,

---

13   Lord Porter at 858.

but in my opinion an ordinarily careful man does not take precautions against every foreseeable risk. He can, of course, foresee the possibility of many risks, but life would be almost impossible if he were to attempt to take precautions against every risk which he can foresee. He takes precautions against risks which are reasonably likely to happen. Many foreseeable risks are extremely unlikely to happen and cannot be guarded against except by almost complete isolation. The ordinarily prudent owner of a dog does not keep his dog always on a lead on a country highway for fear it may cause injury to a passing motor cyclist, nor does the ordinarily prudent pedestrian avoid the use of the highway for fear of skidding motor cars. It may very well be that after this accident the ordinarily prudent committee man of a similar cricket ground would take some further precaution, but that is not to say that he would have taken a similar precaution before the accident.[14]

Bolton v Stone suggests that precautions should be taken against those risks which are 'reasonably likely' to result in harm, if a negligence action is to be avoided. This is not, however, the end of the story: the gravity of the foreseeable harm likely to result is also a factor that is taken into account in making a decision about how reasonable a defendant's behaviour was in the circumstances. This is illustrated most clearly by the following case of *Paris v Stepney Borough Council* [1951].

KEY CASE

Paris v Stepney Borough Council [1951] AC 367

The claimant was the employee of the defendant and had, to its knowledge, only one good eye; the sight in his other eye being seriously compromised by cataracts. Whilst trying to remove a rusted metal bolt during the course of his employment, the claimant was struck in his good eye by a piece of metal, and incurred serious injury to it. He claimed that his employer was in breach of its duty of care by not providing him with goggles as part of a safe system of work. The question for the House of Lords was whether it was reasonable for the defendant not to have provided goggles. In doing so, the House considered whether it was material that the defendant knew the claimant's sight to be already restricted, meaning that the risk of an eye injury had graver consequences for this claimant than for employees with two fully functioning eyes:

The duty of an employer towards his servant is to take reasonable care for the servant's safety in all the circumstances of the case. The fact that the servant has only one eye if that fact is known to the employer, and that if he loses it he will be blind, is one of the circumstances which must be considered by the employer in determining what precautions if any shall be taken for the servant's safety. The standard of care which the law demands is the care which an ordinarily prudent employer would take in all the circumstances. As the circumstances may vary infinitely it is often impossible to adduce evidence of what care an ordinarily prudent employer would take. In some cases, of course, it is possible to prove that it is the ordinary practice for employers to take or not to take a certain precaution, but in such a case as the present, where a one-eyed man has been injured, it is unlikely that such evidence can be adduced. The court has, therefore, to form its own opinion of what precautions the notional ordinarily prudent employer would take. In the present case the question is whether an ordinarily prudent employer would supply goggles to a one-eyed workman whose job was to knock bolts out of a chassis with a steel hammer while the chassis was elevated on

---

14   Lord Oaksey at 863.

a ramp so that the workman's eye was close to and under the bolt.[15]

On these facts, the House of Lords decided that the defendant employer had been in breach of its duty of care to this particular employee. This was because a reasonably prudent employer, knowing that the gravity of such an injury occurring to someone with only one eye was far higher than that which would occur in the case of someone with good sight in both eyes, would have taken precautions. This is a form of cost–benefit analysis: evaluating the cost of preventing or reducing a risk of harm, on the one hand, against the likelihood of that harm occurring and the gravity of the harm should it occur, on the other.[16]

Paris v Stepney Borough Council shows the importance of not confusing the objective nature of the standard of care with an approach which does not take into account the subjective facts of the situation at hand. *Paris* demonstrates how the defendant's behaviour is measured against what would be objectively reasonable (i.e. what a reasonable employer would do, rather than what this employer was capable of), but in the particular circumstances known to him (i.e. what a reasonable employer would do on these specific facts).

PROBLEM QUESTION TECHNIQUE

Gina could have tested the operation of the code rigorously across all makes of phone, but it would have cost her £2,000, and taken her an extra six months, to have done so.

On arriving home and encountering the fire, Harj pulls onto his drive and, in his rush to get out of the car, forgets to put on the handbrake. Consequently, a minute later, the car rolls down the sloping driveway and into the road, where it hits Ian, a passing cyclist. Ian dies as a result of his injuries.

▸ In deciding whether Gina has breached her standard of care, weigh up the costs to her of taking further precautions against the risks of not doing so, as in *Bolton* and *Paris*.

▸ What would a reasonable person have done in these circumstances? Consider Watt and take into account the fact that Harj was acting in emergency circumstances. You might here also want to think about the fact that there was unlikely to have been anyone in the house (given that he was using the app in the first place), so he was trying to save property rather than human life.

5.3 The standard to be applied to children

The standard of care for adults is the same, regardless of how old they are. However, the same is not true of children. It is important to note that the standard still remains objective. For those who are not yet adults, the expectations of what is reasonable will be adjusted according to what is typical for their age, but the standard will not be adjusted for the capacity of any particular defendant. This is aptly demonstrated by *Mullin v Richards* [1998].

---

15   Lord Oaksey at 384.

16   A similar exercise is referred to in the United States as the Learned Hand formula, after the judge who set it out in *United States v Carroll Towing Co*, 159 F.2d 169: (B = PL), according to which liability turns on the relation between costs of precaution (B) and the product of the probability (P) and magnitude (L) of harm resulting from the accident. If PL exceeds B, the defendant has not acted reasonably in the circumstances. If B equals or exceeds PL, then the defendant has acted reasonably. English courts engage in the same reasoning in substance, but generally do not use such explicitly mathematical language.

KEY CASE

Mullin v Richards [1998] 1 WLR 1304

The 15-year-old claimant was injured whilst engaged in a plastic ruler 'swordfight' with a classmate of the same age. At first instance, damages were awarded against her fellow pupil (subject to a 50% reduction for contributory negligence), but the Court of Appeal reversed that decision. Hutchison LJ explained how the concept of what is reasonably foreseeable requires account to be taken of the defendant's age:

> So far as negligence is concerned, the relevant principles are well settled ... I would summarise the principles that govern liability in negligence in a case such as the present as follows. In order to succeed the plaintiff must show that the defendant did an act which it was reasonably foreseeable would cause injury to the plaintiff, that the relationship between the plaintiff and the defendant was such as to give rise to a duty of care, and that the act was one which caused injury to the plaintiff. In the present case, as it seems to me, no difficulty arose as to the second and third requirements because Teresa and Heidi were plainly in a sufficiently proximate relationship to give rise to a duty of care and the causation of the injury is not in issue. The argument centres on foreseeability. The test of foreseeability is an objective one; but the fact that the first defendant was at the time a 15-year-old

schoolgirl is not irrelevant. The question for the judge is not whether the actions of the defendant were such as an ordinarily prudent and reasonable adult in the defendant's situation would have realised gave rise to a risk of injury, it is whether an ordinarily prudent and reasonable 15-year-old schoolgirl in the defendant's situation would have realised as much. In that connection both counsel referred us to, and relied upon, the Australian decision in *McHale v Watson* (1966) 115 C.L.R. 199 and, in particular, the passage in the judgment of Kitto J., at pp. 213-214. I cite a portion of the passage I have referred to ...:

> 'The standard of care being objective, it is no answer for him, [that is a child] any more than it is for an adult, to say that the harm he caused was due to his being abnormally slow-witted, quick-tempered, absent-minded or inexperienced. But it does not follow that he cannot rely in his defence upon a limitation upon the capacity for foresight or prudence, not as being personal to himself, but as being characteristic of humanity at his stage of development and in that sense normal. By doing so he appeals to a standard of ordinariness, to an objective and not a subjective standard.'

Since children have a capacity for gauging risks and behavioural outcomes that is different to that of adults, and different indeed to that of children within other age groups, it makes sense to accommodate this when setting the appropriate standard of care. Were the courts to apply a standard of what would be reasonably foreseeable for an adult in the same situation, it would not be making an authentic judgement about what is reasonable in the circumstances. To the extent that tort law is about providing incentives for behaviour,[17] this makes sense because there is little point in holding all children to a standard that they are, as a class, incapable of attaining: holding them liable for outcomes they are unable to prevent is not obviously consistent with the objective of deterrence.

■ VIEWPOINT

If we regard the principal objective of tort as aiming to compensate those who have been injured as a result of another's breach of duty, do you think the allowance made for a defendant's age is

---

17 See Chapter 1 (Introduction) and 1.3 (Aims of tort law).

constructive? Why should a claimant bear her own loss because she happened to have suffered loss as a result of a child's, rather than an adult's, actions?

Figure 5.1 demonstrates just how comprehensive the objective standard of care is: it gives a few examples, in each case, of individual characteristics and circumstances ('longitudinal characteristics') which make no difference to the courts' determination of what the defendant should have done. Instead, the judgement of whether the duty of care has been breached will be made entirely on the basis of the content of the box.

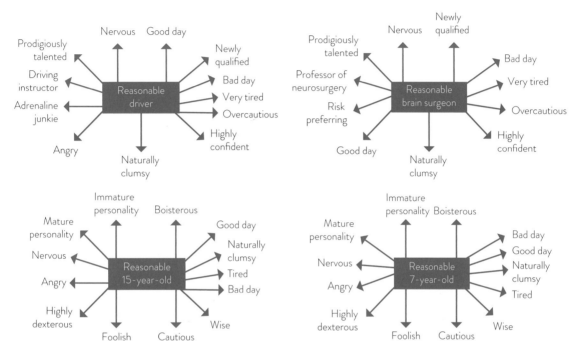

Figure 5.1: The implications of an objective standard of care

DIFFERENT PERSPECTIVES on the objective standard of care

Tony Honoré, 'Responsibility and Luck: The Moral Basis of Strict Liability' (1988) 104 (Oct) LQR 530–53

Honoré here argues that the objective standard of care, which amounts in effect to strict liability for those unable to reach that standard (such as the learner driver in *Nettleship v Weston*), is justifiable. He calls the phenomenon of being responsible in law for the consequences of one's actions (whether or not those actions are in themselves defective) outcome-responsibility, and says that we cannot do away with it without denying our status as persons. Honoré explains this by saying that the law is merely backing up outcomes which would occur anyway for, by example, imposing liability on someone who has injured another. Such an individual would, simply by virtue of the act of injuring, incur discredit, and the law adds a sanction to this. This is acceptable overall, he says, because we take credit for the positive outcomes of our actions as well, thereby forming something like a balance sheet of luck, on which most people will be in credit overall.

Lord Sumption, 'Abolishing Personal Injuries Law – A project' (2018) 34(3) Professional Negligence 113–21

In this lecture, Lord Sumption outlines his personal views about the problems with employing a fault-based system at all in order to deal with personal injuries. He makes the point that a fault-based standard in negligence has a diluted deterrent effect at best since those who cause harm by falling below the objective standard set rarely do so as a result of considered decision-making, and so are unlikely to have reflected on the consequences. Lord Sumption supposes that the most realistic reason for the fault-based system to have been accepted for so long, despite being so expensive and unwieldy, is that the notion of individuals making good the damage they have caused accords most closely with people's intuitions about what the response to such accidents should be.

5.4 The standard to be applied to professionals

In certain cases – specifically where the defendant is purporting to exercise a specialist professional skill at the time of the alleged breach, such as a surgeon performing surgery using a particular method – judges will not necessarily be in a position to say what would have been reasonable or otherwise on a given set of facts:

> I must tell you what in law we mean by 'negligence.' In the ordinary case which does not involve any special skill, negligence in law means a failure to do some act which a reasonable man in the circumstances would do, or the doing of some act which a reasonable man in the circumstances would not do; and if that failure or the doing of that act results in injury, then there is a cause of action. How do you test whether this act or failure is negligent? In an ordinary case it is generally said you judge it by the action of the man in the street. He is the ordinary man. In one case it has been said you judge it by the conduct of the man on the top of a Clapham omnibus. He is the ordinary man. But where you get a situation which involves the use of some special skill or competence, then the test as to whether there has been negligence or not is not the test of the man on the top of a Clapham omnibus, because he has not got this special skill. The test is the standard of the ordinary skilled man exercising and professing to have that special skill. A man need not possess the highest expert skill; it is well established law that it is sufficient if he exercises the ordinary skill of an ordinary competent man exercising that particular art.[18]

A judge, who is legally, but not medically, trained, will not easily be able to determine whether a course of conduct was reasonable in such a context. In circumstances such as these, therefore, the courts employ an approach which has come to be known as the *Bolam* test, after the words of McNair J in the case of *Bolam v Friern Hospital Management Committee* [1957], in which he said that a person would not be liable

> in negligence if he has acted in accordance with a practice accepted as proper by a responsible body of medical men skilled in that particular art … Putting it the other way round, a man is not negligent, if he is acting in accordance with such a practice, merely because there is a body of opinion who would take a contrary view.[19]

This *Bolam* test, therefore, is employed when trying to determine whether a professional, or at least someone purporting to exercise a professional skill, has breached her duty of care. First, '[t]he test is the standard of the ordinary skilled man exercising and professing to have that special skill'; what is expected is the ordinary level of competence of someone in that particular specialty of that profession.[20] Then, is the defendant able to identify an established body of professional opinion which would regard his conduct as

18   McNair J in *Bolam v Friern Hospital Management Committee* [1957] 1 WLR 582 at 586.
19   *Bolam v Friern Hospital Management Committee* [1957] 1 WLR 582 at 587.
20   *Bolam* at 586.

reasonable in the circumstances? Note that this body of opinion need not be the only voice on the matter, or even the dominant one: even if there are other bodies of opinion that would take a contrary view, this is not necessarily determinative of the claimant's case (see *Bolitho v City of Hackney Health Authority* [1998], below). Although now firmly established as an integral element of the negligence inquiry in the context of professional activity, the *Bolam* test has not been without its critics.[21] As Lord Scarman said in *Sidaway v Bethlem Royal Hospital* [1985], 'The law imposes the duty of care: but the standard of care is a matter of medical judgment.'[22] Therefore, by asking the profession itself to take a view on whether the defendant's conduct was reasonable in the circumstances, the court could be said to be delegating an important part of its judicial function. It is very difficult to suggest, however, a way in which a court could realistically take a view on what amounts to reasonable conduct in a specialised sphere of activity in which none of its members has any training or experience. Note also that you do not need to apply the *Bolam* test to every action performed by a professional: only those professional activities for which specialist knowledge or training is required. If, for instance, a dentist is cycling to work, any potential breach of her duty as a cyclist falls to be assessed on ordinary, non-*Bolam* principles.

The potential conceptual difficulties with the *Bolam* test, and the medical protectionism which it could be said to stand for, have in more recent years been mitigated by the House of Lords' subsequent decision in *Bolitho v City of Hackney Health Authority* [1998].

KEY CASE

Bolitho v City of Hackney Health Authority [1998] AC 232

A 2-year-old boy died after suffering a cardiac arrest and respiratory failure. He had, prior to the attack that killed him, suffered two previous respiratory failures whilst in the care of the defendant's hospital. On neither of the previous two occasions did a doctor attend the boy, despite nurses having requested such attendance. The claimant argued that, had a doctor attended, and had the boy been intubated as a result of these earlier episodes, the final respiratory failure and cardiac arrest could have been prevented. The doctor argued that, even had she attended, she would not have intubated the boy in the circumstances.[23] The question for the court, therefore, was whether omitting to intubate a child in this situation was a reasonable course of action for a doctor to take. Lord Browne-Wilkinson said:

[I]n cases of diagnosis and treatment there are cases where, despite a body of professional opinion sanctioning the defendant's conduct, the defendant can properly be held liable for negligence (I am not here considering questions of disclosure of risk). In my judgment that is because, in some cases, it cannot be demonstrated to the judge's satisfaction that the body of opinion relied upon is reasonable or responsible. In the vast majority of cases the fact that distinguished experts in the field are of a particular opinion will demonstrate the reasonableness of that opinion. In particular, where there are questions of assessment of the relative risks and benefits of adopting a particular medical practice, a reasonable view necessarily presupposes that the relative risks

---

21   See, e.g., K. Norrie, 'Medical Negligence: Who Sets the Standard?' (1985) 11 JME 135. See also the critical literature referred to in M. Brazier and J. Miola, 'Bye-Bye Bolam: A Medical Litigation Revolution?' (2000) 8 *Med Law Review* 85 at fn 2.

22   [1985] AC 871 at 881. Note, however, that here Lord Scarman was dissenting from the House of Lords' application of the *Bolam* test to the question of whether a doctor should inform her patient of the risks of a given procedure. The Supreme Court has since departed from the approach in *Sidaway*, preferring Lord Scarman's perspicacious preference for patient self-determination: see *Montgomery v Lanarkshire Health Board* [2015] AC 1430 (below, at 5.5 (Failure to warn patients of risks)).

23   Given the particular context of the situation, and her professional judgement in relation to it.

and benefits have been weighed by the experts in forming their opinions. But if, in a rare case, it can be demonstrated that the professional opinion is not capable of withstanding logical analysis, the judge is entitled to hold that the body of opinion is not reasonable or responsible.

I emphasise that in my view it will very seldom be right for a judge to reach the conclusion that views genuinely held by a competent medical expert are unreasonable. The assessment of medical risks and benefits is a matter of clinical judgment which a judge would not normally be able to make without expert evidence … [I]t would be wrong to allow such assessment to deteriorate into seeking to persuade the judge to prefer one of two views both of which are capable of being logically supported. It is only where a judge can be satisfied that the body of expert opinion cannot be logically supported at all that such opinion will not provide the benchmark by reference to which the defendant's conduct falls to be assessed.[24]

Bolitho itself was not deemed to be one of the rare cases to which Lord Browne-Wilkinson referred, and the court was willing to accept as reasonable and logical the expert opinion which supported the doctor's actions in not intubating the deceased. The decision is nonetheless a significant one in terms of its signalling that the court remains the final arbiter on questions of breach. Whether it was ever really necessary to articulate this so explicitly, and whether the case has had any substantive impact on the law, is a different question: nothing that McNair J said (or could have said) in *Bolam* ever precluded judicial rejection of any professional opinion offered to the court. This is clear if we put his words in the context in which they were originally uttered (bearing in mind that, as it was 1957, he was giving guidance to a civil jury, a thing which no longer exists in this jurisdiction):

[W]here you get a situation which involves the use of some special skill or competence, then the test as to whether there has been negligence or not is not the test of the man on the top of a Clapham omnibus, because he has not got this special skill. The test is the standard of the ordinary skilled man exercising and professing to have that special skill. A man need not possess the highest expert skill; it is well established law that it is sufficient if he exercises the ordinary skill of an ordinary competent man exercising that particular art. … in the case of a medical man, negligence means failure to act in accordance with the standards of reasonably competent medical men at the time. That is a perfectly accurate statement, as long as it is remembered that there may be one or more perfectly proper standards; and if he conforms with one of those proper standards, then he is not negligent … In a recent Scottish case, *Hunter v Hanley*, Lord President Clyde said:

'In the realm of diagnosis and treatment there is ample scope for genuine difference of opinion and one man clearly is not negligent merely because his conclusion differs from that of other professional men, nor because he has displayed less skill or knowledge than others would have shown. The true test for establishing negligence in diagnosis or treatment on the part of a doctor is whether he has been proved to be guilty of such failure as no doctor of ordinary skill would be guilty of, if acting with ordinary care … I myself would prefer to put it this way, that he is not guilty of negligence if he has acted in accordance with a practice accepted as proper by a responsible body of medical men skilled in that particular art … Putting it the other way round, a man is not negligent, if he is acting in accordance with such a practice, merely because there is a body of opinion who would take a contrary view. At the same time, that does not mean that a medical man can obstinately and pig-headedly carry on with some old technique if it has been proved to be contrary to what is really substantially the whole of informed medical opinion.'[25]

24   At 243.
25   Lord President Clyde in *Hunter v Hanley* [1955] S.L.T. 213 at 217.

Taken as a whole, and with particular reference to the section highlighted above, McNair J's statement does not obviously require the *Bolitho* qualification. It is important, nevertheless, that when you use the *Bolam* test, you do so alongside the formal gloss on that test provided by *Bolitho*, since this accurately represents the positive law position as it now stands.

PROBLEM QUESTION TECHNIQUE

One morning, Harj puts a raw chicken in the oven, and uses Gina's app to set a time of 5pm for the appliance to come on, an hour and a half before he is due to arrive home. The app, however, turns his oven on at midday because its default internal clock is set to Toronto time. This happens because Gina had followed one of the coding protocols from her group's library, which suggested that, once downloaded, the app would update its clock based on the time zone in which the phone was operating. This did not work in Harj's case, and, by the time he gets home, his kitchen has caught fire, causing serious damage to his home.

▶ The question of Gina's breach here involves an issue of professional judgement. You can identify such issues by asking yourself whether a judge would know what was reasonable to do in the circumstances. Since these facts require an evaluation of what would have been a reasonable way to develop a computer program, it is unlikely that a judge would be able to conduct that inquiry. Consequently, the *Bolam* test needs to be applied.

▶ Remember, the *Bolam* test does not require that the whole profession, or even the greater part of the profession, agrees with what the defendant did. It asks instead whether the defendant is able to point to an established body of professional opinion which deems the conduct reasonable. The question would be whether Gina's group's library would amount to that reasonable body of opinion, and whether the court, through *Bolitho*, would be prepared to accept it as such.

> **Reasonable person professing to exercise specialist skill**
> Court ascertains whether there is an acceptable body
> of professional opinion which would have performed the same risk-cost
> analysis as the defendant (and reached the same conculsion)

> **Reasonable person**
> Court performs risk-cost analysis as it would occur to a
> person in the defendant's position

> **Reasonable person in emergency situations**
> Court performs risk-cost analysis as it would occur to a
> person in the defendant's situation

> **Reasonable child of x years old in a given situation**
> Court performs risk-cost analysis as it would occur to a
> child of the defendant's age

Figure 5.2: Standards of care

5.5 Failure to warn patients of risks

This aspect of the doctor–patient relationship requires consideration in its own right. It has never been straightforward, and has recently been the subject of a significant shift in judicial direction. The case of *Montgomery v Lanarkshire Health Board* [2015] is the authority with which you now need to be familiar.

KEY CASE

Montgomery v Lanarkshire Health Board [2015] AC 1430

The claimant in this case suffered from diabetes and had a small physical frame. Both of these characteristics increased the risk of something called shoulder dystocia (referring to the increased probability of her baby's shoulders getting stuck in the birth canal and causing a possible emergency) during the process of her giving birth. This is in fact what did ensue, and her baby son suffered serious injuries as a result. Whilst Mrs Montgomery had expressed concern in the past about the size of her baby, she did not ask about specific risks and her doctor did not volunteer information about the risk of shoulder dystocia and its consequences. The doctor's decision was based on her judgement that the risk to the baby was small and that, were the mother to be made aware of it, she would likely opt for delivery by caesarean section, something which would not be in her overall interests. Had the claimant been made aware of the risks, she would have opted for a caesarean delivery, it would have been made available to her, and the injuries to her son would not, on the balance of probabilities, have occurred.[26]

The claimant's case had failed in the lower courts on the issue of breach, with those courts applying *Sidaway*[27] to conclude that the question of whether a doctor had breached her duty in not informing her patient of risks pertaining to treatment was to be decided by application of the *Bolam* test. Such a failure to disclose would not, therefore, amount to a breach of duty if an established body of professional opinion would deem it to have been a reasonable course of action to have taken. The Supreme Court, however, departed from the *Sidaway* approach for the purposes of risk disclosure, and made a clear distinction between a doctor's conduct in providing diagnosis or treatment, to which the *Bolam* test *will* apply, and a doctor's conduct in advising patients about risks and alternative treatments, in relation to which Lords Kerr and Reed said:

> An adult person of sound mind is entitled to decide which, if any, of the available forms of treatment to undergo, and her consent must be obtained before treatment interfering with her bodily integrity is undertaken. The doctor is therefore under a duty to take reasonable care to ensure that the patient is aware of any material risks involved in any recommended treatment, and of any reasonable alternative or variant treatments. The test of materiality is whether, in the circumstances of the particular case, a reasonable person in the patient's position would be likely to attach significance to the risk, or the doctor is or should reasonably be aware that the particular patient would be likely to attach significance to it.

This approach is subject to two exceptions:

> The doctor is however entitled to withhold from the patient information as to a risk if he reasonably considers that its disclosure would be seriously detrimental to the patient's health. The doctor is also excused from conferring with the patient in circumstances of necessity, as for example where the patient requires treatment urgently but is unconscious or otherwise unable to make a decision. It is unnecessary for the purposes of this case to consider in detail the scope of those exceptions.

---

26 The claimant had lost on the causation issue in the lower courts, but the Supreme Court found in her favour on the basis that, had the doctor discharged her duty, the availability of the caesarean section as an alternative method of delivery would have been offered.

27 As they were bound to.

The ultimate success of the claimant's action in *Montgomery*, and the clear judicial willingness to give greater recognition to patient autonomy, reflects a change in social attitudes; moving towards self-determination and away from medical paternalism.

■ VIEWPOINT

- Do you think this is a positive development?
- Is it a good idea to prioritise the full autonomy of patients, even in a situation in which they might, through lack of specialist knowledge, not be able to judge what is in their best interests?
- If individual autonomy is so important, why does the law require people to wear seatbelts when in a car?

DIFFERENT PERSPECTIVES on the *Bolam* test

John-Paul Swoboda, 'Bolam: going, going ... gone' (2018) 1 JPI Law 9

In this article, Swoboda argues that the *Bolam* test should be consigned to common law history, that its effect has already been significantly diluted, particularly in relation to advising patients about risks (*Montgomery*), and that common law development would be better in its absence. He first traces the history of the *Bolam* test, and shows how it has increasingly become less appropriate as a judicial device. He points out, for example, that at the time *Bolam* was decided, civil juries were still in use, and it made sense to simplify the decision they had to make. There is no reason, however, why a judge cannot assess the evidence in front of her to determine whether a defendant's conduct was reasonable in the circumstances.

Clark Hobson, 'No (,) more Bolam please: Lanarkshire v Montgomery Health Board' (2016) 79(3) MLR 488–503

Hobson argues that the relevance of the *Bolam* test survives *Montgomery*, and remains applicable in certain clinical situations: those giving rise to the 'therapeutic privilege', in which medical professionals are entitled to withhold information about risks where to do otherwise would be seriously detrimental to the patient's health. His point is that this category of cases is too potentially significant for *Bolam* to be written off as nothing more than a piece of legal history.

5.6 Social Action, Responsibility and Heroism (SARAH) Act 2015

Any discussion of breach of duty should now make reference to the Social Action, Responsibility and Heroism (SARAH) Act 2015, which was formulated in response to the perception of a growing compensation culture. A press release issued soon after the Act was passed stated that it

> is designed to bring some common sense back to Britain's health and safety culture ... The government is taking action to support the millions of people who volunteer and carry out good deeds every year. An important part of this is to make sure they are not put off from participating by worries about risk and liability if something goes wrong ... Changes are being made to counteract the growing perception that people risk being successfully sued if they do something for the common good – like leading a school trip, organising a village fete, clearing snow from a path in front of their home or helping in an emergency situation.[28]

---

28   https://www.gov.uk/government/news/grayling-law-must-protect-everyday-heroes: last accessed 31 January 2019.

> ## KEY LEGISLATION
>
> ### Social Action, Responsibility and Heroism (SARAH) Act 2015
>
> The SARAH Act 2015 is very short. For the purposes of this chapter, the relevant sections are as follows:[29]
>
> 1 When does this act apply?
>
> This Act applies when a court, in considering a claim that a person was negligent or in breach of statutory duty, is determining the steps that the person was required to take to meet a standard of care.
>
> 2 Social action
>
> The court must have regard to whether the alleged negligence or breach of statutory duty occurred when the person was acting for the benefit of society or any of its members.
>
> 3 Responsibility
>
> The court must have regard to whether the person, in carrying out the activity in the course of which the alleged negligence or breach of statutory duty occurred, demonstrated a predominantly responsible approach towards protecting the safety or other interests of others.
>
> 4 Heroism
>
> The court must have regard to whether the alleged negligence or breach of statutory duty occurred when the person was acting heroically by intervening in an emergency to assist an individual in danger.

To date, the effect of the SARAH Act 2015 on reported case law has been negligible. It has generated mixed views as to its likely effects. The dominant view appears to be that it amounts to little more than a restatement of the common law position, and is therefore unlikely to have much of a substantive impact. Others, such as James Goudkamp, take the view that it has the potential to have a wide-ranging effect, and one which is not even limited to the law of tort.[30]

5.7 *Res ipsa loquitur*

The phrase *res ipsa loquitur* means 'the thing speaks for itself'. It is employed in cases in which the circumstances are such that they can amount to evidence of carelessness in their own right, without the need for the claimant (who retains the burden of proof) to adduce further evidence.

The most famous account of this principle was given by Erle CJ in *Scott v The London and St Katherine Docks Company* [1865], a case in which some bags of sugar fell and injured the claimant as they were being loaded by the defendant's crane:[31]

> There must be reasonable evidence of negligence … But where the thing is shewn to be under the management of the defendant or his servants, and the accident is such as in the ordinary course of things does not happen if those who have the management use proper care, it affords reasonable evidence, in the absence of explanation by the defendants, that the accident arose from want of care.

---

29 There is not much more to the whole statute than what is set out here.

30 See J. Goudkamp, 'Restating the common law? The Social Action, Responsibility and Heroism Act' (2015) 37(4) *Legal Studies* 577.

31 [1865] H & C 596.

When dealing with *res ipsa loquitur*, it is important not to make the common mistake of describing it as a means of shifting the burden of proof from the claimant to the defendant. The claimant retains the burden of proof, but is merely held to have satisfied that burden by adducing factual evidence which would be very hard to explain in the absence of carelessness.[32]

5.8 CHAPTER SUMMARY

One of the principal aims of this chapter has been to make clear the crucial distinction between establishing the existence of a duty of care (Chapter 2) and deciding whether it has been breached. It is essential to a correct and coherent understanding of the tort that the two questions are seen as separate and independent inquiries, yet the elision of these two concepts is a very common mistake made by students. This chapter has also explained the objective nature of the reasonableness standard in negligence, and how and when this can vary, according to the scene of the activity, but *not* the individual defendant. The *Bolam* test for professional standards of reasonableness has also been introduced, along with the limitations on its use and the academic criticism which has been levelled at it. The *Bolam* test has already been curtailed in its application to situations involving informing patients of risk: it might be that, in an era in which individual autonomy is increasingly prioritised, the significance of the test decreases further still.

FURTHER READING

J. Gardner, 'Obligations and Outcomes in the Law of Torts' in P. Cane and J. Gardner (eds), *Relating to Responsibility: Essays for Tony Honoré* (Hart 2001)

R. Kidner, 'The Variable Standard of Care, Contributory Negligence and *Volenti*' (1991) 11 *Legal Studies* 1

N.J. McBride, *The Humanity of Private Law* (Hart, 2019), ch 6

M. Moran, *Rethinking the Reasonable Person* (OUP, 2003)

D. Nolan, 'Varying the Standard of Care in Negligence' (2013) 72 *CLJ* 651

---

32   See also K. Williams, 'Res Ipsa Loquitur Still Speaks' (2009) 125 LQR 567.

Roadmap: What would a reasonable agent do in the circumstances?

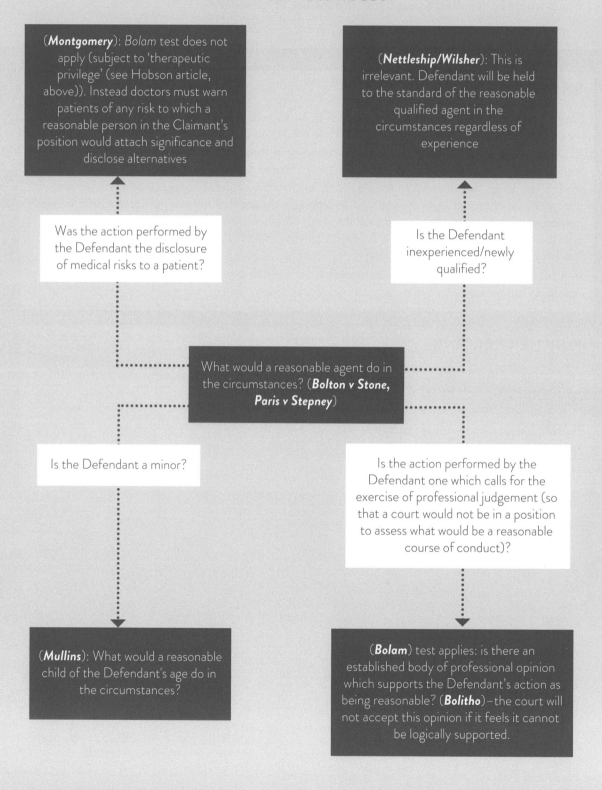

(**Montgomery**): *Bolam* test does not apply (subject to 'therapeutic privilege' (see Hobson article, above)). Instead doctors must warn patients of any risk to which a reasonable person in the Claimant's position would attach significance and disclose alternatives

(**Nettleship/Wilsher**): This is irrelevant. Defendant will be held to the standard of the reasonable qualified agent in the circumstances regardless of experience

Was the action performed by the Defendant the disclosure of medical risks to a patient?

Is the Defendant inexperienced/newly qualified?

What would a reasonable agent do in the circumstances? (**Bolton v Stone, Paris v Stepney**)

Is the Defendant a minor?

Is the action performed by the Defendant one which calls for the exercise of professional judgement (so that a court would not be in a position to assess what would be a reasonable course of conduct)?

(**Mullins**): What would a reasonable child of the Defendant's age do in the circumstances?

(**Bolam**) test applies: is there an established body of professional opinion which supports the Defendant's action as being reasonable? (**Bolitho**) – the court will not accept this opinion if it feels it cannot be logically supported.

CAUSATION

CHAPTER CONTENTS

6.1 Introduction   106
6.2 Why is the causal inquiry significant and what role does it play?   107
6.3 But for causation   108
    6.3.1 Basic but for causation   108
    6.3.2 Divisible and indivisible injuries   110
    6.3.3 Successive factors   112
    6.3.4 Material contribution to injury   115
    6.3.5 Loss of a chance of avoiding an adverse physical outcome   118
6.4 Exceptions to the but for test   123
    6.4.1 Loss of a chance of achieving a better financial outcome   123
    6.4.2 Overdetermination   125
    6.4.3 Material contribution to risk   126
    6.4.4 Single agent   132
    6.4.5 Failure to warn   138
6.5 Chapter summary   140
Further reading   141
Roadmap   142

PROBLEM QUESTION

Alastair works for Badbury Estates as a gardener. One day, whilst attempting to erect a pergola, the (company) ladder he is using collapses without warning, and he is thrown to the ground, causing him severe spinal injuries. Dr Cook, to whom he is referred, informs Alastair that he will never walk again. This means, inevitably, that Alastair will no longer be able to work as a gardener.

Danny, a young apprentice working for Badbury Estates, was standing underneath the ladder when it gave way. His right arm is broken in the accident. Before the accident happened, that arm was in a sling because he had broken his right collarbone playing rugby the previous weekend when a scrum collapsed. A month later, Danny gets into a fight outside a nightclub and his right arm, which had started to heal, is broken for a second time. The man responsible is never identified.

Evie, Alastair's wife, was made redundant the year before the accident. She developed an anxiety disorder as a result of the loss of her job. When she learns of Alastair's paralysis, her anxiety escalates into depression, and she is unable to leave the house.

Fred also works for Badbury Estates, and has done so for 38 years. As a heating engineer, he spent much of that time dealing with Toximent, an insulating material commonly used in the industry until it was found to be carcinogenic. It was banned in 1981. Badbury Estates withdrew it from their sites in 1987. Before he worked for Badbury Estates, Fred did similar work for another firm, which also used Toximent. That firm has not existed for 15 years. Fred recently discovered that he has developed mesothelioma, and has been given nine months to live. Toximent has been linked with the development of this disease, but very little is known about precisely how this happens.

Two years after Alastair's accident, his friend Harry, who is a doctor, tells Alastair about some research he has found which casts doubt on Dr Cook's original diagnosis. This research, which was available at the time of Alastair's accident, suggests that, in the case of injuries such as those Alastair sustained, paralysis is not in fact an inevitable result and that, in 35% of cases, immediate and regular physiotherapy can lead to the resumption of limb movement, and the prevention of paralysis.

Since he did not know about this, Alastair has since consulted Kris, an orthopaedic surgeon in the US, who advised him to undergo an experimental procedure pioneered by Kris himself. If successful, it can reverse the effects of a patient's paralysis almost entirely.

At his consultation, Alastair had said, 'There must be a catch – it sounds too perfect.'

Kris had replied, 'Well, yes, there is a bit of a downside. There is a risk of ...'

Alastair had interrupted him, 'No, no, don't tell me – just do it.'

There is actually a 5% risk of the operation, howsoever performed, leaving the patient paralysed, but in greater pain than before. This risk decreases as time goes by, so that the longer the period between the injury occurring and the operation, the smaller the chance it will be unsuccessful. Kris, keen to test out his procedure, decides to respect Alastair's wish not to know this, and performs the operation competently. Sadly, the 5% risk materialises and Alastair remains paralysed, and in greater pain than before.

6.1 Introduction

Causation is made up of two parts, variously referred to as 'cause in fact and cause in law' (or 'factual causation and legal causation') or 'causation and remoteness'. This book uses the terms causation and remoteness because they permit a more straightforward analogy with comparable concepts in contract and, to some extent, criminal law. This chapter will look at causation and the following chapter will cover remoteness. Causation is often regarded as the most difficult element of the negligence inquiry due to the thorny question of what we mean by 'cause' in a legal sense. There is also a potentially confusing maze of case law that has arisen in this area. However, separating the case law carefully into categories, and applying it appropriately to different factual situations, gets rid of many of the apparent complications. This chapter aims to categorise the relevant case law and show how and when each approach should be applied. It will, for instance, make clear the crucial difference between material contribution to injury and material contribution to risk – two categories which must be distinguished. It will also examine the concept of lost chances in tort, and explain why this set of cases in particular divides opinion, both academic and judicial. Finally, this chapter deals with overdetermination and failure to warn situations, neither of which generate much case law but both of which present potential challenges to the function of the causal inquiry.

6.2 Why is the causal inquiry significant and what role does it play?

Why is causation important in tort law? One reason is that to insist on causal connection between conduct and harm ensures that in general we impose liability only on those who, by intervening in the world, have changed the course of events for the worse.[1]

This is one of the clearest statements of the role causation plays in tort and, if kept in mind, can help to make sense of even the least straightforward causal tests. It also says much about the corrective justice implications of the causal inquiry: that is, ensuring that the party responsible for any given injury is the one who provides compensation to the person who incurs the loss. This is in contrast to systems which ensure that victims of harm are compensated from, say, a social or insurance fund. The latter spreads the risk of harm amongst a group of potential harm causers, rather than insisting on compensation coming from the specific individual who actually caused the harm. This would be a distributive justice approach and, whilst perfectly legitimate (and some would say preferable to a negligence system), is very different to that adopted by the tort of negligence. Under a corrective justice framework, the establishment of a causal link between a particular breach and a particular harm is crucial.

A correlatively structured remedy responds to and undoes an injustice only if that injustice is itself correlatively structured. In bringing an action against the defendant the plaintiff is asserting that they are connected as doer and sufferer of the same injustice. As is evidenced by the judgment's simultaneous correction of both sides of the injustice, what the defendant has done and what the plaintiff has suffered are not independent items. Rather, they are the active and passive poles of the same injustice, so that what the defendant has done counts as an injustice only because of what the plaintiff has suffered and vice versa.[2]

The tort system is unwieldy and relatively inefficient. It is certainly not the simplest or the most effective way of ensuring that those who have suffered loss receive compensation for it:

[T]he administrative expenses of the system as a whole amount to about 85 per cent of the value of the sums paid out, or about 45 per cent of the total costs of the system. So … we can say that about 55 pence of the insurance premium pound is paid out to injured victims, and 45 pence is swallowed up in administration … no other compensation system is anything like as expensive to operate as the tort system. The social security system, for instance, runs at a cost of about 12 per cent of the total amounts paid out.[3]

If securing compensation *tout court* is the priority, then either some type of social welfare scheme, or a system of first party insurance is the best means of achieving that.[4] Tort, on the other hand, is

---

1   A. Honoré, 'Necessary and Sufficient Conditions' in D. Owen (ed.), *Philosophical Foundations of Tort Law* (Clarendon Press, 1995), 385.

2   E. Weinrib, *Corrective Justice* (Oxford University Press 2012), 17. See also E. Weinrib, 'Correlativity, Personality, and the Emerging Consensus on Corrective Justice' (2002) 2 *Theoretical Inquiries in Law* 107.

3   P. Cane, *Atiyah's Accidents, Compensation and the Law*, 8th edn (Cambridge University Press 2013), 392–3.

4   See, e.g., J. Stapleton, 'Tort, Insurance and Ideology' (1995) 58(6) *MLR* 820, R. Merkin, 'Tort, Insurance and Ideology: Further Thoughts' (2012) 75(3) *MLR* 301, and J. Morgan, 'Tort, Insurance and Incoherence' (2004) 67(3) *MLR* 384.

not concerned solely with prioritising such distributive concerns. Rather, its expensive and often torturous processes are justified by its aim of achieving some form of corrective justice:

> Compensation is, of course, the principle underlying the assessment of tort damages. Even so, there is a sense in which compensation is a subsidiary goal of tort law, in that personal injury attracts compensation in tort only if a responsible defendant can be found to pay it. Tort law focuses primarily on the obligation of the defendant to pay rather than the entitlement of the claimant to be paid compensation. The fundamental goal of tort law … is corrective justice or fairness – in other words, the aim is to redress the balance of fairness or justice between the parties, which has been upset by the tortious behaviour of the defendant.[5]

This is why the causal inquiry is so crucial: the existence of a duty-breaching defendant and an injured claimant tells us nothing about why or whether *that* defendant should compensate *that* claimant. Only the causal inquiry can do that.

The best way to understand the various means of analysing causation is to see them applied to a concrete set of facts. The problem question (above) includes all of the key issues discussed in this chapter, and it will be broken down throughout in order to help you understand how the law should be applied to each issue in turn.

6.3 But for causation

6.3.1 Basic but for causation

The basic device for establishing causation in tort is the but for test. This is the simple, practical means of establishing whether, as Tony Honoré put it above, the defendant has intervened in the claimant's life and made it worse. The test asks, 'But for the defendant's breach of duty, would the claimant's injury have occurred?'[6] Crucially, it does so on the balance of probabilities, asking whether it is *more likely than not* that the defendant's breach of duty was a but for cause of the claimant's injury.

6.3.1.1 THE STANDARD OF PROOF IN CIVIL LAW VS CRIMINAL LAW

The standard of proof in civil law is that of the **balance of probabilities**. The claimant, on whom the *burden* of proof lies,[7] has to persuade the court that it is more likely than not that her version of events is correct. In statistical terms, this means that a claimant must show that it is >50% likely that her account is a true representation of what happened. This is to be clearly distinguished from the standard of proof in criminal cases, which is that of **beyond reasonable doubt**. In the latter, the burden of proof is on the prosecution. Note that in neither case does the competing account have to be *dis*proved, as long as the proffered account is 'proved'. The burden of proof is on the claimant, but if and when the claimant establishes that it is more likely than not that the defendant caused her injury, the court proceeds as if this were proved as a certainty. Conversely, the case of any claimant who fails to prove her causal submission to this standard, even if she comes very close to the threshold, will be treated as a total failure of proof.

---

5   P. Cane, *Atiyah's Accidents, Compensation and the Law*, 8th edn (Cambridge University Press 2013), 477.

6   Technically, there should be more to this question, i.e. 'But for the defendant's breach of duty, would the claimant's injury have occurred *when it did*?' As we will see later in this chapter, the time at which the injury occurs is material and, after all, we are all going to die one day.

7   Note the essential difference between the standard of proof and the burden of proof: the *burden* refers to the party who has the task of persuading the court of the truth of her account; the *standard* is the degree to which that proof has to be established.

The law operates a binary system in which the only values are 0 and 1. If the evidence that something happened satisfies the burden of proof … then it is assigned a value of 1 and treated as definitely having happened. If the evidence does not discharge the burden of proof, the event is assigned a value of 0 and treated as definitely not having happened. There is no forensic space for the conclusion that something which has to be proved may have happened.[8]

This all or nothing approach to causation, in which certainty will almost always be fictional to some extent, raises several interesting issues and will be discussed in greater depth later in this chapter. Whilst there are several instances in which it will not be helpful (or even possible) to apply a but for causal test, it should always be the starting point for any causal analysis.

The clearest and simplest example of but for causation is *Barnett v Chelsea and Kensington Hospital Management Committee* [1969].

KEY CASE

Barnett v Chelsea and Kensington Hospital Management Committee [1969] 1 QB 428

The claimant's husband was a night watchman who became ill after drinking tea during his shift. Having attended the defendant's hospital, he was sent home without appropriate diagnosis and treatment, an action which amounted to a breach of the hospital's duty of care. He died a few hours later of what transpired to be arsenic poisoning. The question for the court was whether the negligent medical treatment made any difference to the deceased's course of events or whether, even with appropriate medical treatment, he would still have died when he did. The medical evidence was such that, on the balance of probabilities, the outcome would have been the same whether or not treatment had been provided. In other words, it was more likely than not that, but for the defendant's breach, the night watchman would still have died. Therefore, the negligence did not intervene in the victim's life to change the course of events for the worse. Consequently, the defendant hospital was not liable to the claimant.

PROBLEM QUESTION TECHNIQUE

Alastair works for Badbury Estates as a gardener. One day, whilst attempting to erect a pergola, the (company) ladder he is using collapses without warning, and he is thrown to the ground, causing him severe spinal injuries. Dr Cook, to whom he is referred, informs Alastair that he will never walk again. This means, inevitably, that Alastair will no longer be able to work as a gardener.

▸ This is a simple but for situation, to which the basic test, as illustrated by *Barnett*, is applicable.

▸ Consider whether, but for Badbury Estates' breach, Alastair would be in the position he is now.

As we will see in the appellate cases with which you will need to be familiar, it is relatively common for there to be an established or accepted breach of duty and an injured claimant, but the absence of a causal link between the two. This is particularly true of medical negligence situations because, by virtue of their function, medical professionals come into contact with individuals who are already injured, ill, weak or otherwise predisposed to adverse physical consequences. Given the nature of

---

8   L. Hoffmann, 'Causation' in R. Goldberg (ed.), *Perspectives on Causation* (Hart Publishing, 2011), 8.

human physiology and the limits of scientific knowledge, it is often incredibly difficult to distinguish in causal terms between the natural deterioration of a person's physical state and the influence of medical intervention.

6.3.2 Divisible and indivisible injuries

Whilst highly effective in situations like *Barnett*, the basic but for test will not always be applicable or helpful on less straightforward facts. One of the most common complications for causal analysis is the presence of multiple potential causal factors. It is crucial to understand the difference between those injuries which are divisible and those which are indivisible in relation to the causal inquiry in this respect.

Divisible injuries are those that can be divided up into constituent parts, and matched up with different causal factors over a period of time. The gravity of these injuries generally exists along a spectrum. A classic example is deafness: an individual can be mildly, moderately, profoundly or completely deaf. As an industrial disease, degrees of deafness can often be attributed to different time periods and therefore different employers. So, for instance, a claimant who has worked for three different employers, all of whom negligently exposed her to excessive noise over her working life, is now profoundly deaf. A court faced with this situation will be able to assign the stages of her deafness to each successive employer as in *Thompson v Smiths Shiprepairers (North Shields) Ltd* [1984][9] (see below). Normally, this makes the causal inquiry simpler than it would be in the case of an indivisible injury caused by multiple causal factors.

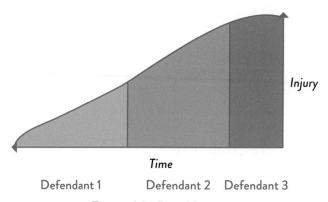

Injury

Time

Defendant 1   Defendant 2   Defendant 3

Figure 6.1: Divisible injury

Indivisible injuries are those that cannot be divided up into constituent parts because they are binary in nature. An individual either suffers from an indivisible injury, or does not; indivisible injuries do not exist in degrees of severity. Examples are death, a broken bone (presuming it is broken in only one place) and, as we will see below, mesothelioma, a cancer which grows on the lining of internal organs, commonly the lungs. It is indivisible because it only has one degree of severity: it is always fatal. Therefore, individuals either have mesothelioma, or they do not; just like an individual is either dead or not dead. These injuries generally pose problems for a court faced with multiple potential causal factors because they cannot easily be divided up between such factors. The various ways in which this has been dealt with will be set out below.

---

9   [1984] QB 405.

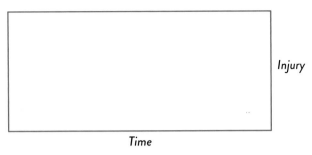

Injury

Time

Figure 6.2: Indivisible injury

Depending on the nature of the claimant's injury, the multiplicity of factors can make things very difficult indeed or it can also be resolved very simply. For instance, where the claimant is suffering from a **divisible** injury, the causal question is simple: the but for test remains applicable but the analysis asks whether the defendant has *caused part* (rather than the entirety) of the claimant's injury.

This illustrates the basic principle of orthodox causation that a defendant will only be liable for the measure of difference which, on the balance of probabilities, she can be determined to have made to the claimant's course of events. Several well-known cases dealing with causation clearly articulate this principle.

KEY CASE

Performance Cars Ltd v Abraham [1962] 1 QB 33

In *Performance Cars Ltd*, the defendant negligently collided with the claimant's Rolls Royce, causing damage necessitating a respray. However, the car had already been damaged in an earlier collision with a third party (against whom the claimant had an unsatisfied judgment). Evershed MR regarded the question of the extent of the defendant's liability as 'interesting and novel',[10] and dealt with it thus:

> I have in the end felt compelled to the conclusion that the necessity for respraying was

not the result of the defendant's wrongdoing because that necessity already existed. The Rolls Royce, when the defendant struck it, was in a condition which already required that it should be resprayed in any event. In my judgment in the present case the defendant should be taken to have injured a motor-car that was already in certain respects (that is, in respect of the need for respraying) injured; with the result that to the extent of that need or injury the damage claimed did not flow from the defendant's wrongdoing.[11]

KEY CASE

Dingle v Associated Newspapers [1961] 2 QB 162

In this libel case, Lord Devlin also discussed the principles of damages for personal injury. His Lordship stated that where

> there is not one indivisible injury but two separate injuries, the second wrongdoer – at any rate in cases where the legal consequences of the first injury are complete and ascertained before the

second injury is done – is liable only for the excess of damage done by the second injury. That excess is not necessarily smaller than the damage done by the first injury. The earning capacity of a man who has lost an eye may be diminished by perhaps 10 per cent. If he loses his other eye, his earning capacity will probably disappear altogether. A defendant who is responsible for the loss of the

---

10   At 37.
11   [1962] 1 QB 33 at 39–40.

second eye will have to pay for much more than half of the consequences of total blindness. In the example I have taken, he will have to pay for 90 per cent of the loss of earnings; but he will not have to pay the full 100 per cent because he can properly plead that the plaintiff's earning capacity was already damaged.[12]

KEY CASE

Thompson v Smiths Shiprepairers (North Shields) Ltd. [1984] QB 405

In *Thompson v Smiths Shiprepairers (North Shields) Ltd.*,[13] the claimants suffered from deafness as a result of industrial exposure by several different employers. Mustill J (as he then was) offered the following succinct account of this basic point:

> [O]ne must consider how this approach can be applied to a case where either (a) there are two successive employers, of whom only the second is at fault, or (b) there is a single employer, who has been guilty of an actionable fault only from a date after the employment began … Employer B has … 'inherited' a workman whose hearing is already damaged by events with which that employer has had no connection, or at least no connection which makes him liable in law. The fact that, so far as the worker is concerned, the prior events unfortunately give him no cause of action against anyone should not affect the principles on which he recovers from employer B. Justice looks to the interests of both parties, not to those of the plaintiff alone. It would be an injustice to employer B to make him liable for damage already done before he had any connection with the plaintiff. His liability, first principles suggest, should be limited to compensation for (a) the perpetuation and amplification of the handicaps already being suffered at the moment when the employment changed hands, and (b) the bringing to fruit in the shape of current hardship those symptoms which had previously been no more than potential.[14]

PROBLEM QUESTION TECHNIQUE

Danny, a young apprentice working for Badbury Estates, was standing underneath the ladder when it gave way. His right arm is broken in the accident. Before the accident happened, that arm was in a sling because he had broken his right collarbone playing rugby the previous weekend when a scrum collapsed.

▸ Consider whether the claimant's injury is divisible between the rugby match as the first causal factor and the ladder collapsing as the second causal factor.

▸ If Badbury is liable, it will only be for the broken arm and its effects, and not for the broken collarbone. This seems an easy distinction to make, but is often overlooked in favour of unnecessarily complicated causal analysis. An application of *Performance Cars* is appropriate here.

6.3.3 Successive factors

Two cases which can often lead to confusion are *Baker v Willoughby* [1970] and *Jobling v Associated Dairies* [1982].

---

12   *Dingle v Associated Newspapers* [1961] 2 QB 162 at 194.
13   [1984] QB 405.
14   *Thompson v Smiths Shiprepairers (North Shields) Ltd* [1984] QB 405 at 438.

KEY CASE

Baker v Willoughby [1970] AC 467

In this case, the claimant's left leg had been injured in a collision caused by the defendant's careless driving. Later, but before his claim came to court, he was shot in the same leg during an armed robbery at the scrap metal yard where he worked, which led to the amputation of his left leg. The robbers, who were the second tortfeasors, were, unsurprisingly, not before the court. The defendant argued that he should not be liable for damages beyond the point at which the leg was amputated, but the House of Lords disagreed, and he remained liable for all of the consequences of the claimant's original injury, as if the intervening event had never occurred. If the defendant's liability ended at the point at which the leg was removed, the claimant would have been worse off as a result of two torts than if he had just been a victim of the defendant's carelessness, since then there would have been no question of his receiving damages for being deprived of the use of a good leg for the rest of his life. This respects orthodox principles of causation; the defendant pays for depriving the claimant of the use of a good leg forever and, were the robbers to have been sued, they would have been liable for the additional damage they caused to an already injured leg.

KEY CASE

Jobling v Associated Dairies Ltd [1982] AC 794

In Jobling, the claimant was injured at work as a result of his employer's breach of duty.[15] His back was damaged and his earning capacity thereby reduced. Three years later, and completely independent of his accident, Jobling developed a back disease which rendered him completely unfit for work. The House of Lords held that the defendant should not be liable for the claimant's consequential losses after the point at which the disease manifested itself. The decision in Baker came in for some criticism along the way, but remained unaffected as a matter of precedent.[16]

According to *Clerk & Lindsell on Torts*, 'Jobling v Associated Dairies cannot be satisfactorily reconciled with *Baker v Willoughby*.'[17] Presumably, this is because, in the former case, the intervening event served to truncate the defendant's liability whilst, in the latter, it did not. However, such a simplistic comparison belies the legal import of the difference between the two factual situations.

It has generally come to be accepted that, as Lords Russell and Keith suggested in Jobling,[18] the *Baker* approach is applicable where the two events are successive torts and the *Jobling* approach appropriate where the subsequent event is not tortious. Since the claimant's ultimate state of affairs in *Jobling* was not worsened by a breach of duty, the case falls outside the remit of the tort of negligence. The facts of *Baker*, on the other hand, do fall within the parameters of the tort because, but for at least one breach of duty, the claimant would not have been in the condition he was at trial. On the basis of the causal inquiry as formulated for the purposes of negligence, the ultimate injury in *Baker* had a legally relevant cause, whereas the injury in Jobling (as it stood at the date of trial) did not. The two cases are thus perfectly easy to reconcile and to understand.

15　A statutory one under the Offices, Shops and Railway Premises Act 1963.

16　See, for instance, Lord Bridge at 821.

17　At 2–76 Although the two were regarded as being consistent with one another by Laws LJ in *Rahman v Arearose* [2001] QB 351 at [32].

18　[1982] AC 794 at 810 and 815, although this was not universally accepted – see Lord Bridge at 819–21.

The result in *Jobling* was further justified by reference to the 'vicissitudes of life' principle. Since damages for personal injury would normally be discounted to recognise the possibility that the claimant would not have led an unimpeded life for her remaining future in any event, all the decision in *Jobling* did was to substitute concrete knowledge of such a vicissitude having happened for the speculation it would normally make.[19] This might lead to the question of why the second tort in *Baker* did not count as the manifestation of such a vicissitude with similar effect. The answer to this is simply that torts are not 'vicissitudes of life' for this purpose and do not count as part of a claimant's 'normal course of events' when evaluating the causal effect of any other breach of duty.

Therefore, despite the fact that *Baker v Willoughby* is almost universally given negative academic and judicial treatment,[20] it is in fact a perfectly good example of basic causation principles being applied to good effect. As Lord Pearson recognised in that case,

> The supervening event has not made the plaintiff less lame nor less disabled nor less deprived of amenities. It has not shortened the period over which he will be suffering. It has made him more lame, more disabled, more deprived of amenities. He should not have less damages through being worse off than might have been expected.[21]

In other words, the effects of both breaches remained operative on the claimant: there was nothing about the second event which neutralised or improved the injury caused by the first, or reduced the duration of the claimant's suffering. The shooting served only to exacerbate the claimant's condition. The infringement of his right (in this case to bodily integrity) did not stop once the second event occurred, and so losses consequent on it did not disappear:

> For the defendant driver, the subject matter of the right infringed was a good leg. The defendant driver must pay for all of the loss consequent upon making a good leg stiff, and infringements of the right to bodily safety by others … do not reduce this loss. The actions of other wrongdoers, both actual and hypothetical, do not reduce the loss consequent upon the infringement of the right.[22]

Basically, this is a situation to which the *Performance Cars* principle would be applied, if the second tortfeasor were before the court. The approach in *Baker* ensures that claimants are not worse off, post-judgment, as a result of suffering multiple torts, than they would be had they suffered fewer. That is not to say that they should be better off either; they should not recover for more than the value of the infringement of their right plus any losses consequent on it,[23] but, as *Baker* demonstrates, this will not happen if each defendant pays only for the losses he caused. It does mean that the only recovery risk faced by claimants is that universal risk of the disappearing defendant (the robbers in *Baker*). Applying this principle, at least the absence of a defendant whose contribution occurred later in the physical sequence of events will not detract from a claimant's ability to recover for the ongoing effects of earlier torts (as would have been the case had the defendant's argument in *Baker* been accepted by the House of Lords). The gap in recovery will then be the difference between the claimant's earlier injured state and her ultimate injured state; not the entire difference between an uninjured claimant and her final injuries. This is clearly preferable to the Court of Appeal's approach to the facts of *Baker*, where the court was prepared to hold the second defendants liable for the whole of the loss on the basis that they had deprived the claimant of his ability to establish a case against the first defendant: where the defendant to whom all liability has been transferred is judgment-proof, the final outcome performs no compensatory or corrective functions at all. The House of Lords' approach, on the other

---

19   See Lord Russell at 810–11.
20   R. Stevens, *Torts and Rights* (Oxford University Press, 2007) at 139.
21   At 495.
22   R. Stevens, *Torts and Rights*, (above) 140–1.
23   See R. Stevens, *Torts and Rights*, (above) 133–4.

hand, made the best of a notoriously difficult situation without under-compensating the claimant, and without either over-burdening or arbitrarily absolving the defendant.

PROBLEM QUESTION TECHNIQUE

Danny, a young apprentice working for Badbury Estates, was standing underneath the ladder when it gave way. His right arm is broken in the accident. Before the accident happened, that arm was in a sling because he had broken his right collarbone playing rugby the previous weekend when a scrum collapsed. A month later, Danny gets into a fight outside a nightclub and his right arm, which had started to heal, is broken for a second time. The man responsible is never identified.

▸ This part of the problem question calls for an application of *Baker v Willoughby*.

▸ There are consecutive torts leading to the same harm, but the harm cannot be divided up according to the *Performance Cars* principle because the second tortfeasor is not before the court.

6.3.4 Material contribution to injury

In some situations, it is not possible to establish whether the defendant has caused part of the claimant's injury. This might be because the injury itself is **indivisible**, or because the causal factors do not operate independently of one another, or both. In such cases, the causal question is not whether the defendant has *caused part* of the injury but whether the defendant has *part-caused* that injury. If the answer is yes, the defendant is found to have **materially contributed to the injury** (to be distinguished clearly from liability imposed for materially contributing to the *risk* of an injury occurring, which will be dealt with below).

The classic example of this category of case is *Bonnington Castings v Wardlaw* [1956].[24]

KEY CASE

Bonnington Castings Ltd v Wardlaw [1956] AC 613

In this case, the claimant contracted pneumoconiosis (a lung disease caused by the inhalation of dust, usually in intensive work environments) during the course of his employment by the defendant. Two factors in the workplace atmosphere were identified as contributing to this disease: first, particles of silica dust that had emanated from swing grinders; and, second, particles of silica dust that had emanated from pneumatic hammers. Whilst both types of workplace machinery were the legal responsibility of the defendants,[25] there was only a breach of their duty in relation to the first, since there was no known or practicable means of reducing the dust escaping from the latter. This meant that there was, in effect, 'guilty' dust and 'innocent' dust, both of

which had affected the claimant. The question for the court in this case was whether the 'guilty' dust had sufficient causal significance to the claimant's injury to establish liability in negligence.

The specific problem posed for the causal inquiry in *Bonnington* stems from the fact that each potential causal factor (the 'innocent' dust and the 'guilty' dust) operated on the claimant concurrently:

The disease is a disease of gradual incidence. Small though the contribution of pollution may be for which the defenders are to blame, it was continuous over a long period. In cumulo, it must have been substantial, though it might remain small in proportion. It was the atmosphere

---

24 Although, as Lord Rodger states in *Fairchild v Glenhaven Funeral Services* [2002] UKHL 22 at [129]: 'The idea of liability based on wrongful conduct that had materially contributed to an injury was … established long before *Wardlaw*. But *Wardlaw* became a convenient point of reference, especially in cases of industrial disease.'

25 Covered specifically by regulation 1 of the Grinding of Metals (Miscellaneous Industries) Regulations 1925.

> inhaled by the pursuer that caused his illness and it is impossible, in my opinion, to resolve the components of that atmosphere into particles caused by the fault of the defenders and particles not caused by the fault of the defenders, as if they were separate and independent factors in his illness. Prima facie the particles inhaled are acting cumulatively, and I think the natural inference is that had it not been for the cumulative effect the pursuer would not have developed pneumoconiosis when he did and might not have developed it at all.[26]

Even though the injury in *Bonnington* is theoretically divisible because it is a disease which develops incrementally, the fact that the dust from two different sources operated on the claimant simultaneously during the same time period meant that, in practice, the court could not divide up and assign different stages of the pneumoconiosis to different sources, as in *Thompson* and *Performance Cars* above.

The defendant in *Bonnington*, therefore, was held liable for materially contributing to the claimant's injury. In other words, but for the 'guilty' dust, the claimant's pneumoconiosis would not have been as it was. The contribution of the negligence was found to have been 'material' and therefore legally relevant, even though it could not be quantified.

Figure 6.3 shows how *Bonnington* could be illustrated.

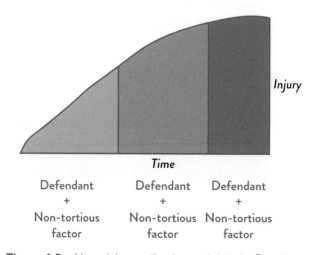

Figure 6.3: Material contribution to injury in *Bonnington*

> *Bonnington* may represent a departure from the ... orthodox approach in the context of a particular evidentiary gap: namely, where it is known that the victim's total condition is a divisible one but there is no acceptable evidentiary basis on which the disability due to the separate insults to the body could be apportioned to the individual sources, the claimant is allowed to recover for the total condition ... the pursuer could prove an orthodox causal connection between breach and a part of the divisible injury, he just could not quantify it.[27]

Therefore, where a claimant's injury is either indivisible, or is divisible into time periods but those time periods have each been affected by more than one factor, as in *Bonnington*, the material contribution to injury approach is appropriate.

26 *Bonnington Castings v Wardlaw* [1956] AC 613 at 626 per Lord Keith.
27 J. Stapleton, 'Unnecessary Causes' (2013) 129 LQR 39 at 52–3. See also J. Stapleton, 'Lords a Leaping Evidentiary Gaps' (2002) 10 *Torts Law Journal* 276 at 283 onwards.

In *Williams v Bermuda Hospitals Board* [2016], the Privy Council relied on *Bonnington* to apply a material contribution to injury analysis to a somewhat different situation.

KEY CASE

Williams v Bermuda Hospitals Board [2016] UKPC 4

The claimant was admitted to the defendant's hospital with acute appendicitis. Later that day, he underwent an appendectomy. He subsequently experienced complications resulting from that surgery, leaving him unwell for several weeks before he made a full recovery. Williams' case was that the defendant's negligence caused his operation to be delayed by two hours and 20 minutes, a delay which caused or materially contributed to the consequent physical issues he suffered. The trial judge, Hellman J, found for the defendant Board on the grounds that the delay had not been proven to have made any difference to the claimant's position. The evidence did not on his reading indicate that, but for the delay, the claimant would more likely than not have avoided the sepsis which prolonged his illness. In a less than straightforward judgment, the Court of Appeal of Bermuda reversed the decision on causation and found that the delay had materially contributed to the claimant's injury. The Privy Council upheld the Court of Appeal decision on causation, asserting that a material contribution to injury analysis did not require potential causal factors to operate simultaneously, but could apply where they operate successively.

It is worth considering whether *Williams* looks more in substance like *Barnett* than it does like *Bonnington*.

As a decision of the Privy Council, *Williams* has persuasive rather than binding effect on English courts, and it is certainly an area on which very interesting discussions might be had, as summarised in 'Different Perspectives' below.

It is very common in tort for both the outcome and the reasoning in cases to seem inconsistent. Remember you are not expected to reconcile the irreconcilable; you *are* expected to be able to formulate a robust and convincing presentation of a tenable viewpoint.

PROBLEM QUESTION TECHNIQUE

Evie, Alastair's wife, was made redundant the year before the accident. She developed an anxiety disorder as a result of the loss of her job. When she learns of Alastair's paralysis, her anxiety escalates into depression, and she is unable to leave the house.

▶ Anxiety and depression are instances of indivisible injury, and the factors of Evie's job loss and Alastair's injury operate interdependently as part of the process leading to such a condition.

▶ There is no way of identifying 'parts' of that illness and no way, therefore, of dividing it up between separate factors, as in *Performance Cars*. It is necessary, therefore, to apply a material contribution to injury analysis.[28]

Once you have a clear understanding of the law in this area, you can move on to thinking about it critically. 'Different Perspectives' below summarises contrasting opinions on the way in which the causal analysis should proceed on facts such as these.

---

28 Although see Sedley LJ in *O2 v Dickins plc* [2008] EWCA Civ 1144.

DIFFERENT PERSPECTIVES on but for causes and contributions

J. Stapleton and S. Steel, 'Causes and Contributions' (2016) LQR 363

This case comment takes the view that the law should recognise a distinction between but for causes and contributions. It defines factors, which are but for causes, as those without which the claimant's injury would not have occurred at all, whereas contributions are factors without which part of a process leading to the claimant's indivisible injury would not have occurred (the problem does not arise where the injury is divisible because the court can apportion causal responsibility, as explained earlier in this chapter). Stapleton and Steel give the example of three defendants who each independently put a drop of poison into a drink. One drop is not sufficient to cause harm, but two drops are. The third defendant's drop of poison is not, therefore, a but for cause of the harm to whomever drinks the tea, since the two previous drops are sufficient to achieve that. According to Stapleton and Steel, the third defendant's action is nonetheless a contribution to the process involved and should be recognised as a legal cause (albeit not a necessary but for cause). Compensatory damages should be available where a defendant has contributed to a process which has led to a claimant being worse off than she would have been in the absence of wrongful behaviour. Applying this to *Williams*, Stapleton and Steel criticise the reasoning of the Privy Council in stating that causation had been established on but for grounds. In fact, this article argues, any liability of the defendant in *Williams* should have been based on its non-necessary contribution to the process leading to the claimant's eventual injury.

S. Green, 'When is a Material Contribution Not a Material Contribution?' (2016) 32(2) Journal of Professional Negligence 169

This case comment takes the view that there should have been no liability in *Williams* because the claimant failed to establish the requisite causal link. It argues that the Privy Council should not have applied *Bonnington* and the material contribution to injury analysis because the facts of the case do not call for it. Rather, the facts of *Williams* bear a closer analogy to *Barnett* and invite the application of the basic and orthodox but for test. In both *Barnett* and *Williams*, factors unrelated to the defendant (the ingestion of arsenic and the appendicitis respectively) occurred and affected the claimant before the claimant sought each defendant's medical assistance and so, by definition, before any breach of duty occurred. Whereas in *Bonnington*, the background factor (the 'innocent' dust) and the breach factor (the 'guilty' dust) operated on the claimant at the same time. The material contribution analysis of *Bonnington* is explained as being relevant only where the breach and non-breach factors operate upon the claimant simultaneously and interdependently. Where this occurs, there is no point in time at which it is possible to say whether the claimant would have been worse off but for the defendant's breach. In *Williams*, however, as in *Barnett*, there was a point, prior to the defendant's breach of duty, where it was possible to ask whether, on the balance of probabilities, the claimant was likely to incur his eventual injury regardless of the defendant's intervention. The basic point here is that the causal issue in *Williams* was far simpler than counsels' arguments and the courts' reasoning suggest.

6.3.5 Loss of a chance of avoiding an adverse physical outcome

This is one of the most interesting issues in causation, dividing opinion possibly more than any other. To think and write about this concept effectively, you will need to have a sound understanding of the balance of probabilities standard of proof and how it operates. Remember that a claimant in a tort action has to persuade the court that it is more likely than not that her account of events is a true representation of what happened. Particularly in medical cases, this often takes the form of providing evidence that it was more than 50% likely that the defendant's breach caused the claimant's loss. Crucially, however, once the claimant has 'proved' her case to >50%, the court treats it as proved with certainty. So, she succeeds and recovers full damages even if the evidence accepted suggests that it was 51% likely that the defendant caused her loss. Correspondingly, if she fails to reach this standard, even with a 49% likelihood, she recovers nothing.

There are two important cases with which you will need to be familiar, although they are not completely analogous with one another. The first is *Hotson v East Berkshire Area Health Authority* [1987] and the second is *Gregg v Scott* [2005].

KEY CASE

Hotson v East Berkshire Area Health Authority [1987] AC 750

In this case, the claimant, a 13-year-old boy, fell from a tree and injured his left hip.[29] The defendant's hospital negligently failed to diagnose or treat him correctly for five days. Ultimately, the claimant suffered avascular necrosis of the epiphysis (which means that the bone tissue in his hip died due to insufficient blood supply), which led to disability of the hip joint with the virtual certainty that osteoarthritis would later develop. At trial, Simon Brown J found that, even if the injury had been properly diagnosed and treated in a timely manner, there remained a 75% risk that avascular necrosis would have developed, but he awarded the claimant damages corresponding to the 25% chance of which the defendant's negligence had supposedly deprived him. Whilst the Court of Appeal concurred, the House of Lords decided in favour of the defendant and held that the trial judge's finding that, at the time of the fall there had already been a 75% chance of avascular necrosis developing, amounted to a finding on the balance of probabilities that the fall was the sole cause of the injury. However, the Court did not expressly exclude the possibility that 'loss of a chance' could ever form the basis of a successful claim in negligence.[30]

KEY CASE

Gregg v Scott [2005] UKHL 2

In this case, the claimant visited the defendant GP in November 1994, complaining of a lump under his left arm, which the defendant diagnosed as a benign growth. It was not until November 1995 that a specialist saw the claimant, following a referral by another GP in August 1995. A biopsy carried out by order of the specialist surgeon revealed that the claimant actually had non-Hodgkin's lymphoma, a form of cancer. By failing to refer the claimant to a specialist at the point of the initial (incorrect) diagnosis, the defendant was held to have been in breach of his duty of care. The trial judge found that the claimant's chance of being 'cured' (defined in this context as a period of ten years' remission) was 42% when he made his visit to the defendant, but that the nine-month delay consequent upon the defendant's negligent failure to diagnose his illness correctly reduced his chance of being cured to 25%. As the claimant had only a 42% chance of a cure in the first place, he was unable to prove on the balance of probabilities that the defendant's negligence caused him to be in a worse state than he would have been in without the delay. In light of this fact, the claimant argued that he had suffered the loss of a chance of being cured as a result of the defendant's negligence. In so doing, he invited the court to address a similar question to that first considered by the House in *Hotson* as to whether or not such a loss should be recoverable.

---

29 More specifically, his left femoral epiphysis.
30 [1987] AC 750 at 786.

By a majority of three to two (Lord Hope and Lord Nicholls dissenting), the House of Lords dismissed the claimant's appeal and held that it was (still) not prepared to extend loss of a chance claims to clinical negligence cases. In essence, Mr Gregg was told that he could not recover from Dr Scott because he could not prove on the balance of probabilities that the latter's negligence caused his life expectancy to be reduced. Whilst, on the facts as found by the trial judge, it had been established that the defendant's breach of duty had reduced the epidemiological likelihood of survival by 17%, the House of Lords refused to recognise this as actionable damage. As Lord Hoffmann put it:

> A wholesale adoption of possible rather than probable causation as the criterion of liability would be so radical a change in our law as to amount to a legislative act.[31]

The court refused to depart from the orthodox approach of establishing a causal link between a defendant's breach of duty and a claimant's actionable damage on the balance of probabilities. In doing so, it recognised that the characteristic common to all causation problems is that of imperfect knowledge. To use Lord Hoffmann's words once more:

> What we lack is knowledge and the law deals with that lack of knowledge by the concept of the burden of proof.[32]

In other words, although the law cannot expect to deal in certainties, the least it can do is expect them to be more likely than not.

The claimants in *Hotson* and *Gregg* were each found to have a less than even chance of recovery even *before* the defendants' negligence intervened in their lives (in *Hotson*, 25% and in *Gregg*, 42%). On the balance of probabilities, they were both (according to fiction of certainty) going to suffer from adverse physical consequences regardless of the actions of the defendants. This was the very reason why counsel in both cases reformulated the claims to be for loss of chance: it was clear that neither was ever going to be able to recover on orthodox grounds. It was an attempt to sidestep the standard burden of proof on the basis that, in having their 'already likely to suffer an adverse outcome' position made into 'even more likely to suffer an adverse outcome' by the defendants' breach, the claimants had lost something of value to them. From a human interest point of view, making this argument is easily understandable, since most individuals would class even the tiniest percentage chance of avoiding an adverse physical outcome as having significant value.[33] In legal terms, however, such a 'chance' is not a prediction of what would have happened to a particular claimant.

One of the main points of contention around the question of lost chances is the interpretation of statistics:

> If it is proved statistically that 25 per cent of the population have a chance of recovery from a certain injury and 75 per cent do not, it does not mean that someone who suffers that injury and who does not recover from it has lost a 25 per cent chance. He may have lost nothing at all. What he has to do is prove that he was one of the 25 per cent and that his loss was caused by the defendant's negligence. To be a figure in a statistic does not by itself give him a cause of action. *If the plaintiff succeeds in proving that he was one of the 25 per cent and the defendant took away that chance*, the logical result would be to award him 100 per cent of his damages.[34]

31 [2005] UKHL 2 at [90].
32 [2005] UKHL 2 at [79].
33 See S. Steel, 'Rationalising Loss of a Chance in Tort' in S. Pitel, J. Neyers and E. Chamberlain (eds), *Challenging Orthodoxy in Tort Law* (Hart Publishing, 2013).
34 *Hotson v East Berkshire Health Authority* [1987] 1 All ER 210, 223 *per* Croom-Johnson LJ (emphasis added).

As Croom-Johnson LJ suggests above, a medical assessment that someone has a 25% chance of recovery means that, out of 100 people with the same condition, 25 will recover and 75 will not. Such statistics do not provide a personalised assessment of a particular claimant's chances; merely a risk ratio across a given population. The effect of the defendant's negligence in such a case is to move a claimant from, say, a 42 in 100 category into a 25 in 100 category. On one view, this does not reduce the chances personal to any individual since, in a deterministic world, the individual is and always has been either one of the 25 or one of the 75 – we just don't know which. This was the point made by Lord Hoffmann above in *Gregg*; every claimant has a destiny, not a constantly shifting percentage 'chance'. The law uses statistics because it is its only means of dealing with its imperfect knowledge of any claimant's fate. Therefore, those statistics are not approximations of the claimant's position, but approximations of the court's chances of being right about what that position is.

On another view, justice demands that recovery be permitted for such lost 'chances'. In *Gregg v Scott*, Lord Nicholls in his dissent said:

> My Lords, this appeal raises a question which has divided courts and commentators throughout the common law world. The division derives essentially from different perceptions of what constitutes injustice in a common form type of medical negligence case. Some believe a remedy is essential and that a principled ground for providing an appropriate remedy can be found. Others are not persuaded. I am in the former camp.
>
> This is the type of case under consideration. A patient is suffering from cancer. His prospects are uncertain. He has a 45% chance of recovery. Unfortunately his doctor negligently misdiagnoses his condition as benign. So the necessary treatment is delayed for months. As a result the patient's prospects of recovery become nil or almost nil. Has the patient a claim for damages against the doctor? No, the House was told. The patient could recover damages if his initial prospects of recovery had been more than 50%. But because they were less than 50% he can recover nothing.
>
> This surely cannot be the state of the law today. It would be irrational and indefensible. The loss of a 45% prospect of recovery is just as much a real loss for a patient as the loss of a 55% prospect of recovery. In both cases the doctor was in breach of his duty to his patient. In both cases the patient was worse off. He lost something of importance and value. But, it is said, in one case the patient has a remedy, in the other he does not.
>
> This would make no sort of sense. It would mean that in the 45% case the doctor's duty would be hollow. The duty would be empty of content. For the reasons which follow I reject this suggested distinction. The common law does not compel courts to proceed in such an unreal fashion. I would hold that a patient has a right to a remedy as much where his prospects of recovery were less than 50-50 as where they exceeded 50-50.[35]

As outlined above, the main point of distinction between whether a claimant on such facts has actually 'lost' a chance is in what the statistical assessments are understood to mean.

■ VIEWPOINT

Do you think the claimants in these cases have lost anything? Are there any convincing arguments in favour of allowing recovery in cases like *Hotson*? Do you think the facts of *Hotson* are materially different from those of *Gregg*?

---

35   At [1]–[4].

PROBLEM QUESTION TECHNIQUE

Two years after Alastair's accident, his friend Harry, who is a doctor, tells Alastair about some research he has found which casts doubt on Dr Cook's original diagnosis. This research, which was available at the time of Alastair's accident, suggests that, in the case of injuries such as those Alastair sustained, paralysis is not in fact an inevitable result and that, in 35% of cases, immediate and regular physiotherapy can lead to the resumption of limb movement, and the prevention of paralysis.

▸ Even if Dr Cook's failure to read and respond to the available research is deemed (on the basis of the *Bolam* test – see Chapter 5) to be a breach of his duty of care, Alastair would be unable to establish on the balance of probabilities that the breach caused his paralysis, since it was only 35% likely that he would have avoided that outcome in any event.

▸ He could make the argument, however, that the breach deprived him of that 35% chance. The initial less than evens probability here points to an application of the loss of chance cases of *Hotson* and *Gregg*, which, as the law stands at the moment, would lead to a conclusion of no liability.

DIFFERENT PERSPECTIVES on loss of a chance

J. Morgan, 'A Chance Missed to Recognise Loss of a Chance in Negligence' (2005) 3(Aug) LMCLQ 281–90

Morgan argues that the House of Lords was wrong not to allow the claim for loss of a chance in *Gregg*. First, Morgan says, the blanket refusal to compensate for lost chances means that a doctor's duty of care is effectively empty of content whenever she is treating a patient who comes to her with a less than evens chance of survival. Morgan also argues that the majority was wrong to reject Lord Hope of Craighead's suggestion that the diminution of life prospects could be deemed to be loss consequential upon the growth of the tumour resulting from the negligent misdiagnosis. Although the case was not pleaded this way in *Gregg*, such growth could amount to personal injury, upon which loss of life expectancy could be deemed consequential. Loss not recognised as actionable in its own right is after all elsewhere in tort recognised as recoverable consequential loss; mere distress is given as an example.

E. Peel, 'Loss of a Chance in Medical Negligence' (2005) 121 LQR 364

Peel takes the view that the House of Lords was correct to reject the loss of chance claims in both *Hotson* and *Gregg* and that it was acceptable to use statistical evidence to do so. He distinguishes loss of chance claims in relation to the avoidance of an adverse physical outcome from those made in relation to losing the chance of a financial gain, suggesting that this distinction could be justified because the financial gain cases turn on the unpredictable action of another human being and/or because it is appropriate to measure financial opportunities in terms of lost gains. Peel disagrees with Lord Hope's suggestion in *Gregg* that the growth of the tumour consequent upon the failure to diagnose could act as a base on which a loss chance claim could be set up as consequential, and states that this would arbitrarily allow the recovery of lost chances for those with a physiological deterioration but not others.

H. Reece, 'Losses of Chances in the Law' (1996) 59 MLR 188

In one of the most insightful articles written on the topic, Reece distinguishes between two different situations: deterministic and 'quasi-indeterministic'. Deterministic situations are those in which, if we had perfect information, we could look at past facts and predict what the result of those facts would be. Quasi-indeterministic situations, by contrast, are those in which, even if we had unlimited information, we could still never predict a future outcome from the facts as we know them. In deterministic situations, the evidence is uncertain. In quasi-indeterministic situations, the world is uncertain. Reece makes the point that, where the evidence is uncertain, courts should stick to the balance of probabilities, to split the risk of error between claimant and defendant. In other words, loss of chance claims should not be allowed in this context. Where neither side could ever prove or disprove causation on the balance of probabilities, loss of chance claims should be allowed. An example of the former is *Hotson* and an example of the latter is *Chaplin v Hicks* [1911][36] (see 'Making Connections' below). In *Hotson*, there was a point at which the state of the claimants' blood vessels would have determined whether he developed avascular necrosis or not. At no point in *Chaplin*, however, did any state of the world determine which contestant the panel in the beauty contest would favour.

S. Green, 'Loss of a Chance as a Commercial Remedy' in G. Virgo and S. Worthington (eds), Commercial Remedies: Resolving Controversies (CUP, 2016)

Green argues that the cases that have historically been argued as 'lost chance' cases are not all analogous, and that a distinction needs to be made between three different types of case. Only in Type 1 cases is it appropriate for a loss of a chance claim to succeed. Type 1 cases are those in which the chance itself is external to the relationship between the parties. It is the interaction between the parties which either allows or prevents access to this chance. For instance, in *Allied Maples v Simmons & Simmons* [1995],[37] detailed below, the solicitors' negligence deprived the claimants of the ability to avail themselves of a bargaining opportunity. The chance or probability of that bargaining activity having a successful outcome was not affected in any way by the relationship between the parties, but access to it was. Where, on the balance of probabilities, a defendant's breach has denied a claimant access to such an external opportunity, the claimant should succeed in recovering the value of the chance lost. In Type 2 situations – as in both *Hotson* and *Gregg* – the 'chance' is determined entirely by the interaction between the parties, because the defendant's action reduced the probability of recovery. In this type of case, the 'chance' formulation is really just an attempt to sidestep the standard of proof requirement and, as such, should not be permitted. Type 3 cases are not really lost chance cases at all. They are simply where causation has been established on the balance of probabilities, but the claimant's consequential losses remain to be quantified. They are not, therefore, about causation at all. For example, if a defendant has negligently injured a promising young cricketer, the main gist of that claim will be the personal injury, but the chances of her going on to play professionally might well also have to be assessed. Type 3 is simply an example of orthodox damage assessment, but is sometimes misleadingly referred to as a lost chance.

6.4 Exceptions to the but for test

6.4.1 Loss of a chance of achieving a better financial outcome

When discussing loss of a chance in law, you should take care to be precise about what has been accepted as recoverable by the courts and what has not. The cases of *Hotson* and *Gregg*, discussed above, cover the particular circumstances of claimants who claim to have lost a chance of *avoiding an adverse physical outcome*. However, in *Allied Maples v Simmons & Simmons*[38] the Court of Appeal allowed a claim for the lost chance of achieving a better *financial outcome*.

---

36 [1911] 2 KB 786.
37 [1995] 1 WLR 1602, CA.
38 [1995] 1 WLR 1602.

KEY CASE

Allied Maples v Simmons & Simmons [1995] 1 WLR 1602

The defendants were solicitors whose negligence in drafting an acquisition contract deprived the claimants of the opportunity to negotiate more advantageous terms. Relying on the negligently drafted agreement, the claimants believed they were protected from liabilities arising from the acquisition when in fact they were not. Had they known of their vulnerability, they would have attempted to acquire protection from the vendor before the contract was concluded. The Court of Appeal decided in favour of the claimants, and determined that damages should be quantified according to the chance that the claimants would have succeeded in this negotiation in the absence of the defendants' negligence. It concluded that, as long as there was a real (as opposed to speculative) chance of success, there was no need for a positive outcome to be more likely than not in order for the claimant to be able to recover.

On this basis, it is often said that it is possible to recover in negligence for the loss of a chance to make a financial gain. However, given that the common law usually prioritises the protection of physical integrity over that of financial welfare, this seems inconsistent with the refusal to allow for 'lost chances' in relation to physical wellbeing. There are several responses to this. First, the House of Lords' decision in *Gregg* left some considerable room for manoeuvre for future lost chance claims concerning physical harm; its position was closer to 'not on these facts' than it was to 'not on principle'. Second, there is the fact that financial counterfactuals are more authentic than physical counterfactuals. In other words, a claimant will often be able convincingly to point to some sort of market-determined outcome which, but for the defendant's negligence, she would have had a chance of benefiting from, such as the price of certain stock, or a particular property. Such phenomena are facts about the world as it now exists. Where the physical outcome of an individual is concerned, the counterfactual state of the world cannot be known. We will simply never know what would have happened to a claimant, had her physical being been treated differently. Finally, there is the view, taken from the judgment of Stuart-Smith LJ himself in *Allied Maples*,[39] that the loss of chance formulation is appropriate where the desired outcome is dependent on the actions of a third party. This explanation would seem to present less of a challenge to priorities of the tort of negligence, in that it does not expressly favour financial gain over physical wellbeing.

MAKING CONNECTIONS

Similarly, it is possible to recover for the loss a chance in the law of contract. Indeed, *Allied Maples* was a claim brought in contract and tort. In the case of *Chaplin v Hicks*,[40] an aspiring actress entered a competition organised by the defendant, for which the prize was a paid position in the defendant's theatre. The claimant was one of 50 entrants, selected from a class of 6,000, to proceed to the second round of the contest, but, as a result of the defendant's breach of contract, she was deprived of the

---

39   At 1611. This is the view which can also be found in M. Jones et al, *Clerk & Lindsell on Torts*, 22nd edn (Sweet & Maxwell, 2017), 2–26 and A. Burrows, *Remedies for Torts, Breach of Contract and Equitable Wrongs*, 4th edn (Oxford University Press, 2019), 67–73.

40   [1911] 2 KB 786.

opportunity to participate further. She claimed, and was awarded, damages for the loss of a chance of winning the competition. This looks similar to a claim in tort for the loss of a chance of financial gain. In the Court of Appeal, Fletcher Moulton LJ said:

> Where by contract a man [sic] has a right to belong to a limited class of competitors, he is possessed of something of value, and it is the duty of the jury [now court] to estimate the pecuniary value of that advantage, if it is taken from him.[41]

Since the defendant was to choose 12 from the final 50 competitors, the claimant's chances were estimated to be 1 in 4 of winning the prize, and her damages estimated accordingly.[42]

■ VIEWPOINT

Do you think it is justifiable for the common law to allow recovery for the lost chance of a financial gain but not for the lost chance of avoiding an adverse physical outcome?

6.4.2 Overdetermination

… the preferable course is to use the causa sine qua non[43] test as the exclusive test of causation. One obvious exception to this rule must be the unusual case where the damage is the result of the simultaneous operation of two or more separate and independent events each of which was sufficient to cause the damage. None of the various tests of causation suggested by courts and writers, however, is satisfactory in dealing with this exceptional case.[44]

Overdetermination refers to situations where there are several potential causal factors, and each on its own would be sufficient to bring about the result in question. In such situations, the but for test is of no use because it generates a logically indefensible answer, which must be wrong in practice.

Take, for example, the much-used example of the two hunters who both negligently fire into the forest, hitting and killing V. Asked of each hunter in turn, the but for test generates the obviously incorrect answer that neither caused the death because, but for either shot, the death would still have occurred. The over-determination problem has a long history in the literature on causation, partly because it exposes in vivid detail the shortcomings of the but for test. However, there is not much case law, particularly in England and Wales, though there are a few examples from other jurisdictions.

The following excerpt is from the infamous case of *Summers v Tice* [1948],[45] decided by the Supreme Court of California, and remarkably similar on its facts to two other cases: *Cook v Lewis* [1951],[46] decided a few years later by the Supreme Court of Canada; and *Oliver v Miles* [1926], another much earlier judgment of the Supreme Court of Mississippi.[47]

---

41 At 798.
42 The Court of Appeal treated the interview panel as if it were independent of the defendant, making this look like an *Allied Maples*-type situation, in which the claimant's chances were dependent upon the actions of a third party. In actual fact, the defendant himself was responsible for making the final decision, which should have meant that loss of chance principles were irrelevant.
43 This is the Latin term for the but for test.
44 Per McHugh J in *March v Stramare* (1991) 171 CLR 506 at 533.
45 33 Cal. 2d 80.
46 [1951] SCR 830.
47 144 Miss. 852, 110 So. 666.

> If two hunters are negligent and liable as independent tortfeasors for firing in the direction of a third hunter who is injured thereby, the innocent wronged hunter should not be deprived of his right to redress where the matter of apportionment of damages is incapable of proof. The wrongdoers should be left to work out between themselves any apportionment.[48]

All three cases concerned the now classic scenario in which multiple defendants each discharged their firearms in breach of duty, injuring a claimant. The problem in each case was that, although it was clear that but for *a* breach the claimant would not have been injured at all, it was not possible for the court to ascertain which of the defendants caused the injuries. In the first two cases, the courts dealt with the overdetermination problem by reversing the burden of proof, and holding both defendants jointly liable until, and to the extent that, each could establish he did *not* cause the claimant's injuries. This is known in the United States as 'alternative liability'.[49] In *Oliver v Miles*, the same result was reached by means of an apparently different method, viewing both defendants as having been engaged in a joint enterprise:

> We think that they were jointly engaged in the unlawful enterprise of shooting at birds flying over the highway; that they were in pursuit of a common purpose; that each did an unlawful act, in the pursuit thereof; and that each is liable for the resulting injury to the boy, although no one can say definitely who actually shot him. To hold otherwise would be to exonerate both from liability, although each was negligent, and the injury resulted from such negligence.[50]

It would seem that courts are unwilling to let defendants benefit from the difficulties in establishing causation which arise from these types of multiple cause situations. Whilst there is no direct English authority on the point, the decisions outlined above at least provide a suggested model for dealing with this particular causal issue. English courts have, however, had to grapple with an even more intractable causal problem; the situation where there are multiple factors, but it is not known whether any one factor, or even combination of factors, would have been enough to cause the harm in its own right. For this purpose, there now exists in English law a very specific exception to orthodox causal analysis variously referred to either as the *Fairchild* principle or as liability for material contribution to risk.

6.4.3 Material contribution to risk

Exceptionally, a link between a defendant's breach and a claimant's damage can be established by finding that the actions of the defendant *materially increased the risk* of the claimant's damage occurring. This method derived originally from *McGhee v National Coal Board* [1973] and developed into the approach taken in *Fairchild v Glenhaven Funeral Services Ltd* [2002].

KEY CASE

McGhee v National Coal Board [1973] 1 WLR 1

The claimant in *McGhee*, whose complaint was dermatitis, was employed by the defendants to work in brick kilns. During this occupation, his skin was inevitably in contact with brick dust, which was the agent identified as the cause of his illness. His employers were not in breach of their duty of

---

48   *Summers v Tice* 33 Cal.2d 80 (Sup Ct Cal, 1948) at (9).
49   US Restatement (Third) §28.
50   110 So. 666 at 668. The reference herein to joint engagement in an unlawful enterprise was presumably the means chosen by the court to ensure that the defendants were jointly, as opposed to severally, liable to the claimant.

care for exposing him to brick dust whilst he was physically in the kilns, but they were in breach for failing to provide washing facilities to enable him to wash the dust off his skin before cycling home. However, the medical experts were unable to determine whether, and if so to what extent, the disease was triggered by brick dust attributable to the breach of duty as opposed to exposure which would have occurred even if showers had been provided for use after work. Therefore they were unable to say whether the dermatitis would have occurred but for the defendant's breach of duty. To deal with this evidentiary gap,[51] the House of Lords held the defendants liable for having materially increased the risk of the claimant's developing dermatitis, since risk was the only medium through which such a conclusion could be reached. Lord Wilberforce summarised the issue:

> [T]he question remains whether a pursuer must necessarily fail if, after he has shown a breach of duty, involving an increase of risk of disease, he cannot positively prove that this increase of risk caused or materially contributed to the disease while his employers cannot positively prove the contrary. In this intermediate case there is an appearance of logic in the view that the pursuer, on whom the onus lies, should fail ... The question is whether

we should be satisfied, in factual situations like the present, with this logical approach. In my opinion, there are further considerations of importance. First, it is a sound principle that where a person has, by breach of a duty of care, created a risk, and injury occurs within the area of that risk, the loss should be borne by him unless he shows that it had some other cause. Secondly, from the evidentiary point of view, one may ask, why should a man who is able to show that his employer should have taken certain precautions, because without them there is a risk, or an added risk, of injury or disease, and who in fact sustains exactly that injury or disease, have to assume the burden of proving more: namely, that it was the addition to the risk, caused by the breach of duty, which caused or materially contributed to the injury? In many cases, of which the present is typical, this is impossible to prove, just because honest medical opinion cannot segregate the causes of an illness between compound causes. And if one asks which of the parties, the workman or the employers, should suffer from this inherent evidentiary difficulty, the answer as a matter of policy or justice should be that it is the creator of the risk who, ex hypothesi must be taken to have foreseen the possibility of damage, who should bear its consequences.[52]

The idea of a defendant being liable in negligence for materially increasing the risk of a claimant incurring damage was a novel development. It was also of fairly minor importance for nearly three decades until the House of Lords employed it in the landmark decision of *Fairchild v Glenhaven Funeral Services*.

KEY CASE

Fairchild v Glenhaven Funeral Services [2002] UKHL 22

The defendants in *Fairchild* were former employers of individuals who had contracted mesothelioma, and had exposed those individuals to asbestos in breach of their duties of care. It was accepted that, for the purposes of the case, any exposure to

asbestos other than that for which the defendants were responsible (such as general environmental exposure) could be discounted. The major complication was that each individual had been exposed to asbestos by more than one employer,

---

51   So characterised by Jane Stapleton in 'Lords a'Leaping Evidentiary Gaps' (2002) 10 *Torts Law Journal* 276.
52   Lord Wilberforce at 1012.

and medical knowledge about the way in which mesothelioma occurred was incomplete. The Court was therefore unable to associate the development of the disease with any particular source of asbestos (in other words, with any particular employer):

> The mechanism by which a normal mesothelial cell is transformed into a mesothelioma cell is not known... There is no way of identifying, even on a balance of probabilities, the source of the fibre or fibres which initiated the genetic process which culminated in the malignant tumour. It is on this rock of uncertainty, reflecting the point to which medical science has so far advanced, that the three claims were rejected by the Court of Appeal and by two of the three trial judges.[53]

This meant that there was an evidentiary gap comparable to that in *McGhee*, and it is hardly

surprising that, after detailed consideration of the earlier case, the House of Lords applied the material increase in risk approach to decide in favour of the claimants in *Fairchild*. However, the Court emphasised the exceptional nature of what it was doing:

> The crucial issue on appeal is whether, in the special circumstances of such a case, principle, authority or policy requires or justifies a modified approach to proof of causation.[54]

This is the crux of the issue in both *McGhee* and *Fairchild*, characterised by Lord Bingham as the 'rock of uncertainty'.[55] Specifically, the crucial uncertainty here is that the nature of mesothelioma makes it impossible (currently) to discern which exposures contributed to the disease and which did not.[56]

The next case to test the limits of the *Fairchild* principle was *Barker v Corus* [2006].

KEY CASE

Barker v Corus [2006] UKHL 20

Barker raised two issues that were bound to require clarification in the wake of *Fairchild*. The late Mr Barker had been exposed to asbestos during three periods of his working life: whilst working for an employer other than the defendant;[57] whilst working for the defendant; and also whilst self-employed. The issue was whether the *Fairchild* principle should apply to situations where an individual has been exposed to asbestos dust during periods of self-employment as well as periods of employment

by others. The House of Lords was also asked to address the question of whether or not a defendant in a *Fairchild*-type situation should be entitled to apportionment of his liability to reflect the extent of exposure for which the defendant was responsible.[58] Ultimately, the *Fairchild* principle was held to apply in such circumstances, but on the basis of liability aliquoted according to relative risk contributions rather than joint and several liability.[59] This distinction is highly significant for defendants

53 Lord Bingham at [7].
54 Lord Bingham at [2].
55 Lord Bingham at [7].
56 It is entirely possible, according to our current state of knowledge, that all but one defendant on the facts of *Fairchild* (or, indeed, no defendant at all, if Stapleton's point that environmental exposure cannot defensibly be discounted, despite what their Lordships decided in *Fairchild* – see Lords a'Leaping at 17–20) could have had no effect whatsoever on the claimant. This is what makes the issue so difficult.
57 Who had since become insolvent.
58 See R. Merkin and J. Steele, *Insurance and the Law of Obligations* (Oxford University Press, 2013), 366.
59 The effect of the latter part of this ruling was reversed in relation to asbestos and mesothelioma by s 3 of the Compensation Act 2006 – see below.

because joint and several liability means that any one defendant can be pursued by the claimant for the full amount of damages. That defendant then has to claim back from its co-defendants their share of the award under the Civil Liability (Contribution) Act 1978. Not only is this time-consuming and expensive, but it puts the risk of any of the other defendants being insolvent or unable to pay on to the defendant who has paid out. Aliquot liability, on the other hand, involves the court allocating a set amount to be recovered from each defendant, which cannot be exceeded. Under this allocation, the risk of any defendant being unable to pay falls on the claimant, and it was this to which Parliament objected, as explained below.

Very soon after the decision in *Barker* had been handed down, Parliament added s 3 to the Compensation Act 2006 in order to reverse the aliquot liability aspect of the decision.[60]

KEY LEGISLATION

Compensation Act 2006

3   Mesothelioma: damages

(1)   This section applies where—

  (a) a person ('the responsible person') has negligently or in breach of statutory duty caused or permitted another person ('the victim') to be exposed to asbestos,

  (b) the victim has contracted mesothelioma as a result of exposure to asbestos,

  (c) because of the nature of mesothelioma and the state of medical science, it is not possible to determine with certainty whether it was the exposure mentioned in paragraph (a) or another exposure which caused the victim to become ill, and

  (d) the responsible person is liable in tort, by virtue of the exposure mentioned in paragraph (a), in connection with damage caused to the victim by the disease (whether by reason of having materially increased a risk or for any other reason).

(2)   The responsible person shall be liable—

  (a) in respect of the whole of the damage caused to the victim by the disease (irrespective of whether the victim was also exposed to asbestos—

    (i)   other than by the responsible person, whether or not in circumstances in which another person has liability in tort, or

    (ii) by the responsible person in circumstances in which he has no liability in tort), and

    (iii) jointly and severally with any other responsible person.

The effect of this section is to make joint and several liability the only possible consequence of an application of the *Fairchild* principle *where the damage is mesothelioma and the harmful agent is asbestos*, regardless of whether there has been any exposure whatsoever[61] other than that resulting from the defendant's breach of duty. Any analogous, but not identical, facts which attract the application

60   The alacrity with which this was achieved can be explained by the fact that the Bill which ultimately became the Compensation Act 2006 was already being considered when the House of Lords decided *Barker*. Section 3 was added after several members of Parliament expressed outrage at the decision. For a detailed discussion, see J. Lee, 'Inconsiderate Alterations in our Laws: Legislative Reversal of Supreme Court Decisions' in *From House of Lords to Supreme Court: Judges, Jurists and the Process of Judging* (Hart Publishing, 2011), 79–86.

61   This is so whether or not the other exposures resulted from (anyone's) breach(es) of duty – s 3(2)(a)(i)and (ii).

of that principle (such as dermatitis and brick dust) remain subject to the common law rule of apportionment derived from *Barker*. This is potentially highly unfavourable from a defendant's point of view, since any one defendant might end up paying the full award of damages (if its co-defendants are insolvent) despite, as a result of the *Fairchild* principle, not having been found on the balance of probabilities to have caused any damage at all. The next case, *Sienkiewicz v Grief (UK) Ltd*,[62] arguably exacerbated the issue.

KEY CASE

Sienkiewicz v Grief (UK) Ltd [2011] UKSC 10

In *Sienkiewicz*, one of the claimants had been exposed to asbestos by the defendant while in its employment. The context differed from *Fairchild* in a significant way: the court accepted that her occupational exposure had been very light. In fact, the trial judge accepted evidence to the effect that her asbestos exposure by the defendant increased her overall risk of developing mesothelioma by only 18%, and that the rest of her exposure was due to background environmental factors not associated with any breach of duty. The major question facing the Supreme Court was whether the exceptional *Fairchild* principle should be applied in situations in which there had been only one exposure to risk as a result of negligence.

As Lord Brown pointed out, this question had been considered in *Fairchild* itself:

Lord Rodger of Earlsferry, for example, expressly recognised (at para 170 of his speech) that 'it can also apply where, as in *McGhee*, the other possible source of the injury is a similar, but lawful, act or omission of the same defendant'. But he immediately then 'reserve[d] [his] opinion as to whether the principle applies where the other possible source of injury is a similar but lawful act or omission of someone else or a natural occurrence'. The point I make is that it is hardly to be thought that had the House, on the occasion of the *Fairchild* hearing, been considering not the facts of those three appeals but instead the facts of the present

appeals the claimants would have succeeded and the law have developed as it has.[63]

The key distinction alluded to here by Lord Brown is that, in *Fairchild*, the evidence showed that the injury had been caused by at least one defendant (because non-occupational exposure was deemed to have been negligible); it just was not possible to say which defendant or defendant was responsible. In *Sienkiewicz*, by contrast, it was entirely possible that the injury was not caused by a breach of duty at all, but by background environmental factors which we know (see e.g. *Jobling* above) are not the concern of the tort of negligence.

Lord Rodger gave this problem an updated[64] account:

In the case of a disease like mesothelioma the claimant will be able to prove on the balance of probability that he is suffering from mesothelioma and that he has suffered loss as a result. He may also be able to prove, on the balance of probability, that a defendant or a number of defendants negligently exposed him to asbestos in the course of his employment with them ... What, however, the claimant will be quite unable to prove, on the balance of probability, in the present state of medical knowledge, is that he developed mesothelioma as a result of inhaling any particular fibre or fibres and that, therefore, a particular defendant was responsible for

62   [2011] UKSC 10 at [139].

63   Lord Brown in *Sienkiewicz* at [179].

64   Necessary because, in the decade separating *Fairchild* and *Sienkiewicz*, the 'single-fibre theory' had been effectively discredited. See *Amaca Pty Ltd v Booth* [2011] HCA 53.

exposing him to the fibre or fibres that caused his illness. Moreover, medical experts are no more able to tell whether the fibre or fibres which triggered the claimant's mesothelioma came from the general atmosphere than they can tell whether they came from exposure during the claimant's work with one or other of a number of employers.

In summary, the *Fairchild* exception will only apply on a very narrow set of facts involving:

- indivisible injuries;

- multiple sources of a single causal agent;

- an evidentiary gap.

However, that is not to say that it is restricted to mesothelioma or to any particular disease. As Lord Phillips recognised in *Sienkiewicz,*

> Of course, the *Fairchild* exception was created only because of the present state of medical knowledge. If the day ever dawns when medical science can identify which fibre or fibres led to the malignant mutation and the source from which that fibre or those fibres came, then the problem which gave rise to the exception will have ceased to exist. At that point, by leading the appropriate medical evidence, claimants will be able to prove, on the balance of probability, that a particular defendant or particular defendants were responsible. So the *Fairchild* exception will no longer be needed. But, unless and until that time comes, the rock of uncertainty which prompted the creation of the *Fairchild* exception will remain.[65]

It is difficult to imagine that there will ever be medical knowledge so comprehensive that the *Fairchild* principle will become redundant. There are already signs[66] that it might not be necessary for much longer in cases involving asbestos exposure and mesothelioma but, just as there was an evidentiary gap in relation to dermatitis 40 years ago, there is bound always to be a similar issue with some disease. Evidentiary gaps are unlikely to disappear, and therefore an appropriate analysis and understanding of the *Fairchild* principle is of more than transitory importance.

Judicial concerns about how the *Fairchild* principle would play out across different fact patterns were first discernible in *Barker*, and were obvious by the time that *Sienkiewicz* reached the Supreme Court. There was a sense in both cases that the decision in *Fairchild* had started a process as much as it had stated a principle, and that, outside of the particular facts of the case in which it was conceived, the principle would have very different and not necessarily favourable implications.[67] In *Sienkiewicz*, Lord Phillips went so far as to describe its effect, combined with s 3 of the Compensation Act 2006, as 'draconian' as far as defendants were concerned:[68] it made it possible for a defendant to have to pay the full amount of a claim, despite the injury in question having been caused by one of its co-defendants. *Sienkiewicz*, coupled with s 3, however, makes it possible for a defendant to be held liable in full for a case of mesothelioma that might not even have been caused by a tort at all.

Lord Brown's speech in *Sienkiewicz* most clearly articulates the troublesome implications of extending *Fairchild* beyond the problem it was originally intended to address in *Barker*:

---

65 At [142].

66 See, e.g., *Jones v Secretary of State for Energy & Climate Change* [2012] EWHC 2936 (QB), at 8.21.

67 See, e.g., Lord Hoffmann at [43], Lord Scott at [61], Lord Walker at [117] and Baroness Hale at [128] in *Barker*.

68 Lord Phillips in *Sienkiewicz* at [58].

[O]ne finds the House having to face up to some of the problems it had left open with *Fairchild* and, as it seems to me, beginning to have second thoughts both as to the juristic basis for this special rule of causation which *Fairchild* held to apply in certain toxic tort cases and as to where the abandonment of the 'but for' principle was taking the law … It is to my mind quite clear that the preparedness of the majority of the court in *Barker* to extend the reach of the *Fairchild* principle this far was specifically dependent upon there being aliquot liability only.[69]

Lord Brown went on to say:

[M]esothelioma cases are in a category all their own. Whether, however, this special treatment is justified may be doubted. The unfortunate fact is, however, that the courts are faced with comparable rocks of uncertainty in a wide variety of other situations too and that to circumvent these rocks on a routine basis—let alone if to do so would open the way, as here, to compensation on a full liability basis—would turn our law upside down and dramatically increase the scope for what hitherto have been rejected as purely speculative compensation claims. Although, therefore, mesothelioma claims must now be considered from the defendant's standpoint a lost cause, there is to my mind a lesson to be learned from losing it: the law tampers with the 'but for' test of causation at its peril.[70]

That is not to suggest that the House of Lords, when formulating the *Fairchild* principle, was unaware of the inevitable pressure that would be exerted upon it by the march of the common law.[71] Lord Bingham explicitly recognised this in what is now one of the most well-known passages in the entire judgment:

It would be unrealistic to suppose that the principle here affirmed will not over time be the subject of incremental and analogical development. Cases seeking to develop the principle must be decided when and as they arise.[72]

6.4.4 Single agent

Since *Fairchild* and *Barker*, there has been much academic focus on a supposedly critical distinction between so-called 'single agent' and 'multiple agent' cases, the suggestion being that the former more readily lend themselves to special rules of causation than the latter. For my part I have difficulty even in recognising the distinction between these categories, at any rate in some cases.[73]

Despite this statement by Lord Brown, it is difficult to see how the distinction between single and multiple agent causes is anything other than critical to the application of the *Fairchild* principle.

---

69 At [181]–[182]. The legislative reversal of only one limb of that decision (that liability should be apportioned rather than joint and several) leaves open the question of whether the House would have reached the same conclusion on the other limb (the applicability of the *Fairchild* principle to such a situation), had joint and several liability been the result. See J. Morgan, 'The English – and Scottish – Asbestos Saga' in R. Goldberg (ed.), *Perspectives on Causation* (Hart Publishing, 2011), 79.

70 At [186].

71 J. Morgan, 'The English – and Scottish – Asbestos Saga' in R Goldberg (ed.), *Perspectives on Causation* (Hart Publishing, 2011), 64–5, where he refers to *Fairchild* as 'an essentially legislative attempt to carve out an exceptional category, doomed to failure by the common law's ineluctable method of reasoning by analogy'.

72 At [34].

73 Lord Brown in *Sienkiewicz* at [187].

'Single agent' means that, although we might not know precisely how the damage was caused, we do know that it was caused by one single source, e.g. asbestos or brick dust. 'Multiple agent', on the other hand, is the label given to those situations, explained below, where the court does not even know which of several different sources was the one that caused the injury. The relevance of this distinction was addressed explicitly by Lord Hoffmann in *Barker*: ultimately, despite failing to recognise its importance in *Fairchild*,[74] his Lordship conceded that, for the exceptional principle to apply, 'the mechanism by which it caused the damage, whatever it was, must have been the same',[75] and that he was 'wrong' to think otherwise.[76]

Lord Rodger, by contrast, had already identified the significance of single, as opposed to multiple, risks at the time the *Fairchild* principle was formulated:

> the principle does not apply where the claimant has merely proved that his injury could have been caused by a number of different events, only one of which is the eventuation of the risk created by the defendant's wrongful act or omission. *Wilsher* is an example.[77]

■ VIEWPOINT

Do you think the *Fairchild* exception is defensible? Have *Sienkiewicz* and s 3 of the Compensation Act 2006 made it more or less so?

KEY CASE

Wilsher v Essex Area Health Authority [1988] AC 1074

In this case, the claimant had been born almost three months early. As a result of his premature birth, in his first few days he suffered from a number of conditions which often affect premature babies. In addition to these unfortunate, but naturally arising, conditions, the defendant's hospital also breached its duty of care to the claimant during his treatment in its special care baby unit by negligently inserting a catheter into an umbilical vein instead of an artery and administering too much oxygen. Shortly after his birth, the claimant developed a condition called Retrolental Fibroplasia (RLF),[78] which left him blind in one eye and with severely impaired vision in the other. The specific problem for the causal inquiry was that RLF could have been caused by

any of the naturally arising conditions from which the claimant suffered, or by the excess oxygen to which he was exposed by the defendant's breach of duty. Whilst both the trial judge and the Court of Appeal were satisfied that a sufficient causal link existed between the defendant's breach and the RLF, the House of Lords disagreed.[79]

The reasoning in *Wilsher* makes it very clear why the claimant failed to establish causation. The crucial element is the fact that no specific causal relationship was established between the effect of the defendant's breach of duty and the claimant's injury. It was a case of indeterminate cause. By contrast, in the material contribution to injury line of cases, the cause was determinate (for example,

---

74 At [73].
75 *Barker* at [24].
76 At [23].
77 Lord Rodger in *Fairchild* at [170].
78 Which is a gathering of excess tissue behind the eye, often leading to severe visual impairment or blindness.
79 The House of Lords did not dismiss the case against the defendant, but rather ordered a retrial of the causation issue in front of a different judge. It concluded that the trial judge had misdirected himself on the correct test to apply to the evidence, but that it would be inappropriate, given the complexity of the evidence and the extent of the disagreements between the relevant experts, for an appellate court with access only to a transcript, to come to any final decision on liability based on causation.

in *Bonnington*, the cause of the pneumoconiosis was accepted as being silica dust) and it was only the *proportion* which resulted from the breach of duty that was indeterminate. Similarly, in the material contribution to risk cases, such as *McGhee*, the cause of the claimant's dermatitis was brick dust, and, although more extensive, the indeterminacy related to the source(s) from which it came rather than the cause itself. Therefore, on both material contribution analyses, a specific causal link was established between a particular agent and the claimant's injury, which was lacking on the facts of *Wilsher*. In the House of Lords, Lord Bridge recognised this in stating that he was 'quite unable to find any fault' with the following dissenting judgment of Sir Nicholas Browne-Wilkinson VC in the Court of Appeal:

> To apply the principle in *McGhee v National Coal Board* [1973] 1 W.L.R. 1 to the present case would constitute an extension of that principle. In the *McGhee* case there was no doubt that the pursuer's dermatitis was physically caused by brick dust: the only question was whether the continued presence of such brick dust on the pursuer's skin after the time when he should have been provided with a shower caused or materially contributed to the dermatitis which he contracted. There was only one possible agent which could have caused the dermatitis, viz., brick dust, and there was no doubt that the dermatitis from which he suffered was caused by that brick dust.
>
> In the present case the question is different. There are a number of different agents which could have caused the RLF. Excess oxygen was one of them. The defendants failed to take reasonable precautions to prevent one of the possible causative agents (e.g. excess oxygen) from causing RLF. But no one can tell in this case whether excess oxygen did or did not cause or contribute to the RLF suffered by the plaintiff. The plaintiff's RLF may have been caused by some completely different agent or agents, e.g. hypercarbia, intraventricular haemorrhage, apnoea or patent ductus arteriosus. In addition to oxygen, each of those conditions has been implicated as a possible cause of RLF. This baby suffered from each of those conditions at various times in the first two months of his life. There is no satisfactory evidence that excess oxygen is more likely than any of those other four candidates to have caused RLF in this baby. To my mind, the occurrence of RLF following a failure to take a necessary precaution to prevent excess oxygen causing RLF provides no evidence and raises no presumption that it was excess oxygen rather than one or more of the four other possible agents which caused or contributed to RLF in this case.
>
> The position, to my mind, is wholly different from that in the *McGhee* case where there was only one candidate (brick dust) which could have caused the dermatitis and failure to take a precaution against brick dust causing dermatitis was followed by dermatitis caused by brick dust. In such a case, I can see the common sense, if not the logic, of holding that, in the absence of any other evidence, the failure to take the precaution caused or contributed to the dermatitis. To the extent that certain members of the House of Lords decided the question on inference from evidence or presumptions, I do not consider that the present case falls within their reasoning. A failure to take preventative measures against one out of six possible causes is no evidence as to which of those six caused the injury.[80]

Despite the various challenges which orthodox causal principles have faced during the years since it was decided, appellate courts have adhered to this decision ever since.[81] *Wilsher*, therefore, remains good law. The issue in that case, in which the defendant's breach was one of six different

---

80   [1987] QB 730 at 779.

81   See, for instance, *AB v Ministry of Defence* [2012] 1 AC 78.

potential causes[82] of the claimant's injury, was that the *agent* of cause was indeterminate. This should be contrasted with the mesothelioma cases (such as *Fairchild, Barker, Sienkiewicz*), in which it is accepted that the causal agent is asbestos, and the *source* of the causal agent is indeterminate. In the mesothelioma cases, therefore, we know more. We know that the defendant's behaviour contributed to *the* risk which came to fruition in the form of the claimant's ultimate injury. In *Wilsher*, this was not known; all that was established was that the defendant had created *a* risk which might have resulted in the claimant's injury. For a distinction that can be communicated by such a minor textual alteration, it has major implications. As Stapleton has pointed out, deciding in favour of liability in *Wilsher*-type situations would effectively mean imposing liability for risk creation, regardless of whether or not that risk actually resulted in injury. Not only would this rail against the law of torts' refusal to award damages for pure risk creation,[83] but, in practical terms, it would mean potentially crushing liability for defendants, particularly those likely to create such risks on a regular basis by dint of their nature, such as the NHS.

It is crucial to note that liability under the *Fairchild* principle is not liability for the creation of risk *simpliciter*. Although, in *Barker*, Lord Hoffmann presented the basis of the principle as one which recognises risk creation, it is clear that this was a means by which the imposition of proportionate liability for an indivisible injury could be both carried out and justified, and would only occur *where that risk has eventuated in damage to the claimant*.[84] In *Durham v BAI (Run-off) Ltd* [2012],[85] Lord Mance provided a definitive confirmation of this:

> In reality, it is impossible, or at least inaccurate, to speak of the cause of action recognised in *Fairchild* and *Barker* as being simply 'for the risk created by exposing' someone to asbestos. If it were simply for that risk, then the risk would be the injury; damages would be recoverable for every exposure, without proof by the claimant of any (other) injury at all. That is emphatically not the law … The cause of action exists because the defendant has previously exposed the victim to asbestos, because that exposure *may* have led to the mesothelioma, not because it did, and because mesothelioma has been suffered by the victim … The actual development of mesothelioma is an essential element of the cause of action. In ordinary language, the cause of action is 'for' or 'in respect of' the mesothelioma, and in ordinary language a defendant who exposes a victim of mesothelioma to asbestos is, under the rule in *Fairchild* and *Barker*, held responsible 'for' and 'in respect of' both that exposure and the mesothelioma.[86]

The crucial distinction between *Wilsher*-type cases, *Bonnington*-type cases and *Fairchild*-type cases is summarised in diagrammatic form in Figures 6.4 to 6.7:

'T' represents a tortious source of risk (defendant's breach)
'N' represents a naturally occurring risk (not the result of breach)
'I' represents the claimant's injury
Dashed lines represent the absence of an established causal link (on the balance of probabilities)
Solid lines represent the presence of an established causal link (on the balance of probabilities)

---

82   The other five of which were not breaches of duty.
83   See *Rothwell v Chemical & Insulating Co Ltd* [2007] UKHL 39 and S. Green, 'Risk Exposure and Negligence' (2006) 122 LQR 386 (a note on the Court of Appeal decision, but referred to by the House of Lords at [55]).
84   At [35], [36] and [48]. This is not the same as liability for risk creation *simpliciter*, where, by definition, no harm has yet befallen the claimant, and may well never do so.
85   [2012] UKSC 14. See also [68], [72], [73], [77], [85], [87] and [90].
86   At [65].

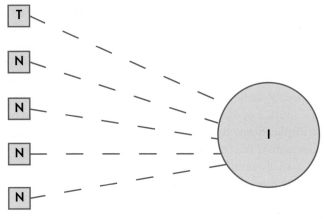

Figure 6.4: *Wilsher*

In Figure 6.4, the defendant's tort was only one of multiple potential agents, all of which *could* have caused the harm, but none of which had been proven on the balance of probabilities to have done so.

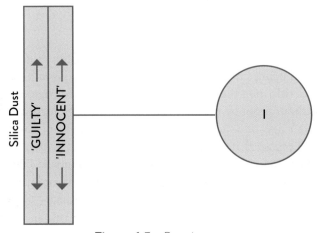

Figure 6.5: *Bonnington*

In Figure 6.5, both tortious and non-tortious factors operated simultaneously on the claimant, such that it was not possible to separate the effects of each and assign them to any particular 'part' of the harm. It was, however, known that both made a material contribution to the eventual result.

In Figures 6.6 and 6.7, the distribution of tortious and naturally occurring risks is intended to be random.

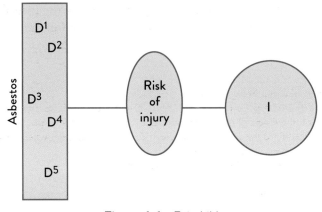

Figure 6.6: *Fairchild*

In Figure 6.6, all of the defendants generated the same risk through exposure to the same single agent (asbestos), but medical knowledge of the disease is not yet able to assign causal relevance (on the balance of probabilities) to any particular exposure.

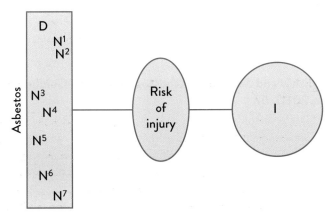

Figure 6.7: *Sienkiewicz*

Figure 6.7 is like 6.6 above, but here the single agent risk is generated not only by defendants, but also by naturally occurring, non-tortious environmental factors.

PROBLEM QUESTION TECHNIQUE

Fred also works for Badbury Estates, and has done so for 38 years. As a heating engineer, he spent much of that time dealing with Toximent, an insulating material used commonly in the industry until it was found to be carcinogenic. It was banned in 1981. Badbury Estates withdrew it from their sites in 1987. Before he worked for Badbury Estates, Fred did similar work for another firm, which also used Toximent. That firm has not existed for 15 years. Fred has recently discovered that he has developed mesothelioma, and has been given nine months to live. Toximent has been linked with the development of this disease, but very little is known about precisely how this happens.

▶ This part of the problem question contains all of the essential ingredients of *Fairchild*: multiple defendants, an apparent evidentiary gap and a single agent.

▶ The key point to grapple with here is that, whilst *Fairchild* should be applied, the question then arises whether liability should be on the joint and several basis directed by s 3 of the Compensation Act 2006 or apportioned according to the decision in *Barker*.

▶ Since these facts involve mesothelioma but not asbestos, it would appear that s 3 would not apply, limited as it is to cases involving mesothelioma and asbestos, leaving liability to be apportioned between potential sources on the basis of *Barker*. This will not be good news for Fred because one of those sources is no longer a going concern, meaning that he will not receive that portion of his damages award.

DIFFERENT PERSPECTIVES on material contribution to risk

L. Hoffmann, 'Fairchild and After' in A. Burrows, D. Johnston and R. Zimmermann (eds), Judge and Jurist: Essays in Memory of Lord Rodger of Earlsferry (OUP, 2013), 64

Writing extra-judicially, here Lord Hoffmann expresses doubt about whether the House of Lords took the right course of action in formulating the *Fairchild* exception to orthodox causal rules. Whilst explaining the decision, both in terms of its Roman Law conceptual basis and in terms of the policy desire not to see defendants escape liability simply on the basis that another defendant had exposed the same claimant to the same risk, Lord Hoffmann nonetheless suggests that it might have been more appropriate for the Court to decline to assist claimants in the way that it did. In doing so, the way would have been left open for Parliament to legislate in order to deal with the very specific problems of mesothelioma and multiple asbestos exposures, creating the sort of statutory exception that would have been far less contentious than that created by the common law.

J. Morgan, 'The English – and Scottish – Asbestos Saga' in R. Goldberg (ed.), Perspectives on Causation (Hart, 2011), 67

Morgan criticises the legal developments in this area, arguing that in *Fairchild* the House of Lords failed to justify what was so unique about the case as to merit a departure from orthodox causal principles. Consequently, he regards the exceptional principle developed therein as arbitrary, and compares it to the unprincipled development of the common law in relation to psychiatric injury, which has been the focus of much academic and judicial criticism.[87] Morgan goes on to suggest that, if policy reasons in favour of such a departure from established rules are so strong, this is the remit of the legislature, rather than the courts: an approach which would also make it easier to contain the exceptions made within acceptable and predictable boundaries.

S. Steel and D. Ibbetson, 'More Grief on Uncertain Causation in Tort' (2011) 70 CLJ 451

Steel and Ibbetson argue that the line of cases culminating in *Sienkiewicz* has left the law in an unprincipled state because certain claimants, such as those who die from a serious illness as a result of a medical misdiagnosis, are still subject to conventional rules of causation, whilst those who develop a skin disease as a result of their employer's negligence have the benefit of the exceptional principle. Steel and Ibbetson also discuss the tension, evident in the progression from *Fairchild* to *Sienkiewicz*, between the need to prove individual causation, and the need for some form of collective justice. The pursuit of individual causation would suggest that the exceptional principle should not be applied because it imposes liability on those who cannot be proven on the balance of probabilities to have caused the claimant's injury. Collective justice, by contrast, requires an application of the exceptional principle, at least on the facts of *Fairchild* itself: without it, claimants who contracted mesothelioma after working for multiple employers will never be able to prove their case on orthodox grounds.

6.4.5 Failure to warn

This is something of a standalone category. Although it is covered by only one House of Lords authority, it is a very well-known and controversial decision. The advantage is that its very particular facts, involving the failure to warn of a risk, are easy to spot in problem questions.

KEY CASE

Chester v Afshar [2004] UKHL 41

In this case, the defendant performed elective surgery to alleviate the claimant's severe back pain. Although he did so without negligence, she suffered significant nerve damage and was consequently left partially paralysed. The defendant breached his duty of care by failing to warn his patient of the 1–2% risk of such paralysis occurring as a result of the operation. The causal problem arose because the claimant did not argue that, had she been warned of the risk, she would never have had the operation, or

---

87 See Chapter 4 (Psychiatric Injury).

even that, duly warned, she would have sought out another surgeon to perform the operation.[88] Her argument was simply that, had she been properly warned of the risks inherent in the procedure, she would not have consented to having the surgery within three days of her appointment, and would have sought further advice on alternatives.

The House of Lords (Lords Bingham and Hoffmann dissenting) held Mr Afshar liable on the basis that, since the ultimate injury suffered by the claimant was due to the very risk of which she should have been warned, it could *be regarded* as having been caused by the failure to warn. This was despite the fact that the defendant's breach had not been established, on the balance of probabilities, to have played any historical role in the claimant's injury because, but for the failure to warn, she would have run exactly the same risk (the 1–2% risk inherent in the procedure itself, however carefully performed) on a different day. In effect, what the House of Lords did was to vindicate the claimant's right of autonomy. Despite the fact that a bare interference with such a right is by no means an established category of actionable damage in negligence,[89] it is difficult to see what else she was being compensated for, since, in negligence, individuals do not have a duty to compensate for damage that they do not cause.

DIFFERENT PERSPECTIVES on failure to warn

S. Green, 'A Game of Doctors and Purses' (2006) 14 Medical Law Review 1

Green criticises the decision in *Chester* as one which sidesteps the requirement for causation on the basis that the defendant's failure to warn made the claimant no worse off than she would have been, had she been warned. The analysis proceeds to show how changing the day on which the operation was performed was the only effect of the defendant's failure to warn, and that this made it no more or less likely that the claimant would succumb to the inherent risks of the operation. This article also argues that the cases of *Gregg v Scott* and *Chester v Afshar* are substantively far more similar than suggested by the way they are often presented. Whilst defending the no-liability outcome in *Gregg*, Green points out that *Chester's* case was even weaker than *Gregg's*, meaning that it was inconsistent of the court to allow the former claim but not the latter: Miss Chester's medical diagnosis and treatment were not negligent, and she was given some choice about how to deal with her condition. Mr Gregg, by contrast, received an incorrect diagnosis, none of the treatment he required and no choice about how to proceed in relation to his condition. Comparing the substance of both cases, rather than the way in which the facts were presented to the court ('failure to warn' vs 'loss of a chance'), shows how their divergent outcomes detract from the coherence of the law in this area.

J. Stapleton, 'Occam's Razor reveals an orthodox basis for Chester v Afshar' (2006) 122 LQR 426

Stapleton argues in favour of the decision in *Chester*, explaining how that result could have been reached more simply by employing a two-step test, asking, first, whether the defendant's breach was a historical factor in the events leading to the claimant's injury and, second, whether a particular consequence should be deemed to be within the scope of the duty breached. The first is a factual inquiry and the second a normative one. Stapleton contends that the finding of liability in *Chester* was no more than an application of orthodox causal analysis because, in her view, the failure to warn was a but for cause of the claimant's injury, meaning that the House of Lords merely had to decide whether or not that injury fell within the

---

88   cf *Chappell v Hart* (1998) 195 CLR 232.

89   Although see *Rees v Darlington Memorial Hospital NHS Trust* [2003] UKHL 52, and D. Nolan, 'New Forms of Damage in Negligence' (2007) 70 *Modern Law Review* 59, 70.

scope of the doctor's duty of care. This analysis is based on the premise that, because the risk of injury was 1–2%, it was more likely than not that, had the claimant had the operation on a different day, that risk would not have materialised (because it is <50% likely that it would have occurred on another day).

PROBLEM QUESTION TECHNIQUE

Alastair has since consulted Kris, an orthopaedic surgeon in the US, who had advised him to undergo an experimental procedure pioneered by Kris himself. If successful, it can reverse the effects of a patient's paralysis almost entirely.

At his consultation, Alastair had said 'There must be a catch – it sounds too perfect.'

Kris had replied 'Well, yes, there is a bit of a downside. There is a risk of ...'

Alastair had interrupted him, 'No, no, don't tell me – just do it.'

There is actually a 5% risk of the operation, howsoever performed, leaving the patient paralysed, but in greater pain than before. This risk decreases as time goes by, so that the longer the period between the injury occurring and the operation, the smaller the chance of its being unsuccessful. Kris, keen to test out his procedure, decides to respect Alastair's wish not to know this, and performs the operation competently. Sadly, the 5% risk materialises and Alastair remains paralysed, and in greater pain than before.

▸ Can you identify a failure to warn here? If breach has been established,[90] there is clearly room for consideration of *Chester v Afshar*.

▸ Always look for any material differences between the facts of the problem question and those of the principal cases to be applied. Here, for instance, a delay does affect the level of inherent risk, so changing the timing of the procedure could well make the patient worse off.

▸ This will not change the outcome since, if liability was imposed on the basis of the facts in *Chester*, it will a fortiori be imposed here, but it is worth making the point that the facts of this problem might, for instance, have served to dispel the reservations of the minority in *Chester* itself.

6.5 CHAPTER SUMMARY

The principal aims of this chapter have been to establish why causation is so important to the negligence inquiry, and to understand the distinctive ways in which the courts have dealt with different factual challenges. The only really effective way to understand causation in negligence, and certainly to be able to answer questions on it, is to have a sound understanding of the case law and how it should be applied. It is a good idea to follow a similar structure to the one presented here: start with the simpler tests and only proceed to the more complicated and exceptional approaches if necessary. A common mistake that students make is to identify a causal issue and attempt *straightaway* to apply a causal test that was not formulated for that scenario. Significantly, this chapter has set out the importance of basic causal principles and the exceptional nature of the *Fairchild* line of cases. It has also sought to demonstrate how conceptually thorny the issue of causation is, and that there are various different ways of analysing the cases and their implications. Causation is known for being one of the most difficult topics on the tort syllabus, but if approached systematically, along the lines suggested by this chapter, and using the roadmap below, most of those difficulties fall away. Some will remain because the case law in this area is not perfectly coherent: such issues can be harnessed as ammunition for writing an incisive critical essay or two.

---

90   For how to do this on these facts, see Chapter 5 (Breach of Duty).

FURTHER READING

S. Green, *Causation in Negligence* (Hart, 2014)

L. Hoffmann, '*Fairchild* and After' in A. Burrows, D. Johnston and R. Zimmermann (eds), *Judge and Jurist: Essays in Memory of Lord Rodger of Earlsferry* (OUP, 2013)

N. Jansen, 'The Idea of a Lost Chance' (1999) *OJLS* 271

J. Lee, 'Inconsiderate Alterations in our Laws: Legislative Reversal of Supreme Court Decisions' in J. Lee (ed.), *From House of Lords to Supreme Court* (Hart, 2010)

R. Merkin and J. Steele, 'Compensating Mesothelioma Victims' (2011) 27 *LQR* 329

J. Morgan, 'Reinterpreting the Reinterpretation of the Reinterpretation of *Fairchild*' [2015] *CLJ* 395

J. Smith, 'Causation: The Search for Principle' [2009] *JPIL* 101

J. Stapleton, 'Cause-in-Fact and Scope of Liability for Consequences' (2003) 119 *LQR* 388

S. Steel, 'Justifying Exceptions to Proof of Causation in Tort Law' (2015) 78 *MLR* 729

Roadmap: Is there a Single Tortious Factor to Consider?

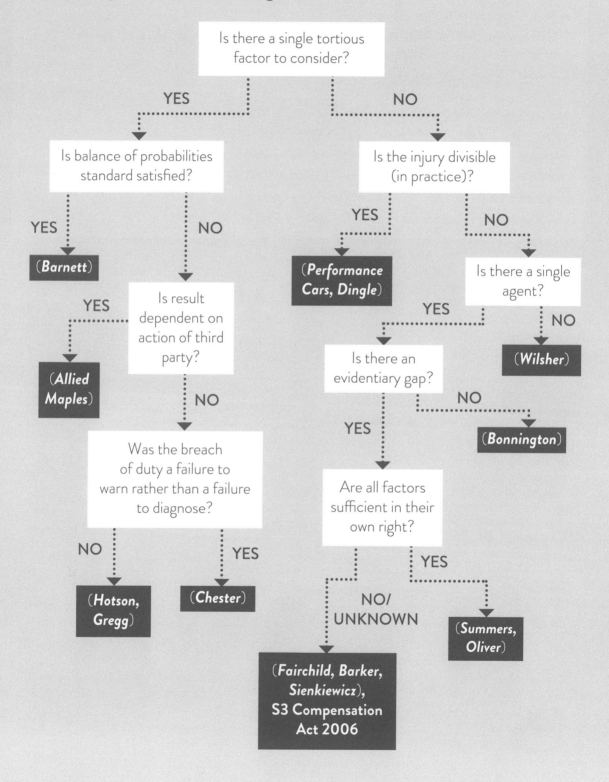

REMOTENESS

LEARNING OBJECTIVES

By the end of this chapter, you should be able to:
· Explain the function of the remoteness inquiry
· Outline the operation of the remoteness inquiry and how it differs between intentional and non-intentional torts
· Contrast the remoteness tests in tort and the remoteness tests in contract, and explain what happens in cases where there is both a tort and a breach of contract
· Summarise how the remoteness inquiry fits with the 'eggshell skull' rule
· Illustrate how the 'scope of duty' analysis functions in relation to the remoteness inquiry

CHAPTER CONTENTS

7.1 Introduction   144
7.2 Basic form   145
7.3 Eggshell skull rule   148
7.4 Scope of duty   149
7.5 *Novus actus interveniens*   155
      7.5.1 Act of a third party   155
      7.5.2 Act of the claimant   156
7.6 Intentional torts   158
7.7 Chapter summary   161
Further reading   161
Roadmap   162

PROBLEM QUESTION

Barbara works as a careers adviser for Arlington School. Carol goes to see Barbara because she wants to be a forensic scientist but is not sure what academic qualifications she will need in order to realise this ambition. On the day before her appointment with Carol, Barbara had been at Wimbledon, watching the tennis. She intended to read up on forensic science careers in the evening on her return, but she had indulged in quite a lot of champagne during the day and ended up falling asleep almost straightaway on her return. Consequently, she did not have time to prepare for the appointment with Carol, and ends up giving her some out of date information, suggesting that she take Fingerprint Analysis[1] as one of her A levels, a subject which has fallen out of favour with those companies offering forensic science apprenticeships. Carol trusts Barbara's advice, takes Fingerprint Analysis and later discovers that, as a result, she cannot get an apprenticeship and cannot, therefore, qualify for her dream job and reach her earning potential as quickly as she otherwise would have done. Also, soon after Carol receives her A Level results, there is a media storm over the Fingerprint Analysis paper because a copy of it was found to have been released on the internet before the exam, allowing many students to cheat. Carol did not cheat, but the value of her qualification is devalued as a result of the scandal, and several employers refuse to acknowledge it. This makes it harder for Carol to get any of the jobs she feels would be appropriate for her level of education. She ends up working as a volunteer in a National Trust Garden and living at home with her dad. It does not look likely that she will ever be able to earn the level of income she could have expected had she qualified as a forensic scientist.

1   This is an entirely fictional A level course and the forensic science community, therefore, has no actual view on it at all.

Duncan also attends Arlington School, but he thinks Barbara is a 'waste of space' and refuses to go to her for careers advice. He does, however, get on well with his Physical Education teacher, Ellie, and so asks her one day which university offers the best degree in Education for those wanting to specialise in PE teaching as a career. Ellie went to Tadchester University, had a fantastic time and found it very easy to get a job afterwards. She tells Duncan this. Her experience, however, was over 20 years ago, and Tadchester's Education Department is now very poor and its students do not have good employment prospects. Duncan does not do any further research, however, and applies on the strength of what Ellie told him. He graduates with a pass degree and fails to get a teaching job. During his degree, Duncan's girlfriend, Fen, lived 200 miles away, working as a zoologist on the Isle of Wight, and he spent most of his time with her rather than attending lectures and seminars at Tadchester. He enjoyed the social life at Tadchester, but just preferred to be with Fen.

Ellie likes Duncan, and she had thought she was being helpful in recommending her former university to him. Ellie does not, however, like Greta, and Greta asks her the same question. Not wanting Greta to succeed, Ellie tells her that she should go to Camberwick University because it has 'an excellent employability profile'. In actual fact, Ellie knows that Camberwick has long been known for neglecting its students, not teaching them well and inflating their grades. Potential employers know this and are very reluctant indeed to employ students from there. Greta goes to Camberwick and, on graduation, realises that she is going to struggle to get the job she has always longed to have. As a result, Greta cannot earn a salary comparable to that she would have earned as a teacher, and consequently develops a depressive illness. One of the symptoms of Greta's illness is that she becomes destructive, and one day she sets fire to her flat. Nobody is injured, but all of her property is destroyed. She then commits suicide.

Harriet is the Domestic Science teacher at Arlington School. Ian is a student in one of her classes. During a session in which the students are learning how to make chicken schnitzel, Harriet is suffering from severe hayfever and is feeling highly irritable. When Ian asks her how to check whether his chicken is cooked, therefore, she snaps at him 'Use your common sense'. Since the chicken looks golden brown on the outside, Ian concludes that it is cooked and eats it on his way home from school. It is not in fact cooked and Ian contracts salmonella as a result. After a week in hospital, Ian's physical recovery is complete, but, as a child who had a longstanding phobia of being sick, he now suffers from an anxiety disorder.

7.1 Introduction

The causal inquiry, as detailed in the previous chapter, tells us whether the defendant's breach had a historical role to play in bringing about the claimant's injury. This is not, however, the end of the inquiry into whether the claim in question is actionable. A further inquiry, sometimes termed 'remoteness' and sometimes termed 'cause in law',[2] also needs to be satisfied before a defendant will be found liable. The principal reason for this is that historical involvement, without more, is a far too inclusive criterion for legal liability. As we saw with the duty inquiry in Chapter 2, the law needs some devices for limiting the reach of the defendant's responsibility in order to avoid excessive liability, particularly for negligence, which is, after all, a non-intentional tort. Unlike those who commit intentional wrongs, under both tort and criminal law, most negligence defendants do not make a conscious choice to cause any harm, or indeed to risk the causing of harm. Whilst, for example, most people could say with reasonable certainty that they will never be a thief or a murderer, they cannot say the same about being

---

2   See J. Stapleton, 'Cause-in-Fact and Scope of Liability for Consequences' (2003) 119 *LQR* 388.

either a negligence defendant or a claimant. There is much to be said, therefore, for the law achieving some balance between compensating the claimant's losses without overburdening defendants. One of the ways in which it achieves this is to say that if the damage caused by the defendant is deemed to be 'too remote' from the breach, liability will not attach to it. There are several ways in which remoteness can operate so as to prevent the imposition of liability, and, as with the duty of care analysis discussed previously, foreseeability plays a significant role.

7.2 Basic form

The basic remoteness test for non-intentional torts comes from the Privy Council decision in *Overseas Tankship v Morts Dock & Engineering Co Ltd (The Wagon Mound No 1)* [1961].[3] It states that a defendant will be held liable for the *type* of damage that was a reasonably foreseeable consequence of his breach, but not for any damage that is of a *type* that was not so reasonably foreseeable. Crucially, note that this test says nothing about the *extent* of the damage which occurs, nor about the *manner* in which it comes about: as we will see below, neither of these elements needs to have been reasonably foreseeable. In order to understand how the courts decide whether damage is or is not of a reasonably foreseeable type, you will need to have a sound knowledge of the case law in the area, starting with *The Wagon Mound (No 1)* itself.[4]

KEY CASE

The Wagon Mound (No 1) [1961] AC 388

The defendant in this case was responsible for the leakage of oil from a ship that was being loaded in Sydney Harbour. The oil formed a film across the surface of the water, which ultimately came into contact with, and damaged, the claimant's wharf. Also in the claimant's wharf, however, was a ship on which welding repair work was being carried out. This work generated some sparks, which eventually combined with some cotton debris floating on the surface of the water and ignited the oil. This caused further damage to the claimant's wharf. Significantly, however, the latter incident caused damage of a different type to the first: the oil leakage caused oil damage, and the burning of the oil caused fire damage. This is the key to understanding the case and the test which derives from it. The trial judge, with whom the Privy

Council agreed, found that, whilst damage by oil was a reasonably foreseeable consequence of the defendant's breach of duty, damage by fire was not reasonably foreseeable. The claimant could only recover, therefore, for the oil damage. In reaching this conclusion, the Privy Council declared that the previous test, derived from *Re Polemis and Furness Withy & Co* [1921],[5] was no longer good law. That test had held that a defendant would be liable for all the consequences which flowed directly from his breach of duty, thereby providing much less of a limit on a defendant's potential liability. The claimant in *The Wagon Mound (No 1)*, for instance, would have been able to recover for its full loss under *Re Polemis*. Note, therefore, that *The Wagon Mound (No 1)* now provides the test for remoteness in non-intentional torts.[6]

3 The same test, for instance, also applies to private nuisance. See Chapter 10 (Nuisance and the Rule in *Rylands v Fletcher*).

4 Also, make sure you distinguish this case from *The Wagon Mound (No 2)*, which dealt with the same sequence of events, but from the point of view of a different claim: in *No 2*, the shipowners were suing the charterers of the ship from which the oil escaped, and they were successful because the damage was on the evidence in that case found to be reasonably foreseeable – see Chapter 5 (Breach of Duty).

5 [1921] 3 KB 560.

6 Although it does not apply to intentional torts – see below at 7.6.

■ VIEWPOINT

Do you think that the common law is correct to distinguish between intentional and non-intentional torts for the purposes of deciding which damage is too remote?

PROBLEM QUESTION TECHNIQUE

Barbara works as a careers adviser for Arlington School. Carol goes to see Barbara because she wants to be a forensic scientist but is not sure what academic qualifications she will need in order to realise this ambition. On the day before her appointment with Carol, Barbara has been at Wimbledon, watching the tennis. She intended to read up on forensic science careers in the evening on her return, but she had indulged in quite a lot of champagne during the day and ended up falling asleep almost straightaway on her return. Consequently, she did not have time to prepare for the appointment with Carol, and ends up giving her some out-of-date information, suggesting that she take Fingerprint Analysis as one of her A levels; a subject which has fallen out of favour with those companies offering forensic science apprenticeships. Carol trusts Barbara's advice, takes Fingerprint Analysis and later discovers that, as a result, she cannot get an apprenticeship and cannot, therefore, qualify for her dream job and reach her earning potential as quickly as she otherwise would have done.

▶ This first part of the problem presents a straightforward question, to which an application of *The Wagon Mound (No 1)* is appropriate. Consider whether pure economic loss is the type of damage which is a reasonably foreseeable consequence of negligently giving career advice.

▶ Note, however, that this is not a complete resolution of Carol's case, since her taking of the Fingerprint Analysis A Level also leads to a general diminution in her career prospects. Whilst this further setback to her interests is not a different type of damage, it needs to be considered further, with an application of the *SAAMCO* principle, below.[7]

It is essential to remember, however, that this test looks forward to the final outcome and asks only whether the ultimate damage is of a type that was reasonably foreseeable. It does not concern itself with whether the events which brought about that damage were in themselves reasonably foreseeable. The authority for this point is *Hughes v Lord Advocate* [1963].[8]

KEY CASE

Hughes v Lord Advocate [1963] AC 837

In this case, the defendant Post Office had left warning paraffin lamps around an unsupervised excavation in the pavement. An 8-year-old boy entered the tent that had been erected around the hole and knocked one of the lamps into the hole. This resulted in an explosion, which caused severe burns to the boy. Although the defendant argued that the damage which the boy suffered was of a different kind to what would have been foreseeable, the House of Lords disagreed: burns are precisely the *type* of damage that is the reasonably foreseeable consequence of leaving paraffin lamps accessible to children. The fact that the way in which those burns came about, and the fact that the injury was ultimately more severe than could reasonably have been foreseen, was irrelevant.[9]

---

7   See 7.4 below.
8   [1963] AC 837.
9   See, along the same lines, *Vacwell Engineering Co Ltd v BDH Chemicals Ltd* [1971] 1 QB 111.

The same point has more recently been considered by the House of Lords in *Jolley v Sutton LBC* [2000].

KEY CASE

Jolley v Sutton LBC [2000] 1 WLR 1082

The claimant, aged 13, and another boy, aged 14, had been playing on a boat abandoned on the defendant's land. The boat, having been propped up with a car jack, fell on the claimant, causing him severe injuries which led to paraplegia. The defendant council had planned to remove the boat but, despite it having been present for nearly two years, had never got around to doing so. The council conceded that it had foreseen that children might suffer minor injuries by standing on the boat which, owing to the rotting of its wood, could well have given way beneath them. Lord Hoffmann in particular noted that this meant that damage which actually occurred was of a reasonably foreseeable type (and pointed out that it would have cost the council the same amount to remove the boat, whatever the potential outcome):

[W]hat must have been foreseen is not the precise injury which occurred but injury of a given description.[10]

Jolley v Sutton consolidates and confirms both *The Wagon Mound (No 1)* and *Hughes v Lord Advocate*.

The next aspect of the remoteness test that is important to understand is the way in which its parameters have been adjusted to some extent, according to what it is the claimant has suffered. In short, the courts have, particularly in recent times, been more willing to treat different manifestations of personal injury as the same *type* of injury for the purposes of remoteness than they have in relation to property damage or to economic loss. This is perhaps unsurprising, given the common law's general propensity to prioritise the protection of physical integrity over proprietary and economic interests. It is important, therefore, to use the most specifically relevant case law when considering how to evaluate 'type' on any given set of facts.

This approach is clearly illustrated by *Corr v IBC Vehicles Ltd* [2008].

KEY CASE

Corr v IBC Vehicles Ltd [2008] UKHL 13

The deceased victim in this case suffered a head injury at work as a result of the defendant's breach of duty. As a consequence, he developed severe depression and, six years after the accident, committed suicide. His widow claimed against the defendant under the Fatal Accidents Act 1976, and one of the questions for the court was whether the deceased's suicide was too remote a consequence of the defendant's breach of duty. Whilst the defendant conceded that the head injury had caused the depressive illness, and that that illness had led to the suicide, a real question of contention was whether the suicide itself was a reasonably foreseeable consequence of the breach. Obviously, the defendant argued that it was not. The House of Lords disagreed, stating that suicide was not an uncommon manifestation of severe depression and that, since severe depression was a foreseeable consequence of causing a head injury, the claimant did not have to establish that suicide itself was reasonably foreseeable. Essentially, the House of Lords treated the depressive illness and the suicide as being the same type of damage, such that the claimant widow was able to recover.

Corr v IBC Vehicles Ltd demonstrates a far more inclusive approach to the interpretation of 'type' than was evident in *The Wagon Mound (No 1)*, in which, as we have seen, the court was willing to distinguish, for the purposes of property damage, between damage by oil and damage by burning oil.

10   Lord Hoffmann at 1091.

7.3 Eggshell skull rule

It is crucial to understand that the *extent* of the damage caused does *not* have to be reasonably foreseeable. This remoteness test does not, therefore, displace the axiomatic 'eggshell' or 'thin skull' rule which says that a tortfeasor takes her victim as she finds him. This rule is best illustrated by *Smith v Leech Brain and Co Ltd* [1962].

KEY CASE

Smith v Leech Brain and Co Ltd [1962] 2 QB 405

As a result of the defendant's breach of duty, the claimant's husband suffered a burn to his lip whilst at work. This burn became cancerous and it turned out that he had had a predisposition to cancer.[11] Although the defendant argued that the cancer was not reasonably foreseeable, the (first instance) court made it clear that *The Wagon Mound (No 1)* did not affect the position that a defendant takes her victim as she finds him. Consequently, as long as the type of damage was reasonably foreseeable, the fact that the victim's pre-existing susceptibility rendered the extent of the damage much greater than it would have been had the victim not had that weakness, is irrelevant.

Whilst it might be argued that a burn is different in type to a cancer, *Smith v Leech Brain and Co Ltd*, along with *Corr*, emphasises the courts' reluctance to distinguish between different types of damage when it comes to personal injury. Once physical injury to a claimant is deemed to be reasonably foreseeable, recall from Chapter 4 (Psychiatric Injury) that the reluctance to distinguish also applies where psychiatric injury is in play.

PROBLEM QUESTION TECHNIQUE

During a session in which the students are learning how to make chicken schnitzel, Harriet is suffering from severe hayfever and is feeling highly irritable. When Ian asks her how to check whether his chicken is cooked, therefore, she snaps at him 'Use your common sense'. Since the chicken looks golden brown on the outside, Ian concludes that it is cooked and eats it on his way home from school. It is not in fact cooked and Ian contracts salmonella as a result. After a week in hospital, Ian's physical recovery is complete, but, as a child who had a longstanding phobia of being sick, he now suffers from an anxiety disorder.

▸ Ian's pre-existing phobia of being sick requires analysis of two different rules. First, would an anxiety disorder, which would be classed as psychiatric injury, be classed as damage of a reasonably foreseeable type? As we saw in Chapter 4, Ian would be classed as a primary victim in this scenario because physical injury to him is a reasonably foreseeable consequence of Harriet's breach. Consequently, an application of *Page v Smith*[12] tells us that his psychiatric injury would be recoverable. The same case also deals with the thin skull point; it is irrelevant that Ian has this particular susceptibility because Harriet has to take her victim as she finds him. *Smith v Leech Brain*, above, could also be applied here to deal with the thin skull issue.

It seemed for a while as if there were a narrow exception to the thin skull rule. In *The Liesboch* [1933],[13] the House of Lords held that losses increased as a result of a claimant's impecuniosity could not be

---

11 The affected tissue had a pre-malignancy.
12 [1996] AC 155.
13 [1933] AC 449.

recovered. In that case, the defendant's negligence damaged the claimant's dredger and put it out of action. The claimant, who did not have the funds to buy a replacement dredger, was forced to hire one at considerable expense in order to avoid a contractual penalty with a third party. Nonetheless, the claimant was not permitted to recover for any part of its loss which occurred only as a result of its impecuniosity: that is, for the extra costs associated with the hire of the replacement ship.

That apparent exception, however, did not survive the House of Lords' decision in *Lagden v O'Connor* [2004].[14] In *Lagden*, the situation was similar, in that the claimant lost the use of her car because of the defendant's negligence and was forced, as a result of having no other financial option, to enter into an expensive credit agreement in order to secure a replacement. The House of Lords decided that *The Liesbosch* was no longer good law, and that the thin skull rule should apply as much to financial vulnerability as it does to any other type of vulnerability.

■ VIEWPOINT

Does the fact that defendants take their victims as they find them lead to fair results? Two defendants could behave in identical ways and yet be liable for vastly different damages, simply by virtue of their moral luck. How can this be justified?

7.4 Scope of duty

Another way in which the defendant's liability might be deemed to be less than the claimant's entire loss is through the application of 'scope of duty' reasoning. This, sometimes referred to as the '*SAAMCO* principle' after the case from which it derives (*South Australia Asset Management Corporation v York Montague Ltd* [1997]), states that a defendant will only be liable for those losses which fall within the scope of his duty. In other words, was it the defendant's duty to protect the claimant from that loss. This is most easily illustrated by *SAAMCO* itself.

KEY CASE

South Australia Asset Management Corporation v York Montague Ltd [1997] AC 191

The defendants were valuers who had negligently overvalued properties on which the claimant lenders had advanced funds. The borrowers of those funds defaulted but, by the time the lenders attempted to sell the properties to realise their assets, the property market had crashed. The lenders, therefore, suffered loss as a result of the properties never having been worth what they advanced on them. They also suffered additional loss because, after the crash, those properties were not even worth what their true market value had been at the time the valuations were performed. They were no longer, therefore, even worth what a correct valuation would have stated. The Court of Appeal allowed the claimants to recover for the full extent of their loss, that is the difference between the negligent valuations and the value of

the properties after the crash. The House of Lords disagreed, and held the defendants liable only for the foreseeable consequences of their valuations being wrong: that is, the lenders were able to recover only the difference between the negligent overvaluation and the true market value of the properties before the crash. The additional fall in value owing to the crash was not held to be within the scope of the defendant's duty, and so not recoverable. The House of Lords made the distinction between a duty to provide information and a duty to advise. In the former case, the defendant will not be responsible for the decision made by the claimant on the basis of the information provided. In the latter case, however, the scope of the defendant's duty in terms of the consequences of the claimant's decision will be wider.

---

14   [2004] 1 AC 1067.

■ VIEWPOINT

In SAAMCO, do you agree with the House of Lords that the consequences of a market fall are not within the scope of a valuer's duty of care?

The Court of Appeal in *SAAMCO* had distinguished between 'no transaction' cases, in which the lender would not have lent anything at all had it been provided with an accurate valuation, and 'successful transaction' cases, in which the lender would still have lent money having been given an accurate valuation, but a lesser sum. Where the lender would have lent nothing at all, the Court of Appeal held that recovery should include the full consequences of the overvaluation, i.e. the full fall including the consequences of the market crash. Where, however, the lender would still have entered into the transaction, but done so by advancing less money, it should be able to recover only the difference between the overvaluation and the true market value before the crash. This is because, on entering the transaction regardless of the negligence, it would still have been affected by the market fall. The House of Lords dismissed this distinction as unhelpful.

■ VIEWPOINT

Which do you think is the better analysis? Is it convincing to say that it is not within the scope of a valuer's duty to provide sufficient information to enable a lender to make a viable judgement about its margin of risk?

The *SAAMCO* principle has recently been scrutinised further by the Supreme Court, in a judgment handed down by Lord Sumption – who was counsel for the appellants in *SAAMCO* itself – in *Hughes-Holland v BPE Solicitors* [2017].

KEY CASE

Hughes-Holland v BPE Solicitors [2017] UKSC 21

The claimant was a trustee in bankruptcy, claiming in relation to losses incurred by G. G had lent £200,000 to a friend, L, believing that those funds were to be used to develop a particular property. In actual fact, L never intended to use those funds for the development of the property, but instead to discharge a bank loan and other debts he had incurred. G's solicitors drew up the loan documentation for him, and negligently included terms which confirmed G's mistaken belief in how the funds were to be used. The development project failed, and G sued his solicitors for the full extent of his loss (which was the full £200,000). At first instance, G succeeded, the judge taking the view that, but for the solicitors' negligence, he would not have lent the money and so not suffered any loss at all. The Court of Appeal reduced his damages to nil on the basis that, even had G's money been used for the purposes which G believed they would be,

the project would still have failed and he would still therefore have lost all of his money. The Supreme Court agreed, and confirmed the *SAAMCO* distinction between a duty to provide information and a duty to advise: where, as here, a defendant had a duty to provide information, it would be liable only for the consequences of that information being wrong. Where, by contrast, a defendant has a duty to advise, it will be liable for the consequences of that course of action being taken. This is so, even where the defendant knows that the information it supplies is critical to the claimant's decision.

At [55] in *Hughes-Holland*, Lord Sumption summarised the effect of the application of *SAAMCO* to the facts of BPE:

On the footing that BPE was not legally responsible for Mr Gabriel's decision to lend the money, but only for confirming his assumption about one of a number of factors in his assessment of the project, the next question is what if any loss was attributable to that assumption being wrong. The answer is that if it had been right, Mr Gabriel would still have lost his money because the expenditure of £200,000 would not have enhanced the value of the property. The development would have been left incomplete, the loan unpaid and the property substantially worthless when it came to be sold into a depressed market under the chargee's power of sale. None of the loss which Mr Gabriel suffered was within the scope of BPE's duty. None of it was loss against which BPE was duty bound to take reasonable care to protect him. It arose from commercial misjudgments which were no concern of theirs.

It is, therefore, essential to distinguish between duties to advise and duties to provide information, and to consider what the function of the defendant's duty is with regards to the claimant's protection. Note here that, in a case we encountered in Chapter 6, *Chester v Afshar*,[15] the majority in the House of Lords referred to the scope of duty analysis set out here to support its decision in favour of liability in that case. For example, Lord Hope said of the doctor's duty in that case:

> The duty was owed to her so that she could make her own decision as to whether or not she should undergo the particular course of surgery which he was proposing to carry out. That was the scope of the duty, the existence of which gave effect to her right to be informed before she consented to it. It was unaffected in its scope by the response which Miss Chester would have given had she been told of these risks.[16]

The problem with applying this analysis to *Chester*, however, is that the scope of duty, as derived from *SAAMCO*, was not supposed to be a substitute for but for causation, but only to be applied once but for causation has been established. It is a limiting device; not an inculpatory tool. See, however, 'Differing Perspectives' on this issue in Chapter 6 (Causation) for views on whether but for causation had been established in that case.

PROBLEM QUESTION TECHNIQUE

Also, soon after Carol receives her A Level results, there is a media storm over the Fingerprint Analysis paper because a copy of it was found to have been released on the internet before the exam, allowing many students to cheat. Carol did not cheat, but the value of her qualification is devalued as a result of the scandal, and several employers refuse to acknowledge it. This makes it harder for Carol to get any of the jobs she feels would be appropriate for her level of education. She ends up working as a volunteer in a National Trust Garden and living at home with her dad. It does not look likely that she will ever be able to earn the level of income she could have expected had she qualified as a forensic scientist.

▸ As with *SAAMCO* and *BPE*, the issue here is not with the type of damage caused because it is all classed as pure economic loss. Rather, the live issue on these facts is whether, notwithstanding that the claimant's ultimate loss is of a type that was a reasonably foreseeable consequence of the defendant's breach, the whole of that loss is within the scope of the defendant's duty of care.

▸ On the facts of this problem question, it is important to refer to the distinction, affirmed by Lord Sumption in *BPE*, between a duty to advise and a duty to provide information. If Barbara's duty is to provide information,

15 [2004] UKHL 41.
16 [2004] UKHL 41 at [55].

she will not be liable for all of the consequences of the course of action taken, but only for the results of that information being wrong, i.e. Carol's inability to get a forensic science apprenticeship. This means that she will not be liable for the poor reputation of the Fingerprint Analysis A level.

▸ If, however, her duty is one to advise, an application of *SAAMCO* and *BPE* suggests that Barbara could be liable for all of the consequences of Carol's taking of that course, which would include the longer term lowered earning capacity. It is not of course certain that a court faced with Carol's case would decide that her full loss falls within the scope of Barbara's duty, but you would need to discuss the similarities between both authorities with the facts of this question, and point out the potential analogy between the market crash in *SAAMCO* and the reputational fall here. Are they analogous? Or do you think that the cheating issue in the problem question could be distinguished from the market fall?

▸ What is the nature of Barbara's duty? She is called a careers adviser, but this label in itself would not be enough to decide the question forensically. Whatever you decide, you need to explain to the examiner why the distinction would be relevant and what the outcome is likely to be for either alternative. A contrast could be made with the following part of the problem question, below.

PROBLEM QUESTION TECHNIQUE

Duncan also attends Arlington School, but he thinks Barbara is a 'waste of space' and refuses to go to her for careers advice. He does, however, get on well with his Physical Education teacher, Ellie, and so asks her one day which university offers the best degree in Education for those wanting to specialise in PE teaching as a career. Ellie went to Tadchester University, had a fantastic time and found it very easy to get a job afterwards. She tells Duncan this. Her experience, however, was over 20 years ago, and Tadchester's Education Department is now very poor and its students do not have good employment prospects. Duncan does not do any further research, however, and applies on the strength of what Ellie told him. He graduates with a pass degree and fails to get a teaching job. During his degree, Duncan's girlfriend, Fen, lived 200 miles away, working as a zoologist on the Isle of Wight, and he spent most of his time with her rather than attending lectures and seminars at Tadchester. He enjoyed the social life at Tadchester, but just preferred to be with Fen.

▸ Here, there would seem to be a much stronger argument for Ellie, in contrast to Barbara, not to have a duty to advise, but only a duty to provide information, since she is not employed by the school specifically to advise its students on careers issues, and it would be constructive for you to make this distinction. (If, indeed, Ellie has any duty at all on these facts: recall that this situation would require an application of *Hedley Byrne & Co v Heller & Partners*.[17])

▸ Were Ellie's duty to be that of providing information as opposed to advice, she would on an application of *BPE* be liable only for the consequences of that information being wrong, and not for all of the consequences of Duncan going to Tadchester University. In any event, the ultimate consequences for Duncan need to be considered in the light of his potential *novus actus interveniens* – see below at 7.5.2 (Act of the claimant).

The case law and the issues here are difficult, rarely suggesting an obvious answer. Try not to be put off by this: a clear explanation of the difficulties, well sustained by a sound knowledge of the authorities, is what you will get credit for – perfect and clear-cut solutions simply do not exist.

17   [1964] AC 465. See Chapter 3 (Pure Economic Loss).

PROBLEM QUESTION TECHNIQUE

Remember:

When answering problem questions, the important thing is always to explain your answer, with reference to the decided case. The conclusion you come to is not as important as the rigour of the analysis you employ in reaching it. As in a maths test, always show your working in a problem question:

▸ Explain why you are applying a certain case.

▸ Explain what the analogies and distinctions are between that case and the facts of the question.

▸ Explain what the implications are for your conclusion.

DIFFERENT PERSPECTIVES on the reasoning in *SAAMCO*

Both of the following perspectives are comments on a particular aspect of the reasoning in *SAAMCO*. Lord Hoffmann justified his restrictions on the claimant's recovery partly on the basis that it would be a paradox for a defendant who had not warranted the truth of his valuation (i.e. someone who owed a duty of care in tort but who had not provided a contractual warranty as to the valuation's accuracy) to be liable to a greater extent than one who had provided such a warranty. In Lord Hoffmann's view, this would happen in the absence of the '*SAAMCO* cap' because the damages available for the breach of a contractual warranty would not exceed the difference between the valuation made by the defendant and the true value of the property at the time of the valuation.

J. Stapleton, 'Negligent Valuers and Falls in the Property Market' (1997) 113 LQR 1

In this comment, Professor Stapleton criticises Lord Hoffmann's analysis, calling this situation a 'false paradox'. There is, she says, nothing problematic about claimants recovering more for the breach of a duty of care in tort than they would for the breach of a contractual warranty: since contract damages aim to put the claimant in the position she would have been in had the contractual duty been properly performed, the risk of that bargain being a bad one falls on the claimant. Since damages for the breach of a duty of care take the claimant in the other direction, that is, back to the position she was in before the breach, the risk of the bargain being a bad one does not fall on the claimant because it will not be enforced, as it would in contract. So, in some factual situations, particularly those in which the claimant has made a bad bargain, tort damages will be more favourable to a claimant than contract damages,[18] but this is just a characteristic of the way the two spheres operate and is not, according to Stapleton, a paradox to be resolved. Another criticism levelled by Stapleton at Lord Hoffmann's analysis is that it can have arbitrary effects. Since the 'cap' is formulated by calculating the difference between the valuation provided by the defendant and the true value of the property at the time of valuation, the size of the gap depends on the extent of the defendant's inaccuracy. From a claimant's point of view, she says, this has an undesirable effect, since two lenders could advance the same funds, suffer the same loss, but have different caps applied to their damages, depending on how far away their valuer's assessment was from the true value of the security.

D.W. McLauchlan, 'Negligent Valuer Liability: The Paradox Remains?' (1997) 113 LQR 421

Here, Professor McLauchlan also takes issue with the paradox identified by Lord Hoffmann, but his objection is a slightly different one. He makes the point in this comment that, if the measure of damages for the breach of a contractual warranty on the facts of *SAAMCO* had been properly calculated, it would have been lower in any event than the capped tort measure actually awarded in that case. This is because, he explains (a point alluded to by Stapleton, above), damages awarded for the breach of a contractual warranty would be limited

---

18   For a more detailed discussion of this point, see Chapter 17 (Damages).

by the quality of the claimant's bargain. If, therefore, there is a fall in the market in which a lender invests, the relevant value to be compared with the negligently given value is not the true value before the fall, but the true value of the property at the time the asset is realised (that is, after the fall). This is because contract damages do not enable a claimant to shift the effect of her bad bargain on to the defendant; it is her risk to bear. McLauchlan's point, therefore, is that, even with the cap as formulated by Lord Hoffmann, the measure of damages for the breach of a valuer's duty to take care is greater than the measure would be for breach of a contractual warranty on the same facts. Should there even be a paradox here therefore (an issue on which he is inclined to agree with Stapleton's doubts), the *SAAMCO* cap has not resolved it.

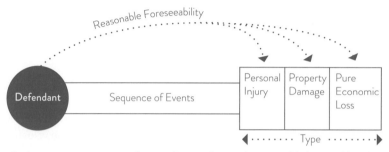

a. Basic test - exact sequence of events does not have to be reasonably foreseeable as long as type of damage is reasonably forseeable

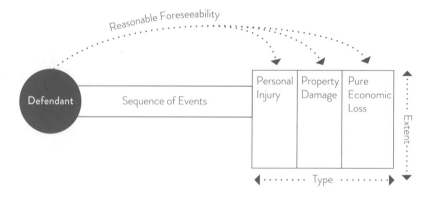

b. Extent of damage irrelevent once type is established to have been reasonably foreseeable

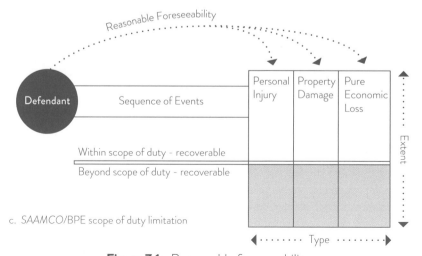

c. *SAAMCO*/BPE scope of duty limitation

Figure 7.1: Reasonable foreseeability

■ VIEWPOINT

Do you think there is a problem with allowing claimants to recover more in tort than they would under a contractual claim on the same facts?

7.5 *Novus actus interveniens*

Sometimes, an intervening factor will operate so as to 'break the chain of causation' between a defendant's breach of duty and a claimant's ultimate injury. In other words, the operative effect of the defendant's breach can be deemed by a court to be superseded by the effect of a subsequent event, meaning that the defendant will not be held liable for the claimant's ultimate damage.

7.5.1 Act of a third party

KEY CASE

Knightley v Johns [1982] 1 WLR 349

The defendant's negligence caused a traffic accident in a road tunnel. The claimant was a police officer who attended the scene and, on the instructions of his senior officer, rode his motorcycle against the flow of traffic coming into the tunnel in order to erect a hazard barrier at the end of the tunnel. In doing so, he was injured in a collision. The question for the court was whether the defendant, who was clearly a but for cause of the claimant's injury, should nonetheless be liable for it. The Court of Appeal held that the intervening act of the senior police officer broke the chain of causation between the defendant's breach and the claimant's injury, so that the defendant was not liable for it. The fact that the senior police officer's actions were unreasonable in the circumstances, and the fact that they were not necessitated by the effect of the defendant's breach, were both referred to by the Court as being relevant considerations. The more negligent the act of the third party, and the more independent the action from the breach of the defendant, the more likely it is that an event will be deemed to intervene and to break the causal link between the claimant and defendant.

KEY CASE

Robinson v Post Office [1974] 1 WLR 1176

The claimant was injured at work as a result of his employer's negligence. Consequently, he sought medical assistance, and was given anti-tetanus serum by a doctor. It transpired that he was allergic to this serum and developed encephalitis as a result. The defendant argued that it should not be liable for the encephalitis because, although its negligence was a but for cause of that occurrence, the doctor's actions functioned as a *novus actus interveniens*, absolving it of liability for it. Whilst the doctor's failure to administer an allergy test was found by the trial judge to have been negligent, the evidence also showed that the claimant would not have shown symptoms in response to such a test in time for it to have altered the doctor's course of action. But for the negligence, therefore, the claimant would still have received the serum and would still have contracted encephalitis. Consequently, the Court of Appeal found that the doctor's negligence was not a *novus actus interveniens* and the defendant remained liable for the claimant's ultimate state.

The potential intervention of a third party is something that we have encountered before in our consideration of duty in Chapter 2. This was one of the questions faced by the House of Lords in *Dorset Yacht v Home Office*,[19] in which the actions of the borstal boys were argued by the Home Office to have operated as an intervening act, sufficient to break the chain of causation between the Home Office employee's negligent failure properly to supervise the boys and the ultimate damage to the claimant's property. Although the actions of the third parties in this case were more than negligent, they were deemed not to be sufficiently independent of the defendant's breach to amount to a *novus actus*. Moreover, the fact that it was one of the purposes of the defendant's duty to stop those third parties from causing harm meant that it was not up to the defendant then to argue that the very actions it was charged with preventing could operate so as to negate its liability. This point was also made by the Supreme Court in *Robinson v Chief Constable of North Yorkshire*[20] in relation to police officers remaining responsible for injuries caused to an innocent pedestrian by their arrest of a suspect in a busy street. The suspect's actions could not break the chain of causation on such facts because their prevention formed part of the police officer's duty.

A similar issue arose in relation to the intervening act of the claimant in *Reeves v Commissioner of Police for Metropolis* [2000].

7.5.2 Act of the claimant

KEY CASE

Reeves v Commissioner of Police for Metropolis [2000] 1 AC 360

L, for whose estate the claimant was claiming, committed suicide whilst in police custody. Although L was a known suicide risk, the police left the hatch on his cell door open, allowing him to hang himself, and so were held to have breached their duty of care. The subject of the appeal, however, was whether the claimant's suicide amounted to a *novus actus interveniens*. The claim failed at first instance on the basis that the defences of *volenti non fit injuria* (consent) and *novus actus interveniens* operated so as to prevent the defendant being liable. The Court of Appeal reversed that decision on the grounds that an action cannot operate as a *novus actus interveniens* where it was the very purpose of the defendant's duty of care to guard against such

an action. The House of Lords (Lord Hobhouse dissenting on the causation point) held that, although persons of sound mind would generally be regarded as being responsible for their own actions, exceptions to this could be recognised in certain situations. The police custody situation provided an example of this potential exception, given the extent of the power exercised by the police over those in their custody, and the stressful nature of being so held. Ultimately, the House held that both the police's breach of duty and the deceased's action were equally causative of the result, and apportioned fault equally, reducing damages by 50% for contributory negligence (for an explanation of which, see Chapter 16 (Defences)).[21]

McKew v Holland & Hannen & Cubitts (Scotland) Ltd [1969] and *Wieland v Cyril Lord Carpets* [1969] are very useful to know and to contrast in order to decide on any given set of facts whether a claimant's action will operate so as to absolve the defendant of liability.

---

19   [1970] AC 1004.
20   [2018] UKSC 4 – see Chapter 2 (Duty of Care).
21   See 16.3.

KEY CASE

McKew v Holland & Hannen & Cubitts (Scotland) Ltd [1969] 3 All ER 1621

The claimant in this case had been injured by his employer's negligence. As a result, his left leg would on occasion give way without warning. Knowing this, the claimant nonetheless attempted to descend, without assistance, a steep staircase which had no handrail. During his descent, his leg collapsed, compelling him to jump down the remaining stairs, severely fracturing his ankle. The House of Lords held that the defendant was not liable for the sprained ankle because the claimant's own act operated as a *novus actus interveniens*. The fact that what the claimant did in these circumstances was unreasonable, and easily avoided, was the significant factor in the decision.

The significance attached to the unreasonableness of the claimant's actions in *McKew v Holland & Hannen & Cubitts* echoes the courts' approach to the unreasonable behaviour of third parties, above. The more unreasonable an action, the more unforeseeable it will be from the defendant's point of view, and the more independent it appears to be from the original breach of duty. This can be contrasted to the facts of *Wieland v Cyril Lord Carpets*.

KEY CASE

Wieland v Cyril Lord Carpets [1969] 3 All ER 1006

As a result of the defendant's negligence, the claimant suffered a neck injury and had to wear a neck brace. Both the neck brace and the stiffness caused by the injury prevented her from using her bifocal spectacles properly, and she consequently fell whilst attempting to descend some stairs. Here, the claimant's own actions were deemed not to amount to a *novus actus interveniens*, and the defendant remained liable for the claimant's ultimate injury, even after the fall. The fact that her actions were not unreasonable, and occurred as an unavoidable result of the injuries caused by the defendant, meant that her fall did not break the chain of causation, but was deemed in effect to be an extension of that original injury.

If the claimant's own actions are deemed by the court to have made some causal contribution to her injury, but not enough to amount to a *novus actus interveniens*, her damages will be reduced proportionately under the Law Reform (Contributory Negligence) Act 1945.[22]

PROBLEM QUESTION TECHNIQUE

During his degree, Duncan's girlfriend, Fen, lived 200 miles away, working as a zoologist on the Isle of Wight, and he spent most of his time with her rather than attending lectures and seminars at Tadchester. He enjoyed the social life at Tadchester, but just preferred to be with Fen.

▶ These facts imply that Duncan's behaviour is not related to his experience of Tadchester specifically, implying that he would have done the same at whichever institution he had attended.

▶ Consider, therefore, whether his intervening neglect of his studies is both unreasonable in itself and independent of Ellie's breach of duty. As such, *McKew* in particular could be used to make the case for Duncan's own behaviour to function as a *novus actus interveniens* sufficient to break the chain of causation between Ellie's breach and Duncan's pure economic loss.

22   See Chapter 16 (Defences).

7.6 Intentional torts

In *Quinn v Leathem* [1901],[23] Lord Lindley said, 'The intention to injure the plaintiff disposes of any question of remoteness.' Thus, the defendant who acts with intention is liable for all the direct consequences of her breach of duty,[24] and the same is true of those defendants who act recklessly.[25] This is defensible on the basis that the potentially limiting effects of the test in *The Wagon Mound (No 1)* are not appropriate where a defendant has acted consciously and deliberately, or recklessly as opposed to inadvertently. It is crucial, therefore, to notice if the facts of a problem question involve any intentional or reckless act.

PROBLEM QUESTION TECHNIQUE

Ellie likes Duncan, and she had thought she was being helpful in recommending her former university to him. Ellie does not, however, like Greta, and Greta asks her the same question. Not wanting Greta to succeed, Ellie tells her that she should go to Camberwick University because it has 'an excellent employability profile'. In actual fact, Ellie knows that Camberwick has long been known for neglecting its students, not teaching them well and inflating their grades. Potential employers know this and are very reluctant indeed to employ students from there. Greta goes to Camberwick and, on graduation, realises that she is going to struggle to get the job she has always longed to have. As a result, Greta cannot earn a salary comparable to that she would have earned as a teacher, and consequently develops a depressive illness. One of the symptoms of Greta's illness is that she becomes destructive, and one day she sets fire to her flat. Nobody is injured, but all of her property is destroyed. She then commits suicide.

▶ These facts contain three different types of damage: pure economic loss, property damage and personal injury.

▶ Were the *The Wagon Mound (No 1)* to be applied here, it would lead to the conclusion that only pure economic loss, as the type of loss that was reasonably foreseeable, is recoverable. Since Ellie acted deliberately here, however, committing the tort of deceit rather than negligence,[26] *The Wagon Mound (No 1)* is not applicable and, on the basis of *Doyle v Olby (Ironmongers) Ltd* [1969][27] and *Smith New Court Securities v Citibank NA* [1997],[28] Greta's estate should be able to recover the full extent of its loss, whether reasonably foreseeable or not.

MAKING CONNECTIONS

The distinction between negligence and intention is important in relation to tortious misstatements, both because of the remoteness issue and because of the very different requirements of the torts of negligence and deceit.[29] It is also, however, a commonly examined issue in contract problem questions concerned with misrepresentation, and it is essential to deal with the remoteness issue properly in both

---

23 [1901] AC 495 at 537.
24 As was the case in negligence before the Privy Council in *The Wagon Mound (No 1)* decided that *Re Polemis* was no longer good law for the purposes of the non-intentional tort. See above, at 7.2.
25 *Scott v Shepherd* (1772) 2 Wm Bl 892.
26 Discussed in detail in Chapter 12 (Intentional Torts Against the Person).
27 [1969] 2 QB 158. See Chapter 12 for more details.
28 [1997] AC 254. See Chapter 12 for more details.
29 See Chapter 3 (Pure Economic Loss) and Chapter 12 (Intentional Torts Against the Person).

contexts. If a party to a contract is induced to enter into that contract as a result of a misrepresentation, this can lead to a claim in either contract or in tort, or both. If the representation is deemed to have been incorporated into the contract as a term, a breach of it will enable the claimant to bring a claim for contractual damages against the defendant, and, as a result of the Misrepresentation Act 1967, such a claimant can also bring a tort claim for misrepresentation. Where the misrepresentation is not incorporated into the contract, the claimant can bring a claim for misrepresentation in tort, and this claim can take several forms. First, a claim for the tort of misrepresentation can be brought under the common law: in negligence, under *Hedley Byrne & Co Ltd v Heller & Partners*,[30] or in deceit under *Derry v Peek*.[31] As has already been established, a defendant under the former will be liable for the reasonably foreseeable types of loss flowing from her breach, whilst a defendant under the latter will be liable for all direct consequences of her breach, foreseeable or not. The fraud measure is, therefore, far more favourable for claimants but does require proof of fraud: that is, proof that the defendant made the misrepresentation knowing it to be false, or being reckless as to whether it was true or false. This is a high threshold.

Significantly, however, the Misrepresentation Act 1967 offers an alternative, and far more attractive, route for claimants who have been induced to enter into a contract by a misrepresentation made to them by the other party to the contract.[32] The wording of s 2(1) of the Misrepresentation Act 1967 is as follows:

> 2   Damages for misrepresentation
> (1)   Where a person has entered into a contract after a misrepresentation has been made to him by another party thereto and as a result thereof he has suffered loss, then, if the person making the misrepresentation would be liable to damages in respect thereof had the misrepresentation been made fraudulently, that person shall be so liable notwithstanding that the misrepresentation was not made fraudulently, unless he proves that he had reasonable ground to believe and did believe up to the time the contract was made the facts represented were true.

This has the effect, therefore, of allowing a claimant under s 2(1) to have the benefit of the intentional tort remoteness test (all direct consequences, whether foreseeable or not) unless the defendant can prove that he had reasonable grounds to believe that his representation was true up until the time the contract was made. This has the dramatic effect of reversing the burden of proving negligence. So, even a defendant who innocently made a misrepresentation could potentially be liable for unforeseeable losses if he cannot prove that he had reasonable grounds for so acting. This is highly favourable to claimants, and has been criticised for the extent to which this is true.[33] This also means that, tasked with advising a claimant in a problem question on this topic, you should always point out the folly of not using the 1967 Act if it applies. Crucially, however, when answering a problem question on this in contract or tort, you should:

- take great care in establishing which claim the victim of a misrepresentation can bring;
- outline clearly which remoteness test applies;
- explain what the implications of this are for the facts of the case at hand.

---

30   [1964] AC 465. See Chapter 3 (Pure Economic Loss).
31   (1889) LR 14 App Cas 337.
32   Where the misrepresentation is made by a third party, the 1967 Act is not applicable, although a common law claim might of course still be available. See the wording of s 2(1) of the 1967 Act: 'Where a person has entered into a contract after a misrepresentation has been made to him by another party thereto …' and *Taberna Europe CDO II Plc v Selskabet (Fomerly Roskild Bank A/S) (In Bankruptcy)* [2016] EWCA Civ 1262.
33   R. Hooley, 'Damages and the Misrepresentation Act 1967' (1991) 107 LQR 547.

PROBLEM QUESTION TECHNIQUE

Consider once again the situation of Ellie and Greta, but this time with the Misrepresentation Act 1967 in mind:

Ellie likes Duncan, and she had thought she was being helpful in recommending her former university to him. Ellie does not, however, like Greta, and Greta asks her the same question. Not wanting Greta to succeed, Ellie tells her that she should go to Camberwick University because it has 'an excellent employability profile'. In actual fact, Ellie knows that Camberwick has long been known for neglecting its students, not teaching them well and inflating their grades. Potential employers know this and are very reluctant indeed to employ students from there. Greta goes to Camberwick and, on graduation, realises that she is going to struggle to get the job she has always longed to have. As a result, Greta cannot earn a salary comparable to that she would have earned as a teacher, and consequently develops a depressive illness. One of the symptoms of Greta's illness is that she becomes destructive, and one day she sets fire to her flat. Nobody is injured, but all of her property is destroyed. She then commits suicide.

▶ We have already seen how, analysing this through the tort of deceit at common law, Greta's estate is entitled to all losses flowing directly from the breach. It should now be clear, however, that, wherever a misrepresentation has been made, it makes sense to consider first whether the Misrepresentation Act 1967 applies because this gives claimants the benefit of a non-restrictive remoteness test without their having to prove fraud.

▶ On these facts, the 1967 Act would not apply because the only contract is the one made between Greta and Camberwick, whereas the misrepresentation was made by Ellie, who is a third party. Greta's estate, therefore, is restricted to its common law claim.

▶ If, on the other hand, the representation about Camberwick's 'excellent employability profile' had come from Camberwick itself, and had induced Greta's entry into her contract with them, Greta would be far better advised to bring a claim under s 2(1) of the 1967 Act.

MAKING CONNECTIONS

Another potential remoteness issue, which exists at the intersection between contract and tort, is that of which test to apply in situations of concurrent liability. Where the claimant is suing the defendant in both contract and tort, the question arises whether the court should apply the tort test of remoteness, or the contract test of remoteness, which is markedly different. Recoverable damages in a contract claim are those

> as may fairly and reasonably be considered either arising naturally, i.e., according to the usual course of things, from such breach of contract itself, or such as may reasonably be supposed to have been in the contemplation of both parties, at the time they made the contract, as the probable result of the breach of it.[34]

This is narrower than *The Wagon Mound (No 1)* test and a fortiori narrower than the *Doyle v Olby* test. In contract, therefore, even losses of a reasonably foreseeable type will not be recoverable by a claimant unless they could reasonably be regarded by the parties as likely to result from the breach. Until the

---

34 Alderson B in *Hadley v Baxendale* (1854) 9 Exch 341, 354. This is the basic rule, which now needs to be read, particularly in unusual circumstances, in the light of *The Achilleas* [2008] UKHL 48.

Court of Appeal decided *Wellesley Partners LLP v Withers LLP* [2015],[35] there was some doubt and some confusion over whether the remoteness test to be applied in such cases should depend upon whether the claim was brought in contract or in tort, or whether it should depend instead on whether the damage suffered was loss of profit or physical damage.[36] *Wellesley*, however, clarified the point: where the tortious duty of care arises alongside a contractual duty, the stricter contractual test of remoteness will apply because parties in a contractual relationship have had the opportunity to bring particular risks to each other's attention in a way that strangers brought together by many tort actions cannot. If, therefore, the parties to a tort claim are also in a contractual relationship which covers the same actions of the defendant, remember to point out that the contractual remoteness test will apply. If, for instance, Arlington School in this chapter's problem question were a private school, all of the duties owed in tort by its employees would also be covered by the contract between the school and the various claimants. The *Hadley v Baxendale* test of remoteness would therefore apply to those. Whilst the contractual test is potentially narrower in its effect, however, this does not mean that a claimant will always recover less under the contractual test than under the tortious test: on the facts of this problem question, for example, some of the losses would meet the *Hadley v Baxendale* requirements in any event. The reputational issue with the A level course, the fire and the suicide would, however, require an application of the more complicated contractual remoteness test in *The Achilleas*,[37] which essentially asks whether the parties to the contract assumed responsibility for the loss in question. Read the details of this last case in a specialist contract textbook.

7.7 CHAPTER SUMMARY

This chapter has set out the rules limiting liability for those who have breached their duty of care and thereby caused actionable damage in a *factual* sense. It has explained how, under certain conditions, such breaches of duty will not necessarily incur liability in negligence where that actionable damage is deemed to be too remote from the breach in question. Sometimes referred to as 'cause in law', this set of rules recognises the difference between intentional and non-intentional torts by imposing a stricter test on the former (which carry with them greater moral censure). The test you will encounter the most during your studies is likely to be the test for negligence: reasonable foreseeability of the *type of loss* ultimately suffered by the claimant. This chapter has also explained how this test fits with the thin skull principle; the idea that you take your victim as you find him. Crucially, this means that the extent of the loss ultimately caused to the claimant does *not* have to be reasonably foreseeable in order to be recoverable in a negligence action.

FURTHER READING

R. Dias, 'Remoteness of Liability and Legal Policy' [1962] *CLJ* 178

D. Howarth, 'Complexity Strikes Back – Valuation in the House of Lords' (2000) 8 *Tort L Rev* 85

J. Stapleton, 'Cause-in-Fact and Scope of Liability for Consequences' (2003) 119 *LQR* 388

M. Stauch, 'Risk and Remoteness of Damage in Negligence' (2001) 64 *MLR* 191

---

35 [2015] EWCA Civ 1146.
36 See, e.g., *Heron II* [1969] 1 AC 350 and *Parsons v Uttley Ingham & Co Ltd* [1978] QB 791 (specifically the judgment of Lord Denning).
37 [2008] UKHL 48.

162

Roadmap: Is the tort in question a misrepresentation? *

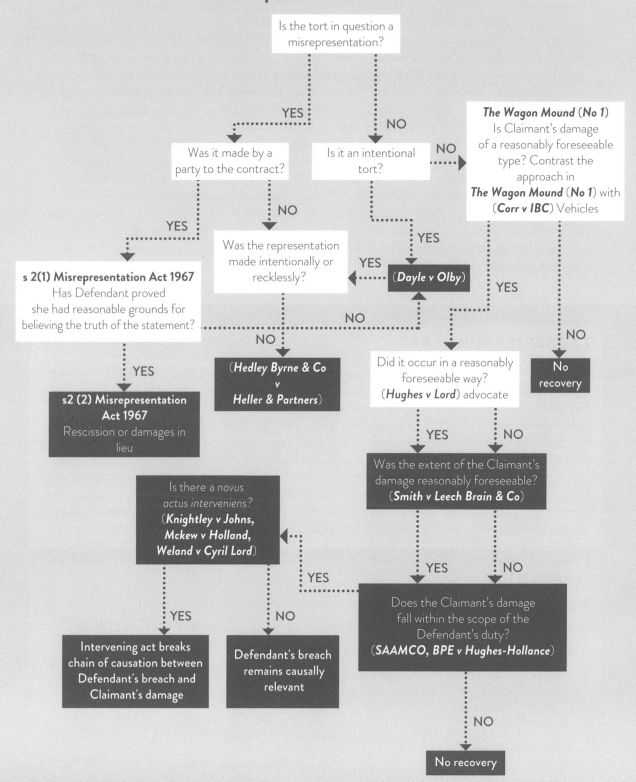

* diagram does not deal with contractual exclusions

TORTS RELATING TO LAND AND GOODS

8.	Occupiers' Liability	164
9.	Product Liability	193
10.	Nuisance and the Rule in *Rylands v Fletcher*	217

Although two of the torts covered in this Part relate to land, they are in fact very different in form. The first, Occupiers' Liability, is a specialised species of negligence, put on a statutory footing. It protects, however, the same principal interests protected by common law negligence: interests in both bodily and (in most cases) property integrity. Unusually for negligence liability, the duty of care of an occupier often requires some positive action to be taken in order to discharge it appropriately. Nuisance and the rule in *Rylands v Fletcher*, on the other hand, protect a completely different interest; they protect claimants' interests in their land. Significantly, those torts protect *only* those interests so, for instance, personal injury is not recoverable in either private nuisance or under the rule in *Rylands v Fletcher*. So, the two torts in this Part are very different in both form and objective, and you should take care to ensure that you understand the conceptual and practical differences between them. In very simple terms, occupiers' liability is concerned with damage caused *by* land,[1] and nuisance is concerned with damage caused *to* the land (and interests in it).

The other tort covered here is similar in some ways to occupiers' liability because it covers damage caused by property, but here it is personal, rather than real, property which is the focus. Product liability is in part covered by the common law of negligence, but is also subject to an (almost) strict liability statutory scheme, as well as having some basis in the law of contract. The addition of a statutory scheme to the common law remedies resulted from a European directive, and is based on the idea that the risk of loss caused by products should be borne mainly by those who produce and supply those products for commercial gain.

---

1   Although, technically, occupiers' liability applies to 'premises', which also includes fixed or moveable structures on the land.

8 OCCUPIERS' LIABILITY

LEARNING OBJECTIVES

By the end of this chapter, you should be able to:

- Outline the statutory scheme for occupiers' liability
- Know when to apply the statutory scheme
- Explain the distinction between the common law and the statutory scheme
- Set out the difference between the Occupiers' Liability Act 1957 and the Occupiers' Liability Act 1984
- Understand how the case law assists in interpreting the provisions of the statutory scheme
- Navigate the case law and the statutory scheme in order to apply both to a given set of facts

CHAPTER CONTENTS

8.1 Introduction	165
8.2 Who is an occupier?	165
8.3 The Occupiers' Liability Act 1957 – liability to 'visitors'	167
8.3.1 Who is a visitor?	167
8.3.2 What are premises?	169
8.3.3 What is the content of the occupier's duty?	170
8.3.4 How can that duty be discharged?	176
8.4 The Occupiers' Liability Act 1984 – liability to those not classed as 'visitors'	183
8.4.1 Who is classed as a non-visitor?	186
8.4.2 In what circumstances will non-visitors be owed a duty?	187
8.4.3 What is the content of that duty?	188
8.4.4 How can that duty be discharged?	189
8.5 Chapter summary	191
Further reading	191
Roadmap	192

PROBLEM QUESTION

Alice's boyfriend, who works overseas, lets her use his flat for her holistic health business, 'Artful Alice'. For these purposes, customers use the living room as a waiting room, and then are called through to the spare bedroom for treatment. There are signs on all the other internal doors of the flat, stating 'Strictly no admittance to customers of Artful Alice'.

The kitchen of the flat is being refurbished and is non-functional. Customers always used to use it on an informal basis to get drinks of water, and since the refurbishment, have taken to using the bathroom instead, where there are several drinking glasses stacked on the washstand. During the refurbishment,

Alice has added another sign to the kitchen door, which reads 'This kitchen is currently unsafe. Artful Alice excludes all liability for any loss, injury or damage resulting from the use of this kitchen by her customers, howsoever caused.'

Bryan, who has treatment from Alice to alleviate the effect of his glaucoma, is sitting in the waiting room one hot afternoon. He decides to get a drink and, not noticing the additional sign on the kitchen door despite its prominent position, enters the room and trips on a loose floorboard. His left leg and arm are seriously injured, and his Rolex watch is smashed.

His screams alert Alice, who is in the middle of treating her 5-year-old nephew, Carl. Alice runs to the kitchen. There, she finds Bryan lying on the floor and Diana, her kitchen fitter's assistant, unconscious. Diana had, ten minutes earlier, been knocked out by a cupboard unit falling on her. She had been asked to fit it by her boss, Eddie, even though he had not trained her how to do it safely. Eddie has rarely been on site since he took on the job. Alice interviewed several contractors and questioned them all extensively before deciding on Eddie because of his excellent credentials and apparently complete paperwork, so she is surprised by the fact that he is often absent, leaving the inexperienced Diana to do most of the work.

Whilst Alice is dealing with Bryan and Diana, Carl, left on his own (since his mum has gone out for the day), goes into the bathroom and drinks a bottle of Alice's essential oils and is violently ill. He needs to be hospitalised for a week, and will have stomach and bowel problems for years.

8.1 Introduction

Occupiers' liability is a statutory form of negligence which imposes positive duties on those who are subject to it. The area is governed by two statutes: the Occupiers' Liability Act (the OLA 1957) and the Occupiers' Liability Act (the OLA 1984). Occupiers' liability arises where a claimant has been injured by the state of an occupier's premises. When, therefore, you identify these facts, you must ensure that you apply whichever of the OLAs is appropriate. The liability of an occupier is based on her control of premises, and her corresponding ability to influence the effect the state of those premises will have on individuals who are on them. It is notable, however, that her duty is to keep such individuals reasonably safe. There is no duty to keep the premises themselves safe: arguably this would be both impossible and undesirable because it is hard, for example, to imagine how one could make a park, a beach or a ski resort 'safe'. 'Premises' is also a category far broader than simply land, since it extends to any 'fixed or moveable structure'. Occupiers' liability is a good topic to learn, both for your degree and for your own purposes; as you will see, everyone who controls any premises will potentially be liable for any injury caused by them. If, for instance, you lend your ladder to a friend, and it is defective in some way, you could be liable for any injury it causes. As far as hypothetical situations go, occupiers' liability can be a relatively straightforward way to get some good marks: it is self-contained and there is little conceptual complexity, which means that a systematic application of the relevant statutes and case law is both possible and highly effective.

8.2 Who is an occupier?

When answering problem questions on this topic, it is essential to distinguish correctly between the 1957 Act (or OLA 1957 as referred to later) and the 1984 Act (or OLA 1984 as referred to later) because each applies to a different type of claimant; the OLA 1957 applies to visitors and the OLA 1984 applies to non-visitors. The identification of the defendant, however, which requires a determination of who the occupier is, is the same for the purposes of both statutes.

KEY LEGISLATION

Occupiers' Liability Act 1957

1   Preliminary

(2)   The rules so enacted shall regulate the nature of the duty imposed by law in consequence of a person's occupation or control of premises and of any invitation or permission he gives (or is to be treated as giving) to another to enter or use the premises, but they shall not alter the rules of the common law as to the persons on whom a duty is so imposed or to whom it is owed; and accordingly for the purpose of the rules so enacted the persons who are to be treated as an occupier and as his visitors are the same (subject to subsection (4) of this section) as the persons who would at common law be treated as an occupier and as his invitees or licensees.

Occupiers' Liability Act 1984

1   Duty of occupier to persons other than his visitors

(2)   For the purposes of this section, the persons who are to be treated respectively as an occupier of any premises (which, for those purposes, include any fixed or movable structure) and as his visitors are—

(a)   any person who owes in relation to the premises the duty referred to in section 2 of the Occupiers' Liability Act 1957 (the common duty of care)...

KEY CASE

Wheat v Lacon [1966] AC 552

The defendant brewers were owners of a pub. The running of the business was entrusted to a manager, who was employed under a service agreement. The manager and his wife lived on the first floor of the pub. Whilst the claimant and her husband were staying on the first floor as paying guests of the manager's wife, the claimant's husband suffered a fatal fall on his way downstairs, caused by a handrail that was too short, and insufficient lighting on the stairs. The question for the court was whether the defendant brewers were liable as occupiers. The House of Lords found that the defendant brewers were indeed occupiers of the first floor, and owed therefore the common duty of care under the 1957 Act (although they were found not to have breached that duty on these facts). Significantly, the defendant brewers and their manager could both be occupiers of the premises simultaneously.

The title of this Act affords a convenient name-tag for the kind of relationship which does give rise to a duty of care – but it is a name-tag which may be deceptive if it leads one to suppose that the criterion of liability is 'occupation' in the sense in which that concept is relevant to the law of property or of landlord and tenant or of fiscal, franchise or rating law.[1]

[W]herever a person has sufficient degree of control over premises that he ought to realise that any failure on his part to use care may result in injury to a person coming lawfully there, then he is an 'occupier' and the person coming lawfully there is his 'visitor' and the 'occupier' is under a duty to his 'visitor' to use reasonable care. In order to be an 'occupier' it is not necessary for a person to have entire control over the premises. He need not have exclusive occupation. Suffice it that he has some degree of control. He may share the control with others. Two or more may be 'occupiers' and whenever this happens, each is under a duty to use care towards persons coming lawfully on to the premises, dependent on his degree of control.[2]

---

1   Lord Diplock at 561.
2   Lord Denning at 578.

As *Wheat v Lacon* shows, the definition of 'occupier' for this purpose is specific, and distinct from the non-legal connotations of occupation because a physical presence is not required, and nor, therefore, is any sort of residence. In fact, residence in itself might not even be sufficient if, for instance, one individual lives on certain premises, but another controls the maintenance and upkeep of those premises. It would be the latter in such circumstances, and not the former, who would be deemed to be the occupier for these purposes. It is a question of degree, however, and, as *Wheat v Lacon* demonstrates, both parties might exercise sufficient control to amount to an occupier. Where this is the case, claimants can choose whom to sue, and they will usually pursue the defendant better able to satisfy judgment; that is, the defendant with the most resources or the best valid insurance policy.

PROBLEM QUESTION TECHNIQUE

Alice's boyfriend, who works overseas, lets her use his flat for her holistic health business, 'Artful Alice'.

▸ Here, you need to analyse, using the relevant case law, whether Alice exercises the requisite degree of control over the flat to be deemed its occupier. Remember, she does not have to be the owner of the flat in order to be deemed the legal occupier for these purposes.

8.3 The Occupiers' Liability Act 1957 – liability to 'visitors'

8.3.1 Who is a 'visitor'?

This wording in s 1(2) of the OLA 1957 – 'persons who would at common law be treated as … his invitees or licensees' (see 'Key Legislation' above) – is not particularly helpful in its own right, and requires an accompanying knowledge of common law interpretations of the term. Basically, a visitor to whom the 1957 Act will apply is someone who has express or implied permission to be on the premises. *McGeown v Northern Ireland Housing Executive* [1995] and *Phipps v Rochester* [1955], however, provide a more nuanced account of what the term 'visitor' means for these purposes.

KEY CASE

McGeown v Northern Ireland Housing Executive [1995] 1 AC 233

The claimant lived with her husband, who was a tenant of the defendant housing authority. There were paths across the housing estate, over which the public had acquired a right of way. The claimant was injured whilst using one of the paths, owing to the fact that its surface had been allowed to lapse into disrepair. The claimant sued the defendant housing authority under the OLA (Northern Ireland) 1957. The House of Lords held that the user of a public right of way was not a visitor for the purposes of the OLA (Northern Ireland) 1957 or the OLA 1957 of England and Wales, since her use was one of right.

A DIFFERENT PERSPECTIVE on visitors

F. Barker and N. Parry, 'Private Property, Public Access and Occupiers' Liability' (1995) 15 Legal Studies 335

These authors make the argument that the exclusion in *McGeown v Northern Ireland Housing Executive* is unjustified, particularly given that non-visitors have the benefit of statutory protection under the OLA 1984 (see below). This article proposes a broadening of the existing statutory regime so as to include users of public rights of way, premised on a generally increased emphasis on inclusive public property rights, as opposed to exclusive, private property rights. In practical terms, the authors suggest that a new comprehensive legislative model, based on the OLA (Scotland) 1960, would be the most effective way of achieving this.

KEY CASE

Phipps v Rochester Corporation [1955] 1 QB 450

A 5-year-old boy, accompanied by his 7-year-old sister, was blackberry-picking on an area of grassland that was at the relevant time a building site being developed by the defendant. The boy fell into a deep trench that had been dug to accommodate a sewer, and was injured. Since children had been known to play on the land, and the defendant had done nothing to prevent this, Devlin J, as he then was, held that children as a class had implied permission to be on the site (although, as we will see when we return to this case below, the defendant was held not to have been in breach of its duty on the facts).

Express permission will usually be easy to spot, but this case is important because it illustrates how the category of visitor also includes those who have implied permission to be on the premises, even if the defendant did not want them to be there. In order to exclude potential claimants from the protection afforded to visitors by the OLA 1957, occupiers need to make the limits of their permission very clear. This means that, if occupiers know of their premises being used other than in accordance with their wishes, they must take steps to stop this: the absence of an express invitation is not sufficient.

KEY CASE

Tomlinson v Congleton BC [2003] UKHL 47

The defendant council was the occupier of a country park. Within the park was a lake in which members of the public were known to swim, despite oral warnings from rangers employed by the defendant, and signs making it clear that swimming was prohibited. The claimant was severely injured when, ignoring the warnings, he dived into the lake and damaged his neck. His claim against the defendant occupier failed in the House of Lords.

Tomlinson v Congleton BC is a very important case, and we will encounter it again, below, when we look at the OLA 1984. For present purposes, it is significant for its clear statement of the principle that a claimant can be a visitor on part of the premises, or for a particular time period, or whilst behaving in a certain way, but become a non-visitor (and so come to be covered by the OLA 1984) once his permission has been exceeded. In *Tomlinson*, for example, the claimant was a visitor whilst on the 'beach' because he was entitled to be there, but he became a non-visitor once he went beyond the limits of the council's permission to those who used the park.

> When you invite a person into your house to use the staircase, you do not invite him to slide down the bannisters.[3]

---

3   Scrutton LJ in *The Calgarth* [1927] P 93.

PROBLEM QUESTION TECHNIQUE

There are signs on all the other internal doors of the flat, stating 'Strictly no admittance to customers of Artful Alice'. Bryan ... decides to get a drink and, not noticing the additional sign on the kitchen door despite its prominent position, enters the room and trips on a loose floorboard.

Alice runs to the kitchen. There, she finds ... Diana, her kitchen fitter's assistant, unconscious.

Whilst Alice is dealing with Bryan and Diana, Carl, left on his own (since his mum has gone out for the day), goes into the bathroom and drinks a bottle of Alice's essential oils and is violently ill.

▸ For all of these potential claimants, you need to consider whether they would have the status of occupiers (and so be owed duties under the OLA 1957) or whether they are non-visitors (in which case their cases would need to be considered under the OLA 1984).

▸ The essential distinction is whether they have the permission of the occupier to be where they are. Such permission can be express or implied.

▸ You must obviously deal with each one separately, since each needs to be considered on its own particular facts: Diana and Bryan, for instance, need to be distinguished in terms of the permission each has in relation to different rooms in the flat.

■ VIEWPOINT

What do you think about visitors to a park being deemed to be non-visitors once they exceed their permission to be there? Do you think the balance of responsibility is properly achieved by *Tomlinson*?

8.3.2 What are 'premises'?

In *Wheeler v Copas* [1981],[4] Chapman J held that a ladder could be premises for the purposes of the OLA 1957. More commonly (and we will see examples of these in the cases below), the 'fixed or moveable structures' concerned are recreational structures such as bouncy castles, bungee runs and similar fairground attractions. Other examples include abandoned boats, fire escapes and scaffolding.

KEY LEGISLATION

Occupiers' Liability Act 1957

1   Preliminary

(3) The rules so enacted in relation to an occupier of premises and his visitors shall also apply, in like manner and to the like extent as the principles applicable at common law to an occupier of premises and his invitees or licensees would apply, to regulate—

(a) the obligations of a person occupying or having control over any fixed or moveable structure, including any vessel, vehicle or aircraft; and

(b) the obligations of a person occupying or having control over any premises or structure in respect of damage to property, including the property of persons who are not themselves his visitors.

---

4   [1981] 3 All ER 405.

8.3.3 What is the content of the occupier's duty?

This is really the essence of this field of liability: what does an occupier have to do in order to discharge her duty? As mentioned above, occupiers' liability imposes positive duties and so is an area in which omissions will be actionable if they have the effect of amounting to a breach of the duty contained in s 2(1), set out below. Note, however, that the duty of an occupier is limited to damage caused *by the state of the premises*. An occupier is not liable, therefore, for all damage which arises or occurs on her premises. Notably, and this will become even more apparent below when we look at potential liability under the OLA 1984, occupiers will not be liable where the damage has been caused by what is being done on the premises (that is, caused by the behaviour of the claimant or of others), rather than by the premises themselves.

KEY LEGISLATION

Occupiers' Liability Act 1957

1 Preliminary

(4) The rules enacted by the two next following sections shall have effect, in place of the rules of the common law, to regulate the duty which an occupier of premises owes to his visitors in respect of dangers due to the state of the premises or to things done or omitted to be done on them.

The facts of *Fairchild v Glenhaven Funeral Services Ltd*[5] are set out in detail in Chapter 6 (Causation). Recall that this was a case in which claimants had contracted mesothelioma as a result of being exposed to asbestos at work. As far as the Court of Appeal, the claim was against both their employers (whom the House of Lords ultimately held liable) and the occupiers of the premises on which they worked. The relevant point for current purposes is that the Court of Appeal found that the occupiers were not liable for the claimants' exposure to asbestos because this was not a result of the state of the premises but rather a result of the employers' work practices. Here, we encounter a recurrent point in judicial responses to occupiers' liability claims: where an occupier has engaged a reputable contractor, he discharges his duty by so doing, and does not have to go further by supervising or intervening in work practices.[6]

As we saw in Chapter 6, *Fairchild* ultimately went to the House of Lords, but the occupiers' liability point went no further than the Court of Appeal, so this is the decision you must cite for this particular point.

KEY CASE

Ferguson v Welsh [1987] 3 All ER 777

A district council contracted with a company, S, to carry out demolition work on its premises, and prohibited subcontracting without permission. S, however, did subcontract to two brothers, W, whose work practices were unsafe. F, the claimant, was working for the W brothers when he was seriously injured. The question for the House of Lords was whether the council was liable as an occupier (since neither S nor W was effectively insured). The House of Lords held that, although the council was an occupier, it had not breached its duty under the OLA 1957 in this case because it was not, in the absence of special circumstances, responsible for the work practices which were implemented by a third party on its premises.

---

5 [2001] EWCA Civ 1881.
6 Fore more detail, see 8.3.4.3 (Engaging contractors).

Ferguson v Welsh is another case which makes the point that there can be more than one occupier of a set of premises. Remember, though, that, as with common law negligence, it is not sufficient for liability to establish that the defendant owes the claimant a duty of care (which is what you do by establishing that the defendant is an occupier vis-à-vis someone on his premises). There is another crucial question which needs to be answered, which is whether this duty has been breached. Despite seeming like an obvious point to make here, this is something which is so often overlooked by students, particularly in exams under time constraints; there is a tendency to assume that, once a duty is owed, the defendant will be liable if a claimant suffers damage. This does not, however, make sense: countless duties of care exist in the world, and only a very small proportion of these are ever breached. This is particularly acute in occupiers' liability, where it may be relatively easy to identify those who have a sufficient degree of control to amount to an occupier but, as several of these cases demonstrate, the existence of this degree of control does not automatically equate to an abuse of it. As *Portsmouth Youth Activities Committee v Poppleton* [2008] shows, the courts in this area are very conscious of the significant and often dominant role played by the behaviour of claimants themselves.

KEY CASE

Portsmouth Youth Activities Committee v Poppleton [2008] EWCA Civ 646

The defendant was the occupier of a climbing wall facility which the claimant was visiting for the fourth or fifth time when he was severely injured. He was attempting to jump from one wall to another when he fell and incurred his injuries, rendering him tetraplegic. He alleged in his claim that the defendant was liable as an occupier because it had failed to supervise his activities, or to provide an appropriate warning that the matting provided, whilst very thick, would not be sufficient to preclude the possibility of all injuries. The Court of Appeal found that the conduct of the claimant was the cause of the claimant's injuries, rather than the state of the premises, and declined therefore to hold the defendant liable.

In policy terms, there is a clear theme in occupiers' liability cases; the courts have for a long time been cognisant of the fact that most injuries will occur on some form of premises, but that the provision or control of such premises is not enough in itself to give rise to liability. Particularly given that making premises available is generally in the public interest, there is much to be said for not disincentivising such provision by imposing extensive liability on those who do so.

■ VIEWPOINT

Does it surprise you that there is no duty on an occupier to make premises safe? Why is this so?

KEY LEGISLATION

Occupiers' Liability Act 1957

2   Extent of occupier's ordinary duty

(1)   An occupier of premises owes the same duty, the 'common duty of care', to all his visitors, except in so far as he is free to and does extend, restrict, modify or exclude his duty to any visitor or visitors by agreement or otherwise.

> (2) The common duty of care is a duty to take such care as in all the circumstances of the case is reasonable to see that the visitor will be reasonably safe in using the premises for the purposes for which he is invited or permitted by the occupier to be there.

Section 2(2) is the pivotal section of the OLA 1957, and contains the core duty. Remember that the duty is to keep the visitor reasonably safe and not the premises themselves. Not only is it fairly impossible to make most premises safe, but it is also undesirable. After all, who would want a landscape without trees, ponds, cliffs, shrubs etc.? Moreover, some premises are attractive precisely because they allow visitors to engage in a reasonable degree of managed risk, such as ski slopes, climbing facilities, water courses and so on. The point is that an occupier needs to make her visitors reasonably safe in the circumstances of her visit. This means not only that the discharge of that duty will depend on the characteristics of each individual visitor and the purposes for which each is there, but the fact that many visitors will voluntarily assume a certain level of risk receives explicit recognition in the statute. The following sections are, therefore, highly significant.

8.3.3.1 CHILDREN

The standard of care owed by an occupier is varied by the statute in relation to children and to people who are acting in the course of their professional expertise. In the case of the former, the duty is higher, given the reduced ability of children to perceive and to manage risks. Conversely, the duty is lower in relation to professionals, since they are held to have an augmented ability to perceive and to deal with the risks *inherent in their professional activities.*

KEY LEGISLATION

Occupiers' Liability Act 1957

2   Extent of occupier's ordinary duty
(3) The circumstances relevant for the present purpose include the degree of care, and of want of care, which would ordinarily be looked for in such a visitor, so that (for example) in proper cases—
     (a) an occupier must be prepared for children to be less careful than adults; ...

KEY CASE

Glasgow Corporation v Taylor [1922] 1 AC 44

The defendant corporation was the occupier of a botanical garden, access to which had not been denied to unaccompanied children. The claimant's 7-year-old son died after eating the berries of a poisonous shrub. The House of Lords held that the occupier's failure to restrict access to children meant that there was a good cause for trial, particularly because the tree could have stood as an allurement or hidden danger to children.

It is in relation to children that the courts seem less sympathetic to occupiers (or, perhaps, merely more sympathetic to claimants). This is understandable, given that occupiers are in a better position than children both to appreciate, and guard against, risks and dangers. Note, however, the effect of the next case. If an occupier knows or has reason to believe that his premises might hold a danger to children, especially if it is in some way particularly alluring (which many dangerous things are to children!), he is expected to take reasonable steps to prevent access to such individuals. Note, however, the effect of the next decision, which we have already encountered above: it is the case that the courts treat children as one homogeneous group. The age of the children concerned, the particular environment or function of the premises, and the likelihood of those children being accompanied, are all highly relevant to the question of whether a duty has been breached on particular facts.

KEY CASE

Phipps v Rochester Corporation [1955] 1 QB 450

The facts of this case are set out above. The relevant finding for these purposes is that, although the defendant occupier had taken no steps to prevent children from accessing its premises, it was also entitled to assume that very little children would be accompanied by a responsible supervisor of some sort, and that this responsibility lay with parents rather than occupiers. Given that this was the case, occupiers had a duty to ensure that dangers were brought to the attention of those accompanying little children, rather than having to accommodate the limitations of little children themselves. There was, therefore, on these facts, no breach of the occupier's duty of care.

As *Glasgow Corporation v Taylor* and *Phipps v Rochester Corporation* show, the degree of precautions that an occupier has to take increases as the age of the children with access to the premises decreases. This is true, however, only up to a point: once the age of such children drops below a certain level, the occupier can expect such children to be accompanied and so the degree of precaution falls once more to a level which is reasonable in relation to those accompanying the children, rather than the children themselves. There are no hard and fast figures available, however, for the age at which children should be accompanied. This is because it is context-dependent. It might, for instance, be reasonable to expect a 5-year-old, for example, to be unsupervised in an enclosed soft-play area, but not at all on a building site. You will need, therefore, to know and apply the case law in this area, and to make a case for whether a particular expectation is reasonable on a given set of facts.

KEY CASE

West Sussex CC v Pierce [2013] EWCA Civ 1230

The claimant had been playing with his brother by a metal water fountain in a school of which the defendant was an occupier. Intending to punch his brother, the claimant instead punched the water fountain and injured his hand. His case against the defendant alleged that it had breached its duty as occupier in not ensuring that the water fountain was safe and, in so doing, not expecting children to be less careful than adults. The Court of Appeal disagreed and rejected the claimant's submissions, finding that, in objective terms, there was nothing about the water fountain itself that was unsafe and that a school does not owe a duty to the children on its premises to prevent all manner of injuries from occurring.

PROBLEM QUESTION TECHNIQUE

Carl, left on his own (since his mum has gone out for the day), goes into the bathroom and drinks a bottle of Alice's essential oils and is violently ill.

▸ It is important to note here both that Carl is a child and that he is 5 years old. Whilst the OLA 1957 tells occupiers that they should expect children to be less careful than adults, the case law, as we have seen, makes it clear that the age of the child is also relevant, since younger children can be expected to be less careful than older children.

▸ We also know from *Phipps* that, below a certain age, children can be expected to be accompanied in some circumstances. Here, therefore, you need to consider whether it was reasonable of Alice to leave a 5-year-old alone in her flat in the circumstances.

▸ It would also be worth asking whether it was reasonable for Carl's mother to leave him with Alice while she was working (presumably knowing that he couldn't be supervised at all times). Remember always to evaluate both the age of the child and the environment/situation in which they have been left.

The case law on children is very valuable to know. Children often appear in occupiers' liability situations, both hypothetical and real.

8.3.3.2 THOSE IN 'EXERCISE OF CALLING'

The OLA 1957 also makes express provision for those who might be regarded as occupying the other end of the spectrum of required care to children: professional visitors, attending premises in the 'exercise of their calling'. In relation to these, occupiers can be expected to do less in terms of guarding against risks which are both more apparent to, and more easily mitigated by, the professionals themselves.

KEY LEGISLATION

Occupiers' Liability Act 1957

2   Extent of occupier's ordinary duty

(3)   The circumstances relevant for the present purpose include the degree of care, and of want of care, which would ordinarily be looked for in such a visitor, so that (for example) in proper cases—

...

(a) an occupier may expect that a person, in the exercise of his calling, will appreciate and guard against any special risks ordinarily incident to it, so far as the occupier leaves him free to do so.

KEY CASE

Roles v Nathan [1963] 1 WLR 1117

The defendant was the occupier of a building heated by an old coke boiler. On one occasion, when the boiler produced a great deal of smoke, a boiler engineer advised that the flues needed cleaning, and two brothers, who were chimney sweeps, were called in. The flues were cleaned, but when the boiler was started again, more smoke escaped. When the defendant called in a second boiler expert, he stated that the boiler room was dangerous and ordered everyone out. The sweeps ignored his warning, but were removed by force and warned by the expert a second time. Nonetheless, the sweeps were later found to be working there. When found, they said that they had nearly completed their work but couldn't quite finish because they had not enough cement to do so. They then said that they would return on Saturday. In fact they returned to complete their work that night, and both were found dead in the boiler room on Saturday morning. Their wives sued the defendant for breach of its duty as occupier. The Court of Appeal held that the warnings given to the chimney sweeps were enough to keep them 'reasonably safe' according to the duty outlined in the OLA 1957 and that they should have had a better professional appreciation of the risks to which they subjected themselves. Lord Denning MR made the point that when an occupier calls a specialist in to his premises to deal with a specific risk, it is reasonable to expect that specialist to guard against the inherent risks of her profession.

The decision in *Roles v Nathan* has to be correct; otherwise householders would be risking liability as occupiers every time they called in a specialist to deal with a dangerous situation, such as faulty wiring, for example. There is nothing to be said for incentivising non-specialist occupiers to try to deal with such dangerous situations themselves in order to avoid a potential occupiers' liability suit.

That is not to say, however, that specialists in the exercise of their calling are held to assume all of the risks of their vocation, and that occupiers will never be liable when such individuals are injured on their premises, as *Salmon v Seafarer Restaurants* [1983] shows.

KEY CASE

Salmon v Seafarer Restaurants Ltd [1983] 1 WLR 1264

The claimant fireman was injured by an explosion which occurred at the defendant's chip shop whilst he was there, fighting a fire. The fire had been caused by the defendant's negligence in failing to extinguish the light under a fryer. Woolf J found the defendant liable, and explained that the duty of an occupier towards specialists was not limited to extraordinary risks, but extended also to those standard risks inherent in the exercise of a particular calling where the defendant has been negligent and where it was foreseeable that a specialist would be injured.

The crucial difference between *Roles v Nathan* and *Salmon v Seafarer Restaurants* lies in the nature of the occupier's behaviour: where an occupier has acted reasonably before the specialist attends the premises, the latter can be expected to assume the risks inherent in her professional calling. A defendant occupier will not, however, be insulated from the effects of her negligent behaviour simply by virtue of the fact that the claimant is brought into the situation by virtue of her calling. On a related point, an occupier will also be potentially liable where a professional is injured as a result of a risk which materialises but which has nothing to do with the risks of her calling. So, if an electrician is injured by a defective loft ladder whilst trying to access a fuse board, this will not engage s 2(3)(b).

PROBLEM QUESTION TECHNIQUE

Diana had, ten minutes earlier, been knocked out by a cupboard unit falling on her. She had been asked to fit it by her boss, Eddie, even though he had not trained her how to do it safely. Eddie has rarely been on site since he took on the job. Alice interviewed several contractors and questioned them all extensively before deciding on Eddie because of his excellent credentials and apparently complete paperwork, so she is surprised by the fact that he is often absent, leaving the inexperienced Diana to do most of the work.

▶ This requires you to analyse whether Diana is working in the exercise of her calling, making it reasonable for Alice to presume that she should be aware of, and able to guard against, risks which are inherent in that.

▶ Consider this question alongside that of the engagement of contractors, outlined below.

8.3.4 How can that duty be discharged?

We have already encountered one of the ways in which this duty can be discharged, namely physically, by restricting access to particular dangers or situations that could be risky for all, or just some visitors. We have also already seen, however, how some premises cannot be made physically safe, or at least not in all circumstances and to all comers.

8.3.4.1 WARNINGS

One of the most common ways to ensure that visitors are reasonably safe, therefore, is to provide effective warnings so that potential claimants can either avoid, or assume, the relevant risks themselves.

KEY LEGISLATION

Any warning must be sufficient to enable the visitor to be reasonably safe

Occupiers' Liability Act 1957

2   Extent of occupier's ordinary duty

(4)   In determining whether the occupier of premises has discharged the common duty of care to a visitor, regard is to be had to all the circumstances, so that (for example)—

(a) where damage is caused to a visitor by a danger of which he had been warned by the occupier, the warning is not to be treated without more as absolving the occupier from liability, unless in all the circumstances it was enough to enable the visitor to be reasonably safe; ...

KEY CASE

Intruder Detection & Surveillance Ltd v Fulton [2008] EWCA Civ 1009

The defendant was refurbishing his family home, and the claimant was an employee of the firm contracted to instal a security system. When the claimant fell from one floor to the other, owing to the absence of a balustrade, he was seriously injured and sued his employer for failing to implement a safe system of work. The employer then sued the defendant occupier for contribution, claiming that he had been in breach of his duty as an occupier by allowing the claimant to work at his home, knowing there to be no balustrade. The defendant had warned the claimant that there was no balustrade, but had done no more than this, and had not supervised the claimant's work. In the circumstances, the Court of Appeal found anyone working on that part of the premises could not be made safe, and so the occupier was partly (25%) to blame for the claimant's injuries.

Warnings will not always suffice to make a visitor 'reasonably safe' but, where they are deemed to be sufficient, s 2(5) of the OLA 1957 will be engaged because claimants will then be deemed voluntarily to have assumed the attendant risks for themselves, thereby absolving the occupier of liability. This is an express statutory statement of the well-known common law defence of *volenti non fit injuria* (a willing person cannot complain of injury thereby caused) and is highly significant, both conceptually and in terms of how often it is applied, in an occupiers' liability context.

KEY LEGISLATION

Assumption of risk by visitor

Occupiers' Liability Act 1957

2   Extent of occupier's ordinary duty

(5)   The common duty of care does not impose on an occupier any obligation to a visitor in respect of risks willingly accepted as his by the visitor (the question whether a risk was so accepted to be decided on the same principles as in other cases in which one person owes a duty of care to another).

KEY CASE

Darby v National Trust [2001] EWCA Civ 189

The claimant's husband was drowned whilst swimming in a pond on the defendant's property. The defendant Trust had put up a sign, warning against bathing and boating, and the deceased had been a competent swimmer. There was also an irregular practice in place of wardens warning people around the ponds of the dangers of catching Weil's disease from the water. The claimant alleged that there should have been specific 'No Swimming' notices in place around the water. The Court of Appeal, however, found that the risks to competent swimmers of swimming in the pool were obvious, and that the defendant had therefore no duty to warn against it. The Court further found that, whilst the defendant could be said to have a duty to warn against the non-obvious dangers of Weil's disease, the deceased's death did not come within the scope of such a duty, caused as it was by such a distinct phenomenon.

KEY CASE

Bunker v Charles Brand & Son Ltd [1969] 2 QB 480

The claimant was working in a tunnel on a cutting machine. As he was walking along the machine to reach the front, his foot slipped and he fell, injuring himself in the process. O'Connor J found that the defendant, as occupier of the machine and the part of the tunnel in which it was situated, was in breach of its common duty of care under s 2(1). It was not enough that the claimant knew of the risks inherent in walking on the machine unless he also had the opportunity to keep himself safe from such risks. The claimant was, however, held to be 50% contributory negligent on these facts because he had not used the handrail provided, and his damages were reduced accordingly.

As with the common law defence of *volenti*,[7] it is not sufficient for the defence to apply that that claimant *knew* of the relevant risks if there is no realistic possibility of avoiding or averting them.

---

7   See Chapter 16 (Defences) at 16.4.

PROBLEM QUESTION TECHNIQUE

During the refurbishment, Alice has added another sign to the kitchen door, which reads 'This kitchen is currently unsafe'.

▶ The question here is, quite simply, whether Alice has done enough to make her visitors reasonably safe for the purposes for which they have been invited to use the premises.

▶ Wherever an occupier purports to do this by using a sign or notice, you need to consider whether this in itself is enough and whether it is feasible for the visitor to follow the guidance on the sign.

▶ Bear in mind on these facts that Bryan has been invited into the flat so that Alice can treat his glaucoma: she knows, then, that his eyesight is not good.

▶ Also remember that it is the visitor, rather than the premises, which needs to be kept reasonably safe.

8.3.4.2 EXCLUSIONS

It is essential to distinguish between warnings and exclusions, and yet omitting to do so is a common mistake made by students when answering problem questions. This is perhaps because both are often included in the same notice provided by the occupier. Be very clear, however, that a warning is an attempt to make the visitor safe and so to prevent liability from arising in the first place. An exclusion, by contrast, is an attempt to exclude any prima facie liability which does arise. We have dealt with the former above. The latter requires some familiarity with another statutory scheme – that covering exclusions and limitations of liability, and is generally found within the law of contract.

Any attempt by an occupier to exclude or restrict his liability will be circumscribed by two pieces of legislation.

(1) Where the relationship is between two entities, both acting in their business capacities, the Unfair Contract Terms Act (UCTA) 1977 will apply. This is so even where there is no contractual relationship between the parties.[8]

(2) Where the relationship is between one party acting in its business capacity (referred to as a 'trader' in the 2015 legislation) and another acting as a consumer, it is the Consumer Rights Act (CRA) 2015 that will apply. Ensure that you apply the correct statute, since to do otherwise is incorrect as a matter of law (although, in substance, the effect of both in this context is much the same).

KEY LEGISLATION

Definition of business liability

Unfair Contract Terms Act 1977

1   Scope of Part I

(3)   ... liability for breach of obligations or duties arising—

   (a) from things done or to be done by a person in the course of a business (whether his own business or another's); or

   (b) from the occupation of premises used for business purposes of the occupier; ...

---

8   See s 1(1)(c) of UCTA 1977.

References to liability are to be read according to s 1(3) of UCTA 1977. But liability of an occupier of premises for breach of an obligation or duty towards a person obtaining access to the premises for recreational or educational purposes, being liability for loss or damage suffered by reason of the dangerous state of the premises, is not a business liability of the occupier unless granting that person such access for the purposes concerned falls within the business purposes of the occupier.

KEY LEGISLATION

Definition of 'trader'

Consumer Rights Act 2015

2   Key definitions

(2)   'Trader' means a person acting for the purposes relating to that person's trade, business, craft or profession ...

It is crucial to establish the capacity in which the occupier allows the visitor access to her premises. If it is within the remit and course of her business or professional operations, the context will be one of business liability, even if the visitor's purpose is educational or recreational. The significance of this is that under both UCTA 1977 (where both parties are acting in the course of their business) and under the CRA 2015 (where one is acting in the course of a business (a trader) and one a consumer[9]), it is *not possible* to limit or restrict liability for death or personal injury caused by negligence. This is dealt with under s 2(1) of UCTA 1977 and under s 65 of the CRA 2015.

KEY LEGISLATION

Unfair Contract Terms Act 1977

2   Negligence liability

(1)   A person cannot by reference to any contract term or to a notice given to persons generally or to particular persons exclude or restrict his liability for death or personal injury resulting from negligence.

(2)   In the case of other loss or damage, a person cannot so exclude or restrict his liability for negligence except in so far as the term or notice satisfies the requirement of reasonableness.

(3)   Where a contract term or notice purports to exclude or restrict liability for negligence a person's agreement to or awareness of it is not of itself to be taken as indicating his voluntary acceptance of any risk.

KEY LEGISLATION

Consumer Rights Act 2015

65   Bar on exclusion or restriction of negligence liability

(1)   A trader cannot by a term of a consumer contract or by a consumer notice exclude or restrict liability for death or personal injury resulting from negligence.

---

9   A 'consumer' for the purposes of the CRA 2015 'means an individual acting for purposes that are wholly or mainly outside that individual's trade, business, craft or profession' – s 2(3).

(2) Where a term of a consumer contract, or a consumer notice, purports to exclude or restrict a trader's liability for negligence, a person is not to be taken to have voluntarily accepted any risk merely because the person agreed to or knew about the term or notice.

(3) In this section 'personal injury' includes any disease and any impairment of physical or mental condition.

(4) In this section 'negligence' means the breach of—

...

(c) the common duty of care imposed by the Occupiers' Liability Act 1957 or the Occupiers' Liability Act (Northern Ireland) 1957, ...

(5) It is immaterial for the purposes of subsection (4)—

(a) whether a breach of duty or obligation was inadvertent or intentional, or

(b) whether liability for it arises directly or vicariously.

Where, however, the visitor has suffered damage that is not death or personal injury, or where death or personal injury has resulted other than from negligence, exclusions and limitations can apply as long as they meet the requirements of 'reasonableness'[10] under UCTA 1977 or 'fairness' under the CRA 2015.[11] Where the visitor has not entered the premises within the course of the occupier's business purposes, neither UCTA 1977 nor the CRA 2015 applies, meaning that, by default, the common law rules apply. Unfortunately, however, it is not clear what these would be in a modern context since most of the case law in this area either concerns business liability, or pre-dates UCTA 1977 (meaning that it was decided before the need to restrict exclusions was recognised, and so is an unreliable gauge of modern legal thinking). Happily, it is not a situation which is likely to arise very often, and certainly has not done so in the past. If it does arise in a problem question, you need to make it clear why neither UCTA 1977 nor the CRA 2015 applies, and explain why there is no directly useful authority to cite. It would be reasonable to suggest that perhaps a court would take a lead from the CRA 2015 and consider whether any purported exclusion or limitation would be fair in the circumstances of the case before it (although it would not of course be *applying* the statutory test). It might also be instructive to look at cases pre-dating UCTA 1977, as long as these are considered alongside an appropriate recognition of their age and the consequently different legal and social environment in which they were decided. Take, for instance, *White v Blackmore* [1972], in which the defendant was a charitable organisation (which means that it is not clear whether UCTA 1977 or the CRA 2015 would today be applied).[12]

KEY CASE

White v Blackmore [1972] 2 QB 651

The claimant's husband was killed while watching jalopy racing organised by the defendant. The deceased had been signed on as a competitor

early in the day, and later took his family along to spectate. Notices were displayed, which both warned the public of the danger of motor

---

10 See s 11 and Sch 2 of UCTA 1977.

11 See s 62 of the CRA 2015.

12 Although the definition of trader in the CRA 2015 does not refer to charities, the Explanatory Notes provide that: 'Not-for-profit organisations, such as charities, mutuals and cooperatives, may also come within the definition of a trader, for example, if a charity shop sells t-shirts or mugs, they would be acting within the meaning of trader.' This could mean that charities will be deemed to be traders when acting in a way which is analogous to standard commercial behaviour, e.g. transacting direct with an individual or individuals. There is, however, no more authoritative guidance currently available.

racing and stated that it was a condition of admission that the organisers were absolved from all liabilities to spectators from accidents 'howsoever caused'. The deceased paid for the admission of his family, and was given programmes with a warning in small print on an inside page.

Whilst watching one of the races, the deceased was catapulted into the air by a boundary rope and was killed.

The Court of Appeal found that the defendant had effectively excluded its liability by the use of the words 'howsoever caused' on the warning notices which they were entitled to do by s 2(1) of OLA 1957. Recall that this section reads: 'An occupier of premises owes the same duty, the "common duty of care", to all his visitors, except in so far as he is free to and does extend, restrict, modify or exclude his duty to any visitor or visitors by agreement or otherwise.'

PROBLEM QUESTION TECHNIQUE

During the refurbishment, Alice has added another sign to the kitchen door, which reads 'This kitchen is currently unsafe. Artful Alice excludes all liability for any loss, injury or damage resulting from the use of this kitchen by her customers, howsoever caused.'

▶ Remember always to distinguish between notices which purport to prevent liability from arising (i.e. those which are phrased so as to try to keep visitors safe) and those which purport to exclude any liability which arises as a result of their not being kept safe.

▶ This particular notice has two parts, and each part has a different aim. The first has been dealt with above, in relation to the safety of visitors. The second, which purports to exclude liability, needs to be considered in the light of the legislation above: the CRA 2015 in relation to consumer claims (Bryan), and UCTA 1977 for non-consumer claims (Diana).

8.3.4.3 ENGAGING CONTRACTORS

Another way in which an occupier can discharge his common duty of care is to engage a reputable contractor to work on the premises. If he does so reasonably so that, for instance, he engages someone for a price around at least market value (as opposed to suspiciously low), about whom he has heard no repeated adverse reports, his duty will in effect be delegated to that contractor.

KEY LEGISLATION

Occupiers' Liability Act 1957

2   Extent of occupier's ordinary duty

(4)   In determining whether the occupier of premises has discharged the common duty of care to a visitor, regard is to be had to all the circumstances, so that (for example)—

...

(b) where damage is caused to a visitor by a danger due to the faulty execution of any work of construction, maintenance or repair by an independent contractor employed by the occupier, the occupier is not to be treated without more as answerable for the danger if in all the circumstances he had acted reasonably in entrusting the work to an independent contractor and had taken such steps (if any) as he reasonably ought in order to satisfy himself that the contractor was competent and that the work had been properly done.

KEY CASE

Maguire v Sefton MBC [2006] EWCA Civ 316

The first defendant council was the occupier of a leisure centre at which several of the second defendant's exercise machines were installed. The second defendant performed an inspection of the machines after three years, and the first and second defendants then entered into a service agreement. Soon afterwards, the claimant, who held membership of the centre, was injured by one of the machines, which turned out to be defective. He sued the council for breach of contract and for breach of its duty as an occupier. He also sued the second defendant in negligence. The Court of Appeal found that the existence of the contract between the first defendant council and the claimant did not affect the standard or nature of the duty owed; it remained the common duty of care. The council did not therefore warrant that any contractor, engaged consistently with the common duty of care, would also take care. By entering into a service agreement with the second defendant, the council had performed its duty as occupier and would not therefore be liable to the claimant.

KEY CASE

Gwilliam v West Hertfordshire Hospitals NHS Trust [2002] EWCA Civ 1041

The first defendant hospital hired, for a fund-raising event, a 'splat-wall', on which participants bounced from a trampoline and stuck to a Velcro wall. The second defendant operated the splat-wall and had been found by the first defendant from the phone book. As part of the agreement between the first and second defendants, the hospital agreed to pay £100 extra to secure both staff to operate the attraction on the day, and also to get the benefit of the second defendant's public liability insurance. When the claimant was injured by the structure, it transpired that the equipment had been negligently set up by the second defendant. Since his public liability insurance had expired four days before the incident occurred, the claimant has to settle her action against him for less than the full amount of her claim. She pursued the first defendant hospital, therefore, for the difference between the sum which she would have recovered from the second defendant had he been insured and the sum she got from her settlement, claiming that the hospital owed a duty to its visitors to exercise reasonable care in the selection of contractors, and that this included a duty to ensure that visitors were covered by public liability insurance, or to warn visitors where this was not the case. The Court of Appeal found that the hospital did owe a duty to inquire into the insurance position of the second defendant in order to confirm his suitability to be engaged for such an event and for such a purpose, but that since it had made such an inquiry, by asking whether the second defendant had relevant insurance, it had thereby discharged its duty as an occupier. It would be unreasonable to expect it to have gone further and checked the policy document.

Maguire v Sefton MBC and *Gwilliam v West Hertfordshire Hospitals NHS Trust* demonstrate clearly the limits of the occupier's duty in engaging independent contractors. The first, *Maguire*, is intuitively easy to accept: if an occupier goes to the trouble and expense of entering into a service agreement in order to keep its machines functional and safe, it could be deemed unreasonable then to hold it liable if that service is not carried out properly by the party to whom it has been entrusted. As far as *Gwilliam* goes, though, do you think it would be unreasonable to expect occupiers to see insurance documents in order to check that the policy will cover the relevant event?

A DIFFERENT PERSPECTIVE on insurance liability in tort

J. Morgan, 'Tort, Insurance and Incoherence' (2004) 67 MLR 384

Morgan here argues that the decision in *Gwilliam* counters the traditional argument that insurance is irrelevant to liability in tort. He makes the point that recognising that the hospital had a duty to inquire into the insurance status of the contractor it engaged elides the concept of an unsafe contractor with that of an uninsured contractor. They are not, in substance, however, the same thing, and requiring an occupier to make such inquiries reshapes its duty to guarding visitors against economic loss rather than against damage caused by the premises. Morgan is not in favour of insurance playing such a substantive role in the development of the common law of tort, and exhorts courts to treat the phenomenon of insurance as irrelevant. In this vein, he praises the approach of the House of Lords in *Tomlinson* for taking the correct approach.

■ VIEWPOINT

Do you think the presence or absence of insurance should have any bearing on liability in negligence? If it becomes relevant, could this be said to change the objectives of the tort as a whole?

PROBLEM QUESTION TECHNIQUE

Diana had, ten minutes earlier, been knocked out by a cupboard unit falling on her. She had been asked to fit it by her boss, Eddie, even though he had not trained her how to do it safely. Eddie has rarely been on site since he took on the job. Alice interviewed several contractors and questioned them all extensively before deciding on Eddie because of his excellent credentials and apparently complete paperwork, so she is surprised by the fact that he is often absent, leaving the inexperienced Diana to do most of the work.

▸ A really helpful case to consider here is *Ferguson v Walsh* because it deals with the issue of the 'extra layer' of occupier between Alice and Diana – in this case, Eddie.

▸ You need, therefore, to decide whether it was reasonable for Alice as an occupier to assume that Eddie would run a safe system of work on her premises. If so, it is likely that Eddie (as an occupier in his own right of the kitchen) would be the party on whom any liability is fixed.

▸ Remember, with each party, that it is not enough simply to state that he or she will be an occupier; you need also to establish that that duty has been breached. Has Eddie acted reasonably here?

8.4 The Occupiers' Liability Act 1984 – liability to those not classed as 'visitors'

The OLA 1984 deals with the liability of occupiers to 'non-visitors'. Broadly, it means that occupiers can be liable to people who are trespassing on their premises. The notion of occupiers being liable to people who are committing a legal wrong against them is not immediately palatable, particularly to non-lawyers. On closer examination, however, it is not as contentious as it might first appear. Historically, occupiers owed no such duty,[13] but in the next case, the House of Lords recognised that those who are technically trespassing will often be children, who cannot always be expected to understand the nuances of boundaries (behavioural or geographical!). This signalled something of a softening in attitude towards trespassers, which later manifested itself in the OLA 1984. It is

---

13 *Robert Addie & Sons (Collieries) Ltd v Dumbreck* [1929] AC 358.

essential to note, however, that the occupiers' liability regime for non-visitors has a palpably different sense to the one in place for visitors. Although both Acts have the same name, and the potential for occupiers to owe a duty to trespassers unquestionably exists, the courts take a markedly different, and far more restrictive, approach to non-visitors. This is obvious from the case law, in which, unless children are involved, the result is one of no liability much more often than not. This approach is explicitly set out by Lord Hoffmann in the leading case in the area, *Tomlinson v Congleton BC*, later in this section.

KEY CASE

British Railways Board v Herrington [1972] AC 877

The defendant railway board was the occupier of an electrified rail line which was fenced off from a meadow to which children had lawful access. At the time of the accident, this fence had been in disrepair for a number of months, and this had led to people taking shortcuts across the line. Despite the defendant having been notified that children had been seen on the electrified line, no action was taken to prevent this or to repair the fence. The claimant was 6 years old when he went on to the rail, through the hole in the fence, and was injured. The House of Lords, in broad agreement with the courts below, held the defendant liable for the claimant's injuries. The decision made it clear that occupiers do not owe trespassers the same duty as they owe to visitors, but that, in an age in which perils such as railway lines were becoming ever more common phenomena, and where space between premises was becoming ever more limited, it was appropriate to recognise that occupiers do owe a 'duty of common humanity' to those who encounter such dangers, particularly children who might find them to be a particular allurement.

The OLA 1984 is a short and relatively simple statute, and its core can be found at s 1(3) and (4), which sets out the only circumstances in which an occupier will be liable to a trespasser.

KEY LEGISLATION

Occupiers' Liability Act 1984

1 Duty of occupier to persons other than his visitors

(3) An occupier of premises owes a duty to another (not being his visitor) in respect of any such risk as is referred to in subsection (1) above if—

  (a) he is aware of the danger or has reasonable grounds to believe that it exists;

  (b) he knows or has reasonable grounds to believe that the other is in the vicinity of the danger concerned or that he may come into the vicinity of the danger (in either case, whether the other has lawful authority for being in that vicinity or not); and

  (c) the risk is one against which, in all the circumstances of the case, he may reasonably be expected to offer the other some protection.

(4) Where, by virtue of this section, an occupier of premises owes a duty to another in respect of such a risk, the duty is to take such care as is reasonable in all the circumstances of the case to see that he does not suffer injury on the premises by reason of the danger concerned.

DIFFERENT PERSPECTIVES on the duty owed to trespassers

M. Jones, 'The Occupiers' Liability Act 1984' (1984) MLR 713

This is an article written very soon after the OLA 1984 had been passed, and analyses its derivation, both from the decision in *Herrington*, and the subsequent referral of the issue to the Law Commission. Jones suggests that the three requirements in s 1(3) could have made it clearer whether the test to be applied to a defendant's knowledge of dangers and the presence of non-visitors should be subjective or objective. He points out that the tenor of the judgment in *Herrington* was that liability in this context should be based on subjective knowledge, whereas the Law Commission favoured an objective standard. Whilst s 1(3)(c) constitutes an objective inquiry, Jones laments the confusion created by the addition of s 1(3)(a) and 1(3)(b) which appear to introduce subjectivity (and therefore confusion).

J. Murphy, 'Public Rights of Way and Private Law Wrongs' [1997] Conv 362

In this article, Murphy draws out the point that occupiers responsible for public rights of way should not necessarily be immune from negligence actions brought by injured users (despite the fact the *McGeown* case, discussed earlier in this chapter, suggests that such liability will be limited). The argument advanced by Murphy here is that the liability of those who control public rights of way should depend on the context of the user's visit. He makes the point that, on the one hand, occupiers who invite users onto their land for commercial purposes, and/or in order to make a gain, should be expected, as a quid pro quo, to bear responsibility for injuries which occur (in the relevant way) as a result. On the other hand, it is not so clear that landowners should be liable for injuries caused by premises which have been used by the public gratuitously and for their own gain. This more nuanced distinction, Murphy argues, is therefore more defensible than any blanket immunity from occupiers' liability for those who control public rights of way.

It is perhaps easy to see why the courts have not found it difficult to restrict liability in this area, where they have felt it necessary to do so. Section 1(3)(c) in particular has a form which allows for a considerable amount of judicial discretion. *Tomlinson v Congleton BC* is a pivotal case for a number of reasons: not only does it set out clearly how to distinguish between visitors and non-visitors for the purposes of the OLAs, but it gives an indispensable insight into the relevant policy concerns which underpin this area of the law. It is a judgment remarkable for its clarity, transparency and overall helpfulness.

KEY CASE

Tomlinson v Congleton BC [2003] UKHL 47

The facts of this case are outlined above. It is instructive here to set out three excerpts from the judgment of Lord Hoffmann, given what it tells us about the interaction between the OLAs:

The duty under the 1984 Act was intended to be a lesser duty, as to both incidence and scope, than the duty to a lawful visitor under the 1957 Act. That was because Parliament recognised that it would often be unduly burdensome to require landowners to take steps to protect the safety of people who came upon their land

without invitation or permission. They should not ordinarily be able to force duties upon unwilling hosts. In the application of that principle, I can see no difference between a person who comes upon land without permission and one who, having come with permission, does something which he has not been given permission to do. In both cases, the entrant would be imposing upon the landowner a duty of care which he has not expressly or impliedly accepted. The 1984 Act provides that even in such cases a duty may exist, based simply upon occupation of land

and knowledge or foresight that unauthorised persons may come upon the land or authorised persons may use it for unauthorised purposes. But that duty is rarer and different in quality from the duty which arises from express or implied invitation or permission to come upon the land and use it. [14]

Parliament has made it clear that in the case of a lawful visitor, one starts from the assumption that there is a duty whereas in the case of a trespasser one starts from the assumption that there is none. [15]

My Lords, as will be clear from what I have just said, I think that there is an important question of freedom at stake. It is unjust that the harmless recreation of responsible parents and children with buckets and spades on the beaches should be prohibited in order to comply with what is thought to be a legal duty to safeguard irresponsible visitors against dangers which are perfectly obvious. The fact that such people take no notice of warnings cannot create a duty to take other steps to protect them. I find it difficult to express with appropriate moderation my disagreement with the proposition of Sedley LJ, ante, p 62b-c, para 45, that it is 'only where the risk is so obvious that the occupier can safely assume that nobody will take it that there will be no liability'. A duty to protect against obvious risks or self-inflicted harm exists only in cases in which there is no genuine and informed choice, as in the case of employees whose work requires them to take the risk, or some lack of capacity, such as the inability of children to recognise danger (*Herrington v British Railways Board* [1972] AC 877) or the despair of prisoners which may lead them to inflict injury on themselves: *Reeves v Comr of Police of the Metropolis* [2000] 1 AC 360.[16]

There was a clear paper trail showing that Congleton Borough Council had acknowledged the need to make physical changes to the area, by removing the beaches and planting vegetation in their place, if it was going to prevent swimming. It had not done so by the time of Tomlinson's accident because of budgetary constraints. This was a point which received more attention in the Court of Appeal (Lord Hoffmann in the House of Lords said that, in his opinion, the financial cost was secondary to the cost of denying others' freedom to use the beaches lawfully), but it is nonetheless an illuminating one. Public bodies have limited budgets, and every time they are required to pay out to one injured individual, they have fewer resources then to spend on making premises safer for the wider community. In terms of occupiers' liability to trespassers, the courts seem particularly conscious of this fact.

8.4.1   Who is classed as a non-visitor?

The OLA1984 is often referred to as being the Act 'for trespassers'. This is largely true, and is fine as an aide-memoire to help you distinguish broadly between the 1957 and 1984 Acts. It is not, however, a technically accurate label because the OLA 1984 also covers those exercising a right of way under the Countryside and Rights of Way Act 2000. This last piece of legislation was passed in an attempt to open up large parts of the countryside to ramblers and recreational walkers. In asking private landowners to grant such access gratuitously to their land, it seems more reasonable to subject them to the level of care expected under the 1984 Act, rather than that expected under the OLA 1957.[17]

---

14   At [13].

15   At [38].

16   At [46].

17   Although see M. Stevens-Hoare and R. Higgins, 'Roam Free?' (2004) NLJ 1856 who observe that, amongst other effects of the incorporation of this group of individuals within the OLA 1984, and the specific limiting provisions which apply to them (see s 1(6A) and (6AA) of the OLA 1984, which essentially prevents liability arising in relation to those exercising a 'right to roam' if they are injured by a natural feature of the landscape or a body of water, whether natural or not, one result is that trespassers are better protected than those exercising such rights.

Those exercising such rights of way are referred to as non-visitors for the purposes of occupiers' liability: they are not trespassers, but neither are they visitors, entitled to OLA 1957 protection.

KEY LEGISLATION

Occupiers' Liability Act 1984

1   Duty of occupier to persons other than his visitors
(1)   The rules enacted by this section shall have effect, in place of the rules of the common law, to determine—
      (a) whether any duty is owed by a person as occupier of premises to persons other than his visitors in respect of any risk of their suffering injury on the premises by reason of any danger due to the state of the premises or to things done or omitted to be done on them; ...

PROBLEM QUESTION TECHNIQUE

There are signs on all the other internal doors of the flat, stating 'Strictly no admittance to customers of Artful Alice'.

Bryan ... decides to get a drink and, not noticing the additional sign on the kitchen door despite its prominent position, enters the room and trips on a loose floorboard.

Carl ... goes into the bathroom and drinks a bottle of Alice's essential oils and is violently ill.

▶ You will have established the answer to this part of the question when you considered whether the parties were visitors (above). Any parties which do not qualify as visitors will fall to be considered as non-visitors under this Act.

8.4.2 In what circumstances will non-visitors be owed a duty?

As we saw above, the answer to this is contained in s 1(3)(a)–(c) of the OLA 1984. In answering a problem question, you must go through these steps each time, making reference to the relevant part of the statute:

• The occupier is aware/has reasonable grounds to believe that danger exists.

• The occupier knows/has reasonable grounds to believe that the non-visitor will come within the vicinity of danger.

• The risk is one against which, in all the circumstances of the case, the occupier can reasonably be expected to offer the non-visitor some protection.

In addition to the restrictions on liability generated by the subsections above, there are two significant exclusions expressly contained in the 1984 Act, and you should be aware of, and ready to apply, both of these where the facts are appropriate:
(1)   OLA 1984, s 1(7) excludes those using the highway.
(2)   OLA 1984, s 1(8) excludes liability for property damage. This is not excluded under the 1957 Act, and reflects the fact that, wherever a duty is owed by an occupier to a non-visitor, it is the basic duty of common humanity. In other words, it covers the most important of basic rights, but does not extend to protecting the property of those injured by premises whilst not entering as visitors.

PROBLEM QUESTION TECHNIQUE

His left leg and arm are seriously injured, and his Rolex watch is smashed.

▸ It is not absolutely clear whether Bryan would be classed as a visitor or as a non-visitor. It would depend upon, inter alia, the severity of his glaucoma, the size of the font on Alice's sign, the availability of water in the waiting room. If, however, his case were to be decided under the OLA 1984, you would need to make it clear that he could not claim for the damage to his watch.

▸ In situations in which it is not clear whether an individual is a visitor or a non-visitor (particularly where not all of the facts are known), it is perfectly acceptable to explain why it is not clear, and what the different implications of each classification would be.

8.4.3 What is the content of that duty?

KEY LEGISLATION

Occupiers' Liability Act 1984

1   Duty of occupier to persons other than his visitors
(4)   Where, by virtue of this section, an occupier of premises owes a duty to another in respect of such a risk, the duty is to take such care as is reasonable in all the circumstances of the case to see that he does not suffer injury on the premises by reason of the danger concerned.

8.4.3.1 OBVIOUS DANGERS

The absence of any need for occupiers to bring the existence of obvious dangers to the attention of non-visitors was made clear by Lord Hoffmann in *Tomlinson*.[18] This raises the question, though, of to whom those dangers must be obvious. There is no express mention of children in the OLA 1984, to correspond to the particular level of care required in relation to them under the OLA 1957. It could be argued that this is because the OLA 1984 was written primarily with children in mind (although there is absolutely nothing in the statute itself to suggest this; it is merely an inference which could be drawn from the way in which the law developed prior to the passing of the Act). It is also because the basic duty of common humanity could be said to apply equally to all people, regardless of age. Nevertheless, the question of whether a danger is obvious to a particular claimant will depend to some extent on the particular characteristics of that claimant, including her age.

KEY CASE

Keown v Coventry Healthcare NHS Trust [2006] EWCA Civ 39

The claimant was 11 years old when he fell from a fire escape on premises of which the defendant was an occupier. He was injured and suffered brain damage as a result. The defendant was aware that children played in the area. The action was brought under the OLA 1984 and included the claim that the fire escape constituted an allurement to children, and that the hospital was aware of this and of the risk it presented. The claimant admitted that he appreciated that his actions were dangerous and that he shouldn't have done what he did. The Court of Appeal found that there was

---

18   At [13], excerpted above.

no liability on these facts: first because the duty of an occupier to a non-visitor is not to guard against injuries which occur as a result of the state of the premises, but only to guard against those caused by the dangerous state of the premises. In this case, the danger had been generated by the claimant's behaviour and not by the inherent state of the premises themselves, which were not deficient or in disrepair. The Court went on to add that it was a question of fact and degree whether premises which were not dangerous from the point of view of an adult could be dangerous for a child, and that, in this case, the dangers of such behaviour should have been apparent to an 11-year-old child.

As with the OLA 1957, there is no discrete age range within which children should be aware of all dangers: whether or not a particular danger or risk is apparent will be depend on the facts of a given situation. *Keown* shows, however, that it will be a relevant consideration for the court, especially when applying s 1(3)(c), and deciding whether it would have been reasonable in the circumstances for the defendant to have provided protection against a particular risk.

8.4.4 How can that duty be discharged?

Section 1 of the OLA 1984 really only tells an occupier that he must behave reasonably in relation to non-visitors. This is not particularly helpful in itself. The more obvious a danger on one's premises, and the more accessible those premises are to non-visitors, particularly children, the more likely it is that an occupier has to take positive steps to mitigate the risks of harm associated with that danger. It will often be difficult to alter any physical attributes of the premises in order to do this, both logistically and financially. One of the best ways in which to discharge the duty is, therefore, to use appropriate warnings where possible.

8.4.4.1 WARNINGS

As with the OLA 1957, if an appropriate and effective warning is provided by the occupier and the claimant has ignored this, it is very likely that the claim will be denied on the basis that the claimant herself assumed the risk voluntarily by not heeding the warning. This is explicitly included within the Act, and is the most common reasons for the failure of claims made under it.

KEY LEGISLATION

Occupiers' Liability Act 1984

1   Duty of occupier to persons other than his visitors
(6)   No duty is owed by virtue of this section to any person in respect of risks willingly accepted as his by that person (the question whether a risk was so accepted to be decided on the same principles as in other cases in which one person owes a duty of care to another).

KEY CASE

Ratcliffe v McConnell [1999] 1 WLR 670

The claimant, aged 19, was injured whilst swimming in a college swimming pool at night, whilst, as he knew, it was closed for the winter season. The pool was enclosed by substantial fences and a gate, which was locked. There was also a sign present, stating that the pool was closed. Nonetheless, the claimant accessed the pool and dived in, hitting his head on the bottom and causing his injuries. The claimant admitted in his evidence that he knew the pool was closed, that he should not have gone into it, and that, even had he seen any warnings, he would have dived in in any event. He also admitted that he was perfectly aware that diving into a body of water without knowing its depth was a risky thing to do. The Court of Appeal held (perhaps unsurprisingly) on these facts that the defendant occupier owed no duty to this particular trespasser to guard him against risks of which he was fully aware himself. By choosing knowingly to run these risks, the claimant had taken himself out of the remit of the limited protection afforded by the OLA 1984.

8.4.4.2 EXCLUSIONS

It seems unlikely that, in formulating the OLA 1984, the legislature intended occupiers to be able to exclude themselves from the basic duty of common humanity, although there is no authority to provide a definitive answer to this.[19] We do know, however, that the OLA 1957 expressly refers to an occupier's liability to exclude or restrict its liability (see s 2(1)), whereas the OLA 1984 makes no reference to such an ability all. There is a strong case for arguing, therefore, that exclusions are unlikely to be effective as against non-visitors in the very limited circumstances in which liability arises at all.

Table 8.1: Overview of the Occupiers' Liability Act 1957 and the Occupiers' Liability Act 1984: similarities and differences

Occupiers' Liability Act 1957	Occupiers' Liability Act 1984
Applies to visitors.	Applies to non-visitors (trespassers and those exercising rights to roam).
Premises are 'any fixed or moveable structure'.	Premises are 'any fixed or moveable structure'.
Occupier defined by *Wheat v Lacon*.	Occupier defined by *Wheat v Lacon*.
Covers property damage.	Excludes property damage.
Duty is owed to all visitors.	Duty only owed where the conditions in s 1(3) are satisfied: the occupier knows or has reasonable grounds to believe that the danger exists, knows or has reasonable grounds to believe that the non-visitor might be in the vicinity of danger, and the risk is one which in all the circumstances of the case the occupier could reasonably be expected to guard against.
Duty to all visitors to take such care that the visitor is reasonably safe while using the premises for the purposes for which they are invited.	Duty to non-visitors to take such care as is reasonable in all the circumstances of the case to see that the non-visitor does not suffer injury on the premises.
Occupier can exclude, restrict or modify its duty insofar as it is able, subject to UCTA 1977 and the CRA 2015.	Uncertain: no express provision and no case law. The lack of provision might be a result of the already minimal duty to which the Act gives rise. It may be that Parliament felt that this minimal duty should not be restricted further.

---

19   Although see M. Jones, 'The Occupiers' Liability Act 1984' (1984) MLR 713 at 723.

8.5 CHAPTER SUMMARY

Occupiers' liability is a self-contained topic, which allows for systematic revision and application of the statutory scheme and its accompanying case law. There is not much that is hugely conceptually difficult or contentious about it, hence the relative paucity of articles written and debates cast in the area. This means that it lends itself particularly well to examination by problem question. If, therefore, you can avoid the obvious pitfalls, it can be a fairly straightforward topic to get under your belt. Unfortunately, if you do not avoid those pitfalls, this can lead to very poor results. You should take great care, for instance, to recognise an issue as being one of occupiers' liability, and so to apply the statutory regime. Although it is unusual to have to do this in tort, ensure that you also apply the *relevant* provisions of the statute (as in the roadmap, below), as well as any applicable common law authority. Even when you have correctly identified the situation as attracting an application of the legislation, always ensure that you are applying the correct Act, having explained why it is that one which is applicable to the claimant in question (or the particular act of the claimant in question, remembering that the same person can be a visitor for some purposes and a non-visitor for others). Finally, when applying the relevant Act, remember how very different the attitude of the courts is to visitors and non-visitors: a reference to Lord Hoffmann's judgment in *Tomlinson* is always valuable on this point, and definitely worth keeping in your mind. A corollary of this is that the OLA 1984, even when it is found to apply, excludes liability for damage to property, and this is often an important distinction to make for the purposes of answering a problem question.

FURTHER READING

S. Bailey, 'Occupiers' Liability: the Enactment of "Common Law" Principles' in T.T. Arvind and J. Steele (eds), *Tort Law and the Legislature* (Hart, 2013)

R. Buckley, 'The Occupiers' Liability Act 1984 – Has Herrington Survived?' (1984) *Conv* 413

R. Kidner, 'The Duty of Occupiers towards Children' (1988) 39 *NILQ* 150

J. Morgan, 'Tort, Insurance and Incoherence' (2004) 67 *MLR* 384

D. Payne, 'The Occupiers' Liability Act' (1958) 21 *MLR* 359

Roadmap: Has the Claimant's damage been caused by defective or dangerous premises?

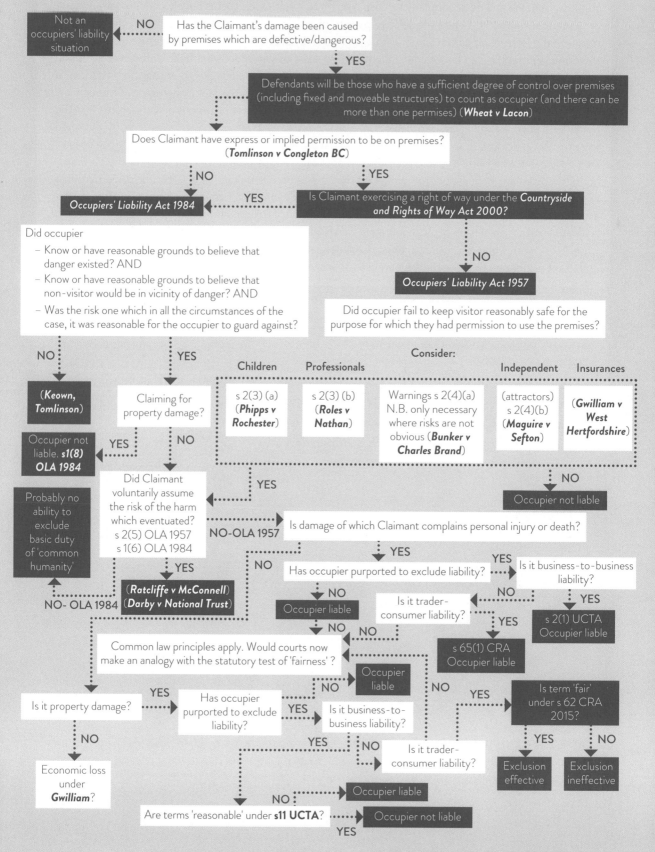

9 PRODUCT LIABILITY

LEARNING OBJECTIVES

By the end of this chapter, you should be able to:

- Outline the three different ways in which the law provides potential redress for harm caused by defective products
- Explain the crucial differences between those different methods, when they are available and when they overlap
- Recognise the relative merits and demerits of each scheme
- Know when to apply the statutory scheme, and how to interpret its provisions
- Analyse the extent to which the statutory scheme meets the objectives which gave rise to it, particularly in comparison to the effectiveness of the common law in this area

CHAPTER CONTENTS

9.1 Introduction	194
9.2 Contractual remedies	195
9.3 Common law negligence	197
9.4 Consumer Protection Act 1987	198
9.4.1 Product	199
9.4.2 Damage	200
9.4.3 Producer	202
9.4.4 Defect	203
9.4.5 Defences	209
9.5 Limitation	212
9.6 Chapter summary	215
Further reading	216

PROBLEM QUESTION

Duleepa is a professional gardener who designs and maintains commercial show gardens. She buys a top-of-the-range lawnmower, aimed at those maintaining ornamental lawns, from Evergreen. Her apprentice, Frieda, sees an advert for a blade accessory for this lawnmower, made by a different firm. The advert says that the blade will enable the mower to cut grass shorter, and in less time, than factory-supplied blades. Having sought Duleepa's agreement, Frieda purchases the blade from Gloria and attaches it to the lawnmower made by Evergreen. Gloria does not know much about the blades, and has nothing to do with their production, but she has agreed to distribute them in England on behalf of her brother, Henri, who is based in Cape Town. When Duleepa is using the mower for the second time since the blade has been attached, the motor overheats and explodes, destroying the mower, burning a large section of expensive turf and causing severe burns to Duleepa. It is not clear whether the overheating was caused by a fault in the original mechanism of the mower, or the later insertion of the accessory blade. Evergreen performed extensive testing on the mower before putting it on the market, but did so in autumn and winter, and not at all during the spring and summer months.

Nine years previously, Duleepa had bought a new strain of fertiliser from Interseed. At the time she bought it, it had been on the market for two years. Since then, she has applied it to the soil in her principal show garden every season. Her roses have been declining in bloom quality ever since, but it only occurs to her and Frieda this summer that the decline started at around the same time that they began to apply the Interseed fertiliser to their soil. When they do an online search to see if they can find any information on this, they find that, in the last year or so, several gardeners who used Interseed fertiliser during the same time period have reported seeing similar declines in their flowering plants.

Interseed claims that they tested the fertiliser for two season cycles before releasing it for sale, and detected no adverse reactions in any plant species. It further claims that there was at that time no research or data available to suggest a different plant response. In actual fact, it turns out that a substance very similar in chemical make-up to the Interseed fertiliser had been used on the small South Pacific island of Tikopia for six successive years prior to the release of Interseed's formulation. It had resulted in the death of several strains of flowering plants. A team of botanists from Tikopia had written a very detailed account of this course of events including data about their initial soil composition, the amount of fertiliser used and the precise effects this had on the flora. They had submitted this in the form of a letter to GardenersUniverse.com, where it was published in the correspondence section the year before Interseed released its product.

9.1 Introduction

There are three potential ways in which a claimant can recover for damage caused by a defective product. One is through the law of contract, using the implied term of quality in the Sale of Goods Act 1979 and the Consumer Rights Act 2015. Another is through common law negligence; *Donoghue v Stevenson*[1] was, after all, a case concerning product liability. The final means is through the Consumer Protection Act (CPA) 1987. Not all of these avenues will be available on every set of facts, although they will sometimes overlap. This chapter will set out the requirements, and discuss the remedial consequences, of each type of claim. This will enable you to analyse the options and assess which is of the greatest benefit to a claimant in a given situation. It is important to understand that the availability of a statutory claim under the CPA 1987 is not necessarily an alternative to a common law claim: depending on the facts of the situation at hand, it might be that a claimant has the option of choosing which one to pursue, or it might be that a claimant has only one option. The statutory scheme, for instance, requires there to be a defect in the product. The common law requires the claimant to establish that the defendant has breached its duty of care. On some facts, both of these elements will be present, but it is perfectly conceivable that there will have been a breach of duty which did not cause a defect (according to the statutory definition) or a defect which was not caused by negligence. It is not, therefore, the same as occupiers' liability, in which the statutory cause of action replaces the common law scheme. The statutory scheme under the CPA 1987 is based on an EU Directive, the intention of which was to create a strict liability platform for producers. Since strict liability requires only that claimants prove that the defendant caused their loss, without having to prove fault, the statutory scheme might at first glance seem to be better for consumers than a common law claim. We will see, however, that this is not necessarily the case, owing to the way in which the UK has implemented the Directive.

Figure 9.1 illustrates the way in which the different avenues of recovery differ and overlap.

---

1   See Chapter 2 (Duty of Care).

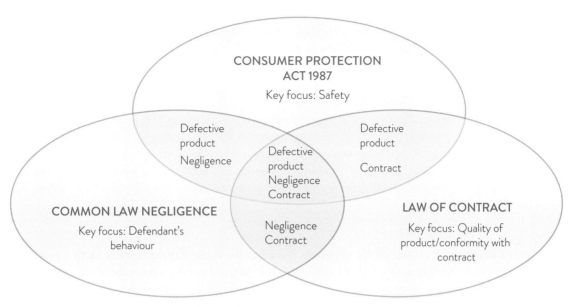

Figure 9.1: Avenues of recovery

Note that the overlapping claims depicted in Figure 9.1 are only *potential*. It will not be the case that all avenues will be available to a claimant on every set of facts.

9.2 Contractual remedies

One of the most straightforward ways to claim for loss caused by a defective product is to sue in contract. A contractual claim is generally easier than having to establish negligence on the part of the defendant, with all its requirements of recognised damage, duty, breach, causation and remoteness. In order to make a contractual claim, the claimant has only to establish that the supply of the defective product amounted to a breach of that contract. In particular, where the claimant purchased the product as a consumer and from a seller acting in the course of a business,[2] the Consumer Rights Act 2015 and the Sale of Goods Act 1979 imply[3] terms into such contracts that products will reach certain standards if the supplier is not to be found to be in breach. Sales law, and particularly consumer sales law, is a broad and increasingly complicated area of contract. There isn't scope to discuss all of its intricacies but it is useful to discuss the main points here.

MAKING CONNECTIONS

For sales made in the course of a business, the Sale of Goods Act 1979 implies that goods sold by description will match that description, that goods will be of satisfactory quality and fit for purpose, and that goods sold by sample will match that sample in quality.[4] Where the goods do not meet these standards, the buyer is able both to reject the goods and to sue for damages.[5] Significantly, damages claimed in contract can cover the cost of damage to the good itself (and so cover replacement or repair)

---

2   That is, not as a private sale.
3   Or, in the language of the Consumer Rights Act 2015, 'treat as included'.
4   Sections 13, 14 and 15 respectively.
5   Since the terms implied by the Sale of Goods Act 1979 are deemed to be conditions of the contract.

as well as any consequential damage caused as a result of the product being sub-standard. The value of the product itself is not something which is recoverable in either common law negligence (since it is classed as pure economic loss)[6] or under the CPA 1987. In this respect, therefore, the contract law remedy may well prove to be preferable for claimants. The Consumer Rights Act 2015, which applies only where the purchaser of the goods in question is 'an individual acting for purposes that are wholly or mainly outside that individual's trade, business, craft or profession' provides that, where goods are not of satisfactory quality or fit for purpose,[7] the consumer can reject the goods and receive a refund,[8] but must resort to the common law for damages or for specific performance. These common law rules on contractual breach are a further avenue for claimants wanting to sue for receiving products which do not match the supplier's contractual obligations where neither statute applies (such as sales between private individuals).

The law of contract gives potentially generous remedies for those damaged by defective products. The principal limitation, however, is that in order for the claimant to take advantage of any contractual avenue of redress, the claimant and defendant must be in contractual privity[9]. As a result, *Donoghue v Stevenson* gave rise to the unified tort of negligence in order to give a remedy to those damaged by a product that was bought by somebody else (with the effect that it also covers those who buy products rendered defective by someone other than the retailer). Without a contractual relationship, claimants will not be able to pursue contractual remedies and must therefore seek a remedy in the common law tort of negligence, or under the CPA 1987.

PROBLEM QUESTION TECHNIQUE

Her apprentice, Frieda, sees an advert for a blade accessory for this lawnmower, made by a different firm ... Having sought Duleepa's agreement, Frieda purchases the blade from Gloria and attaches it to the lawnmower made by Evergreen ...When Duleepa is using the mower for the second time since the blade has been attached, the motor overheats and explodes, destroying the mower, burning a large section of expensive turf and causing severe burns to Duleepa.

▸ This issue requires recognition of the fact that Duleepa, the person who has been injured and who has suffered loss, has no contractual privity with the supplier of the blade. Were the blade to have been the cause of her loss, therefore, she would have no remedy in contract.

▸ If, however, the loss turns out to have been caused by a faulty mechanism in the mower, Duleepa is in contractual privity (i.e. has a contract with) Evergreen, the supplier of the mower, and so could pursue a remedy in contract. Remember to consider how this remedy differs from those offered by the common law or under the CPA 1987 because it will allow Duleepa to claim for the value of the mower itself as well as the consequential loss she suffers.

---

6   See Chapter 3 (Pure Economic Loss).
7   Sections 9 and 10 respectively.
8   Sections 20, 22 and 24.
9   Or the claimant must be able to take the benefit of the contract under the provisions of the Contracts (Rights of Third Parties) Act 1999, which is unlikely to happen very often, given that she 'must be expressly identified in the contract by name, as a member of a class or as answering a particular description' in order to do so.

9.3 Common law negligence

Whilst this might seem rather obvious, common law negligence is an important potential avenue of redress for claimants, and it should always be considered in problem questions in which damage has been caused by a defective product. The temptation, on identifying a fact pattern involving product liability, is to focus exclusively on the CPA 1987 (which is covered in detail at 9.4) since that statute is the most recent development in this area of law and can appear to give claimants advantages over and above their common law rights. The CPA 1987 does not, however, *displace* the common law action, and so the relative merits and demerits of each type of action should always be considered in the first instance (even if, on the facts, one or both are eventually dismissed).

There is, of course, no need for a contract in order to claim at common law, but a claimant must be able to establish negligence. The key principles of the tort of negligence are covered in detail in Chapters 2 to 7. Product liability at common law is merely an application of those rules and principles. To summarise in brief, this means, in the usual way, that the claimant has the burden of proving that the defendant owed her a duty of care in relation to the provision of the product, that the defendant breached that duty of care, that the breach caused the harm of which the claimant complains, and that that harm was not too remote from the breach.

To recall some of the salient reasoning in *Donoghue v Stevenson*:

> You must take reasonable care to avoid acts or omissions which you can reasonably foresee would be likely to injure your neighbour. Who, then, in law is my neighbour? The answer seems to be – persons who are so closely and directly affected by my act that I ought reasonably to have them in contemplation as being so affected when I am directing my mind to the acts or omissions which are called in question. This appears to me to be the doctrine of *Heaven v Pender*, as laid down by Lord Esher (then Brett M.R.) when it is limited by the notion of proximity introduced by Lord Esher himself and A. L. Smith L.J. in *Le Lievre v Gould*. Lord Esher says: 'That case established that, under certain circumstances, one man may owe a duty to another, even though there is no contract between them. If one man is near to another, or is near to the property of another, a duty lies upon him not to do that which may cause a personal injury to that other, or may injure his property.' So A. L. Smith L.J.: 'The decision of *Heaven v Pender* was founded upon the principle, that a duty to take due care did arise when the person or property of one was in such proximity to the person or property of another that, if due care was not taken, damage might be done by the one to the other.' I think that this sufficiently states the truth if proximity be not confined to mere physical proximity, but be used, as I think it was intended, to extend to such close and direct relations that the act complained of directly affects a person whom the person alleged to be bound to take care would know would be directly affected by his careless act. That this is the sense in which nearness of 'proximity' was intended by Lord Esher is obvious from his own illustration in *Heaven v Pender* of the application of his doctrine to the sale of goods. 'This' (i.e., the rule he has just formulated) 'includes the case of goods, etc., supplied to be used immediately by a particular person or persons, or one of a class of persons, where it would be obvious to the person supplying, if he thought, that the goods would in all probability be used at once by such persons before a reasonable opportunity for discovering any defect which might exist, and where the thing supplied would be of such a nature that a neglect of ordinary care or skill as to its condition or the manner of supplying it would probably cause danger to the person or property of the person for whose use it was supplied, and who was about to use it. It would exclude a case in which the goods are supplied under circumstances in which it would be a chance by whom they would be used or whether they would be used or not, or whether they would be used before there would probably be means of observing any defect, or where the goods would be of such a nature that a want

of care or skill as to their condition or the manner of supplying them would not probably produce danger of injury to person or property.' I draw particular attention to the fact that Lord Esher emphasizes the necessity of goods having to be 'used immediately' and 'used at once before a reasonable opportunity of inspection.' This is obviously to exclude the possibility of goods having their condition altered by lapse of time, and to call attention to the proximate relationship, which may be too remote where inspection even of the person using, certainly of an intermediate person, may reasonably be interposed.[10]

What is important in this context is how the principles of negligence compare to, and contrast with, the other avenues of claiming for loss caused by defective products.

PROBLEM QUESTION TECHNIQUE

Evergreen performed extensive testing on the mower before putting it on the market, but did so in autumn and winter, and not at all during the spring and summer months.

▸ This should be an inquiry which is familiar to you from Chapter 5 (Breach of Duty). It is simply a question of whether Evergreen breached its duty of care by falling below the standard of what a reasonable lawn mower manufacturer would have done in the circumstances, taking into account the risks generated and the costs of avoiding them.

▸ It is material to note that testing was not done at the time of year that most lawn mowers are normally used, and you need to consider how much additional cost such testing is likely to have incurred.

9.4 Consumer Protection Act 1987

The CPA 1987 constituted the UK's implementation of EU Council Directive 85/374/EEC (the Product Liability Directive). The aim of the Directive was the creation of a scheme to make producers of products strictly liable for any damage caused by defects in those products. However, the effect of the UK's implementation of the Directive has been to dilute the strictness of that liability.

We have seen that a claim in contract requires an enforceable contract between claimant and defendant, and that a claim in common law negligence requires negligence on the part of the defendant which has caused the claimant's damage or loss. In order to bring a claim under the CPA 1987, the claimant must establish that the product in question is defective, and that the defect has caused the loss of which he complains. This is not the same as proving that the defendant's negligence caused his harm, although it will sometimes be possible to establish both on the same facts. In order to deal satisfactorily with the CPA 1987, you will need to be familiar with the (relatively sparse) case law in the area, so that you know how its significant concepts function in practice. Specifically, you will need to understand the following concepts, which will each be examined in more detail below:

- what a product is;

- what damage is;

- who can be classified as a 'producer';

- what a 'defect' is;

- the defences under the CPA 1987, and how one defence in particular does not appear to conform to the scheme intended by the Directive.

---

10   Lord Atkin at 580–2.

9.4.1 Product

The relevant parts of the CPA 1987 are as follows:

KEY LEGISLATION

Consumer Protection Act 1987

1   Purpose and construction of Part I

(2)   … 'product' means any goods or electricity and (subject to subsection (3) below) includes a product which is comprised in another product, whether by virtue of being a component part or raw material or otherwise; …

(3)   For the purposes of this Part a person who supplies any product in which products are comprised, whether by virtue of being component parts or raw materials or otherwise, shall not be treated by reason only of his supply of that product as supplying any of the products so comprised.[11]

45   Interpretation

(4)   … 'goods' includes substances, growing crops and things comprised in land by virtue of being attached to it and any ship, aircraft or vehicle; …

There are several important points to note here about products incorporated within other products: component parts of larger products are, for these purposes, legally separate from those larger products, and so it is the producer of the component itself who will be liable for any defectiveness in it. This liability, however, extends only to the party who suffers consequential loss as a result of the defective component product, and *it does not extend to cover any damage done to the product in which the component is incorporated*. Both the producer of the component and the producer of the finished product in which it is comprised, however, can be jointly and severally liable[12] for damage caused by that finished product to a third party.[13] Nonetheless, if the producer of a component part can show that the defect in the final product was 'wholly attributable' to the design of the finished product, or to compliance with instructions issued by the producer of the finished product, she will have a defence under s 4(1)(f) of the CPA 1987.

PROBLEM QUESTION TECHNIQUE

Duleepa is a professional gardener who designs and maintains commercial show gardens. She buys a top-of-the-range lawnmower, aimed at those maintaining ornamental lawns, from Evergreen. Her apprentice, Frieda, sees an advert for a blade accessory for this lawnmower, made by a different firm. The advert says that the blade will enable the mower to which it is fixed to cut grass shorter, and in less time, than factory-supplied blades … It is not clear whether the overheating was caused by a fault in the original mechanism of the mower, or whether the malfunction was caused by the later insertion of the accessory blade.

---

11   As a result of the BSE ('mad cow' disease) crisis, the definition of 'product' was expanded to include primary agricultural produce – see Consumer Protection Act 1987 (Product Liability) (Modification) Order 2000 (SI 2000/2771).

12   See Chapter 17 (Damages).

13   CPA 1987, s 2(5).

▶ As with the contract point above, the identification of the relevant 'product' will depend on what was the cause of the damage. You cannot know this from the facts provided in the question, and so you simply need to make the point that the component blade can be regarded as a separate product from the mower. Consequently, once it is established what was the cause of the damage, either the producer of the mower as a product, or the producer of the blade as a separate product, will be liable.

9.4.2 Damage

The damage which may be the subject of a claim is dealt with under s 5 of the CPA 1987.

KEY LEGISLATION

Consumer Protection Act 1987

5   Damage giving rise to liability

(1)   Subject to the following provisions of this section, in this Part 'damage' means death or personal injury or any loss of or damage to any property (including land).

(2)   A person shall not be liable under section 2 above in respect of any defect in a product for the loss of or any damage to the product itself or for the loss of or any damage to the whole or any part of any product which has been supplied with the product in question comprised in it.

(3)   A person shall not be liable under section 2 above for any loss of or damage to any property which, at the time it is lost or damaged, is not—

(a) of a description of property ordinarily intended for private use, occupation or consumption; and

(b) intended by the person suffering the loss or damage mainly for his own private use, occupation or consumption.

(4)   No damages shall be awarded to any person by virtue of this Part in respect of any loss of or damage to any property if the amount which would fall to be so awarded to that person, apart from this subsection and any liability for interest, does not exceed £275.

(5)   In determining for the purposes of this Part who has suffered any loss of or damage to property and when any such loss or damage occurred, the loss or damage shall be regarded as having occurred at the earliest time at which a person with an interest in the property had knowledge of the material facts about the loss or damage.

(6)   For the purposes of subsection (5) above the material facts about any loss of or damage to any property are such facts about the loss or damage as would lead a reasonable person with an interest in the property to consider the loss or damage sufficiently serious to justify his instituting proceedings for damages against a defendant who did not dispute liability and was able to satisfy a judgment.

(7)   For the purposes of subsection (5) above a person's knowledge includes knowledge which he might reasonably have been expected to acquire—

(a) from facts observable or ascertainable by him; or

(b) from facts ascertainable by him with the help of appropriate expert advice which it is reasonable for him to seek;

but a person shall not be taken by virtue of this subsection to have knowledge of a fact ascertainable by him only with the help of expert advice unless he has failed to take all reasonable steps to obtain (and, where appropriate, to act on) that advice.

Under the CPA 1987, claimants can recover only for death, personal injury, or damage to other property caused by the defective product. Notably, as in common law negligence, loss or damage to the product itself is not recoverable, and is regarded as pure economic loss.[14] However, the law in this area distinguishes between component parts which are supplied in the first instance with a product, and those which are added later. If a part is added to a product at a time after its production, and causes damage to that product as a result of being defective, damage to the product itself *is* recoverable under the CPA 1987. Take, for example, the purchase of a bicycle. Any parts which are supplied with the bike when it is purchased will be considered as component parts. Should the brakes, for example, be defective and cause the bike to crash, the claimant will not be able to recover for damage to the bike itself; only for her personal injury and for any consequential damage to other property caused by the crashed bike. Had the claimant in this situation replaced the factory-installed brakes with another set after purchase, any damage to the bike itself caused by defectiveness in those brakes would be recoverable. This is the consequence of the wording of s 5(2): 'any product which has been *supplied with the product in question comprised* in it'.

■ VIEWPOINT

Do you think that this is anomalous and/or problematic? Why should it make a difference whether the component part is supplied at the same time as the product in which it is incorporated, or added at a later date?

It should also be noted that recovery under the CPA 1987 is only possible in relation to goods ordinarily supplied for private use, *and also* intended for private use by the user. This condition requires both subparagraphs (a) and (b) of s 5(3) to be satisfied and this is hardly surprising, given the name of the Act and the intention of the Directive on which it is based. This is a measure aimed at protecting the interests of consumers, rather than commercial parties, since the latter are presumably regarded as being better able to look after their own interests (probably through the greater contractual leverage they have).

Subsection (4) provides that the value of the claim must exceed £275 and is intended to prevent the courts having to deal with very minor claims. In 1987, however, when the Act was passed, £275 was worth considerably more than it is today. Taking inflation into account, an equivalent amount in 2019 would be around £730. It is worth asking whether this provision still serves it purpose, because very minor claims can now still be brought under the CPA 1987 without being excluded by s 5(4).

PROBLEM QUESTION TECHNIQUE

Duleepa is a professional gardener who designs and maintains commercial show gardens. She buys a top-of-the-range lawnmower, aimed at those maintaining ornamental lawns, from Evergreen ... Having sought Duleepa's agreement, Frieda purchases the blade from Gloria and attaches it to the lawnmower made by Evergreen ... When Duleepa is using the mower for the second time since the blade has been attached, the motor overheats and explodes, destroying the mower itself, burning a large section of expensive turf and causing severe burns to Duleepa.

---

14   Which is why it is recoverable in contract (in which most claims are for loss which is purely economic), but not in tort.

▸ Consider the two products: the blade was not supplied with the lawnmower and so, were the blade to be the cause of the explosion, the producer of the blade could potentially be liable for damage caused to the mower. And vice versa (were such a claim to exceed the minimum value set out above).

▸ There is an important question about whether Duleepa's claim would be actionable at all under the CPA 1987, seeing as she bought and used the mower for commercial use, rather than for the private use specified in s 5(3). Consider subparagraphs (a) and (b); whilst a lawnmower might be something 'ordinarily intended' for private use, you need then to go on and ask whether Duleepa bought it, intending to use it for private or for commercial purposes. If the latter, she will not be able to recover under the CPA 1987.

9.4.3 Producer

A 'producer' for the purposes of product liability is defined in s 1 of the CPA 1987:

KEY LEGISLATION

Consumer Protection Act 1987

1   Purpose and construction of Part I

(2)   In this Part, except in so far as the context otherwise requires—

'producer', in relation to a product, means—

(a) the person who manufactured it;

(b) in the case of a substance which has not been manufactured but has been won or abstracted, the person who won or abstracted it;

(c) in the case of a product which has not been manufactured, won or abstracted but essential characteristics of which are attributable to an industrial or other process having been carried out (for example, in relation to agricultural produce), the person who carried out that process;

2   Liability for defective products

(1)   Subject to the following provisions of this Part, where any damage is caused wholly or partly by a defect in a product, every person to whom subsection (2) below applies shall be liable for the damage.

(2)   This subsection applies to—

(a) the producer of the product;

(b) any person who, by putting his name on the product or using a trade mark or other distinguishing mark in relation to the product, has held himself out to be the producer of the product;

(c) any person who has imported the product into a member State from a place outside the member States in order, in the course of any business of his, to supply it to another.

(3)   Subject as aforesaid, where any damage is caused wholly or partly by a defect in a product, any person who supplied the product (whether to the person who suffered the damage, to the producer of any product in which the product in question is comprised or to any other person) shall be liable for the damage if—

(a) the person who suffered the damage requests the supplier to identify one or more of the persons (whether still in existence or not) to whom subsection (2) above applies in relation to the product;

(b) that request is made within a reasonable period after the damage occurs and at a time when it is not reasonably practicable for the person making the request to identify all those persons; and

(c) the supplier fails, within a reasonable period after receiving the request, either to comply with the request or to identify the person who supplied the product to him.

(4) Where two or more persons are liable by virtue of this Part for the same damage, their liability shall be joint and several.

As we can see from the provisions above, liability under the Act is narrower than at common law, in that the CPA 1987 specifies nominate parties rather than simply requiring a duty of care to be established. It is nonetheless not limited to those who actually make or manufacture the products concerned (although manufacturers are the most straightforward category of defendant). In line with the consumer protection concerns of the Act, the combined effect of ss 1(2) and 2 is to maximise the chances that there will be an answerable party for the damage caused by a defective product, even if the manufacturer of the product is hard to identify, contact or pursue, or if the product was not the result of a manufacturing process at all. We can see from these provisions that those who import products into the EU[15] and those who present products under their 'own brand' are potential defendants in claims for product liability. As a further avenue of potential redress, claimants may also sue those who supplied them with the defective product where those suppliers have failed to identify the producer of the product, or the party from whom they themselves acquired it. This aims to ensure that claimants will be able to trace the producer through the supply chain, and, where this is not possible, to sue instead an intermediate supplier. Where a defective product is made up of several component parts, and one of those parts is defective, s 2(5) tells us that the manufacturers of both the end product and the component part will be jointly and severally liable for any damage thereby caused. Whilst the implications of joint and several liability have been explored in full elsewhere,[16] this means essentially that a claimant can claim full damages from either defendant, and it is then up to the defendant to seek contribution from the other under the Civil Liability (Contribution) Act 1978.

PROBLEM QUESTION TECHNIQUE

Having sought Duleepa's agreement, Frieda purchases the blade from Gloria and attaches it to the lawnmower made by Evergreen. Gloria does not know much about the blades, and has nothing to do with their production, but she has agreed to distribute them in England on behalf of her brother, Henri, who is based in Cape Town.

▸ This part of the problem question is concerned with the identity of the defendant. Here, although Gloria does not manufacture the blades, she can be liable under the CPA 1987 as the party who has imported them into a member state (thereby making it easier for the claimant to pursue a remedy).

9.4.4 Defect

The meaning of 'defect' is probably the least straightforward aspect of the statutory scheme, although – or maybe because – it is the issue on which most of the case law has arisen. Section 3 of the CPA 1987 contains the relevant provisions.

---

15 Again, the objective of this provision is to fortify consumer protection; this time by preventing claimants from having to pursue producers outside of the member states.

16 See Chapter 6 (Causation) and Chapter 17 (Damages).

KEY LEGISLATION

Consumer Protection Act 1987

3   Meaning of 'defect'

(1)   Subject to the following provisions of this section, there is a defect in a product for the purposes of this Part if the safety of the product is not such as persons generally are entitled to expect; and for those purposes 'safety', in relation to a product, shall include safety with respect to products comprised in that product and safety in the context of risks of damage to property, as well as in the context of risks of death or personal injury.

(2)   In determining for the purposes of subsection (1) above what persons generally are entitled to expect in relation to a product all the circumstances shall be taken into account, including—

(a) the manner in which, and purposes for which, the product has been marketed, its get-up, the use of any mark in relation to the product and any instructions for, or warnings with respect to, doing or refraining from doing anything with or in relation to the product;

(b) what might reasonably be expected to be done with or in relation to the product; and

(c) the time when the product was supplied by its producer to another;

(3)   and nothing in this section shall require a defect to be inferred from the fact alone that the safety of a product which is supplied after that time is greater than the safety of the product in question.

The test of whether there is a defect in the product for the purposes of the CPA 1987 is linked to safety and based on the idea of 'what persons generally are entitled to expect' in terms of safety. To a layperson, the phrasing 'what persons generally are entitled to expect' might appear to be reasonably clear and determinate. However, from a legal perspective, this provision leaves open many questions. Nolan has said that 'the test of defectiveness in s 3 is essentially an empty vessel to be filled by judicial analysis'.[17] For a start, are the 'persons generally' the users, or intended users, of the product, or are they those who manufacture the product – or both? Whilst it might seem apparent that 'persons generally' is intended to cover both, this does not dispose of the interpretative difficulty in practice, because it is not at all clear that both of those groups will have the same expectations in terms of the safety of products. It is highly likely, for instance, that users of products will feel that they are entitled to expect a higher level of safety than the producers of those products feel that they are entitled to expect.[18] Section 3(2) is important because it provides specific guidance on what will affect those expectations (although it provides no obvious means of aligning the expectations of users and producers). Section 3(2)(a) and (b) in particular set out the criteria which will be considered by a court trying to benchmark the expectations of 'persons generally', all of which are fairly intuitive. It is relevant, for example, what the product is marketed, and intended to be used, for. This has to form part of any safety assessment because some products are, by their very nature, inescapably less safe than other products, but this does not mean that they are defective. A blowtorch, for example, is unlikely ever to be as 'safe' in absolute terms as a plush teddy bear, but its potential to cause harm is, in effect, a necessary part of its make-up and functionality. It is really only

17 D. Nolan, 'Strict Product Liability for Design Defects' (2018) 134(Apr) *LQR* 176–81, 181.

18 Interestingly, the Directive on which the CPA 1987 is based defines 'defective' in its Article 6 as a product which 'does not provide the safety which a person is entitled to expect, taking all circumstances into account …'. This, more than the wording adopted by the UK implementation, could be construed as focusing the evaluation of expectations on the person using the product. It is not, however, without ambiguity on the point, and might still be taken to refer to any person as a representative of the general public.

if the risks generated by the blowtorch are unreasonable in the context of such tools, rather than in the context of objects generally, that it might be deemed to be less safe than persons generally are entitled to expect. Section 3(2)(a) makes it clear that the instructions or warnings included with the product will also be considered as part of this equation: whilst persons generally are not entitled to expect blowtorches not to be intrinsically dangerous, they are entitled to expect producers clearly to identify the relevant risks, and to provide information about the best way in which those risks can be minimised. There are echoes here of occupiers' liability:[19] we cannot expect premises to be made 'safe', since this would be neither possible nor desirable, but we can expect occupiers (or producers) to make premises (or products) reasonably safe for the purposes for which they are intended to be visited (or used). This analogy (and the fact that occupiers' liability is a specialised form of negligence) suggests that the CPA 1987 liability regime for defective products is not strict in the way that the Directive was formulated to achieve.

Whilst you will need clear knowledge of the statute and its provisions in relation to an action under the CPA 1987, you will also need to be familiar with the small number of cases which have been decided in the area,[20] most of which relate to the question of what amounts to a defect. In *Richardson v LRC Products Ltd* [2000],[21] for example, the claimant was unsuccessful in her action against the manufacturers of a condom which had split during intercourse with her husband, resulting in an unplanned pregnancy. This case is nicely illustrative of the point that imperfection and defectiveness are not the same thing: the fact that the condom had ruptured was not sufficient to prove that it had been defective as a product. After all, 'persons generally' are not entitled to expect condoms to be 100% effective as a means of preventing pregnancy. The case also provides a reminder that, as with common law claims, a causal link between the fault and the damage must be proved. It was observed in *Richardson* that such a link would have been challenged on the facts of the case because the claimant had failed to avail herself of the option of taking the morning after pill. In a similar context, in *Worsley v Tambrands Ltd* [2000],[22] the claimant sued the manufacturer of tampons which she alleged had caused her to contract toxic shock syndrome. In deciding in favour of the defendant on the basis that the tampons were not defective products, the court disagreed with the claimant's arguments that the warnings accompanying the tampons were insufficient.

The next case provides a trickier source of analysis, and, as its effects on the law in this area have been enduring, it is an important decision to understand.

KEY CASE

A v National Blood Authority [2001] 3 All ER 289

The claimants in this case had all contracted Hepatitis C, a disease affecting the liver, as a result of transfusions of blood supplied by the National Blood Authority. They claimed that the blood was a defective product because there was a known risk[23] that any of the blood products supplied could have been infected with the disease, even though at that time there were no means available to test for its presence, and so the defendants could not have identified which products were affected. The

---

19 See Chapter 8 (Occupiers' Liability).

20 On one view, it is remarkable how little litigation has been generated by the CPA 1987. On another, it is not surprising, given that it could be said to add little to the existing remedies in English law. Another point to make is that the very existence of a statute intended to make the liability of producers stricter than it is at common law could have led either to more efforts being made by producers to avoid making defective products, or by more cases being settled out of court.

21 [2000] Lloyd's Rep Med 280.

22 [2000] PIQR P95.

23 Not publicly known, but medically known.

facts of this case, therefore, provided an effective test for the relevance of producer fault in cases decided under the CPA 1987, particularly since the Authority had an obligation to provide blood products to hospitals. Significantly, Burton J expressly considered the language of Article 6[24] of the Directive in order to assist his interpretation of what amounts to 'defective'. Article 6 defines a defective product as one which 'does not provide the safety which a person is entitled to expect, taking all circumstances into account ...'. Burton J concluded that the absence of avoidability has no bearing on the concept of defectiveness because it does not affect the safety of the product concerned, and that persons generally were entitled to expect clean blood to be supplied.[25] He also made the point that notions of fault were not part of the fabric of the regime envisaged by the Directive, and that the scheme was intended to allocate risks such as those in this case to producers, rather than to users, of products.

Burton J made the important distinction between standard and non-standard products (or 'lemons');

that is, those products which are examples of how that type of product should be, and those which are deficient versions. This distinction is significant, for example, when dealing with products which are inherently dangerous but perfectly functional and well-made, like a very sharp chef's knife, and those which create a risk simply because they are poorly produced, like a child's toy with a faulty battery compartment. The defendants argued that the bags of blood were standard products, since they all carried the same risk of being infected with Hepatitis C. This argument was rejected, and the defendants found liable for supplying defective blood, because those bags which were infected could not, in the judge's view, be described as standard products. Since they contained the pathogens, they were different from bags of clean blood and therefore non-standard products. Even if they had been standard products, the risks attributable to them should only be borne by users if and when they were known to those users.[26]

In the wake of *A v National Blood Authority*, it is likely to be easier to establish defectiveness in relation to non-standard products than it is in relation to standard products. A defect in a standard product is one that will exist in all versions and instances of the product. Note that this does *not* mean that such products cannot be defective; just that the assessment of their safety will require a broader consideration of their characteristics, taking into account the way in which they compare to other similar products in the market or industry. *Abouzaid v Mothercare (UK) Ltd* [2000] and *Tesco Stores Ltd v Pollard* [2006] give further indication of how the concept of defectiveness operates in practice, although they may be regarded as giving conflicting guidance.

KEY CASE

Abouzaid v Mothercare (UK) Ltd [2000] All ER (D) 2436

The 12-year-old claimant was trying to strap a sleeping cover to a buggy when the strap sprung back, severely injuring his eye. The defendant

manufacturer of the cover argued that the product was not defective because there were no reports of any such accidents in existence at the time, meaning

---

24   And Article 7(e), relating to the development risks defence, which will be dealt with below.

25   It was relevant to this consideration that, although the medical profession was aware of the risk of infected blood, this was not something which the public could have been expected to be aware of, given the information available in the public domain at the time.

26   Either because of information in the public domain, or because the risks in question are obvious – see the infamous 'hot coffee' cases such as *Bogle & Others v McDonald's Restaurants Ltd* [2002] EWHC 490 (QB), in which hot drinks which caused injuries when spilt were deemed *not* to be defective.

that it could not have known this was a possibility. Whilst the court accepted this was the case, it made a distinction between liability at common law (for which that consideration would have been material) and liability under the CPA 1987. Under the latter, the manufacturer's knowledge, or ability to gain knowledge, about the possibility of a particular outcome occurring was not relevant where the safety of the product did not meet the level of what persons generally are entitled to expect.

KEY CASE

Tesco Stores Ltd v Pollard [2006] EWCA Civ 393

In this case, a 13-month-old child was injured by eating dishwasher powder sold by the defendants in a bottle which had a child resistant closure. The trial judge had found the bottle to be defective on the basis that the child resistant cap did not meet the British Standard certificate level, and Tesco appealed against that decision. The Court of Appeal reversed the decision, finding that the bottle was not defective because it did meet the standard of safety that persons generally are entitled to expect. Primarily, this was because it was harder to open than a standard screw top, and the Court felt that entering into deliberations about gradations of difficulty beyond that would be too fraught with difficulty in terms of a generic standard of public expectation.

It is not immediately obvious why the two decisions in *Abouzaid v Mothercare* and *Tesco Stores v Pollard* have different outcomes. This is particularly so, given that, in *Abouzaid*, there was no benchmark of safety available, and the defendant was held liable nonetheless, whereas, in *Pollard*, there was just such a benchmark in the form of the British Standard, and the defendant was found not to be liable even though its product did not meet that standard.[27] A means of distinction could be that, in *Pollard*, the defendant had undoubtedly taken steps to make the product safer for children than it would have been in standard packaging, whereas there was no evidence of such steps having been taken in *Abouzaid*. Also, the injury in *Abouzaid* was arguably as likely to happen to an adult as to a child, which could not really be said of *Pollard*, meaning that the product threatened greater potential for harm. For the purposes of academic legal analysis, what really matters is that you know both cases, and you are familiar with the factual differences between them and the means by which they can be distinguished. This way, you will be able to find the closest analogy with the facts in front of you and apply them as appropriate to problem questions. You will also be able to refer to them in an essay discussion, by analysing their implications for the law in this area, with support or criticism according to your opinion of them.

After a long time with no further judicial consideration of these issues, Hickinbottom J gave judgment in the following case, which provides something of a gloss on the analysis in the earlier decisions, rather than making any dramatic changes or developments.

KEY CASE

Wilkes v DePuy International Ltd [2016] EWHC 3096 (QB)

The claimant sued the defendant in common law and under the CPA 1987, alleging that his artificial replacement hip, which had been produced by the defendant, was defective. Specifically, the hip had suffered a fracture three years after its placement, and the claimant argued that this was the result of the way in which the neck of the joint had been designed. The principal issue was whether this amounted in law to a defect. The court decided that it did not.

27 This standard did not provide a legal requirement for such products, but was instead a guideline.

Inevitably, Hickinbottom J made reference in his judgment to the analysis conducted by Burton J in *A v National Blood Authority*. The facts of *Wilkes*, however, were different to the earlier decision in that the characteristic of the artificial hip which was alleged by the claimant to be defective was an aspect of its *design*, rather than of its *manufacture*. In Burton J's terminology, the hip was therefore a standard product: it had been produced exactly as it should have been and was not a 'lemon' or a bad example of its design. Whilst Hickinbottom J did not adhere to the standard/non-standard distinction in the form that it is found in *A v National Blood Authority*,[28] he based his analysis on the distinction between design and manufacturing defects, which arguably amounts to the same thing. What is significant about this later decision is that it emphasises the need for the court to consider the safety of the product, taking into account any relevant regulatory safety standards to which it should conform (in this case, the hip exceeded the level benchmarked by British Standards), as well as any competing considerations inherent in the product's function. The claimant in *Wilkes*, for example, argued that the risk of the artificial hip fracturing could have been avoided by an alteration in the design of its 'C-Stem' connection. The judge found, however, that the design of that C-Stem had sufficient advantages so as to outweigh any benefit that might be achieved by altering it: 'whether a product has an acceptable level of safety … necessarily involves some balancing of risks and potential benefits including, of course, potential utility'.[29] Hickinbottom J also found that the warnings of fracture supplied with the product were sufficient to prevent that risk from rendering the product defective for the purposes of the CPA 1987. It is also noteworthy that these conclusions were reached through an express analysis of the wording of the OLA 1987, and not the Directive (the latter had formed the basis of Burton J's analysis; an approach that had attracted some criticism).

PROBLEM QUESTION TECHNIQUE

When Duleepa is using the mower for the second time after the blade has been attached, the motor overheats and explodes, destroying the mower, burning a large section of expensive turf and causing severe burns to Duleepa.

… several gardeners who used Interseed fertiliser during the same time period have reported seeing similar declines in their flowering plants …

▸ Here you need to address the issue of defectiveness. In terms of the mower, it is easy to answer the question of whether the explosion of a mower that has been used for the second time is as safe as 'persons generally are entitled to expect', but there remains the causal question of whether the mower would have exploded were it not for the insertion of the new blade. If it wouldn't have done so, it is the blade which fails the test and the claim should be made against Gloria.

▸ In relation to Interseed, the same question needs to be asked – is a fertiliser that kills surrounding plantlife as safe as persons generally are entitled to expect?

▸ Is the batch of fertiliser purchased by Duleepa a standard or a non-standard product? This is not determinative of whether it is defective or not, but, under *A v National Blood Authority* and *Wilkes*, different issues arise. If it is a non-standard product, it is somewhat simpler to demonstrate a defect, since the product was not made as it should have been. Where, however, it is a standard version, the question arises whether the design is defective, taking into account its relative risks and benefits. Is it possible that a fertiliser that kills surrounding flora can be a worthwhile product?

---

28 Describing it as 'unnecessary and undesirable' at [94].
29 At [13].

DIFFERENT PERSPECTIVES on the defect test

D. Nolan, 'Strict Product Liability for Design Defects' (2018) 134 LQR 176–81

Nolan analyses the decision in *Wilkes* in a light which is generally favourable, concluding that its analysis is broadly in line with what had gone before. He points out, for example, that Hickinbottom's approach is to be preferred in relation to three points: first, his clear delineation of the difference between the identification of a defect and the finding of a causal link between that and the claimant's damage; second, his retreat from describing the test in s 3 as being one of 'legitimate expectation'; and, third, his focus on the wording of the CPA 1987 itself, rather than on the Directive on which the Act is based. Nolan does, however, go on to level some criticism at the *Wilkes* approach: first, at Hickinbottom's analysis of the risk–benefit analysis in terms of a specific patient, as opposed to a global evaluation; and, second, at the judge's apparent hostility towards the standard/non-standard product distinction, which Nolan regards as both substantively helpful and difficult to avoid if a proper analysis is to be carried out.

J. Eisler, 'One Step Forward and Two Steps Back in Product Liability: The Search for Clarity in the Identification of Defects' (2017) 76(2) CLJ 230–3

Eisler is less enamoured of *Wilkes*. He is critical of what he regards as the rejection in that case of the 'firmer structure' provided by *A v National Blood Authority*, with specific reference to Hickinbottom J's scepticism about the standard/non-standard product distinction. He also takes the view that the analysis in *Wilkes* relies too heavily on consumer preference as a means of identifying when a product is defective (by, for example, taking into account the extent to which consumers will choose to continue using a product, even after its risks have been made known), at the risk of making the inquiry a circular one. Ultimately, Eisler regards the *Wilkes* analysis as being too flexible to provide much helpful guidance to the courts in identifying defectiveness in products, and argues that the best way forward is to synthesise the best parts of the reasoning in both *A v National Blood Authority* and in *Wilkes*. On this final point, his perspective is perhaps not so different from Nolan's.

9.4.5 Defences

Section 4 of the CPA 1987 lists the defences available to defendants, should their products be deemed to be defective under s 3.

KEY LEGISLATION

Consumer Protection Act 1987

4 Defences

(1) In any civil proceedings by virtue of this Part against any person ('the person proceeded against') in respect of a defect in a product it shall be a defence for him to show—

(a) that the defect is attributable to compliance with any requirement imposed by or under any enactment or with any EU obligation; or

(b) that the person proceeded against did not at any time supply the product to another; or

(c) that the following conditions are satisfied, that is to say—

(i) that the only supply of the product to another by the person proceeded against was otherwise than in the course of a business of that person's; and

(ii) that section 2(2) above does not apply to that person or applies to him by virtue only of things done otherwise than with a view to profit; or

(d) that the defect did not exist in the product at the relevant time; or

> (e) that the state of scientific and technical knowledge at the relevant time was not such that a producer of products of the same description as the product in question might be expected to have discovered the defect if it had existed in his products while they were under his control; or
>
> (f) that the defect—
>
>   (i) constituted a defect in a product ('the subsequent product') in which the product in question had been comprised; and
>
>   (ii) was wholly attributable to the design of the subsequent product or to compliance by the producer of the product in question with instructions given by the producer of the subsequent product.
>
> (2) In this section 'the relevant time', in relation to electricity, means the time at which it was generated, being a time before it was transmitted or distributed, and in relation to any other product, means—
>
>   (a) if the person proceeded against is a person to whom subsection (2) of section 2 above applies in relation to the product, the time when he supplied the product to another;
>
>   (b) if that subsection does not apply to that person in relation to the product, the time when the product was last supplied by a person to whom that subsection does apply in relation to the product.

Most of these defences are intuitively reasonable and have caused little, if any, concern. For instance, the defence in s 4(1)(a) absolves a defendant from liability where the defect arose because the product was produced in compliance with another legal requirement. The defences in s 4(1)(b), (c) and (d) set out the circumstances in which the defendant will be deemed to fall outside the remit of the Act: either because (b) the supply was not made at all, (c) was not made in the course of business, or (d) because the defect occurred after the defendant had supplied the product. The defence in (e), however, has been the cause not just of controversy, but of infringement proceedings brought by the European Commission[30] in the European Court of Justice. The Commission was of the view that the defence in s 4(1)(e) of the CPA 1987, known as the 'development risks defence', was excessively broad and did not therefore represent a proper implementation of Article 7(e) of the Directive, which reads as follows:

> The producer shall not be liable as a result of this Directive if he proves:
>
> ...
>
> (e) that the state of scientific and technical knowledge at the time when he put the product into circulation was not such as to enable the existence of the defect to be discovered.

Compare this to s 4(1)(e) of the CPA 1987, under which a defendant must show:

> that the state of scientific and technical knowledge at the relevant time was not such that a producer of products of the same description as the product in question might be expected to have discovered the defect if it had existed in his products while they were under his control.

The Commission's point was that the wording of s 4(1)(e) demands less of producers because what they can be expected to discover is a lower bar than what is *possible* for them to discover. The UK version also narrows the field of discoverability to those producers in a particular industry, not

---

30 *Commission v United Kingdom* [1997] All ER (EC) 481.

producers generally. However, the European Court of Justice found that the UK transposition of the defence did not amount to an infringement of the Directive because there was no inconsistency in substance between the two versions of the provision, and there was no evidence (because there was no case law) that the UK intended to implement the defence by looking to the subjective knowledge of producers. The High Court has since decided *A v National Blood Authority*, and Burton J's reading of the defence in s 4(1)(e) would undoubtedly have pleased both the European Commission and the ECJ.[31] In response to the National Blood Authority's argument that it should be able to avail itself of the development risks defence because at the relevant time there was no means of identifying the defective blood and removing it from supply, the judge held that this is not relevant so long as the risk itself is known. In his view, the Directive aimed to put the unknown product risks on users, and known product risks on producers. Allowing the National Blood Authority to rely on a known risk in establishing a defence would therefore contravene the objective of the statutory scheme. Although it was not relevant in that case, the legislation does in fact go further and include within the defence not just risks which are known, but also risks which are knowable. What exactly is meant by knowable is something which was considered explicitly by Advocate General Tesauro in *Commission v UK*:[32] the defence does not fail to apply wherever there is some knowledge somewhere in the world, but only where that knowledge is accessible to the defendant. This will be a matter to be assessed on the merits of each particular case, but the tenor of the regime suggests that lack of accessibility will only assist a defendant where the relevant knowledge is available solely in obscure, niche, or far-flung locations.[33]

PROBLEM QUESTION TECHNIQUE

It further claims that there was at that time no research or data available to suggest a different plant response. In actual fact, it turns out that a substance very similar in chemical make-up to the Interseed fertiliser had been used on the island of Tikopia (a small island in the South Pacific) for six successive years prior to the release of Interseed's formulation. It had resulted in the death of several strains of flowering plants. A team of botanists from Tikopia had written a very detailed account of this course of events including data about their initial soil composition, the amount of fertiliser used and the precise effects this had on the flora. They had submitted this in the form of a letter to GardenersUniverse.com, where it was published in the correspondence section the year before Interseed released its product.

▶ This requires you to assess whether the defendant can avail itself of the development risks defence under s 4(1)(e). This means you need to consider whether the Tikopia research relating to the effect of its chemically similar substance was accessible to the defendant at the time it released it product.

DIFFERENT PERSPECTIVES on the development risks defence

C. Hodges, 'Development Risks: Unanswered Questions' (1998) 61 MLR 560

Hodges is critical of the wording of the defence in the Directive itself. Discoverability is, in his view, a concept which sets so high a bar that the defence is unworkable if interpreted literally. If the defence is not to undermine any incentives for producers to innovate (and he makes the point that much innovation

---

31 Not least because he referred directly to the Directive, rather than to the CPA, in his analysis.
32 [1997] All ER (EC) 481.
33 Publication in Manchuria was the example given by the Advocate General.

is carried out by small and medium enterprises, on whom broad liability could have a significant impact), it needs to be read as including an element of reasonableness in terms of balancing resources and costs. Hodges criticises the reasoning of the European Court of Justice in *Commission v UK* for failing to have proper regard for the way in which scientific knowledge exists and develops: knowledge of a certain set of scientific facts which might relate in some way to a product does not necessarily equate to knowledge about the way in which that product might be defective. Since such knowledge develops incrementally and not in a straight line, he argues for an interpretation of the development risks defence which does not require a producer to 'prove that the defect was undiscoverable on the basis of the most advanced level of scientific and technical knowledge'.

M. Mildred and G. Howells, 'Comment on "Development Risks: Unanswered Questions"' (1998) 61 MLR 570

Mildred and Howells take an avowedly different view in this, their comment directly on Hodges' article. Their position has more sympathy with the position of consumers (which, they argue, given the title of the OLA 1987, is more appropriate) than it does with the effects of the regime on producers. In fact, they suggest that, in line with some other European member states, the defence could usefully be completely removed from the regime. One of the reasons offered in support of this position is that, under the CPA 1987, consumers already bear the burden of having to prove that a product is defective and that it caused the damage of which they complain. A narrow interpretation of a relevant defence is a reasonable counterbalance to this, particularly in an age in which internet-enabled databases will assist producers in accessing a wide range of acquired knowledge and research.

9.5 Limitation

Product liability receives unusual treatment in terms of the limitation of actions – and this has some unfortunate implications. See s 11A of the Limitation Act 1980.

KEY LEGISLATION

Limitation Act 1980

11A   Actions in respect of defective products

(1)   This section shall apply to an action for damages by virtue of any provision of Part I of the Consumer Protection Act 1987.

(2)   None of the time limits given in the preceding provisions of this Act shall apply to an action to which this section applies.

(3)   An action to which this section applies shall not be brought after the expiration of the period of ten years from the relevant time, within the meaning of section 4 of the said Act of 1987; and this subsection shall operate to extinguish a right of action and shall do so whether or not that right of action had accrued, or time under the following provisions of this Act had begun to run, at the end of the said period of ten years.

(4)   Subject to subsection (5) below, an action to which this section applies in which the damages claimed by the plaintiff consist of or include damages in respect of personal injuries to the plaintiff or any other person or loss of or damage to any property, shall not be brought after the expiration of the period of three years from whichever is the later of—

(a) the date on which the cause of action accrued; and

(b) the date of knowledge of the injured person or, in the case of loss of or damage to property, the date of knowledge of the plaintiff or (if earlier) of any person in whom his cause of action was previously vested.

...

There are two principal points to take from s 11A of the Limitation Act 1980. First, under s 11A(4), actions for personal injuries and property damage caused by defective products must be brought within three years of the cause of action accruing. 'Accruing' for these purposes means either when the damage is caused, or when it becomes reasonably discoverable by the claimant.[34] This is not an unusual limitation for contract and tort claims, but it is then coupled with a 'long-stop' period under s 11A(3) of ten years *after the product was put into circulation*. Significantly, the wording of this section states that, after the expiration of the ten-year period, the right of action is 'extinguished'. This *is* unusual in the context of contract and tort because limitation usually operates to bar the remedy but not the right. In other words, limitation does not normally alter the claimant's legal rights; it just prevents her from enforcing them. Section 11A(3), however, actually removes the right itself, and this effect was expressly mandated by Article 11 of the Product Liability Directive. Add to this the fact that product liability claims are also outside of the application of s 33 of the Limitation Act 1980, which means that the court is unable, in the case of personal injuries, to grant a discretionary extension to the limitation period, and we see that limitation periods can be very limiting indeed for product liability claimants. The claimant in *O'Byrne v Aventis Pasteur MSD Ltd* [2010][35] experienced this acutely. Having suffered brain damage following a vaccination, the claimant alleged that the vaccine had been defective and had caused his injuries. However, in the first instance, the batch number of the vaccine he received was incorrectly associated with the defendant's subsidiary, rather than the defendant itself, and proceedings issued accordingly. It was only after the expiration of the ten-year long-stop period that the mistake came to light, and the claimant then tried to substitute the defendant for its subsidiary. Following two separate references on the matter to the European Court of Justice, the Supreme Court finally decided against the claimant, and refused his request to substitute a defendant after the end of the long-stop period.

The point of this long-stop is of course to prevent producers from being exposed to liability a long time after they have put their products into circulation. Given the strictness of the rest of the regime,[36] this could be regarded as a means of balancing out the interests of producers and users. After all, producers exposed to excessive liability for an indeterminate time will have fewer incentives to research, innovate and create.

---

34   See s 14 of the Limitation Act 1980.

35   [2010] UKSC 23.

36   Note also that s 7 prevents defendants from limiting or excluding their liability for defective products. Contributory negligence is, however, applicable to claims under the CPA 1987 – see s 6(4).

PROBLEM QUESTION TECHNIQUE

Nine years previously, Duleepa had bought a new strain of fertiliser from Interseed. At the time she bought it, it had been on the market for two years. Since then, she has applied it to the soil in her principal show garden every season. Her roses have been declining in bloom quality ever since, but it only occurs to her and Frieda this summer that the decline started at around the same time that they began to apply the Interseed fertiliser to their soil.

▸ If Duleepa bought the product nine years ago, and it had already been on the market for two years at that point, the long-stop period under s 11A(3) means that her right to claim is time-barred.

■ VIEWPOINT

Do you think the limitation rules for product liability are too restrictive? Or are they appropriate for a strict liability regime? Bear the discussion below in mind when you conduct your analysis.

Strict liability can be regarded, particularly in contrast to negligence liability, as being 'harsh' or as holding defendants out as hostages to bad luck. Remember, though, that when evaluating legal frameworks, it is always instructive to consider the interests of all parties involved. Negligence liability serves several purposes; chief amongst them are the compensation of certain forms of loss and the optimisation of risk-taking amongst members of a civil society. Strict liability, on the other hand, usually has very different purposes, not least because it is applied in areas in which the need for compensation is elevated above the need to take into account the nature of the defendant's behaviour. As Peter Cane has said:

> Philosophical discussions of responsibility often seem to assume that strict liability is responsibility in the absence of fault. However, legal regimes of strict liability are typically created in order to improve protection of the interests of potential plaintiffs … an important justification for strict legal liability is to increase the chance that those at fault will be held liable in the face of difficulties of proof … responsibility for fault rests on a judgment that the responsible person failed to meet a specified standard of conduct, whereas strict liability rests on no such judgment … Fault liability is liability for conduct that fails to measure up to relevant specified standards of conduct. Strict liability is liability for conduct regardless of whether it falls short of specified standards of conduct.[37]

In dealing with potential claims under the CPA 1987, it is a good idea to be systematic in approaching your analysis. Unusually for tort (although in common with occupiers' liability), you will need to have more focus on statutory provisions than you will on case law. Whilst the small amount of case law that exists in this area is essential for you to use in order to interpret the language of the statute, the building blocks of your analysis need to come from the Act. The following diagram provides a clear framework for ensuring that you examine all the relevant elements of a claim.

---

37 P. Cane, 'Responsibility and Fault' in P. Cane and J. Gardner (eds), *Relating to Responsibility* (Hart Publishing, 2001), 100.

☐ Has DAMAGE been caused to something other than the product itself?

☐ Is the PRODUCT goods or electricity, whether in its own right, or incorporated into another product?

☐ Did the defendant PRODUCER manufacture, process or abstract the product, put its own brand on it, or import it from outside the member States of Europe? Alternatively, was the PRODUCER a supplier of a product who failed to identify within a reasonable time the person who supplied the good to it?

☐ Is the product DEFECTIVE in that its safety is not such as persons generally are entitled to expect?

☐ Can the defendant avail itself of a DEFENCE? Most notably, was knowledge of the risk of harm generated by the product accessible to producers in that industry at the time of supply?

☐ Has the claim been brought within the LIMITATION period of three years from the accrual of the cause of action and within ten years of the product being put into circulation?

Figure 9.2: Consumer Protection Act 1987 Checklist

9.6 CHAPTER SUMMARY

This chapter has dealt with the three ways in which claimants can recover for loss or damage resulting from defective products: a claim in contract, common law negligence and under the CPA 1987. Because contract law is covered in detail separately on your law course, and the principles of common law claims have been covered by the chapters of this book dealing with negligence, the greater part of this chapter's focus has been on the CPA 1987 and its subsequent interpretation by the courts. It is clear from this analysis that the statutory scheme differs significantly from the common law approach. In common law negligence, the behaviour of the defendant is the concern of the court. In the CPA 1987, however, the conduct of the defendant yields to the safety of the product, and liability will attach to defendants wherever the safety of their products is not such as persons generally are entitled to expect. In evaluating the safety of products, which has been acknowledged by the courts to be a relative concept, judicial reasoning has distinguished between defects in design (standard products) and defects in manufacture (non-standard products), making it clear that both can be actionable. Whilst it is absolutely clear that the statutory scheme gives rise to a stricter liability than a common law action in negligence, it also appears to be the case that the scheme is less strict than envisaged by those who formulated the Directive on which the CPA 1987 is based. It has, however, survived a challenge on this basis by the European Commission and remains good law. In any event, the parameters of the CPA 1987 will be defined to a large extent by the way in which its terms are interpreted by the courts. The scarce case law generated by the statute does not really suggest that UK courts are disposed to unduly favouring the interests of producers over those of users.

FURTHER READING

D. Fairgrieve and G. Howells, 'Rethinking Product Liability: A Missing Element in the European Commission's Third Review of the Product Liability Directive' (2007) 70(6) *MLR* 962

C. Hodges, 'Product Liability: Suppliers, Limitation and Mistake' (2006) 122 *LQR* 393

G. Howells and M. Mildred, 'Infected Blood: Defect and Discoverability. A First Exposition of the EC Product Liability Directive' (2002) 65(1) *MLR* 95

C. Johnston QC, 'A Personal (and Selective) Introduction to Product Liability Law' (2012) *JPI Law*, 1

C. Newdick, 'The Future of Negligence in Product Liability' (1987) 103 *LQR* 288

J. Stapleton, 'Bugs in Anglo-American Product Liability' in D. Fairgrieve (ed.), *Product Liability in Comparative Perspective* (CUP, 2005), 295

10 NUISANCE AND THE RULE IN *RYLANDS V FLETCHER*

LEARNING OBJECTIVES

By the end of this chapter, you should be able to:

- Understand what is significant about a tort to protect interests in land
- Map out the parameters of the torts of private nuisance, public nuisance, the rule in *Rylands v Fletcher* and trespass to land, and explain distinctions between them
- Recognise the distinctions between private nuisance and negligence
- Demonstrate how the rule in *Rylands v Fletcher* fits within the scheme of protecting interests in land, i.e. as a sub-species of private nuisance
- Analyse what the rule in *Rylands v Fletcher* means in a contemporary context
- Establish what amounts to an unreasonable interference with interests in land
- Give the particular remedies applicable to actions in private nuisance and apply the latest common law principles to determine what these might be on a given set of facts

CHAPTER CONTENTS

10.1 Introduction	218
10.2 What is private nuisance?	219
10.2.1 Title to sue and nature of damage suffered	219
10.2.2 What amounts to an unreasonable interference	221
10.3 Remedies	226
10.3.1 Injunction v damages	226
10.3.2 Abatement	229
10.4 Defences in private nuisance	229
10.4.1 Prescription	229
10.4.2 Act of a stranger	230
10.4.3 Statutory authority	230
10.5 The rule in *Rylands v Fletcher*	231
10.5.1 Defences to the rule in *Rylands v Fletcher*	234
10.6 Public nuisance: a very different thing	237
10.7 Trespass to land	239
10.8 Chapter summary	240
Further reading	240
Roadmap	241

PROBLEM QUESTION

Ridhi buys a house on a new residential estate in Streetsville. Sergei buys the houses either side of Ridhi's. He lives in one of the houses himself, and lets the other out to Trey. Behind the back gardens of this row of houses is Ursula's abattoir. The area used to be highly agricultural, but as farming became increasingly unprofitable, local farmers sold much of their land to property developers. The local supply to Ursula's abattoir has therefore dwindled. Ursula has managed to stay in business, however, by bringing animals from farms further afield. Owing to the increased distances that now need to be travelled, farmers send their animals to her in larger groups, so she has more live (and noisy) animals on site than she did before. Since it is cheaper for Ursula to use her electricity at night, she receives her deliveries (which need to be electronically tagged and sorted) between 8pm and midnight on six days of the week. The animal delivery trucks are very large and loud, and the livestock they unload generates high levels of noise and unpleasant smells. As a result, Ridhi, Sergei and Trey find that they are unable to enjoy sitting in their gardens in the evenings. Trey, who is allergic to cows, starts to suffer from seizures. Sergei has been trying to train his pet ferrets, who live in a cage in his garden, to dance. He is hoping for success on 'Streetsville's Got Talent'. The temperament of the ferrets, however, is such that they don't feel like dancing when they are regularly exposed to loud noises, such as those emanating from Ursula's property.

Ridhi, Trey and Sergei all experience poor wi-fi speeds because the presence of Ursula's abattoir has prevented any provider from installing high-speed cables. Ridhi's daughter, Violet, often gets bored and frustrated with the slow wi-fi and so occupies herself by squirting Trey's roses with her Super Soaker water pistol over their dividing fence. This regularly knocks all the flower heads off.

Sergei has spent hundreds of thousands of pounds on a top-of-the-range ferret cage. It is the most expensive model available and is marketed as being 100% escape and tamper-proof. One of its layers of security, however, is a real-time sensor feed to a central monitor. The poor wi-fi signal delays the feed, meaning that the central monitor is not notified of a circuit breach, caused by one of the ferret's collars getting caught on the lockpad. The interference confuses the lock into disengaging, and Sergei's ferrets (of which there are 50) escape into Ridhi's garden, where they destroy her plants and the expensive camping equipment she has just purchased. Ridhi had always loved Sergei's ferrets, regularly asking about them. In fact, she had encouraged him to buy his last litter from a friend of hers who breeds them.

Meanwhile, the drains connected to Trey's house have become blocked, and Streetsville council is digging up the road to fix them. On excavation, the workers find several significant problems, all of which will take a long time to rectify. The road to Ridhi's and Sergei's houses is therefore unpassable for three months. There are five houses on the road but, because of where the works are, only Ridhi's and Sergei's are affected. Ridhi does not drive and so does not mind very much, but Sergei works from home as a physiotherapist, and many of his clients, who can no longer park nearby, have taken their business elsewhere.

10.1 Introduction

The crucial thing to understand in relation to nuisance is that it is a tort to protect interests in land. It is, therefore, completely separate from the tort of negligence and, as such, has very different rules, requirements and results. First, an action in the tort of nuisance is only available to those who have a sufficient interest in the land affected. Also, it is not possible to claim in the tort of nuisance for personal injury, since this does not amount to an interference with an interest in land. The remedies for nuisance also differ from those generally granted in negligence actions: the default remedy in nuisance is an injunction, rather than compensatory damages (although the latter might be available alternatively or in addition). This is because, in general, if someone is interfering with your ability to exercise your rights over your land, such as emitting noxious fumes which prevent you from being able to sit in your garden, what you really want as a claimant is for the action to stop. This is what an injunction does, by giving the defendant an order from the court. Technically, there are two principal types of nuisance: private and public. The latter is not strictly a tort but will be dealt with briefly in this chapter, as it is in most tort courses, for the sake of contrasting it with private nuisance. The material which follows will also explain how trespass to land fits within the common law scheme of protecting interests in land. Finally, no analysis of private nuisance would be complete without an account of the rule in *Rylands v Fletcher*, a nominate tort which has come to form a subset of private nuisance, with specific application to isolated escapes resulting from ultra-hazardous uses of land.

10.2 What is private nuisance?

One of the principal concerns of the courts when dealing with the tort of private nuisance[1] is the balancing of interests between neighbouring landowners. It is inevitable, particularly in the relatively crowded landmass that makes up England and Wales, that the exercise of the right to use any land will to some extent, and sometimes, interfere with neighbours' rights to do the same. The idea of the tort of private nuisance, therefore, is to protect those with interests in land from unreasonable interferences with it. It is, therefore, this concept of *unreasonable interference* that is pivotal to common law reasoning on the subject.

10.2.1 Title to sue and nature of damage suffered

Given that private nuisance is a tort to protect interests in land, it is an action which is only available to those with interests in land, and only for damage caused to those interests. *It is not, therefore, available to remedy personal injuries.*

The next case is one of the most important nuisance cases in recent times: not only does it contain a broad restatement by the House of Lords of the general principles of private nuisance; it reaffirms the requirement for a claimant to have a sufficient interest in the land affected[2] and makes clear that claimants cannot recover in private nuisance for personal injuries. These two points clearly set the parameters of the tort and emphasise its exclusive proprietary focus. *Hunter* is an invaluable judgment to read and to be familiar with in order to understand this tort, and to engage with its implications and policy considerations.

KEY CASE

Hunter v Canary Wharf Ltd [1997] AC 655

This case arose out of the extensive construction work involved in renovating Canary Wharf in London. The action in nuisance was brought in relation to interference with television reception caused by the construction of the Canary Wharf Tower. In an age before cable and wi-fi, this had the potential significantly to disrupt people's enjoyment of their homes. The claimants appealed against the Court of Appeal's decision that no action lay in private nuisance for interference with a television signal caused by the presence of a building on neighbouring land. The defendants cross-appealed against the Court of Appeal's ruling that the mere occupation of property as a home entitled an occupier to sue in private nuisance.

The House of Lords reaffirmed that a person who had no right in the affected land could not sue for private nuisance, following *Malone v Laskey* [1907],[3] and overruling *Khorasandjian v Bush* [1993][4] (in so far as it decided that a mere licensee could sue in private nuisance). The only exception to this that the House of Lords was willing to recognise is where a claimant, although unable to prove title to the land in question, is nonetheless in exclusive possession of it. Nor could a person sue who had suffered anything except an injury to an interest in land.

With regards to the interference with television reception, the Court held that an owner was entitled to put up whatever she

---

1   And its sub-species, the rule in *Rylands v Fletcher* – see below at 10.5.
2   Although there remains the potential for a claimant to challenge this under the European Convention on Human Rights, Article 8(1): 'Everyone has the right to respect for his private and family life, his home and his correspondence' (Human Rights Act 1988, Sch 1, Pt 1). After all, a house is a 'home' to more people than just those with a proprietary interest in the estate.
3   [1907] 2 KB 141.
4   [1993] QB 727.

chose on her own land even though this might interfere with her neighbour's reception or view. Whilst both such interferences might be highly inconvenient and detrimental to the land and its value, they nevertheless give rise to no action in private nuisance. Were it to be otherwise, landowners might not be able to put up any substantial structures at all, and this would amount to too great a restriction of property owners' autonomy.

The core principles of *Hunter* were reiterated by the Court of Appeal very recently in the following case. This case is perhaps notable for the way in which an undoubtedly troublesome and life-affecting interference was nonetheless deemed by the Court not to amount to a private nuisance. As in *Hunter*, the reasoning in this case focuses on the balancing act that society has to perform between the competing interests in different uses of land: protecting one party's right not to suffer an interference will almost always infringe another's right to use her own land as she wishes. It is easy to see, particularly in a crowded space such as London, why making the overlooking of another's property an actionable nuisance would quickly lead to a huge amount of litigation as well as significant restrictions on development. Note that the Court does *not* say that the flat owners' interests should not be legally protected; just that private nuisance is not the most appropriate vehicle through which to do so.

KEY CASE

Fearn and others v Board of Trustees of the Tate Gallery [2020] 2 WLR 1081

Flat owners here sought an injunction to close part of the Tate Modern art gallery's new viewing platform on the basis that it overlooked their living spaces. Visitors to the platform frequently looked into their flats, which had floor-to-ceiling windows, and had also been known to use binoculars and cameras to do so. The flat owners' argument was that the use of certain sections of the viewing gallery unreasonably interfered with their interests in their flats, and therefore amounted to a nuisance. They also argued that the use of that viewing gallery infringed their rights under Article 8 of the European Convention of Human Rights, and that the Tate, as a public authority, was therefore in breach of s 6 of the Human Rights Act 1998.

The Court of Appeal dismissed the flat owners' appeal on the basis that the overwhelming weight of judicial authority indicated that the mere overlooking of a property was not capable of giving rise to a cause of action in private nuisance, and there was no existing authority to suggest that it could. The Court pointed to *Hunter v Canary Wharf Ltd* as an authoritative demonstration of the point that the law does not provide redress for every annoyance to a landowner. In deciding whether to extend private nuisance to cover overlooking,

the Court considered that there exist other ways of protecting landowners from overlooking, such as planning laws and control. In essence, the issue in cases of overlooking is closer in substance to invasion of privacy more than it is damage to interests in property, and there are other laws which protect this interest. Ultimately, the Court of Appeal felt that it would be more appropriate for Parliament to formulate a means of protecting landowners from overlooking, should it be deemed appropriate, than for it to extend the tort of private nuisance to do so.

Similarly, there had never been a Strasbourg case in which it had been held that mere overlooking amounted to a breach of Article 8. In reaching its conclusion on this basis, the Court went on to consider, in *obiter dicta*, that it would not be constructive to try and overlay the tort of private nuisance with Article 8 rights in this respect, principally because private nuisance is a tort exclusively to protect interests in land, whereas Article 8 protects anyone who has a reasonable expectation of privacy. Since the considerations involved in assessing these two forms of protection do not overlap, it would be counter-productive to try and align them in the way suggested by the flat owners in this case.

PROBLEM QUESTION TECHNIQUE

Ridhi buys a house on a new residential estate in Streetsville. Sergei buys the houses either side of Ridhi's. He lives in one of the houses himself, and lets the other out to Trey...

Trey, who is allergic to cows, starts to suffer from seizures ...

Ridhi, Trey and Sergei all experience poor wi-fi speeds because the presence of Ursula's abattoir has prevented any provider from installing high-speed cables. Ridhi's daughter, Violet, often gets bored and frustrated with the slow wi-fi ...

▸ First, you need to consider the ability of the various parties to sue in private nuisance: do they all have the requisite interest in land?

▸ You then need to deal with the type of damage suffered by each: personal injury and poor wi-fi. This requires an application of *Hunter*.

▸ All of these issue go to the heart of nuisance as a tort to protect interests in land, so remember to keep that at the forefront of your mind when answering a problem question.

10.2.2 What amounts to an unreasonable interference?

One of the most common mistakes made by students tackling a question on private nuisance is to miss out the vital step of establishing just what amounts to such a nuisance. It is tempting to jump straight to discussions about remedies and defences, or to limit an enquiry to whether the facts of a question lend themselves better to private nuisance, public nuisance, trespass or the rule in *Rylands v Fletcher*. Remember, however, that, even once you have established that the situation is potentially one to which private nuisance will apply, and before you get as far as remedies and possible defences, you need to establish whether or not an unreasonable interference, amounting to a private nuisance, *has actually occurred*. As ever, you need to do this by applying the relevant case law. On this point, there are several considerations that courts take into account. The list is not exhaustive, and neither is it a list of requirements, all of which need to be satisfied in order to identify a nuisance. Rather, it is a list of indications of what amounts to unreasonable interference. So, you need to be very familiar with these cases and considerations, in order to apply them to any facts with which you are presented.

As outlined above, the proximity of many landowners to their neighbour's land means that some interference is inevitable. Nuisance is not concerned with every such interference, but only those that amount to an interference which is unreasonable, and which the claimant should not be expected to tolerate. Ad hoc interferences, therefore, such as a 21st birthday party that goes on long into the night, or a wedding reception, will not be actionable in private nuisance as individual events. If, however, noisy celebrations go on for many days, or happen frequently, this might well engage the tort of private nuisance. There is no explicit criterion, such as '5 days' or 'music until 4am on three days a week'; rather it is a matter of making analogies with decided cases, in order to establish whether a particular interference is unreasonable in its context.

When deciding what amounts to an unreasonable interference, there are six key areas to take into account:
(1) Duration and extent
(2) Time of day
(3) Locality (only where damage is intangible)
(4) Motivation
(5) Interference with a right
(6) Claimant's hypersensitivity

The sections below consider each of these areas in turn.

10.2.2.1 DURATION AND EXTENT

The longer the interference continues, and/or the higher its level, the more likely it is to be deemed unreasonable.

KEY CASE

Andreae v Selfridge & Co Ltd [1938] Ch 1

The claimant in this case was successful in her action because the defendant's demolition work interfered unreasonably with her hotel business. The Court of Appeal recognised that the defendant was entitled to carry out demolition work in its own property, but it made the point that such activities should not be carried out without due regard for the interests of neighbours, and that the methods and manner of that work should be such as is reasonable, given the equipment and practices available at any given time. On the facts of this particular case, the Court felt that the defendant was charging ahead with its demolition work, trying to complete it as quickly and crudely as possible and that, had it been done more carefully, the interference with the claimant's interests need not have been unreasonable.

10.2.2.2 TIME OF DAY

The more anti-social the time of day at which the interference occurs, the more likely it is to be deemed unreasonable. Note that this consideration is particularly context-specific: what is regarded as unreasonably early in, say, an area of student accommodation is unlikely to be regarded as unreasonable in an agricultural area. Similarly, noise interference until late evening in a city centre is to be expected, but less so in a rural village (see 'Locality' below).

KEY CASE

De Keyser's Royal Hotel v Spicer Bros Ltd (1914) 30 TLR 257

Here, the defendant was pile-driving in order to prepare foundations for a building. The action was brought because it carried out this activity through the night, and the claimant was consequently unable to sleep. The Court granted an injunction to prevent the defendant from continuing its activity, but only between the hours of 10pm and 6:30am, thereby indicating that it was this element of the work that was unreasonable, not the entire activity.[5]

PROBLEM QUESTION TECHNIQUE

Ursula has managed to stay in business, however, by bringing animals from farms further afield. Owing to the increased distances that now need to be travelled, farmers send their animals to her in larger groups, so she has more live (and noisy) animals on site than she did before. Since it is cheaper for Ursula to use her electricity at night, she receives her deliveries (which need to be electronically tagged and sorted) between 8pm and midnight on six days of the week. The animal delivery trucks are very

---

5   See also *Halsey v Esso Petroleum* [1961] 2 All ER 145.

large and loud, and the livestock they unload generates high levels of noise and unpleasant smells. As a result, Ridhi, Sergei and Trey find that they are unable to enjoy sitting in their gardens in the evenings.

▶ Here, you need to consider both the duration and extent of the interferences, and the time of day at which they occur, using the cases outlined above.

10.2.2.3 LOCALITY (ONLY WHERE DAMAGE IS INTANGIBLE)

The nature of the locality in which the claimant's and the defendant's property is situated can play a role in establishing whether the interference is an unreasonable one. This is not an independent consideration, but has a bearing on how other elements of an interference are evaluated. What is reasonable in one location, for instance, in terms of noise, fumes or smells, might be unreasonable in another: 'What would be a nuisance in Belgrave Square would not necessarily be so in Bermondsey.'[6]

Importantly, the nature of any given locality can change over time – see the Supreme Court decision in *Coventry v Lawrence* [2014], below.[7] The locality criterion is important in terms of a court's ability to balance competing interests: if a claimant has chosen to live in an industrial area, she should expect more industrial effects than if she has chosen to live in the middle of the rural countryside. Note, however, that, whilst the effect of this consideration is that claimants should expect a higher level of intangible interference in some locations than others, an interference which has a tangible effect on property can never be justified by the nature of the locality.

KEY CASE

St Helen's Smelting Co v Tipping (1865) 11 HL Cas 642, HL

Emissions from the defendant's copper smelting factory damaged the claimant's crops, trees and plants. In response to the defendant's argument that the area was an industrial one, and that such emissions were therefore an intrinsic characteristic of the locality, the Court held that the locality consideration was irrelevant where the damage caused to the claimant's interests was tangible.

KEY CASE

Gillingham BC v Medway (Chatham) Dock Ltd [1993] QB 343

The claimants were residents whose interests in land were affected by the activities of a local commercial dock which operated every hour of the day and night. Their action in private nuisance was unsuccessful because, in the view of Buckley J, the development of what had been a naval dockyard into a 24-hour commercial dock had changed the nature of the locality, with the result that the disruption caused by its operation was a reasonable part of the local environment.

PROBLEM QUESTION TECHNIQUE

Behind the back gardens of this row of houses is Ursula's abattoir. The area used to be highly agricultural, but as farming became increasingly unprofitable, local farmers sold much of their land to property developers ...

---

6 Thesiger LJ in *Sturges v Bridgman* (1879) 11 Ch D 852, 865.
7 [2014] UKSC 13 – see 10.3.1 (Injunction v damages).

> ▸ This is a question of locality, requiring an application of the cases outlined in the section directly above. Remember to distinguish between tangible and intangible damage for the purposes of this criterion.

■ VIEWPOINT

How fair do you think the locality consideration is, given that, for many people, the location of where they live might not be a matter of pure choice, but dictated instead by financial demands and/or logistical work reasons?

10.2.2.4 MOTIVATION

The reason for the defendant's behaviour can be relevant to the reasonableness inquiry. At one end of the spectrum, the courts have decided that making 'normal use' of one's property will not amount to a nuisance. At the other end, there is clear authority that creating an interference with malicious intent will be a very strong indication that the interference is an unreasonable one. This makes sense: nuisance is about the balancing of competing property interests and establishing what is reasonable. It is very hard to argue that the deliberate creation of an interference with a neighbour's interests is reasonable or an inevitable consequence of using one's land in the ordinary way.

KEY CASE

Southwark LBC v Mills [2001] 1 AC 1

The claimant in this case was complaining about the fact that her neighbours' use of their flats amounted to a nuisance because the poor soundproofing between properties meant that she could hear all of their day-to-day activities. Since, however, the neighbours were merely going about their lives and using their property in the normal way, there was no nuisance.

KEY CASE

Christie v Davey [1893] 1 Ch 316

The defendant lived next door to a music teacher, whose lessons caused a noise that annoyed him. In response, the defendant took to banging loudly on household implements and the party wall, and wailing in a purported imitation of the music emanating from his neighbour's house. This maliciously created interference was held to amount to an actionable nuisance.

KEY CASE

Hollywood Silver Fox Farm v Emmet [1936] 2 KB 468

The claimant in this case bred rare silver foxes. The defendant, its neighbour, deliberately discharged shotguns at the border of his land nearest to the pens, thereby interrupting the foxes' breeding. Since this was done with the intention of interfering with the breeding programme, it was deemed to be an unreasonable interference and therefore an actionable nuisance.

PROBLEM QUESTION TECHNIQUE

Ridhi's daughter, Violet, often gets bored and frustrated with the slow wi-fi and so occupies herself by squirting Trey's roses with her Super Soaker water pistol over their dividing fence. This regularly knocks all the flower heads off.

▶ This requires an examination of Violet's motivation, in the light of the cases listed in this section. There is also, however, a question of the nature of the interference, which is direct rather than indirect, which should make you think about trespass rather than nuisance.[8]

10.2.2.5 INTERFERENCE WITH A RIGHT

It is clear that, in order to amount to an actionable private nuisance, the defendant's activity must interfere with an established right of the claimant's.

KEY CASE

Bradford Corp v Pickles [1895] AC 587

The defendant wanted the claimant to purchase his land. In order to try and compel it to do so, he drained his land so as to prevent water percolating beneath it from reaching the claimant's land. Although he therefore acted intentionally and maliciously to create an interference, his actions were nonetheless not actionable in private nuisance because the claimant had no right to receive the water supply in the first place.

10.2.2.6 CLAIMANT'S HYPERSENSITIVITY

It was once clear that an interference would not be deemed by a court to be a nuisance because its level of interference had an unreasonable effect simply by virtue of that's claimant's particular sensitivity. Unless the interference would be unreasonable in the context of a user of average sensitivities, it would not have been a nuisance. This was a longstanding rule in the tort of private nuisance. Relatively recently, however, the notion of 'hypersensitivity' in its own right has been deemed to be 'outmoded', and to be dealt with better as an aspect of foreseeability. Bear in mind, then, that 'hypersensitivity' is a dynamic, rather than a static, concept.

KEY CASE

Robinson v Kilvert (1889) 41 Ch D 88

The claimant stored brown paper in its premises above those of the defendant. The defendant's use of its premises generated hot and dry air, which permeated the claimant's floor above and damaged the paper stored there. The claimant was unable to recover on these facts because, in the view of the court, it had chosen to use its premises in a delicate manner, and could not thereby impose a higher expectation of behaviour on its neighbour by doing so.

Note that in *McKinnon Industries v Walker* [1951],[9] it was confirmed that, where the interference would have amounted to a nuisance even to a non-sensitive user of land, the hypersensitive user could not only recover, but could recover the full extent of its loss, despite the fact that its loss

---

8   See 10.7 (Trespass to land) below.
9   (1951) 3 DLR 577.

was greater because of its hypersensitivity. In that case, the claimant's hypersensitive orchids were damaged by fumes and smuts from the defendant's factory. It was established, however, that since even non-delicate flowers would have been adversely affected by the emissions, the claimant could succeed, and could recover for the full loss of losing the particularly valuable orchids.

The cases in the 'Key Cases' above now need to be read and understood in the light of the following Court of Appeal judgment, which suggests that the relevance of the claimant's level of sensitivity is now to be evaluated as an aspect of foreseeability.

KEY CASE

Morris v Network Rail [2004] EWCA Civ 172

Here, the defendant's railway line interfered with the claimant's use of sensitive recording equipment in his studio. The defendant, in appealing against its liability in nuisance, argued that the extent of interference on these facts was a result of the claimant's hypersensitivity, and that it could not reasonably have foreseen such damage occurring to this claimant as a result of its operations. The Court of Appeal allowed the appeal, taking a broader approach than the traditional inquiry into hypersensitivity, preferring instead to look at foreseeability as an element of reasonableness. Although it accepted that the use of sensitive recording equipment was not a hypersensitive use of property in a contemporary setting, the Court nonetheless found that it was not reasonable to expect Network Rail to have foreseen such damage occurring, given the information available to it at the time.

Hypersensitivity remains an important consideration in establishing whether an interference has been unreasonable. The *Morris* judgment, however, indicates that courts will evaluate such potential hypersensitivity in a contemporary light.

PROBLEM QUESTION TECHNIQUE

Sergei has been trying to train his pet ferrets, who live in a cage in his garden, to dance. He is hoping for success on 'Streetsville's Got Talent'. The temperament of the ferrets, however, is such that they don't feel like dancing when they are regularly exposed to loud noises, such as those emanating from Ursula's property.

▶ This is a question of potential hypersensitivity in relation to the ferrets, and now needs to be dealt with under the principle enunciated in *Robinson*, and through the lens of foreseeability in *Network Rail*, above.

10.3 Remedies

10.3.1 Injunction v damages

As outlined above, the default remedy in the tort of private nuisance is an injunction, rather than the award of compensatory damages. This is because, generally, claimants who are experiencing an interference with their interests in their land want that interference to stop, rather than wanting to be given money in exchange for their suffering, and an injunction enables a court to compel a defendant to behave in a certain way.[10] In recent times, the bright line nature of this rule has been somewhat diluted, at least in theory, by the decision of *Coventry v Lawrence* (see below), in which the Supreme Court stated that a court's discretion to award damages instead of an injunction should not be fettered. Even before the decision in *Coventry*, there were situations in which courts did not think it appropriate to injunct the defendant's behaviour. In the following case, this was because the interest of national security was deemed to be superior to private property interests.

KEY CASE

Dennis v Ministry of Defence [2003] EWHC 793 (QB)

The claimant owned and lived on an estate adjacent to RAF Wittering and alleged that noise emanating from it constituted a nuisance. Harrier jet pilots were trained at the base, and their aircraft flew directly over the claimant's estate, making a noise that the claimant described as deafening. In addition to alleging that this constituted a nuisance at common law, Dennis also brought a claim under the Human Rights Act 1998 for breach of Article 1, Protocol 1 and Article 8 of the ECHR. The defendant argued that the training was necessary for national security and that nothing could reasonably be done to alter the situation for the better. The defendant further claimed that it had acquired the right to commit nuisance by prescription because it had carried out this activity since 1969. The case raised, therefore, the question of the extent to which the public interest could amount to a defence to a claim in nuisance.

Buckley J in the High Court held that, whilst the noise emanating from the military base constituted a nuisance, the public interest required that the training activity should nonetheless continue. Both national security and the cost of moving the military base meant that the public interest here weighed against the claimant's private rights. It would not be just, however, to give effect to the public interest without compensating the claimant. Since there had been an interference with the claimant's human rights under Article 1, Protocol 1 and Article 8 (the peaceful enjoyment of property and the right to private and family life respectively), an award of damages at common law would be appropriate in lieu of an injunction.[11] In acknowledging the exceptional nature of this case, the court awarded damages assessed at £950,000 for the reduction in the market value of the property as a result of the nuisance, for the loss of amenity and for the loss of commercial opportunities consequent upon it. The defendant had not acquired the right to commit a nuisance by prescription because the claimant had not consented to it at any stage.

Particularly since it predates *Coventry*, this is a bold decision by Buckley J. Except for the appealing, but legally quaint, view of the majority in the earlier case of *Miller v Jackson* [1977][12] that an injunction should not be used to prevent a village club from playing cricket, the position pre-*Coventry* clearly

---

10   Specifically, a prohibitory injunction is the means by which a court orders a defendant to desist from certain actions or behaviour.

11   Perhaps surprisingly, the Human Rights Act 1998 has so far had very little effect on the common law of nuisance. In *Marcic v Thames Water Utilities* [2003] UKHL 66, for example, a claim was brought under Article 8 and Article 1 of Protocol 1 (as well as in nuisance) against a public authority for failing to prevent the claimant's home from flooding with foul water during heavy rain. The House of Lords rejected both the common law claim and the claim under the HRA 1998 on the basis that a finding of liability would be inconsistent with the statutory scheme under the Water Industry Act 1991, which provided for an independent regulator to balance competing interests in such situations. See also *Dobson v Thames Water Utilities* [2009] EWCA Civ 28, in which it was held that damages under the 1998 Act would not be necessary where the rights concerned would be protected by a common law action in nuisance.

12   [1977] QB 966.

recognised that injunctions were necessary to stop private individuals from shouldering the burden of the public interest and having to 'take one for the team' by compromising their own property interests for the sake of the many.[13] Now that *Coventry* has been decided, Buckley J's decision appears prescient.

KEY CASE

Coventry v Lawrence [2014] UKSC 13

One defendant operated a speedway and stock car racing stadium that had been functioning since 1976, and another operated a motocross track behind that stadium. Both the speedway racing and the motocross activities had been granted planning permission, and the stock car racing had a certificate of lawful use. In 2006, the claimant moved into a bungalow nearby. The Court of Appeal found that the noise coming from the defendants' activities amounted to a nuisance, and the claimants appealed to the Supreme Court to determine the following issues:

(i) whether a defendant could argue that she had established a prescriptive right to commit what would otherwise be a nuisance by means of noise;

(ii) whether a defendant could rely in her defence on the fact that the claimant 'came to the nuisance';

(iii) whether a defendant could invoke the use made of her premises when assessing the character of the locality;

(iv) whether the grant of planning permission for a particular use had any bearing on whether that use was a nuisance;

(v) what approach a court should adopt when deciding whether to grant an injunction to restrain a nuisance or whether to award damages instead.

The Supreme Court allowed the claimant's appeal, and held the following:

(i) It is possible to obtain by prescription a right to commit what would otherwise be a nuisance by noise.

(ii) It remains the case that a defendant cannot argue in his defence that a claimant moved to the nuisance. It might, however, be possible for a defendant to argue in his defence that, in changing the use of her land, the claimant made the defendant's pre-existing activities into a nuisance.

(iii) A defendant can argue that his activities constitute part of the nature of the locality, but only in relation to any activities which do not in themselves amount to a nuisance. The same is true of other neighbourhood activities.

(iv) The fact that an activity has been the subject of a grant of planning permission does not prevent it from being deemed to be an actionable nuisance. The existence of planning permission might, however, be relevant in deciding whether an activity is of benefit to the wider public, and whether therefore an injunction should be granted.

(v) Whilst it remained the prima facie position that an injunction should be granted as a remedy in private nuisance, the court's discretion to award damages instead should not be fettered by the application of the four tests in *Shelfer v City of London Electric Lighting Co (No 1)* [1895].[14]

(vi) Although it would normally be right to refuse an injunction where those four tests were satisfied, an injunction would not necessarily be granted where those tests were not satisfied (which had historically been the presumption).

(vii) The public interest, i.e. the extent to which others in addition to the claimant were affected by the nuisance, would be relevant to the court's decision as to whether to grant an injunction.

---

13   See below, 'Different Perspectives', for further discussion of the relevance of the public interest to the allocation of liability in private nuisance.

14   [1895] 1 Ch 287.

After *Coventry*, the default position remains that an injunction should be granted, unless the defendant produces enough evidence to show why it should not. Each case needs to be considered on its individual facts and evidence, and Lord Neuberger preferred a continued role for the tests which had been laid down by A.L. Smith LJ in *Shelfer v City of London Electric Lighting Co*:

> (1) If the injury to the plaintiff's legal rights is small, (2) And is one which is capable of being estimated in money, (3) And is one which can be adequately compensated by a small money payment, (4) And the case is one in which it would be oppressive to the defendant to grant an injunction – then damages in substitution for an injunction may be given.[15]

The increased judicial discretion which *Coventry* offers stems from the Supreme Court's direction that damages can still be awarded in lieu of an injunction, even where some of these conditions remain unsatisfied. Before the decision in *Coventry*, these four conditions were regarded as a minimum requirement for a damages award.

■ VIEWPOINT

Should an injunction be the remedy for all private nuisances, other than in very exceptional circumstances? Or do you think defendants should be able to pay compensation and continue to cause a nuisance, effectively 'buying' the right to interfere with another's property interests?

10.3.2 Abatement

This is a potential, non-judicial remedy for nuisance. It is a form of self-help in which claimants do what they can to address the nuisance themselves. Sometimes, it is very simple, such as the cutting of branches overhanging a garden from a neighbouring property, and it is unproblematic as long as the party responsible for the interference does not object (which is what happens in many everyday scenarios). It does, however, expose the abating claimant to the risk of infringing another's property rights and so being liable either for conversion (a tort which protects parties' interests in their personal property)[16] or trespass. The risk of such liability must be balanced against the costs of bringing a legal action for what might be an annoying, but relatively minor, interference with property interests.

10.4 Defences in private nuisance

There are several defences potentially available to defendants in private nuisance.

10.4.1 Prescription

Prescription refers to a defendant's ability to acquire a right to perform certain actions, which would otherwise be unlawful, as a result of having done so for a period of at least 20 years. The defendant must show that, during that time, the activity in question interfered with the claimant's interest in her land. The interference during that time must have been uninterrupted, and have occurred without stealth, without force and without the permission of the landowner. If complaints were made about the activity during

---

15 [1895] 1 Ch. 287, 322-323.

16 If, for instance, one party lops overhanging branches of her neighbour's tree, the neighbour may well have a claim in trespass to goods for damage to his tree, or conversion for any part of the tree that is removed or killed. Trespass to goods provides a remedy where personal property (all property other than land) has been damaged or harmed. Conversion provides a remedy where property belonging to one party has been used by another as her own. For more detail, see S. Green and J. Randall, *The Tort of Conversion* (Hart Publishing, 2009).

the period, but were ignored, prescription cannot be established – the defence requires that the defendant acted as of right. The well-known case that illustrates how difficult it is to establish prescription (and how rare its success is likely to be) is *Sturges v Bridgman* [1879]:[17] the claimant was a doctor who built a consulting room at the bottom of his garden, being aware that his neighbour, who was a confectioner, used large pestles and mortars in his own garden, which were noisy and caused significant vibrations, and had done for more than 20 years. It was only when the claimant started to use his new building, however, that the activities of the defendant caused an interference with the use of his land, leading to his claim in nuisance. The defendant confectioner was unable to rely on the defence of prescription because his actions had not amounted to a nuisance for longer than 20 years.

10.4.2 Act of a stranger

In *Sedleigh-Denfield v O'Callaghan* [1940],[18] the House of Lords ruled that a defendant will be liable for the actions of a trespasser, which lead to the commission of a nuisance, where the defendant adopts or continues that nuisance. In essence, this means that, where a defendant knows about the actions of the trespasser and uses them to her own advantage, or fails to address them where it would be reasonable to do so, the act of a stranger defence will fail. In *Sedleigh-Denfield*, the third party local authority had, without permission, installed a drainage pipe under the defendant's land, but had done so without properly protecting it against blockages. When it blocked and led to flooding of the claimant's land, the defendant was held liable in nuisance because he had relied on the pipe to drain his land, and had taken no steps to prevent it interfering with his neighbour's interest in land. This approach is not limited to the physical state of the land: landowners, for instance, can also be liable for the actions of tenants, or even for the actions of those present on their land whom they have failed to evict. In *Lippiatt v South Gloucestershire CC* [2000],[19] for example, the defendant council was held liable for the repeated acts of destruction carried out to neighbouring properties by travellers resident on its land.[20]

10.4.3 Statutory authority

This is the most significant, and in principle straightforward, of the defences available for nuisance. Basically, if the action in question has been authorised by Parliament, and has been carried out in a reasonable way, it will not give rise to a successful action in nuisance. Questions arise, as they inevitably do, in relation to the interpretation of a given statute, and whether it does in fact cover the activity in question.

Note that it is no defence to a nuisance that the claimant moved to the nuisance,[21] that the defendant's activities have social utility,[22] or that someone else has a greater interest in the land than the claimant.[23]

---

17 (1879) 11 Ch D 852.
18 [1940] AC 880.
19 [2000] QB 51.
20 Although note the potential tension between this decision and the earlier case of *Hussain v Lancaster City Council* [2000] QB 1 (which was distinguished in *Lippiatt v South Gloucestershire Council* [2000] QB 51), in which the defendant council was not held liable for a series of racist attacks carried out by some of its tenants on other residents of the same estate. The distinction seems to lie (although Staughton LJ in *Lippiatt* was not entirely convinced) in the fact that, in *Hussain*, all of the interferences occurred within the same estate, and there was no 'emanation' from one property to another (on the emanation point, see Lord Hoffmann in *Hunter v Canary Wharf Ltd* [1997] AC 655 at 685).
21 As we have seen above – *Miller v Jackson* [1977] QB 966, *Sturges v Bridgman* (1879) LR 11.
22 The tort of private nuisance prioritises private property interests over the public good, unless the public good in question has been deemed by legislation to be superior to private rights (the statutory authority defence). See also Maria Lee's article below.
23 Once a claimant has a *sufficient* proprietary interest (exclusive possession being the general rule of thumb), this will be protected. Otherwise, for instance, the argument could be taken to its logical conclusion, and tenants could be prevented from claiming because they have an 'inferior' property right to their landlord (although such an argument rests on a contentious debate about relativity of title, which cannot be examined here).

DIFFERENT PERSPECTIVES on the collective interest

M. Lee, 'The Public Interest in Private Nuisance: Collectives and Communities in Tort' (2015) 74(2) CLJ 329–58

In this article, Lee examines the interrelationship between private and public interests in the law of tort and identifies a complex set of tensions. One of the problems, which can be seen in some of the recent case law, is that there is no consistent means of defining or setting out what the public, or collective, interest is, and how this is distinct from the private interests with which courts deciding tort cases are more familiar. Lee's point is not that this interest should be a driving force in private nuisance but that, given the inevitable relevance of the public interest to decisions in this area, the courts should at least be explicit and clear in the way that they deal with it. Lee proceeds to argue that the Supreme Court in *Coventry* assumed the existence of a strong public interest in the case, without ever explaining or exploring what that interest was. In her view, the Court was more resolute on the relevance of the public interest to the remedies point than it was on its relevance to liability. The article concludes by suggesting that, as a means of making discussions of the collective interest in tort more explicit and robust, a cautious reference could be made to the way in which administrative decisions are made.

S. Steel, 'The Locality Principle in Private Nuisance' (2017) 76(1) CLJ 145–67

The locality principle means that, in certain geographical areas, some interferences are not actionable in nuisance because they are deemed to be a reasonable consequence of the nature of the local environment. Here, Steel argues that the collective interest is not always sufficient to justify the application of this principle, particularly in the absence of compensation to the individuals who are left to suffer the interference. He points out, for example, that the level of acceptable interference varies from locality to locality, which means that people are likely to enjoy unequal rights. What is more, the making of liability decisions based on issues which are external to the relationship between claimant and defendant is not consistent with the norms of corrective justice. Steel also points to a logical fallacy in Lord Neuberger's reasoning around the nature of the locality: that the defendant's use of its land can be relevant to the character of the locality only insofar as it does not amount to a nuisance. This consideration in itself, however, requires knowing what amounts to the nature of the locality; otherwise we do not know which elements of the defendant's use do or do not amount to a nuisance.

10.5 The rule in *Rylands v Fletcher*

This tort, now a subset of private nuisance, is underpinned by a very particular fact pattern which it is important to remember. Fortunately, it is also fairly memorable!

KEY CASE

Rylands v Fletcher (1868) LR 3 HL 330

The defendant was a mill owner, who had built a reservoir on his land. Underneath the reservoir there were disused mine shafts which connected with the claimant's mine. The reservoir flooded the disused shafts and the claimant's mine. The question for the House of Lords was whether the defendant was liable for this damage as a result of using his land in the way that he did. In deciding in favour of the claimant, it made a distinction between a natural use of land, and the activity of bringing onto one's land something that does not naturally occur there, and is likely to cause damage if it escapes. Where a defendant has done the latter, she does so at her own risk, meaning that she will be liable if that non-naturally occurring thing escapes and does damage. To use the famous words of Blackburn J in the Court of Exchequer Chamber, the rule in *Rylands v Fletcher* is that a person who, for his own purposes, brought on his land and collected and kept there anything likely to do mischief if it escaped, had to keep it in at his peril; and if he did not do so, he was *prima facie* answerable for all the damage which was the natural consequence of its escape.

KEY CASE

Cambridge Water v Eastern Counties Leather plc [1994] 2 AC 264

The defendant operated a tannery close to the claimant's borehole. The defendant stored solvent at its tannery, which seeped into the ground and contaminated the water in the borehole. This rendered the water unfit for human consumption. The claimant brought alternative actions in negligence, nuisance and the rule in *Rylands v Fletcher*. The first two were dismissed at trial because it was found that the defendant could not reasonably have foreseen the damage. The *Rylands v Fletcher* claim was dismissed at first instance because the storage of the solvent was held to be a natural use of the defendant's land. The Court of Appeal found in the claimant's favour, but not on the basis of the rule in *Rylands v Fletcher*: it found instead that there was a parallel rule of strict liability in nuisance.

The House of Lords allowed the defendant's appeal, finding that, in both nuisance and under the rule in *Rylands v Fletcher*, foreseeability of harm of the relevant type is a prerequisite of recovery. Since such damage was not reasonably foreseeable on the facts of the instant case, the defendant was not liable under the rule, despite its use of its land being non-natural.

The decision in *Cambridge Water v Eastern Counties Leather* was highly significant for the application of the rule in *Rylands v Fletcher* because it means that, although a defendant will be liable under the rule even in the absence of fault, he will only be so liable for damage which is of a reasonably foreseeable type. Note also that *the escape itself* does *not* have to be reasonably foreseeable; only the damage which ultimately results. This might be said to dilute the modern purpose of the rule, which is to make those who use their land in an ultra-hazardous way effective insurers of any damage thereby caused to neighbouring properties – see 'Viewpoint' questions below.

Figure 10.1 offers a clear depiction of the foreseeability requirements which are now essential elements of both private nuisance and the rule in *Rylands v Fletcher*.

Private Nusiance	Rylands v Fletcher
Was this type of damage foreseeable to this claimant?	Was the ultimate damage to the claimant foreseeable?
(subsumes traditional inquiry into hypersensitivity)	(the escape itself does NOT have to be foreseeable)
Morris v Network Rail	*Cambridge Water v Eastern Counties Leather*

Figure 10.1: Foreseeability requirements

PROBLEM QUESTION TECHNIQUE

Sergei has spent hundreds of thousands of pounds on a top-of-the-range ferret cage. It is the most expensive model available and is marketed as being 100% escape and tamper-proof. One of its layers of security, however, is a real-time sensor feed to a central monitor. The poor wi-fi signal delays the feed, meaning that the central monitor is not notified of a circuit breach, caused by one of the ferret's collars getting caught on the lockpad. The interference confuses the lock into disengaging, and Sergei's ferrets (of which there are 50) escape into Ridhi's garden, where they destroy her plants and the expensive camping equipment she has just purchased.

▶ Here, you need to consider the crucial distinction between the foreseeability of the ultimate damage and the foreseeability of the escape, following *Cambridge Water*. Treat them as separate issues and remember that it is the former that needs to be foreseeable in order for the defendant to be liable, and not the latter.

KEY CASE

Transco plc v Stockport MBC [2003] UKHL 61

The defendant local authority owned a block of flats. Water had escaped from a pipe supplying the block of flats, although this was not due to any negligence on the part of the defendant. The claimant owned a gas pipe in a nearby railway embankment. When this embankment collapsed as a result of the water damage caused by the defendant's leaking water supply, the claimant claimed the cost of taking remedial measures to protect its gas pipe from damage. Its case was that the local authority was liable for damage caused by the escape of the water even in the absence of negligence. The House of Lords had to decide whether the local authority had brought onto its land something likely to cause damage if it escaped, and whether its use of land was a natural one. It found in favour of the defendant, and outlined the appropriate test as being whether the defendant had brought something on to its land:

(i) which it recognised, or ought reasonably to have recognised, judged by the standards appropriate to the place and time, as giving rise to an exceptionally high risk of danger if it should escape, and

(ii) recognised, or ought to have recognised, as being quite out of the ordinary for the place and time.

On the facts in the case before it, the Court held that the piping of a water supply was commonplace in a contemporary context, and would not reasonably have been regarded as being ultra-hazardous. Since the defendant in this case had not accumulated any water but had instead set up a means of supplying the residential building it owned, this was not analogous with the facts of *Rylands v Fletcher*.

One of the interesting aspects of *Transco* was the fact that the House of Lords was asked, in addition to deciding the questions which arose in the case itself, to consider getting rid of the rule in *Rylands v Fletcher* as a separate tort, and instead subsuming it within negligence liability, as the High Court of Australia had done in *Burnie Port Authority v General Jones Pty Ltd* [1994].[24] The House decided not to do this, but instead to retain the rule in *Rylands v Fletcher* to cover instances in which defendants use their land in an ultra-hazardous or extraordinary way. In essence, the Court decided that strict liability should continue to apply to those landowners who choose to

---

24   (1994) 179 CLR 520.

expose their neighbours to a particularly high risk of damage caused by the escape of something harmful. Lord Bingham made it clear that it should be difficult to fulfil the conditions attaching to the rule, but that there was nonetheless a clear case for retaining it. Lord Hoffmann seemed to think that the rule in *Rylands v Fletcher* is now far narrower in its influence than it has been in the past, owing to the fact that statutes now deal with many of the instances of accumulation that would historically have been the concern of the common law. His rationale for retaining the rule was a very pragmatic one: in his view, strict liability has a role to play in relation to risks that are not readily insurable by the claimant, thereby explaining his characterisation of the rule as being one to apply in extraordinary circumstances only.

PROBLEM QUESTION TECHNIQUE

Sergei's ferrets (of which there are 50) escape into Ridhi's garden …

▶ This is a question of whether, following the reasoning in *Transco*, the keeping of 50 ferrets on one's land counts as an ultra-hazardous use in the modern age, thereby engaging the rule in *Rylands v Fletcher*.

■ VIEWPOINT

- Do you think that the House of Lords was right to retain the rule in *Rylands v Fletcher* as a separate tort, holding those who use their land in an ultra-hazardous way to a higher standard of liability than negligence? Imagine that your neighbour stores vast quantities of a harmful chemical which, if it escapes, will poison the contents of your garden: do you think liability should depend on how hard your neighbour tried to prevent the escape?

- Do you think that the *Cambridge Water* requirement that the damage needs to be of a reasonably foreseeable type before it is recoverable fits with the overall development of the rule? That is, if ultra-hazardous use of land is to be met with strict liability in terms of a defendant's actions, should it matter whether the damage was reasonably foreseeable or not?

10.5.1 Defences to the rule in *Rylands v Fletcher*

There are several defences potentially available to a claim under the rule in *Rylands v Fletcher*.

10.5.1.1 CONSENT

This is fairly straightforward; a nuisance will not be actionable where a claimant consented to the action or situation which causes the interference. That consent, however, need not be explicit and can be implied from context. In *Peters v Prince of Wales Theatre* [1943],[25] for example, the claimant's shop was damaged by water from his defendant landlord's sprinkler system, the operation of which had been triggered by a severe frost (and, materially, not through any negligence of the landlord's). His *Rylands v Fletcher* claim was unsuccessful because he was deemed to have consented to the presence of the sprinkler system: not only was its presence declared in the lease, but it also accrued to his benefit to have such precautions against fire in place.

---

25   [1943] KB 73.

10.5.1.2 ACT OF GOD

This is a defence of very limited application in a modern world in which technology enables us to predict natural occurrences with a considerable degree of accuracy. The point of the defence is to excuse defendants where the interference in question was the result of extraordinary and unpredictable natural forces which could not have been prepared for. It was last applied in *Nichols v Marsland* in 1876,[26] to an exceptionally heavy episode of rainfall which destroyed four bridges. Given both our increased ability to predict such happenings, and our greater knowledge of how to guard against their effects, it is likely that this defence will apply only in very rare circumstances in the future, if it ever applies at all.

10.5.1.3 CLAIMANT'S OWN FAULT

This applies where the interference occurs as a result of the claimant's own fault or action. In the old case of *Ponting v Noakes* [1894],[27] the claimant's horse ate poisonous leaves from the defendant's tree and subsequently died. Since the horse had reached over the dividing fence to take the leaves from the defendant's property, the claim failed. (This overlaps, here, with the issue of escape; something which arguably did not occur on these facts.)

10.5.1.4 ACT OF A STRANGER

In order to function as a valid defence, such an act must have been unforeseeable from the defendant's point of view. Had the defendant foreseen the likely intervention of a third party, it should have taken steps to prevent such an occurrence. In *Ribee v Norrie* [2001],[28] the claimant's home caught fire when a blaze spread from an adjoining property of which the defendant was landlord. The evidence suggested that one of the tenants had left a cigarette burning on a sofa, which had led to the fire. Because the landlord was deemed to have the ability to control his tenants, and to foresee such an eventuality, he could not escape liability simply because the act in question was carried out not by him but by someone else. In *Rickards v Lothian* [1913],[29] by contrast, in which the claimant's property was flooded as a result of an overflowing sink in a property above, the defendant successfully invoked this defence. In this case, the tap had been turned on, and the drain deliberately blocked, by an unknown stranger. On these facts, the defendant was held not to have been in a position either to foresee, or to prevent, such an action.

10.5.1.5 STATUTORY AUTHORITY

As with nuisance, this is the most significant of the defences available to an action in *Rylands v Fletcher*, and its ability to constrain the tort was emphasised by the House of Lords in *Transco*. If a statute, as construed by the court, imposes a statutory duty on the defendant to carry out the activity in question, that party will, in the absence of negligence, not be liable under *Rylands v Fletcher* for damage which occurs as a result.[30] Some statutes, however, contain an express clause, providing that they do not protect the party carrying out the activity from a claim in nuisance.[31] Obviously, statutory authority will not be a valid defence in such cases.

26 (1876) 2 Ex D1.
27 [1894] 2 QB 281.
28 [2001] PIQR P8.
29 [1913] AC 263.
30 See *Dunne v North Western Gas Board* [1964] 2 QB 806.
31 As in *Charing Cross Electricity Supply Co v Hydraulic Power Co* [1914] 3 KB 772.

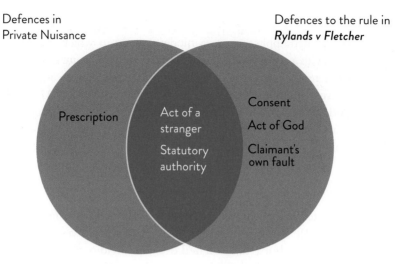

Figure 10.2: Defences in private nuisance and defences to the rule in *Rylands v Fletcher*

PROBLEM QUESTION TECHNIQUE

Ridhi had always loved Sergei's ferrets, regularly asking about them. In fact, she had encouraged him to buy his last litter from a friend of hers who breeds them.

▶ This is a straightforward question of whether any of the potential defences outlined above would apply to Ridhi.

DIFFERENT PERSPECTIVES on the rule in *Rylands v Fletcher*

R. Bagshaw, 'Rylands Confirmed' (2004) 120(Jul) LQR 388–92

In this article, Bagshaw argues that, in choosing not to subsume the rule in *Rylands v Fletcher* into the tort of negligence (as has happened in Australia), and in retaining it instead as a 'sub-species' of private nuisance, the House of Lords made it into 'a more incoherent relic than it was before'. Specifically, Bagshaw highlights the exclusion of recovery for personal injury from the tort, which, as he points out, means that liability without fault is retained for interferences with real property interests but not for interferences with bodily integrity. Given the common law's usual order of protection, this is hard to defend. Bagshaw goes on to criticise the way in which the House of Lords dealt with the distinctive feature of *Rylands v Fletcher* liability: the nature of the defendant's use of the land. There is, he says, inconsistency in their Lordships' choice of terminology, with the result that it is not clear whether liability under the rule now attaches to uses of land which are 'unusual' or 'extraordinary', or whether that use needs to give rise to 'an exceptionally high risk of danger'. Since the concepts of unusual and unreasonable are not the same, this might well lead to problems in application to certain factual situations, particularly those in which hazardous activities are commonplace (such as an area containing several factories using chemicals).

K. Amirthalingam, 'Rylands Lives' (2004) 63(2) CLJ 273–6

In this article, Amirthalingam argues that, in narrowing the parameters of the rule in *Rylands v Fletcher*, the House of Lords 'saved it from disrepute'. For instance, he approves of the way in which the decision adheres to the historical approach of not requiring the escape of the dangerous thing to be reasonably foreseeable: this, Amirthalingam contends, is in keeping with the strict liability basis of the rule. This article also supports the majority's view on the proprietary interest necessary for a claim under the rule in *Rylands v Fletcher*: the claimant in *Transco* in fact had only an easement over the defendant's land, but this was deemed by four of their Lordships to be sufficient. What is more, it was on the land subject to that easement that the damage occurred, and so there was, on one potential view, no 'escape' from the defendant's land. The fact that only Lord Scott took this view in *Transco* is in Amirthalingam's view a good thing. Otherwise, he argues, liability under the rule would be subject to geographical chance.*

■ VIEWPOINT

- Is it not the case that all cases in nuisance and *Rylands v Fletcher* are, to a greater or lesser extent, subject to geographical chance?
- Does it make sense to keep the rule in *Rylands v Fletcher* as a separate tort, or would it make more sense to do what Australia has done, and to subsume it within the tort of negligence? If you were someone who used your land for ultra-hazardous purposes, such as the manufacture of explosives, would you prefer a negligence regime or one that used the rule in *Rylands v Fletcher*?

10.6 Public nuisance: a very different thing

Public nuisance, protecting as it does the wider public good as opposed to interests in land, is not just a tort. It is primarily a crime, and can only be brought as a civil action by a private individual in very specific circumstances. It is dealt with briefly here because it is worth knowing how it fits alongside private nuisance. It frequently appears, for instance, as a minor element in problem questions on private nuisance, in order to draw out the distinction between private and public interests.

Public nuisance is quite simple to address in two stages. First, has the interference in question 'materially affect[ed] the reasonable comfort and convenience of life of a class of Her Majesty's subjects .... the question whether the local community within that sphere comprises a sufficient number of persons to constitute a class of the public is a question of fact in every case.'[32] There are no numerical indications in the case law as to what amounts to the requisite 'class' of people, and this is understandable. The key element is the *proportion* of those affected: in a tiny village, an interference might affect only a handful of people, but if this group is representative of the public interest in that particular area, this might well be sufficient.[33]

Second, an individual claimant must establish that she has suffered 'special' damage above and beyond that suffered by the rest of the class of people affected. This is what makes such a claim distinct from straightforward crimes of public nuisance, which affect a public interest, but which generate no individual claim for damages. The point is effectively illustrated by *Tate & Lyle Industries Ltd v GLC* [1983],[34] in which a section of the Thames had silted up as a consequence of the defendants' building of ferry terminals. This affected all users of the river, which brought the claim within the first stage outlined above; it affected a class of people. The claimants in that case, however, incurred considerable expense as a result of having to dredge the river so that their vessels could access a jetty, something which was necessary for their commercial operations. In this, they had suffered particular damage, above that suffered by the rest of the class of people so affected, and so could claim damages from the defendants for their loss.

---

32 Romer LJ in *Attorney General v PYA Quarries* [1957] 2 QB 169.

33 In *PYA Quarries*, Denning LJ made the point that a public nuisance is one which affects such a broad and indiscriminate range of people that it would be unreasonable to expect a single individual to bring an action in her own right in order to address it.

34 [1983] 2 AC 509.

In *Corby Group Litigation* [2008],[35] the Court of Appeal highlighted a significant distinction between private nuisance (of which *Rylands v Fletcher* is a species) and public nuisance. In deciding that damages for personal injury *could* be recovered in public nuisance, the Court decided that it was not bound to follow *Hunter v Canary Wharf*,[36] the case in which the House of Lords confirmed that damages for physical injury could not be recovered in *private* nuisance. This was partly because the Court decided that it was bound by authority specific to public nuisance which held that personal injury damages were recoverable (and that this was, in fact, a 'long-established principle') and partly because the nature and objectives of public nuisance made such recovery appropriate:

> … it is difficult to see why a person whose life, safety or health has been endangered and adversely affected by an unlawful act or omission and who suffers personal injuries as a result should not be able to recover damages. The purpose of the law which makes it a crime and a tort to do an unlawful act which endangers the life, safety or health of the public is surely to protect the public against the consequences of acts or omissions which do endanger their lives, safety or health. … *The purpose of this law is not to protect the property interests of the public. It is true that the same conduct can amount to a private nuisance and a public nuisance. But the two torts are distinct and the rights protected by them are different.*[37]

It is essential, therefore, that you distinguish between the two torts and their very different underlying objectives and functions. As Dyson LJ points out above, public nuisance is *not* an action to protect interests in land, whereas private nuisance is *solely* about that. It is perhaps unfortunate, given the significance of the distinction between the two actions, that they bear the same name.

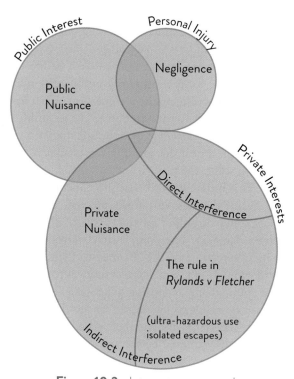

Figure 10.3: Interests protected

---

35 *Corby Group v Corby BC* [2008] EWCA Civ 463.
36 Above at 10.2.1.
37 Dyson LJ in *Corby Group* at [30] (emphasis added).

Figure 10.3 shows the interests protected by the different actions that can be engaged by interferences with interests in land. Its purpose is to show where there can be factual crossover and where there cannot, such as the fact that negligence and public nuisance allow recovery for personal injury where private nuisance does not.

PROBLEM QUESTION TECHNIQUE

Meanwhile, the drains connected to Trey's house have become blocked, and Streetsville council is digging up the road to fix them. On excavation, the workers find several significant problems, all of which will take a long time to rectify. The road to Ridhi's and Sergei's houses is therefore unpassable for three months. There are five houses on the road but, because of where the works are, only Ridhi and Sergei's are affected. Ridhi does not drive and so does not mind very much, but Sergei works from home as a physiotherapist, and many of his clients, who can no longer park nearby, have taken their business elsewhere.

▸ The important point to notice here is that the land directly affected is public, and the same is true of the interest affected.

▸ This then requires an analysis of public nuisance to decide whether the two stages described above are satisfied.

▸ Remember to take each potential claimant in turn, as the facts might mean that one is likely to be successful, whilst the case for the other is much weaker.

10.7 Trespass to land

Although this is a tort which, like nuisance, protects interests in land, it is crucial to understand how the two torts differ. Thankfully, trespass is a fairly straightforward tort, and its principal elements can be outlined briefly:

(1) *Lack of permission.* A trespass is only committed where the landowner does not consent to, or authorise, the defendant's action, or where there is no statutory authority for the defendant to be on the premises. The Police and Criminal Evidence Act 1984, for example, allows police to enter land without permission where it is necessary to do so in order to make an arrest.

(2) *Intention.* Trespass to land, like trespass to the person and trespass to goods, is a tort which can only be committed intentionally. Significantly, however, it is the action that must be intentional; there is no requirement that the defendant intends to commit a tort by so acting. For example, standing by the boundary of the claimant's land and tripping over a tree root so that one falls onto the claimant's land is not an intentional act, meaning that the defendant will not be liable for this in trespass. The defendant who deliberately steps onto the claimant's land, however, even believing that she is still on her own land, *will* be liable for trespass: her action was intentional, even though her wrong was not.

(3) *Direct interference.* Where nuisance deals with indirect interferences with land, such as the emanation of noise, smells or vapours, or the overhanging of tree branches, trespass covers those situations in which the interference is direct, such as walking on land, straying beyond permitted boundaries, or putting physical items on the land without the owner's consent.

(4) *Actionable per se.* Torts that are actionable *per se*, as trespass is, are those which are actionable without proof of consequential damage. In other words, they are actionable simply because a right has been infringed, regardless of whether this has made the claimant factually worse off. So, if a defendant steps over a boundary line, so that he is on another's land without permission, it is no answer to a claim in trespass that the land has not been harmed or altered in any way by his presence. The tort of trespass protects a titleholder's right to exclude others from her property, and so nothing more than an infringement of that right to exclude need be shown.

Note also that necessity provides a defence to the tort of trespass. This occurs where the defendant's action is deemed necessary to have protected a superior interest, or to have avoided a greater harm.[38]

10.8 CHAPTER SUMMARY

This chapter has examined the suite of torts that protect interests in land, and explored the differences between them. It has set out the direct interference required for trespass, as compared to the indirect interference covered by private nuisance, as well as explaining the contemporary judicial attitude towards developing the rule in *Rylands v Fletcher* as a species of private nuisance. The discussion has also included an account of public nuisance, both in terms of the potential factual overlap with private nuisance and in terms of the significant distinctions between the two actions: in essence, private nuisance protects private interests in land, whilst public nuisance protects the public interest. Along with an analysis of the balancing exercise inherent in judicial decisions regarding private nuisance, the chapter has also examined the defences and remedies available for nuisance, with a particular emphasis on the recent apparent willingness of the Supreme Court to make damages less of an exceptional remedy in nuisance cases, for which the traditional response has been injunctive relief. It should be clear from the material in this chapter that nuisance, in all its forms, is to be clearly separated from negligence, with which so much of most undergraduate courses is concerned. Nuisance, unlike negligence, takes its lead from the effect of the defendant's behaviour on the claimant's interests in land, rather than being determined by the nature of that behaviour itself. This *must* be borne in mind when answering questions on nuisance: doing so will help you to remember, for instance, that claimants cannot claim in private nuisance for personal injury, and that they must have a sufficient interest in land. Whilst foreseeability does play a part in nuisance (and arguably, increasingly so), the defendant's fault in the negligence sense is not the driving force behind the development and application of the land torts.

FURTHER READING

A. Beever, The Law of Private Nuisance (Hart, 2014)

M. Lee, 'What is Private Nuisance?' (2003) 119 *LQR* 298

M. Lee, '*Hunter v Canary Wharf Ltd* (1997)' in C. Mitchell and P. Mitchell (eds), *Landmark Cases in the Law of Tort* (Hart, 2010)

J. Murphy, 'The Merits of *Rylands v Fletcher*' (2004) 24 *Oxford Journal of Legal Studies* 643–69

J. Murphy, *The Law of Nuisance* (OUP, 2015)

B. Pontin, 'Private Nuisance in the Balance: *Coventry v Lawrence (No 1) and (No 2)*' (2015) 27(1) *J Env L* 119–37

A.W.B. Simpson, 'Victorian Judges and the Problem of Social Cost: *Tipping v St Helen's Smelting Company* (1895)' in *Leading Cases in the Common Law* (OUP, 1995)

---

38 The most well-known example of this is *Esso Petroleum v Southport Corporation* [1956] AC 218, in which the defendant's actions in discharging oil into the ocean were deemed to have been necessary in order to prevent the endangerment of the ship and her crew: the direct and immediate protection of human life was identified by the courts as a greater priority than the prevention of pollution. As Devlin J said at first instance, 'The safety of human lives belongs to a different scale of values from the safety of property. The two are beyond comparison and the necessity for saving life has at all times been considered a proper ground for inflicting such damage as may be necessary upon another's property.'

Roadmap: Private Nuisance

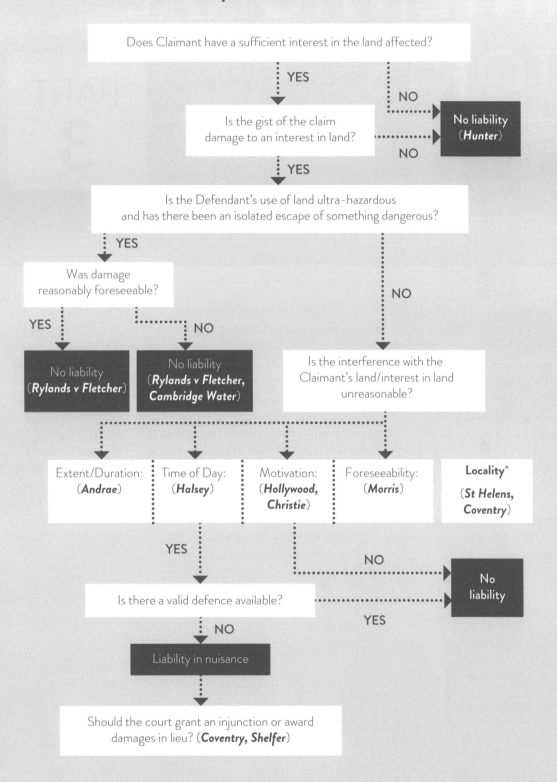

Does Claimant have a sufficient interest in the land affected?

YES → Is the gist of the claim damage to an interest in land?

NO → No liability (*Hunter*)

NO → No liability (*Hunter*)

YES → Is the Defendant's use of land ultra-hazardous and has there been an isolated escape of something dangerous?

YES → Was damage reasonably foreseeable?

YES → No liability (*Rylands v Fletcher*)

NO → No liability (*Rylands v Fletcher, Cambridge Water*)

NO → Is the interference with the Claimant's land/interest in land unreasonable?

Extent/Duration: (*Andrae*)

Time of Day: (*Halsey*)

Motivation: (*Hollywood, Christie*)

Foreseeability: (*Morris*)

Locality* (*St Helens, Coventry*)

YES → Is there a valid defence available?

NO → No liability

NO → Liability in nuisance

YES → No liability

Should the court grant an injunction or award damages in lieu? (*Coventry, Shelfer*)

* Only relevant where damage is intangible

INTENTIONAL TORTS

TORTS

PART

3

11. The Economic Torts   243

12. Intentional Torts against the Person   260

This Part covers a wide range of torts that protect a vast array of different interests. Whilst there are many more differences than similarities between these torts, what brings them together is that they protect the claimant from *intentional* infliction of harm. In the Economic Torts chapter, the causes of action provide redress for intentional infliction of economic loss. The chapter is strongly focused on the landmark House of Lords decision in *OBG v Allan*, which provided some level of clarity to a confusing and incoherent area of law. Whilst there is a wide range of economic torts, the chapter focuses on inducing breach of contract, causing loss by unlawful means and conspiracy. The second chapter in this Part addresses intentional torts to the person, which protect the bodily autonomy of individuals. In many ways this is less controversial than the protection of economic interests; however, the area has its own complexities. The chapter focuses on the three 'trespass to the person' torts – assault, battery and false imprisonment – but includes a discussion of the lesser known intentional torts to the person, *Wilkinson v Downton*, the Protection from Harassment Act 1997 and malicious prosecution. These torts raise a range of historical and novel challenges. Whilst trespass of the case is the oldest tort established in English common law, the current tort actions have a number of more modern usages and contexts, such as stalking, harassment and application to the #MeToo movement.

LEARNING OBJECTIVES

By the end of this chapter, you should be able to:

- Explain how the economic torts differ from, and fit alongside, other torts
- Understand the reasons for the existence of the economic torts
- Trace the historical development of this suite of torts, and see how this is relevant to their contemporary status
- Outline the separate economic torts and identify where the distinctions between them lie
- Identify the common themes that run through what could be regarded as a set of disparate legal actions

CHAPTER CONTENTS

11.1 Introduction		244
11.2 The distinction made by the House of Lords in *OBG*		245
	11.2.1 Inducing breach of contract	247
	11.2.2 Causing loss by unlawful means	249
11.3 (The former tort of) intimidation – now covered by causing loss by unlawful means		251
11.4 Conspiracy		252
	11.4.1 Lawful means conspiracy (or simple conspiracy)	252
	11.4.2 Unlawful means conspiracy	253
11.5 Chapter summary		257
Further reading		257
Roadmap		258

PROBLEM QUESTION

Hang owns a restaurant, The Kingfisher, in Eastville. Iris is the landlord of The Star, a gastropub in the same village, owned by Jekyll Brewery. Lennie is an experienced chef who has just moved to the area. He has worked with Hang in the past, and she offered him a job as soon as he arrived in Eastville. This has meant a pay cut for Lennie, but he is good friends with Hang, and really wants to work near his new home, so he agrees and signs a contract to work for her. He and his boyfriend, Matteo, go to The Star, their new local pub, to celebrate Lennie's new job. Despite what they have heard to the contrary, the food is terrible and the men go to the bar to complain. Iris apologises, but says that her chef has just walked out, leaving her and two other employees to do all of the cooking and manage the bar. Lennie feels sorry for Iris and offers to cook for the evening. Iris is so impressed with Lennie's work that she begs him to come and work for her. Lennie refuses, and explains his situation with Hang. Iris has known Hang for a while, and likes her a lot, but she also thinks that sentiment has no place in business. 'Whatever she is paying, I will double it', Iris tells Lennie. Lennie still refuses out of a sense of loyalty, but Matteo is furious with his response: 'Think what we could do with the extra cash! If you don't take this job, I will destroy your vintage record collection when we get home.' Lennie has spent over 20 years and tens of thousands of pounds on that collection, which is also his pride and joy. He is also quite scared of Matteo, so he reluctantly agrees to work for Iris and phones Hang to let her know that he can no longer work for her. As a result, Hang has no chef until she can find a replacement, and loses £20,000.

Hang, worried about her financial affairs, falls into a state of deep depression and starts to have suicidal thoughts. She knows what she needs to do in such a situation, as it has happened before, so she goes straight to see her psychotherapist, Nia, and begs for an emergency appointment. Nia has treated Hang for a long time, and so knows that immediate treatment is needed. She accedes to Hang's request and consequently fails to turn up and give a keynote lecture at an International Symposium for Psychotherapists, organised by Psychotherapy UK. Many delegates at the conference, who had booked to hear Nia, are now demanding refunds for the conference fee that they paid to Psychotherapy UK.

Iris and Jekyll have for a while been concerned about the expansion and increased success of Kali's Eastfield Delicatessen, which has taken more and more custom from their pub over the past year. They decide to teach Kali a lesson. 'Let's be clever about it, though', says Iris to Jekyll. 'Let's not do anything that can get us into trouble – just something that will make Kali's life miserable.' They decide, therefore, to stop the pub's bulk purchase of Kali's vegetable crisps. Since The Star had been the main customer for these, Kali is no longer able to produce them profitably, even for her own direct customers, and loses £700 a month.

When Hang and Kali realise that they have both suffered significant losses as a result of Iris's actions, they decide to get their revenge. They cut the cable leading from The Star's satellite dish to its television several times: each time, Jekyll repairs the cable, only for Hang and Kali to cut it again. Sports TV had long been one of the main attractions of The Star, and the frequent interruptions to service drive most customers to the local competitor pub, The Sun. Within six months, The Star has to close, with losses of over £800,000.

11.1 Introduction

The economic torts perform a very important function, but they also give rise to some considerable conceptual difficulties: they make up a group of what might be regarded as disparate actions with no obvious coherent theme, and the harm against which they protect is not obviously something which should always be the concern of the law. In order to understand the economic torts in their modern state, you need to have a sound knowledge of the decision of the House of Lords in *OBG v Allan* [2007].[1] This was a landmark decision, which served to restructure, and to bring clarity to, an area of the common law that had developed in a piecemeal and confusing way over many years.[2]

The underlying function of the economic torts is to provide redress for the intentional infliction of economic loss, but this simple description provides a clue as to what the first issue is: in a modern, market-based society,[3] parties are not only generally free intentionally to inflict economic loss on others, but are encouraged to do so. It is considered a positive thing, for example, for providers of, say, food, to be subject to competition from other providers. Without such competition, monopolies

---

1   [2007] UKHL 21.
2   For more detail on this, see H. Carty, 'The Economic Torts in the 21st Century' (2008) 124(Oct) LQR 641–74. In particular, a 'hybrid' tort had developed during the 20th century, known as 'unlawful interference with contractual relations'. This required no actual breach of contract, and sat somewhere between inducing breach of contract and causing loss by unlawful means, as described below. The House of Lords in *OBG* made it clear that there was to be no such tort.
3   As we saw in Chapter 3 (Pure Economic Loss).

arise and monopolies lead, in general, to higher prices for consumers. Competition, on the other hand, incentivises efficiency, the provision of good quality goods and services, and the availability of choice. Competing commercial parties act to increase their market share and, in so doing, usually deprive their competitors of custom, thereby causing pure economic loss. In many circumstances, this is not wrongful and is not the concern of the law of tort. Rather, the limits and the restrictions on these competitive practices are the focus of the economic torts. In other words, at what point does healthy and legitimate competition yield to the wrongful infliction of loss? This is the question that the economic torts seek to answer.

KEY CASE

Allen v Flood [1898] AC 1

The claimants in this case were shipwrights; craftsmen who worked with both iron and wood. The problem arose when they were employed to carry out repairs to a ship on which ironworkers were also engaged. The ironworkers objected to the fact that shipwrights worked on both wood and metal and threatened to walk out unless their employers dismissed the shipwrights. Allen, the defendant delegate, communicated this to the employers, who duly dismissed the shipwrights to prevent a walkout by the ironworkers. The shipwrights then sued Allen for intentionally causing them economic loss.

Since there had been no breach of contract, either by the employers (they were entitled to dismiss the shipwrights at will)[4] or by the ironworkers (who were not contractually obliged to continue work), the question was whether any wrong had been committed.

A majority of the House of Lords found that the presence of intention was of no relevance where there had been no action that was unlawful in itself. After reviewing the authorities, Lord Watson concluded:

> But none of these cases tend to establish that an act which does not amount to a legal wrong, and therefore needs no protection, can have privilege attached to it; and still less that an act in itself lawful is converted into a legal wrong if it was done from a bad motive.[5]

KEY CASE

Lumley v Gye (1853) 2 E&B 216

The claimant, who was the manager of Her Majesty's Theatre, had engaged the opera star, Johanna Wagner, to perform exclusively at his venue. The defendant operated a rival opera house in Covent Garden, and he persuaded Wagner[6] to breach her contract with the claimant by coming to sing for him instead. In recognising this set of facts as giving rise to a cause of action, the court fashioned the tort of inducing (or procuring) breach of contract.

11.2 The distinction made by the House of Lords in *OBG*

OBG v Allan was a landmark case, and one which had a defining impact on the economic torts.

---

4   There was, therefore, no induced breach as in *Lumley v Gye*.
5   [1898] AC 1 at 92.
6   By offering her a large sum of money.

KEY CASE

OBG Ltd v Allan; Douglas v Hello! Ltd; Mainstream Properties Ltd v Young [2007] UKHL 21

Two directors of a property company had, in breach of their contracts, diverted a development opportunity to a joint venture in which they had an interest. The defendant knew of their contractual obligations in this respect, but mistakenly believed that their pursuit of the development opportunity would not amount to a breach. He therefore provided them with finance for the venture. The claimant therefore argued that the defendant was liable for inducing breach of contract.

In a conjoined appeal, the defendants had been appointed as receivers under a charge which turned out to be invalid. They had been acting in good faith, therefore, when they had taken control of the claimant's business and assets. The claimant brought actions in both unlawful interference with its contractual relations and in conversion.

In the final conjoined appeal, the claimants were well-known celebrities, Catherine Zeta-Jones and Michael Douglas, who had contracted with OK! magazine for the exclusive publication of their wedding photographs. The defendant, a rival lifestyle magazine, published photographs that had been taken secretly at the event, thereby preventing the claimants from having photographs published exclusively in a single outlet. The claimants therefore alleged that this amounted to interference by unlawful means with its contractual relations (as well as a breach of its equitable right to confidentiality).

The House of Lords held that the tort of intentionally inducing a breach of contract was conceptually distinct from the tort of inflicting harm by unlawful means, although in some factual situations they might overlap. If the breach of contract was neither an end in itself nor a means to an end, but merely a foreseeable consequence, then it could not be said to have been intended.

- Liability for interference with contractual relations requires a breach of contract and, without such a breach, there will be no liability.
- 'Unlawful means' refers to those acts which are unlawful as against a third party, and which are intended to cause loss to the claimant by interfering with the freedom of a third party.
- Acts against a third party are regarded as 'unlawful means' only if they are actionable at the suit of the third party.

On the facts of the case before the Court, the defendant who provided financial assistance to the directors honestly believed that the joint venture would not involve breaches of their contracts. Since he could not be said to have been indifferent to whether there was a breach of contract, or to have made a conscious decision not to inquire further, he did not intend to cause a breach of contract, and the conditions for accessory liability were therefore not satisfied in his case. Furthermore, there was no question of his having caused loss by unlawful means because he neither intended to cause loss to the claimant nor used any unlawful means.

The defendant receivers were not liable for inducing breach of contract or for causing loss by unlawful means.[7] There was no breach of contract to which accessory liability could attach, and the defendants neither employed unlawful means nor intended to cause the claimant any loss.

Finally, the Douglases' unlawful interference claim failed because the defendant in that case had not used unlawful means to interfere with the freedom of the third party publisher, despite having the necessary intention to cause loss.

---

7   Or for conversion, since this was, according to the Court, an action restricted to tangible property. Since conversion is not an economic tort, however, there is no need to comment further on it here.

The principal effect of the House of Lords' decision in *OBG v Allan* was clearly to separate the torts of inducing breach of contract and causing loss by unlawful means. Prior to *OBG*, these two claims were often elided with one another, and there was in general no coherent framework on which the economic torts could be set out. Whilst there remains some doubt about whether *OBG* has provided such a framework for *all* economic torts (more on this below), there can be little doubt that its separation of inducing breach of contract and causing loss by unlawful means has brought at least partial clarity to a difficult area. Take care, then, particularly when answering problem questions, to distinguish between these two claims; once you know the criteria, it is relatively straightforward.

11.2.1 Inducing breach of contract

- This is a species of accessory liability. This means that the liability of the tortfeasor is parasitic on someone else's wrong – the wrong of the contracting party in breaching the contract.

- The essence of the tort is therefore that the person inducing the breach of contract combines with the contracting party to bring about the breach. It is not enough for the defendant merely to have facilitated the breach: she must join with the breaching party and actively 'do or secure the doing'[8] of acts which amount to breach.

- There is, as we saw above, no liability unless the contract is actually breached.

- The person alleged to have induced the breach must have had the requisite intention to cause the breach. There need be no intention to cause loss itself, as long as the breach is intended. To intend to cause the breach, all of the following criteria must therefore be satisfied:

(1) *She must know of the existence of the contract.*[9]

(2) *She must know that the induced action will lead to its breach.*[10] This will include situations in which the court finds that the defendant deliberately 'turned a blind eye' to the relevant provisions of a contract: that is, for instance, not reading the contract, even though it is available for her to do so, and there are reasons (such as industry practice) to believe that the relevant information is contained therein.

(3) *The breach must be either an ends or a means to achieving that end (as opposed to merely being a by-product of a particular action).*[11] In other words, a defendant might want a builder to build a conservatory on his house in the next two months. Owing to the builder's prior contractual commitments, this will require the builder to breach her existing contract with another party. The defendant might be completely indifferent about whether that other party suffers loss or might, even, be sad about it,[12] but nonetheless proceed with inducing the breach because he is determined to get his own building work done. This is sufficient intention: the breach is a means to an end. There will also be rarer cases where depriving the other party of the benefit of the contract is the end in itself, and this will a fortiori constitute the requisite intention. Where, however, the defendant is, say, a supplier, who has been unable to supply the builder with the materials necessary to complete the building work under the original contract, this

---

8   Lord Toulson in *Fish & Fish Ltd v Sea Shephard UK* [2015] AC 1229 at [210].
9   See Lord Nicholls in *OBG v Allan* [2007] UKHL 21 at [192].
10 See *One Money Mail Ltd v Ria Financial Services* [2015] EWCA Civ 1084.
11 In *OBG*, Lord Hoffmann referred to this as being the distinction between 'ends, means and consequences'.
12 See Lord Hoffmann in *OBG* at [42].

could well lead to a breach, but there will be no tort of inducing breach of contract where the breach was merely an incidental effect or consequence of the supplier's actions.[13]

(4) *Negligent interference is not sufficient.*[14]

11.2.1.1 A NOTE ON INDUSTRIAL ACTION

The development of the economic torts owes much to industrial action and trade union activity. Historically, the economic torts were regarded as a necessary means of protecting employers from loss caused by workers trying to improve their pay and conditions by reducing their output in some way. In the modern era, the attitude of the law has changed, and industrial action has become a far more accepted, and legally protected, activity. For instance, strike action by members of a trade union could clearly be regarded[15] as a prima facie instance of the union having induced workers to breach their contract of employment. The Trade Union and Labour Relations (Consolidation) Act 1992, s 219, however, provides a statutory immunity against tort liability for strike organisers.

KEY LEGISLATION

Trade Union and Labour Relations (Consolidation) Act 1992

219   Protection from certain tort liabilities

(1)   An act done by a person in contemplation or furtherance of a trade dispute is not actionable in tort on the ground only—

(a) that it induces another person to break a contract or interferes or induces another person to interfere with its performance, or

(b) that it consists in his threatening that a contract (whether one to which he is a party or not) will be broken or its performance interfered with, or that he will induce another person to break a contract or interfere with its performance.

(2)   An agreement or combination by two or more persons to do or procure the doing of an act in contemplation or furtherance of a trade dispute is not actionable in tort if the act is one which if done without any such agreement or combination would not be actionable in tort.

Essentially, trade unions and strike organisers will be covered by this immunity provided that the tort they have committed is covered by the statute and that they have acted 'in contemplation or furtherance of a trade dispute'. Amongst other requirements, this means that any industrial action taken has complied in full with balloting and notice provisions.[16] This is, for obvious reasons, a highly significant defence in the contemporary economic environment.

---

13 See *Millar v Bassey* [1994] EMLR 44, in which Shirley Bassey breached her recording contract with her record company so as to free herself from her obligations to them. This led to the company having to breach its contract with a producer and musicians, who had already been contracted to make the next record. In *OBG*, the House of Lords regarded this situation as being one of consequences, rather than ends or means, meaning that Ms Bassey did not, in such a situation, have the requisite intent.

14 Remember that this is an intentional tort.

15 See A. Davies, *Employment Law* (Pearson, 2015), 466.

16 There is more to the restrictions than this, but a full discussion is beyond the remit of the current text. For a highly accessible specialist account, see A. Davies (above).

PROBLEM QUESTION TECHNIQUE

Lennie is an experienced chef who has just moved to the area. He has worked with Hang in the past, and she offered him a job as soon as he arrived in Eastville. This has meant a pay cut for Lennie, but he is good friends with Hang, and really wants to work near his new home, so he agrees and signs a contract to work for her. He and his boyfriend, Matteo, go to The Star, their new local pub, to celebrate Lennie's new job. Despite what they have heard to the contrary, the food is terrible and the men go to the bar to complain. Iris apologises, but says that her chef has just walked out, leaving her and two other employees to do all of the cooking and manage the bar. Lennie feels sorry for Iris and offers to cook for the evening. Iris is so impressed with Lennie's work that she begs him to come and work for her. Lennie refuses, and explains his situation with Hang. Iris has known Hang for a while, and likes her a lot, but she also thinks that sentiment has no place in business. 'Whatever she is paying, I will double it', Iris tells Lennie. Lennie still refuses out of a sense of loyalty, but Matteo is furious with his response: 'Think what we could do with the extra cash! If you don't take this job, I will destroy your vintage record collection when we get home.' Lennie has spent over 20 years and tens of thousands of pounds on that collection, which is also his pride and joy. He is also quite scared of Matteo, so he reluctantly agrees to work for Iris and phones Hang to let her know that he can no longer work for her. As a result, Hang has no chef until she can find a replacement, and loses £20,000.

Hang, worried about her financial affairs, falls into a state of deep depression and starts to have suicidal thoughts. She knows what she needs to do in such a situation, as it has happened before, so she goes straight to see her psychotherapist, Nia, and begs for an emergency appointment. Nia has treated Hang for a long time, and so knows that immediate treatment is needed. She accedes to Hang's request and consequently fails to turn up and give a keynote lecture at an International Symposium for Psychotherapists, organised by Psychotherapy UK. Many delegates at the conference, who had booked to hear Nia, are now demanding refunds for the conference fee that they paid to Psychotherapy UK.

▸ You need to acknowledge the existence of the contract between Hang and Lennie, and its breach.

▸ You also need to consider Iris's knowledge of the contract and her intention – is the breach an end or a means to an end for her?

▸ Acknowledge that it is Lennie who commits the primary wrong of breach, but Iris whose action is parasitic on that wrong.

▸ Look at Matteo's actions as well here – consider his knowledge and intention in the same way as you do for Iris. Note that Matteo's actions can also be considered under other headings, as these facts give rise to the potential overlap acknowledged by the House of Lords – see below.

▸ Hang has caused Nia to breach her contract with Psychotherapy UK, but does she have the requisite knowledge and/or intention? Is the breach an end, a means to an end, or just a foreseeable consequence of her actions?

11.2.2 Causing loss by unlawful means

> Unlawful means … consists of acts intended to cause loss to the claimant by interfering with the freedom of a third party in a way which is unlawful as against that third party and which is intended to cause loss to the claimant. It does not in my opinion include acts which may be unlawful against a third party but which do not affect his freedom to deal with the claimant.[17]

---

17   Lord Hoffmann in *OBG* at [51].

Prior to *OBG*, the activities now covered by this 'umbrella' tort were referred to either as 'intimidation' or as 'interference with contractual relations'. The three constituent elements of the newly consolidated tort are:
(1) The defendant must affect a third party's freedom to deal with the claimant.
(2) The defendant's actions in so doing must be 'unlawful'.
(3) The defendant must have the requisite intention.

11.2.2.1 THE DEFENDANT MUST AFFECT A THIRD PARTY'S FREEDOM TO DEAL WITH THE CLAIMANT

This element covers those acts which would previously have been seen as intimidation. Note that this means the 'causing loss by unlawful means tort' is one of *primary* liability – that is, it is *not* parasitic on another's wrong in the way that 'inducing breach of contract' is, but is committed by striking at one party (the claimant) through actions directed at another (the third party). Those actions must have an impact on the third party's ability to deal with the claimant and thereby cause the loss. This requirement is what has prevented claimants in 'bootlegging' cases from being able successfully to sue defendants for causing loss by unlawful means: where a defendant makes and distributes material without the necessary consents ('bootleg' or 'pirate' recordings), it is easy to see why this causes loss to a licensed distributor, but it does not, according to the common law, do so by preventing any third party from dealing with the claimant.[18] A similar distinction was made by Lord Hoffmann in relation to the Douglases' claim in *OBG*: the unlicensed photographs taken at the wedding had not affected the claimants' ability to deal with the third party; they had *reduced the value of that contract*, which is a different thing in law:

> Hello! did [not do] anything to interfere with the liberty of the Douglases to deal with OK! or perform their obligations under their contract. All they did was to make OK!'s contractual rights less profitable than they would otherwise have been.[19]

11.2.2.2   THE DEFENDANT'S ACTIONS IN SO DOING MUST BE 'UNLAWFUL'

The use of this word is rarely straightforward, and it does not even have a consistent meaning across the economic torts.[20] Ensure, therefore, that you adopt the correct analysis for the correct tort. In *OBG*, the House of Lords defined 'unlawful' for current purposes as referring only to *those acts which would be independently actionable by the party on the receiving end of them*. (To this must be added Lord Hoffmann's gloss that such acts would still be unlawful for these purposes, even if they ultimately cause no loss.)[21] The requirement of independent actionability was deemed by the Court to be necessary so as to prevent *any* unlawful act from being sufficient, even where it was not directed against, and arguably did not harm, the third party. The famous example given by Lord Walker is that of a pizza delivery business, which increases its share of the market by delivering pizzas faster than its rivals, but does so by exceeding speed limits and ignoring traffic restrictions. Such wrongs would not be independently actionable by any third party, and so would *not* be the concern of this tort. The point is to focus on the effects of the defendant's behaviour on the third party, and not simply on any wrongs committed by the defendant.[22]

---

18 See, e.g., *RCA Corp v Pollard* [1983] Ch 135.
19 Lord Hoffmann in *OBG* at [129].
20 Its meaning here differs from its meaning for the purposes of 'unlawful means conspiracy', for example.
21 And so would not strictly be independently actionable where the tort concerned requires damage to have been caused.
22 See Lord Walker in *OBG* at [269].

11.2.2.3 THE DEFENDANT MUST HAVE THE REQUISITE INTENTION

For this tort, the defendant must intend to cause the claimant loss through the mechanism of affecting a third party. In other words, the defendant must intend to 'strike at' the claimant through the third party.

There is no doubt that the issue of intention is a thorny one, and arguably remains so even after the House of Lords' decision in *OBG*. A majority of the House of Lords took a different view of intention from that expressed (at some length) in the Court of Appeal: in making a more concise statement of what is required, it left some questions unanswered, as Carty explains below:

> [I]t is to be regretted that the House of Lords – or rather Lord Hoffmann and Lord Nicholls – spent relatively little time on this issue … neither Lord Hoffmann nor Lord Nicholls was prepared to adopt the usual terminology that the claimant must be 'targeted' or 'aimed at' by the defendant's conduct. Rather they both required the courts to identify 'ends' and 'means to ends' and to distinguish them from mere 'consequences'. So intentional harm is to be defined for the economic torts as either a desired end or the means of achieving a desired end … The 'end or means to an end' test may move the definition of intention for these torts further along the spectrum, widening the chance of liability …[23]

As with inducing breach of contract, above, the simplest way to analyse intention is to distinguish between 'ends, means and consequences', with only the first two sufficing for liability:

> One intends to cause loss even though it is the means by which one achieves the end of enriching oneself.[24]

Thus, in *Barretts & Baird (Wholesale) Ltd v IPCS* [1987],[25] members of the defendant union went out on strike in breach of their employment contracts. When their employer was, as a result, unable to comply with statutory obligations to the claimant, the claimant's claim against the union failed because the damage, although an inevitable by-product of the strike, did not result from any intention to injure it.

11.3 (The former tort of) intimidation – now covered by causing loss by unlawful means

KEY CASE

Rookes v Barnard [1964] AC 1129

The defendants were union officials in a context in which the union and the employer, BOAC, had an informal agreement that all employees would be members of the union. When the claimant left the union, the defendants threatened BOAC with an unlawful strike unless it dismissed him. BOAC did so, and because it brought the claimant's contract to an end in a way which was lawful, the claimant had no legal redress against it. He therefore brought an action against the defendants, who were found by the House of Lords to be liable for the tort of intimidation. This tort was made out where the defendant threatened to use unlawful means in order to get a third party to act in a way which causes loss to the claimant.

---

23   H. Carty, 'The Economic Torts in the 21st Century' (2008) 124(Oct) LQR 641–74.
24   Lord Hoffmann in *OBG* at [62].
25   [1987] IRLR 3.

In the wake of *OBG*, this situation no longer requires the attention of a separate tort of intimidation because it contains all the ingredients of the post-*OBG* 'genus' tort of causing loss by unlawful means: the threatened strike action was unlawful, the conduct was directed against a third party (the employer) and the intention was to cause the claimant loss (in the sense that such loss was a means to their end of ensuring that the whole workforce was unionised).

PROBLEM QUESTION TECHNIQUE

Lennie still refuses out of a sense of loyalty, but Matteo is furious with his response: 'Think what we could do with the extra cash! If you don't take this job, I will destroy your vintage record collection when we get home.' Lennie has spent over 20 years and tens of thousands of pounds on that collection, which is also his pride and joy. He is also quite scared of Matteo, so he reluctantly agrees to work for Iris and phones Hang to let her know that he can no longer work for her. As a result, Hang has no chef until she can find a replacement, and loses £20,000.

▸ You might have established already that Matteo could be liable for inducing breach of contract, but you also need to consider whether he has caused loss by unlawful means.

▸ Consider his intention: as above, was the loss to Hang an end or a means to an end in his enriching himself?

▸ Was he using a third party (Lennie) to strike at the claimant (Hang)?

▸ Was his action unlawful in the sense that it would be independently actionable by the third party if it were carried out (see Lord Hoffmann in *OBG*, above)?

▸ Would this be a situation that, pre-*OBG*, would have been covered by the (old) tort of intimidation?

11.4 Conspiracy

This was not one of the torts examined by the House of Lords in *OBG*, although it came to the attention of that court very soon afterwards in *Total Network SL v Customs & Excise Commissioners* [2008][26] analysed below. Essentially, there are two types of conspiracy at common law: lawful means conspiracy (or simple conspiracy) and unlawful means conspiracy.

11.4.1 Lawful means conspiracy (or simple conspiracy)

To the modern eye, this may well look like a strange concept. It is based on the idea that even action which would otherwise be lawful will attract the censure of the law of tort if it is carried out by several parties, combining with the intention of causing loss to another. It hints at a common law haunted by a historical aversion to collective action (in particular, a fear of trade unions exercising their disruptive might in order to harm the interests of employers). This is now something of an anachronism, given the very different context in which modern employment relationships function, and in which industrial action is both protected and limited by statute.[27] Its relevance might also be questioned in an era of global commerce: can it really be said, for instance, that two small family businesses combined will generate a disproportionate threat to the interests of a multinational company?[28]

---

26 [2008] UKHL 19.
27 Mostly by the Trade Union and Labour Relations (Consolidation) Act 1992.
28 See Lord Diplock, to whom this point was already clear nearly four decades ago, in *Lonrho Ltd v Shell Petroleum Co Ltd* [1983] AC 173.

11.4.2 Unlawful means conspiracy

All that said, this is a very difficult tort to establish, and claimants have rarely been successful. One of the reasons for this is that it requires the claimant's loss to be the defendant's *direct* motive. In the language of *OBG*, this means that the defendant's ends in themselves must have been the claimant's loss; neither means nor consequences will be sufficient. It differs therefore, in terms of intention, from both inducing breach of contract and causing loss by unlawful means. The well-known authority in which it was established, *Quinn v Leathem* [1901],[29] is over a hundred years old, and there is little else to suggest that it will be engaged in any but the rarest of factual situations. The defendants in *Quinn* were butchers who lawfully refused to continue selling the claimant's meat because he was employing non-union workers. What was material in this case was that the defendants were not found to have been operating in the genuine pursuit of a trade dispute, but were acting with the predominant and particular aim of causing the claimant economic loss. On the facts, it was clear to the Court that the claimant had no objection to his employees joining the union, and had in fact offered to pay for them to do so:

> I do not think that the acts done by the defendants were done 'in contemplation or furtherance of a trade dispute between employers and workmen.' So far as I can see, there was no trade dispute at all. Leathem had no difference with his men. They had no quarrel with him. For his part he was quite willing that all his men should join the union. He offered to pay their fines and entrance moneys. What he objected to was a cruel punishment proposed to be inflicted on some of his men for not having joined the union sooner … the defendants conspired to do harm … to Leathem, and so enable them to wreak their vengeance on Leathem's servants who were not members of the union.[30]

On this point, it is useful to contrast *Quinn* with *Crofter Hand Woven Harris Tweed Co Ltd v Veitch* [1942],[31] in which the defendants refused (lawfully) to deal with the claimant's machine-spun yarn. Here, they did so because they wanted to maintain the demand for hand-spun yarn, and thereby protect the incomes of their union's members. This, rather than the causing of harm to the claimant, was their 'predominant purpose', meaning that they were not liable for lawful means conspiracy.

PROBLEM QUESTION TECHNIQUE

Iris and Jekyll have for a while been concerned about the expansion and increased success of Kali's Eastfield Delicatessen, which has taken more and more custom from their pub over the past year. They decide to teach Kali a lesson. 'Let's be clever about it, though', says Iris to Jekyll. 'Let's not do anything that can get us into trouble – just something that will make Kali's life miserable.' They decide, therefore, to stop the pub's bulk purchase of Kali's vegetable crisps. Since The Star had been the main customer for these, Kali is no longer able to produce them profitably, even for her own direct customers, and loses £700 a month.

▸ The fact that we have here two defendants acting together means that you should start thinking about conspiracy.

▸ It is material that the course of action they choose to take is a perfectly lawful one: they are within their rights to choose not to buy from a particular supplier (presuming this is not a breach of any ongoing contract).

---

29   [1901] AC 495.
30   Lord MacNaghten at 511–12.
31   [1942] AC 435.

▶ Even in the absence of unlawful acts, however, simple conspiracy can be actionable.

▶ It does, however, require the harm caused to the claimant to be an end in itself. Unlike the two *OBG*-defined torts, dealt with above, it is not sufficient for the harm to have been a means to that end.

■ VIEWPOINT

● Do you think the distinction made between *Quinn* and *Crofter* is satisfactory? Does it really come down to the presence of malice? After all, could it not be argued that the defendants in *Quinn* were also trying to promote the interests of their union?

● Do you think it is justifiable to have a different test for intention across different economic torts?

● Do you think the threshold in lawful means conspiracy is too high? Or is it defensible on the basis that lawful means conspiracy is anomalous in other ways, i.e. for making something unlawful simply because it is done in combination with another party?

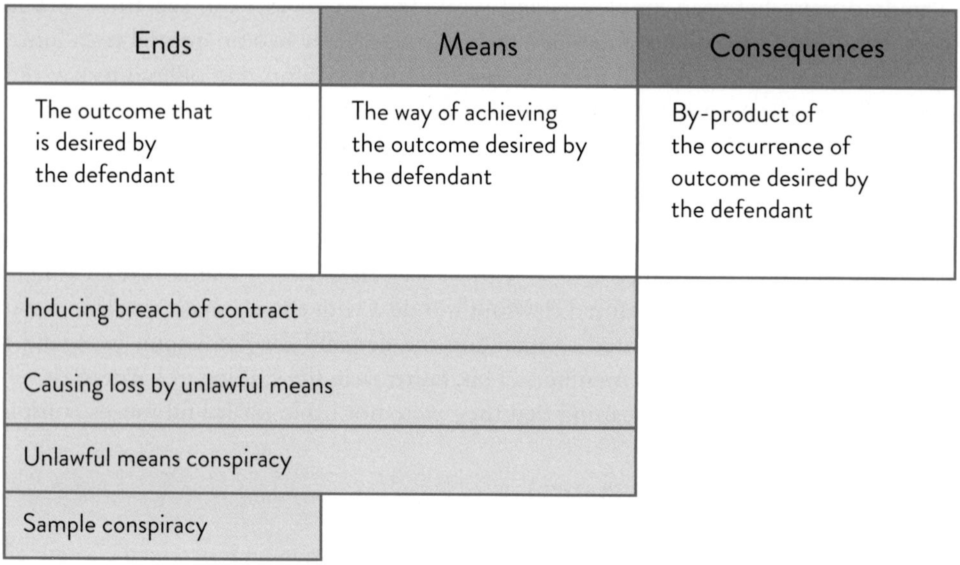

Ends	Means	Consequences
The outcome that is desired by the defendant	The way of achieving the outcome desired by the defendant	By-product of the occurrence of outcome desired by the defendant
Inducing breach of contract		
Causing loss by unlawful means		
Unlawful means conspiracy		
Sample conspiracy		

Figure 11.1: Intention in the economic torts

KEY CASE

Total Network SL v Customs & Excise Commissioners [2008] UKHL 19

The claimant commissioners claimed that the defendant was liable in unlawful means conspiracy for claiming, by means of a 'carousel fraud', VAT rebates to which it was not entitled. The House of Lords was faced with the question of whether it was an essential requirement of the tort of unlawful means conspiracy that the 'unlawful means' in question should be independently actionable in tort against at least one of the conspirators. In its view, it was perfectly clear from the relevant authorities that criminal conduct engaged in as a means of inflicting harm on the claimant was actionable as the tort of conspiracy, whether or not that conduct, if carried out by an individual alone, would be actionable as a tort. In other words, criminal conduct could constitute unlawful means, provided that it was indeed the means of intentionally inflicting harm.

As a result of this decision of the House of Lords, it is clear that 'unlawful means' has a wider meaning in the tort of conspiracy than it has in causing loss by unlawful means. This has been confirmed more recently by the Supreme Court in *JSC BTA Bank v Ablyazov* [2018],[32] in which it was held that contempt of court could constitute unlawful means for the purposes of conspiracy. This means that we now have different criteria for unlawful means and for intention across the economic torts. The threshold for intention is not even consistent across both types of conspiracy: we know from *Lonrho Plc v Fayed* [1992][33] that, for unlawful means conspiracy, *OBG*-type intention (for which the harm being a means to an end, as opposed to being the end in itself) is sufficient. Simple conspiracy is the anomaly in terms of intention, being the only one of the torts discussed here which requires the defendant to have intended the claimant's harm as an end in itself.

PROBLEM QUESTION TECHNIQUE

When Hang and Kali realise that they have both suffered significant losses as a result of Iris's actions, they decide to get their revenge. They cut the cable leading from The Star's satellite dish to its television several times: each time, Jekyll repairs the cable, only for Hang and Kali to cut it again. Sports TV had long been one of the main attractions of The Star, and the frequent interruptions to service drive most customers to the local competitor pub, The Sun. Within six months, The Star has to close, with losses of over £800,000.

▸ Again, the combination of defendants should lead you to consider conspiracy.

▸ Here, the actions are in themselves unlawful. Since the actions are both civilly actionable (trespass to goods) and a crime (criminal damage), you need to consider whether this meets the 'unlawful means' requirement, as extended by *Total Network*.

▸ Once more, the intention of the defendants here is relevant – because this is an example of unlawful means conspiracy, remember it is sufficient if the harm to the claimant is a means to an end (so its being an end in itself certainly meets the threshold).

■ VIEWPOINT

● Does the existence of these differing criteria have the potential to generate incoherence and confusion? Or could it be viewed as the common law using its flexibility to be responsive to different situations and policy demands?

● Is the 'economic torts' label simply an umbrella term that has been applied to several different actions? Would it therefore be a case of the tail wagging the dog, were they to be developed in sync with one another just because they share a textbook chapter?

---

32 [2018] UKSC 19.
33 [1992] 1 AC 448.

DIFFERENT PERSPECTIVES on the economic torts

H. Carty, 'The Economic Torts in the 21st Century' (2008) 124(Oct) LQR 641–74

In this article, Carty is broadly in favour of the House of Lords' development of the economic torts in *OBG*. In her view, the Court was absolutely right to get rid of the 'hybrid' tort of unlawful interference with contractual relations, which required no breach of contract, but instead an unlawful act of the defendant, directed towards affecting the contractual actions of the claimant. This, Carty explains, resulted from an erroneous understanding of several 20th-century decisions, and ignored the basic framework for the economic torts, set out in *Allen v Flood*. She agrees with what she terms the 'abstentionist' judicial approach to economic wrongdoing, evident in *Allen* and re-emphasised in *OBG*, that the common law is not the place to develop rules about fair competition. Carty does, however, outline some uncertainties which remain following the decision: first, she thinks that widening the definition of intention whilst narrowing the concept of unlawful means was an 'unduly complex' way of achieving a result that was historically achieved by asking whether what the claimant suffered was 'targeted harm'. Carty also laments the fact that the decision provided no unanimous definition of 'unlawful means'. Carty's conclusion is that, whilst *OBG* made some good progress in clarifying this area of the law, the House of Lords later arrested this positive development through its later decision in *Total Network*.

S. Deakin and J. Randall, 'Rethinking the Economic Torts' (2009) 72 MLR 519

Here, Deakin and Randall make the case (as the title suggests) for reconceptualising the economic torts – not as a means principally of dealing with intentional harm, or for addressing accessory liability, but as a way of regulating competition. The revised framework, which they set out and defend in this article is based on the economic interests protected by the torts, the behaviour that triggers them and the considerations that should function as legitimate defences to them. They argue that saying that the economic torts maintain the integrity of the competitive process is not the same thing as saying that they have taken a strong position on what constitutes 'fair' or 'unfair' competition. Whilst this question of what is 'fair' in this context is usually now one answered by statute, Deakin and Randall maintain that tort nonetheless retains a role in working out the nuances of that answer. Whilst agreeing with Carty that *OBG* clarified some matters whilst giving rise to further questions, the authors of this piece suggest that the best way to proceed in this area is not to focus on intentional infliction of harm or on secondary liability for wrongs, but instead for the common law to concentrate on 'interests' (such as economic damage or contractual expectation), 'interferences' (such as knowing and intentional procurement of breach or combination coupled with intention to harm) and 'justifications' (such as collective economic self-interest or pre-existing contracts). This, they say, will lead to a more coherent development of the economic torts in the future.

11.5 CHAPTER SUMMARY

This chapter has examined the torts which are grouped together as a category referred to as the economic torts. It has also explained the various ways in which the different torts within that group have developed over time and changed quite markedly in relatively recent years. These changes have challenged the idea that there is a coherent thread running through this whole category, giving rise to questions about whether the differences between the torts should be left to develop, or be minimised. In particular, the analysis has focused on the way in which the House of Lords' decision in *OBG* has served as the most important case in this area in over a century, and how it has produced a clear dichotomy between inducing breach of contract (a form of accessory liability) and causing loss by unlawful means (in which the defendant strikes at the claimant through a third party). Not only, however, did *OBG* leave some questions unanswered, it generated some of its own, particularly in terms of the judicial definition of 'unlawful means'; an issue which was exacerbated by the later decision of the House of Lords in *Total Network*. What should be abundantly clear, having read and digested this chapter, is that a thorough knowledge of *OBG* is absolutely essential if you are going to understand the shape of the economic torts in the 21st century. It is also the case, however, that *OBG* did not deal with all of the economic torts, so, whilst it is necessary knowledge, it is not sufficient. You must also know and understand the relevant authorities on both unlawful means and lawful means (or 'simple') conspiracy.

FURTHER READING

R. Bagshaw, 'Can the Economic Torts be Unified?' (1998) 18 *OJLS* 729

C. Banfi, 'Defining the competition torts as intentional wrongs' (2011) 70(1) *CLJ* 83

H. Carty, *An Analysis of the Economic Torts*, 2nd edn (OUP, 2010)

H. Carty, 'The modern functions of the economic torts: reviewing the English, Canadian, Australian, and New Zealand positions' (2015) 74(2) *CLJ* 261

P. Davies and P. Sales, 'Intentional Harm, Accessories and Conspiracies' (2018) 134 *LQR* 6

J. Lee, 'Restoring Confidence in the Economic Torts' (2007) 15 *Tort L Rev* 172

J. Lee and P. Morgan, 'The Province of *OBG* Determined: The Economic Torts Return to the House of Lords' (2008) *KLJ* 338

J. Murphy, 'Understanding Intimidation' (2014) 77(1) *MLR* 33

Roadmap: Conspiracy Liability

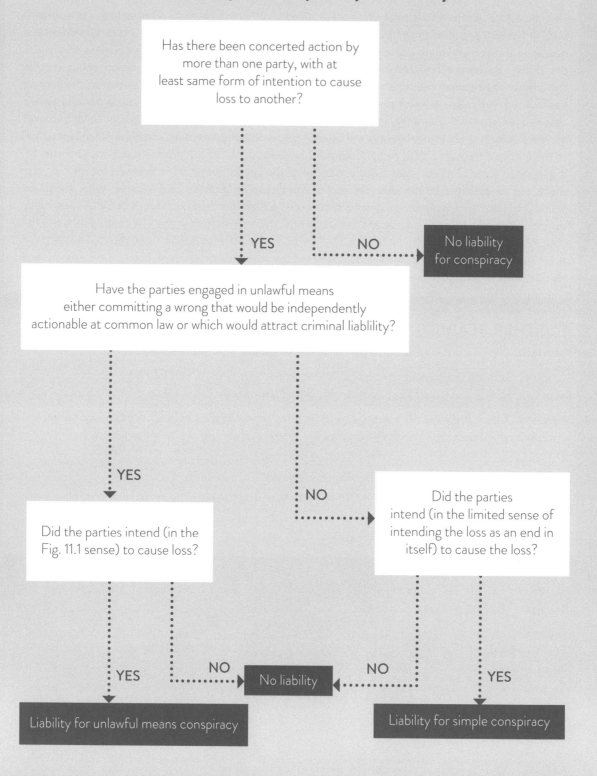

Roadmap: *OBG v Allan*

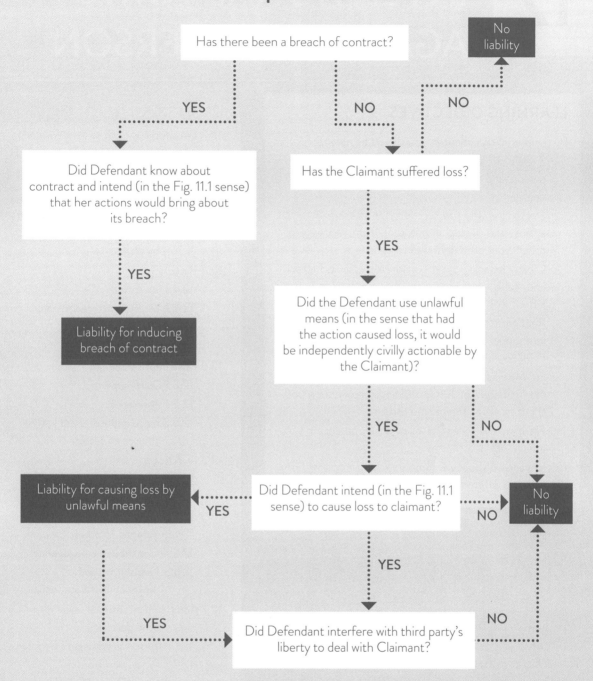

12 INTENTIONAL TORTS AGAINST THE PERSON

LEARNING OBJECTIVES

By the end of this chapter, you should be able to:

- Explain the basis for intentional torts against the person, and how they relate to fault, intention and negligence
- Determine why the recovery for intentional torts against the person is different from recovery of other types of fault-based torts
- Clearly establish what constitutes assault, battery and false imprisonment, and understand the differences between these torts
- Recognise and explain the defences available to intentional torts against the person
- Understand the interrelation between the tort in *Wilkinson v Downton*, the Protection from Harassment Act 1997, malicious prosecution and the trespass to the person torts
- Navigate the recent case law developments in this area
- Engage with policy arguments arising in connection with the different torts

CHAPTER CONTENTS

12.1 Introduction	261
12.2 Comparing the torts	262
12.3 Assault	265
12.3.1 Intentional threat	265
12.3.2 Immediate and direct violence	266
12.3.3 Reasonable expectation by claimant	267
12.4 Battery	268
12.4.1 Intention	268
12.4.2 Direct and immediate force	268
12.4.3 Without consent	270
12.4.4 Hostility?	270
12.5 False imprisonment	272
12.5.1 Confinement	272
12.5.2 Awareness	274
12.5.3 False imprisonment within the prison system	275
12.6 Defences	278
12.6.1 Consent	278
12.6.2 Necessity	279
12.6.3 Self-defence (including defence of others)	281
12.6.4 Contributory negligence	282
12.6.5 Lawful arrest and detention/lawful authority	282
12.7 Additional intentional torts against the person	283
12.7.1 The tort in *Wilkinson v Downton*	284
12.7.2 Protection from Harassment Act 1997	287
12.7.3 Malicious prosecution	292
12.8 Chapter summary	294
Further reading	294
Roadmap	295

PROBLEM QUESTION

Amira, Betty and Claire went to a football match at their local stadium to watch their favourite team, the Walruses, against the Carpenters. At the match there was a group of Carpenters fans who were drinking excessively. As the game progressed, the Walruses took the lead and the Carpenters fans became increasingly drunk and angry at the referee. They all started a team chant, which included waving their arms around quite violently. One of the men hit Amira on the back of the head during the chant. She fell forward, knocking out one of her teeth on the back of a seat. During half-time, two of the Carpenters fans saw Betty leaving to get a drink. They were upset that their team was losing, so they followed Betty, cornered her and started hurling verbal abuse at her. This included violent and sexually explicit comments that made Betty fearful of returning to her seat. She therefore left the match without telling anyone. Betty was previously a victim of a violent assault, and the comments caused her to develop serious anxiety and post-traumatic stress disorder.

The organisers of the match heard a rumour that some people without tickets had got in through a broken security door. In order to locate these individuals, the security guards locked everyone in the stadium – including Amira and Claire – informing people that they were unable to leave until they had provided evidence that they had a valid ticket. Claire, who had lost an uncle in the Hillsborough disaster, became very distraught when she was unable to leave the stadium. She started to panic and ran past the guard to escape. Two of the male security guards saw this and jumped on Claire. They held her down, pulled off her bag and coat, and demanded that she show them her ticket. She could not produce it since Amira was holding everyone's tickets. The security guards then roughly escorted Claire to the head office, locked her inside and refused to let her leave until Amira came down and provided the tickets. Amira eventually found Claire, and they were both released when Amira showed them the tickets. Amira was suffering from concussion after the fall and did not recall being detained in the stadium.

Advise Amira, Betty and Claire of any claims they may have in tort.

12.1 Introduction

This chapter discusses intentional torts against the person. These torts care about the *intention* of the defendant, as opposed to carelessness and negligence. However, whilst there *is* a single tort of 'negligence', there *is no* single tort of 'intention'. There is a multitude of torts, which combine long-standing and established legal issues (*trespass vi et armis*, the historic action for trespass of the case, is the oldest tort established under English common law) with novel and modern contexts, such as the #MeToo movement and the increased concern to protect people from harassment. This chapter discusses six causes of action; three of these clearly fall under the label of trespass to the person torts (assault, battery and false imprisonment), and three which are often described as related or *sui generis* causes of action (the tort in *Wilkinson v Downton*, the Protection from Harassment Act 1997 and malicious prosecution). These torts are connected by a focus on protecting individual autonomy and integrity and on the requirement to show intention of some kind. There are, however, significant differences between the various categories of torts: they serve different purposes, have different elements and do not always provide the same remedies. These differences must be borne in mind when reading through the chapter.

MAKING CONNECTIONS – INTENTIONAL TORTS AND NEGLIGENCE

At one time, it was accepted that you could commence a claim in both negligence and trespass to the person for conduct committed carelessly. This is no longer the case, and there is a now clear distinction between intentional torts and negligence. In *Letang v Cooper* [1965], the claimant was sunbathing on a patch of grass that was also used as a car park, and the defendant drove his car over her legs. The claimant commenced an action for negligence and trespass to the person. At first instance, the claimant was awarded damages for trespass to the person as her claim for negligence was statute-barred by s 2(1) of the Law Reform (Limitations of Actions, etc.) Act 1954. The defendant appealed the decision to the Court of Appeal. Denning MR confirmed the decision in *Fowler v Lanning* [1959],[1] stating: 'when the injury is not inflicted intentionally, but negligently ... the only cause of action is negligence and not trespass. If it were trespass, it would be actionable without proof of damage; and that is not the law today.'[2]

This case therefore reaffirmed the distinction set up in *Fowler v Lanning*; trespass to the person requires intention, and negligence requires negligence or carelessness. If there is no intentional act, the claim will need to be brought in negligence. There is also significant difference in the purpose of negligence when compared with intention to the person torts. The former tort is focused on compensation, whereas the latter are designed to protect personal autonomy and rights of the claimant.[3]

12.2 Comparing the torts

This chapter considers six different torts: assault, battery, false imprisonment, the tort in *Wilkinson v Downton*, the Protection from Harassment Act 1997 and malicious prosecution. These six torts are linked together as they are all 'intentional torts'. There are, however, important differences between the six torts on whether they are trespass to the person torts, actionable *per se* and whether recklessness is a sufficient basis for liability.

Table 12.1: Summary of intentional torts

Cause of Action	Definition	Intentional Tort?	Trespass to the Person Tort?	Actionable *Per Se*?	Recklessness Sufficient?
Assault	An intentional threat causing reasonable expectation of immediate and direct violence	Yes	Yes	Yes	Yes
Battery	Intentionally touching another person without their consent	Yes	Yes	Yes	Yes
False Imprisonment	Confining another against their will without lawful justification	Yes	Yes	Yes	Yes

---

1   [1959] 1 All ER 290.
2   [1965] 1 QB 232, 240.
3   See comments by Lord Scott in *Ashley v Chief Constable of Sussex Police* [2008] 2 WLR 975, 986.

Cause of Action	Definition	Intentional Tort?	Trespass to the Person Tort?	Actionable *Per Se*?	Recklessness Sufficient?
Tort in *Wilkinson v Downton*	Intentional infliction of physical harm or emotional distress	Yes	No	No, need to show physical harm or recognised psychiatric illness	No, specific intention must be shown
Protection from Harassment Act 1997	A course of conduct which the tortfeasor knows or ought to know involves harassment	Yes	No	No, need to show 'harassment'	Yes
Malicious prosecution	The commencement of criminal proceedings against someone without reasonable grounds	Yes	No	Yes	No, malice must be shown

There is no single definition of 'intention' in tort law; however, an element of intention is required in each of the torts. It is therefore insufficient to show merely that harm has been caused by the actions of another. The claimant must also show an intentional action by the defendant. The requirement to show intention was confirmed in *Fowler v Lanning* [1959],[4] where a statement of claim for trespass to the person alleged that the 'defendant shot the plaintiff' resulting in personal injuries. The defendant raised an objection that the statement of claim did not disclose a cause of action, as the claimant did not allege that the shooting was intentional or negligent.[5] Diplock J agreed and held that an intentional tort will not be committed if 'the injury to the plaintiff, although the direct consequence of the act of the defendant, was caused unintentionally'.[6] The different aspects of intention for each cause of action will be considered in more depth below.

Like trespass to land,[7] trespass to the person torts (assault, battery and false imprisonment) and malicious prosecution are actionable *per se*. This means that, provided the claimant can prove the elements of the tort, proof of damage is not required. The wrongful act of the defendant is sufficient to justify damages, as the aim of these torts is to protect the claimant's freedom from interference. The classification of a tort as actionable *per se* is, however, likely to be more important in theory than in practice. If the claimant cannot show that a loss has been suffered – even though all the elements of the tort have been fulfilled – the court will only award nominal or minimal damages.[8] The torts in *Wilkinson v Downton* and the Protection from Harassment Act 1997 are not actionable *per se*, and a specific type of harm must be shown for these torts to be successful.

For the majority of the intentional torts, it is sufficient merely to show that the defendant acted with a reckless disregard for the claimant. Recklessness is 'a word capable of different shades of meaning. In everyday usage, it may include thoughtlessness about the likely consequences in circumstances where there is an obvious high risk.'[9] A number of cases had previously held that recklessness was

4 [1959] 1 All ER 290.

4   [1959] 1 All ER 290.
5   [1959] 1 All ER 290, 292.
6   [1959] 1 All ER 290, 297.
7   See discussion in section 10.7.
8   See, for example, in *R (Lumba) v Secretary of State for the Home Department* [2012] 1 AC 245 and *Walker v Commissioner of Police of the Metropolis* [2015] 1 WLR 312.
9   *Rhodes v OPO* [2016] AC 219, 253.

sufficient for most intentional torts, including assault and battery,[10] false imprisonment[11] and under the Protection from Harassment Act 1997.[12] A crucial element of malicious prosecution is that the defendant acted with malice, so recklessness is not a sufficient basis for this tort.[13] The Supreme Court in *Rhodes v OPO* [2016] also relatively recently confirmed that recklessness is an insufficient basis on which to impose liability for the tort in *Wilkinson v Downton*, and instead specific intention is necessary.[14] If and when recklessness can be sufficient for trespass to the person torts therefore appears to be unsettled. It could be that the Supreme Court comments in *Rhodes v OPO* have changed the approach of the previous (lower court) cases, or it could be that recklessness is sufficient for most intentional torts but not the tort in *Wilkinson v Downton*. Given the difficulties of showing subjective intention for the specific requirement of 'intentional infliction of harm' in the tort in *Wilkinson v Downton*, it appears that the latter approach is favourable,[15] but this will have to be confirmed in future cases.

■ VIEWPOINT

How do you think the courts should approach the requirement of intent for trespass against the person torts? Does it make sense to have differing tests for different torts? Should recklessness ever be sufficient?

MAKING CONNECTIONS – INTENTIONAL TORTS AND CRIMINAL LAW

Many of the torts considered in this chapter have closely related criminal law counterparts. For example, the tort of battery (non-consensual touching of another person) is closely related to criminal battery, which occurs when unlawful violence is exerted on another person. The tort of assault also mirrors the crime of common assault, which occurs when the accused causes another to apprehend immediate violence. Accordingly, a number of cases concerning these counterpart criminal offences are considered in the course of this chapter. It is important, however, to be aware of the key distinctions that remain between the civil and criminal law. This includes different court processes and evidentiary rules and the distinct standard of proof. Furthermore certain, seemingly common, defences (such as self-defence) are available on different bases in criminal and civil matters. Tort law and criminal law also have very different purposes, with the former aiming to achieve compensation and protection of individual rights, while the latter focuses on deterrence, punishment and rehabilitation. It therefore cannot be assumed that the principles found in criminal cases can automatically be applied to tort matters.

---

10   *Breslin v McKevitt* [2011] NICA 33 at [19] as per Higgins LJ who referred to the fact that recklessness was sufficient in the criminal law and stated that 'there can be no logical exclusion of civil liability for the reckless infliction of injury'; *Prichard v Co-operative Group Ltd* [2012] QB 320, 330–1 per Aikens LJ; and *Haystead v Chief Constable of Derbyshire* [2000] 3 All ER 890, 896 where the Court actually categorised the tort as 'a case of reckless and not intentional battery'.

11   [2010] 2 All ER 663, 680 as per Smith LJ, 'in the criminal law, a reckless disregard of the consequences is taken as sufficient to satisfy the requirement of intention. I think that a similar standard should be applied in the tort of false imprisonment.'

12   Protection from Harassment Act 1997, s 1(1)(b).

13   *Juman v Attorney General* [2017] 2 LRC 610 at [17]–[19].

14   [2016] AC 219, 254.

15   For further discussion, see F.A. Trindade, 'Intentional Torts: Some Thoughts on Assault and Battery' (1982) 2(2) *Oxford Journal of Legal Studies* 211, 223–4.

12.3 Assault

The tort of assault is defined by Goff LJ in *Collins v Wilcock* [1984] as 'an act which causes another person to apprehend the infliction of immediate, unlawful force on his person'.[16] It protects individuals from threats of violence which cause them to *fear* immediate harm. The harm remedied by assault is not damage to the claimant's physical self; rather the focus is on protecting their mental integrity.

KEY CASE

Stephens v Myers (1830) 4 Car & P 349

This case highlights the wide scope of assault. The facts were outlined by Tindal LJ:

> It appeared, that the plaintiff was acting as chairman, at a parish meeting, and at the head of a table, at which table the defendant also sat, there being about six or seven persons between him and the plaintiff. The defendant having, in the course of some angry discussion, which took place, been very vociferous, and interrupted the proceedings of the meeting, a motion was made, that he should be turned out, which was carried by a very large majority. Upon this, the defendant said, he would rather pull the chairman out of the chair, than be turned out of the room; and immediately advanced with his fist clenched toward the chairman, but was stopt by the churchwarden, who sat next but one to the chairman, at a time when he was not near enough for any blow he might have meditated to have reached the chairman; but the witnesses said, that it seemed to them that he was advancing with an intention to strike the chairman.[17]

His Honour summed up to the jury that: 'It is not every threat, when there is no actual personal violence, that constitutes an assault, there must, in all cases, be the means of carrying the threat into effect'.

The jury held that there was an actionable assault. As the tort is actionable *per se*, the claimant did not have to show specific harm to obtain damages. However, the jury must have believed that any harm caused was very minor, as damages of only 1 shilling were awarded.

The claimant must show there was an intentional threat that gave them the reasonable expectation of immediate and direct violence. This can be divided into the following three elements:

(1) intentional threat;
(2) immediate and direct violence;
(3) reasonable expectation by claimant.

12.3.1 Intentional threat

The first element is that the defendant must have made an intentional threat to the claimant. The relevant intention is not an intention to actually use the violence; it is an intention (or possibly recklessness[18]) to produce an expectation or fear that violence is about to be used. Whilst the expectation of violence is highly likely to cause fear, the claimant does not actually have to be frightened for the tort to be actionable.[19] For example, if the person makes very violent and aggressive threats to a black-belt karate champion in an attempt to make them fearful, they could potentially be liable for assault even though the claimant (because of their personal abilities) was not scared by the threats made.

---

16 [1984] 1 WLR 1172, 1177.
17 (1830) 4 Car & P 349, 349.
18 *R v Venna* [1976] QB 421; *Bici v Ministry of Defence* [2004] EWHC 786 (QB); see also earlier discussion on whether recklessness is sufficient.
19 *R v Norden* (1755) Fost 129.

12.3.2 Immediate and direct violence

The threat must be related to an immediate use of force, and not something in the remote future. The victim must fear immediate and direct violence from the threat experienced. This must be more than passive obstruction of the claimant.[20] It was previously unclear whether mere words alone were sufficient for this fear to arise, or whether the verbal threat needed to be accompanied with actions.[21] This was settled by *R v Ireland* [1998], where the House of Lords held that – in certain circumstances – words alone could constitute an assault. The decision actually went further and stated that silent calls (i.e. a lack of words) could also be sufficient to produce an expectation of fear or violence.

KEY CASE

R v Ireland [1998] AC 147

This case concerned two appeals. In the first appeal, the defendant made repeated silent telephone calls to three women, mostly at night. As a result of these calls, the women suffered psychiatric illness. He was convicted of three counts of assault occasioning actual bodily harm on the basis that repeated telephone calls of a menacing nature could cause victims to apprehend immediate and unlawful violence. In the second appeal, the defendant had harassed the victim for eight months, and this harassment included making silent and abusive telephone calls, distributing offensive cards in the street in which she lived, visiting her place of work and home, taking photographs of her and her family and sending her a menacing note. The victim was fearful of personal violence and as a result was suffering from a severe depressive illness. The defendant was convicted of unlawfully and maliciously inflicting grievous bodily harm.

Lord Steyn stated:

> It is to assault in the form of an act causing the victim to fear an immediate application of force to her that I must turn. Counsel argued that as a matter of law an assault can never be committed by words alone and therefore it cannot be committed by silence. The premise depends on the slenderest authority, namely an observation by Holroyd J to a jury that 'no words or singing are equivalent to an assault' (see *Meade's and Belt's Case* (1823) 1 Lew CC 184 at 185, 168 ER 1006). The proposition that a gesture may amount to an assault, but

> that words can never suffice, is unrealistic and indefensible. A thing said is also a thing done. There is no reason why something said should be incapable of causing an apprehension of immediate personal violence, e.g. a man accosting a woman in a dark alley saying 'come with me or I will stab you'. I would, therefore, reject the proposition that an assault can never be committed by words.

> That brings me to the critical question whether a silent caller may be guilty of an assault. The answer to this question seems to me to be 'Yes, depending on the facts'. It involves questions of fact within the province of the jury. After all, there is no reason why a telephone caller who says to a woman in a menacing way 'I will be at your door in a minute or two' may not be guilty of an assault if he causes his victim to apprehend immediate personal violence. Take now the case of the silent caller. He intends by his silence to cause fear and he is so understood. The victim is assailed by uncertainty about his intentions. Fear may dominate her emotions, and it may be the fear that the caller's arrival at her door may be imminent. She may fear the possibility of immediate personal violence. As a matter of law the caller may be guilty of an assault: whether he is or not will depend on the circumstance and in particular on the impact of the caller's potentially menacing call or calls on the victim.[22]

The convictions of both defendants were upheld by the House of Lords.

---

20 *Innes v Wylie* (1844) 1 C & K 257, 263.
21 *Meade's & Belt's Case* (1823) 1 Lew CC 184.
22 [1998] AC 147, 162.

12.3.3 Reasonable expectation by claimant

The actions of the defendant must give the claimant a reasonable expectation that force will be used against them. For example, in *Tuberville v Savage* [1669],[23] no assault was found when the words used were, 'if it were not assize time,[24] I would not take such language from you', even though they were combined with the defendant placing his hand on his sword. The court held that, as it was assize time, the claimant did not have a reasonable expectation of violence and no assault occurred. This approach was followed in *Thomas v National Union of Miners (South Wales Area)* [1986],[25] where a claim for assault was rejected as the threats and insults were made from behind a police cordon and the non-striking miners were in a bus; therefore there was no reasonable fear of immediate and direct violence.

The focus is on a reasonable expectation of force. Therefore, the key question is not whether a person actually felt threatened, but whether a reasonable person would feel threatened in the same circumstances. It would be unreasonable for people to be held liable if, for example, a person experiencing a paranoid delusion were threatened by the entirely innocent actions of, say, a pedestrian on the same pavement as her.

It also does not matter if the threat of violence cannot in fact be fulfilled. It will suffice that a reasonable person in the position of the claimant would have had a reasonable expectation of force. For example, threatening someone with a fake, highly realistic knife could induce such worry (provided the claimant was unaware it was a toy knife). The criminal law has clearly held that holding an unloaded gun at someone will amount to an assault.[26] This was further confirmed in *R v Ireland*, where the focus was not on whether the maker of the silent phone calls was in a position to commit violence, but whether the victim had a reasonable expectation of violence arising from the phone calls.

PROBLEM QUESTION TECHNIQUE

During half-time, two of the Carpenters fans saw Betty leaving to get a drink. They were upset that their team was losing, so they followed Betty, cornered her and started hurling verbal abuse at her. This included violent and sexually explicit comments that made Betty fearful of returning to her seat. She therefore left the match without telling anyone.

▸ You will have to examine the elements of assault to determine whether the tort has been committed.

▸ First, decide whether the Carpenters fans made an intentional threat.

▸ Then, consider whether the victim feared immediate and direct violence from the threat experienced. There were no threatening actions included, but take into account *R v Ireland*.

▸ Finally, did the victim's fear amount to a reasonable expectation of force? Even though there were words uttered in the absence of threatening acts in this case, they were the threatening words of two drunk men directed towards a single female.

---

23 (1669) 2 Keb 545.
24 Meaning that judges were in the town for court sessions.
25 [1986] Ch 20, 26; see also *Mbasogo v Logo Ltd (No 1)* [2007] QB 846.
26 *R v St George* (1840) 9 C & P 483, 493; *Logdon v DPP* [1976] Crim LR 121.

12.4 Battery

Battery is a tort protecting an individual's bodily integrity. It prevents people from intentionally touching another person without their consent and consists of the following elements:

(1) intention;
(2) direct and immediate force;
(3) without consent;
(4) hostility?

12.4.1 Intention

The defendant must have intended to touch the claimant, or at least touch someone in the immediate vicinity of the claimant.[27] The test for intention is whether the touching in question occurred as a result of a voluntary act of the defendant. Touching of a person in a sleepwalking state or due to physical force being exerted by a third party are not voluntary acts and therefore could not constitute battery. The intention does not have to be an intention to harm the victim; a mere purposeful touching will suffice. In *Williams v Humphrey* [1975],[28] a 16-year-old boy deliberately pushed the 49-year-old claimant into a pool as a practical joke. Unfortunately, the claimant fell in an awkward manner and sustained very serious injuries from the fall requiring multiple surgeries. The claim for battery succeeded, even though there was no intention to injure him.

A battery will only occur so long as the intention to touch is present at the time of the touching. The amusing case of *Fagan v Metropolitan Police Commissioner* [1969][29] provides an excellent example of the way that the touching and intention must coincide. The defendant accidentally stopped his car on a police officer's foot. When he realised what had happened, the defendant delayed driving off. The court held that while there was no intention at the time of the initial running over of the police officer's foot, the intention was nonetheless present when the defendant delayed in driving off it. There was therefore a battery from the moment that the defendant declined to drive off the officer's foot.

12.4.2 Direct and immediate force

According to orthodoxy, the force directed at the victim of the battery must be 'direct and immediate'. However, at least for the purposes of the criminal law, the meaning ascribed to 'direct contact' is rather a broad one. The High Court of Australia has recently held that the use of tear gas to control detainees in a youth detention centre was an actionable battery.[30] In *Haystead v Chief Constable of Derbyshire* [2000],[31] the defendant punched a woman in the face while she was holding her 12-month-old baby. The baby then fell from her arms and hit his head on the floor. The defendant was convicted of criminal battery, but appealed on the basis that he had made no direct contact with the baby. The appeal was unsuccessful, as the Court of Appeal held that the mother's action 'whereby she lost hold of the child was entirely and immediately the result of the appellant's action in punching her. There is no difference in logic or good sense between the facts of this case and one where the defendant might have used a weapon to fell the child to the floor.'[32]

---

27   *James v Campbell* (1832) 5 C & P 372; *Bici v Ministry of Defence* [2004] EWHC 786 (QB).
28   *Williams v Humphrey* (1975) *The Times*, 20 February.
29   [1969] 1 QB 439; see also *R v Millar* [1983] 2 AC 161.
30   *Binsaris v Northern Territory; Webster v Northern Territory; O'Shea v Northern Territory; Austral v Northern Territory* [2020] HCA 22 (3 June 2020).
31   [2000] 3 All ER 890.
32   *Haystead v Chief Constable of Derbyshire* [2000] 3 All ER 890, 896.

In *Breslin v McKevitt* [2011],[33] the Court of Appeal of Northern Ireland held that a delay of approximately 35 minutes between the planting of a bomb and its explosion did not prevent a finding of direct and immediate force, with Higgans LJ stating:

> If a defendant plants a bomb designed to explode with the intention of injuring a person, common sense leads to [the] conclusion that this would be as unlawful as hitting the injured person or throwing a stone or firing a bullet at him.[34]

The notion of directness was further stretched in *DPP v K* [1990].[35] In this case, a 15-year-old schoolboy was carrying out an experiment with sulphuric acid. He accidentally splashed some acid on his hand and was given permission to go to the bathroom to wash it off. He took with him a test-tube of acid with the purpose of testing its reaction to toilet paper. When he heard footsteps, the defendant poured the acid into the hot air drier to conceal it. He intended to return later and remove it. In the meantime, another pupil used the drier, and acid from the machine was ejected into his face causing a permanent scar.

The conviction of the defendant was upheld on the grounds that recklessness was sufficient for a finding of battery; however, there was no analysis of whether the force was 'direct and immediate'. The time between the defendant leaving the acid and the other schoolboy being injured is an important aspect of the cause of action. The failure to consider this issue is surprising, especially as the facts specifically state that 'the case stated does not reveal how much later [the second schoolboy turned on the drier]'.[36] The timing was surely an important aspect of identifying that direct and immediate force had been used.

KEY CASE

Scott v Shepherd [1558-1774] All ER Rep 295

The facts of the case are as follows:

> The defendant threw a lighted squib [a small explosive firework made from gunpowder] from the street into the market-house which was a covered building supported by arches and enclosed at one end, but open at the other and both the sides, where a large concourse of people were assembled. The lighted squib fell in the stall of one William Yates, who sold gingerbread, etc. One James Willis instantly, and to prevent injury to himself and the wares of Yates, took up the lighted squib from off the stall and then threw it across the market-house where it fell on another stall there of one Ryal, who sold the same sort of wares. He instantly and to save his own goods from being injured took up the lighted squib from off the stall and then threw it to another part of the market-house and, in so throwing it, struck the plaintiff then in the markethouse in the face therewith, and the combustible matter then bursting, put out one of the plaintiff's eyes.[37]

The majority of the Court of Common Pleas held that the defendant was liable for battery. It was apparently not necessary for the defendant to personally touch the claimant, and the injury suffered was held to be the result of the direct and immediate act of the defendant. Blackstone J dissented, stating that the harm suffered was only consequential and not direct. The actions of the two other people had rendered the application of force an indirect one.

33 [2011] NICA 33.
34 [2011] NICA 33, [16].
35 [1990] 1 All ER 331.
36 [1990] 1 All ER 331, 333.
37 [1558-1774] All ER Rep 295, 296.

PART 3

There can also be a spatial distance between the defendant's actions and the victim's harm. In *R v Lydsey* [1995], the Court of Appeal held that spitting constituted a battery as it resulted in 'physical contact of the body'.[38] Throwing an item that goes on to strike someone will also be treated as applying direct and immediate force.[39]

12.4.3 Without consent

The touching needs to occur without the consent of the victim. The claimant must therefore prove there was no agreement to the touching that gave rise to the battery.[40] This element does, however, pose difficulties. There are a lot of situations in which someone touches another person without obtaining specific consent – shaking hands with someone you have just met, walking along a crowded street and bumping into others, sitting next to people on public transport and playing contact sports are all examples.[41] It would be unreasonable if these instances could give rise of a claim of battery, but how does the law deal with the lack of consent? In *Collins v Wilcock* [1984], it was held that these activities are all 'generally acceptable in the ordinary conduct of everyday life', and therefore parties are taken to 'impliedly consent' to this type of touching.[42] This is, however, far from ideal, and the defences section below further discusses the challenges posed by consent.

PROBLEM QUESTION TECHNIQUE

Claire, who had lost an uncle in the Hillsborough disaster, became very distraught when she was unable to leave the stadium. She started to panic and ran past the guard to escape. Two of the male security guards saw this and jumped on Claire. They held her down, pulled off her bag and coat, and demanded that she show them her ticket.

▶ Whilst the main aspect of this factual scenario is false imprisonment, some of the actions of the security guards might also constitute a battery against Claire.

▶ You need to consider the four main elements of battery and determine whether they are all met.

12.4.4 Hostility?

This element has been included with a question mark, because it is unclear what, if any, role hostility plays in the tort of battery. The starting point here is Lord Holt CJ's statement in *Cole v Turner* [1704] that 'the least touching of another in *anger* is a battery'.[43]

KEY CASE

Wilson v Pringle [1986] 2 All ER 440

The claimant and the defendant were in the same class and were both aged 13. The claimant alleged that he was seriously injured when the defendant intentionally jumped on him. The defendant argued that he merely pulled the claimant's schoolbag off his shoulder in the course of 'ordinary horseplay'

38 [1995] 3 All ER 654, 657.
39 See example given by Fortescue CJ in *Reynolds v Clarke* (1725) 1 Stra 634, 636.
40 *Freeman v Home Office (No 2)* [1983] 3 All ER 589; affirmed by the Court of Appeal in [1984] QB 524.
41 See comments from Holt CJ in *Cole v Turner* (1704) 6 Mod Rep 149.
42 *Collins v Wilcock* [1984] 1 WLR 1172, 1177.
43 (1704) 6 Mod Rep 149; 90 ER 958 (emphasis added).

and that the claimant had then fallen to the ground and sustained injuries. Judge Wilson Mellor QC held that a battery was committed on the grounds that the defendant admitted intentionally touching the claimant in a direct and immediate manner without his consent. This decision was appealed to the Court of Appeal which held that, in addition to these elements, the touching needed to have a 'hostile' nature. Croom-Johnson LJ stated:

> In our view, the authorities lead one to the conclusion that in a battery there must be an intentional touching or contact in one form or another of the plaintiff by the defendant. That touching must be proved to be a hostile touching. That still leaves unanswered the question 'when is

a touching to be called hostile?' Hostility cannot be equated with ill-will or malevolence. It cannot be governed by the obvious intention shown in acts like punching, stabbing or shooting. It cannot be solely governed by an expressed intention, although that may be strong evidence. But the element of hostility, in the sense in which it is now to be considered, must be a question of fact for the tribunal of fact. It may be imported from the circumstances.

As in this case the touching occurred during juvenile 'horseplay', there was not the relevant hostility required for battery. The Court of Appeal therefore allowed the appeal and held that no battery had occurred.

Wilson v Pringle raised the question of whether hostility is an essential element of the tort of battery, and the Court of Appeal held that the touching in question must indeed go beyond being merely 'intentional' and be hostile too. In the course of so holding, the court used the requirement of hostility to distinguish an incidental touching from an actionable battery. As Croom-Johnson LJ put it: 'although we are all entitled to protection from physical molestation, we live in a crowded world in which people must be considered as taking on themselves some risk of injury (where it occurs) from the acts of others which are not in themselves unlawful.'[44] The requirement of hostility was confirmed by Lord Hoffmann in *Wainwright v Home Office* [2004][45] where battery was defined as touching someone with 'hostile intent'.

Nonetheless, insisting that a touching be hostile appears to challenge the core point that the mere touching of another person without consent or lawful excuse is battery.[46] Accordingly, the requirement of hostility was severely criticised by Lord Goff in the House of Lords in *Re F*, where he stated:

> In the old days it used to be said that, for a touching of another's person to amount to a battery, it had to be a touching 'in anger' (see *Cole v Turner* (1794) 6 Mod. 149 per Holt CJ); and it has recently been said that the touching must be 'hostile' to have that effect (see *Wilson v Pringle* [1987] QB 237, 253). I respectfully doubt whether that is correct. A prank that gets out of hand; an over-friendly slap on the back; surgical treatment by a surgeon who mistakenly thinks that the patient has consented to it — all these things may transcend the bounds of lawfulness, without being characterised as hostile. Indeed the suggested qualification is difficult to reconcile with the principle that any touching of another's body is, in the absence of lawful excuse, capable of amounting to a battery and a trespass.

Whilst Lord Goff accurately highlights the complexities of requiring 'hostility', not every touching of another person's body without consent could possibly constitute an actionable battery. As previously discussed, there are many circumstances where we intentionally touch others without consent that cannot be reasonably classified as battery.

---

44   [1986] 3 WLR 1, 11.
45   [2004] 2 AC 406. See discussion of this case at 12.7.1 below.
46   See, for example, Lord Goff's comments in *Re F* [1990] 2 AC 1.

Whilst the decision in *Wilson v Pringle* makes plain that a mere incidental touch will not amount to an actionable battery, the requirement of 'hostility' seems dubious. Hostility does not capture the 'essence' of the wrong that the tort of battery is seeking to address. Kissing someone without consent[47] and performing lifesaving surgery against a patient's religious beliefs are not acts that are motivated by a 'hostile' intention, but they both clearly constitute a battery.

■ VIEWPOINT

Should hostility ever be a requirement for battery? What are the courts looking for when requiring that the touching be 'hostile' in nature?

PROBLEM QUESTION TECHNIQUE

At the match there was a group of Carpenters fans who were drinking excessively. As the game progressed, the Walruses took the lead and the Carpenters fans became increasingly drunk and angry at the referee. They all started a team chant, which included waving their arms around quite violently. One of the men hit Amira in the back of the head during the chant. She fell forward, knocking out one of her teeth on the back of a seat.

▶ This requires an examination of whether the actions of the Carpenters fans went beyond what would normally be expected at a football match.

▶ If you take Lord Goff's view in *Re F* that any 'any touching of another's body is, in the absence of lawful excuse, capable of amounting to a battery', this is clearly actionable.

▶ If, however, *Wilson v Pringle* is still good law, then the action of the team chant and waving arms around could be considered to lack the necessary 'hostility'.

12.5 False imprisonment

The tort of false imprisonment recognises and protects personal autonomy and freedom of movement. It prevents people from confining others against their will without lawful justification for doing so, and it is one of the three remaining civil actions where the claimant is entitled to trial by jury. False imprisonment by the government can overlap with the protection of liberty under Article 5(1) of the European Convention on Human Rights (ECHR). No force or physical conduct is required, but false imprisonment often occurs in conjunction with an assault or a battery. It is therefore important to remember that the same scenario can potentially lead to both false imprisonment *and* assault or battery.

12.5.1 Confinement

The claimant must be confined in a way that restricts their liberty. The confinement must be complete and amount to more than a mere obstruction forcing a person to follow an undesired route. This is evidenced in *Bird v Jones* [1845],[48] where the claimant was unable to use his false imprisonment as a defence to a charge for breach of the peace. A part of Hammersmith Bridge in London was sectioned off without due permission. The claimant refused to go back and use the public footpath, instead choosing to climb over the fence. He was then prevented from doing so and arrested.

---

47   *R v Chief Constable of Devon and Cornwall, ex parte Central Electricity Generating Board* [1982] QB 458, 471 (Lord Denning citing Salmon and Henston's *Law of Torts*).

48   (1845) 7 QB 742.

Can the defendant confine the claimant for the purpose of ensuring that the claimant fulfils her contractual obligations? The Privy Council considered this question in *Robertson v Balmain New Ferry Co* [1910].[49] The defendant ran a harbour steam ferry and charged customers for entering and exiting the wharf (as opposed to charging for the use of the ferry). There were turnstiles on the premises that prevented people from leaving without paying the charge and a sign clearly stating, 'Notice. A fare of one penny must be paid on entering or leaving the wharf. No exception will be made to this rule, whether the passenger has travelled by the ferry or not.' The claimant entered the wharf and paid his penny, intending to get the ferry. When he discovered that there was a 20-minute wait, he decided to exit, but employees of the defendant prevented him from leaving until payment was made. The Privy Council held that notice of the terms and conditions had been given to the claimant and formed part of his contract with the defendant. The toll was reasonable, and the defendant was entitled to resist forcible fare evasion by the claimant. The claim for false imprisonment therefore failed.

This approach was (controversially) applied in *Herd v Weardale Steel, Coal and Coke Co Ltd* [1915].[50] The claimant was a miner who worked in the defendant's coal mines. He descended into the mine at 9.30am in the morning for the purposes of working until the shift finished at 4pm. The miner wanted to be brought to the surface at 11am as he felt that the work was dangerous. The employer refused to do this until 1.30pm, and the miner made a claim for false imprisonment for the period that he was unable to leave the coal mine. The defendant company was able to defend a claim for false imprisonment on the basis that he had consented to the restrictions on his liberty. It is, however, important to note that this decision was made over 100 years ago, and (fortunately) employee rights have advanced significantly since then under both common law and statute.

It can often be difficult to find consistency within the decisions on what constitutes confinement. One particularly complex case is *R v Bournewood Community and Mental Health NHS Trust, ex parte L* [1998].

KEY CASE

R v Bournewood Community and Mental Health NHS Trust, ex parte L [1998] UKHL 24

The claimant in this matter had extreme intellectual disabilities and was incapable of consenting to medical treatment. He became distressed and was taken by ambulance to the Accident and Emergency Department of a local hospital. He was then sedated and detained in an unlocked mental health ward in the behavioural unit at the hospital. It was determined that there was no requirement to detain him under the provisions of the Mental Health Act 1983 as he was fully compliant and did not resist admission. The claimant was admitted informally.

The Court of Appeal found that the claimant had been falsely imprisoned, and stated that

'a person is detained in law if those who have control over the premises in which he is have the intention that he shall not be permitted to leave those premises and have the ability to prevent him from leaving'.[51]

The Trust successfully appealed this decision. The majority of the House of Lords held that the actions of the Trust did not constitute false imprisonment. The claimant showed no desire to leave, and it was held that the deprivation of liberty must be actual, rather than potential. The House of Lords relied on the comments of Lord Macnaghten in *Syed Mahamad Yusuf-ud-Din v Secretary of State for India in Council* [1903][52] that

---

49   [1910] AC 295 (also referred to as *Robinson v Balmain New Ferry Co Ltd*).
50   [1915] AC 67.
51   [1998] 1 All ER 634, 639.
52   (1903) 19 TLR 496, 497.

'nothing short of actual detention and complete loss of freedom would support an action for false imprisonment'.

This case seems to conflict with other cases, especially as the claimant was sedated, and, if he had tried to leave, the Trust would have applied for an order for detention under the Mental Health Act 1983. Quite unsurprisingly, the House of Lords' decision was overturned by the European Court of Human Rights in *HL v United Kingdom* [2004]. The Strasbourg court rejected the House of Lords' distinguishing between 'actual restraint of a person (which would amount to false imprisonment) and restraint which was conditional upon his seeking to leave (which would not constitute false imprisonment)'.[53] This distinction was held not to apply for the purpose of the ECHR, and therefore the defence in Article 5(1)(e) was not enlivened. The European Court of Human Rights determined that the NHS did not have adequate procedural processes in place to ensure that there was no breach of Article 5.

This case highlights the potential for a distinction between the common law claim for false imprisonment and a claim for deprivation of liberty under Article 5 ECHR. The law on this relationship is still unsettled. It could be held that Article 5 now 'covers the field' and replaces the common law action in cases against public defendants. The English courts do not, however, seem to have accepted this, as in *Austin v Metropolitan Police Commissioner* [2009],[54] it was held that confinement could be justified on the basis of necessity.[55]

The tort of false imprisonment is again actionable *per se*, so the claimant can obtain a remedy without proof of damage. If the imprisonment is only a very limited one, then nominal damages only are available. In *R (Lumba) v Secretary of State for the Home Department* [2011],[56] the Supreme Court held that a victim of false imprisonment was only entitled to nominal damages. This is because even though they had been detained under an unlawful policy, they had suffered no loss. If the Department had followed the correct policy, the claimant would have been detained anyway. This meant that the claimant did not suffer any loss and only nominal damages were awarded.[57]

This case can be compared with *Walker v Commissioner of Police of the Metropolis* [2015],[58] where a police officer detained the claimant in the doorway for 'a matter of seconds'. The Court of Appeal held that there had been false imprisonment, but the claimant was entitled to minimal damages of £5 for 'the brief and "technical" imprisonment immediately before his own unlawful violence and initial [lawful] arrest'.[59]

12.5.2 Awareness

The tort of false imprisonment will be actionable even if the claimant was unaware of the confinement.[60] In *R v Bournewood Community and Mental Health NHS Trust, ex parte L*, there was no suggestion that the claimant's unawareness of his confinement could prevent a finding of false

---

53 (App No 45508/99) (2004) 81 BMLR 131, 162.
54 [2009] UKHL 5.
55 See further discussion below for defences at 12.6.5.
56 [2011] UKSC 12.
57 This case is discussed further at 12.5.3 below.
58 [2015] 1 WLR 312.
59 [2015] 1 WLR 312, 329. The Court of Appeal defined these damages as 'nominal', but it is respectfully submitted that they cannot actually be nominal damage as some (exceptionally minimal) loss was suffered by the claimant as opposed to *R (Lumba) v Secretary of State for the Home Department*, where no loss at all was suffered.
60 See discussion in *Meering v Grahame-White Aviation Co Ltd* (1920) 122 LT 44, 53 per Atkin LJ.

imprisonment. It was simply accepted that awareness of imprisonment is not an ingredient of the tort. This approach is in line with other trespass against the person torts. In just the same way that a sexual assault committed against an unconscious person will count as a battery, so too will imprisonment of the unconscious result in liability for false imprisonment. It is therefore hard to see why it would be any different for false imprisonment. This was discussed by Lord Griffiths who stated that 'the law attaches supreme importance to the liberty of the individual and if he suffers a wrongful interference with that liberty it should remain actionable even without proof of special damage'.[61]

There are, however, some cases that appear to challenge the principle that the claimant does not need to be aware of the confinement. For example, in *Herring v Boyle* [1834],[62] a student was detained in a private school until his mother had paid the outstanding account. The court held that there was no false imprisonment because the student was unaware that he was restrained. This case was decided almost 200 years ago, and it has arguably been superseded by subsequent developments. Alternatively, it could be justified on the basis of *Robinson v Balmain Ferry*, that reasonable confinement is allowed to ensure fulfilment of contractual obligations – in this case outstanding payments to the school.

PROBLEM QUESTION TECHNIQUE

Amira was suffering from concussion after the fall and did not recall being detained in the stadium.

▸ Intentional torts are actionable without proof of damage.

▸ It is important here to recognise that Amira's lack of awareness of her detention does not prevent her from making a claim for false imprisonment.

▸ Minimal damages can, however, be awarded – see *Walker v Commissioner of Police of the Metropolis*.

12.5.3 False imprisonment within the prison system

False imprisonment within the prison system is quite a complicated issue. As the potential claimant has already been lawfully imprisoned by the State, it is important to determine if and when they can be falsely imprisoned *in addition* to their existing lawful imprisonment. This was discussed in *Weldon v Home Office* [1990], with Fox LJ stating:

> There is no reason, apparent to me, why the nature of the tort, evolved by the common law for the protection of personal liberty, should be held to be such as to deny its availability to a convicted prisoner whose residual liberty should, in my judgment, be protected so far as the law can properly achieve unless statute requires otherwise.[63]

As seen in *R v Governor of Brockhill Prison; ex p Exans* [2001],[64] continuing imprisonment beyond the sentence imposed constitutes false imprisonment.

Not every error made within the prison system will result in an actionable false imprisonment. The courts are sensitive to the need for prison authorities to balance multiple competing factors.

---

61   *Murray v Ministry of Defence* [1988] 1 WLR 692, 704.
62   (1834) 1 CM & R 377; 149 ER 1126.
63   [1990] 3 All ER 672, 681
64   [2001] 1 AC 19.

In *R v Deputy Governor of Parkhurst Prison, ex p Hague* [1991],[65] it was held that a breach of the Prison Rules making the prisoner subject to continued segregation did not amount to confinement sufficient for false imprisonment. Whilst this may seem a slightly unfair or harsh outcome for the prisoner involved, to find otherwise would potentially mean that any technical breach of the internal rules could give rise to a claim for false imprisonment.[66] This does not give prison authorities complete discretion to ignore the prison rules and legal rights of those incarcerated. It would be a question of fact and degree whether the actions in question are sufficient to justify the courts finding against the authority.

KEY CASE

R (Lumba) v Secretary of State for the Home Department [2011] UKSC 12

In this case, five foreign national prisoners, including the two claimants, were detained under the Immigration Act 1971 following the completion of their prison sentences. The process for detaining the prisoners occurred as a result of an unpublished policy on the detention of convicted foreign nationals following the completion of their prison sentences and did not occur in accordance with the published process.

The claimants argued that they had been unlawfully detained by the Secretary of State as the unpublished policy was inconsistent with the published policy. The Supreme Court found that the claimants had been unlawfully detained and that their claims for false imprisonment should succeed. The claimants claimed they were entitled to vindicatory or exemplary damages, but the majority of the Supreme Court held that they were entitled to no more than nominal damages, as they had suffered no loss or damage.

R v Deputy Governor of Parkhurst Prison, ex p Hague was relied on in the Court of Appeal in *Iqbal v Prison Officers Association* [2010].[67] In the latter case, the prisoner was serving a 15-year prison sentence but was entitled to leave his prison cell during the day for certain activities (exercise, cleaning work, contacting family members etc.). The Prison Service went on strike, and the Governor decided that prisoners should remain in their cells throughout the strike. The strike lasted a day, but broke the prisoner's usual routine. He sought an action for false imprisonment on the basis that his inability to leave his prison cell that day amounted to confinement for six hours. Judge Spencer QC accepted the argument and assessed damages at £5. The defendant was successful on appeal, with the majority of the Court of Appeal stating that there was no false imprisonment. First, confinement required a positive act, and the actions of the prison offers only amounted to an omission (a failure to unlock and open the prisoner's cell).[68] Secondly, the cause of the confinement was the Governor's order and not the strike, and therefore the officers could not be held liable for the claimant's ongoing imprisonment. In contrast, in *R (on the application of Jalloh) v Secretary of State for the Home Department* [2020][69], the Supreme Court held that a curfew and home detention were sufficient constraints on the claimant's liberty to constitute false imprisonment.

---

65 [1991] 3 All ER 733.
66 [1991] 3 All ER 733, 744.
67 [2010] QB 732.
68 [2009] EWCA Civ 1312, [22].
69 [2020] UKSC 4.

KEY CASE

R (on the application of Jalloh) v Secretary of State for the Home Department [2020] UKSC 4

This case considered whether a curfew and home detention were sufficient constraints to constitute false imprisonment. The claimant was granted asylum in 2003, but convicted of various offences in 2006, and a deportation order was made against him in 2008. There was a further conviction in 2013, and, when the custodial sentence was completed, the claimant was issued with a document headed 'NOTICE OF RESTRICTION'. This imposed a number of restrictions on him, including reporting to an immigration officer three times a week, living in a specified address, electronic monitoring and staying at home between 11pm and 7am every day. If he did not comply with these restrictions, there was a potential penalty of £5,000 and/or six months' imprisonment.

The curfew was in place for 891 days. Although there were a number of occasions when the claimant breached the curfew, either for the entire night or part of it, he generally sought to comply with the restrictions. In 2016, the curfew was lifted when the Court of Appeal held that the Secretary of State did not have the power to impose a curfew by way of restriction.

The claimant successfully sued for false imprisonment and was awarded £4,000. The Secretary of State appealed this decision to the Court of Appeal and then Supreme Court, contending that the curfew did not amount to imprisonment at common law.

In the Supreme Court, the Secretary of State made five arguments as to why the curfew did not amount to false imprisonment. First, imprisonment requires constraint on a person's freedom of movement, and this usually occurs with physical or human barriers. The claimant's voluntary compliance with the curfew was therefore insufficient to amount to false imprisonment. Secondly, if the constraint is not by physical barriers, it must be sufficient to keep the detained person in the same place. Thirdly, the constraint must result in a 'total' or 'complete' restriction on the individual (referring specifically to *Bird v Jones*). Fourthly, it is not false imprisonment if the individual can leave by another route, even if that is not the way he wants and the route involves trespassing. Finally, it is not sufficient that the act of leaving would trigger an adverse response, such as prosecution or arrest. On the basis of these arguments, the Secretary of State stated the claimant's situation cannot be compared with being detained in an open prison or psychiatric hospital. As the claimant was not locked in his home, there was nothing preventing him from leaving, he broke the curfew on a number of occasions and he was not physically constrained, the curfew did not result in false imprisonment.

The Supreme Court rejected all of these arguments. It distinguished the curfew from cases like *Bird v Jones* where the claimant could cross the bridge by another route, or *Robinson v Balmain* where the claimant merely had to pay the agreed fare to leave. The Court held that the defendant had defined the place that the claimant had to stay between the hours of 11pm and 7am. The claimant did not voluntarily comply with curfew, and instead the restrictions were forced on him with electronic monitoring and threats of punishments in the event of a breach. Lady Hale commented that 'all of this was backed up by the full authority of the State, which was claiming to have the power to do this. The idea that the claimant was a free agent, able to come and go as he pleased, is completely unreal.'[70]

The Supreme Court therefore dismissed the appeal, holding that the home detention and curfew amounted to false imprisonment. In doing so, it referred to the 2007 House of Lords decision in *Secretary of State for the Home Department v JJ* [2007] which commented that a curfew enforced by electronic tagging, clocking in and clocking out, and arrest or imprisonment for breach was a 'classic detention or confinement'.[71]

---

70   [2020] UKSC 4 at [27].
71   [2007] UKHL 45 at [59].

PART 3

False imprisonment within the prison system is intimately bound up with the defence of lawful authority, which is discussed in more detail below. It is worth noting at this stage that the burden of proof is on the *claimant* to show that the use of legal discretion was not reasonable.

■ VIEWPOINT

What challenges does the court need to address when considering whether a claimant has been falsely imprisoned whilst incarcerated? Is the law achieving the correct balance of the competing tensions?

12.6 Defences

For a detailed analysis of tort law defences, see Chapter 16 of this book. This section focuses on certain defences that apply differently in the context of intentional torts, including trespass to the person.[72] The following defences will be considered:

(1) Consent
(2) Necessity
(3) Self-defence
(4) Contributory negligence
(5) Lawful authority

12.6.1 Consent

There is a general requirement for assault, battery and false imprisonment that the wrongdoing occurred without the consent of the victim.[73] Consent is central to the operation of the trespass torts considered in this section. It is therefore not a 'true' defence; the claimant has the burden of proving that consent was not given.[74]

There are limits to consent. The first is whether the consent is 'genuine' and therefore capable of precluding a successful action against the defendant. The consent obtained must be sincerely given and not induced by fraud or misrepresentation.[75]

The second limitation occurs in a medical situation, in which consent to a treatment may not be sufficient if the doctor has not given the patient adequate information about the procedure in question. Information about the general risks will be sufficient to find that consent has been given.[76] Consent will, however, not be valid where the claimant's assent was induced by the provision of false information, or information given in bad faith. In *Appleton v Garrett* [1995], the claimant had consented to dental work being completed. Yet, it was unnecessary treatment performed solely for the financial gain of the defendant. A claim in battery was upheld as the consent given was not 'suitably informed consent'.[77] The Supreme Court held in *Montgomery v Lanarkshire* [2015][78] that doctors must ensure that patients are able to make 'informed decisions'. This involves having a dialogue so that the patient understands the seriousness of her condition, the anticipated benefits and risks of the proposed treatment and any reasonable alternatives.

---

72 There are some other defences, such as provocation, that have been held not to be a valid defence to trespass to the person torts: see *Lane v Holloway* [1968] 1 QB 379, cf Lord Denning's comments in *Murphy v Culhane* [1977] 1 QB 94.

73 *Freeman v Home Office (No 2)* [1984] QB 524, cf comments from Clarke MR in *Ashley v Chief Constable of Sussex Police* [2007] 1 WLR 398, 410.

74 *Freeman v Home Office (No 2)* [1984] 1 QB 524, 537–9 (McCowan J), 557 (Sir John Donaldson MR).

75 *R v Williams* [1923] 1 KB 340; *Chatterton v Gerson* (1980) 1 BMLR 80, particularly 89–90.

76 *Chatterton v Gerson* (1980) 1 BMLR 80; *Sidaway v Bethlam Royal Hospital* [1985] AC 871.

77 *Appleton v Garrett* (1995) 34 BMLR 23 at 25.

78 [2015] AC 1430.

Finally, consent may be negatived by the application of public policy. In *Re F* [1989], Lord Griffiths held that 'although the general rule is that the individual is the master of his own fate the judges through the common law have, in the public interest, imposed certain constraints on the harm that people may consent to being inflicted on their bodies'. The most famous example of this is *R v Brown* [1994], where the House of Lords held that – in a criminal law setting – individuals could not consent to serious injuries inflicted during sexual practices.[79] The application of this restriction on tort law claims is, however, questionable.[80]

12.6.2 Necessity

The nature of trespass to the person torts raises interesting questions for potential rescuers and providers of medical assistance. If you provide CPR to someone who is unconscious, you clearly meet the requirements of (1) an intentional touching, that is (2) direct and immediate, and (3) without consent. The same could be said for a doctor providing lifesaving medical care to very young children,[81] or performing sterilisation on a person with severe learning difficulties who would be unable to physically or emotionally handle pregnancy.[82] In some circumstances, an individual will not be in a position to give consent to physical contact, even if that touching occurs so as to provide life-saving assistance or medical treatment. A defence of necessity is therefore available – but in very limited circumstances.

Necessity is a well-established defence to trespass to the person tort, and it is particularly important to understand how it works in relation to the tort in question. The requirements were laid out by Lord Goff in *Re F*:

> To fall within the principle, not only (1) must there be a necessity to act when it is not practicable to communicate with the assisted person, but also (2) the action taken must be such as a reasonable person would in all the circumstances take, acting in the best interests of the assisted person.

The unique factual scenario of this case, however, highlighted the intersection between the defence of necessity and public interest.

KEY CASE

Re F (sterilisation) [1989] 2 WLR 1025

F was a 36-year-old woman who resided in a mental hospital as a voluntary in-patient. She had delayed mental development, but had formed a sexual relationship with a male patient. The staff at the hospital and F's mother believed that she would be unable to cope with the impact of pregnancy and childbirth, but all other forms of contraception were unsuitable. The mother therefore issued an originating summons requesting a declaration from the court that the operation would not amount to an unlawful act due to the absence of F's consent.

Scott Baker J at first instance made a declaration of the lawfulness of the proposed operation as it was held to be in the best interests of F. The jurisdiction of the court to make such an order was, however, unsettled and this matter was appealed to the House of Lords.

---

79 [1994] 1 AC 212. Other situations where the defence of consent may not be effective due to public policy considerations could include particularly dangerous fighting or entering into a contract allowing someone to injure another for their own personal pleasure.

80 In *Ashley v Chief Constable of Sussex Police* [2008] 1 AC 962, 973, Lord Scott focused on the differing applications of defences to criminal and civil matters on the basis that 'the function of the civil law of tort is different'.

81 *Re A (Children) (Conjoined Twins: Surgical Separation)* [2001] Fam 147.

82 *Re F (Sterilisation)* [1989] 2 WLR 1025.

The House of Lords held that the court had an inherent jurisdiction to make a declaration that a proposed operation was in the patient's best interests. The Court upheld the declaration of lawfulness. The complex and interrelated nature of the defences to trespass to the person was highlighted by Lord Griffiths, who stated:

> I agree that those charged with the care of the mentally incompetent are protected from any criminal or tortious action based on lack of consent. Whether one arrives at this conclusion by applying a principle of 'necessity' as do Lord Goff of Chieveley and Lord Brandon of Oakbrook or by saying that it is in the public interest as did Neill LJ in the Court of Appeal, appear to me to be inextricably interrelated conceptual justifications for the humane development of the common law. Why is it necessary that the mentally incompetent should be given treatment to which they lack the capacity to consent? The answer must surely be because it is in the public interest that it should be so.[83]

The defence of necessity is limited to circumstances where the person cannot practically communicate, such as when people are unconscious or are mentally ill.[84] If the individual is not of sound mind, the relevant test is found in the Mental Capacity Act (MCA) 2005.

KEY LEGISLATION

Mental Capacity Act 2005

1   The principles

(1)   The following principles apply for the purposes of this Act.

(2)   A person must be assumed to have capacity unless it is established that he lacks capacity.

(3)   A person is not to be treated as unable to make a decision unless all practicable steps to help him to do so have been taken without success.

(4)   A person is not to be treated as unable to make a decision merely because he makes an unwise decision.

(5)   An act done, or decision made, under this Act for or on behalf of a person who lacks capacity must be done, or made, in his best interests.

(6)   Before the act is done, or the decision is made, regard must be had to whether the purpose for which it is needed can be as effectively achieved in a way that is less restrictive of the person's rights and freedom of action.

2   People who lack capacity

(1)   For the purposes of this Act, a person lacks capacity in relation to a matter if at the material time he is unable to make a decision for himself in relation to the matter because of an impairment of, or a disturbance in the functioning of, the mind or brain.

The MCA 2005 creates a distinction between people who have capacity (and therefore are deemed to be able to consent) and those who do not have capacity (and therefore cannot consent). The threshold test for capacity is whether the person is able, at the material time, to make a decision

---

83   [1989] 2 WLR 1025, 1079–80.

84   *Airedale NHS Trust v Bland* [1993] 1 All ER 821.

for him- or herself. This is further explained in s 3, which states that a person is unable to make a decision if they are unable to:

(a)   understand the information relevant to the decision; or

(b)   retain that information; or

(c)   use or weigh that information as part of the process of making the decision; or

(d)   communicate the decision (whether by talking, using sign language or any other means).[85]

There are significant challenges to the application of the Act in many circumstances. As outlined by Herring and Wall, the MCA 2005 'typically seeks to determine the minimum necessary for autonomy and treats the person as autonomous once they cross that threshold'.[86] It is therefore a blunt instrument, and often cannot respond adequately to challenges posed by trespass to the person torts.

If the individual does fall within the statutory definition of incapacity, they will be deemed to have the capacity to make their own decisions, including consenting (and withholding consent). A person with sound mind is entitled to refuse to accept life-saving treatment, even if it will result in the death of themselves[87] (and – in the relevant circumstances – their unborn baby[88]). Necessity does not extend to circumstances where an adult of sound mind clearly refuses medical treatment[89] and, arguably by extension, refuses being rescued from dangerous situations.

12.6.3 Self-defence (including defence of others)

Trespass to the person is justified if it is necessary for reasonable self-defence. The defendant must establish that they acted in an honest *and* reasonable belief. This is a more stringent test than its criminal law counterpart, since the latter only requires the defendant's belief to have been honestly held.[90] The self-defence must also be reasonable and within proportion to the original threat. In *Lane v Holloway* [1993],[91] the 23-year-old defendant was found not to be acting in self-defence when, in response to a punch on the shoulder, he hit the 64-year-old claimant with such force that he had multiple stitches and was hospitalised for a month. In relation to the latter limitation, the courts do not insist on *exact* proportionality. Rather, they will give significant leeway to the defendant as decisions about what amounts to a proportionate response are difficult to make with precision where the defendant has been forced to make a decision on the 'spur of the moment'.[92]

Defence of another may also be used to justify a trespass to the person tort. Trinidade provides the examples of holding down a motorist who is about to attack and injure another motorist after an accident, or holding a person back from running into her burning house. These instances would be sufficient to ground a defence against a potential claim for battery or false imprisonment.[93]

---

85   MCA 2005, s 3(1).

86   J. Herring and J. Wall, 'Autonomy, Capacity and Vulnerable Adults: Filling the Gaps in the Mental Capacity Act' (2015) 35 *Legal Studies* 698 and N. Knauer, 'Defining Capacity: Balancing the Competing Interests of Autonomy and Need' (2003) 12 *Temple Political & Civil Rights Law Review* 321.

87   *St George's Healthcare NHS Trust v S; Re B (Adult: Refusal of Treatment)* [2002] 1 All ER 449.

88   *Re MB (Caesarean Section)* [1997] 2 FLR 426 (where consent was eventually given by the patient).

89   *Re F* [1989] 2 WLR 1025.

90   *Ashley v Chief Constable of West Sussex Police* [2008] 1 AC 962.

91   *Lane v Holloway* [1968] 1 QB 379.

92   *Cross v Kikby* (2000) *The Times*, 5 April.

93   F.A. Trindade, 'Intentional Torts: Some Thoughts on Assault and Battery' (1982) 2(2) *Oxford Journal of Legal Studies* 211, 227.

12.6.4 Contributory negligence

The defence of contributory negligence will be considered in depth at 16.3. There is some limited authority that contributory negligence could apply to intentional torts. In *Murphy v Culhane* [1976], Lord Denning MR held, in *obiter*, that damages under the Fatal Accidents Act may be reduced by contributory negligence if the result of the death was partly the fault of the defendant.[94] This view, however, has been heavily criticised in subsequent cases.[95] It also does not accord with the definition of 'fault' in the Law Reform (Contributory Negligence) Act 1945 (the 1945 Act).[96] Contributory negligence under the 1945 Act is defined as the test that existed at common law prior to 1945, which held that the contributory negligence defence did not apply to intentional torts.[97]

It is therefore difficult to see how Lord Denning could have concluded that contributory negligence may apply to intentional torts. Whilst there has been no direct case on trespass to the person and contributory negligence, *Standard Chartered Bank v Pakistan* [2003][98] confirms that the defence cannot apply for actions of deceit or fraudulent misrepresentations (both of which are intentional torts).[99] Therefore whilst *Murphy v Culhane* appears to state that the defence of contributory negligence could apply to trespass to the person torts, this is highly unlikely to be correct.

12.6.5 Lawful arrest and detention/lawful authority

The lawful arrest of a suspect will likely involve both a battery and confinement. If the police or other law enforcement officers are fulfilling their everyday duties, this will generally ground a defence to any trespass to the person torts that may otherwise arise. There are, however, limits to this power, particularly imposed by the ECHR. Therefore, if the defendant's actions go beyond their powers, they may be liable under tort.[100]

The Courts are generally sensitive to the competing obligations of law enforcement officers and the fact that their decisions are often taken in the heat of the moment. An example of this is *Austin v Metropolitan Police Commissioner* [2009].[101] In this case, the police confined approximately 3,000 protestors in a 'closed cordon' of approximately 50 metres in London as some participants in the protest were becoming violent. The police were fearful for the safety of the general public. The claimant was caught amongst the protesters and was unable to move for several hours. She made a claim against the police for a breach of Article 5 of the ECHR (right to liberty). The House of Lords held that, whilst the actions may amount to false imprisonment, the police's actions were not in contravention of Article 5: they were lawful and in proportion to the threat at hand. This decision was subject to considerable criticism, but was upheld by the Grand Chamber of the European Court of Human Rights. The Court held that it was possible to bring a claim against the police for false imprisonment but that, in this case, the actions were proportionate and were the least restrictive

---

94 [1976] 3 All ER 533, 536.
95 See *Standard Chartered Bank v Pakistan* [2003] 1 AC 959 and *Co-operative Group (CWS) Ltd v Pritchard* [2012] 1 All ER 205, 219, which states that the 'remarks of Lord Denning are problematical'.
96 Law Reform (Contributory Negligence) Act 1945, s 4.
97 *Co-operative Group (CWS) Ltd v Pritchard* [2012] 1 All ER 205, 214–15 per Aikens LJ. For further discussion, see J. Murphy, 'Misleading Appearances in the Tort of Deceit' (2016) 75(1) *Cambridge Law Journal* 301. This was because the defence at common law was a complete defence, and it was considered inappropriate to have a complete defence against someone who had committed a deliberate wrong. See G. Williams, *Joint Torts and Contributory Negligence* (London 1951), 198 and Murphy's criticism of this analysis in J. Murphy (above) 326–9.
98 [2003] 1 AC 959.
99 [2003] 1 AC 959, 965–6.
100 *Collins v Wilcock* [1984] 3 All ER 374.
101 [2009] UKHL 5.

means available. It did, however, note that if 'the "type" of measure would have been different, its coercive and restrictive nature might have been sufficient to bring it within Article 5'.[102]

The relationship between the common law tort of false imprisonment and deprivation of liberty under Article 5 was considered by the Supreme Court in *R (on the application of Jalloh) v Secretary of State for the Home Department* [2020].[103] In this case the Secretary of State argued that the time had come to align the common law concept of false imprisonment with the concept of deprivation of liberty under Article 5. The Supreme Court rejected this suggestion, emphasising that the ECHR distinguishes between the deprivation and restriction of liberty, and that the multi-factorial approach to Article 5 is very different from the approach of the common law tort of false imprisonment.[104] The Supreme Court held that aligning the two concepts would not develop the common law, but would actually result in a step backwards, and

> restrict the classic understanding of imprisonment at common law to the very different and much more nuanced concept of deprivation of liberty under the ECHR. The Strasbourg court has adopted this approach because of the need to draw a distinction between the deprivation and the restriction of physical liberty. There is no need for the common law to draw such a distinction and every reason for the common law to continue to protect those whom it has protected for centuries against unlawful imprisonment, whether by the State or private persons.[105]

The clear distinction between the common law tort of false imprisonment and deprivation of liberty under Article 5 has therefore been retained.

PROBLEM QUESTION TECHNIQUE

The organisers of the match heard a rumour that some people without tickets had got in through a broken security door. In order to locate these individuals, the security guards locked everyone in the stadium – including Amira and Claire – informing people that they were unable to leave until they had provided evidence that they had a valid ticket.

▸ This requires an examination of the actions of the organisers of the football match in attempting to locate the people who had not purchased a ticket.

▸ Were the actions a reasonable and proportionate approach to the potential threat?

▸ This is very different situation to *Austin v Metropolitan Police Commissioner*, especially as the security guards do not have the legal powers of the police.

12.7 Additional intentional torts against the person

The three trespass to the person torts (assault, battery and false imprisonment) have been considered in the first part of this chapter. There are, however, related causes of action and other intentional torts to the person. Whilst a full consideration of all other intentional torts is beyond the scope of this book, three relevant causes of action and their elements will be considered:

---

102 *Austin v United Kingdom* (Application No 39692/09).
103 [2020] UKSC 4.
104 [2020] UKSC 4 at [29].
105 [2020] UKSC 4 at [33].

(1)   The tort in *Wilkinson v Downton*
(2)   Protection from Harassment Act 1997
(3)   Malicious prosecution

12.7.1 The tort in *Wilkinson v Downton*

The tort in *Wilkinson v Downton* [1897][106] provides a cause of action for the intentional infliction of physical harm or emotional distress. Prior to this case, *Victorian Railways Comrs v Coultas* [1888][107] had established that mere sudden upset or terror unaccompanied by physical injury could not result in a cause of action. In *Victorian Railways*, the claimant and her husband were in a horse-drawn buggy, the gatekeeper negligently opened the train barrier gates for them to cross, and they only just missed being hit by an oncoming train. The claimant was not physically injured but suffered emotional harm from the shock of seeing the train approaching and fearing that she would be injured or killed. The restriction created by this case was, however, doubted by the Court of Appeal[108] and outrightly rejected in Ireland.[109] The decision was then questioned in *Wilkinson v Downton* which held, in certain circumstances, a cause of action could exist to recover for mental shock unaccompanied by physical injury.

KEY CASE

Wilkinson v Downton [1897] 2 QB 57

The claimant's husband attended a race meeting. That evening, the defendant visited the claimant's house and informed her that her husband had been in an accident and broken both of his legs. He further stated that the claimant's husband was lying in The Elms public house at Leytonstone, and that he had been sent to fetch the claimant and take her to her husband. All of these statements were false, and the claimant's husband was fine. The claimant, however, believed the comments and became seriously ill from what was at the time called 'nervous shock', entailing weeks of suffering and medical expenses. The claimant also incurred the cost of railway fares to see her husband. The defendant stated that the comments were only made as a 'practical joke'. He further claimed that the damage caused to the claimant by way of nervous shock could not be supported as the consequence was too remote.

Wright J found for the claimant and awarded damages for both the railway fares and a much larger sum for her nervous shock. His Honour reviewed the authorities on awarding damages for mental shock, including *Victorian Railways Comrs v Coultas*, and held that they did not prevent an award in the current case. In this matter the defendant had 'wilfully done an act calculated to cause physical harm to the plaintiff—that is to say, to infringe her legal right to personal safety, and has in fact thereby caused physical harm to her'. This was sufficient for a 'good cause of action, there being no justification alleged for the act. This wilful injuria is in law malicious, although no malicious purpose to cause the harm which was caused nor any motive of spite is imputed to the defendant'.[110]

We started this chapter with a discussion of the need within these torts for some element of 'intention'. However, the meaning ascribed to intention varies quite significantly from one tort to the next. Whilst it is clear that in *Wilkinson* the defendant did not intend to cause the claimant to suffer the specific injuries that she suffered, Wright

---

106 [1897] 2 QB 57.
107 (1888) PC 21.
108 *Pugh v The London, Brighton and South Coast Railway Co* [1896] 2 QB 248, 250 per Lord Esher MR.
109 *Bell v Great Northern Railway Co of Ireland* (1890) 26 LR Ir 428 per Palles CB.
110 [1897] 2 QB 57, 59.

J nonetheless held that intention could be imputed by the Court. His Honour stated that the action by the defendant was 'so plainly calculated to produce some effect of the kind which was produced that an intention to produce it ought to be imputed to the defendant'.[111]

The specific elements of the present tort were not clearly outlined by Wright J. Happily, the Supreme Court in *Rhodes v OPO* [2015] has since clarified that there are three elements to the tort in *Wilkinson v Downton*:

(a) the conduct element requiring words or conduct directed at the claimant for which there is no justification or excuse;

(b) the mental element requiring an intention to cause at least severe mental or emotional distress; and

(c) the consequence element requiring physical harm or recognised psychiatric illness.[112]

PROBLEM QUESTION TECHNIQUE

During half-time, two of the Carpenters fans saw Betty leaving to get a drink. They were upset that their team was losing, so they followed Betty, cornered her and started hurling verbal abuse at her. This included violent and sexually explicit comments that made Betty fearful of returning to her seat. She therefore left the match without telling anyone. Betty was previously a victim of a violent assault and the comments caused her to develop serious anxiety and post-traumatic stress disorder.

▸ As outlined above, these actions are highly likely to constitute the tort of assault.

▸ Could they also fulfil the requirements of the tort in *Wilkinson v Downton*?

▸ The Supreme Court in *Rhodes v OPO* held that there are three elements: (a) a conduct element, (b) a mental element and (c) a consequence element.

▸ The conduct element is clearly fulfilled; the individuals made 'comments directed to [Betty] for which there is no justification or reasonable excuse' and they 'infringe[d] her legal right to personal safety'.

▸ The mental element is also probably met as the comments were likely to have the intention of causing emotional distress.

▸ The consequence element is equally likely to be satisfied since Betty, whilst not suffering from any physical injury, has clearly suffered a recognised psychiatric illness from the actions.

The rule in *Wilkinson v Downton* therefore created a tort for intentional infliction of harm. Whilst it is a unique tort that arose from an 1897 first instance decision, it has been upheld in a number of more recent cases[113] and is clearly good law. It is often referred to as a *sui generis* (unique) trespass to the person tort; however, this is not uniformly accepted. For example, Lord Hoffmann in *Wainwright v Home Office* [2004] commented that intentional infliction of harm 'has nothing to do with trespass to the person'.[114]

---

111 [1897] 2 QB 57, 59.
112 [2015] 4 All ER 1, 23.
113 *Janvier v Sweeney [1919] 2 KB 316; Khorasandjian v Bush* [1993] QB 727; *Wong v Parkside Health NHS Trust* [2001] EWCA Civ 1721; C v D [2006] EWHC 166 (QB); *Sullivan v Boylan* [2013] IEHC 104.
114 [2004] 2 AC 406, 426.

KEY CASE

Wainwright v Home Office [2004] 2 AC 406

Mrs Wainwright and one of her sons visited another of her sons in prison. During their visit, they were subjected to a strip search. This was due to a drug-smuggling problem in the prison. They both agreed to the process but found the experience very upsetting, and the son suffered from post-traumatic stress disorder as a consequence. They both commenced an action against the Home Office for damages. It was found that the strip search was not a proper use of the powers conferred under the Prison Rules 1964, as it was an invasion of their privacy and was not necessary and proportionate to deal with the drug-smuggling problem.

At first instance, the trial judge held that the actions constituted trespass to the person. The Court of Appeal allowed the defendant's appeal on the basis that there was no trespass to the person. This was then appealed to the House of Lords, with the claimants arguing both invasion of privacy and intentional infliction of harm.

The House of Lords affirmed the Court of Appeal's decision. It held that there is no common law tort of invasion of privacy, which will be discussed in Chapter 14 (Privacy). The Court further held that there is no remedy under intentional infliction of harm if the claimant only suffered humiliation and distress. Lord Hoffmann stated that the tort in question 'does not provide a remedy for distress which does not amount to recognized psychiatric injury'.[115]

This requirement in *Wainwright v Home Office* was approved by the majority in the Supreme Court in *Rhodes v OPO*, which stated that intentional of infliction harm included a consequence element requiring physical harm or recognised psychiatric illness. The restriction was, however, questioned in obiter by Lord Neuberger. The limitation on recovering damages for mere grief and distress is often premised on the basis that these are 'part of normal life, whereas psychiatric illness is not'. Lord Neuberger, however, indicated that there is a 'powerful case' for saying that when comments are made with the intent to cause distress, the suffering of a 'significant distress' alone should be actionable.[116]

In *Rhodes v OPO*, the Supreme Court took the opportunity to question the scope and application of the tort in *Wilkinson v Downton*.[117]

KEY CASE

Rhodes v OPO [2015] 4 All ER 1

In this case, Rhodes, a well-known concert pianist, wrote a personal memoir that described severe abuse he had experienced as a child and his subsequent mental health challenges and issues with addiction. His ex-wife sought an injunction preventing publication of the memoir (or a requirement that significant parts be deleted before publication) on the basis that the publication would cause severe emotional distress and harm to their 'psychologically vulnerable' son. The specific question was whether the tort could be used to prevent a person from publishing true information about himself.

The Supreme Court held that the facts of the case did not fulfil the requirements of the tort in *Wilkinson v Downton* as there was no intentional infliction of harm, and it was not enough to show imputed intention or recklessness. As discussed

---

115 [2004] 2 AC 406, 426.
116 [2015] 4 All ER 1, 32.
117 [2015] 4 All ER 1.

above, it was held that recklessness is an insufficient basis on which to impose liability for the tort in *Wilkinson v Downton*, and instead specific intention is necessary.[118]

The Court did, however, make a number of useful comments about its applicability to modern day issues. In relation to the mental element, it was held in *obiter* that imputed intention or recklessness was no longer sufficient. Lady Hale and Lord Toulson held that a defendant would need to have intended to cause severe distress to the claimant but not a recognised psychiatric illness. Although such intention could not be imputed, it might nevertheless be inferred from the facts of the case. The Supreme Court commented that

> *Wilkinson v Downton* has been a source of much discussion and debate in legal textbooks and academic articles but seldom invoked in practice. This may be due to the development of the law of negligence in the area of recognised illness resulting from nervous shock.[119]

The Court did, however, comment that in 'the last 25 years [the tort] has had a modest resurgence in the context of harassment'.[120]

Therefore, whilst the tort in *Wilkinson v Downton* is still part of the English common law, there has been a movement away from it. This is likely to do with the increased use of negligence for these types of behaviour, and the enactment of the Protection from Harassment Act 1997, which will be discussed below.

12.7.2 Protection from Harassment Act 1997

In the 1990s, there was an increased understanding, and awareness, of the danger of harassment and stalking. Tort law's remit at the time was generally considered insufficient to respond to these threats, and further action was necessary. As outlined by Mr Howard, the Secretary of State for the Home Department, in the Second Reading Speech, 'a number of highly publicised stalking cases have come to public attention. They have highlighted the need to give the courts more effective powers to deal with stalkers.'[121]

The Protection from Harassment Act (PHA) 1997 includes both a civil remedy for harassment[122] and a criminal offence of harassment.[123] The victim of the harassment will be entitled to damages for anxiety and any financial loss resulting from the harassment[124] and may seek an injunction to protect themselves from harassment,[125] restraining orders on conviction[126] and potential conviction for breach of any injunction awarded.[127] It therefore has a number of mechanisms to protect victims from the harmful actions of harassment, as well as to financially compensate anyone who has suffered from these activities. Unlike the tort in *Wilkinson v Downton*, victims do not need to suffer a recognised psychiatric illness to make a claim under the PHA 1997.

---

118 [2016] AC 219, 254.
119 [2015] 4 All ER 1, 17.
120 [2015] 4 All ER 1, 18.
121 HC Deb 17 December 1996 vol 287 cc781–862, 781.
122 PHA 1997, s 3.
123 PHA 1997, s 4.
124 PHA 1997, s 3(2).
125 PHA 1997, s 3A.
126 PHA 1997, s 5.
127 PHA 1997, s 3(3).

KEY LEGISLATION

Protection from Harassment Act 1997

1   Prohibition of harassment

(1)   A person must not pursue a course of conduct—

      (a) which amounts to harassment of another, and

      (b) which he knows or ought to know amounts to harassment of the other.

3   Civil remedy

(1)   An actual or apprehended breach of section 1(1) may be the subject of a claim in civil proceedings by the person who is or may be the victim of the course of conduct in question.

(2)   On such a claim, damages may be awarded for (among other things) any anxiety caused by the harassment and any financial loss resulting from the harassment.

Since its enactment, the PHA 1997 has been frequently invoked. Whilst the Act was originally enacted to protect people from stalking activities, the legislation has been widely used in a number of other, very different, circumstances, including libel and slander,[128] unwanted sexual advances in the workplace,[129] neighbourhood disputes,[130] banks inundating customers with telephone calls,[131] homophobic remarks and threats,[132] protests against the construction of a facility designed for the conducting of experiments on live animals,[133] publication of personal details of a convicted sex offender,[134] and gas companies threatening to cut off gas supplies and report customers to a credit rating agency.[135] The House of Lords has held that employers can also be vicariously liable for harassment committed by employees during their course of employment.[136]

The passing of the Human Rights Act (HRA) 1998 meant that the PHA 1997 needs to be interpreted in light of the rights protected by the HRA 1998. The relevant provisions are Articles 10 and 11 of the ECHR – rights to freedom of expression and association. The complex relationship between these two pieces of legislation was explored in *Thomas v News Groups Newspapers* [2002][137] and *Rhodes v OPO*.[138]

Under s 1 of the PHA 1997, the Act will apply if a defendant pursues a course of conduct that amounts to harassment of another, when they know (or ought reasonably to know) that the

---

128 *Triad Group plc v Makar* [2019] EWHC 423 (QB); *Levi v Bates* [2015] EWCA Civ 206; *Law Society v Kordowski* [2011] All ER (D) 46 (Dec).

129 *Piepenbrock v London School of Economics and Political Science* [2018] ELR 596.

130 *Worthington v Metropolitan Housing Trust Ltd* [2018] EWCA Civ 1125; *Sheffield City Council v Shaw* [2007] HLR 374.

131 *Roberts v Bank of Scotland plc* [2013] All ER (D) 88 (Jun).

132 *Jones v Ruth* [2012] 1 All ER 490.

133 *Chancellor, Masters and Scholars of the University of Oxford v Broughton* [2006] All ER (D) 78 (Aug). For similar facts, see *Daiichi UK Ltd and others v Stop Huntingdon Animal Cruelty* [2003] All ER (D) 194 (Oct), which also involved 'threatening letters and telephone calls, letters containing offensive material such as excrement, criminal damage, firebombings and intimidatory home visits'.

134 *CG v Facebook Ireland Ltd* [2015] NIQB 28.

135 *Ferguson v British Gas Trading Ltd* [2009] 3 All ER 304.

136 *Majrowski v Guy's and St Thomas's NHS Trust* [2006] 4 All ER 395.

137 [2002] EMLR 78.

138 [2016] AC 219. For further analysis of this issue, see E. Finch, 'The Relationship between Freedom of Expression and Harassment' (2002) 66 *J Cr Law* 134.

actions in question would amount to harassment of another. To obtain a remedy under the Act, the following elements must be shown:

(1) a 'course of conduct';
(2) that amounts to harassment of another; and
(3) that the perpetrator knows or ought to know amounts to harassment.

12.7.2.1 A 'COURSE OF CONDUCT'

The PHA 1997 is not designed to protect people from individual episodes of inappropriate behaviour, as a course of conduct is required. This is defined as 'conduct on at least two occasions',[139] meaning that an element of repeated behaviour is needed to fulfil the definition of 'harassment'. The courts have also indicated that 'at least' gives them discretion to find that two or more instances may *not* be sufficient for a finding of a course of conduct, and they will look at the particular incidents in question in determining whether they fit the definition.[140] This occurred in *Conn v Sunderland City Council* [2008],[141] where the Court of Appeal held that despite two instances of alleged harassment, the actions of the defendant did not amount to a course of conduct. The Court emphasised that the touchstone of the Act was whether the conduct was of such gravity that it could justify criminal sanctions.

How can the PHA be used to protect people against image-based and internet-based misconduct? For example, if someone takes an inappropriate photo of a victim or posts revenge porn on a single occasion, can they be caught by the legislation? On first reading, it would seem that a single incident does not fulfil the definition of a 'course of conduct', and therefore victims would not have any remedy under the Act. The courts have, however, held that, in certain circumstances, a single publication of a harassing nature can constitute a 'course of conduct'. In the case of *Law Society v Kordowski* [2011], the claimant sought an injunction stopping the defendant from including his details on a 'name and shame' part of its website which encourages members of the public to expose wrongdoing within the legal profession. Even though the details of the claimant were posted once, Tugendhat J held that a course of conduct was present if the alleged harasser submitted the material 'in the knowledge that such publications will inevitably come to their attention on more than one occasion and on each occasion cause them alarm and distress constituting harassment'.[142] The judge went even further and stated that if the publication is ongoing and on a prominent website, 'the distress and alarm caused by the publication will also be continuous. It is reasonable to infer in every case that the victims would suffer such distress and alarm on at least two occasions.'[143]

This case is therefore authority for the point that one harassing publication *may* constitute a course of conduct if the courts feel able to 'infer' that the victim would suffer distress and alarm on at least two occasions. This provides a powerful tool for victims of revenge porn or similar incidents to take a claim against their harasser under the PHA 1997.

---

139 PHA 1997, s 7(3).
140 Elias LJ in *James v Crown Prosecution Service* [2009] EWHC 2925 (Admin) at [11] stating 'the fewer incidents there are and the further in time they are apart, the less likely it will be that they can properly be treated as constituting a course of conduct'.
141 [2008] IRLR 324.
142 *Law Society v Kordowski* [2011] All ER (D) 46 (Dec) at [61].
143 Ibid at [64].

12.7.2.2 AMOUNTS TO HARASSMENT OF ANOTHER

Whilst there is no specific definition of 'harassment' in the PHA 1997, there is guidance. For example, it states that 'references to harassing a person include alarming the person or causing the person distress'.[144] As the relevant wording is 'include', courts are clearly entitled to consider consequences beyond causing alarm and distress. The lack of a statutory definition was discussed in *Thomas v News Group Newspapers Ltd*, with the Court of Appeal stating that 'harassment is … a word which has a meaning that is generally understood'.[145] There is, however, a contextual aspect of harassment: 'what might not be harassment on the factory floor or in the barrack room might well be harassment in the hospital ward'.[146] The ability of the courts to decide whether something constitutes harassment without legislative guidance was confirmed by Baroness Hale in *Majrowski v Guy's and St Thomas's NHS Trust* [2006]. She emphasised that the principal purpose of the act was prevention and protection, as opposed to compensation. The definition of harassment was therefore left deliberately wide and open-ended, and 'a great deal is left to the wisdom of the courts to draw sensible lines between the ordinary banter and badinage of life and genuinely offensive and unacceptable behaviour'.[147]

PROBLEM QUESTION TECHNIQUE

During half-time, two of the Carpenters fans saw Betty leaving to get a drink. They were upset that their team was losing, so they followed Betty, cornered her and started hurling verbal abuse at her. This included violent and sexually explicit comments that made Betty fearful of returning to her seat.

This definition (or lack of it) of harassment can understandably be frustrating for students, particularly when they need to apply the law to a problem question applying the PHA 1997. The best way to approach these types of questions is therefore to know the relevant cases and reason by analogy. The marker will be aware that the courts have refused to provide strict criteria, and it is therefore important to show that you are aware of this limitation and can apply the law as it is currently stands.

▸ It may appear that there is harassing behaviour here on the part of the Carpenters fans.

▸ You need to remember the requirement for a 'course of conduct' under s 7(3) and apply this to the situation.

▸ In this case, there was a single incident, so it will not come within the Act.

The reference to 'another' does not mean that the harassing conduct must be directed at the victim in question. The claimant can bring an action for harassment even if the defendant's actions were aimed at a different party (for example a friend or family member).[148]

12.7.2.3 KNOWS OR OUGHT TO KNOW AMOUNTS TO HARASSMENT

The PHA 1997 shields defendants from harassment actions where the alleged victim subjectively feels harassed, but a reasonable person would not, in such circumstances, have considered herself to have suffered harassment. A victim's paranoia, for example, cannot transform an otherwise innocent course of conduct into an actionable tort.

---

144 Protection from Harassment Act 1997, s 7(2).
145 [2001] EWCA Civ 1233 at [30].
146 *Sunderland CC v Conn* [2007] EWCA Civ 1492 at [12].
147 [2007] 1 AC 224, 245.
148 *Levi v Bates* [2016] 1 All ER 625.

The Act also makes it clear that the defendant need not intend to harass the victim. The test is whether they knew or *ought to have known* that the actions in question would amount to harassment. In creating these requirements, the aim was to ensure

> the balance right between the need to protect victims from the destructive behaviour of stalkers and the need to prevent the courts from being used for the pursuit of frivolous claims. A victim would have to show that harassment had been caused, and that the stalker ought to have known that that would be the effect of his actions – and stalkers will no longer be able to claim as a defence that they did not intend to harass their victims.[149]

Whilst it is a useful step that the victim no longer has to prove intent, there are admittedly some difficulties with this approach. The first, as outlined above, is the fact that the courts have refused to provide clear guidance on what does or does not constitute harassing behaviour. It could therefore seem unfair to base the test on what the defendant 'ought to know' if this test is not clear or transparent. The approach has also been questioned by Conaghan, who argues that the Act 'is a singularly inappropriate technique for distinguishing between legitimate and illegitimate activity in an area so dogged by controversy and disagreement'.[150] The test ensures that the standard is that of 'reasonable harasser' as opposed to the experiences of a 'reasonable harassee'.[151] She therefore argues that the Act gives considerable power to the courts and law enforcement agencies while at the same time taking such power away from the victim.

12.7.2.4 HARASSMENT IN THE 21ST CENTURY

Even though the PHA 1997 is increasingly used to cover a wide variety of different scenarios, it is clearly not providing an adequate deterrent effect. The #MeToo movement highlighted the disturbing prevalence of harassment, particularly sexual harassment, in the workplace. The TUC in collaboration with the Everyday Sexism Project undertook a quantitative review of sexual harassment in the workplace in England. It reported that 52% of women have experienced some form of sexual harassment at their work, including nearly 20% experiencing unwanted sexual advances and 10% reporting unwanted sexual touching. Out of these complainants, 80% did not report the sexual harassment to their employer. Of those who did complain, only 6% reported that it was taken seriously and dealt with satisfactorily and 16% stated they were treated worse after making the complaint.[152]

The Act provides a useful mechanism and potential remedy for a large number of people. However, it is clear that a great many victims are not utilising the legislation. The Act also only deals with the consequences of the harassing activity, and does little to prevent offending actions in the first place. More needs to be done to first prevent the harassment from occurring and then provide support and assistance for people who want to make a claim against their harasser.

In conclusion, there are clear links between the 1897 case of *Wilkinson v Downton* and the legislation passed exactly 100 years later. Has the PHA 1997 overtaken the 'seldom invoked' common law tort? In *Wainwright v Home Office*, Lord Hoffmann (echoing comments by Hale LJ (as she then was) in *Wong v Parkside Health NHS Trust* [2001][153]) commented that the passing of the PHA 1997 'leaves *Wilkinson v Downton* with no leading role in the modern law'.[154] The Act, however, has

---

149 HC Deb 17 December 1996 vol 287 cc781–862, 783.
150 J. Conaghan, 'Enhancing Civil Remedies for (Sexual) Harassment: s 3 of the Protection from Harassment Act 1997' (1999) 7(2) *Feminist Legal Studies* 203, 207.
151 J. Conaghan (above), 207.
152 TUC in Association with the Everyday Sexism Project, *Still Just a Bit of Banter? Sexual Harassment in the Workplace in 2016* (2016).
153 [2001] EWCA Civ 1721 at [29].
154 [2003] 3 WLR 1137, 1148.

specific requirements that do not exist in the common law tort, such as the need for a 'course of conduct'. This element would have prevented the actual case of *Wilkinson* producing a remedy had the course of conduct element formed part of the common law. In addition, it is clear from cases since 1997 that the implementation of the statute has not 'covered the field', and that the common law tort of *Wilkinson v Downton* is still very much a relevant part of the English law landscape.

■ VIEWPOINT

What role does the tort of intentional infliction of emotional distress have now that the Protection from Harassment Act 1997 has been passed? What are the key differences between these two causes of action?

DIFFERENT PERSPECTIVES on the Protection from Harassment Act 1997

P. Giliker, 'A New Head of Damages: Damages for Mental Distress in the English Law of Torts' (2000) 20 Legal Stud 19

In this article, Giliker explores the ability of claimants to recover damages for mental distress in the English law of torts. She argues that mental distress has been a neglected part of tort law and that it should be recognised as a distinct head of damages under the common law. Despite the fact that the courts do not openly recognise mental distress, damages of this nature are commonly awarded in a variety of different ways. Whilst the article does not focus specifically on the PHA 1997, Giliker does mention the impact that the legislation could have on the court's approach to awarding damages for mental distress. In light of the House of Lords decision in *Hunter v Canary Wharf* that claims for harassment should no longer be brought in private nuisance, but under the Act, Giliker contends that the PHA 1997 will have an impact on the approach taken by the courts when dealing with various aspects of damages for mental distress.

J. Conaghan, 'Enhancing Civil Remedies for (Sexual) Harassment: s 3 of the Protection from Harassment Act 1997' (1999) 7 Feminist Legal Studies 203

Conaghan's article is less optimistic about the ability of the PHA 1997 to be a vehicle for positive change. She notes that it 'may become a political "own goal" in that it is capable of being used to suppress rather than enhance the rights and dignities of individuals and groups'. As the definition of harassment is left so unclear and there is a lack of legislative guidance, there is considerable opportunity for the common law to fall back on the existing categories of conduct when determining liability under the PHA 1997. Conaghan also argues that many important questions have been left unanswered, including the role of consent, the role of trust or power, the conflict with civil rights and – most importantly – whether the common law torts continue to have a role in remedying acts of harassment. On the basis of these issues, Conaghan argues that the common law will still be invoked to 'plug the gaps', and the courts need to ensure that interpretation of the Act develops in a manner that balances women's rights with the legitimate interests of others.

12.7.3 Malicious prosecution

The final action to consider is malicious prosecution, which has a number of similarities to false imprisonment as both torts are focused on liberty and autonomy. Unlike false imprisonment, malicious prosecution is not actionable *per se* and the claimant must show damage. In a malicious prosecution claim, the focus is not upon the party who has directly detained the claimant, but instead on a third party who has caused the claimant to be falsely prosecuted. For example, if an individual with a personal vendetta arranges for another to be arrested by planting evidence or lying to the police, should the victim have a cause of action against the person who caused their imprisonment? There is clearly embarrassment and potential reputation damage arising from an unjustified prosecution, and tort law has responded by way of the tort of malicious prosecution.[155] This will, however, only apply if the arresting party has acted as an agent for the defendant or did not exercise any independent discretion.[156]

With malicious prosecution, the 'wrong' committed by the tortfeasor is that they set a false prosecution in motion. There are four elements to such a claim:

(1) the prosecution of the victim was initiated by the defendant;
(2) the prosecution was terminated in the claimant's favour;
(3) there was an absence of reasonable and probable cause to commence the prosecution; and
(4) the process was fuelled by malice.

It can be difficult to determine when the first element is fulfilled as prosecutions are generally conducted by a completely separate third party. However, in certain circumstances, the defendant can be so obviously involved in the process that the court will find that they are responsible for the initiation of the prosecution. In *Martin v Watson* [1995] the plaintiff and defendant were neighbours with a history of mutual antagonism. The defendant made a complaint to the police that the claimant had indecently exposed himself to her, which caused him to be arrested and charged. The magistrate dismissed the charge, however, as no evidence was offered by the prosecutor. The judge at first instance found for the claimant and stated that the defendant had been active and instrumental in setting the law in motion and could therefore be regarded as the prosecutor. The claimant was awarded £3,500 for malicious prosecution. The Court of Appeal overturned this decision, holding that the mere action of bringing a false allegation to police was not sufficient to ground the tort of malicious prosecution. The claimant then appealed to the House of Lords which allowed the appeal. Lord Keith commented that this case went beyond merely providing false information, stating that:

> where an individual falsely and maliciously gives a police officer information indicating that some person is guilty of a criminal offence and states that he is willing to give evidence in court of the matters in question, it is properly to be inferred that he desires and intends that the person he names should be prosecuted. Where the circumstances are such that the facts relating to the alleged offence can be within the knowledge only of the complainant, as was the position here, then it becomes virtually impossible for the police officer to exercise any independent discretion or judgment, and if a prosecution is instituted by the police officer the proper view of the matter is that the prosecution has been procured by the complainant.[157]

The mere reporting of false information will not be sufficient for malicious prosecution. The court will look closely at the factual scenario and determine what role the defendant had in the resulting prosecution. In *Davidson v Chief Constable of North Wales* [1994], a store detective incorrectly suspected that the claimant and her friend had stolen a cassette from a Woolworths store. The detective then followed the pair and informed the police of their whereabouts and suspected activities. The police approached the claimant and her friend and arrested them for shoplifting. When no receipt could be produced, they were taken to the police station and questioned. The police then spoke to the shop assistant who sold them the item and they were released. The pair had, however, suffered embarrassment and humiliation as a result of the incident. The claimant commenced an action against the police and against the store detective. As the police had acted lawfully and had reasonable grounds for arresting the claimant and her friend, this claim was unsuccessful. The court also withdrew the case against the store detective on the grounds that she 'did not arrest, imprison, detain or restrain the plaintiff's liberty directly in any way'.[158] Her role in the arrest was merely the provision of information, which was acted on by the police.

---

155 *Clark v Chief Constable of Cleveland* [2000] CP Rep 22.
156 *Harnett v Bond* [1925] All ER Rep 110.
157 [1995] 3 All ER 559, 567–8.
158 [1994] 2 All ER 597, 600.

Whilst malicious prosecution is still a valid tort, it is becoming more difficult to prove the required elements. There are increasing regulatory requirements outlining the steps that law enforcement agents and prosecutors must take when performing their prosecutorial duties, and they are now required to form their own judgment about the charge before arresting or prosecuting.

12.8 CHAPTER SUMMARY

This chapter has provided an outline of six intentional torts against the person – assault, battery, false imprisonment, the tort in *Wilkinson v Downton*, the Protection from Harassment Act 1997 and malicious prosecution. These are a group of torts linked together by the need to show an 'intentional' act, as opposed to a negligent or careless one. There are, however, a number of important differences, and these need to be kept in mind when considering how to answer problem questions and essays on these torts. The first three torts (assault, battery and false imprisonment) are 'trespass to the person' torts, which are the oldest and most established torts in the English common law. The majority of the torts are actionable *per se*, meaning that there is no need to show specific damage for a successful claim. This does not, however, apply to the tort in *Wilkinson v Downton* (where the claimant must show physical harm or a recognised psychiatric illness) or the Protection from Harassment Act 1997 (where the claimant needs to show 'harassment'). Despite the strong historical basis of most of the torts considered in this chapter, all of the causes of action have had to develop in a way that tackles modern challenges, including increased understanding of psychiatric illness, human rights developments and the increasing awareness of sexual harassment.

FURTHER READING

P. Cane, 'Mens Rea in Tort Law' (2000) 20 *Oxford Journal of Legal Studies* 533

J. Conaghan, 'Enhancing Civil Remedies for (Sexual) Harassment: s 3 of the Protection from Harassment Act 1997' (1999) 7 *Feminist Legal Studies* 203

M. Fordham, 'False Imprisonment and Prisoners: A Question of Justice or Law?' [2003] *Singapore Journal of Legal Studies* 444

M. Lunney, 'False Imprisonment, Fare Dodging and Federation – Mr Robertson's Evening Out' (2009) 31 *Sydney LR* 537

N. Moreham 'Harassment by Publication' in N. Moreham and M. Warby (eds), *The Law of Privacy and the Media*, 3rd edn (OUP, 2016), 393

D. Reìaume, 'The Role of Intention in the Tort in *Wilkinson v Downton*', in J. Neyers, E. Chamberlain and S. Pitel (eds), *Emerging Issues in Tort Law* (Hart, 2007)

F.A. Trindade, 'Intentional Torts: Some Thoughts on Assault and Battery' (1982) 2(2) *Oxford Journal of Legal Studies* 211

Roadmap: Intentional Torts to the Person

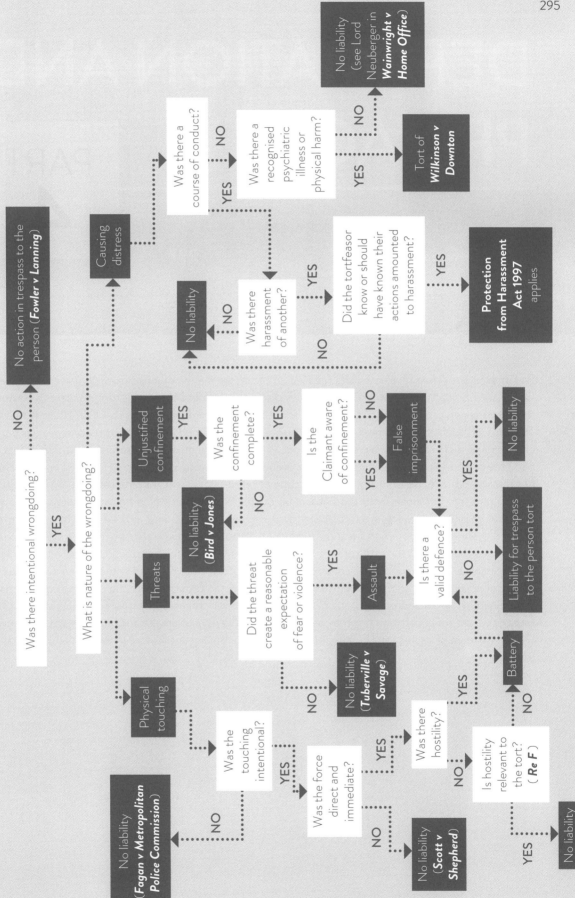

DEFAMATION AND PRIVACY

13. Defamation   297

14. Privacy   338

PART 4

Defamation and privacy are both torts focused on the dissemination of information, but in different ways. Defamation protects the reputation of people and some companies. Under this tort, claimants are entitled to seek damages, or a restraint of publication, for the publication of statements that injury their reputation. This area of law has transformed considerably over a short period of time, with two legislative regime changes and many common law developments. The development of the internet and social media has also provided novel challenges for defamation laws, and the relevant legal principles are still being finalised. Defamation protects parties from the publication of *untrue* statements and representations. In contrast, privacy protects individuals from the publication of *true* information which has a confidential or private nature. A chapter on 'privacy' in a tort law textbook can be a bit misleading, as there is no freestanding tort protecting privacy. The common law and Parliament have both continually refused to develop the law in this way, stating that it is not their role or that there is no need for enhanced protection of individuals' privacy. The equitable breach of confidence cause of action (or as it has been referred to more recently, the tort of misuse of private information) has been expanded to protect information with the requisite confidential or private nature. Defamation and privacy have both been heavily impacted by the Human Rights Act 1998, with both causes of action requiring the courts to balance the right to private and family life (ECHR, Article 8) with freedom of expression (ECHR, Article 10). This balancing act features heavily in both chapters in this Part.

LEARNING OBJECTIVES

By the end of this chapter, you should be able to:

- Recognise and explain the historical distinction between libel and slander, as well as the impact that recent legislative amendments has had on the distinction
- Understand the impact of the Defamation Act 2013 on the common law of defamation
- Recognise when parties can and cannot sue in defamation, and why these restrictions are in place
- Clearly establish what constitutes defamation and apply the relevant elements of a defamation action
- Recognise and explain the defences available to defamation actions, under both the common law and statute
- Engage with the policy arguments and challenges that arise from defamation law in modern society

CHAPTER CONTENTS

13.1	Introduction	298
13.2	Defamation structure	299
	13.2.1 Was the publication *defamatory*?	300
	13.2.2 Is the publication *defensible*?	300
	13.2.3 What *damages* should be awarded?	300
13.3	Initial issues to consider	300
	13.3.1 Legislative reform	301
	13.3.2 Libel and slander	302
	13.3.3 Who can sue?	304
13.4	Elements of defamation	309
	13.4.1 Was the publication defamatory?	309
	13.4.2 The statement referred to the claimant	316
	13.4.3 The statement was published to a third party	317
13.5	Defences	319
	13.5.1 Truth	320
	13.5.2 Honest opinion	321
	13.5.3 Privilege and public interest	323
	13.5.4 Operators of websites	327
	13.5.5 Consent	328
13.6	Remedies	329
	13.6.1 Damages	329
	13.6.2 Other remedies	330
13.7	Challenges	330
	13.7.1 Human rights and defamation	331
	13.7.2 Defamation and social media	332
	13.7.3 Society's views and defamation	333
13.8	Chapter summary	335
	Further reading	335
	Roadmap	336

PROBLEM QUESTION

Michael failed a mid-term tort law examination. Unable to take responsibility for the grade, he blamed the following people:

▸ His teacher, Professor Matilda Honey, on the grounds that it was unfair that tort lectures started at 9am on Monday mornings;

▸ His study group peers, Mr Bruce Bogtrotter and Ms Amanda Thripp, as they met on Friday mornings to go over study notes which interfered with Michael's Thursday night clubbing plans;

▸ The company that manufactured his pencils, Wormwood Pty Ltd, on the basis that they slowed down his writing in the exam; and

▸ His local authority, Pasadena Borough Council, for not providing all university students with free public transport.

In an attempt to get even with these parties, Michael spent his vacation undertaking the following:

▸ Posting a very insulting picture of Professor Honey on the Law Faculty library noticeboard which made it appear that she accepted bribes from a variety of different people. Professor Honey asked the Law Faculty to take it down, but they refused as they thought it was positive that students were visiting the library to view the picture;

▸ Sending a number of tweets about Bruce and Amanda, calling them the 'nerd girl' and 'nerd guy', and stating that they were bad friends for preferring to study than go out clubbing with him;

▸ Writing a negative blog about Wormwood pencils and how they made students write slower in exams. His blog has been read 15 times (mostly by his family members), and he has successfully convinced his mother to no longer buy pencils from Wormwood Pty Ltd; and

▸ Distributing a number of educational leaflets accusing the Pasadena Borough Council of not supporting university students and calling it a 'toytown Hitlerism local government'.

Michael believes that he will not be held liable for defamation on the grounds that:

▸ The picture of Professor Honey does not explicitly state that she is accepting bribes and could be interpreted as implying that she is so nice that lots of people want to give her money;

▸ The tweets were merely playful, friendly banter, and people cannot be held liable in defamation for comments made on Twitter; and

▸ He honestly believes that the Wormwood pencils made him write slower, although he has no factual basis for his belief.

Advise all parties about any potential claims in defamation.

13.1 Introduction

The law of defamation aims to protect the reputation of individuals and certain corporations, such as trading corporations, whose reputation or goodwill are valuable. It allows people defamed to obtain damages for statements that injure reputation, as well as restrain publication of these statements. There are two key forms of defamation: libel and slander. Slander involves transient publications, such as a conversation. This type of defamation is only actionable if it results in actual damage to the claimant. In contrast, libel is publication in a permanent (i.e. written) form or on stage, screen or electronically. Whilst the distinction between libel and slander had a strong historical basis, it has been criticised and altered by legislation which deems some oral defamations to be libels. Also, the distinction has been overtaken by the requirement in the Defamation Act 2013 that the statement be likely to cause 'serious injury' to the claimant's reputation.

For an action in defamation to be successful, it must be shown that a defamatory statement referring to the claimant was published to a third party. There are a number of defences available to the defendant under both common law and statute. Once a claim is successful, the claimant is entitled damages and possibly an injunction against further publication. Unlike almost all other torts, defamation cases have historically been heard by juries. This was justified on the ground that the harm suffered is that the claimant's reputation in the general community has been lowered, and therefore representatives of the community are best placed to determine if this has occurred and, if so, what damages should be awarded. As will be discussed below, recent legislative amendments have significantly reduced the scope for jury trials in defamation cases.

Defamation law is complex. It has changed considerably over a reasonably short period of time. There have been two different legislative regimes (Defamation Act 1996; Defamation Act 2013). The European Convention on Human Rights (ECHR) (particularly the tension created by the rights to freedom of expression under Article 10 and respect for private and family life under Article 8) has influenced judge-made law and statutory reforms. The internet and social media have profoundly affected how information is published and generate issues about whether and when content hosts, like Facebook, should be liable for communicating defamatory content.

13.2 Defamation structure

The law of defamation is complicated. Judge-made law developed over the centuries has been amended by legislation to reflect modern conditions and the importance of freedom of expression in a democratic society. Complex, technical terms like 'libel and slander'[1] and 'true innuendo'[2] are still commonly used. Some entities cannot sue; others have to show different thresholds to be able to sue. Despite these complications, the elements of defamation can be simplified into the **3Ds**:

(1) Was the publication **defamatory** of the claimant because the meaning it conveyed was likely to cause serious injury to the claimant's reputation?
(2) If so, is the publication **defensible** under a statutory or common law defence?
(3) If not, what **damages** should be awarded?

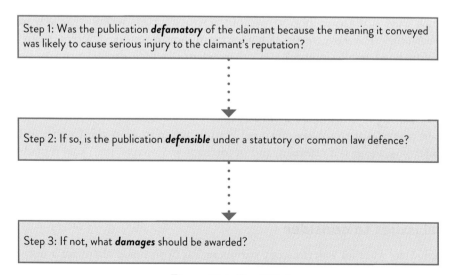

Figure 13.1: The '3Ds'

---

1   See discussion at 13.3.2.
2   See discussion at 13.4.1.2.

13.2.1 Was the publication *defamatory*?

For this first requirement, the claimant must show that:

(a)   the statement was defamatory;

(b)   the statement referred to the claimant by name or otherwise; and

(c)   the statement was published to a third party.

These elements may be easily proved where the publication names the claimant and says something obviously defamatory, for example 'X is a thief'. Difficult issues arise where the meaning is debatable, for example, 'X was fired from his job after money went missing'. Do those words mean that X is guilty of theft, that he was reasonably suspected of being a thief or simply that he was suspected by his employer of taking the money? Depending on which meaning the court finds would have been understood by a hypothetical 'ordinary, reasonable reader', a defence of truth may be available. The publisher may not be able to prove that X was guilty, but it may be able to prove that X was suspected on reasonable grounds of stealing.

The statement also needs to refer to the claimant in some way. A person may, however, be defamed without being specifically named or without the publisher intending to defame him or her (by, for example, referring to another person of the same name). The claimant may be identified by a reasonable reader who knows certain things that are mentioned in a publication which does not identify the claimant by name. Is it enough if the publication in fact referred to the claimant, by name or otherwise? What if the publisher intended to refer to someone else with the same name?

13.2.2 Is the publication *defensible*?

Defamation is a law of strict liability. Liability does not depend on the intentions of the publisher, or proof of carelessness. Liability may exist without the publisher intending to convey any meaning about the claimant or intending a different meaning to the one the court finds was conveyed. It is sufficient if the publication in fact conveyed a defamatory meaning about the claimant to a third party. The publisher's intention and other states of mind, such as malice, and the reasonableness of its conduct may become relevant to a defence.

The interest in protecting reputation must be balanced against other interests. For example, an undeserved reputation will not be protected if the defendant proves that the defamatory meaning was substantially true. The public interest in the free flow of information and opinions also justifies defences which leave a defamed person without a remedy, even when what was published was untrue and harmful. The law creates defences for honest opinion, different kinds of privilege (absolute, qualified and public interest) and other defences which protect primary publishers and intermediaries from liability.

13.2.3 What *damages* should be awarded?

If the claimant proves that the defendant's publication was read by a third party, and conveyed a defamatory meaning about the claimant, and no defence is available, the usual remedy is damages. These aim to vindicate the claimant's reputation and to compensate for the hurt and suffering experienced by an individual claimant.

13.3 Initial issues to consider

Prior to establishing whether a defamatory statement has been made, there are a number of initial issues to consider, namely:

(1)   recent legislative reform;

(2)   the distinction between libel and slander; and

(3)   who can sue for defamation?

These issues will be discussed before moving on to the steps needed to establish the tort of defamation.

13.3.1 Legislative reform

Prior to the implementation of the Defamation Act 2013, there had been significant criticism of the state of English defamation law. There were specific concerns about the large damages awards from juries,[3] the potential for England and Wales to become a destination for 'defamation tourism', the impact on the previous legal regime on free speech and civil liberties, the tension between English common law and human rights, the liability of internet hosts and service providers, and the rights of corporations to sue in defamation.[4] The state of law was eloquently outlined by Lord Sumption in *Lachaux v Independent Print Ltd* [2019]:

> The tort of defamation is an ancient construct of the common law. It has accumulated, over the centuries, a number of formal rules with no analogue in other branches of the law of tort. Most of them originated well before freedom of expression acquired the prominent place in our jurisprudence that it enjoys today. Its coherence has not been improved by attempts at statutory reform. Statutes to amend the law of defamation were enacted in 1888, 1952, 1996 and 2013, each of which sought to modify existing common law rules piecemeal, without always attending to the impact of the changes on the rest of the law. The Defamation Act 2013 is the latest chapter in this history. Broadly speaking, it seeks to modify some of the common law rules which were seen unduly to favour the protection of reputation at the expense of freedom of expression.[5]

The 2013 Act enacted a wide range of amendments. Whilst the reforms have generally been supported, there have been some notable criticisms. As discussed above, one of the key issues is the complexity of the current regime, which has a complicated mixture of legislation and common law and a myriad of detailed rules and procedures.

The different legislative reforms will be discussed throughout the chapter, but the key amendments of the Defamation Act 2013 were:

- abolishing 'defamation tourism' – a case can now only be brought against a non-EU citizen if England and Wales is clearly the most appropriate jurisdiction;

- restricting the use of juries – defamation cases will now be tried without a jury unless the court orders otherwise;

- increasing the threshold for defamation – a statement will now not be defamatory unless the publication has caused or is likely to cause 'serious harm' to the reputation of the claimant;

- requiring trading corporations to show 'serious financial loss';

- amending the defences – the defences of justification and fair comment have been replaced by defences of truth and honest opinion;

- the introduction of new defences – the defence of public interest replaced the defence in *Reynolds v Times Newspapers Ltd*, and a new defence was added for operators of websites;

- extending qualified privilege to statements in peer-reviewed journals and extending a number of categories of statutory privilege;

- removing the offer of amends procedure under s 2(2) of the Defamation Act 1996; and

- providing additional remedy powers – a court can now order a summary of its judgment to be published by the defendant.

---

3   See, for example, the £1.5 million jury award in *Tolstoy Miloslavsky v United Kingdom* (1995) 20 EHRR 442.

4   For more information on this see, J. Price QC and F. McMahon, *Blackstone's Guide to the Defamation Act 2013* (Oxford University Press 2013), ch 1; A. Mullis and A. Scott, 'Something Rotten in the State of English Libel Law? A Rejoinder to the Clamour for Reform of Defamation' (2009) 14(6) *Communications Law* 173.

5   [2019] UKSC 27 at [1].

13.3.2 Libel and slander

As previously outlined, there are two forms of defamation – libel and slander. The distinction between these two is generally based on whether the defamatory statements are made in a permanent or transient fashion. There are historical reasons for the distinction between libel and slander in the English common law. In the 17th century, it was held that written statements (i.e. libel) showed particular malice, and therefore could be actionable against the publisher without the need to show special damages.[6]

Whilst the distinction between slander and libel is often thought of as 'unwritten/written', it is now no longer that straightforward. Many verbal comments will be treated as libel – for example, s 166 of the Broadcasting Act 1990 states that words, pictures, visual images and gestures on radio and television are to be treated as libel, and s 4(1) of the Theatres Act 1968 states that defamatory words in the course of a performance of a play are also to be treated as libel. The common law had, however, developed this approach to libel prior to the enactment of the legislation.[7] In 1894 Lopes LJ commented in *Monson v Tussauds Ltd* [1894] that

> libels are general in writing or printing, but this is not necessary and the defamatory matter may be conveyed in some other permanent form. For instance, a statue, a caricature, an effigy, chalk-marks on a wall, signs or pictures may constitute a libel.[8]

In this case, a wax figure of the claimant was included as part of a 'Chambers of Horrors' which featured notorious murderers, as well as relics from and models of murder scenes. The claimant had shot a young man and was tried for murder, but the jury returned a verdict of 'Not Proven'. It was held that the wax figure was clearly libel as it implied that the claimant was guilty of murder, which resulted in 'an actionable wrong, tending to disparage and injure'.[9]

PROBLEM QUESTION TECHNIQUE

Michael posted a very insulting picture of Professor Honey on the Law Faculty library noticeboard which made it appear that she accepted bribes from a variety of different people.

▸ Can the picture of Professor Honey constitute libel, despite the fact that there was no writing?

▸ Remember that the picture will still need to fulfil the three requirements of defamation (which will be discussed below).

Historically, libel was similar to trespass to the person torts in that the claimant did not have to show damage for a successful action. The Defamation Act 2013 has reduced the importance of this distinction, with the new requirement for all claimants to show they have or are likely to suffer 'serious harm' as a result of the alleged statement.[10]

A victim of a slander, on the other hand, must show 'special damage' for the action to be successful.[11] This is classified as some sort of material loss, beyond mere reputational or social damage. There is, however, a fine line between what the law will consider special damage and mere

---

6   *King v Lake* (1667) 1 Hardres 470.

7   In *Youssoupoff v MGM Ltd* (1934) 50 TLR 581 the court addressed a 'novel problem [of] whether the product of the combined photographic and talking instrument which produces these modern films does, if it throws upon the screen and impresses upon the ear defamatory matter, produce that which can be complained of as libel or slander'.

8   [1894] 1 QB 671, 692.

9   [1894] 1 QB 671, 677.

10 Defamation Act 2013, s 1(1), discussed in more detail below. Previously, it had been held in *Jameel v Down Jones & Co Ltd* [2005] QB 946 that the presumption of damage was compatible with Article 10 of the ECHR.

11 The term 'special damage' is, however, misleading and not consistent with how the term 'special damage' is used in other contexts. 'Actual damage' is a more accurate description: see J.A. Jolowicz, 'The Changing use of "Special Damage" and its Effect on the Law' (1960) 18(2) CLJ 214.

reputational or social damage. For example, the loss of employment arising from reputational issues or the loss of hospitality because of ruined friendships are both forms of special damage.[12] The requirement to show special damage has been strongly criticised, and there is no clear justification for the different approaches and the additional requirements for slander claims.

Traditionally there were four types of slander that were actionable without the need to show special damage:

(1)   the imputation of a criminal offence that was punishable by imprisonment;[13]
(2)   the imputation of professional unfitness or incompetence;[14]
(3)   the imputation of a contagious disease;[15] and
(4)   the imputation of unchastity or adultery by a female.

Fortunately, the outdated imputations of a contagious disease and unchastity or adultery by a female have now been abolished by the Defamation Act 2013.[16]

13.3.2.1 CRITICISM OF THE DISTINCTION

The ongoing utility of the distinction between libel and slander has been widely criticised, and there are very relevant questions on whether it holds any utility, particularly in light of the Defamation Act 2013. The distinction between the two has a strong historical component, as not everyone was able to make written statements; therefore slander was more common. Technological developments – the telephone, recording devices, film, internet – have challenged the utility of distinguishing between these two forms of defamation.

The libel/slander distinction has been considered by two official reports: the Porter Committee (*Report of the Committee on the Law of Defamation*, 1948, Cmd 7536) and the Faulks Committee (*Report of the Committee on Defamation*, 1975, Cmnd 5909). The first Report supported the retention of the distinction on the basis that

> slander is often trivial, not infrequently good-tempered and harmless …. If all slander were actionable *per se*, the scope of trivial but costly litigation might be enormously increased …. A change in the law in England and Wales at the present date would, we think, be likely to encourage frivolous actions.[17]

This can be contrasted with the Faulks Committee Report which commented that the distinction had created law that was 'unreasonable and unnecessarily complicated and refined, carrying a host of rules and exceptions, derived partly from precedent and partly from statute, which are illogical, difficult to learn, and … unjust'.[18] On this basis, the Committee recommended that the distinction between the two causes of action be abolished and that slander should be assimilated into libel.[19]

As outlined above, the Defamation Act 2013 has further questioned the ongoing validity of the distinction. However, unlike the Faulks Committee Recommendation (that the law of slander be assimilated into libel), the Act has resulted in the claimant having to show evidence of serious harm for both causes of action.[20] The two causes of actions do, however – at least in theory – remain separated.

---

12   *Moore v Meagher* (1807) 1 Taunt 39; *Davies v Solomon* (1871) LR 7 QB 112; *McManus v Beckham* [2002] 1 WLR 2982.
13   *Webb v Beavan* (1883) 11 QBD 609.
14   *Jones v Jones* [1916] 2 AC 481.
15   The last reported case regarding the imputation of a contagious disease was *Bloodworth v Gray* (1844) 7 Man & Gr 334.
16   Defamation Act 2013, s 14.
17   *Report of the Committee on the Law of Defamation*, 1948, Cmnd.7536 at [38]-[40].
18   *Report of the Committee on Defamation*, 1975, Cmnd. 5909 at [86].
19   Report of the Committee on Defamation, 1975, Cmnd. 5909 at [91].
20   Defamation Act 2013, s 1.

■ VIEWPOINT

Do you think there is ongoing utility in the distinction between libel and slander?

13.3.3 Who can sue?

Before considering the three elements of defamation, it is important to consider *who* can sue. This covers three key issues:

(1) geographical limitations;
(2) body corporates; and
(3) public authorities.

13.3.3.1 GEOGRAPHICAL LIMITATIONS

There is now a geographical element to the right to sue for defamation. One of the main amendments of the Defamation Act 2013 is that s 9 addressed the increasing concern of 'defamation tourism'.[21] If the defendant is not from the United Kingdom or the EU, or a member of the Lugano Convention, the court does not have jurisdiction to hear claims for defamation *unless* England and Wales is clearly the most appropriate place to bring the action.

KEY LEGISLATION

Defamation Act 2013

9   Action against a person not domiciled in the UK or a Member State etc.

(1)   This section applies to an action for defamation against a person who is not domiciled—

(a) in the United Kingdom;

(b) in another Member State; or

(c) in a state which is for the time being a contracting party to the Lugano Convention.

(2)   A court does not have jurisdiction to hear and determine an action to which this section applies unless the court is satisfied that, of all the places in which the statement complained of has been published, England and Wales is clearly the most appropriate place in which to bring an action in respect of the statement.

The test for determining the 'most appropriate' jurisdiction was outlined in the Explanatory Notes:

This means that in cases where a statement has been published in this jurisdiction and also abroad the court will be required to consider the overall global picture to consider where it would be most appropriate for a claim to be heard. It is intended that this will overcome the problem of courts readily accepting jurisdiction simply because a claimant frames their claim so as to focus on damage which has occurred in this jurisdiction only. This would mean that, for example, if a statement was published 100,000 times in Australia and only 5,000 times in England that would be a good basis on which to conclude that the most appropriate jurisdiction in which to bring an action in respect of the statement was Australia rather than England. There will however be a range of factors which the court may wish to take into account including, for example, the amount of damage to the claimant's reputation in this jurisdiction compared to elsewhere, the

---

21   The practice of people from outside the UK commencing an action for defamation in the UK court system, largely on the basis of its perceived claimant-friendly defamation laws.

extent to which the publication was targeted at a readership in this jurisdiction compared to elsewhere, and whether there is reason to think that the claimant would not receive a fair hearing elsewhere.[22]

13.3.3.2 COMPANIES

All natural persons have the right to sue in defamation, although this action does not survive death.[23] There is a debate on whether defamation should be limited to natural persons.

DIFFERENT PERSPECTIVES on defamation of corporations

J. Oster, 'The Criticism of Trading Corporations and their Right to Sue for Defamation' (2011) 2 JETL 255–79

Oster draws on both English and German law to analyse the right that trading corporations have to sue for defamation. He emphasises that 'due to their socio-cultural and political influence, multinational corporations are subject to close public scrutiny and criticism'.[24] The author comments that there are three rationales for the protection of reputation: honour, dignity and property. Trading corporations are created for one specific purpose – to make a profit. On this basis, they do not have honour or dignity, and the only protection that should be afforded to corporations is to their property rights. As an extension, the protection under the ECHR should not be under Article 8(1), which protects private life, family life, home, and correspondence, but under Article 1 of the First Protocol to the ECHR, which protects property.

Whilst the article does recognise that the reputation of a company is something of value, Oster argues that companies cannot suffer 'hurt feelings or mental distress'. He also comments that there is significant value in criticism of companies in public speech, and their right to reputation needs to be balanced against the right to freedom of expression and free speech protection.

A. Mullis and A. Scott, 'Something Rotten in the State of English Libel Law? A Rejoinder to the Clamour for Reform of Defamation' (2009) 14(6) Communications Law 173–83

Mullis and Scott are much more hesitant about removing or significantly restricting a corporation's right to sue in defamation. Whilst corporate bodies would still have the right to sue for malicious falsehood, this tort has a very high burden and requires the claimant to prove malice, falsehood and special damages. The authors note that Australia is the only major jurisdiction that has prevented corporations from suing in defamation. In contrast, the European Court of Human Rights has held that a large, multinational company suing in defamation does not constitute a breach of Article 10, and in many cases in the United States a corporation is to be treated as a private figure for the purposes of defamation.

There are also some 'arguably very good reasons' for corporations to have the right to sue in defamation. The name of a company and its reputation is something of value. If a company is defamed, there is a risk that it will struggle to attract investors, employees and customers. The authors even cite Warren Buffett's famous quote, 'it takes 20 years to build a reputation and five minutes to ruin it.' The article concludes by recommending a middle route – instead of removing the right for companies to sue in defamation, there should be a requirement that they show that they have suffered, or are likely to suffer, financial loss.

---

22 Defamation Act 2013, Explanatory Notes, section 9 at [66].
23 Law Reform (Miscellaneous Provisions) Act 1934, s 1(1).
24 J. Oster, 'The Criticism of Trading Corporations and their Right to Sue for Defamation' (2011) 2 *JETL* 255–79, 255.

> Despite their different opinions on the general protection that corporations should be afforded, both articles generally come to the same conclusion: corporations should be entitled to sue for defamation, but only if they can prove that serious financial loss has been suffered.

In 1975, the Faulks Committee recommended that companies should not have the right to sue unless they can show financial harm.[25] There is a long and complex history of what rights corporations have in relation to defamation and what damage they need to prove, which is further complicated by the implementation of the ECHR.[26] This has been clarified to some extent by s 1(2) of the Defamation Act 2013, which requires a body that trades for profit to show that the defamatory publication has caused or is likely to cause it 'serious financial loss'. When interpreting this section in *Brett Wilson LLP v Persons Unknown* [2015],[27] Warby J emphasised that the question on whether the loss is serious must depend on the context. His Honour held that, in this case, the defamatory comments had caused the claimant to lose one potential client and were likely to deter multiple others, and therefore serious financial loss had occurred.

PROBLEM QUESTION TECHNIQUE

Unable to take responsibility for the grade, Michael blamed the company that manufactured his pencils, Wormwood Pty Ltd, on the basis that their pencils slowed down his writing in the exam. In an attempt to get even, Michael spent his vacation writing a negative blog about Wormwood pencils and how they made students write slower in exams. His blog has been read 15 times (mostly by his family members), and he has convinced his mother to no longer buy pencils from Wormwood Pty Ltd.

▶ Is Wormwood Pty Ltd a body that trades for profit? If so, it will only be entitled to sue Michael in defamation if the company can show that it has suffered 'serious financial loss'.

▶ Considering that Michael's blog has only been read 15 times and the only person that has clearly been impacted is his mother, would the company be able to fulfil the requirements of the Defamation Act 2013?

▶ An analogy could, however, be drawn with *Brett Wilson LLP v Persons Unknown* where the loss of one client and the likely deterrence of another was considered serious financial loss. Warby J emphasised the context of the loss, so you need to consider whether losing one client from purchasing pencils is the same as a law firm losing one client?

13.3.3.3 PUBLIC AUTHORITIES

There has been an ongoing debate about whether public authorities should be able to sue for defamation. In *Manchester Corporation v Williams* [1891][28] and *Bognor Regis Urban District Council v Campion* [1972], it was held that local government corporations could. This view was criticised as an unjustified restriction on freedom of speech. The House of Lords then held in *Derbyshire County Council v Times Newspapers* [1993] that government bodies cannot sue in defamation, as this would result in an undermining of the democratic process.

---

25 Faulks Committee, [342].
26 For discussion of this see J. Oster, 'The Criticism of Trading Corporations and their Right to Sue for Defamation' (2011) 2(3) *Journal of European Tort Law* 255–79.
27 [2015] EWHC 2628 (QB).
28 [1891] 1 QB 94.

DIFFERENT PERSPECTIVES on defamation of public authorities

Bognor Regis UDC v Campion [1972] 2 QB 169

Bognor Regis Urban District Council brought an action for damages for libel and an injunction against Eric Campion. The issue arose from a leaflet that the defendant distributed at a meeting held at the village hall on 24 January 1969. The leaflet was titled 'Save Bognor Group, Leaflet No.4' and made a number of severe accusations against the District Council and described it as a 'toytown Hitlerism local government'. The defendant appeared in person and pleaded the defences of privilege, justification and fair comment. The only issue in front of the judge was whether a local government corporation could sue for defamation.

Brown J outlined that the District Council was a 'statutory corporation' by virtue of s 31 of the Local Government Act 1933 and had power to bring legal proceedings through s 276 of this Act. There was no argument that corporations (trading and non-trading) could sue for defamation, so the issue was whether statutory corporations had the same ability. His Lordship relied on *National Union of General and Municipal Workers v Gillian* [1945][29] as a case where a trade union was entitled to sue for libel and was treated no differently to a company under the Companies Act.[30] The basis of allowing companies and trade unions to sue in defamation was that they have a 'trading reputation' which they are entitled to protect. Brown J then stated that:

> Just as a trading company has a trading reputation which it is entitled to protect by bringing an action for defamation, so in my view the plaintiffs as a local government corporation have a 'governing' reputation which they are equally entitled to protect in the same way.[31]

The District Council was therefore entitled to sue in defamation. Brown J held that the leaflet contained certain defamatory statements and rejected the defences of privilege, justification and fair comment. His Lordship awarded the District Council £2,000 in damages, an injunction and costs.

J.A. Weir 'Local Authority v Critical Ratepayer – A Suit in Defamation [1972] CLJ 238–46

Weir is scathing of the decision in *Bognor Regis UDC v Campion*. His article starts:

> It's a free country, is it? A man says that his local council is behaving in a dictatorial and undemocratic manner. He is tried for it, fined £32,000[32] and threatened with imprisonment if he ever says such a thing again. It couldn't happen? It did happen, in England, in 1972.[33]

In his discussion, Weir draws a distinction between the tort of malicious falsehood, where a body can obtain compensation for a loss that has resulted from a false statement improperly made by the defendant, and defamation, where an institution enjoys the benefit of all the legal rules protecting its reputation and esteem.

The article is generally critical of the ability for companies to sue in defamation, as they have 'no feelings which might have been hurt and no social relations which might have been impaired'[34] by defamatory statements. Weir is, however, particularly concerned with the ability of government bodies to sue in defamation, as he sees this as undermining the fundamental distinction between public law and private law. Governments should be required to put up with criticism, as this is a critical part of the democratic process.

29 [1945] 2 All ER 593.
30 See the Court of Appeal decision in this case at [1946] KB 81, 87 per Scott LJ.
31 [1972] 2 QB 169, 175.
32 Weir later states that legal costs would have been 'perhaps £30,000' so adds this to the £2,000 award for libel.
33 [1972] CLJ 238, 238.
34 [1972] CLJ 238, 240.

Weir recognises that local governments are distinct from central government, but states that, 'functionally speaking, the Bognor Regis Urban District Council is government, though doubtless of a very low order'.[35] Despite the fact that Mr Campion was 'tiresome', 'extreme' and 'a nuisance' to the District Council, he had a right to question the local government on any matters of public interest. Weir finishes by commenting on the dangers of letting government bodies sue critics (at the taxpayers' expense), as this will inevitably result in undermining our democratic system.

Derbyshire County Council v Times Newspapers Ltd [1993] AC 534

Weir's forceful arguments were upheld (but surprisingly not referred to) in *Derbyshire County Council v Times Newspapers Ltd*. In this case, the House of Lords overruled *Bognor Regis UDC v Campion* and held that public authorities and government bodies could not sue in defamation. The basis of this case was Derbyshire County Council suing in libel for two newspaper articles that questioned investments made for its superannuation fund. The first instance judge dismissed the defendant's application to strike out the statement of claim on the basis that local authorities could not sue in libel in respect of governmental and administrative functions. This dismissal of the strike out application was appealed and, when it reached the House of Lords, the question had 'opened out into an investigation of whether a local authority can sue in libel at all'.[36]

Lord Keith, delivering the main judgment of the House of Lords, summarised the authorities on whether government bodies can sue for defamation. His Lordship concluded by holding that the authorities established that a trading corporation is entitled to sue for defamatory matters which can be seen as having a tendency to damage its business, giving examples of credit-worthiness and the ability to obtain loans and recruitment of qualified workers.

A sharp distinction was drawn between corporations and democratically elected government bodies, with His Lordship commenting that:

> It is of the highest public importance that a democratically elected government body, or indeed any governmental body, should be open to uninhibited public criticism. The threat of a civil action for defamation must inevitably have an inhibiting effect on freedom of speech.[37]

Instead of utilising the jurisprudence on the European Convention on Human Rights, the House of Lords based its decision on case law from the United Kingdom and the United States. The decision of *New York Times Co v Sullivan* (1964) 376 US 254 from the Supreme Court of the United States was cited in support of the proposition that every citizen must be able to criticise a government without fear of civil or criminal prosecution. This applies to government bodies that are statutorily created corporations, and his Lordship outlined that many departments of the UK central government are statutory corporations, including the Secretaries of State for Defence, Education and Science, Energy, Environment and Social Services.

In conclusion, Lord Keith regarded

> it as right for this House to lay down that not only is there no public interest in favouring the right of organs of the government, whether central or local, to sue for libel, but that it is contrary to the public interest that they should have it. It is contrary to the public interest because to admit such actions would place an undesirable fetter on freedom of speech.[38]

Derbyshire County Council v Times Newspapers therefore held that a local authority – and by implication any government body – does not have the right to sue in defamation.

---

35   [1972] CLJ 238, 242.
36   [1993] AC 534, 542.
37   [1993] AC 534, 547.
38   [1993] AC 534, 549.

The finding in *Derbyshire County Council v Times Newspapers* was applied to political parties in *Goldsmith v Bhoyrul* [1996][39] to stop the Referendum Party from suing in defamation. It does not, however, apply to individual politicians, who still generally have rights to sue in defamation (and, indeed, have previously commenced actions[40]).

■ VIEWPOINT

Defamation is a cause of action designed to protect the claimant's reputation and esteem. Can and should companies and public authorities be able to sue in defamation?

PROBLEM QUESTION TECHNIQUE

Unable to take responsibility for the grade, Michael blamed his local authority, Pasadena Borough Council, for not providing all university students with free public transport. In an attempt to get even, Michael spent his vacation distributing a number of educational leaflets accusing the Pasadena Borough Council of not supporting university students and calling it a 'toytown Hitlerism local government'.

▸ As the Pasadena Borough Council is a public authority, would it be able to sue Michael in defamation?

▸ Despite the factual similarities to *Bognor Regis UDC v Campion*, the ratio in *Derbyshire County Council v Times Newspapers* should be applied.

13.4 Elements of defamation

As outlined in the initial discussion, the elements of the tort of defamation can be simplified into the **3Ds**:

(1) Was the publication **defamatory** of the claimant because the meaning it conveyed was likely to cause serious injury to the claimant's reputation?

(2) If so, is the publication **defensible** under a statutory or common law defence?

(3) If not, what **damages** should be awarded?

13.4.1 Was the publication defamatory?

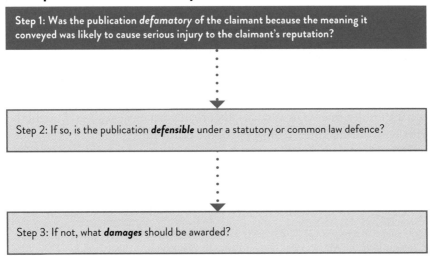

Step 1: Was the publication *defamatory* of the claimant because the meaning it conveyed was likely to cause serious injury to the claimant's reputation?

Step 2: If so, is the publication *defensible* under a statutory or common law defence?

Step 3: If not, what *damages* should be awarded?

Figure 13.2: Step 1

Once it has been concluded that the claimant has standing to sue and the defendant can be sued, it must be determined whether defamation has actually occurred. The first of the **3Ds** to consider is whether the publication was **defamatory**. For this requirement, the claimant must show that:

(a) the statement was defamatory;

(b) the statement referred to the claimant by name or otherwise; and

(c) the statement was published to a third party.

This next sections will consider each of these elements in turn.

13.4.1.1 THE STATEMENT WAS DEFAMATORY

The Defamation Act 2013 does not include any definition of 'defamation', and therefore the courts have continued to rely on the common law to define what constitutes defamatory material. The Act does, however, increase the threshold required, as s 1(1) states that for a statement to be defamatory, it must have 'caused or is likely to cause serious harm to the reputation of the claimant'. This test was considered by the Supreme Court in *Lachaux v Independent Print Ltd*, which stated that:

> Although the Act must be construed as a whole, the issue must turn primarily on the language of s 1. This shows, very clearly to my mind, that it not only raises the threshold of seriousness above that envisaged [by the common law], but requires its application to be determined by reference to the actual facts about its impact and not just to the meaning of the words.[41]

This case involved a number of potentially defamatory statements, including that the claimant had been violent and abusive towards his wife, hidden their son's passport to stop his removal from the UAE and deprived his wife of custody and contact with their son. In finding that these statements had fulfilled the 'serious harm' test under the 2013 Act, the Court considered a range of factors, including: the scale of the publications, the fact that the statements had come to the attention of at least one person who knew the claimant, that they were likely to come to the attention of other people who knew the claimant or would come to know him in the future, the gravity of the statements and the meaning attributed to them.[42]

Defamation is not concerned with the intentions of the party making the statement, but on whether defamation has occurred.[43] The focus at common law is on whether the statement would tend to injure the claimant's reputation or expose them to hatred, contempt or ridicule or lower them in the esteem of right-thinking members of society.[44] The statement will also be defamatory if it causes the claimant to be shunned or avoided.[45] The emphasis is on how a 'right thinking' person would interpret the statement and react to it.

Two issues arise: what is the meaning, and would this meaning lower the reputation of the claimant? Both are decided according to standards set by a 'hypothetical referee'. This means the ordinary, reasonable reader, listener or viewer, rather than what *actual* readers thought the publication meant and whether it affected their estimation of the claimant.

---

41 [2019] UKSC 27 at [12].

42 [2019] UKSC 27 at [21].

43 *Cassidy v Daily Mirror Newspapers Ltd* [1929] 2 KB 331, 354 per Russell LJ.

44 *Parmiter v Coupland* (1840) 6 M&W 105, 108 (per Parke B); *Sim v Stretch* [1936] 2 All ER 1237, 1240 (per Lord Atkin).

45 *Youssoupoff v MGM Pictures Ltd* (1934) 50 TLR 581.

The first is the question of meaning: what meaning would have been conveyed about the claimant to an ordinary reasonable reader (or listener/viewer). The ordinary, reasonable reader is not 'unduly suspicious' or 'avid for scandal',[46] but they do have a capacity to read between the lines and engage in a degree of loose thinking. The meaning reached may therefore be drawn from implications, rather than strict logical thinking. Courts deciding what meaning would be conveyed to an ordinary reasonable reader or viewer consider the circumstances in which an item would be read or heard. With a transient publication like a television programme which cannot be reviewed by the viewer, the general impression left will be important. This may, however, be different for television programmes that can be re-watched, such as those on Netflix, Amazon Prime or BBC iPlayer.

The second issue at common law is whether that meaning would lower the reputation of the claimant in the estimation of the ordinary reasonable reader. This involves the assumption that the ordinary reasonable reader has the standards of 'ordinary decent folk in the community'[47] and that there is a common standard. This may be so for many statements, for example, statements which impute crime, corruption or other obvious wrongdoing. However, in a pluralist society there may be different attitudes towards behaviour. Is it defamatory to report that a doctor performs abortions? Some would think that performing a legal medical procedure is incapable of being defamatory. In some sections of the community, performing an abortion would be frowned upon. Social attitudes change, and so what is defamatory changes as a result. Once it was thought to be defamatory to impute that a woman had been the victim of rape (*Youssoupoff v MGM Pictures Ltd*[48]). It was also defamatory to impute that someone was homosexual (*R v Bishop*[49]). These views no longer reflect the views of 'right thinking' members of society, taken as a whole.

This standard can cause some difficulties. An example of this was the case of *Byrne v Deane*.[50] Here, the allegedly defamatory statement was a notice put on a public noticeboard that imputed that the claimant had informed the police about the use of illegal gambling machines at a golf club. The court held that this was not defamatory, as reporting illegal activity to police would not lower Byrne's reputation in the eyes of 'right thinking' members of society. Whilst it is understandable that the courts may want to find that allegations of reporting crimes to the police are not capable of defamation, it is clear from the evidence given that the claimant had suffered distress and been isolated as a result of the notice. This brings into question whether the test really should be based on 'right thinking' people, or whether it would be more appropriate to focus on what impact it would have on the views and reactions of 'ordinary' members of our society.

The question of whether a statement is defamatory is far from straightforward; there is a wide variety of cases that consider this complex question. Table 13.1 below summarises a number of these cases and whether or not the court found the statement in question to be defamatory. When reviewing these cases, please keep in mind that each individual situation needs to be considered in the specific context and on its own merits. It is also important to remember that attitudes, opinions and beliefs of society – especially around issues such as homosexuality and adultery – have changed significantly since a number of these decisions. The impact of this is discussed further at 13.7 (Challenges) below.

46   *Lewis v Daily Telegraph* [1964] AC 234.
47   *Gardiner v John Fairfax & Sons Pty Ltd* (1942) 42 SR (NSW) 171, 172 per Jordan CJ.
48   (1934) 50 TLR 581. For more discussion, see Treiger-Bar-Am, 'Defamation law in a changing society: the case of *Youssoupoff v Metro-Goldwyn Mayer*' (2000) 20(2) *Legal Studies* 291.
49   *R v Bishop* [1975] QB 275.
50   [1937] 1 KB 818.

Table 13.1: Key cases on whether statements are defamatory

Case	Statement(s) Made	Were the Statement(s) Defamatory?
Monson v Tussauds Ltd [1894]	A wax figure of the claimant was included as part of an exhibit called the 'Chambers of Horrors' which featured predominately notorious murderers, but also relics and models of murder scenes. The claimant shot a young man and was tried for murder, but the jury returned a verdict of 'Not Proven'.	The wax figure was defamatory. The defendant unsuccessfully argued that the figure was exhibited simply because the claimant was a notorious person and it did not insinuate anything further. The House of Lords rejected this claim and held that the figure and circumstances resulted in 'an actionable wrong, tending to disparage and injure the plaintiff'.
Myroft v Sleight [1921]	The defendant said that the claimant, who was a member of the Trade Union, voted in favour of a strike, but then asked the employer for work.	The statement was defamatory, as 'an ordinary member of a trade union may claim that the duty of honesty and loyalty rests upon him' and the statement implies that the claimant acted dishonestly.
Cassidy v Daily Mirror Newspapers Ltd [1929]	The claimant's husband was featured in a newspaper with another woman stating that they were engaged to be married.	The statement was defamatory, as it conveyed the meaning that the claimant and her husband were not legally married and in 'immoral cohabitation'.
Tolley v JS Fry & Sons Ltd [1931]	The defendant published an advertisement without the claimant's consent. The advertisement made it appear that the claimant, who was a famous amateur golfer, had agreed to advertise the defendant's products for gain and reward.	The statement was defamatory. People who knew of the claimant's status of an amateur golfer would believe that he had accepted some sort of consideration from the defendant, and therefore was 'guilty of conduct unworthy of his status as an amateur golfer'.
Blennerhassett v Novelty Sales Services Ltd [1933]	The defendant published an advertisement stating that the claimant, a member of the London Stock Exchange for over 30 years, had such a fascination with the defendant's yo-yo that he became addicted to it.	The statement was not defamatory. Even though the claimant was subjected to a certain level of good-natured teasing at the London Stock Exchange, the advertisement was not serious enough to constitute a defamatory statement.
Youssoupoff v MGM Pictures Ltd [1934]	The claimant had been seduced by and/or raped by Rasputin.	It was defamatory to impute that a woman had been the victim of rape. Even though there is no moral turpitude on the victim, the statement could cause her to be shunned or avoided.
Byrne v Deane [1937]	The defendant said, 'He who gave the game away, may he byrnn in hell and rue the day', imputing that the claimant had informed the police about the use of illegal gambling machines.	The statement was not defamatory as reporting illegal activity to the police would not lower the claimant's reputation in the eyes of 'right thinking' members of society.
Lewis v Daily Telegraph [1964]	The claimants were being investigated for fraud and whether that imputed that the claimants were guilty of fraud.	The statements were defamatory, but did not impute that the claimants were guilty of the fraud as a reasonable person would not 'infer guilt of fraud merely because an inquiry is on foot'.
R v Bishop [1975]	An allegation of a homosexual affair.	It was defamatory to impute that someone was homosexual.

Case	Statement(s) Made	Were the Statement(s) Defamatory?
Shah v Akram [1981]	The claimant, a man of the Muslim faith, 'satirically passed such frivolous remarks in the presence of some reliable persons on the respected personality of the Prophet ... that cannot be written down and which are unbearable for a proud Muslim to hear'. The claimant admitted he made a statement the Prophet having married his fourth wife when she was eight years old, but denied it was made satirically.	The statement was defamatory. The Court of Appeal stated that 'the ordinary member of the public, even if he had no religious views of his own or no strongly held views, would not approve of anyone insulting the religious beliefs of others; and anyone who did insult the religious beliefs of other people would, in my judgment, be lowering himself in the estimation of right thinking people'.
Charleston v News Group Newspapers Ltd [1995]	A series of digitally manipulated images of the claimants (popular actors in a soap opera) in pornographic poses including bondage and sodomy.	The statement was not defamatory as the corresponding text made it clear that the images had been made without the consent of the claimants. The images had to be considered as a whole.
Berkoff v Burchill [1996]	That the claimant was 'hideous-looking' and that Frankenstein's monster is 'marginally better-looking' than the claimant.	The statement was defamatory not because it is defamatory that someone is ugly but because the wording could cause the claimant to suffer 'contempt, scorn or ridicule' and/or 'will cause him to be shunned or avoided'.
Cruise v Express Newspapers plc [1999]	The claimant, a married man, was referred to as 'gay'.	This statement was defamatory as it implied that the marriage was a sham to cover up the claimant's homosexuality.
Church v MGN Ltd [2012]	The claimant, a famous singer-songwriter, had proposed to her partner after consuming too much alcohol at a karaoke venue.	The statement was defamatory as it attributed drunken behaviour to the claimant. The judge emphasised, however, that whether a statement was defamatory 'depends on the context', so the statement may not have been defamatory if made against another individual.
Monroe v Hopkins [2017]	A tweet stating '@MsJackMonroe scrawled on any memorials recently? Vandalised the memory of those who fought for your freedom. Grandma got any more medals?' This was held to mean that the claimant condoned and approved of vandalising war memorials and/or monuments commemorating those who fought for the claimant's freedom.	The statement was defamatory. The judge commented that we live 'in a diverse society, there are many with views of which some people approve and some disapprove'. Regardless, it was held that an accusation of vandalising war memorials would lower the claimant's reputation in right thinking members of society as it undermines 'the shared values of our society.'
Lachaux v Independent Print Ltd [2019]	A number of statements, including that the claimant had been violent and abusive towards his wife, hidden their son's passport to prevent his removal from the UAE and deprived his wife of custody and contact with her son.	The statements were defamatory, as they fulfilled the 'serious harm' test under s 1(1) of the Defamation Act 2013.
Stocker v Stocker [2019]	Stated on her Facebook page that her husband 'tried to strangle' her.	The judge at first instance relied on the dictionary definition of strangle, which stated that 'strangle' must mean try to kill. The Supreme Court held that this was a mistake and the statement did not mean to convey that the husband had attempted to kill the claimant. Therefore, the statement was not defamatory.

PROBLEM QUESTION TECHNIQUE

In an attempt to get even, Michael posted a very insulting picture of Professor Honey on the Law Faculty library noticeboard which made it appear that she accepted bribes from a variety of different people. He also sent a number of tweets about Bruce and Amanda, calling them the 'nerd girl' and 'nerd guy', and stating that they were bad friends for preferring to study than go out clubbing with him.

▸ Do the comments made by Michael fulfil the 'serious harm' test?

▸ Would they be sufficient to constitute defamatory statements under the Defamation Act 2013?

▸ Can tweets constitute defamatory statements (remember *Monroe v Hopkins*)?

▸ With the picture of Professor Honey, specifically consider whether the imputation that an academic would accept bribes would be likely to lower Professor Honey's reputation in the eyes of the 'right thinking' members of society.

▸ In contrast, is the imputation that Bruce and Amanda were bad friends for preferring to study than go clubbing unlikely to lower their reputation on the basis of the same test? Right thinking members of society are (hopefully) going to think more highly of them for their dedication to their studies. Could the comments 'nerd girl' and 'nerd guy' be classified as 'mere vulgar abuse' (*Berkoff v Burchill*) or do they go further?

Interestingly, the claimant does not need to prove that the statement was false. Provided that the allegation is deemed to be defamatory, it will be presumed to be false. The burden then shifts on to the defendant to prove that the statement was true, which now occurs through the defence of 'truth' under s 2 of the Defamation Act 2013.[51]

13.4.1.2 INNUENDO

It is important to consider the role of innuendo when determining whether a statement is defamatory. It may be relatively straightforward to determine whether a statement is defamatory if the words impute wrongdoing or something adverse to the claimant's reputation according to their literal meaning. The issue becomes more complex if the words convey a meaning by implication or inference. In the context of defamation, this is referred to as an 'innuendo' and there are two different types. A true (or legal) innuendo occurs where the statements themselves are not sufficient, and the claimant must show that the recipients of the allegations have additional information that would make the statements defamatory.[52] A false (or popular) innuendo occurs where reasonable members of society with general knowledge could infer the defamatory nature of the statement if they 'read between the lines'.[53] In both cases, the claimant will have to prove the facts to support a case of defamation by innuendo. This distinction is often difficult to determine, so an example may be helpful.

For example, '*I've seen Joe come out of 54 Young Street many times*' is not defamatory in and of itself, but it may be a defamatory innuendo. It would be a true innuendo if only some members of society knew that 54 Young Street was an illegal drug house, as that statement may imply that Joe is an illegal drug user. It would be a false innuendo if the term '54 Young Street' was widely known and commonly used slang for an illegal drug house.

Courts often have difficulty interpreting statements that have a range of possible meanings as, in reality, different, reasonable readers will derive different meanings. For example, a report of a police investigation may suggest to some readers that the claimant is guilty, but others may infer the less

---

51 See below for further discussion of this defence.
52 See *Tolley v JS Fry & Sons Ltd* [1931] AC 333 for an example of a true innuendo.
53 See *Lewis v Daily Telegraph Ltd* [1964] AC 234 for an example of a false innuendo.

serious meaning that the claimant has attracted the suspicion of police. The law operates, however, on the assumption that the 'ordinary reasonable reader' derives a single meaning. Lord Reid in *Lewis v Daily Telegraph* considered this task, stating that:

> Ordinary men and women have different temperaments and outlooks. Some are unusually suspicious and some are unusually naive. One must try to envisage people between these two extremes and see what is the most damaging meaning they would put on the words in question.[54]

KEY CASE

Lewis v Daily Telegraph [1964] AC 234

In this case, the *Daily Telegraph* and *Daily Mail* published reports on their front pages stating that Officers of the Fraud Squad were inquiring into the affairs of Rubber Improvement Ltd, with the headlines 'Inquiry on Firm by City Police' and 'Fraud Squad Probe Firm'. The claimants commenced an action for defamation on the ground that 'the defendants meant and were understood to mean that the affairs of the plaintiffs and/or its subsidiaries were conducted fraudulently or dishonestly or in such a way that the police suspected that their affairs were so conducted'.[55]

The defendants accepted that the publication was defamatory, but argued that the ordinary person would not interpret the statement to mean that the claimants were guilty or suspected of a breach of criminal law. The question therefore was whether there was evidence to support meanings pleaded in the innuendo and whether ordinary people would understand the difference between being investigated for fraud and being guilty of fraud.

The first instance decision held that the jury should be entitled to consider the matter, but this was overturned by the Court of Appeal, and the House of Lords upheld the Court of Appeal's decision. Lord Reid commented

> So let me suppose a number of ordinary people discussing one of these paragraphs which they had read in the newspaper ... What the ordinary man, not avid for scandal, would read into the words complained of must be a matter of impression. I can only say that I do not think that he would infer guilt of fraud merely because an inquiry is on foot. And, if that is so, then it is the duty of the trial judge to direct the jury that it is for them to determine the meaning of the paragraph but that they must not hold it to impute guilt of fraud because as a matter of law the paragraph is not capable of having that meaning.[56]

Jeynes v News Magazines Ltd [2008][57] provides a more recent example of drawing innuendo from newspaper articles. In this case, the defendant published a magazine which had the words 'BB'S LISA "THE GEEZER" My fake boobs fell out on a date with James Hewitt!' on the front cover. The claimant argued that these words had

> the natural and ordinary (alternatively the inferential meaning) that the Claimant (who is and was born a woman) is in truth a man posing as a woman, alternatively that the Claimant is a transgendered or transsexual person, who was born a man but has become a woman.[58]

The Court of Appeal rejected this argument. Sir Anthony Clarke MR emphasised that the governing principle is reasonableness, and agreed with the trial judge's finding that no reasonable magazine

---

54 [1964] AC 234, 259.
55 [1964] AC 234, 238.
56 [1964] AC 234, 259–60.
57 [2008] EWCA Civ 130.
58 [2008] EWCA Civ 130 at [3].

reader could conclude that the women in the photo 'was deceiving people, or intending to deceive people, into believing that she was a woman when she was in fact a man or a transsexual'.[59]

■ VIEWPOINT

Consider the statement, 'Hannah has been arrested for serious criminal offences.' Is that defamatory? Think through whether it is capable of imputing guilt of the offences charged and whether an ordinary reasonable reader is likely to adopt the presumption of innocence (which is the basis of the criminal law).

13.4.2 The statement referred to the claimant

The next issue to consider is whether the statement referred to the claimant. The defamatory statement must identify the claimant to at least some of the recipients of the publication. Where the claimant is not specifically named, he or she may be identified by a description in the article which coincides with things known to readers about the claimant, for example any distinctive physical features, professional positions or biographical details. Identification may occur explicitly, implicitly or through the use of a second publication to identify the claimant.[60] The last example occurred when a publication about 'a leading Conservative politician' was combined with a tweet stating, 'Why is Lord McAlpine trending?' to identify Lord McAlpine.[61]

An unnamed person may also be described in a publication and identified by a reasonable reader, who knows that the claimant matches that description. In *Morgan v Odhams Press* [1971], Lord Donovan warned against 'expecting too high a standard of reasonableness in the readers of a popular newspaper'.[62] A newspaper article's headline made it seem like Morgan was part of a dog-doping gang, although if the entire article was read, it was clear that Morgan was not, in fact, involved. The question was whether a reasonable reader would have looked at the entire article. On the basis of the particular facts of this case, there may have been no defamation 'if one were dealing with a readership composed of Fellows of All Souls, the readers of "The Sun" are not in that class. They scan the headlines, skim the reading matter, and subject whatever attracts any deeper attention to no careful analysis.'[63]

It is possible to have unintentional defamation of the claimant, as the focus of defamation is on the harm to the claimant, not the intention of the defendant. The issue is therefore not whether the publisher intended to identify the claimant, but whether a reasonable reader would in fact identify the claimant.[64] This may occur where a person is named, but someone else with the same name is identified. In *Newstead v London Express Newspapers Ltd* [1940],[65] it was held that a report stating that 'Harold Newstead, a thirty-year-old Camberwell man' had been convicted of bigamy was defamatory, even though it referred unintentionally to the claimant, who was also called Harold Newstead and who lived in Camberwell. This is because it would not have been unduly onerous on the newspaper to check whether there was anyone else who fitted that definition before publishing the statement.

Whilst it is possible to have unintentional defamation, in *O'Shea v MGN Ltd* [2001][66] it was held that the publishing of pornographic pictures that have a strong resemblance to a particular individual is not defamation. This is because it would require the publisher to check whether the picture

---

59 [2008] EWCA Civ 130 at [19].
60 *Hayward v Thompson* [1982] QB 47.
61 *The Lord McAlpine of West Green v Sally Bercow* [2013] EWHC 1342 (QB).
62 [1971] 1 WLR 1239, 1265.
63 [1971] 1 WLR 1239, 1264–5.
64 *Cassidy v Daily Mirror Newspapers Ltd* [1929] 2 KB 331, 354 per Russell LJ.
65 [1940] 1 KB 377.
66 [2001] EMLR 40.

resembled anyone before publishing it. The judge held that this obligation would be contrary to Article 10 of the ECHR as the burden on the press would be unjustifiability high.

13.4.3 The statement was published to a third party

The third element to consider is whether the statement was published to a third party. 'Publication' is a key criterion because the aim is to judge the actual or likely effect of publication on the recipient's estimation of the claimant. Despite the fact that this element refers to 'publishing', there is no requirement for a formal publication of the statement. For publication to occur, the statement needs to be communicated to a third party; merely making a defamatory statement to the claimant herself is not sufficient. Making a statement which is not read or otherwise comprehended by a third party is not a 'publication'. There are a number of specific rules for publication:

- Generally, a positive act of publication is required. In certain limited circumstances, a failure to remove a defamatory statement may also be deemed a publication. For example, in *Byrne v Deane* [1937][67] managers of a club could have been held liable in defamation for not removing an allegedly defamatory poem from a public noticeboard.

- Communication between spouses is not considered 'publication', on the (questionable) basis of the unity between husband and wife.

- Public posting of documents or open postcards will generally be deemed to be publication.[68]

- Merely placing information on the internet is not sufficient proof of publication, and the claimant will need to show either actual publication to identifiable third parties or ask the court to draw an inference based upon facts admitted or proved.[69]

PROBLEM QUESTION TECHNIQUE

In an attempt to get even with these parties, Michael posted a very insulting picture of Professor Honey on the Law Faculty library noticeboard which made it appear that she accepted bribes from a variety of different people. Professor Honey asked the Law Faculty to take it down, but they refused, as they thought it was positive that students were visiting the library to view the picture.

▸ The liability of Michael has already been considered.

▸ Consider also whether the Law Faculty could also be held liable for defamation on the grounds that they refused to take down the defamatory picture from the public noticeboard even though it was in their control (remember the test in *Byrne v Deane*)?

13.4.3.1 REPUBLICATION

In determining whether there has been publication of the defamatory statement, the potential liability for *re*publication of defamatory material must be considered. The law of defamation was developed over the centuries to protect individuals from untrue and hurtful allegations. If someone repeated an allegation or rumour, it was no defence that they were accurately repeating what they had been told. This party could be liable for 'republishing' a defamatory allegation. In certain circumstances, someone

---

67   [1937] 1 KB 818.
68   *Theaker v Richardson* [1962] 1 WLR 151.
69   *Loutchansky v Times Newspapers* [2001] EMLR 876; *Al-Amoudi v Brisard* [2006] EWHC 1062 (QB).

who publishes an indefensible defamation may be liable not only for its publication, but for its repetition or republication by the person to whom it was published, for instance where the republication was the natural and probable consequence of making the publication. For instance, if someone reports to a school principal that a teacher assaulted a student, a natural and probable consequence will be that the principal will report the allegation to authorities like the police. The original accuser can be held liable for this republication, as well as the original publication to the principal.

The law of defamation has struggled to deal with liability for republication of a defamatory statement. Under the common law, a new cause of action arose each time the statement was republished.[70] This rule was substantially changed by s 8 of the Defamation Act 2013, which introduced a 'single publication' rule. This rule prevents an action being brought for the publication of the same material by the same publisher after a one-year limitation period from the first publication. It does not apply to publication that is materially different,[71] or when the court exercises its discretion to extend the limitation period.[72]

KEY LEGISLATION

Defamation Act 2013

8   Single publication rule

(1)   This section applies if a person—

(a) publishes a statement to the public ('the first publication'), and

(b) subsequently publishes (whether or not to the public) that statement or a statement which is substantially the same.

(2)   In subsection (1) 'publication to the public' includes publication to a section of the public.

(3)   For the purposes of section 4A of the Limitation Act 1980 (time limit for actions for defamation etc) any cause of action against the person for defamation in respect of the subsequent publication is to be treated as having accrued on the date of the first publication.

(4)   This section does not apply in relation to the subsequent publication if the manner of that publication is materially different from the manner of the first publication.

(5)   In determining whether the manner of a subsequent publication is materially different from the manner of the first publication, the matters to which the court may have regard include (amongst other matters)—

(a) the level of prominence that a statement is given;

(b) the extent of the subsequent publication.

The single publication rule only applies, however, to the *same publisher* and does not address republication by a third party.

A party who makes a publication will not be liable for damages resulting from republication of the statement, provided it is committed by a third party and it has no control over the actions of this third party.[73] It will, however, be liable in the following circumstances:

70 *Duke of Brunswick v Harmer* (1849) 14 QB 185.
71 Defamation Act 2013, s 8(4).
72 Defamation Act 2013, s 8(6)(a).
73 *Stocker v Stocker* [2019] UKSC 27.

- if the republication was authorised or intended;[74]

- if the original publication was made to a person who was under a moral duty to republish the statement; [75] or

- where republication was the natural and probable result of the original publication.[76]

The limits of republication were questioned in *McManus v Beckham* [2002].[77] In this case, the wife of the footballer David Beckham entered a memorabilia shop and commented that a signed photo of her husband was a forgery. Unsurprisingly, her comments received significant publicity, and the owner of the shop brought a claim in defamation against Ms Beckham. The question for the Court of Appeal was whether the republication of the comments was a natural and probable result of her original statement. The Court rejected the earlier test of reasonable foresight[78] as this would place an unfair burden on the defendant. It was held that the original publisher would be liable if they were aware that the statement was likely to be reported or there was a significant risk that the comment would be repeated in whole or in part by the press and that this would increase the harm suffered by the claimant.[79] If it can be shown that the defendant made a defamatory statement that referred to the claimant and was published, the claimant will be liable in defamation (subject to the application of any relevant defence(s)).

This section has considered the first of our **3Ds** – was the publication **defamatory** of the claimant because the meaning it conveyed was likely to cause serious injury to the claimant's reputation? There are three elements to consider: was the statement defamatory and did it cause serious harm to the claimant, did it refer to the claimant and was it published to a third party. These elements are very broad – for example, there is no need to show fault, malice, intention or even that the statement was false. This means that there is a strong role for the second of our **3Ds**, **defences**, which will be considered at 13.5.

PART 4

13.5 Defences

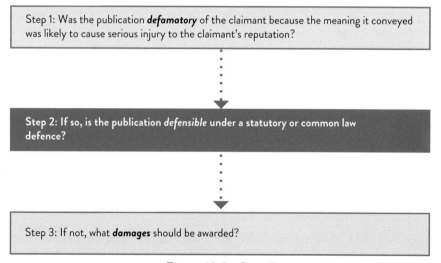

Figure 13.3: Step 2

---

74   *Speight v Gosnay* (1819) 60 LJQB 231.
75   *Slipper v BBC* [1991] 1 QB 283.
76   *McManus v Beckham* [2002] 1 WLR 2982.
77   [2002] 1 WLR 2982.
78   from *Slipper v BBC* [1991] 1 QB 283.
79   [2002] 1 WLR 2982, 2998 (per Waller LJ).

This section considers the second of our **3Ds**, whether there is an applicable **defence**. Defences in defamation law have a very strong role to play in balancing the competing interests of reputation and freedom of speech. The following sections will summarise the main defences applicable to defamation under both the common law and the Defamation Act 2013. The Act made significant changes to the defences available in a claim in defamation, and the following defences will be used:

(1) Truth
(2) Honest opinion
(3) Privilege and public interest
(4) Operators of website
(5) Consent

13.5.1 Truth

There is no requirement for the claimant to show that the statement made was false. Provided that the elements of defamation are made out (including that the statement was defamatory), it will be presumed that the statement was false. The defendant may seek to rely on the defence of truth, which prior to the Defamation Act 2013 was referred to as 'justification'.

Section 2 of the Defamation Act 2013 abolishes the previous common law defence of justification and repeals s 5 of the Defamation Act 1952 (justification). It holds that it is a defence to an action for defamation if the defendant can show that the imputation conveyed by the statement is 'substantially true'.[80] The defendant will need to provide some evidence supporting their assertion of truth, and this must be more than their mere belief in the statement's correctness. For example, the repeating of a rumour that the defendant honestly believes is true will not provide a defence to defamation.[81]

KEY LEGISLATION

Defamation Act 2013

2   Truth

(1)   It is a defence to an action for defamation for the defendant to show that the imputation conveyed by the statement complained of is substantially true.

(2)   Subsection (3) applies in an action for defamation if the statement complained of conveys two or more distinct imputations.

(3)   If one or more of the imputations is not shown to be substantially true, the defence under this section does not fail if, having regard to the imputations which are shown to be substantially true, the imputations which are not shown to be substantially true do not seriously harm the claimant's reputation.

(4)   The common law defence of justification is abolished and, accordingly, section 5 of the Defamation Act 1952 (justification) is repealed.

The Defamation Act 2013, however, amended the test to require that the defendant show that the statement was 'substantially true', not that it was completely true. For example, if the publication was to state that 'Anne defrauded 30 families out of £3 million of their hard-earned savings' but, in reality, she defrauded 29 families out of £2.9 million of their savings, the defamatory comment is

---

80   Defamation Act 2013, s 2(1).
81   *Cookson v Harewood* [1932] 2 KB 478.

not *completely* true. The defence of truth is, however, highly likely to succeed as the statement was substantially true. This is generally in line with the common law as minor inaccuracies in specific points would not have defeated the defence in common law.[82] The Explanatory Notes for s 2 of the Act explain that the section 'is intended broadly to reflect the current law while simplifying and clarifying certain elements'.

Special rules apply if the statement complained of could possibly convey two or more distinct imputations. If one or more of the imputations is not shown to be substantially true, the defence will not fail if – having regard to the imputations which are shown to be substantially true – the imputations that are not substantially true do not seriously harm the claimant's reputation.[83]

13.5.2 Honest opinion

Section 3 of the Defamation Act 2013 provides the defence of 'honest opinion', which resembles in some respects the common law defence of 'fair comment'. For the 'honest opinion' defence, the defendant has to prove that:

(a)   the statement complained of was a statement of opinion and not fact;[84]

(b)   the statement made clear, whether in general or specific terms, the basis of the opinion; and

(c)   an honest person could have held the opinion.[85]

KEY LEGISLATION

Defamation Act 2013

3   Honest opinion

(1)   It is a defence to an action for defamation for the defendant to show that the following conditions are met.

(2)   The first condition is that the statement complained of was a statement of opinion.

(3)   The second condition is that the statement complained of indicated, whether in general or specific terms, the basis of the opinion.

(4)   The third condition is that an honest person could have held the opinion on the basis of—

   (a) any fact which existed at the time the statement complained of was published;

   (b) anything asserted to be a fact in a privileged statement published before the statement complained of.

(5)   The defence is defeated if the claimant shows that the defendant did not hold the opinion.

(6)   Subsection (5) does not apply in a case where the statement complained of was published by the defendant but made by another person ('the author'); and in such a case the defence is defeated if the claimant shows that the defendant knew or ought to have known that the author did not hold the opinion.

   ...

(8)   The common law defence of fair comment is abolished and, accordingly, section 6 of the Defamation Act 1952 (fair comment) is repealed.

---

82   *Henry v BBC* [2006] EWHC 386; *Chase v News Group Newspapers Ltd* [2002] EWCA Civ 1772.

83   Defamation Act 2013, s 2(3).

84   *Joseph v Spiller* [2010] UKSC 53.

85   Defamation Act 2013, s 3(2)–(4).

There are a number of requirements on the defendant's opinion for the defence to apply. First, it has to be based on true facts.[86] The defendant will have the obligation to prove the true facts on which their opinion is based. If they cannot do this, the defence will not succeed. For example, in *London Artists Ltd v Littler* [1969],[87] the defence of fair comment failed as the defendant was unable to prove that the underlying facts were true. Second, the opinion also has to be one that an honest-minded person could make on the facts.[88] Third, if the defendant does not actually hold the belief, the defence will be defeated.[89] The distinction between fact and opinion is often difficult to assess, as shown by *British Chiropractic Association v Singh* [2010].

KEY CASE

British Chiropractic Association v Singh [2010] EWCA Civ 350

This case highlights the complex relationship between fact and opinion in the context of allegedly defamatory comments.

The defendant was a scientist and science writer. He published an article which included this passage:

The British Chiropractic Association claims that their members can help treat children with colic, sleeping and feeding problems, frequent ear infections, asthma and prolonged crying, even though there is not a jot of evidence. This organisation is the respectable face of the chiropractic profession and yet it happily promotes bogus treatments.

The claimant sued for defamation, and the defendant argued that the defence of honest opinion applied. At trial, the judge held that the statement should be classified as containing factual assertions as opposed to mere expression of opinions.

The defendant successfully appealed to the Court of Appeal. It was held that the references to 'bogus treatments' and 'not a jot of evidence' were both best characterised as 'value judgments'; therefore they were statements of opinions made by the claimant.

Similar to the truth defence, the Defamation Act 2013 abolishes the previous common law defence, in this case the defence of fair comment, and repeals s 6 of the Defamation Act 1952 (fair comment). The common law requirement that the defence would be defeated if the statement was made with malice therefore no longer applies.[90] This means that an honest opinion can now be made maliciously, provided that the three elements of the statutory defence have been made out. There is also no requirement for the opinion to be made on a matter of public interest or opinion.

PROBLEM QUESTION TECHNIQUE

Michael believes that he will not be held liable for defamation as he honestly believes that the Wormwood pencils made him write slower, although he has no factual basis for his belief.

▸ Does Michael have a basis for his claim? If not, his defence of truth will fail, even if it is honestly held.

▸ Is the statement presented as an assertion of fact, as opposed to an expression of opinion? What impact does this have on the defence of honest opinion?

86 *Grech v Odhams Press Ltd* [1958] 2 QB 275.
87 [1969] 2 QB 375.
88 (1888) 20 QBD 275.
89 Defamation Act 2013, s 3(5).
90 *Thomas v Bradbury, Agnew & Co Ltd* [1906] 2 KB 627.

13.5.3 Privilege and public interest

The law recognises that on occasions it is for the public good that individuals are not deterred from communicating information and opinions. For example, the legitimate interest in prospective employers to obtain a frank assessment of the character or qualifications of potential employees creates an occasion of qualified privilege at common law for persons to communicate such an assessment, provided they act without malice. The public interest in solving crime is advanced by giving citizens protection to report suspicious activities, even where the suspicions later prove to be unfounded. The importance in a democracy of robust discussion on matters of public interest warrants legal protection for such communications.

13.5.3.1 PRIVILEGE

The defence of privilege is concerned with situations where the public interest of the statement is determined to be more important than the claimant's reputation. It is a defence that protects people's ability to speak without fear of defamation in situations where the law deems it important to do so. There are two types of privilege: absolute privilege and qualified privilege. Absolute privilege gives people complete freedom to speak without fear of defamation in any circumstance, whereas qualified privilege only protects individuals who communicate without an improper motive. The privilege is 'qualified' because it will be lost if the claimant proves that the publisher was actuated by malice or some other improper motive.

Absolute privilege covers a number of situations, namely:

- Statements made in Parliament: This is linked to important democratic principles and the idea that 'the freedom of speech and debate or proceedings in Parliament ought not to be impeached or questioned in any court or place out of Parliament'.[91]

- Reports, papers, proceedings and votes ordered to be published by either House of Parliament:[92] Abstracts of parliamentary papers or reports of parliamentary proceedings only receive qualified privilege (see discussion below).

- All admissible evidence in judicial proceedings: The right to a fair trial is paramount, and threats to sue in defamation may restrict or impact a witness's ability to give evidence at trial. There is therefore complete privilege given to judge, jury, lawyers, witnesses and the parties themselves.[93] Communications between lawyers and clients for the purposes of litigation are also covered by absolute privilege.

- Reports of court proceedings: The Defamation Act 2013 extended the scope of this privilege to cover fair and accurate reports of proceedings before any court in the UK; the European Court of Justice; the European Court of Human Rights; any international criminal tribunal established by the Security Council of the United Nations or by an international agreement to which the UK is a party; any court established under the law of a country or territory outside the UK; and any international court or tribunal established by the Security Council of the United Nations or by an international agreement.[94]

---

91   Bill of Rights 1689, Art 9.
92   Parliamentary Papers Act 1840, s 1.
93   See restrictions on expert witnesses under *Jones v Kaney* [2011] UKSC 13; cf *Stanton v Callaghan* [1998] 4 All ER 961.
94   Explanatory Notes, section 7, [50].

- Communications between certain Officers of State: This category of absolute privilege ensures that important Officers of State are able to undertake their professional duties without fear of a defamation suit against them.[95]

In these situations, the person making the statement cannot be sued in defamation, even if the statement is malicious and/or false.

Qualified privilege is more complicated. It applies to a wider number of situations, but has some limitations. Qualified privilege will apply in the following circumstances:

- Where there is a legal or moral obligation to provide the information, and the person receiving the information has a corresponding duty or interest to receive it.[96]

- Abstracts of parliamentary papers or reports of parliamentary proceedings.[97]

- Communications between solicitor and client that are not related to judicial proceedings.[98]

- Statements made in peer-reviewed articles in scientific or academic journals. This is a new category of qualified privilege under the Defamation Act 2013. For this defence to apply, the statement must relate to a scientific or academic matter, and it must be published in a journal where an independent review of the merit was carried out by a qualified individual.[99]

The defence of qualified privilege will not apply if the claimant can show that the defendant was acting with malice, which has been defined as a 'dominant or improper' motive.[100]

The *Reynolds* defence of 'responsible journalism' was previously considered a category of qualified privilege; however, this is now replaced by the public interest defence in s 4 of the Defamation Act 2013.

13.5.3.2 PUBLICATION ON MATTERS OF PUBLIC INTEREST

The test of public interest is not premised on the actual interests of the general public. Instead, public interest is defined as what a judge believes that people should be legitimately interested in or concerned with. Prior to the Defamation Act 2013, this issue was dealt with through the '*Reynolds* defence'.

KEY CASE

Reynolds v Times Newspapers Ltd [2001] 2 AC 127

Albert Reynolds sued the Times Newspapers Ltd in defamation for an article about the 1994 political crisis in Ireland. The article suggested that Reynolds had deliberately misled the Irish Parliament and his cabinet colleagues. Times Newspapers Ltd pleaded, inter alia (among other things), qualified privilege at common law. The matter went to the House of Lords, where the defendants argued that there should be a separate category of qualified privilege for the reporting of 'political information'.

The House of Lords unanimously rejected creating a new category, holding that the current

---

95 *Chatterton v Secretary of State for India* [1895] 2 QB 189.
96 *Watt v Longsdon* [1930] 1 KB 130.
97 *Wason v Walter* (1868) LR 4 QB 73.
98 Although this is not absolutely settled; *Minter v Priest* [1930] AC 558.
99 Explanatory Notes, section 6, [45].
100 *Horrock v Lowe* [1975] AC 135.

defences provided adequate protection and that there was no need to provide special protection for political information. Lord Nicholls emphasised the need to balance the importance of freedom of expression by the media on matters of public concern, but stated that it would be 'unsound in principle' to distinguish political discussion from other matters of public concern. He further commented:[101]

> Depending on the circumstances, the matters to be taken into account include the following. The comments are illustrative only. 1. The seriousness of the allegation. The more serious the charge, the more the public is misinformed and the individual harmed, if the allegation is not true. 2. The nature of the information, and the extent to which the subject-matter is a matter of public concern. 3. The source of the information. Some informants have no direct knowledge of the events. Some have their own axes to grind, or are being paid for their stories. 4. The steps taken to verify the information. 5. The status of the information. The allegation may have already been the subject of an investigation which commands respect. 6. The urgency of the matter. News is often a perishable commodity. 7. Whether comment was sought from the plaintiff. He may have information others do not possess or have not disclosed. An approach to the plaintiff will not always be necessary. 8. Whether the article contained the gist of the plaintiff's side of the story. 9. The tone of the article. A newspaper can raise queries or call for an investigation. It need not adopt allegations as statements of fact. 10. The circumstances of the publication, including the timing.
>
> This list is not exhaustive. The weight to be given to these and any other relevant factors will vary from case to case. Any disputes of primary fact will be a matter for the jury, if there is one. The decision on whether, having regard to the admitted or proved facts, the publication was subject to qualified privilege is a matter for the judge. This is the established practice and seems sound. A balancing operation is better carried out by a judge in a reasoned judgment than by a jury. Over time, a valuable corpus of case law will be built up.

Lord Nicholls made a number of further points, including that a newspaper's unwillingness to disclose the identity of its sources should not be weighed against it, journalists have to act without the benefit of hindsight and that the press discharges 'vital functions as a bloodhound as well as a watchdog'.[102] His Lordship therefore reiterated the fact that courts should be slow to find that a publication was not in the public interest when it is in the field of political discussion.

■ VIEWPOINT

What do you think Lord Nicholls meant when he stated that the press discharges 'vital functions as a bloodhound as well as a watchdog'? Do you agree?

The defence under s 4 requires the publication to be on a matter of public interest and that the defendant reasonably believed it was a matter of public interest.[103] When determining what is in the public interest, the court '*must* have regard to all the circumstances of the case'[104] and '*must* make

---

101 [2001] 2 AC 127, 204-205.
102 [2001] 2 AC 127, 205.
103 Defamation Act 2013, s 4(1).
104 Defamation Act 2013, s 4(2) (emphasis added).

such allowance for editorial judgement as it considers appropriate'.[105] The defence applies to both statements of fact and statements of opinion.[106]

The public interest defence under the Defamation Act 2013 abolishes the common law *Reynolds* defence,[107] but interestingly the defence 'is based on the existing common law defence established in *Reynolds v Times Newspapers* and is intended to reflect the principles established in that case and in subsequent case law'.[108]

The relationship between the common law and statutory defence is explained further in the Explanatory Notes, which state that the abolition of the common law defence occurred because the statutory defence is intended essentially to codify the common law defence. While abolishing the common law defence means that the courts would be required to apply the words used in the statute, the current case law would constitute a helpful (albeit not binding) guide to interpreting how the new statutory defence should be applied. 'It is expected the courts would take the existing case law into consideration where appropriate.'[109]

KEY LEGISLATION

Defamation Act 2013

4   Publication on matter of public interest

(1)   It is a defence to an action for defamation for the defendant to show that—

(a) the statement complained of was, or formed part of, a statement on a matter of public interest; and

(b) the defendant reasonably believed that publishing the statement complained of was in the public interest.

(2)   Subject to subsections (3) and (4), in determining whether the defendant has shown the matters mentioned in subsection (1), the court must have regard to all the circumstances of the case.

(3)   If the statement complained of was, or formed part of, an accurate and impartial account of a dispute to which the claimant was a party, the court must in determining whether it was reasonable for the defendant to believe that publishing the statement was in the public interest disregard any omission of the defendant to take steps to verify the truth of the imputation conveyed by it.

(4)   In determining whether it was reasonable for the defendant to believe that publishing the statement complained of was in the public interest, the court must make such allowance for editorial judgement as it considers appropriate.

(5)   For the avoidance of doubt, the defence under this section may be relied upon irrespective of whether the statement complained of is a statement of fact or a statement of opinion.

(6)   The common law defence known as the Reynolds defence is abolished.

There have been a significant number of cases, including multiple Court of Appeal decisions, considering the scope and application of the public interest defence. The large number of topics

---

105 Defamation Act 2013, s 4(4) (emphasis added).

106 Defamation Act 2013, s 4(5).

107 Defamation Act 2013, s 4(6).

108 Explanatory Notes, section 4, [29].

109 Explanatory Notes, section 4, [35].

covered by these cases[110] means that it is difficult to get a clear understanding of how the common law has interpreted 'public interest' in light of the Defamation Act 2013. Some clarification has been provided by the Supreme Court's comments in *Serafin v Malkiewicz* [2020]. The Court emphasised that whilst the rationale of the *Reynolds* defence and the 'public interest' defence under s 4 is similar, there are still relevant and considerable differences between the two defences.[111] The Supreme Court also held that while the ten different factors outlined in *Reynolds* may be relevant when applying the s 4 defence, they should no longer be used as a 'checklist' by the courts.[112]

13.5.4 Operators of websites

Under the common law, both the parties who actively published or republished defamatory material (i.e. authors, editors and publishers) and the parties who merely distributed the information (internet service providers (ISPs), distributors, booksellers, libraries etc.) could be held liable for the republication of defamatory material.[113]

The Defamation Act 1996 drew a distinction between these two groups and provided a defence for parties who merely disseminated or distributed defamatory information. This distinction is, however, often difficult to apply in practice. For example, in *Tamiz v Google* [2013], the Court of Appeal held that there was an arguable case that Google could be a publisher of a blog hosted by a blogger 'London Muslim'. Richards LJ commented that Google provided 'a platform for blogs, together with design tools and, if required, a URL; it also provides a related service to enable the display of remunerative advertisements on a blog. It makes the Blogger service available on terms of its own choice and it can readily remove or block access to any blog that does not comply with those terms'.[114] It therefore facilitates the publication of the blogs and any comments posted on them. This case was, however, struck out on the basis that the allegedly defamatory statements were too trivial to justify continuing the proceedings.

Section 1 of the Defamation Act 1996 created the 'innocent defamation defence'. This applied to those parties involved in printing, producing, distributing or selling material[115] (including film or sound recordings or any electronic medium[116]), broadcasters of live programmes,[117] and 'the operator of or provider of access to a communications system by means of which the statement is transmitted, or made available, by a person over whom he has no effective control'[118] (i.e. ISPs and websites such as Twitter and Facebook). The defence of innocent defamation would apply if the party could show that it took all reasonable care in relation to the publication of the statement and did not know (or could not have known) that what they did caused or contributed to the publication of a defamatory statement.[119]

---

110 For example, trade union membership (*Turley v Unite the Union* [2019] EWHC 3547 (QB); blogs and social media (*James v Saunders* [2019] EWHC 3265 (QB)) and false rape claims/perverting the course of justice (*Economou v de Freitas* [2018] EWCA Civ 2591).
111 *Serafin v Malkiewicz* [2020] UKSC 23 at [68], [72].
112 *Serafin v Malkiewicz* [2020] UKSC 23 at [69], [77].
113 *Godfred v Demon Internet* [1999] 4 All ER 342.
114 [2013] EWCA Civ 68 at [24].
115 Defamation Act 1996, s 1(3)(a).
116 Defamation Act 1996, s 1(3)(b) and (c).
117 Defamation Act 1996, s 1(3)(d).
118 Defamation Act 1996, s 1(3)(e).
119 Defamation Act 1996, s 1(1).

KEY LEGISLATION

Defamation Act 2013

5   Operators of websites

(1)   This section applies where an action for defamation is brought against the operator of a website in respect of a statement posted on the website.

(2)   It is a defence for the operator to show that it was not the operator who posted the statement on the website.

(3)   The defence is defeated if the claimant shows that—

(a) it was not possible for the claimant to identify the person who posted the statement,

(b) the claimant gave the operator a notice of complaint in relation to the statement, and

(c) the operator failed to respond to the notice of complaint in accordance with any provision contained in regulations.

(4)   For the purposes of subsection (3)(a), it is possible for a claimant to 'identify' a person only if the claimant has sufficient information to bring proceedings against the person.

....

(11) The defence under this section is defeated if the claimant shows that the operator of the website has acted with malice in relation to the posting of the statement concerned.

(12) The defence under this section is not defeated by reason only of the fact that the operator of the website moderates the statements posted on it by others.

10   Action against a person who was not the author, editor etc

(1)   A court does not have jurisdiction to hear and determine an action for defamation brought against a person who was not the author, editor or publisher of the statement complained of unless the court is satisfied that it is not reasonably practicable for an action to be brought against the author, editor or publisher.

This defence was enhanced by the Defamation Act 2013, ss 5 and 10. Under s 10, a court cannot hear an action for defamation brought against a person who is not the author, editor or publisher of the statement, unless the court is satisfied that it was not reasonably practicable for an action to be brought against the author, editor or publisher.

The defence available for operators of websites therefore attempts to strike a balance between allowing freedom of speech on the internet and the protection of reputation. Operators of websites will generally be free from liability if they ensure that parties posting statements can be identified, they respond appropriately to complaints and do not act with any malice.

13.5.5 Consent

Just as consent is a general defence to many (but not all) torts, it is also a defence in defamation. If the claimant has consented to the defamatory statement, there will be no cause of action available.[120]

This section has considered the second of our **3Ds** – whether there is an applicable **defence**? As the elements of showing a **defamatory** statement are so broad, it is important that there is a wide range of applicable **defences** to assist the balance between protecting the claimant's reputation whilst also preventing unjustified restrictions on the freedom of speech.

---

120 See *Chapman v Lord Ellesmere* [1932] 2 KB 431.

13.6 Remedies

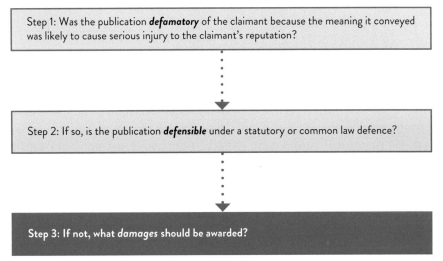

Figure 13.4: Step 3

This section considers the last of our **3Ds**, what **damages** should be awarded. This element is only relevant if the claimant can show (a) that a **defamatory** statement was made, and (b) there are no applicable **defences**. If the claimant can show all the elements of defamation and the defendant is unable to make out a defence, there is a successful claim in defamation. The court will then need to determine what remedies are appropriate. Whilst the main remedy for defamation is damages, there is also the potential for an injunction and publication of the court's judgment.

13.6.1 Damages

Damages are the primary remedy for defamation claims. Traditionally, the amount of damages awarded for defamation was decided by a jury. Whilst determining levels of compensation is always difficult, the amount awarded was designed to compensate the claimant for the damage to their reputation. Damages are intended to vindicate reputation and provide consolation for hurt feelings, distress and embarrassment. There were a number of issues with this approach, and juries could often award very large damages which may not have been seen as fair compared with awards for personal injuries. Vick and Macpherson argued that the dramatic rise in damages awarded against media defendants had detrimental consequences for press freedom.[121] The authors commented that the two key characteristics of modern defamation litigation are the expenses involved in the claim and the threat of a large award of damages (as well as legal costs). They therefore argued that this has created a system that unfairly advantages the rich and powerful, and

> the irony is that the law deters critical reporting of precisely those whose activities most directly affect the public interest. Those who can afford libel litigation are also most likely to be the subject of legitimate comment or journalistic investigation, and are in the best position to rebut negative publicity without needing to resort to the bludgeon of English libel law.[122]

Those with resources do, however, often give in to the temptation to use the threat of defamation proceedings to control their press coverage and to discourage investigation into their activities.

---

121 D. Vick and L. Macpherson, 'An Opportunity Lost: The United Kingdom's Failed Reform of Defamation Law' (1996) 49(3) *Federal Communications Law Journal* 621, 626.

122 Vick and Macpherson (above), 627–8.

This is further exacerbated by the fact that legal aid is not available in defamation cases. The level of damages awarded also has a human rights element. In *Tolstoy Miloslavsky v United Kingdom* [1995],[123] the European Court of Human Rights overturned a £1.5 million libel award on the grounds that the extent of the award was a breach of Article 10.

The extent of these awards was significantly curtailed by the Courts and Legal Services Act 1990 which gives the Court of Appeal the power to substitute an excessive jury award for 'such sum as appears to the court to be proper'.[124] This happened in *John v MGN Ltd* [1996][125] where the jury award of £350,000 was reduced to £75,000. Whilst judicial oversight of jury awards was a positive step forward, courts would only interfere if it was thought that the award was manifestly excessive,[126] and the process still meant that parties were subject to the additional stress and expenditure of an appeal. There was therefore a further reduction of the jury's role in the Defamation Act 2013. Section 11 removed the presumption in favour of trial by jury for defamation cases. This section amended the Senior Courts Act 1981 and the County Courts Act 1984 so that defamation cases will be tried without a jury unless the court orders otherwise.

13.6.2 Other remedies

In addition to the main remedy of **damages**, there are other potential remedies available. The claimant can apply for an injunction to prevent the publication of defamatory material before it occurs or to prevent further publication of the defamatory material. The courts will only grant a pre-trial or interim injunction 'in exceptional circumstances'.[127] If the claimant succeeds at trial and there is a threat that the defendant will continue to publish the defamatory matter or matter to the same effect, then a permanent injunction on further publication may be ordered by the court.[128]

Under s 12 of the Defamation Act 2013, the court can also order a summary of its judgment to be published by the defendant.

The steps for determining whether the claimant has the standing to sue and a successful defamation claim have been outlined. The next section expands on specific relevant legal principles to engage with some of the challenges of modern-day defamation law.

13.7 Challenges

The basis of defamation law is the tension between, on one hand, an individual's interest in protecting their reputation and, on the other, the freedom of other people to express their opinions and the broader social interest in a free flow of information. This tension creates a number of complexities and challenges. The threat of defamation liability may deter individuals from communicating in good faith information which they believe to be true to someone with an interest in receiving it, such as a candid assessment to a prospective employer of the character and qualities of a job applicant. The public good in a free flow of information gave rise to the defence of qualified privilege at common law for such cases, and protects persons who, without malice, communicate information which they are unable or unwilling to prove is true. The dangers of excessive self-censorship on matters of public interest saw the development of the *Reynolds* defence and the 2013 statutory public interest

---

123 (1995) 20 EHRR 442.
124 See Rules of Court made by s 8 of this Act.
125 [1996] 2 All ER 35.
126 See *Kiam v MGN Ltd* [2003] QB 281.
127 *Bonnard v Perryman* [1891] 2 Ch 269.
128 See, for example, *Tolstoy Miloslavsky v United Kingdom* (1995) 20 EHRR 442.

defence. Whilst a full analysis of the challenges associated with modern defamation law is clearly beyond the scope of the current chapter, three specific issues will be briefly discussed:
(1) human rights and defamation;
(2) defamation and social media; and
(3) the utilisation of society's views as a basis for defamation.

13.7.1 Human rights and defamation

One of the most significant challenges faced by the tort of defamation is how it interacts with human rights in general, and the ECHR specifically.[129] In particular, there is a tension between the elements of defamation and the right to freedom of speech under Article 10 which protects the right to 'hold opinions and to receive and impart information and ideas without interference by public authority'. This right is now part of the English law through the Human Rights Act 1998, specifically s 6 which states that public authorities (including courts) cannot act in a way that is incompatible with a Convention right.

Whilst the rights under Article 10 are not unlimited, the courts have a difficult balance to strike between free speech and individual reputation. This need for balance comes up in a number of elements of defamation, including whether a statement will be defamatory, the extent of the defences, and the awards of damages.[130] The tensions associated with the final issue were highlighted in the European Court of Human Rights' decision in *Tolstoy Miloslavsky v United Kingdom*.

KEY CASE

Tolstoy Miloslavsky v United Kingdom (1995) 20 EHRR 442

A pamphlet entitled 'War Crimes and the Wardenship of Winchester College' was circulated to parents, boys, staff and former members of the Winchester school, as well as Members of Parliament, Members of the House of Lords and the press. This pamphlet accused Lord Aldington of being a major war criminal and stated that his 'activities merit comparison with those of the worse butchers of Nazi Germany or Soviet Russia'.

Lord Aldington commenced proceedings for libel. The defendant exercised his right for trial by jury and defended the comments on the grounds of 'justification' and 'fair comment'. The jury unanimously held that libel had been committed and awarded Lord Aldington damages in the amount of £1,500,000, and an injunction was granted preventing further publication of defamatory statements.

There was an attempt to appeal the jury's decision, but the court held that £124,900 would need to be paid as security for costs before an appeal could be held. This decision was appealed to the European Court of Human Rights on the basis that the jury's decision was in violation of Article 10 of the ECHR.

The Court held that the size of the award (which was over three times greater than the next highest award for libel) was a disproportionate interference with the applicant's rights under Article 10. The injunction was held to be reasonable and not wider than necessary to protect Lord Aldington's reputation.

---

129 There is a wealth of literature available from multiple jurisdictions; see, for example, A. Nicol, G. Millar and A. Sharland, *Media Law and Human Rights*, 2nd edn (Oxford University Press, 2009); P. Mitchell, 'Dario Milo, Defamation and Human Rights' (2009) 1(2) *Journal of Media Law* 289–94; D. Kozlowski, ''For the Protection of the Reputation or Rights of Others: The European Court of Human Rights' Interpretation of the Defamation Exception in Article 10(2)' (2006) 11(1) *Communication Law and Policy* 133–78; B. Docherty, 'Defamation Law: Positive Jurisprudence' (2000) 13 *Harvard Human Rights Journal* 263–88.

130 Human Rights Act 1998, s 12 states that when considering whether to grant any relief which may impact the exercise of freedom of expression, the court must balance the importance of free speech and the public interest.

There are also concerns that threats to sue in defamation could be used by powerful and wealthy individuals to supress legitimate allegations and reporting of wrongdoing by both media and the victims. Examples of this can be seen in *Lachaux v Independent Print Ltd*[131] (allegations of domestic violence, child kidnapping, assault) and *Starr v Ward* [2015][132] (allegations of sexual abuse). The seriousness of these types of allegations means that the requirement to show 'serious harm' is unlikely to be a hurdle in these cases. A number of people accused of sexual offences have 'hit back' at the accusers by threatening, or even commencing, defamation suits. There are very real concerns that the mere threat of being sued in defamation could prevent victims from coming forward, particularly when the accused is a wealthy or powerful individual.

■ VIEWPOINT

In light of the important #MeToo movement, should people being accused of sexual harassment and other offences be entitled to sue their accusers in defamation? How does this relate to the ongoing debate between protecting an individual's reputation and encouraging freedom of speech?

In addition to the tension between the tort of defamation and Article 10, there are also tensions with Article 8 (the right to private and family life). There are questions on whether Article 8 gives a freestanding right to privacy[133] and, if so, how that interacts with the law of defamation. These issues will be discussed further in Chapter 14 (Privacy).

13.7.2 Defamation and social media

A second challenge to consider is the role of defamation in the context of social media. Online publications and social media present huge challenges for the law of defamation. Someone who posts a defamatory publication, intending that their words be read by a few friends, may find that their words are republished to thousands or even millions of recipients.

Comments made on social media clearly have the potential to be defamatory. In 2013, Lord McAlpine made claims against a number of people for tweets that implied his involvement in child sexual abuse.[134] The widely reported case of *Monroe v Hopkins*[135] further highlighted the potential for 'tweets' to be statements sufficient to ground a case in defamation. In this case the columnist Katie Hopkins made two tweets implying that Jack Monroe, a British journalist and activist, had taken part in vandalism of a war memorial as part of an anti-austerity protest. Warby J held that the tweets were defamatory and rejected the argument that tweets were less credible than traditional forms of publication. His Honour held that Hopkins' tweets fulfilled the 'serious harm' test and therefore awarded Monroe £24,000 in damages.

The recent jury decision in the United States shows a different approach to the issues of defamation and Twitter. In this case, Vernon Unsworth sued Californian billionaire Elon Musk for a tweet calling him a 'pedo' guy. The judge of the Los Angeles Court closed the courtroom (i.e. did not allow members of the general public to attend, therefore the exact nature of the argument is not known), but a jury found that no defamation had occurred. Whilst it is difficult to determine why the jury made their decision, Dave Lee, the BBC's North American technology reporter, emphasised

---

131 [2019] UKSC 27.
132 [2015] EWHC 1987 (QB).
133 *Douglas v Hello!* (No 3) [2005] EWCA Civ 595.
134 *McAlpine v Bercow* [2013] EWHC 1342 (QB).
135 [2017] 4 WLR 68.

the impact of the 'JDart defence', which is roughly equivalent to a joke made on Twitter, followed by an apology and responsive tweets.[136]

It has yet to be seen how the law will respond to the challenges of social media and defamation, but it is clear that this is going to continue being an issue. There have been multiple defamation cases focused on statements made on Twitter,[137] but also Facebook,[138] blogs,[139] a TED Talk,[140] a YouTube video[141] and WhatsApp group discussions.[142] The number of these cases is sharply increasing, with almost 30 cases focusing on defamation and Twitter in 2019 alone, more than double the previous year. The courts will therefore have to develop further mechanisms to deal with the issue or potentially face a floodgate of claims in the future.

■ VIEWPOINT

How should the law deal with defamation and social media? Should publications in these formats be considered as less credible than traditional forms of publication?

13.7.3 Society's views and defamation

As discussed above, there are some difficulties with the current test for defamation, specifically that the courts use 'right thinking' members of society as a basis for what is defamatory.[143] On one hand, the use of 'right thinking' members of society means that claimants who suffer damage because of the actions of members of society who are not so honourable may not have a claim in defamation. On the other hand, the use of another test, such as that of 'ordinary' members of society, may allow the law to perpetuate harmful views and beliefs.

The case of *Byrne v Deane*[144] offers an example of the former. The allegedly defamatory statement was a notice put on a public noticeboard that implied that the claimant had informed the police about the use of illegal gambling machines at a golf club. The court held that this was not defamatory, as reporting illegal activity to police would not lower Byrne's reputation in the eyes of 'right thinking' members of society. Whilst it is understandable that the courts may want to find that allegations of reporting crimes to the police are not capable of being defamatory, it was clear from the evidence given that the claimant had suffered distress and been isolated from the club as a result of the notice.

The second issue – the perpetuation of harmful views and beliefs – is particularly relevant for allegations of homosexuality or the commission of adultery. Both of these allegations were historically criminal offences and also considered morally questionable, but society's views on these matters have changed considerably. Allegations of adultery historically were clearly capable of being

---

136 https://www.bbc.co.uk/news/world-us-canada-50695593: last accessed 11 August 2020.
137 *Kirkegaard v Smith* [2019] EWHC 3393 (QB); *Chandler v O'Connor* [2019] EWHC 3181 (QB).
138 *Fentiman v Marsh* [2019] EWHC 2099 (QB); *Stocker v Stocker* [2019] UKSC 17; *Richardson v Facebook* [2015] EWHC 3154 (QB). Although defamation actions against Facebook are restricted by s 5 of the Defamation Act 2013.
139 *Turley v UNITE the Union & Anor* [2019] EWHC 3547 (QB); *Baker v Hemming* [2019] EWHC 2950 (QB); *Fox v Wiggins & Ors* [2019] EWHC 2713 (QB).
140 *Banks v Cadwalladr* [2019] EWHC 3451 (QB).
141 *Al-Ko Kober Ltd & Anor v Sambhi* [2019] EWHC 2409 (QB).
142 *Abdulrazaq v Hassan* [2019] EWHC 2930 (QB); *Al Sadik (aka Riad Tawfiq Mahmood Al Sadek Aka Riad Tawfik Sadik) v Sadik* [2019] EWHC 2717 (QB).
143 *Skuse v Granada Television* [1996] EMLR 278.
144 [1937] 1 KB 818.

PART 4

the basis of defamation. An example of this is *Cassidy v Daily Mirror Newspapers Ltd* [1929],[145] where the newspaper published a photo of Mr Cassidy and a woman with an announcement of their engagement. Mr Cassidy was, in fact, already married to a different woman. The newspaper was liable in defamation, as there was an innuendo that the woman was Mr Cassidy's mistress, and was ordered to pay £500 in damages. Would this still be the case? On one hand, society has arguably become more liberal and tolerant of sex outside of marriage – particularly in relation to celebrities. On the other hand, allegations of adultery could have a significantly negative effect on the reputation of many people in the public eye, such as celebrities, politicians and sports players. How the law should balance this tension is a difficult question.

Allegations of homosexuality raise similar, but in many ways more challenging, questions. When homosexual activity was a criminal offence, it was understandable that allegations of homosexuality could be defamatory. But what about after the removal of the criminal offence? Despite the fact that homosexual activity was legalised in the Sexual Offences Act 1967, in 1975 it was still held that many people considered it morally offensive.[146] In 1992, the actor Jason Donovan sued *The Face* magazine over allegations that he was homosexual, and he was awarded £200,000 and an apology. We now live in a society where it is illegal to discriminate against people on the grounds of homosexuality, and homosexual couples can marry, adopt and have children. Surely allegations of homosexuality could not have a defamatory aspect in today's modern world? Unfortunately, this may not be the case.[147] In some sections of society (clearly not those that are 'right thinking'!), allegations of homosexuality could result in the claimant's reputation being lowered, and them being shunned or avoided. Therefore, unfortunately, it seems like not much has changed since *R v Bishop* and – 45 years later – accusations of homosexuality or homosexual behaviour may still injure the claimant's reputation or expose them to hatred, contempt or ridicule (if it does not lower them in the esteem of *right thinking* members of society).

These challenges go back to whether the test for defamation should be based on an 'ordinary' or a 'right thinking' member of society, as these can clearly differ. For example, should the law take the moral high ground that decent people should not, and therefore would not, think less of someone who has a serious mental health condition, and therefore it is not defamatory to say that someone has been diagnosed with such a condition? Or should the law take the realistic view that ordinary, but not right thinking, people may think less of such individuals and they may suffer detriment because of the statement? For example, this has been shown in the unfair stigma and discrimination that people with mental health conditions have been subjected to when obtaining and continuing in employment.[148]

■ VIEWPOINT

How should the law determine what is defamatory? Should judges determine the impact of statements on the 'general public' or on a particular section of the community in which the claimant lives and whose estimation is important to the claimant?

---

145 [1929] 2 KB 331.

146 *R v Bishop* [1975] QB 275.

147 As an example of this in pop culture, see the lyrics of Macklemore & Ryan Lewis in their song 'Same Love' which effectively highlights how 'gay' has continued to be used as an insult in many parts of society.

148 See, for example, research by the Royal College of Psychiatrists, *Mental Health and Work* (commissioned by the cross-government Health, Work and Wellbeing Programme, 2008), particularly Part 2.

13.8 CHAPTER SUMMARY

The tort of defamation concerns the tension between a person's individual right to protect their hard-earned reputation and the public interest in freedom of expression, including the free flow of information, which can include information that may be untrue and hurtful. The law has developed in a piecemeal way over the centuries, with judge-made law and legislation reforming the common law which is seen not to reflect modern conditions in a democratic society. This has resulted in a complex legal regime with both statutory and common law rules, despite the reforms achieved by the enactment of the Defamation Act 2013.

To establish a successful claim in defamation, the **3Ds** must be considered. First, in order to succeed in a claim for defamation, claimants must now show that they have suffered or are likely to suffer serious harm to their reputations as a result of the defamatory statement. They must also show the three elements of a **defamatory** publication – that the statement was defamatory, that it referred to the claimant and that it was published. Once these hurdles are overcome, the defendant has a range of potential **defences** under both the common law and statute which can defeat a claim in defamation. The nature of defamation law raises many challenges and difficulties when applying these defences. Finally, if there are no applicable defences, an appropriate amount of **damages** must be determined.

The law of defamation raises a number of interesting tensions and debates, particularly around the balance between protecting an individual's reputation and freedom of speech/freedom of the press. This makes the tort elements complex and is one of the main reasons that the law has changed considerably over such a short period of time, from both a statutory and common law basis. The balance has also been adjusted with the enactment of the Defamation Act 2013, particularly the requirement for 'serious harm' under s 1. Whilst there is a wide range of potential debates to consider, this chapter has touched on three specific challenges associated with defamation and modern-day society – human rights and defamation, defamation and social media, and the utilisation of society's views as a basis for defamation.

FURTHER READING

T. Gibbons, 'Defamation Reconsidered' (1996) 16 *OLJS* 587

J. Kaye, 'Libel and Slander – Two Torts or One?' (1975) 91 *LQR* 524

I. Loveland, 'A New Legal Landscape?' [2000] *EHRLR* 476

J. Price and F. McMahon (eds), *Blackstone's Guide to the Defamation Act 2013* (OUP, 2013)

C. Sewell, 'More serious harm than good? An empirical observation and analysis of the effects of the serious harm requirement in section 1(1) of the Defamation Act 2013' (2020) 12(1) *Journal of Media Law* 47

J. Townend, 'Freedom of Expression and the Chilling Effect' in H. Tumber and S. Waisbord (eds), *The Routledge Companion to Media and Human Rights* (Routledge, 2017)

K. Treiger-Bar-Am, 'Defamation Law in a Changing Society: The Case of *Youssoupoff v Metro-Goldwyn Mayer*' (2000) 20(2) *Legal Studies* 291

D. Vick and L. Macpherson, 'An Opportunity Lost: The United Kingdom's Failed Reform of Defamation Law' (1996) 49(3) *Federal Communications Law Journal* 621

Roadmap: Defamation

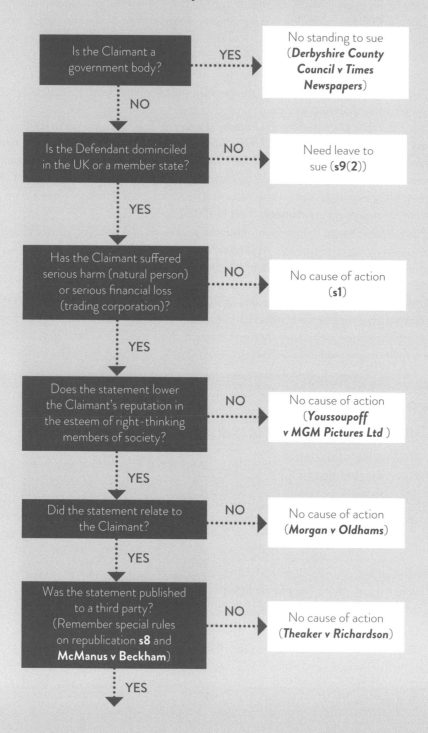

Is the Claimant a government body? — **YES** → No standing to sue (*Derbyshire County Council v Times Newspapers*)

NO ↓

Is the Defendant dominciled in the UK or a member state? — **NO** → Need leave to sue (**s9(2)**)

YES ↓

Has the Claimant suffered serious harm (natural person) or serious financial loss (trading corporation)? — **NO** → No cause of action (**s1**)

YES ↓

Does the statement lower the Claimant's reputation in the esteem of right-thinking members of society? — **NO** → No cause of action (*Youssoupoff v MGM Pictures Ltd*)

YES ↓

Did the statement relate to the Claimant? — **NO** → No cause of action (*Morgan v Oldhams*)

YES ↓

Was the statement published to a third party? (Remember special rules on republication **s8** and **McManus v Beckham**) — **NO** → No cause of action (*Theaker v Richardson*)

YES ↓

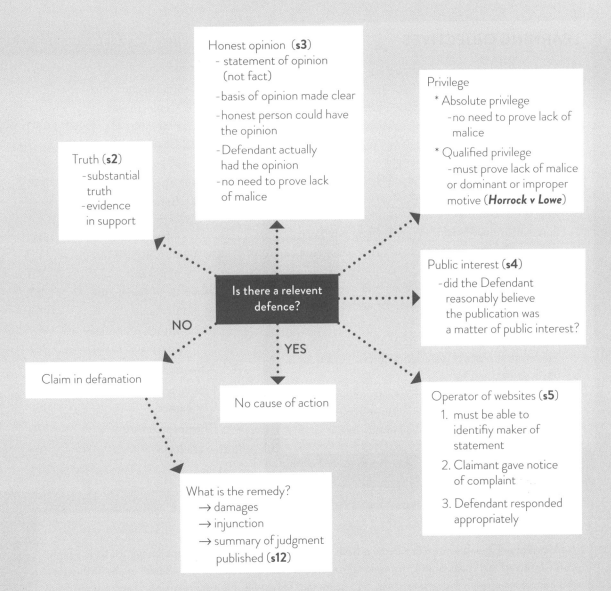

Honest opinion (**s3**)
- statement of opinion (not fact)
- basis of opinion made clear
- honest person could have the opinion
- Defendant actually had the opinion
- no need to prove lack of malice

Privilege
* Absolute privilege
  - no need to prove lack of malice
* Qualified privilege
  - must prove lack of malice or dominant or improper motive (***Horrock v Lowe***)

Truth (**s2**)
- substantial truth
- evidence in support

Public interest (**s4**)
- did the Defendant reasonably believe the publication was a matter of public interest?

Is there a relevent defence?

NO

YES

Claim in defamation

No cause of action

Operator of websites (**s5**)
1. must be able to identifiy maker of statement
2. Claimant gave notice of complaint
3. Defendant responded appropriately

What is the remedy?
→ damages
→ injunction
→ summary of judgment published (**s12**)

LEARNING OBJECTIVES

By the end of this chapter you should be able to:

- Explain the historical issues associated with privacy, particularly in relation to actions of the press
- Understand how a range of common law causes of action and statutory provisions provide limited protection of certain privacy rights
- Outline the role that the Human Rights Act 1998 has had in the development of privacy rights in English common law
- Summarise how breach of confidence has been developed to respond to some of the challenges of privacy
- Establish what constitutes a breach of confidence action, and what remedies may be awarded for a successful action
- Explain the hesitancy of both the courts and legislature to enact freestanding protection of privacy rights
- Recognise the arguments for and against increasing protection of privacy, particularly through the development of a freestanding privacy tort

CHAPTER CONTENTS

14.1	Introduction	339
14.2	Current protection of privacy	340
	14.2.1 Common law protection of privacy	340
	14.2.2 Government regulation of privacy rights	344
14.3	Breach of confidence	348
	14.3.1 Breach of confidence or 'misuse of private information'?	350
	14.3.2 Reasonable expectation of privacy	351
	14.3.3 Unauthorised use	357
	14.3.4 Remedies	360
	14.3.5 Breach of confidence: concluding remarks	362
14.4	A freestanding privacy tort?	363
14.5	Privacy protection in the 21st century	369
14.6	Chapter summary	370
	Further reading	371
	Roadmap	372

PROBLEM QUESTION

The Hassans are a well-known family who have actively sought to be in the public eye. Basia is a high-profile motivational speaker and professional rower, and her husband Haris is a social media 'influencer' who advocates a clean (vegan, organic, non-stimulant) lifestyle. He receives significant money from endorsement deals, and also has his own line of vegan organic children's food. Basia and Haris have two children, 8-year-old twins Malik and Nia, who frequently appear in public with them for photo opportunities. Haris often uses Malik and Nia in advertisements for his food, stating that they are so healthy and intelligent because of their organic vegan lifestyle. Basia and Haris both speak often about their 'perfect' marriage and family, and it is a large part of their public appeal. Basia is currently pregnant with their third child and, whilst stating that the pregnancy is going 'perfectly' thanks to her healthy lifestyle, has asked the public for privacy regarding the health and progress of her unborn child.

The Hassans become aware that a number of stories about their family are about to be published. *Goodbye!* is running a story about Haris's multiple infidelities, after being involved in a sex party with both male and female partners and during which he is seen consuming alcohol and illegal drugs. His actions were covertly recorded by prostitutes attending the party, who sold the footage to the newspaper. The second story is from *Bonjour*, a gossip magazine owned by *Goodbye!*, and is about Basia's pregnancy, stating that the stress of Haris's infidelity has caused health complications with the baby. This includes information about her antenatal care and photos of her leaving a health centre for women who are having difficult pregnancies. Finally, a competitor newspaper, *The End of the World*, is running a story about how the family's apparent clean lifestyle is a lie. This includes photos of Basia taking her children to meat-based fast food restaurants and Haris smoking cigarettes.

Advise Basia and Haris of any rights they may have regarding these stories.

14.1 Introduction

Unlike defamation, which protects individuals from the publication of *untrue* statements and representations, privacy rights are designed to protect individuals from the publication of *true* information that has a confidential or private nature. Whilst there is no definitive and widely agreed definition of privacy, a useful starting point is the 'right to determine for oneself how and to what extent information about oneself is communicated to others'.[1] There is currently no freestanding tort protecting invasions of privacy in English common law; however, confidential information is generally effectively protected by the equitable breach of confidence cause of action, and private information can be protected by the tort of misuse of private information.

The first part of this chapter considers the different ways in which privacy rights of individuals are protected, under the common law, statute and government regulations. These rights are protected in an ad hoc manner through a variety of common law mechanisms, including trespass, defamation and malicious prosecution. There are also various pieces of legislation that provide additional assistance, the most important of which is the Human Rights Act 1998, as Article 8 of Schedule 1 ensures protection of privacy and family life. This must, however, be weighed against the importance of freedom of expression which is enshrined in Article 10 and s 12. There are also a range of regulatory mechanisms, particularly around the regulation of the press, that provide additional protection for certain privacy rights. These legal mechanisms do not, however, provide full coverage, and many 'gaps' still exist in the protection of privacy rights.

The second part of the chapter outlines the background to and elements of the breach of confidence cause of action. The courts have relatively recently developed breach of confidence in a manner that provides protection against the publication of private information. For a successful action, the claimant must show that the information (1) had a reasonable expectation of privacy, and (2) that there was unauthorised use of that information by the defendant. This part will also outline how the courts are required to engage in a balancing exercise for the second element, looking specifically at the competing obligations under Article 8 (private and family life) and Article 10 (freedom of expression).

The chapter concludes by considering whether breach of confidence adequately protects privacy rights in the UK. This raises other interesting questions. Is the development of a freestanding tort of the protection of privacy justified? And if further protection is deemed necessary, should this occur

---

1   Committee on Privacy, Younger Report (Cmnd 5012, July 1972), 10.

through common law or statutory mechanisms? Privacy law is at a crossroads with no clear path forward; it is a complex and complicated area, and the principles are far from settled.

14.2 Current protection of privacy

The main way that privacy is currently protected is through the relatively recently developed breach of confidence action. A detailed discussion of this cause of action, including its elements and relationship with human rights, occurs later in this chapter. The current section focuses on the other ways that privacy is protected by the common law and statute. This includes a consideration of how various torts address privacy interests, as well as statutory protection under the Human Rights Act 1998 and a variety of other government regulations.

14.2.1 Common law protection of privacy

As will be discussed in more detail below, there is no freestanding tort protecting invasions of privacy, and the courts have continually rejected calls to 'find' that such a tort exists – arguing that this is a role for Parliament. In *Malone v Metropolitan Police Commissioner* [1979], Sir Robert Megarry VC considered whether there was a privacy right to hold a telephone conversation in one's home without interference. The judge refused to recognise a new privacy right, stating that 'it is no function of the courts to legislate in a new field. The extension of the existing laws and principles is one thing, the creation of an altogether new right is another.'[2]

In *Wainright v Home Office* [2004], the House of Lords again refused to recognise a freestanding tort of invasion of privacy. In coming to this decision, the Court emphasised the range of protections that are already in place in English law.

KEY CASE

Wainwright v Home Office [2004] 2 AC 406

The facts of this case have already been discussed at length in Chapter 12 and do not need repeating here. In addition to the claim for trespass to the person and the tort in *Wilkinson v Downton*, the claimants argued that their right to privacy had been infringed. It was therefore argued that the House of Lords should declare that there is a freestanding tort of invasion of privacy.

Lord Hoffmann dealt with this claim in significant detail, stating:

> My Lords, let us first consider the proposed tort of invasion of privacy. Since the famous article by Warren and Brandeis ('The Right to Privacy' (1890) 4 Harvard LR 193), the question of whether such a tort exists, or should exist, has been much debated in common law jurisdictions.

Warren and Brandeis suggested that one could generalise certain cases on defamation, breach of copyright in unpublished letters, trade secrets and breach of confidence as all based upon the protection of a common value which they called privacy or, following Judge Cooley (Cooley on Torts, 2nd ed (1888), p 29) 'the right to be let alone'. They said that identifying this common element should enable the courts to declare the existence of a general principle which protected a person's appearance, sayings, acts and personal relations from being exposed in public.[3]

His Lordship then undertook a detailed review of the many ways that privacy is already protected by English law, stating that:

---

2   [1979] Ch 344, 372.
3   [2004] 2 AC 406, 418–19 (Lord Hoffmann).

Common law torts include trespass, nuisance, defamation and malicious falsehood; there is the equitable action for breach of confidence and statutory remedies under the Protection from Harassment Act 1997 and the Data Protection Act 1998. There are also extra-legal remedies under Codes of Practice applicable to broadcasters and newspapers. But there are gaps; cases in which the courts have considered that an invasion of privacy deserves a remedy which the existing law does not offer. Sometimes the perceived gap can be filled by judicious development of an existing principle. The law of breach of confidence has in recent years undergone such a process: see in particular the judgment of Lord Phillips of Worth Matravers MR in *Campbell v MGN Ltd* [2003] QB 633. On the other hand, an attempt to create a tort of telephone harassment by a radical change in the basis of the action for private nuisance in *Khorasandjian v Bush* [1993] QB 727 was held by the House of Lords in *Hunter v Canary Wharf Ltd* [1997] AC 655 to be a step too far. The gap was filled by the 1997 Act.

What the courts have so far refused to do is to formulate a general principle of 'invasion of privacy' (I use the quotation marks to signify doubt about what in such a context the expression would mean) from which the conditions of liability in the particular case can be deduced.[4]

The judgment then proceeded to discuss a number of cases where the absence of a cause of action for privacy was acknowledged, and the courts refused, for various reasons, to find that English law needed one. Finally, Lord Hoffman argued that the enactment of the Human Rights Act 1998 weakened the need for a general tort of invasion of privacy. If a person's right to privacy under Article 8 had been infringed by a public authority, there would be a statutory remedy in place.

Lord Hoffmann's analysis and discussion was specifically supported by Lord Scott, who stated:

> The important issue of principle is not, in my opinion, whether English common law recognises a tort of invasion of privacy. As Lord Hoffmann has demonstrated, whatever remedies may have been developed for misuse of confidential information, for certain types of trespass, for certain types of nuisance and for various other situations in which claimants may find themselves aggrieved by an invasion of what they conceive to be their privacy, the common law has not developed an overall remedy for the invasion of privacy.[5]

The House of Lords in *Wainright v Home Office* emphasised that there was no need to develop a freestanding tort to protect privacy. Lord Hoffmann, for example, drew a distinction between privacy as a value which should underlie the existence of a rule of law as opposed to privacy as a principle of law itself. The English common law is familiar with the underlying value of privacy, but this does not require the creation of a freestanding tort protecting privacy.[6]

Lord Hoffmann outlined in *Wainwright v Home Office* that the English common law already protects some aspects of individuals' privacy in a number of ways, including trespass, private nuisance, defamation and malicious prosecution. Whether this works in practice is, however, another question.

---

4   [2004] 2 AC 406, 419–20 (Lord Hoffmann).
5   [2004] 2 AC 406, 429 (Lord Scott).
6   [2004] 2 AC 406, 423 (Lord Hoffmann).

Table 14.1: Common law protections of privacy

Tort in Question	Nature of Right Protection	Potential Privacy Protection	Limitations	Case Example(s)
Defamation	Protects individuals from the publication of untrue statements and representations	Prevents the publication of private information that is defamatory in nature	* Generally restricted to publications of *untrue* statements * Does not provide adequate protection for true but private information	*Cassidy v Daily Mirror Newspapers Ltd* [1929] 2 KB 331
Trespass to Land	Protects people from unwanted intrusion onto land	Prevents individuals from entering the property of others (i.e. to take photographs)	* Does not protect people from photographs taken in public spaces or other information (i.e. phone tapping, email hacking etc.) * Can still take photos from outside or above property without committing trespass	*Bernstein v Skyviews & General Ltd* [1977] EWHC QB 1 *Richard v British Broadcasting Corporation* [2018] 3 WLR 1715
Trespass to Person (battery)	Protects the bodily autonomy of individuals	Prevents unwanted touching of others that could constitute an invasion of privacy (i.e. unjustified strip searches)	* Very limited in scope – only protects the privacy of individuals to the extent that physical touching is necessary	*Wainwright v Home Office* [2003] UKHL 53
Tort of Telephone Harassment	Provides protection for verbal threats and persistent / harassing telephone calls	Prevents unwanted telephone calls that invade the privacy of the recipient	* Considered a 'step too far' in later cases, therefore no longer applicable	*Khorasandjian v Bush* [1993] QB 727 *Hunter v Canary Wharf Ltd* [1997] AC 655
Protection from Harassment Act 1997	Provides for tort liability and criminal sanctions for harassing behaviour	Prevents harassment of individuals in an attempt to obtain information or harassing acts that invade the privacy of others (i.e. following to take photographs, stalking etc.)	* Invasion of privacy must be so severe as to constitute 'harassment' * Actions need to result in a 'course of conduct'	*Hunter v Canary Wharf Ltd* [1997] AC 655 *Fearn v Board of Trustees of the Tate Gallery* [2020] EWCA Civ 104
Nuisance	Protects people from unreasonable interference with their use and enjoyment of land	Prevents people from unreasonably interfering with rights to enjoy land, which can expand to privacy rights when on the land	* Needs a proprietary interest in the land * Recent developments moving away from privacy protection	*Thomas v News Group Newspapers Ltd* [2001] EWCA Civ 1233 *Law Society v Kordowski* [2011] All ER (D) 46 (Dec)

Tort in Question	Nature of Right Protection	Potential Privacy Protection	Limitations	Case Example(s)
Malicious Falsehoods	Protects people from the malicious publication of false statements which cause financial harm	Prevents the publication of some sorts of private information	* Protected information needs to be of the type that causes financial harm * Only relates to false information, therefore does not prevent the publication of true but private information	*Kaye v Robertson* (1991) FSR 62
Breach of Confidence	If people had a reasonable expectation of privacy, it protects them from the unauthorised use of information	Prevents the publication of private information by individuals or the press more generally	* Provides for the protection of private information only – does not protect other forms of privacy * Need to show that there was (a) a reasonable expectation of privacy, and (b) unauthorised use of this information	*Campbell v MGN Ltd* [2004] 2 WLR 1232

Whilst these different causes of action provide some protection, they do not provide anything close to a coherent cause of action. The limitation of the ability for other torts to adequately protect privacy interests was recently confirmed by the Court of Appeal in *Fearn v Board of Trustees of the Tate Gallery* [2020], which focused specifically on the interaction between privacy and nuisance.

KEY CASE

Fearn and others v Board of Trustees of the Tate Gallery [2020] EWCA Civ 104

The residents of Neo Bankside apartments brought a claim in nuisance and under the Human Rights Act 1998 for protection of their 'rights of privacy'. Their living areas are extensively glassed, and look directly onto the new extension of the Tate Modern viewing gallery. The people on the viewing gallery could therefore see directly into their windows, and this was a breach of their privacy. The residents sought an injunction for the closure of the viewing gallery.

Mann J held that the tort of nuisance could be used to protect privacy rights, but further stated that 'whether anything is an invasion of privacy depends on whether, and to what extent, there is a legitimate expectation of privacy. That inquiry is likely to be closely related to the sort of inquiry that has to take place in a nuisance case into whether a landowner's use of land is, in all the circumstances and having regard to the locality, unreasonable to the extent of being a nuisance.'[7]

After reviewing the specific facts of the case, Mann J held that the owners did not have a reasonable expectation of privacy, and therefore there was no cause of action in nuisance or under the Human Rights Act 1998. The judge noted that the residents of the apartments were able to undertake a range of protective measures, including installing solar blinds, privacy films or net curtains, or even placing plants in the windows.[8] His Honour stated that the flat owners 'could choose to leave his or her view open, with the concomitant ability for outsiders to look in, or the owner could adopt remedial measures'.[9]

---

7   [2019] EWHC 246 (Ch) at [175].
8   [2019] EWHC 246 (Ch) at [214].
9   [2019] EWHC 246 (Ch) at [203].

The residents appealed this decision to the Court of Appeal, and it was dismissed. The Court of Appeal, however, disagreed with the approach taken by Mann J, and held that the tort of nuisance cannot, in the absence of statute, protect invasions of privacy. The privacy right in this case was the 'overlooking' by the visitors of the Tate Gallery into the residents' living space. The Court commented that:

> Unlike such annoyances as noise, dirt, fumes, noxious smells and vibrations emanating from neighbouring land, it would be difficult, in the case of overlooking, to apply the objective test in nuisance for determining whether there has been a material interference with the amenity value of the affected land. While the viewing of the claimants' land by thousands of people from the Tate's viewing gallery may be thought to be a clear case of nuisance at one end of the spectrum, overlooking on a much smaller scale may be just as objectively annoying to owners and occupiers of overlooked properties. The construction of a balcony overlooking a neighbour's garden which results in a complete or substantial lack of privacy for all or part of the garden, with particular significance in the summer months, and which may even diminish the marketability or value of the overlooked property, would appear to satisfy the objective test. There would also be a question whether, in such a case, it makes any difference if there was more than one balcony or more than one family using the balcony or balconies. It is difficult to envisage any clear legal guidance as to where the line would be drawn between what is legal and what is not, depending on the number of people and frequency of overlooking.[10]

The judges therefore held that any protection from overlooking is better dealt with by planning laws and regulations, as opposed to an extension of the common law of private nuisance.

Whilst this decision does not completely overrule the ability for nuisance to provide some level of protection against invasions of privacy, it is a strong indication that this cause of action will not be used to protect privacy rights in and of themselves without evidence of interference with other protected rights. As the common law does not provide a complete protection of privacy, it now must be considered what additional statutory safeguards exist.

The courts have referred to the multiple ways that existing tort law causes of action protect privacy interests, and then used these protections as a justification for why there is no need to develop a freestanding tort protecting privacy. The development of breach of confidence has been, by far, the most effective mechanism for privacy protection. Whilst there are several other causes of action that can also assist potential claimants – including, defamation, trespass, nuisance, Protection from Harassment Act 1997, and malicious falsehoods – these do not provide coherent or consistent protection. Recent cases, such as *Fearn v Board of Trustees of the Tate Gallery* and *Hunter v Canary Wharf Ltd,* have also seen a movement away from privacy protection. In light of these limitations, the next section will consider the multiple ways that government regulation protects privacy rights.

14.2.2 Government regulation of privacy rights

Given that the existing torts offer inadequate protection for privacy interests, there are a number of statutes that have provided significant protection for invasions of privacy. The first is the Protection from Harassment Act 1997, providing for civil and criminal penalties for harassment, which is defined to include publication of private information by individuals.[11] The Data Protection Act 2018 also

---

10   [2020] EWCA Civ 104 at [81] (Sir Terence Etherton MR, Lord Justice Lewison and Lady Justice Rose DBE).
11   See detailed discussion of this Act at 12.7.2.

provides a remedy for invasion of privacy occurring through either the publication of information or the processing of data.

By far the most important piece of legislation is the Human Rights Act (HRA) 1998, which has had a profound impact on the development of laws protecting an individual's privacy rights. Section 6 of the HRA 1998 makes it unlawful for a public authority to act in a manner that is incompatible with a Convention right. In terms of privacy, Article 8 is particularly important as it creates a right to private and family life. It is, however, a qualified right, and must be balanced against the right to freedom of expression in Article 10 and s 12. The rights and obligations in the HRA 1998 regarding privacy have been enshrined into existing common law causes of action, particularly breach of confidence (discussed in more depth below). Lord Woolf in *A v B Plc* [2003] commented that the courts absorb 'the rights which Articles 8 and 10 protect into the long-established action for breach of confidence. This involves giving a new strength and breadth to the action so that it accommodates the requirements of those articles.'[12] The balancing exercise of the courts is discussed in more detail when reviewing breach of confidence later in the chapter.

The protection of privacy has been a source of debate and frustration, with Parliament struggling to strike the correct balance between privacy and freedom of expression. There have been a number of attempts to either directly enact further legislation protecting against invasions of privacy, or to at least review whether the law would benefit from further development of privacy rights. Since the end of the Second World War, there have been five pieces of unsuccessful legislation and six official reports focused on privacy. Whilst the significant issues relating to press invasion and privacy were consistently recognised in these processes, the government has consistently rejected further protection through legislation or the common law.

The Press Council was established in 1953 to govern the behaviour of media and the press, with the aim to ensure high standards of ethics in journalism in Britain. The limitations of this organisation were quickly recognised, and soon after the Press Council's establishment there were attempts to provide further protection. The Committee on Privacy was appointed in 1970 by the Home Secretary, the Lord Chancellor and the Scottish Secretary. This Committee was led by the Rt. Hon. Kenneth Younger, and was given the task of considering 'whether legislation is needed to give further protection to the privacy of individuals and companies against intrusions from other individuals and companies'. The final report was published in June 1972. It was outlined that 'the concept of privacy cannot be satisfactorily defined',[13] and a single and comprehensive definition of 'privacy' or 'invasion of privacy' should not be attempted.[14] Despite this, the Committee itself provided a useful definition of privacy as the 'right to determine for oneself how and to what extent information about oneself is communicated to others'.[15]

The Committee also outlined the importance of privacy,[16] noting that there were already significant protections in place for privacy, including through legislation, multiple tort law actions (namely defamation, malicious falsehood, trespass to land and nuisance), breach of contract, copyright and the criminal law.[17] In light of the definitional difficulties, protections that existed in other areas of the law, and experiences in other jurisdictions, the Committee decided that any general development or extension of the law of privacy was neither necessary nor justified.

---

12 [2003] QB 195, 202.

13 Committee on Privacy, Younger Report (Cmnd 5012, July 1972), 17.

14 Younger Report, 22.

15 Younger Report, 10.

16 Younger Report, ch 6.

17 Younger Report, ch 5. In the conclusion, the Committee held: 'Looking at the field as a whole, we have expressed the view that the existing law provides more effective relief from some kinds of intrusion into privacy than is generally appreciated': 203.

Two years after the Younger Report was published, the Third Royal Commission on the Press was established with the aim of inquiring 'into the factors affecting the maintenance of the independence, diversity and editorial standards of newspapers and periodicals and the public freedom of choice of newspapers and periodicals, nationally, regionally and locally'. This final report was published in 1977[18] and recognised the significant issues experienced with privacy rights and the press. The considerable limitations of the Press Council were also outlined.[19] The final report recommended a number of reforms, including the requirement for the Press Council to have a written code of behaviour, although the existing focus on self-regulation was continued. These recommendations were not binding, and the implementation of a written code was duly rejected by the Press Council.[20]

Two further Bills aiming to provide increased privacy rights were presented in the 1980s, and they both failed. In 1989 Sir Haris Calcutt QC was appointed to lead a Committee investigating the continued but growing concerns over invasions of privacy by the press. This Committee produced two reports. The first report, the Calcutt Report of the Committee on Privacy and Related Matters, recommended abolishing the Press Council. The report rejected the need for a tort of privacy, and instead recommended establishing a new Press Complaints Commission. This occurred, but did not provide an adequate solution to the issues raised, and the Press Complaints Commission has been subject to significant criticisms since its establishment, including by the Second Calcutt Report.[21] The Second Report recommended the creation of a Press Complaints Tribunal, but this was seen as a step too far by many people and did not occur. The issues with the Press Complaints Commission continued, and the Commission was closed down in 2014.

The death in 1997 of Diana, Princess of Wales also had a significant impact on the debate regarding privacy rights, and resulted in an increased public demand for regulation of press behaviour. As a result, reforms to the Editors' Code of Practice were introduced with effect from 1 January 1998. These also proved ineffective as they were frequently ignored or not enforced.[22]

In 2005, the London Metropolitan Police commenced an investigation into alleged phone tapping by *News of the World* journalists. By early 2006, evidence was uncovered showing that thousands of celebrities, politicians, sports personalities and members of the royal family had been victims of phone tapping and hacking. Following this scandal, it became very clear that self-regulation of the press was not working adequately. The Media Standards Trust submission to the Leveson Inquiry commented that:

> self-regulation on its own, without any greater independence or enhanced powers, does not provide adequate protection for the public or for journalists – is based in large part on an historical analysis of the continued failure of the various voluntary self-regulatory bodies that have existed since the first Royal Commission on the Press published its report in 1949.[23]

As a result, the then Prime Minister David Cameron announced a public inquiry into the issues under the Inquiries Act 2005. This was led by Lord Justice Leveson, and aimed to inquire 'into the culture practices and ethics of the press', which was inherently linked to invasions of privacy. Whilst the Levenson Inquiry made a significant number of recommendations (92 in total!), it did

---

18 Third Royal Commission on the Press (Cmnd 6810, July 1977).
19 Third Royal Commission on the Press, ch 20.
20 For further information, see Leveson Inquiry, *An Inquiry into the Culture, Practices and Ethics of the Press Report* (November 2012), 203–5.
21 For further information on the history and concerns of the Press Complaints Commission, see Leveson Inquiry, Part D, ch 1.
22 Leveson Inquiry, *An Inquiry into the Culture, Practices and Ethics of the Press Report* (November 2012), 214–15.
23 Leveson Inquiry, 195.

not make any specific recommendations for increasing privacy rights or creating a freestanding right against invasions of privacy. The final report did, however, recommend that there should be a 'review of damages generally available for breach of data protection, privacy, breach of confidence or any other media-related torts, to ensure proportionate compensation including for non-pecuniary loss'.[24] There were also specific recommendations on the availability of aggravated and exemplary damages.[25]

In 2014, the Press Complaints Commission was replaced by the Independent Press Standards Organisation (IPSO), which defines itself as 'the independent regulator of most of the UK's newspapers and magazines'. IPSO's Editors' Code of Practice sets out the rules that newspapers and magazines have agreed to follow. There have been a number of different versions of the Code of Practice, with the latest version coming into effect on 1 July 2019. The Code addresses a wide range of reporting issues, including accuracy of reporting, invasions of privacy, protection from harassment, intrusion into grief or shock, reporting suicide, rights of children, reporting of crime, victims of sexual assaults and dealing with confidential sources. If these guidelines are breached, IPSO has the power to issue fines and/or require apologies and corrections to be made to the victim(s).

KEY GUIDELINES

IPSO Code of Practice

The code sets the framework for the highest professional standards that members of the press subscribing to the Independent Press Standards Organisation have undertaken to maintain. ... It balances both the rights of the individual and the public's right to know.

To achieve that balance, it is essential that an agreed Code be honoured not only to the letter, but in the full spirit. It should be interpreted neither so narrowly as to compromise its commitment to respect the rights of the individual, nor so broadly that it infringes the fundamental right to freedom of expression – such as to inform, to be partisan, to challenge, shock, be satirical and to entertain – or prevents publication in the public interest.

It is the responsibility of editors and publishers to apply the Code to editorial material in both printed and online versions of their publications. They should take care to ensure it is observed rigorously by all editorial staff and external contributors, including non-journalists.

1. Accuracy

i)   The Press must take care not to publish inaccurate, misleading or distorted information or images, including headlines not supported by the text.

ii)   A significant inaccuracy, misleading statement or distortion must be corrected, promptly and with due prominence, and — where appropriate — an apology published. In cases involving IPSO, due prominence should be as required by the regulator.

2. Privacy

i)   Everyone is entitled to respect for his or her private and family life, home, health and correspondence, including digital communications.

ii)   Editors will be expected to justify intrusions into any individual's private life without consent. In considering an individual's reasonable expectation of privacy, account will be taken of the

---

24   Leveson Inquiry, 1813.

25   Ibid.

complainant's own public disclosures of information and the extent to which the material complained about is already in the public domain or will become so.

iii) It is unacceptable to photograph individuals, without their consent, in public or private places where there is a reasonable expectation of privacy.

6. Children

ii) They must not be approached or photographed at school without permission of the school authorities.

iii) Children under 16 must not be interviewed or photographed on issues involving their own or another child's welfare unless a custodial parent or similarly responsible adult consents.

iv) Children under 16 must not be paid for material involving their welfare, nor parents or guardians for material about their children or wards, unless it is clearly in the child's interest.

v) Editors must not use the fame, notoriety or position of a parent or guardian as sole justification for publishing details of a child's private life.

There are, however, still questions on whether the existence of an independent regulator is sufficient to adequately protect people from intrusions by the press. There are many recent examples of journalists unfairly intruding into people's lives, even with the added protection afforded by IPSO, for example the BBC's broadcasting of the police search of Sir Cliff Richard's residence and the press coverage of Caroline Flack's assault charge, which tragically resulted in her suicide.

It is clear that privacy rights – particularly those related to press invasions – have attracted considerable government attention. There have been numerous attempts to create legislation enshrining privacy rights, all of which have failed. There have also been frequent government reviews and inquiries. Whilst these have all highlighted the inadequacies of the available privacy protections, none have recommended direct protection of privacy rights.

14.3 Breach of confidence

The development of a cause of action for breach of confidence is the closest example of protection of privacy in English common law. Claimants have a right to protect their information if: (a) the information had a 'necessary element of confidence', (b) the defendant was obliged to keep this information confidential, and (c) the information was used in an unauthorised manner.[26]

MAKING CONNECTIONS

Breach of confidence is traditionally a remedy in equity that prevents unauthorised disclosure of information obtained when there is a duty of confidentiality. This was originally limited to situations where the two parties were in a 'genuine relationship of confidence', and the information had the necessary 'quality of confidence'. The requirement of a relationship of confidence would clearly limit its scope for privacy-related situations, especially as the majority involve the press and therefore no relationship of confidence exists. In light of the lack of a tort protecting privacy, the court has taken a very generous interpretation of the traditional equitable remedy of breach of confidence to try and 'fill the gap'.

---

26   *Coco v AN Clark (Engineers) Ltd* [1969] RPC 41.

The application of breach of confidence to press-related privacy intrusions was developed by the House of Lords in *Campbell v MGN Ltd* [2004], where it was held that when considering the protection of privacy, there were two limbs of a breach of confidence action:

(1)   Did the claimant have a reasonable expectation of privacy?
(2)   Was there unauthorised use of this information? Specifically, were the benefits achieved by the information's publication proportionate to the harm that may be done by the interference with the right to privacy?

It is interesting to note that the requirement put forward was a reasonable expectation of *privacy* and not a reasonable expectation of *confidentiality*. This shows the steps made to protect information that is private as well as information that is confidential. If the breach of confidence action is successful, the court then has to determine an appropriate remedy. This can be a challenge, particularly if the information is already out in the public domain.

KEY CASE

Campbell v MGN Ltd [2004] 2 WLR 1232

The House of Lords considered whether publication of substantially true information about supermodel Naomi Campbell's drug addiction and medical treatment with Narcotics Anonymous was a breach of the claimant's confidence. The Mirror newspaper published an article entitled 'Naomi: I am a drug addict' which included details of Ms Campbell's drug addiction and subsequent attendance at Narcotics Anonymous meetings and counselling sessions. The article included photos of her attending these meetings and quotes from sources about her addiction and recovery. There was also discussion of an occasion where she was rushed to hospital after an overdose, which Ms Campbell had explained as an allergic reaction to antibiotics. Lord Nicholls described the articles as generally having a sympathetic and supportive tone, but with a slight 'undertone of smugness' that she had been caught out by the newspaper.[27]

The claimant argued that the publication of this information was a breach of confidence. At first instance, Morland J upheld the claim and awarded £2,500 compensation and £1,000 aggravated damages. This was overturned by the Court of Appeal, which discharged the judge's order. The matter was then appealed to the House of Lords.

Whilst it was agreed that in English law 'there is no over-arching, all-embracing cause of action for "invasion of privacy"',[28] the information published could be protected by the development of breach of confidence.

There were five separate pieces of information published by the defendant:

(1)   the fact of Miss Campbell's drug addiction;
(2)   the fact that she was receiving treatment;
(3)   the fact that she was receiving treatment at Narcotics Anonymous;
(4)   some details of the treatment – including how long she had been attending meetings, how often she went, how she was treated within the sessions themselves, the extent of her commitment, and the nature of her entrance on the specific occasion; and
(5)   the visual portrayal of her leaving a specific meeting with other addicts.[29]

Of these pieces of information, it was accepted that the claimant's 'public lies' meant that she lost any protection for categories (1) and (2). This was because she had frequently made public comments that she did not take drugs, and by making these assertions she had lost the reasonable

---

27   [2004] 2 WLR 1232, 1232–4.
28   [2004] 2 WLR 1232, 1236.
29   [2004] 2 WLR 1232, 1239.

expectation that this aspect of her life was private. The defendant's public disclosure that she did take drugs and was receiving treatment was therefore not disclosure of private information.[30]

In making their determination, the House of Lords highlighted the traditional constraints of breach of confidence, and how the focus of this case was more on the misuse of private information. As highlighted by Lord Nicholls:

> This cause of action has now firmly shaken off the limiting constraint of the need for an initial confidential relationship. In doing so it has changed its nature. In this country this development was recognised clearly in the judgment of Lord Goff of Chieveley in *Attorney-General v Guardian Newspapers Ltd (No 2)* [1990] 1 AC 109, 281. Now the law imposes a 'duty of confidence' whenever a person receives information he knows or ought to know is fairly and reasonably to be regarded as confidential. Even this formulation is awkward. The continuing use of the phrase 'duty of confidence' and the description of the information as 'confidential' is not altogether comfortable. Information about an individual's private life would not, in ordinary usage, be called 'confidential'. The more natural description today is that such information is private. The essence of the tort is better encapsulated now as misuse of private information.[31]

The House of Lords came to different judgments on whether these pieces of information were confidential. The majority of the court held that the details of the treatment and accompanying photographs were confidential information. It also held that there was unauthorised publication of this information in breach of the claimant's rights, and she was entitled to damages.

14.3.1 Breach of confidence or 'misuse of private information'?

As highlighted in *Campbell v MGN Ltd,* the traditional breach of confidence cause of action has developed significantly and now covers a broad array of information. Despite the basis of the cause of action being the protection of confidentiality, the first step now considers whether there was a reasonable expectation of *privacy*. The House of Lords therefore emphasised that 'the essence of the tort is better encapsulated now as misuse of private information'.[32] This has led many people to the conclusion that the relevant cause of action is actually a tort of 'misuse of private information' as opposed to breach of confidence.

The relationship between these two causes of action is contentious and far from clear, but they appear to protect different types of information. Lord Nicholls in *OBG Ltd v Allan* [2007] stated:

> As the law has developed breach of confidence, or misuse of confidential information, now covers two distinct causes of action, protecting two different interests: privacy, and secret ('confidential') information. It is important to keep these two distinct. In some instances information may qualify for protection both on grounds of privacy and confidentiality. In other instances information may be in the public domain, and not qualify for protection as confidential, and yet qualify for protection on the grounds of privacy. Privacy can be invaded by further publication of information or photographs already disclosed to the public. Conversely, and obviously, a trade secret may be protected as confidential information even though no question of personal privacy is involved.[33]

The relationship between the two causes of action was also discussed by Lord Phillips in *Douglas v Hello! Ltd (No 3)* [2005], where he commented that misuse of private information has been

---

30   [2004] 2 WLR 1232, 1239–40.
31   [2004] 2 WLR 1232, 1237.
32   [2004] 2 WLR 1232, 1237.
33   [2007] UKHL 21 at [255].

'shoehorned' into the laws on breach of confidence.[34] Whilst not universally accepted as a freestanding tort, misuse of private information has been referred to as a 'tort' in a number of subsequent cases.[35]

These developments led Tugendhat J to declare in *Vidal-Hall v Google Inc* [2014] that 'misuse of private information is a tort'.[36] Whilst this was a Queen's Bench decision, the finding was upheld by the Court of Appeal which held that 'misuse of private information should now be recognised as a tort … [t]his does not create a new cause of action. In our view, it simply gives the correct legal label to one that already exists.'[37] The Court of Appeal recognised that this finding would have 'broader implications' and create a range of difficulties, but that these would have to be determined by future decisions.[38] In 2016, the Supreme Court in *PJS v News Group Newspapers* [2016][39] emphasised that different considerations apply depending on whether the claimant is seeking a remedy under breach of confidence or the tort of misuse of private information.

There is therefore an ongoing debate about the relationship between breach of confidence and misuse of private information. The former protects *confidential* information, whereas the latter is focused on *private* information – whilst this sounds relatively straightforward, information can often be both confidential and private. Whilst the developments are important to recognise and understand, for the sake of simplicity, the remainder of this chapter will refer to the relevant cause of action as 'breach of confidence'.

14.3.2 Reasonable expectation of privacy

In determining whether or not a breach of confidence (or, as discussed above, misuse of private information) has taken place, the first thing to consider is whether or not the claimant had a reasonable expectation of privacy. The court will look at a number of different factors when determining this, including - the nature of the information, the actions of the claimant and the form of the information. One way that the claimant can have a reasonable expectation of privacy is if there was a relationship of confidence between the parties, for example close friends, employee/employer, a therapist or other confidant.[40]

The majority of the time, however, the expectation of privacy arises from the nature of the information in question, as opposed to the relationship between the parties. There are certain types of information which are generally private, such as physical and mental health,[41] sexual behaviour and orientation,[42] and financial affairs.[43] The categories are expanding; in *Douglas v Hello! Ltd*, breach of confidence was invoked regarding the publication of covertly taken wedding photos of the celebrities Michael Douglas and Catherine Zeta-Jones. The existence of a confidentiality or non-disclosure agreement can be used in support of a claim of an expectation of privacy. The Court of Appeal in *ABC v Telegraph Media Group Ltd* [2018], however, emphasised that these contractual arrangements would not always protect the claimant.

---

34 [2005] EWCA Civ 595 at [53].
35 *Secretary of State for the Home Office v British Union for the Abolition of Vivisection* [2008] EWHC 892 (QB), [28] (Eady J); *Imerman v Tchenguiz* [2010] EWCA Civ 908 at [65] (Lord Neuberger MR) and *Walsh v Shanahan* [2013] EWCA Civ 411 at [55] (Rimer LJ).
36 [2014] EWHC 13 (QB) at [70].
37 [2015] 3 WLR 409, 427.
38 [2015] 3 WLR 409, 427.
39 [2016] UKSC 26.
40 See, for example, *McKennitt v Ash* [2006] EWCA Civ 1714.
41 *Venables v News Group Newspapers Ltd* [2001] Fam 430.
42 *PG and JH v United Kingdom* (ECtHR), Application No 44787/98, Judgment 25 September 2001). See ABK v KDT [2013] EWHC 1192 (QB) for the utilisation of privacy rights to obtain an injunction for 'revenge porn'.
43 *Lykiardopulo v Lykiardopulo* [2010] EWCA Civ 1315.

KEY CASE

ABC v Telegraph Media Group Ltd [2018] EWCA Civ 2329

The claimants were two companies and a senior executive. Five employees of the companies had previously made serious allegations against the executive. After receiving independent legal advice, the complainants were given substantial payments under settlement agreements. All of these settlements included a non-disclosure agreement to keep the relevant information confidential. A journalist from the defendant media group contacted the claimants to obtain their comments on a story about the complainants' allegations, the settlement and the non-disclosure agreements. The claimants believed that confidential information had been disclosed, and commenced proceedings preventing the publication of the information, arguing that it was a breach of confidence.

The trial judge refused to grant an interim injunction on the grounds that (a) the information was reasonably credible, (b) there could be little or no reasonable expectation of confidentiality or privacy in respect of the information, (c) a considerable amount of the information was already in the public domain, (d) it had not been demonstrated that the information had been obtained in breach of the non-disclosure agreements, and (e) publication of the information was in the public interest. The claimants appealed the refusal of an injunction.

The Court of Appeal allowed the appeal and ordered an interim injunction. It held that there was a real prospect that the publication would cause immediate, substantial and potentially irreversible harm to the claimants. The fact that the complainants had entered into settlements which included non-disclosure agreements could be used to support the claim that there was a reasonable expectation of privacy. Sir Terence Etherton MR, Underhill V-P LJ and Henderson LJ gave a joint decision, commenting that:

> the weight which should be attached to an obligation of confidence may be enhanced if the obligation is contained in an express contractual agreement. One type of situation where this consideration is likely to have a significant influence on the balancing exercise which the court has to perform is where the obligation in question is contained in an agreement to compromise, or avoid the need for, litigation, whether actual or threatened. Provided that the agreement is freely entered into, without improper pressure or any other vitiating factor, and with the benefit (where appropriate) of independent legal advice, and (again, where appropriate) with due allowance for disclosure of any wrongdoing to the police or appropriate regulatory or statutory body, the public policy reasons in favour of upholding the obligation are likely to tell with particular force, and may well outweigh the article 10 rights of the party who wishes to publish the confidential information.

Contractual agreements can therefore be evidence of a party's reasonable expectation of privacy, although this is not absolute. It will only form part of the balancing exercise conducted by the court, and it will have to be shown that the agreement was freely entered into without any improper pressure and with access to independent legal advice.

There are restrictions and limitations on the privacy of this information. The private nature can be 'lost', particularly when the claimant has acted in an immoral or abusive manner.[44] Specifically, individuals can lose their rights to private information by making 'public lies'. If this occurs, the defendant will usually have a right to disclose otherwise private information to rebut the lies made by the claimant. This occurred in *Campbell v MGN Ltd*, where the claimant frequently made public comments that she did not take drugs and, by making these assertions, she lost the reasonable expectation that this aspect of her life was private.[45]

---

44   *Goodwin v NGN Ltd* [2011] EWHC 1437 (QB); *Trimingham v Associated Newspapers Ltd* [2012] EWHC 1296 (QB).
45   See also *Ferdinand v MGN Ltd* [2011] EWHC 2454 (QB).

Public figures in general must also expect and accept that their actions will be subject to increased scrutiny by the media. As shown in *A v B Plc*, this will be particularly the case if the individual has actively 'courted' the publicity and notoriety.[46]

KEY CASE

A v B Plc [2003] QB 195

In this case, a married footballer sought an interim injunction preventing publication of information about affairs he had with two different women. This was originally granted, but was overturned by the Court of Appeal.

Woolf CJ handed down judgment of the Court, providing a number of guidelines that judges should use when considering whether an injunction should be awarded. This included Guideline XII, which stated:

Where an individual is a public figure he is entitled to have his privacy respected in the appropriate circumstances. A public figure is entitled to a private life. The individual, however, should recognise that because of his public position he must expect and accept that his actions will be more closely scrutinised by the media. Even trivial facts relating to a public figure can be of great interest to readers and other observers of the media. Conduct which in the case of a private individual would not be the appropriate subject of comment can be the proper subject of comment in the case of a public figure. The public figure may hold a position where higher standards of conduct can be rightly expected by the public. The public figure may be a role

model whose conduct could well be emulated by others. He may set the fashion. The higher the profile of the individual concerned the more likely that this will be the position. Whether you have courted publicity or not you may be a legitimate subject of public attention. If you have courted public attention then you have less ground to object to the intrusion which follows. In many of these situations it would be overstating the position to say that there is a public interest in the information being published. It would be more accurate to say that the public have an understandable and so a legitimate interest in being told the information. If this is the situation then it can be appropriately taken into account by a court when deciding on which side of the line a case falls. The courts must not ignore the fact that if newspapers do not publish information which the public are interested in, there will be fewer newspapers published, which will not be in the public interest.[47]

Therefore, whilst celebrities can expect some intrusion into their lives, this is not complete and they are 'still entitled to a private life'.

This decision has, however, been questioned and, as discussed in *McKennitt v Ash* [2006],[48] there is no automatic assumption that public figures should enjoy less privacy. The court therefore needs to determine whether the status of the claimant as a public figure has any impact on the level of privacy they are afforded. In *CDE v MGN Ltd* [2010],[49] Eady J granted an injunction preventing the disclosure of information about an extra-marital relationship of the claimant, who was a television personality. During the decision, the judge emphasised that while the claimant was a public figure, he had never actively sought fame and had guarded his family's private life closely. In contract, in

46 *Axel Springer AG v Germany* (2012) 55 EHRR 6.
47 [2003] QB 195, 208. This does, however, appear to go against the approach taken by many European countries which provide protection for public figures and their sexual lives: *Craxi (No 2) v Italy* (2004) 38 EHRR 47; *Tammer v Estonia* (2003) 37 EHRR 43.
48 [2006] EWCA Civ 1714.
49 [2010] EWHC 3309 (QB).

Von Hannover v Germany (No 2) [2012], the court held that photos of Princess Caroline and her family during a family skiing vacation were not private or confidential, largely on the basis that she was an 'undeniably very well known' person.[50]

There is, however, difficulty in determining who counts as a 'public figure'. Whilst celebrities are clearly public figures and this impacts their privacy rights, to whom else might this apply? The public interest in the lives of people clearly goes beyond celebrities, and can include children of celebrities (i.e. *Murray v Express Newspapers Plc* [2008][51]), politicians (i.e. *AAA v Associated Newspapers Ltd* [2013][52]), members of the royal family and their extended family (i.e. *Von Hannover v Germany (No 2)* [2012][53]; *Middleton v Persons Unknown* [2016][54]), elite athletes (i.e. *A v B Plc* [2012][55]), victims or perpetrators of particularly shocking crimes (i.e. *Jane Doe v ABC*,[56] *Venables & Thompson v News Group Newspapers, X (formerly known as Mary Bell) & Y v News Group Newspapers Ltd* [2003][57]), musicians (i.e. *OPA v MLA* [2014][57]), and social media 'influencers'. Many of these people will not have actively sought fame, but they still attract a significant amount of public interest. It can therefore be quite difficult to determine when these people have a reasonable expectation to privacy, and over what type of information.

■ VIEWPOINT

Do you believe that public figures should have different rights to privacy than ordinary individuals? If so, how would you define a 'public figure'?

The form of information published may also be relevant to whether the information is private. For example, covertly taken photos of individuals or secret recordings are likely to be seen as particularly intrusive or confidential.[58] Individuals are entitled to a certain level of privacy, even in public spaces.[59] In *Elizabeth Jagger v John Darling* [2005], the court held that the claimant (Elizabeth Jagger, daughter of Mick Jagger) was entitled to privacy even in the public area 'inside the closed front door' of a well-known nightclub, where she engaged in a sexual activity with her boyfriend. This area was monitored by CCTV, and the defendant published the footage to a number of third parties. Bell J held that the claimant did not realise that her conduct would be observed or electronically recorded, and therefore she had a 'legitimate expectation of privacy'.[60]

PROBLEM QUESTION TECHNIQUE

The Hassans become aware that a number of stories about their family are about to be published. Goodbye! is running a story about Haris's multiple infidelities, after being involved in a sex party with both male and female partners and during which he is seen consuming alcohol and illegal drugs. His actions were covertly recorded by prostitutes attending the party, who sold the footage to the

50 (2012) 55 EHRR 15 at [120].
51 [2008] EWCA Civ 446.
52 [2013] EWCA Civ 554.
53 [2012] 55 EHRR 15.
54 [2016] EWHC 2354 (QB).
55 [2002] EWCA Civ 337.
56 In this case substantial damages were awarded to a rape victim for the publication of her identity by the defendant.
57 [2014] EWCA Civ 1277.
58 [2003] EWHC 1101 (QB).
59 *Douglas v Hello! Ltd* [2005] EWCA Civ 595 (photos); *Mosley v News Group Newspapers Ltd* (2008) EMLR 20 (secret recordings).
60 [2005] EWHC 683 (Ch) at [13].

newspaper. The second story is from Bonjour, a gossip magazine owned by Goodbye!, and is about Basia's pregnancy, stating that the stress of Haris's infidelity has caused health complications with the baby. This includes information about her antenatal care and photos of her leaving a health centre for women who are having difficult pregnancies. Finally, a competitor newspaper, The End of the World, is running a story about how the family's apparent clean lifestyle is a lie. This includes photos of Basia taking her children to meat-based fast food restaurants and Haris smoking cigarettes.

▸ Have Basia and Haris lost their right to keep the majority of this information confidential? Consider the impact of their engagement in a number of 'public lies' about their lifestyle and the state of their marriage.

▸ By placing themselves in the public eye, have Basia and Haris implicitly allowed a certain level of intrusion into their lives, even when undertaking everyday activities? If so, would The End of the World be entitled to publish information of Basia eating fast food and Haris smoking cigarettes, if it was used to combat public lies about their lifestyle?

▸ Are there any limits on the disclosures that can be made? Must they be kept in proportion to the public lies made? What impact would this have on publication of the specific details of Basia's antenatal care and photos of her leaving the health centre?

▸ Will Haris be able to prevent the general information of his alleged infidelities from being published? Remember the decision in Mosley v News Group Newspapers Ltd about covert recording of private activities.

14.3.2.1 PRIVACY RIGHTS OF CHILDREN

The courts have consistently ensured additional protection for children's privacy rights.[61] For example, in *Murray v Express Newspapers Plc* [2008],[62] the Court of Appeal held that children of celebrities had an expectation of privacy above that of their famous parents. The additional protection afforded to children prevented the publication of a photo of J.K. Rowling's 19-month-old child being pushed down the street in a pushchair while they were out in public. Similar protection was afforded to Paul Weller's children (aged 16 years and 10-month-old twins), which prevented publication of photos taken of the family when they were in the United States.[63]

The privacy rights of children can also be used to prevent the publication of confidential information relating to their parents or other family members. For example, in *PJS v News Group Newspapers Ltd* [2016],[64] the rights of the celebrity's children were an important factor in preventing the publication of the information in question.

PROBLEM QUESTION TECHNIQUE

Haris is a social media 'influencer' who advocates a clean (vegan, organic, non-stimulant) lifestyle. He receives significant money from endorsement deals, and also has his own line of vegan organic children's food. Basia and Haris have two children, 8-year-old twins Malik and Nia, who frequently appear in

---

61 See discussion in *AAA v Associated Newspapers Ltd* [2013] EWCA Civ 554. This is supported by ISPO Guidelines 6(v), see discussion above at 14.2.2.
62 [2008] EWCA Civ 446.
63 *Weller v Associated Newspapers Ltd* [2014] EWHC 1163 (QB).
64 [2016] UKSC 26.

public with them for photo opportunities. Haris often uses Malik and Nia in advertisements for his food, stating that they are so healthy and intelligent because of their organic vegan lifestyle.

The End of the World is running a story about how the family's apparent clean lifestyle is a lie. This includes photos of Basia taking her children to meat-based fast food restaurants and Haris smoking cigarettes.

▶ Do the children have a reasonable expectation of privacy? Make sure to balance the different relevant factors, including the fact that the family have actively sought fame and publicity, but that the law will still provide additional protection for children.

▶ Refer specifically to the fact that the twins Malik and Nia are significantly older than the child in *Murray v Express Newspapers Plc* (a 19-month-old toddler).

▶ Have the photographs lost their quality of confidence in light of the fact that they are being used to counter the 'public lies' of the family?

▶ It may be useful to draw an analogy to *Von Hannover v Germany (No 2)*, where photos of Princess Caroline and her family during a family skiing vacation were not private or confidential largely on the basis that she was an 'undeniably very well known' person.

This protection is more controversial when the privacy is needed to prevent people from retaliation against crimes committed when they were children. The most famous example of this is *Venables & Thompson v News Group Newspapers Ltd* [2001], where an injunction was awarded to protect the privacy rights of two criminals who killed a 2-year-old boy when they were both 10 years old (as discussed in the Key Case box later in this chapter).[65] A similar order was granted in *A & B v Person Unknown* [2016], where two young boys were convicted of serious physical assaults against three other children. After undertaking a balancing exercise of the relevant Articles in Schedule 1 to the HRA 1998, the judge awarded a permanent (i.e. lifelong) order of anonymity. In making this decision, Sir Geoffrey Vos noted that

> the public calls for revenge and for harm to be done to the claimants are, in my judgment, to be taken very seriously indeed. The witness evidence, the press coverage, and the posts on the internet all point one way: if the identities of the claimants were to be revealed, they would be at extremely serious risk of physical harm. That is to say nothing of the undoubted fear and actual psychological harm that would undoubtedly follow any lifting of the existing anonymity orders.[66]

The prevention of publication can extend beyond the individual who committed the crime, and include their family members. In *X (formerly known as Mary Bell) & Y v News Group Newspapers Ltd* [2003],[67] the first applicant (X) was formerly known as Mary Bell. She was convicted of the manslaughter of two children when she was 11 years old. Her name was disclosed to the public during the trial, but she was given a new identity when she was released. Her real identity was discovered a number of times, and X and her daughter (the second applicant, Y) had to relocate five times. The two applicants therefore applied to the court for lifetime anonymity from media

---

65   This case is discussed in more detail below at 14.3.3. Similar restrictions were put in place in *Ex parte British Broadcasting Corporation: R v F* [2016] EWCA Crim 12, which prevented publication of the details of the alleged crime by both users of social media and the press. The focus in this case was, however, on the fact that publication could have prejudiced the criminal proceedings, as opposed to the privacy of the individuals in question.

66   *A & B v Person Unknown* [2016] EWHC 3295 (Ch) at [36].

67   [2003] EWHC 1101 (QB).

intrusions, and the prevention of any disclosure of their identity. After considering the exceptional circumstances of the case, guidance given by the courts in earlier case law and special features of the case, Dame Elizabeth Butler-Sloss P granted injunctions *contra mundum* (to the world at large) to protect the anonymity of X and of Y.

14.3.3 Unauthorised use

The second element of a breach of confidence action is whether there was unauthorised use or publication of the private information. This involves a balancing of the interests protected by Article 8 against those protected by Article 10 and s 12.

KEY LEGISLATION

Human Rights Act 1998

Schedule 1

Article 8 – Right to respect for private and family life

1. Everyone has the right to respect for his private and family life, his home and his correspondence.
2. There shall be no interference by a public authority with the exercise of this right except such as is in accordance with the law and is necessary in a democratic society in the interests of national security, public safety or the economic well-being of the country, for the prevention of disorder or crime, for the protection of health or morals, or for the protection of the rights and freedoms of others.

Article 10 – Freedom of expression

1. Everyone has the right to freedom of expression. This right shall include freedom to hold opinions and to receive and impart information and ideas without interference by public authority and regardless of frontiers. This Article shall not prevent States from requiring the licensing of broadcasting, television or cinema enterprises.
2. The exercise of these freedoms, since it carries with it duties and responsibilities, may be subject to such formalities, conditions, restrictions or penalties as are prescribed by law and are necessary in a democratic society, in the interests of national security, territorial integrity or public safety, for the prevention of disorder or crime, for the protection of health or morals, for the protection of the reputation or rights of others, for preventing the disclosure of information received in confidence, or for maintaining the authority and impartiality of the judiciary.

12   Freedom of expression

(1) This section applies if a court is considering whether to grant any relief which, if granted, might affect the exercise of the Convention right to freedom of expression.
(2) If the person against whom the application for relief is made ('the respondent') is neither present nor represented, no such relief is to be granted unless the court is satisfied—
    (a) that the applicant has taken all practicable steps to notify the respondent; or
    (b) that there are compelling reasons why the respondent should not be notified.
(3) No such relief is to be granted so as to restrain publication before trial unless the court is satisfied that the applicant is likely to establish that publication should not be allowed.
(4) The court must have particular regard to the importance of the Convention right to freedom of expression and, where the proceedings relate to material which the respondent claims, or which

> appears to the court, to be journalistic, literary or artistic material (or to conduct connected with such material), to—
>
> (a) the extent to which—
>
> (i) the material has, or is about to, become available to the public; or
>
> (ii) it is, or would be, in the public interest for the material to be published;
>
> (b) any relevant privacy code.

Whilst Article 8 appears to provide a straightforward right, it needs to be balanced with the right to freedom of expression under Article 10 and s 12. When undertaking this balancing exercise, freedom of expression may appear to be a 'trump card that always wins'.[68] This is particularly the case when considering the wording in s 12(4) where the court 'must have particular regard to the importance of the Convention right to freedom of expression'.

The Articles have, however, been interpreted as being of equal value, with neither having precedence over the other. This is confirmed by Lord Nicholls' statement in *Campbell v MGN Ltd*, that 'the case involves the familiar competition between freedom of expression and respect for an individual's privacy. Both are vitally important rights. Neither has precedence over the other.'[69] Further guidance was given by the House of Lords in *Re S (A child)* [2004] which provided four clear propositions when considering the interplay between Articles 8 and 10:

> First, neither article has as such precedence over the other. Secondly, where the values under the two articles are in conflict, an intense focus on the comparative importance of the specific rights being claimed in the individual case is necessary. Thirdly, the justifications for interfering with or restricting each right must be taken into account. Finally, the proportionality test must be applied to each.[70]

More recently in *PJS v News Groups Newspapers Ltd*, the Supreme Court confirmed there is no one right that 'trumps' the other; these two rights must work together, and the law needs to find a way to balance the competing interests protected by the two Articles.[71] An infamous and controversial example of this balancing occurred in *Venables & Thompson v News Group Newspapers*.

KEY CASE

Venables & Thompson v News Group Newspapers Ltd [2001] EWHC 32 (QB)

This case involved the privacy rights of two criminals who killed a 2-year-old boy when they were both 10 years old. They were convicted of the murder and detained. When they turned 18 years old, the four newspaper groups applied to the High Court for clarification on reporting restrictions on the identity and whereabouts of Venables and Thompson. The newspapers emphasised that there was a presumption in favour of freedom of expression, and this was a primary right in a democracy.[72]

In making her decision, Dame Elizabeth Butler-Sloss P emphasised that the combination of Article 10 and s 12 gives an enhanced importance to freedom of expression, and consequently to the

---

68 *R v Central Independent Television plc* [1995] 1 FCR 521.

69 [2004] 2 WLR 1232, 1237.

70 [2004] UKHL 47 at [17].

71 For further discussion of a 'human rights tort', see P. Giliker, 'A Common Law Tort of Privacy?: The Challenges of Developing a Human Rights Tort' (2015) 27 *SAcLJ* 761, 775–83.

72 [2001] 1 All ER 908, 914.

right of the press to publish information about individuals. In particular, s 12(4) states that courts 'must have particular regard to the importance of the Convention right to freedom of expression'. Freedom of expression must therefore only be limited in accordance with the exceptions set out in Article 10(2). This is a high threshold, and

> [t]he onus of proving the case that freedom of expression must be restricted is firmly upon the applicant seeking the relief. The restrictions sought must, in the circumstances of the present case, be shown to be in accordance with the law, justifiable as necessary to satisfy a strong and pressing social need, convincingly demonstrated, to restrain the press in order

to protect the rights of the claimants to confidentiality, and proportionate to the legitimate aim pursued.[73]

After considering the 'real and substantial' threat that disclosure of the information could have on Venables and Thompson, Dame Elizabeth Butler-Sloss P held that the exception in Article 10(2) was made out. After a detailed review of the evidence, it was determined that both individuals were at risk of death or serious harm both in detention and on release if people were able to recognise them. The value of rehabilitation and the importance of allowing the men an opportunity to live as normal lives as possible in the circumstances were also emphasised.

Whilst Article 10 and s 12 emphasise freedom of expression and provide the defendant of a breach of confidence claim with an opportunity to 'tell their story', they do not provide free rein to publish information relating to other people. This was highlighted in *McKennitt v Ash* [2006].[74] In this case, the claimant was a famous but very private Canadian folk singer. The defendant published a book entitled *Travels with Loreena McKennitt: My Life as a Friend*, which involved personal and private information relating to the claimant. This included information about her personal and sexual relationships, her feelings about her deceased fiancé, matters about her health and diet, her emotional vulnerability, and information about a dispute between the claimant and the defendant.[75]

The claimant commenced an action against the defendant for breach of confidence. The defendant argued that the book was not merely about the claimant, but also detailed the defendant's own experiences. Because of this, she was entitled to 'tell her own story that includes her various experiences' with the claimant.[76] This argument was rejected in the first instance, and by the Court of Appeal. Buxton LJ stated that the defendant 'cannot undermine their confidential nature by the paradox of calling in aid the confidential relationship that gave her access to the information in the first place'.[77]

It is therefore clear that while there is a strong emphasis on freedom of expression, the courts will look at the situation in its entirety and balance the defendant's right to freedom of expression with the claimant's right to privacy.

It can often be difficult to determine what specific issues the courts will consider when undertaking this balancing exercise. In *Von Hannover v Germany (No 2)* [2012], the European Court of Human Rights provided a number of relevant criteria:

(a) whether the information contributed to a debate of general interest;

(b) how well known is the person concerned, and the subject of the report;

---

73 [2001] 1 All ER 908, 922.
74 [2006] EWCA Civ 1714.
75 [2006] EWCA Civ 1714 at [12].
76 [2006] EWCA Civ 1714 at [28].
77 [2006] EWCA Civ 1714 at [32].

(c)   the prior conduct of the person concerned;

(d)   consent, form and consequences of the publication; and

(e)   the circumstances in which the information was obtained.[78]

There is therefore clear and considerable overlap between these factors, and they are taken into account in determining whether or not the information in question has a quality of confidence.

PROBLEM QUESTION TECHNIQUE

Basia and Haris both speak often about their 'perfect' marriage and family, and it is a large part of their public appeal.

Goodbye! is running a story about Haris's multiple infidelities, after being involved in a sex party with both male and female partners and during which he was seen consuming alcohol and illegal drugs. His actions were covertly recorded by prostitutes attending the party, who sold the footage to the newspaper.

The second story is from Bonjour, a gossip magazine owned by Goodbye!, and is about Basia's pregnancy, stating that the stress of Haris's infidelity has caused health complications with the baby. This includes information about her antenatal care and photos of her leaving a health centre for women who are having difficult pregnancies. ... The End of the World is running a story about how the family's apparent clean lifestyle is a lie. This includes photos of Basia taking her children to meat-based fast food restaurants and Haris smoking cigarettes.

▸ For the information that has not lost the reasonable expectation of privacy, the court will undertake a balancing exercise to see whether there has been a breach of confidence.

▸ Whilst there is often no clear answer, some relevant factors to consider are:

   – The family, in particular Haris, have actively sought the public eye and therefore their actions could contribute to a debate of general interest.

   – The children are likely to be innocent and therefore publication of photographs of them will be protected.

   – Haris and Basia have both engaged in public deception and lies about their lifestyle and relationship.

   – Basia is in a vulnerable position regarding her pregnancy. Lying about the state of your pregnancy may be seen differently from lying about taking illegal drugs (cf Campbell v MGN Ltd). She had also specifically asked for privacy regarding the health and progress of her baby.

   – Some of the information was obtained covertly, but most appeared to be photographs taken in public without any secrecy.

14.3.4 Remedies

The requested remedy for breach of confidence cases generally depends on whether the information has already been published. If it has, the claimant is likely to seek damages and an injunction granted to prevent further publication. If the information has yet to be published, it is highly likely that an injunction will be sought. As seen in *Venables & Thompson v News Group Newspapers Ltd* [2001][79], there can be the award of an injunction *contra mundum* (against the world at large). Whilst the courts are generally hesitant to award interim injunctions, there is an increasing acceptance of this if the information is in respect of personal information and where damages may be an inadequate

---

78   *Von Hannover v Germany (No 2)* (Application Nos 40660/08 and 60641/08) [2012] ECHR 40660/08 at[108]–[113].

79   [2001] EWHC 32 (QB), [2001] Fam 430, [2001] 1 All ER 908.

remedy.[80] An example of this was *ABC v Telegraph Media Group Ltd* [2018][81], where the court awarded an interim injunction preventing the publication of information contained in employment settlement agreements which included non-disclosure agreements. An injunction can be awarded even if the information is already partly in the public domain. In *PJS v News Group Newspapers Ltd* [2016][82], the Supreme Court upheld an order preventing the disclosure of the details of a three-way sexual encounter involving the claimant, even though the details had already been published in other countries and on social media. The Supreme Court specifically considered the impact further publication could have on the claimant's children when making its determination.

If the confidential information has already been published, the courts are limited in the potential remedies that can be awarded. As will be discussed in Chapter 17, the aim of remedies in tort law is to put the individual, as far as possible, in the position they would have been in had the breach of confidence not occurred. With damages for breach of confidence, the courts have tended to take a rather conservative approach when making awards. For example, in *Campbell v MGN Ltd* [2004][83] the claimant was awarded £2,500 in compensation, and in *Douglas v Hello! Ltd* (No. 3) [2003][84] the claimants were each awarded £3,750.[85] Despite the court's condemnation of the defendant's actions in *McKennitt v Ash* [2006][86], only £5,000 was awarded for the publication of a book detailing significant amounts of private and sensitive information. These awards highlight the limited nature of breach of confidence claims, and the inherent restrictions when an attempt is made to use them to protect privacy rights. In breach of confidence cases, there is the possibility of further aggravated damages, as seen in *Campbell v MGN Ltd* [2004][87]– although in this case the award was limited to £1,000.

There was a change in approach to the award of damages in *Mosley v News Group Newspapers Ltd* [2008][88], when the claimant was awarded £60,000 for the publication of information about the claimant's involvement in Nazi-themed sado-masochistic sexual practices.[89] The judge, Eady J, emphasised the harmful nature of the specific breach of confidence in that case when making this unusually generous award. The *News of the World* phone tapping scandal was such a shocking breach of privacy rights that the court awarded even higher damages for particularly egregious breaches.[90] More recently, in *Richard v BBC* [2018], Mann J awarded Sir Cliff Richard £210,000 in damages for the BBC's coverage of the police search of his residence.

KEY CASE

Richard v BBC [2018] 3 WLR 1715

In 2014 the South Yorkshire Police commenced an investigation of Sir Cliff Richard in relation to allegations of a historic sex offence. This resulted in a search of Sir Cliff's residence. The BBC became aware of the investigation and search, giving it prominent and extensive television coverage both in real time and after the event. This included

filming into his home from both the ground and by helicopter, and taking photographs of the officers searching the apartment. No charges were laid, and the investigation was dropped in 2016.

Sir Cliff commenced an action for damages against the BBC. He claimed that the broadcasting of the police search of his residence had breached

80 *Coco v AN Clark (Engineers) Ltd* [1969] RPC 41, 50.
81 [2018] EWCA Civ 2329, [2019] 2 All ER 684.
82 [2016] UKSC 26.
83 [2004] UKHL 22, [2004] 2 WLR 1232.
84 [2003] EWHC 786 (Ch).
85 For detailed discussion of *Douglas v Hello! Ltd*, see Chapter 11 (Economic Torts).
86 [2006] EWCA Civ 1714.
87 [2004] UKHL 22, [2004] 2 WLR 1232.
88 [2008] EMLR 20.
89 [2008] EMLR 20.
90 *Guluti v MGN Ltd* [2015] EWHC 1482 (Ch) where awards ranging from £72,500 to £260,250 were made.

his right to privacy under Article 8 of Schedule 1 to the HRA 1998. Mann J held that there had been an infringement and that Sir Cliff was entitled to damages, awarding him £190,000 compensation damages and £20,000 exemplary damages. When determining an appropriate level of compensation, Mann J commented that

> awards of damages are not to be such as to have a chilling effect on the right of freedom of expression. I do not consider that an award of that amount should have a chilling effect of the kind which is to be avoided. A claimant is entitled to proper compensatory damages and the figure I have specified is a proper figure for that purpose. I do not consider that it requires any modification on the footing that such figures would have a chilling effect on the exercise of a newspaper's right of freedom of expression. It is not an excessive figure; there is no punitive element; it is a genuine compensatory figure; the reason that the story existed as a story was because information was acquired in breach of a right of privacy in the first place, and then confirmed by less than straightforward means by the BBC's reporter; and it was entirely the decision of the BBC to present the story at all, and then to present it as it did. One of the main motivations of the BBC was the excitement of its scoop. None of that requires any modification of damages otherwise properly payable to Sir Cliff on the basis that responsible journalism would be disincentivised.[91]

This case highlights that the balancing of competing rights enshrined in Article 8 with those in Article 10 and s 12 is therefore relevant for both the finding of a breach of confidence and also when determining an appropriate remedy for any breach that occurs.

PROBLEM QUESTION TECHNIQUE

Advise Basia and Haris of any rights they may have regarding these stories.

▸ What is the impact of the fact that some of the information that will be published is likely to be protected by breach of confidence? Will Basia and Haris be able to obtain an injunction to prevent publication?

▸ If the articles have already been published, would the family would be entitled to damages? In this case, consider what damages they are likely to be awarded. Think about the similarities and differences between this case and *Mosley v News Group Newspapers Ltd*.

▸ Would Basia be able to obtain aggravated damages for the publication of information about her pregnancy (similar to *Campbell v MGN Ltd*)?

14.3.5 Breach of confidence: concluding remarks

Breach of confidence is the main way that the common law currently protects privacy rights. There are two limbs to this cause of action:

(1) Did the claimant have a reasonable expectation of privacy?

(2) Was there unauthorised use of this information? Specifically, were the benefits achieved by the information's publication proportionate to the harm that may be done by the interference with the right to privacy?

The court also has to determine an appropriate remedy, which creates a range of difficulties – particularly if the confidential information is already in the public domain. The development of

---

91 [2018] 3 WLR 1715 at 1764.

breach of confidence has been significantly impacted by the Human Rights Act 1998, and there is an ongoing tension between privacy rights in Article 8 and freedom of expression enshrined in Article 10 and s 12.

The refusal of both the courts and Parliament to develop privacy laws, such as the creation of a freestanding tort protecting privacy, has resulted in the stretching of the traditional scope of breach of confidence. The decision in *Douglas v Hello!* that wedding photos can be 'confidential information' protected by a breach of confidence claim highlights the significant overlap it has with privacy. This 'stretching' means that breach of confidence provides significant protection, and goes a long way to fill the 'privacy' gap currently existing in the law, but does not provide complete protection. It is still limited to 'confidential information', and therefore other forms of privacy – such as physical interferences in the form of strip searches – are not protected. This raises the question of whether the law should develop a freestanding tort of privacy that could protect a wider range of privacy interests.

14.4 A freestanding privacy tort?

Whilst there are a number of protections available for people who have had their privacy invaded, these individual pieces do not provide full coverage. The restrictions of the existing tort law, under both the common law and government regulations, have created increased calls for the development of a freestanding privacy tort. Having a separate specific tort would provide individuals with clearer and arguably stronger privacy rights. There are, however, concerns that such a development could negatively impact freedom of speech, another important right in English common law. Other arguments against privacy reform include that there is already adequate protection, the difficulties of defining privacy, the potential for frivolous or vexatious claims, and complexities when awarding remedies.

Table 14.2: Arguments against privacy developments

Argument against Privacy Development	Limitations of Argument	Case Examples / Other Resources
Importance of freedom of speech	The common law has developed effective ways to balance privacy protection against freedom of expression	*Re S* [2004] UKHL 47 *PJS v News Group Newspapers Ltd* [2016] UKSC 26
Adequate protection already provided by existing legal mechanisms	Whilst breach of confidence (also known as misuse of private information) protects confidential or private *information*, other privacy rights, such as the right to privacy of your bodily autonomy, are not covered by this cause of action	*Wainwright v Home Office* [2004] 2 AC 406
Difficulties defining privacy	Many legal concepts are hard to define. Workable definitions of privacy have been provided by academia ('the right to be left alone'[92]) and the government ('right to determine for oneself how and to what extent information about oneself is communicated to others'[93]). The common law can develop these definitions further.	Warren and Brandeis 'The Right to Privacy' (1890) 4 *Harvard LR* 193 The Committee on Privacy, Younger Report (Cmnd 5012, July 1972)

---

92 S. Warren and L. Brandeis, 'The Right to Privacy' (1890) 4 *Harvard* LR 193, 193.
93 Committee on Privacy, Younger Report (Cmnd 5012, July 1972), 22.

Argument against Privacy Development	Limitations of Argument	Case Examples / Other Resources
The potential for claimants to bring frivolous or vexatious claims	The law already has mechanisms to deal with frivolous or vexatious claims, as this is a concern not only limited to privacy. As with defamation, a 'serious harm' requirement could be included in the requirements for any breach of privacy claim.	Defamation Act 2013, s 1 Civil Procedure Rules, Practice Direction 3A – Striking Out a Statement of Case, para 7 (Vexatious Litigants)
Complexities of awarding remedies	The complexity of awarding remedies is an issue in many areas of tort law.[94] To prevent the publication of confidential information, the court has the power to award injunctions, as well as issue interim injunctions and injunctions to the world at large. If the information is already in the public realm, an injunction can be awarded to stop further publication, and if that will not assist, damages can be awarded to the claimant.	*Venables & Thompson v News Group Newspapers Ltd* [2001] EWHC 32 (QB) *RocknRoll v News Group Newspapers Ltd* [2013] EWHC 24 (Ch) *Douglas v Hello! Ltd* [2001] 2 WLR 992 *ABC v Telegraph Media Group Ltd* [2018] EWCA Civ 2329

The multiple justifications often used to argue against further development of privacy rights are therefore not as convincing as they may seem at first blush. It should also be remembered that many other countries have stronger privacy rights, including a specific right to privacy, and they have managed to address these potential concerns. The answer is therefore far from clear. The benefits and potential detriments of a freestanding tort protecting privacy have been the basis of very interesting analyses, with different academics coming to very different conclusions.

DIFFERENT PERSPECTIVES on privacy

P. Giliker, 'A Common Law Tort of Privacy?: The Challenges of Developing a Human Rights Tort' (2015) 27 SAcLJ 761

In this article, Giliker outlines the significant difficulties associated with the development of a freestanding tort protecting individual privacy. The author highlights that when developing tort law, common law jurisdictions have avoided radical departures from existing laws and instead generally chosen incremental development of the law. She comments that:

> This approach is reflected in the case law ... the courts rejecting a tort of privacy per se as far too vague and broad-ranging, but accepting that aspects of privacy are worthy of protection, notably the publication of private or personal information and intrusion into the private affairs of another.[95]

If a new tort protecting the invasion of privacy was to be created, there would be a number of practical and conceptual challenges. First, English law would need to identify the extent to which existing European Court of Human Rights (ECtHR) case law would impact on the existing English approach to liability. As the development of a tort protecting privacy would be heavily influenced by the obligations under Articles 8 and 10 of the ECHR, English law would need to engage with the ECtHR case law when determining the scope and application of any tort developed. There are some practical difficulties associated with this, including the fact that the nature of ECtHR cases often means that common law

---

94 For further discussion, see Chapter 17 (Damages).
95 P. Giliker, 'A Common Law Tort of Privacy?: The Challenges of Developing a Human Rights Tort' (2015) 27 *SAcLJ* 761, 774.

courts struggle to find clear guidance from these decisions.[96] In addition, the rights under Article 8 have been interpreted differently across some jurisdictions, with some extending privacy rights clearly beyond what has been recognised by English courts. Giliker highlights how these types of decisions create difficulties for judges, commenting that 'ECHR jurisprudence adopts a wide interpretation of Art 8 which goes beyond protection of private information to include freedom from interference with one's physical and psychological integrity and with the right to develop one's own personality and identity and live one's life in the manner of one's choosing'.[97]

The second challenge would be the requirement to integrate the newly created tort within the existing common law torts. Giliker highlights that some academic commentators, notably Nolan and Bagshaw, have argued that it would be difficult to implement the concepts of Articles 8 and 10 into the current tort law framework as they have different purposes and processes. This view also had some support from the Supreme Court in *Michael v Chief Constable of South Wales Police* [2015].[98] The development of a new tort would require the courts to consider the appropriate scope and whether it would just be limited to information, or whether broader rights would be protected (such as invasive strip searches in *Wainwright v Home Office*).

Giliker concludes by outlining that, despite the significant challenges involved, the current situation is untenable and reform must occur. The existing law is unsuitable and cannot be sustained, but unfortunately neither the courts nor legislature are willing to take this much-needed step. She argues that the difficulties experienced so far mean that 'relying on the courts to continue to develop incrementally this area of law is unlikely to provide the certainty and structure expected in the common law legal tradition. Intervention is needed. The referral of this matter to the Law Commission of England and Wales is a necessary first step towards resolving the substantive and constitutional issues.'[99]

H Kalven Jr, 'Privacy in Tort Law – Were Warren and Brandeis Wrong' (1966) 31 Law & Contemporary Problems 326

In contrast, Kalven argues against the development of a freestanding privacy tort. The author comments that 'although privacy is for me a great and important value, tort law's effort to protect the right of privacy seems to me a mistake'. The author describes a number of practical problems associated with recognising such a tort, including the fact that it 'has no legal profile. We do not know what constitutes a prima facie case, we do not know on what basis damages are to be measured, we do not know whether the basis of liability is limited to intentional invasions or includes also negligent invasions and even strict liability.'[100]

It is also difficult to determine what the scope of any potential tort would be, and what interests may be protected. A formula of preventing 'conduct which outrages the common decencies' would limit the tort to exceptional circumstances, whereas restricting disclosures that 'would be offensive and objectionable to a reasonable man' may be too wide. Kalven also highlights that awarding damages for a freestanding tort 'is equally vague and mysterious'. There are a number of other issues explored by the author. What role does fault have to play in a finding of liability? Is it important if the defendant was aware that the disclosure would be offensive? Or if they meant to refer to the claimant at all? What is the relationship between defamation and privacy?

---

96 Giliker (above), 778.
97 Giliker (above), 780–1.
98 [2015] UKSC 2.
99 Giliker (above), 787.
100 H. Kalven Jr, 'Privacy in Tort Law – Were Warren and Brandeis Wrong' (1966) 31 *Law & Contemporary Problems* 326, 333.

In addition to the practical difficulties, Kalven highlights the importance of public interest in the news. Any development of the law of privacy may undermine the right of the value of publishing information of public or general interest. The author questions whether newspapers could safely publish pictures of a train wreck or airplane crash if any of the victims were recognisable, or would their privacy rights prevent this disclosure?

The final point made by Kalven is the issue of who is going to actually utilise a newly created tort of privacy? He guessed that 'the victims on whose behalf the privacy tort remedy was designed will not in the real world elect to use it and that those who will come forward with privacy claims will very often have shabby, unseemly grievances and an interest in exploitation'.[101]

The author therefore argues that, whilst the cause of action on paper looks attractive and meritorious, the victims that society has in mind to be protected by privacy are unlikely to be the ones who actually utilise the remedy provided by any newly created tort.

■ VIEWPOINT

Do you think that the development of a freestanding tort protecting the invasion of privacy is a useful development for English tort law? Has the enactment of the Human Rights Act 1998 has weakened the need for a freestanding tort of privacy? Or is it the opposite – that there is now a need to develop a tort that specifically protects the rights under the Human Rights Act 1998?

If a freestanding privacy tort was to be developed, there is ongoing debate about whether this should occur through the common law or Parliament. Numerous courts have explicitly commented that it is not for the common law to develop such protection; rather it should be left to Parliament. In *Malone v Metropolitan Police Commissioner (No 2)* [1979], Sir Robert Megarry VC considered whether the ECHR should provide the claimant with rights of property privacy and confidentiality. He refused to do this, stating:

> I readily accept that if the question before me were one of construing a statute enacted with the purpose of giving effect to obligations imposed by the Convention, the court would readily seek to construe the legislation in a way that would effectuate the Convention rather than frustrate it. However, no relevant legislation of that sort is in existence. It seems to me that where Parliament has abstained from legislating on a point that is plainly suitable for legislation, it is indeed difficult for the court to lay down new rules of common law or equity that will carry out the Crown's treaty obligations, or to discover for the first time that such rules have always existed.[102]

The role of Parliament was again explicitly noted by Glidewell LJ in *Kaye v Robertson* [1991]. In this case, Bingham LJ also discussed his dissatisfaction with the inadequate protections the existing law gives to privacy rights.

---

101 Kalven Jr (above), 338.

102 [1979] Ch 344, 379. This approach was explicitly supported by Lord Hoffmann in *Wainwright v Home Office*: 'For the reasons so cogently explained by Sir Robert Megarry V-C in *Malone v Metropolitan Police Comr* ... this is an area which requires a detailed approach which can be achieved only by legislation rather than the broad brush of common law principle': [2003] 3 WLR 1137, 1146.

KEY CASE

Kaye v Robertson [1991] FSR 62

The claimant was a well-known actor who had a car accident and needed extensive surgery and ongoing hospitalisation. The defendants, two employees of 'The Sunday Sport' tabloid, gained access to his private hospital room despite notices prohibiting any unauthorised entry. They interviewed the claimant at length and took flash photographs of him before being removed by security staff. The claimant sought an injunction against the publication of any story based on the interview or the photographs on the basis of malicious falsehood, libel, passing off and trespass to the person. The defendants argued that the claimant had consented to the interview, despite the fact that he clearly had not been in a fit state to consent, and a short time after the 'interview' he could not recall the incident. An injunction was granted and the defendants appealed to the Court of Appeal. The appeal was denied and the injunction upheld.

Glidewell LJ gave the main judgment of the Court, holding that it was 'arguably libellous' to imply consent had been given for publication. His Lordship held that there was no actionable right of privacy in English law, but that all elements of malicious falsehood had been made out, thereby justifying an injunction. Glidewell LJ emphasised that this should be a role for Parliament.

It is well-known that in English law there is no right to privacy, and accordingly there is no right of action for breach of a person's privacy. The facts of the present case are a graphic illustration of the desirability of Parliament considering whether and in what circumstances statutory provision can be made to protect the privacy of individuals.[103]

Bingham LJ used the case as an opportunity to express his dissatisfaction with the state of the law, commenting that:

This case nonetheless highlights, yet again, the failure of both the common law of England and statute to protect in an effective way the personal privacy of individual citizens ... The defendants' conduct towards the plaintiff here was 'a monstrous invasion of his privacy' ... If ever a person has a right to be let alone by strangers with no public interest to pursue, it must surely be when he lies in hospital recovering from brain surgery and in no more than partial command of his faculties. It is this invasion of his privacy which underlies the plaintiff's complaint. Yet it alone, however gross, does not entitle him to relief in English law.

The plaintiff's suggested cause of action in libel is in my view arguable, for reasons which Glidewell L.J. has given. We could not give interlocutory relief on that ground. Battery and assault are causes of action never developed to cover acts such as these: they could apply only if the law were substantially extended and the available facts strained to unacceptable lengths. A claim in passing off is hopeless. Fortunately, a cause of action in malicious falsehood exists, but even that obliges us to limit the relief we can grant in a way which would not bind us if the plaintiff's cause of action arose from the invasion of privacy of which, fundamentally, he complains. We cannot give the plaintiff the breadth of protection which I would, for my part, wish. The problems of defining and limiting a tort of privacy are formidable, but the present case strengthens my hope that the review now in progress may prove fruitful.[104]

Interestingly (but also potentially frustratingly), the Court of Appeal in this case criticised the lack of legal protections for privacy rights, but then also refused to develop further protection under the common law.

---

103 *Kaye v Robertson* [1991] FSR 62, 66.
104 *Kaye v Robertson* [1991] FSR 62, 70.

More recently, the Court of Appeal in *Fearn v Board of Trustees of the Tate Gallery* confirmed that any further development of privacy protection should not occur through the common law. Sir Terence Etherton MR, Lord Justice Lewison and Lady Justice Rose DBE gave a joint judgment stating that:

> It may be said that what is really the issue in cases of overlooking in general, and the present case in particular, is invasion of privacy rather than (as is the case with the tort of nuisance) damage to interests in property. There are already other laws which bear on privacy, including the law relating to confidentiality, misuse of private information, data protection (Data Protection Act 2018), harassment and stalking (Protection of Harassment Act 1997). This is an area in which the legislature has intervened and is better suited than the courts to weigh up competing interests: cf. *Wainwright v Home Office* [2003] UKHL 53, [2004] 2 AC 406, esp. at [33], in which the House of Lords held that there is no common law tort of invasion of privacy and that it is an area which requires a detailed approach which can be achieved only by legislation rather than the broad brush of common law principle.
>
> For all those reasons, we consider that it would be preferable to leave it to Parliament to formulate any further laws that are perceived to be necessary to deal with overlooking rather than to extend the law of private nuisance.[105]

Whilst the courts have argued that privacy development should occur through the Parliament, this has been unsuccessful. The government has been unwilling to take steps towards the creation of a privacy tort. In the 1960s, no less than three Bills aimed at increasing the existing privacy rights were presented for consideration, none of which were successful. Lord Mancroft's 1961 attempt was withdrawn because of the lack of government support; Alexander Lyon's 1967 Bill was rejected on the basis that it was too limited, and Brian Waldon's 1969 attempt was rejected as it was widely perceived to encroach too far into freedom of expression. As discussed above, the 1972 Younger Report also rejected the development of legislation to give further protection to the privacy rights. In the 1980s, two further Bills aimed at providing enhanced privacy rights failed.

The government has also repeatedly contended that the development of the law of privacy is the responsibility of the common law and not Parliament. This was particularly evident in the debate regarding the Human Rights Bill, where it was clearly stated that the development of privacy rights was to occur by the common law as opposed to statute.[106] Similar comments were made by the government in its written submissions in *Spencer v United Kingdom* [1998]. In this case, the government argued that there was no need for further statutory development of privacy rights because

> the domestic system as a whole (including remedies in breach of confidence and against trespass, nuisance, harassment and malicious falsehood together with the Press Complaints Commission) provides adequate protection to individuals and an appropriate balance between the often competing rights.[107]

However, as the earlier sections of this chapter have highlighted, the existing regime does not provide a coherent framework for the protection of privacy rights. The general law of privacy is therefore at a crossroads. It is widely believed that further development is necessary, but both the courts and Parliament are refusing the responsibility of taking this forward.

---

105 [2020] EWCA Civ 104 at [84]–[85].
106 HL Hansard, 24 November 1997, col 771. See also the submissions of the government as a respondent in the ECtHR case of *Spencer v United Kingdom* (1998) 25 EHRR CD 105.
107 *Spencer v United Kingdom* (1998) 25 EHRR CD 105.

■ VIEWPOINT

If there is to be increased recognition of privacy rights, do you think that this should occur through the common law or by Parliament?

14.5 Privacy protection in the 21st century

Modern developments – such as social media outlets, the increasing breadth of people considered 'celebrities', and the increased monitoring and recording of lives – have created enhanced challenges for privacy protection. We are more likely to have our private life monitored, and there are now many more ways that this information can be disseminated to the wider community.

The challenges associated with privacy, particularly the impact of the Human Right Act 1998, was recently highlighted by the Supreme Court case of *Sutherland v Her Majesty's Advocate* [2020].[108] Sutherland was convicted of various child sexual offences after being caught by members of the public acting as 'paedophile hunters'. He appealed against his conviction on the basis that the evidence obtained by these paedophile hunters was in breach of his right to private life and respect for correspondence under Article 8(1). The Supreme Court upheld the criminal convictions on two separate bases. First, the appellant's sexual communications (with a person he believed was a 13-year-old boy) were not worthy of respect for the purposes of the ECHR. Second, the appellant had no reasonable expectation of privacy in relation to these communications, and therefore enjoyed no protection under Article 8(1). The communications could therefore be disclosed and used by public authorities in criminal proceedings, and the convictions were upheld.

Another recent example of unfair intrusion into the life of a potentially vulnerable individual was the press coverage of celebrity Caroline Flack after she was charged with assaulting her partner. When she tragically committed suicide, the media were quick to lay the blame at the feet of the prosecutors who decided to charge Flack with the assault. The press, however, has to share in some of the blame. A review of the coverage of Flack before her death highlights the unacceptable level of press scrutiny she endured in the months leading to her suicide. It was described as a 'media frenzy', with 387 stories published in the six months before her death, a quarter of these taking a negative tone against Flack.[109] She received further negative publicity from multiple social media outlets as well as the 'traditional' media. Was it foreseeable that this level of scrutiny and publicity – arguably bordering on harassment and bullying – would result in suicide? This concern is made even worse by the fact that Flack was the fourth contestant from the reality TV show Love Island to commit suicide since the show's commencement in 2015.

There is also a gendered dimension to privacy protection. Privacy has the ability to both enhance and potentially further undermine the rights of women and other vulnerable groups. On one hand, increased protection of privacy allows people greater control over the publication of their personal information. This can assist with issues of hacking, and the publication of private photographs and tackling revenge pornography, both of which are more likely to be issues experienced by women. In *Middleton v Persons Unknown* [2016],[110] Pippa Middleton obtained an urgent injunction preventing the publication of photos – some of which were intimate – that were obtained through the hacking of her iCloud account. In this case, the defendant obtained the images through illegal

PART 4

---

108 [2020] UKSC 32.

109 N. McIntyre, L. al-Khalaf, J. Murray and P. Duncan, 'Caroline Flack: Scale of negative media coverage before death revealed', *The Guardian Online*, 21 February 2020 (https://www.theguardian.com/tv-and-radio/2020/feb/21/caroline-flack-negative-media-coverage-before-death-revealed), accessed 10 June 2020.

110 [2016] EWHC 2354 (QB).

means, although the protections can also extend to 'revenge porn' situations (i.e. where the private information was sent to an individual who, at a later time, discloses or threatens to disclose it to other people). For example, in *ABK v KDT* [2013],[111] Tugendhat J made an order preventing the defendant from disclosing personal photographs and information that had been sent by the claimant during their affair.

On the other hand, privacy can undermine the rights of women. MacKinnon discussed the challenges of privacy in *Toward a Feminist Theory of the State* (Cambridge University Press, 1989). She highlights how privacy can undermine women's rights as it can be used to cover up harm suffered by women, including discrimination, bullying and domestic violence. There are examples of privacy laws being utilised in this manner. In *ABC v Telegraph Media Group Ltd*, an interim injunction was awarded preventing the dissemination of allegations of improper conduct that would have breached non-disclosure agreements. In 2019, the magic circle law firm Linklaters obtained an injunction against one of its former employees, preventing the publication of information about sexual harassment and the treatment of women at the firm. In *Linklaters LLP v Mellish* [2019],[112] when balancing the right of the firm to maintain confidentially against the public interest in sexual harassment and the actions of large firms, Warby J held that Linklaters had a 'legitimate interest' in preventing the publication of this information. Both of these cases received significant criticisms for allowing privacy laws to be used in a way to silence victims and allow perpetrators to shield themselves from public accountability.

These issues are discussed in more detail in the Richardson article included in the Further Reading list. Whilst there is no clear answer on these challenges, it is important for policy makers and the courts to be aware of these issues if and when further development of privacy laws is considered.

■ VIEWPOINT

Does privacy help or hinder the development of equality and women's rights in the 21st century? What further reforms are appropriate or necessary?

14.6 CHAPTER SUMMARY

Ironically, given this is a 'Privacy' chapter in a tort law textbook, the UK has not yet recognised a freestanding tort protecting privacy. Rights to privacy are now enshrined in Article 8 of Schedule 1 to the Human Rights Act 1998, although this has to be balanced with the freedom of expression rights in Article 10. The underlying principles associated with privacy have been protected by a range of other common law, statutory and regulatory mechanisms, but unlike a number of other countries, there is still no 'tort of invasion of privacy' in English common law. There have, however, been huge developments that provide a strong level of protection for confidential and/or private information.

The equity-based breach of confidence tort has provided some relief and assistance for people who have had their privacy invaded, particularly as there is now recognition of a tort of 'misuse of private information'. Under the breach of confidence action, claimants will have a right to damages or an injunction if they can show that there was a reasonable expectation of privacy, and that there has been unauthorised use of this private information. The tests for both of these elements involve a balancing activity by the courts, where a wide array of issues are considered.

---

111 [2013] EWHC 1192 (QB).
112 [2019] EWHC 177 (QB).

The debates around privacy have attracted a lot of government and public attention, especially in light of issues such as Princess Diana's death and other widely publicised press harassment of celebrities, the *News of the World* phone tapping scandal, the suicide of a celebrity who was subject to a 'media frenzy' around her activities, and the recent attempts by residents of multi-million pound apartments to close down part of the Tate Modern's viewing gallery. Recent developments, such as increased use of social media, the changing notion of a 'celebrity' and general enhanced monitoring and recording of everyday life, have also had significant implications in terms of people's reasonable expectations of privacy. There is also a complex gendered aspect to privacy; the courts can be used to protect victims from hacking and revenge porn, but can also shield perpetrators as it has been used to prevent the disclosure of information contained in settlements and non-disclosure agreements.

Multiple government reviews and legislative attempts have suggested stronger and/or clearer protection of privacy rights, particularly regarding the actions of the press, but these have generally resulted in more regulatory requirements or stricter self-regulation and not in any freestanding privacy rights. These common law developments – while taking great strides forward – still do not provide full protection. The focus remains on privacy of information, and other forms of privacy, such as towards bodily autonomy, are still not adequately protected. These limitations raise the question of whether a freestanding tort of privacy should be created. There have been a number of arguments put forward about why this is unnecessary (or even harmful), but these are often unconvincing. The courts have repeatedly stated that it is the role of statute, and government bodies have said on multiple occasions that any development should occur through the common law – so it appears that English law is at a crossroads.

FURTHER READING

T. Aplin, 'The Development of the Action for Breach of Confidence in a Post-HRA Era' [2007] *IPQ* 19

T. Chen, '*PJS* and the Tort of MOPI' (2016) 11 *JIPLP* 892

D. Feldman, 'Secrecy, Dignity or Autonomy? Views of Privacy as a Civil Liberty' (1994) 47(2) *Current Legal Problems* 41

D. Kaspar, 'The Evolution (or Devolution) of Privacy' (2005) 20 *Sociological Forum* 72

B. Markesinis, 'The Right to be Left Alone versus Freedom of Speech' [1986] *PL* 67

J. Morgan, 'Privacy, Confidence and Horizontal Effect: "Hello" Trouble' (2003) 62(2) *CLJ* 444

N. Moreham, 'Unpacking the Reasonable Expectation of Privacy Test' (2018) 134 *LQR* 651

H. Nissenbaum, 'Privacy as Contextual Integrity' (2004) 79(1) *Washington Law Review* 101

G. Philipson, 'Transforming Breach of Confidence? Towards a Common Law Right of Privacy under the Human Rights Act' (2003) 66(5) *MLR* 726

J. Richardson, 'If I Cannot Have Her Everybody Can: Sexual Disclosure and Privacy Law' in Richardson and Rackley (eds), *Feminist Perspectives on Tort Law* (Routledge, 2012) 145

S. Warren and L. Brandeis 'The Right to Privacy' (1890) 4 *Harvard LR* 193

J. Whitman, 'The Two Western Cultures of Privacy: Dignity Versus Liberty' (2004) 113 *The Yale Law Journal* 1153

Roadmap: Privacy

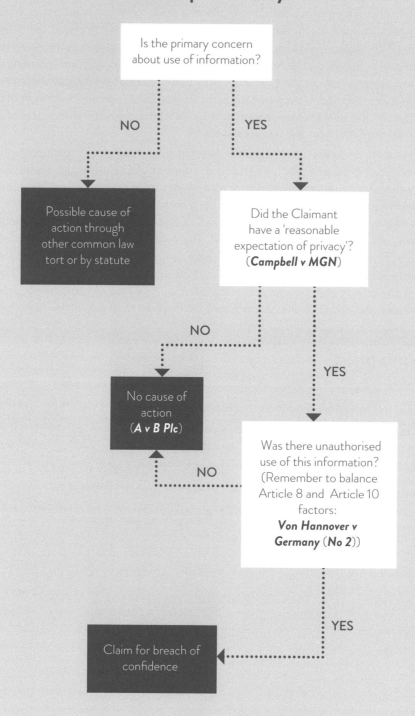

Is the primary concern about use of information?

NO → Possible cause of action through other common law tort or by statute

YES → Did the Claimant have a 'reasonable expectation of privacy'? (*Campbell v MGN*)

NO → No cause of action (*A v B Plc*)

YES → Was there unauthorised use of this information? (Remember to balance Article 8 and Article 10 factors: *Von Hannover v Germany (No 2)*)

NO → No cause of action (*A v B Plc*)

YES → Claim for breach of confidence

GENERAL MATTERS

PART 5

15. Vicarious Liability   374

16. Defences   391

17. Damages   421

The final Part covers a range of topics that apply generally to the torts considered in the previous chapters. Once a tort cause of action is successful, it must be determined who is liable for damages and how much they need to pay. The first chapter deals with vicarious liability, which is secondary liability – meaning the defendant will be liable for torts committed by another. The most common example of this is where the tortfeasor is an employee of the defendant, but there have been numerous developments increasing the scope beyond employees to cover those who are 'akin to an employee'. In contrast, non-delegable duties are associated with primary liability, but the breach is caused by a third party and therefore it is generally considered along with vicarious liability. Both vicarious liability and non-delegable duties raise the philosophical challenge of holding one party liable for wrongs committed by another party, and a range of justifications for this have been discussed in the case law and academic literature. The second chapter considers three defences to a tort claim: contributory negligence, *volenti non fit injuria* and illegality. Unlike the elements of a tort action, defences are pleaded by the defendant, who also has the burden of proof. The three defences have very different elements and rationales, with contributory negligence resulting in the apportionment of damages between the parties, whereas *volenti* and illegality are 'complete defences' – meaning the claimant receives no damages from the defendant. The final chapter addresses the complex world of tort law damages. Once a tort law claim is successful, provided it has not been defeated by a defence, the court must decide on an appropriate remedy. The main remedy is damages, which is the payment of money by the defendant which aims to put the claimant in the position she would have been in had the tort not been committed against her. Damages is a complicated area of law, with students needing to grapple with multiple different 'heads of damages' and complicated statutes. There is also a theoretical aspect to tort law damages, as this topic is closely linked with the different purposes of the law of torts.

15 VICARIOUS LIABILITY

LEARNING OBJECTIVES

By the end of this chapter, you should be able to:

- Understand the theoretical and practical justifications for vicarious liability
- Apply the correct tests for identifying where vicarious liability can be imposed
- Analyse the specific policy considerations behind vicarious liability and its recent developments
- Explain how the concept of a non-delegable duty fits with, and affects, the concept of vicarious liability
- Critically appraise the development of the law in this area

CHAPTER CONTENTS

15.1	Introduction	375
15.2	The development of the principle	375
15.3	Relationships of employment	376
	15.3.1 The relationship	377
	15.3.2 The connection	381
15.4	Non-delegable duties	385
15.5	Chapter summary	388
Further reading		389
Roadmap		390

PROBLEM QUESTION

Enzo regularly volunteers as a porter for Greasdale NHS Trust. One day, just as his shift is coming to an end, he takes 50 boxes of painkillers he has stolen from the hospital storeroom and hides them under thick blankets on the trolley he uses to move patients around the hospital. He then heads towards the back door into the car park, where he is due to meet his friend, Terry, and hand over the drugs in return for cash. As he is still in uniform, and the route is one he takes several times on a daily basis, he arouses no suspicion. On the way, he encounters Les, leaving one of the treatment rooms. Enzo and Les each support rival football teams and hate each other. Enzo's team lost to Les's team the previous weekend, and Les can't help but taunt Enzo about this defeat. Enzo, who is easily angered, rams the trolley into Les, smashing both of his kneecaps. Les is a keen recreational runner, but will, as a result of the injuries to his knees, never be able to participate in the sport again at any level.

Situated next to the hospital at which Enzo works is 'The Glades', the on-site nursery for children of hospital employees. Every Wednesday, the children are taken into the nearby woods by Forest Academy, a company set up by Danny to educate children how best to interact with nature. On excursions, there is always a maximum of three children for each adult supervisor. One week, during a foraging exercise, Niamh, who is 4 years old, picks some poisonous berries. Anna, the supervisor of Niamh's group, had been momentarily distracted by another child, Han, who had been stung by a wasp. Han is allergic to wasp stings, meaning that Anna had to administer an epi pen immediately. Niamh dies as a result of ingesting the poison, and her parents sue The Glades.

15.1 Introduction

This area of tort law deals with secondary liability. In other words, it deals with liability for torts committed by another.[1] In most situations, this will apply where the tortfeasor is the employee of the defendant, although the ambit of the doctrine has expanded in recent times to cover relationships which, whilst not technically contracts of employment, function in broadly analogous ways.[2] This idea of holding one party liable for wrongs committed by another calls for some justification,[3] and this occupies much of the literature in this area. Non-delegable duties are often discussed in the same space as vicarious liability, even though they are a species of primary, rather than secondary, liability. Since, however, a non-delegable duty is one that is breached by a third party, it makes sense to deal with it in this chapter. The interesting and often contentious policy issues connected to vicarious liability are often examined through essay questions, so it is a good idea to have a strong sense of the arguments that have been made, and what your view on them is. This species of liability is also one which arises often in problem questions, so it is advisable to have a sound understanding of the case law in this area, and to know how to apply it.

15.2 The development of the principle

Vicarious liability has, over the last couple of decades in particular, been characterised by progression and by expansion. In this sense, it reflects changes in both social mores and in the world of work. For example, the principles of vicarious liability have evolved to recognise that working patterns and relationships often look very different now to how they did 25 years ago, and to reflect a greater social willingness to address historic sexual abuse.

Despite these significant changes, there remains a core of requirements, as illustrated by the diagram below. It is the means of establishing the existence of these that has been subject to significant judicial development in recent times.

It goes without saying that, in order for any tortious liability to exist, a tort must have been committed by someone. The presence of a relationship which might give rise to vicarious liability, therefore, does not detract from the basic requirement of establishing the commission of a tort. Always remember, therefore, when answering problem questions, to address this issue in the first instance.

Once it is clear that a tort has occurred, the next question is whether there exists between the wrongdoer and the defendant a relationship capable of giving rise to vicarious liability. It is fair to say that the form and features of this relationship have been the subject of some of the most significant common law revisions of the last few years. Historically, the common law required the wrongdoer to be an employee of a defendant in order for the latter to be vicariously liable for his torts. The important distinction was one between contracts for services, under which the wrongdoer would be deemed an independent contractor, for whose torts the defendant would not be vicariously liable; and contracts of employment, under which the wrongdoer was classified as an employee, for whose torts his employer could be vicariously liable. The modern approach, developed over the course of this century, is to include quasi-employment relationships within the category in which vicarious

PART 5

---

1   The imposition of vicarious liability does not remove the liability of the wrongdoer, but gives the claimant the choice of suing either the primary wrongdoer or the vicariously liable defendant. A claimant cannot, however, recover twice for the same wrong.
2   It also covers, for instance, the liability of a firm for torts committed by its partners.
3   Although it is possible in principle (*Lister v Romford Cold Storage* [1957] AC 555) for an employer to seek to recover damages from the employee who committed the tort, this is not something that generally happens in practice, as insurers generally refrain from doing so.

liability can be imposed. These developments are partly a result of the changing nature of working relationships: the 'gig economy', the increase in remote and autonomous working facilitated by digitisation, and the widespread proliferation of highly skilled roles, all of which dilute the traditional 'control' exercised by employers over employees. The same developments are also partly a result of the courts' increasing willingness to compensate those harmed by individuals engaged in non-conventional working arrangements.

15.3 Relationships of employment

Even before the relatively recent disruptions to traditional working patterns, it was not always straightforward for courts to determine whether individuals were employees or independent contractors. One of the reasons for this is that, in terms of tax liability, it can be beneficial for workers not to be classified as employees. The parties might therefore give the impression that there is no formal employment relationship between them, despite the fact that, in reality, the substance of their relationship is one of employment. Two helpful cases that illustrate the way in which the courts will deal with this are *Ready Mixed Concrete v Minister of Pensions and National Insurance* [1968][4] and *Market Investigations v Minister of Social Security* [1969].[5] In the former case, the 'owner-drivers' were described in their contracts as independent contractors, they had to buy and maintain their own lorries, and they were paid fixed mileage rates. They were, however, required to wear company uniform, abide by company rules, and they were not allowed to use their vehicles for service outside of the company. They were deemed by McKenna J *not* to be employees on the ground that they bore their own risk of loss (and, correspondingly, also had the opportunity to make their own profit). Conversely, in the latter case, interviewers working part time in market research were held to be employees because, according to Cooke J, they lacked the autonomy over their working hours and arrangements to qualify as independent contractors. The extent to which those for whom they worked exercised control over their activities was, in the court's view, significant but not wholly determinative. This has to be correct: in my role as a Law Professor, I am undoubtedly an employee of the university, but it would not be true to say that my employer exercises a significant amount of control over my day-to-day activities (telling me what to write, what to tell students etc.).

In the following highly significant decision, the Supreme Court both expanded the category of relationships which can give rise to vicarious liability, and clearly set out the requirement to engage in a two-stage inquiry:

(1)   Does the requisite relationship exist on the facts?
(2)   Was the wrongdoer's action sufficiently closely connected to that relationship?

KEY CASE

Catholic Child Welfare Society v Various Claimants [2012] UKSC 56

The Institute of the Brothers of the Christian Schools (an unincorporated association of lay brothers of the Catholic Church) had supplied headteacher and teachers to a residential school managed by the claimant board. The board had already been held vicariously liable for alleged physical and sexual abuse carried out against pupils at the school, and it challenged in the Supreme Court the finding of the Court of Appeal that the Institute was not also vicariously liable.

The Supreme Court found that the imposition of vicarious liability called for a two-stage test.

---

4   [1968] 2 QB 497.
5   [1969] 2 QB 173.

First, it is necessary to consider the relationship between the defendant and the tortfeasor to see whether it was one that was capable of giving rise to vicarious liability. Once that has been established, there needs to be a connection between that relationship and the commission of the tortious act.

Stage 1: The relationship

Lord Phillips identified five factors that make it fair, just and reasonable to impose liability on an employer:

(1) The employer is more likely to have the means to compensate the victim than the employee and can be expected to have insured against that liability.
(2) The tort will have been committed as a result of activity being taken by the employee on behalf of the employer.
(3) The employee's activity is likely to be part of the business activity of the employer.
(4) The employer, by employing the employee to carry on the activity, will have created the risk of the tort committed by the employee.
(5) The employee will, to a greater or lesser degree, have been under the control of the employer.

Lord Phillips went on to explain that where the defendant and the tortfeasor are not bound by a contract of employment, but their relationship is characterised by the same five factors, that relationship can properly give rise to vicarious liability on the ground that it is 'akin to that between an employer and an employee'.

On the facts of *Catholic Child Welfare Society* (hereafter *CCWS*), the relationship between the teaching brothers and the Institute was deemed to be sufficiently analogous to that of employer and employees to satisfy the first stage of the test: the teaching activity of the brothers, and the manner of its conduct, was directed by the Institute, and it was undertaken by the brothers as an integral part of the objective, or mission, of the Institute.

Stage 2: The connection

The Supreme Court recognised that this is still a developing common law concept, but held that vicarious liability should be imposed where a defendant put the abuser in a particular position to further its own interests, and did so in a way which generated a significantly increased risk of the relevant abuse taking place. This amounted to a close connection and a strong causative link. Here, it was relevant that the standing that the brothers enjoyed as members of the Institute led the school managers to comply with the decisions of the Institute as to who should fill the positions of responsibility, and it was particularly significant that the Institute provided the headmasters of the school.

The common law has developed principles relating to both stages of the inquiry. It makes sense to analyse them in turn.

15.3.1 The relationship

Cox v Ministry of Justice [2016] and *Armes v Nottinghamshire CC* [2017] are highly significant for the way in which they have broken down the traditional boundary between those relationships which are capable of giving rise to vicarious liability, and those which are not. There is no doubt that both decisions represent a departure from the courts' traditional approach to establishing vicarious liability.

KEY CASE

Cox v Ministry of Justice [2016] UKSC 10

The Ministry of Justice appealed against a decision of the Court of Appeal that it was vicariously liable for injury caused by the negligence of a prisoner undertaking work in the prison kitchen.

The Ministry argued that the relationship between the Prison Service and prisoners was fundamentally different from an employment relationship because the primary function of the Service was prisoners' rehabilitation, rather than commercial profit, and that prisoners worked for their own development, rather than to further the Prison Service's objectives.

The Supreme Court found that the approach in *CCWS* extended the scope of vicarious liability beyond employment relationships. In order to be held vicariously liable, a defendant did not have to be acting in pursuit of profits; it was sufficient that it was acting in the furtherance of its own interests. Defendants could not, therefore, avoid liability by strict technical distinctions between employees and non-employees.

On the facts of this case, the *CCWS* criteria had been met and the Ministry was vicariously liable. The Prison Service carried on activities in furtherance of its aims, albeit that those aims were not commercial but instead served the public interest. Prisoners working in the kitchens were integral to the operation of the prison, and had been placed in positions, under the direction of prison employees, which gave rise to the risk that they could commit tortious acts. The prisoners' activities formed part of the operation of the prison and were of benefit to the Prison Service itself. The court recognised that the *CCWS* criteria were designed to ensure that vicarious liability was imposed where it was fair, just and reasonable to do so, regardless of whether a relationship of employment existed.

Cox v Ministry of Justice arguably took the *CCWS* analysis a step further away from traditional employment relationships. In *CCWS*, the Christian Brothers at least fulfilled a function (teaching in a school) which is often based on an employment relationship. In *Cox*, by contrast, the relationship at issue was not one which is ever really conceived of as one of employment. The fact that the objective of the Prison Service is the public good of rehabilitation, rather than commercial profit, was deemed not to be relevant to the inquiry. Instead, what was significant for the court was the fact that the prisoners' activities were integral to the running of the prison, and were, therefore, part of its overall function. Similar reasoning was employed to reach the result in the following case.

KEY CASE

Armes v Nottinghamshire CC [2017] UKSC 60

The appellant, who had been physically and sexually abused by her foster parents, claimed that the local authority should be vicariously liable for the actions of her foster parents. There was no argument in this appeal that the authority had been negligent in its selection of her foster parents. The Supreme Court held the local authority vicariously liable for the activities of those foster parents. The Court considered that the principles outlined in *Cox v Ministry of Justice* pointed towards the imposition of vicarious liability on the local authority for the torts committed by the foster parents. Specifically, this was because they committed the relevant torts in the course of an activity carried on for the benefit of the local authority, and because the local authority exercised a significant degree of control over how the foster parents carried out their responsibilities. The Court also considered it to be material that most foster parents would have insufficient means to be able to meet a substantial award of damages, and that local authorities would more likely be able to compensate the victims of abuse.

Armes restates that what is important is the extent to which the wrongdoer's role was integral to pursuing the defendant's purpose (whatever that purpose might be – educational, rehabilitative or commercial). This is combined with the need for the defendant to exert some form of control over the wrongdoer; a criterion that has long been part of judicial reasoning in this area. Whilst the lack of control does not, as we saw above, preclude the imposition of such liability, the exertion of control is good evidence that the wrongdoer's actions are integral to the defendant's pursuit of its purpose. *Armes* also contains express judicial consideration of distributive issues: the Supreme Court took the arguably modern approach of acknowledging the need for the victims of such wrongs to receive compensation, as well as recognising that they are unlikely to be able to get it from the perpetrators themselves. Given the fact that this reasoning produced a fairly open-textured inquiry, it was unlikely that it would be the end of the line of judicial developments on this point.

Sure enough, in *Barclays Bank Plc v Various Claimants* [2020], the Supreme Court revisited the issue.

KEY CASE

Barclays Bank Plc v Various Claimants [2020] UKSC 13

The defendant bank appealed against a finding of vicarious liability in relation to alleged sexual assaults perpetrated by a doctor who carried out medical examinations on its prospective employees over a number of years. The bank directed its candidates to the doctor, provided the form on which the results of the examinations were to be recorded, and paid a fee for each procedure carried out. There was no retainer paid and the examinations were carried out on the doctor's private premises. The bank's argument was simply that, despite the recent perceived expansion of vicarious liability in recent years, it remains the case that employers are not vicariously liable for wrongs committed by independent contractors. The claimants, by contrast, argued that the policy factors outlined by the Supreme Court in recent cases (*CCWS*, *Cox* and *Armes*) had generated a more nuanced approach to the question, which approximated more closely to an inquiry into whether it was fair, just and reasonable to impose vicarious liability on a given set of facts.

In allowing the defendant's appeal, the Supreme Court stated that the essential legal distinction for the purposes of vicarious liability remains one between those wrongdoers who are acting in the furtherance of their own business, and those whose actions are integral to another's business. The Court went on to clarify that it would only be necessary to consider the five policy considerations outlined in *CCWS* in borderline cases in which the distinction between an employee and an independent contractor was not clear. On the facts of this case, it was clear that the doctor had been acting in the furtherance of his own business, and was not in a relationship with the defendant bank that was either one of employment or one 'sufficiently akin'[6] to employment for vicarious liability to be imposed.

This judgment in *Barclays Bank Plc v Various Claimants* is to be welcomed for its clarification and simplification of the common law approach to vicarious liability. Whilst the changing nature of employment relationships in the modern age means that some flexibility to the employment test was called for,[7] it was perhaps inevitable that the Supreme Court would at some point have to make it clear just how far that expansion goes. *Barclays Bank* sets out in an accessible way just how important the independent contractor distinction remains, and emphasises that it is not undermined by the expansion of the 'akin to employment' category. It is crucial, therefore, that you read and analyse *CCWS*, *Cox* and *Armes* in the light of this most recent judgment.

---

6   *E v English Province of Our Lady of Charity* [2012] EWCA Civ 938.

7   Which was what happened in *CCWS, Cox and Armes*.

PROBLEM QUESTION TECHNIQUE

Enzo regularly volunteers as a porter for Greasdale NHS Trust.

▸ Consider whether Enzo, as a volunteer, would come within the quasi-employment category of relationship.

▸ Consider the principles outlined in *CCWS*, *Cox* and *Armes*, as analysed in *Barclays Bank*: was Enzo in pursuit of his own purposes, or engaged in furthering those of the hospital? Is this a borderline case, which requires an application of the five principles in *CCWS*?

▸ Remember that, even if the requisite relationship is found to exist, this is not sufficient for liability unless and until it has been established that there is a sufficiently close connection between the wrongful act and the relationship.

The following case – *Viasystems v Thermal Transfer Ltd* [2005] – *predates* the previous *Armes* and *Barclays Bank* cases but deals with a different element of the relationship inquiry. Until this case was decided, it appeared to be the case that vicarious liability for a wrongdoer's action could be imposed either on one defendant or on another. In situations in which a wrongdoer is 'lent' by one potential defendant to another, courts had always attempted to select just one of those defendants to carry liability, whilst absolving the other.[8] In *Viasystems v Thermal Transfer Ltd* [2005], the Court of Appeal departed from this approach.

KEY CASE

Viasystems Ltd v Thermal Transfer Ltd [2005] EWCA Civ 1151

Here, the Court of Appeal was faced with the question of whether dual vicarious liability could be imposed. The claimant's factory had been damaged by a flood negligently caused by a fitter's mate supplied by the third defendant, but working under the supervision of the second defendant (the first defendant had been engaged by the claimant to fit air-conditioning into its factory, and it sub-contracted the ducting work to the second defendant). At first instance, the third defendant had been held vicariously liable for the negligent actions of the fitter's mate, but the Court of Appeal held that, correctly formulated, the question to determine vicarious liability was who was entitled to exercise control over the relevant act of the tortfeasor. A focus on the transfer of a contract of employment was misleading and not directly material to the question. On the facts of this case, the fitter's mate's employment was not transferred. Any inquiry into vicarious liability should analyse the negligent action, and ask who was in a position to prevent it: who was obliged to give orders as to how the work should be carried out. There was no need to identify entire and absolute control. On the facts of this case, both the second defendant and the third defendant had been entitled, and were in a position, to prevent the mate's negligence. Furthermore, whilst it had been assumed since the early 19th century that vicarious liability for the tort of an employee lent by one employer to another had to rest on the shoulders of just one of those employers, the point had never been tested. The court was therefore entitled to find that dual vicarious liability was legally possible, and both the second and third defendants were vicariously liable in equal measures for the mate's negligence.

8   See, for example, *Mersey Docks and Harbour Board v Coggins and Griffith (Liverpool) Ltd* [1947] AC 1.

The reasoning in *Viasystems Ltd v Thermal Transfer Ltd* gave the concept of control a contemporary twist, and arguably brought it more into line with 21st-century thinking about working practices. It signifies a definite move away from using the formal contract of employment as a determinative factor, and instead looks at the practicalities of the various relationships. It therefore takes the factual, rather than the legal, characteristics of the situation as being the most significant for the purposes of imposing vicarious liability.

■ VIEWPOINT

Given that it is possible for primary liability to be joint, meaning that it can be imposed on several defendants at once,[9] do you think that it is right for the same to apply to vicarious liability? Does the Supreme Court's recent prioritisation of the need for claimants to have compensation from some source have any bearing on your thinking?

15.3.2 The connection

The first significant shift in terms of the connection inquiry occurred at the beginning of this century, when the House of Lords moved away from the traditional Salmond test[10] for establishing vicarious liability. This test had required:

(1)   a wrongful act authorised by the master; or
(2)   a wrongful and unauthorised mode of doing some act authorised by the master.

The problem with this test, as highlighted in *Lister v Helsey Hall Ltd* [2001], is that it will not cover some of the most serious wrongs committed by an employee, even if their commission could not have happened outside of the employment relationship. For instance, an employee of a computer repair company, who uses her position to take and misuse customer banking information, is clearly not doing an act authorised by her master. She only has easy access to that information, however, because of the role in which her employer has placed her. It is not clear, therefore, that employers should escape liability on this basis. Given the nature of the wrongs perpetrated in *Lister*, the point was even more acute.

KEY CASE

Lister v Hesley Hall Ltd [2001] UKHL 22

The claimant appealed against a decision of the Court of Appeal that the owner of a care home in which he had been a resident was not vicariously liable for the sexual abuse inflicted upon him by the warden of the home (the employee of the owner). The Court of Appeal had been bound by *T v North Yorkshire CC* [1999],[11] which held that sexual abuse could not be considered to be an unauthorised means of carrying out an authorised act. The House of Lords in *Lister* held that what was important in deciding whether to impose vicarious liability on an employer was the existence of a close connection between the employee's duties and the wrongful act. Since the warden had been entrusted with the welfare of the children in the home, it would be fair and just to impose vicarious liability on the owner for the intentional torts committed as a result.

9   See 17.9 (Contribution and apportionment).
10   Formulated by John William Salmond: R.F.V. Heuston and R.A. Buckley, *Salmond and Heuston on the Law of Torts* (Sweet & Maxwell, 1996), 443.
11   [1999] IRLR 98.

Lord Steyn in *Lister* referred in his judgment to the reasoning of McLachlin J in the Canadian case of *Bazley v Curry* [1999]:[12]

> The employer puts in the community an enterprise which carries with it certain risks. When those risks materialise and cause injury to a member of the public despite the employer's reasonable efforts, it is fair that the person or organisation that creates the enterprise and hence the risk should bear the loss.

This justification for the imposition of vicarious liability is often referred to as the enterprise liability argument, and it has had a continuing influence on English law developments of the close connection test.[13]

It was perhaps the apparent simplicity of the close connection test which led to the difficulties of interpretation in the most recent case on the point, *Mohamud v WM Morrison Supermarkets Plc* [2016], a decision which has not received universal academic approval.[14]

KEY CASE

Mohamud v WM Morrison Supermarkets Plc [2016] UKSC 11

The defendant supermarket employed K to deal with the day-to-day running of the petrol station and to serve its customers. The claimant was a customer who approached K with an enquiry, and was met first with verbal abuse by K, followed by a violent physical assault. The customer brought proceedings against the supermarket, claiming that it was vicariously liable for the assault. At both trial and in the Court of Appeal, there was found to be an insufficiently close connection between the role in which K was employed, and his actions in abusing the customer: whilst his job was a customer-facing position, there was nothing inevitable about that leading to the commission of an assault, or other abusive acts.

The Supreme Court allowed the customer's appeal. In doing so, it expressly approved of the close connection test, and attempted to simplify it by identifying two basic questions:

(a) what functions had been entrusted by the employer to the employee (which had to be addressed broadly); and

(b) whether there was sufficient connection between the employee's wrongful conduct and the position in which he was employed to make it right for the employer to be fixed with vicarious liability.

Previous cases in which a sufficiently close connection had been identified were those in which the employee had used or misused his position in order to commit the tort.[15] On the facts of the instant case, it was K's job to respond to customer inquiries. The manner in which he dealt with the claimant's request was inexcusable but remained within the remit of his role, even when he followed the claimant on to the forecourt. The fact that his verbal address to the claimant included an order to leave his employer's premises was not immaterial, since he was at least purporting to act in the furtherance of his employer's business.

Here, the defendant's liability was based on the fact that it had *entrusted* the wrongdoer with a position entailing a range of activities in which he was dealing directly with the general public. In the view of the Supreme Court, this generated a risk of K abusing that position. The fact therefore that,

---

12 [1999] 2 SCR 534 at [31].
13 See also Lord Nicholls in *Dubai Aluminium Co Ltd v Salaam* [2002] UKHL 48.
14 See Different Perspectives box, p. 402.
15 See, e.g., *Mattis v Pollock (t/a Flamingo's Nightclub)* [2003] EWCA Civ 887.

in committing the wrong, K had been motivated by personal inclination rather than the pursuit of his employer's business, did not make it any less fair or just to impose vicarious liability on the defendant.

The Court's approach in this case must, however, now be read in the light of the following analysis by the Supreme Court.

KEY CASE

WM Morrison Supermarkets Plc v Various Claimants [2020] UKSC 12

In this case, the defendant employer appealed against a finding that it was vicariously liable to its employees in respect of the disclosure of their personal information by a former employee, who had worked for the employer as an internal IT auditor. Whilst in that position, he took and copied the personal data of a large number of employees and uploaded it to a publicly accessible file-sharing website. As a result, he was convicted of various criminal offences. The employees whose data he had shared claimed damages from the employer for misuse of private information, breach of confidence, and breach of statutory duty under the Data Protection Act 1998, s 4(4).

In allowing the defendant's appeal, the Supreme Court closely analysed the reasoning of Lord Toulson in *Mohamud*. In particular, it paid close attention to his references to the connection between the employee's conduct and his employment, which the lower courts in this case appeared to have regarded as referring to an unbroken temporal or causal chain of events, and his Lordship's statement that the employee's motive was irrelevant. Were such an interpretation to be correct, *Mohamud* would have effected a major change in the law. In the view of the Supreme Court, this was not the consequence of *Mohamud*: the general principle, as set out in *Dubai Aluminium Co Ltd v Salaam* [2002][16] remained definitive: the wrongful conduct had to be so closely connected with acts the employee was authorised to do that, for the purposes of the liability of the employer to third parties, it might fairly and properly be regarded as done by the employee while acting in the ordinary course of his employment. In this way, Lord Toulson's comments that there was 'an unbroken sequence of events' and 'a seamless episode' did not refer to the temporal or causal connection between employment and action, but between the capacity in which the employee was acting and the events which took place. His statement that motive was irrelevant should not be read in isolation, and he was saying that the reason for the employee's actions in that case could not make a material difference.

On the facts of this particular case, the disclosure of employee data was not deemed to form part of the employee's functions or field of activities. The Supreme Court also reiterated that the five policy factors in *CCWS* were not relevant considerations here, since they were concerned with the distinct question of whether the relationship between the wrongdoer and the defendant was sufficiently akin to employment to engage vicarious liability. By contrast, the question in the instant case was whether there was a sufficient connection between that relationship and the wrongdoing. Finally, although there was a close temporal link and an unbroken chain of causation between the employee being given the data and his disclosing it on the internet, this did not in itself satisfy the close connection test: rather, that test required a consideration of whether the substance and nature of the employee's position was connected with the wrong he committed. In answering this question, the employee's motive was not irrelevant: whether he was acting on his employer's business or for purely personal reasons was highly material. When he disclosed the data, the employee in question was pursuing a personal vendetta and not acting in the furtherance of his employer's business. As such, it was not so closely connected with acts which he was authorised to do that it could fairly and properly be regarded as done by him while acting in the ordinary course of his employment.

---

16 [2002] UKHL 48.

WM Morrison Supermarkets Plc v Various Claimants (hereafter *WM Morrison*) achieves two principal things. First (and this is perhaps unsurprising, given that it was considered by an identically constituted Supreme Court alongside *Barclays Bank* above), it emphasises the *crucial* distinction that must be made between the questions outlined earlier in this chapter: the requisite relationship between the wrongdoer and the defendant, and the separate question of whether, given that relationship, the action of the wrongdoer had a sufficiently close connection to his employment (or quasi-employment). Secondly, it arguably restricts the expansion of the scope of vicarious liability that *Mohamud* was seen by many to represent. Given that the decision in *WM Morrison* is very recent, and presents a significant interpretation of another Supreme Court judgment, it is essential to understand its implications, and to form a view about these. It is also important, of course, to know how to apply it in a problem question. In recent years, assessment questions on this topic have tended to focus on the perceived expansion of vicarious liability over the last decade or so. It is therefore a good idea to think carefully about what effect these two 2020 cases have on that trend.

■ VIEWPOINT

Do you think *Mohamud* expanded the close connection test too far? *CCWS* and *Lister* can perhaps be justified on the basis that teachers are employed with an express objective to safeguard pupils' welfare, but to what extent can this be said to apply to retail employees with customer-facing roles? Do you find the Supreme Court's analysis of *Mohamud* in *WM Morrison* to be convincing, and do you think the approach taken in the latter case is to be preferred?

PROBLEM QUESTION TECHNIQUE

One day, just as his shift is coming to an end, [Enzo] takes 50 boxes of painkillers he has stolen from the hospital storeroom and hides them under thick blankets on the trolley he uses to move patients around the hospital. He then heads towards the back door into the car park, where he is due to meet his friend, Terry, and hand over the drugs in return for cash. As he is still in uniform, and the route is one he takes several times on a daily basis, he arouses no suspicion. On the way, he encounters Les, leaving one of the treatment rooms. Enzo and Les each support rival football teams and hate each other. Enzo's team lost to Les's team the previous weekend, and Les can't help but taunt Enzo about this defeat. Enzo, who is easily angered, rams the trolley into Les, smashing both of his kneecaps. Les is a keen recreational runner, but will, as a result of the injuries to his knees, never be able to participate in the sport again at any level.

▸ This is the stage at which you need to assess the closeness of the connection between the wrong and the relationship.

▸ Consider the principles outlined in *Lister*, *CCWS* and *Mohamud*; ensure that you do so in the light of the reasoning and interpretation of those cases in *WM Morrison*.

▸ Think about the position that Enzo was placed in by the hospital – a role which gave him access to highly marketable drugs and allowed him easily to remove them from the hospital.

▸ It is also necessary to divide Enzo's two wrongs up and consider them separately: is the connection between his relationship with the hospital and the wrongdoing as close in the case of his assault of Les as it is to his drug dealing? It may be that, applying the relevant case law, you come to different conclusions on the hospital's liability in relation to each wrong.

▸ Is there, for instance, an analogy to be made between Enzo's role and K's role in *Mohamud*? Or is there scope to distinguish this from *Mohamud* in terms of what Enzo was employed to do, given the Supreme Court reasoning in *WM Morrison* in relation to the connection between what he was employed to do and his wrongdoing (including his motivation for the wrong)?

15.4 Non-delegable duties

The concept of a non-delegable duty is independent from that of vicarious liability. This is because it is a form of primary, rather than secondary, liability. This means that, when a non-delegable duty has been breached, it is the defendant itself who has committed the wrong. This does not mean that the defendant has performed the action, but that the action is a wrong which is attributed to the defendant (because the responsibility for it cannot be delegated to anyone else). This is different to vicarious liability, in which the wrong is *not* attributed to the defendant: under vicarious (secondary) liability, the defendant is required to compensate the victim for the effects of someone else's wrong.

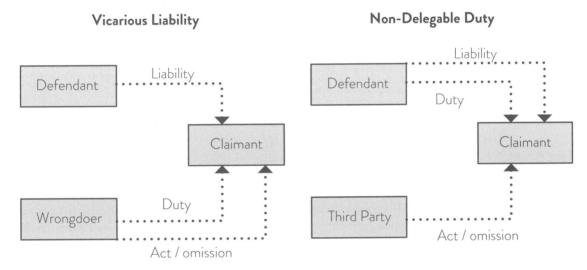

Figure 15.1: Vicarious liability vs non-delegable duties

Since, however, the breach of a non-delegable duty results from the actions of a third party, it makes sense to discuss it here. It is also often litigated alongside vicarious liability. As we have seen, a defendant will not be vicariously liable for the actions of an independent contractor, but might, depending on the facts of the case, be found to be in breach of a non-delegable duty as a result of the actions of an independent contractor. This is what happened in *Woodland v Essex CC* [2013] – a highly significant case.

KEY CASE

Woodland v Essex CC [2013] UKSC 66

In this case, the Supreme Court set out the criteria which would give rise to the existence of a non-delegable duty of care. The claimant had suffered brain injuries during a swimming lesson which, whilst being part of her school curriculum, was taught by an instructor and supervised by a lifeguard, both of whom had been provided to the local authority by an independent contractor. The Court of Appeal had found that the local authority did not owe the claimant a non-delegable duty of care, but the Supreme Court disagreed and held the local authority liable for her injuries.

The criteria identified by the Supreme Court as being necessary for the existence of a non-delegable duty of care were as follows:

- The claimant is for some other reason especially vulnerable, or is dependent on the defendant for protection from injury.
- There was between the claimant and the defendant a pre-existing relationship which was independent of the negligent act, and which imposed on the defendant a positive duty to protect the claimant from harm (rather than being merely a duty to refrain from harming the claimant). Such relationships will be characterised by some degree of control over the claimant, which will be particularly acute in the case of the relationship between schools and their pupils.
- The claimant has no control over how the defendant performs the relevant obligations.

- The defendant has delegated to a third party some function which was an integral part of the positive duty which it owed to the claimant; and that third party was exercising the defendant's care and control over the claimant.
- The third party had been negligent in the very performance of the function assumed by the defendant and delegated by the defendant to it.

The Supreme Court found that these criteria had been satisfied in the present case: the local authority had assumed a duty to ensure that W would be safe during her swimming lessons, and that they would be carefully conducted. The alleged negligence occurred in the course of the very functions in relation to which the school had a duty, and which it had delegated to those it contracted to teach and to supervise.

Like recent developments in vicarious liability, this decision represents a broader interpretation of the concept of non-delegable duties than was previously the case. It arguably fills a gap that would otherwise be created by the relationship required for vicariously liability to be imposed: had the swimming lessons in *Woodland* been provided by an employee, the local authority would have been vicariously liable. Were a non-delegable duty not to be identified in such cases, defendants could *delegate* their responsibility by outsourcing risky activities to independent contractors. This would have seriously adverse consequences for those harmed during those activities, who are the very people defendants in such situations are supposed to protect.

PROBLEM QUESTION TECHNIQUE

Situated next to the hospital at which Enzo works is 'The Glades', the on-site nursery for children of hospital employees. Every Wednesday, the children are taken into the nearby woods by Forest Academy, a company set up by Danny to educate children how best to interact with nature. On excursions, there is always a maximum of three children for each adult supervisor. One week, during a foraging exercise, Niamh, who is 4 years old, picks some poisonous berries. Anna, the supervisor of Niamh's group, had been momentarily distracted by another child, Han, who had been stung by a wasp. Han is allergic to wasp stings, meaning that Anna had to administer an epi pen immediately. Niamh dies as a result of ingesting the poison, and her parents sue The Glades.

▸ This is a question of non-delegable duties, and so requires an application of *Woodland*.

▸ You need to step through each of the principles outlined by the Supreme Court in that case.

▸ Take care to consider on these facts the question of whether the third party, Forest Academy, has been negligent in its carrying out of the function assigned to it by The Glades.

DIFFERENT PERSPECTIVES on vicarious liability[17]

J. Plunkett, 'Taking Stock of Vicarious Liability' (2016) 132 LQR 556–62

In this article, Plunkett is generally critical of the approach taken in the Supreme Court in both *Cox* and *Mohamud*, particularly in terms of enterprise liability. In his view, the Court ignored the limitations inherent in the enterprise liability justification of vicarious liability, and failed therefore to explain why vicarious liability should apply on the facts of these cases, but not to independent contractors. Plunkett also points out that enterprise liability offers very limited guidance on when a tort can be sufficiently connected to the relationship between wrongdoer and defendant; it requires there to be some connection, but does not have much to say about the closeness of that connection. Plunkett then discusses the idea of the relationship giving rise to the risk of the wrong which ultimately occurs. This risk, he argues, should be normatively, rather than merely causally, linked to the relationship between defendant and wrongdoer. In other words, it should be a risk which is inherent in, incidental to, or associated with, that relationship, rather than the relationship simply providing the opportunity for that risk to arise.

A.J. Bell, 'Vicarious Liability: Quasi-employment and Loose Connection' (2016) 32(2) PN 153–7

In this piece, Bell is less critical than Plunkett of the Supreme Court's approach in the companion cases of *Cox* and *Mohamud*. He sees its analysis of the requisite relationship between defendant and wrongdoer as being 'flexible and principled', and one which moves away from reasoning which has historically been based on the narrow semantics of what employment is. In his view, this is a necessary and welcome development, since it reflects a marked change in society's business relationships, since these no longer fit the rigid categories that once defined employment. In this sense, he regards the Court's approach as being pragmatic, and the better for it. In terms of the second stage of the *CCWS* inquiry, Bell approves of the Supreme Court's reluctance to be moved from the traditional closeness of connection test, although questions the way in which the criterion of continuity was applied to the facts of *Mohamud* in particular. This, he argues, leaves uncertainty around the application of the continuity requirement for establishing closeness of connection.

P. Giliker, 'Analysing Institutional Liability for Child Sexual Abuse in England and Wales and Australia: Vicarious Liability, Non-delegable Duties and Statutory Intervention' (2018) 77(3) Cambridge Law Journal 506–35

In this article, Giliker contends that English law has developed vicarious liability too far, and that a more cautious, incremental approach is to be preferred. She refers specifically to the developments in *Mohamud* and *Cox* (above). Her analysis is a comparative one, and she considers the corresponding development of Australian law on the point. Whilst both, in her view, require reform, the current Australian treatment of vicarious liability is better than the English approach because it is more restrictive and has been slower to expand. Principally, the difference can be seen in the relationships regarded by each jurisdiction as being capable of giving rise to vicarious liability: Australia has adhered to employment status as a requirement for the imposition of vicarious liability, whilst English law has removed the 'bright line' that once existed in this context between employees and independent contractors. Whilst Giliker does not argue that vicarious liability should be confined to employment

---

17 Given that both *Barclays Bank and WM Morrison* were handed down only just before the manuscript for this book needed to be submitted, no commentary on them was at that time available to include in the Different Perspectives section. Once such analyses have been published, they will be available on the companion website. Please bear in mind in the meantime that the views presented here were expressed and published in relation to the cases decided pre-2020.

relationships, she makes the case for developing the law in this whole area in a more controlled and incremental way than is currently happening.

A.J. Bell, 'Double, Double Toil and Trouble': Recent Movements in Vicarious Liability' (2018) 4 JPI Law 235–47

Whilst Bell is also critical of the overall expansion in the remit of vicarious liability demonstrated in the recent cases of *Cox*, *Armes*, *CCWS* and *Mohamud*, he makes the specific point that the willingness of the courts to depart from a formalistic view of employment is a good thing, given that it better reflects modern working practices. Bell goes on to emphasise that it is this relationship, rather than compensatory policy, that should drive the formulation of the law in this area, suggesting that some recent common law developments have given rise to the notion that vicarious liability functions to fill a gap where primary liability had failed to compensate a claimant (because the tortfeasor is untraceable, insolvent or dead). In discussing the justification for vicarious liability as a doctrine, Bell makes the important point that it does not necessarily equate to the imposition of liability on an innocent party, and that the concept is more complicated than that. Employers and those entrusting activities integral to their enterprise to others have a corresponding responsibility to reduce the risk of harm generated by their enterprise, and this idea underpins the idea of vicarious liability. Defendants in this context are not, therefore, necessarily blameless, even though the particular tort in question was not committed by them.

■ VIEWPOINT

Do you think the law is right to impose liability on one entity for wrongs committed by another? Can this be justified, given the emphasis placed by so much of the law of tort on principles of corrective justice?

15.5 CHAPTER SUMMARY

This chapter has examined crucial recent common law developments in vicarious liability. Specifically, it has examined the ways in which the parameters of this type of liability have expanded in very recent times, and what the social, economic and policy reasons underlying this expansion might be. Specifically, we have seen how the imposition of vicarious liability now involves a two-stage inquiry, looking first at the nature of the relationship between the wrongdoer and the defendant, and then the closeness of the connection between that relationship and the wrong itself. Whilst the close connection test has been confirmed as the appropriate means of analysing these situations, it has itself arguably undergone an expansion of its own in the contentious case of *Mohamud*. This chapter has also set out recent judicial developments of the concept of the non-delegable duty, and how these fit with the corresponding common law movements in vicarious liability. Policy discussion has focused on the extent to which the imposition of liability on one party for actions committed by another can be justified, and whether the recent evolution of the common law in this context has been positive and constructive.

FURTHER READING

C. Beuermann, 'Disassociating the Two Forms of So-Called "Vicarious Liability"' in S. Pitel, J. Neyers and E. Chamberlain (eds), *Tort Law: Challenging Orthodoxy* (Hart, 2013)

P. Giliker, *Vicarious Liability in Tort: a Comparative Perspective* (CUP, 2010)

P. Giliker, 'Vicarious Liability, Non-delegable Duties and Teachers: Can you Outsource Liability for Lessons?' (2015) 31 *PN* 259

Lord Hope, 'Tailoring the Law on Vicarious Liability' (2013) *LQR* 514

R. Kidner, 'Vicarious liability: For Whom should the "Employer" be Liable? (1995) 15 *LS* 47

E. McKendrick, 'Vicarious Liability and Independent Contractors – a Re-examination' (1990) 53 *MLR* 770

R. Stevens, 'Vicarious Liability or Vicarious Action?' (2007) 123 *LQR* 522

R. Stevens, 'Non-delegable Duties and Vicarious Liability' in J. Neyers et al (eds), Emerging Issues in Tort Law (Hart, 2007), 331

G. Williams, 'Liability for Independent Contractors' [1956] CLJ 180

Roadmap: Vicarious Liability

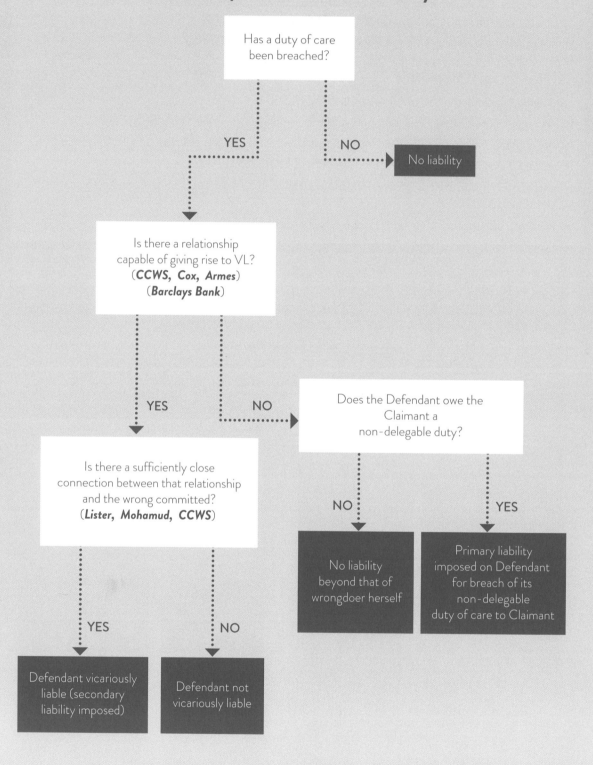

16 DEFENCES

LEARNING OBJECTIVES

By the end of this chapter, you should be able to:

- Describe how defences differ from elements of tort causes of action
- Explain the impact that the Law Reform (Contributory Negligence) Act 1945 has had on the previous common law approach to the doctrine
- Establish what constitutes contributory negligence and apply the relevant elements of the defence
- Understand the philosophical basis of *volenti non fit injuria* (*volenti*) and the role that consent plays in the defence
- Establish what constitutes *volenti* and apply the relevant elements of the defence
- Engage with the policy arguments and challenges that arise from the application of the *volenti* defence
- Understand the rationales behind the defence of illegality and the different debates on its suitability as a defence in tort law
- Identify the relevant factors that a court will consider when determining whether the defence of illegality will apply to a tort action, and be able to apply the factors to a scenario
- Engage with the policy arguments and challenges that arise from the application of the illegality defence

CHAPTER CONTENTS

16.1	Introduction	392
16.2	What is a defence?	393
16.3	Contributory negligence	394
	16.3.1 Historical approach to contributory negligence	394
	16.3.2 Elements of contributory negligence	397
	16.3.3 Contributory negligence: concluding remarks	401
16.4	*Volenti non fit injuria*	402
	16.4.1 *Volenti* and consent	403
	16.4.2 Elements of *volenti*	403
	16.4.3 *Volenti*: concluding remarks	408
16.5	Illegality	409
	16.5.1 Rationale of illegality	409
	16.5.2 Elements of illegality	410
	16.5.3 Illegality: concluding remarks	418
16.6	Chapter summary	418
Further reading		419
Roadmap		420

PROBLEM QUESTION

Anja is a having a very difficult day. She is the oldest of four siblings and has always been the responsible one. She is also a law student, and family members often come to her for advice on their problems. Anja's brother Bruno has just called her from hospital after being involved in a serious car accident. He was riding his bike along High Street and was hit by a drunk driver, who was also speeding and not paying attention to the road. Bruno was riding his bike responsibly but was not wearing a helmet. This was because he had just spent £85 on an expensive haircut, and he did not want to 'ruin the look' before going on a big date that night. He has suffered significant head injuries, which would have been completely avoided had he been wearing a helmet.

Anja's sister Darya is currently working at Carpenters-R-Us, the local joinery. Carpenters-R-Us has specific rules and regulations in place for the safety of the employees, including that two employees are needed to lift any items over 25kg. Failure to abide by these rules results in disciplinary action. Carpenters-R-Us pays the employees relatively high wages because of the dangerous nature of the work; however, it reduces employees' pay if they do not complete the required number of furniture pieces per day. Last week, Darya injured herself lifting a 26kg piece of furniture and is now unable to work for at least six weeks. Carpenters-R-Us is refusing to pay compensation and has threatened Darya with termination for breaching the health and safety rules. On the day that Darya injured herself, there was no other employee available to assist her, and the workshop scales were broken.

Anja's niece Eliska is 17 years old. She is trying to save money for a trip to Australia. She lied about her age and used a fake ID to get a job working in a bar, as that paid her more than her current work filling supermarket shelves. During her employment, the owner of the bar subjects Eliska to sustained sexual harassment and then fires her when she will not return his advances. When Eliska threatens the employer with a claim for sexual harassment and unlawful dismissal, he states that it 'was all her own fault for lying about her age'.

How should Anja advise her family? Assume in each case that the relevant tort cause of action has been established, and focus only on the applicability of any relevant defences.

16.1 Introduction

Once the tortious cause of action has been established, the defendant is entitled to raise any potential defences. Unlike the elements of a tort action, defences need to be pleaded by the defendant – therefore the onus of proof is on the defendant and not the claimant. This chapter covers defences that can be applied generally to tort law causes of actions.[1] In addition to the three defences covered by this chapter, a number of other defences applicable to specific torts have already been covered in previous chapters and will not be repeated here. For these torts, you should always focus on applying the more specific defence if it is available, as that is more relevant to the cause of action than the general defences considered in this chapter. The torts already considered include:

- nuisance – prescription, acts of a stranger and statutory authority;[2]

- trespass to the person – consent, necessity, self-defence and lawful authority; and[3]

- defamation – truth, honest opinion, public interest, operation of websites, privilege and consent.[4]

It is important to recognise that there are significantly more tort law defences than can be covered by a tort law textbook. Goudkamp discusses a total of 38 different defences in his book *Tort Law Defences* – ranging from mistake, self-defence, Foreign State immunity, public necessity and *res judicata* to death and bankruptcy.[5] One particularly important defence to be aware of, but which cannot be covered in this chapter, is the Limitation Act 1980. This Act provides strict time limits on when claimants must commence their actions. If these time limits are not met, the court will refuse to hear the case (subject to certain specific discretionary extensions).[6] This chapter will concentrate

---

1   Apart from contributory negligence, which is excluded from torts of intention. See discussion in Chapter 12.
2   See 10.4.
3   See 12.6.
4   See 13.5.
5   See specifically 'Table 3: Application of the Taxonomy': J. Goudkamp, *Tort Law Defences* (Hart Publishing, 2013), 135.
6   See 17.7.

on the three that are almost universally included in tort law syllabuses in the United Kingdom, namely contributory negligence, *volenti non fit injuria* (*volenti*) and illegality.

Contributory neglifgence is the most common and most successful defence, allowing the court to reduce the damages paid to the claimant on the basis that their actions contributed to the harm suffered. Under common law, the defence worked as a complete bar to a claim, although the Law Reform (Contributory Negligence) Act 1945 has changed the approach and created a system of apportionment between the claimant and the defendant. In contrast, *volenti* and illegality work as complete defences – barring the claimant from a successful tort law claim.

Volenti is based on the consent of the claimant and requires the defendant to show that the claimant voluntarily agreed to take the risk, knowing the full nature and extent of the risk involved. Unlike contributory negligence, *volenti* is a complete defence and results in the claimant receiving no damages from the defendant. Whilst the defence is still a valid part of tort law, it rarely succeeds in modern day tort law cases. *Volenti* also raises important philosophical questions about the ability of people to consent to negligence, particularly in cases of physical injury.

Finally, the illegality defence is founded on public policy and prevents a claimant from basing a cause of action on their own illegal act. Like *volenti*, illegality works as a complete defence to a tort claim. There has been a significant amount of case law on the defence; the approach to, and rationale of, illegality is still highly debated. The most recent Supreme Court case has confirmed a discretionary 'range of factors' approach to the defence; however, the exact application of this test will have to be determined by future case law.

The first issue that will be considered in this chapter is what constitutes a defence, followed by the background of, basis for, and elements of the three key defences.

16.2 What is a defence?

The first issue that must be determined is what is a 'defence'. Whilst this can mistakenly appear straightforward, it is actually quite a complex concept. As outlined by Goudkamp:

> The word 'defence' bears numerous meanings in the tort law context, and a considerable amount of confusion has been spawned by the widespread failure of legal scholars, judges and legislators to indicate what they mean by the word. This situation is a significant impediment to clear thinking in relation to tort law.[7]

There are many different ways that a defendant can respond to a claim against them:

- denying an element of the tort in question (e.g. no duty of care is owed to the claimant);
- pleading a liability-defeating rule external to the elements of the tort in question (e.g. *volenti non fit injuria*);
- pleading a principle that diminishes the claimant's relief (i.e. illegality); and
- invoking a rule that the defendant must plead and prove in order to reduce damages or remove liability (i.e. contributory negligence).

There is an ongoing debate about which of these can be described as 'true' defences, with Goudkamp arguing that they should be limited to 'liability-defeating rules that are external

---

7 J. Goudkamp, *Tort Law Defences* (Hart Publishing 2013), 135.

to the elements of the claimant's action'.[8] There are, for example, strong arguments that contributory negligence is not a defence, but actually a rule on what remedy the claimant is able to receive.[9] These debates, however interesting, are beyond the scope of the current chapter. For ease and simplicity, this chapter will proceed on the widely accepted view that contributory negligence is a defence, and refer to all three doctrines (contributory negligence, *volenti* and illegality) as defences.

16.3 Contributory negligence

Contributory negligence is a defence that works not by the defendant justifying or denying their negligent behaviour, but by contending that the claimant has also been negligent – and that this justifies a reduction in the amount of damages to be paid. There are three elements to contributory negligence:

(1) Was the claimant contributorily negligent?
(2) Did the contributory negligence contribute to the damage suffered?
(3) By how much should the damages be reduced as a consequence of the claimant's actions?

Contributory negligence is frequently raised in litigation, with Steele commenting that 'in cases of tort liability involving personal injury, the … defence is used on a daily basis. It is applied regularly by courts, but is used much more frequently by parties (including of course insurers) negotiating settlements.'[10] Despite this practical importance, there had until recently been very little empirical research into the role of contributory negligence in a practical sense.[11]

16.3.1 Historical approach to contributory negligence

Historically, contributory negligence worked on an 'all or nothing approach'. This meant that if the defendant could show that the claimant had also been negligent and this contributed to the damage, the claimant would be barred from suing. This was clearly shown in the case of *Butterfield v Forrester* [1809], where the careless actions of the claimant prevented a successful cause of action against a negligent defendant.

---

8   J. Goudkamp, *Tort Law Defences* (Hart Publishing 2013), 2–7. See also A. Dyson, J. Goudkamp and F. Wilmot-Smith, Defences in Tort (Hart Publishing, 2015); J. Goudkamp, 'Rethinking Contributory Negligence' in S. Pitel, J. Neyers and E. Chamberlain (eds), *Tort Law: Challenging Orthodoxy* (Hart Publishing, 2013), 337; D.G. Owen, 'The Five Elements of Negligence' (2007) 35 *Hofstra Law Review* 1671.

9   J. Goudkamp, 'Rethinking Contributory Negligence' in S. Pitel, J. Neyers and E. Chamberlain (eds), *Tort Law: Challenging Orthodoxy* (Hart Publishing, 2013), 337; N. McBridge and R. Bagshaw, *Tort Law*, 4th edn (Pearson Education, 2012), 743; A. Dyson, J. Goudkamp and F. Wilmot-Smith, 'Introduction' in Dyson, Goudkamp and Wilmot-Smith (eds), *Defences in Tort* (Hart Publishing, 2015), 10.

10   J. Steele, 'Law Reform (Contributory Negligence) Act 1945: Collisions of a Different Sort' in T. Arvind and J. Steele (eds), *Tort Law and the Legislature: Common Law, Statute and the Dynamics of Legal Change* (Hart Publishing, 2013), 165. See also P. Cane and J. Goudkamp, *Atiyah's Accidents, Compensation and the Law*, 9th edn (Cambridge University Press, 2018), 255.

11   J. Goudkamp and D. Nolan, *Contributory Negligence: Principles and Practice* (Oxford University Press, 2018), 2. See also J. Goudkamp and D. Nolan, *Contributory Negligence in the Twenty-First Century* (Oxford University Press, 2019).

KEY CASE

Butterfield v Forrester (1809) 103 ER 926

The claimant was riding along a road at approximately 8pm in the evening when there was limited light after leaving a 'public house'. The defendant had been making some repairs to his house and had put a pole across part of the road. The claimant rode into the pole and was injured. The judge directed the jury to consider whether a person who had been riding with reasonable and ordinary care would have seen and avoided the obstruction. He commented that if the jury was satisfied that the claimant had been riding without ordinary care, they should find for the defendant.[12] The jury did find for the defendant and dismissed the claim.

The claimant sought a new trial against this decision, but it was denied. Lord Ellenborough CJ held that:

> A party is not to cast himself upon an obstruction which has been made by the fault of another, and avail himself of it, if he do not himself use common and ordinary caution to be in the right. In cases of persons riding upon what is considered to be the wrong side of the road, that would not authorise another purposely to ride up against them. One person being in fault will not dispense with another's using ordinary care for himself. Two things must concur to support this action, an obstruction in the road by the fault of the defendant, and no want of ordinary care to avoid it on the part of the plaintiff.[13]

This case highlighted that under the old common law approach, there was a requirement for the claimant to show both that there was a cause of action in negligence and that they did not themselves contribute to the harm suffered.

■ VIEWPOINT

Why do you think that contributory negligence originally resulted in a complete defence to a cause of action in negligence? Do you agree with this principle?

The potential unfairness of this approach led to the development of the common law 'rule of last opportunity'. If both parties were negligent *but* the defendant had the last chance to avoid the accident completely, the claimant would have a successful claim and would be able to recover in full. For example, in *Davies v Mann* [1842],[14] it was held that the claimant's negligent actions of hobbling his donkey and leaving it on a highway did not prevent him from recovering damages when it was injured by the defendant driving horses without due care. The court held that the negligence was not relevant at the time of the accident, and therefore was not part of the cause of the mischief. The defendant had the 'last opportunity' to avoid the accident and the claimant was entitled to recover damages.

This was clearly an unsatisfactory state of affairs. It allowed defendants to get away with their negligent actions as long as they showed that the action of the claimant in some way contributed to the harm. The 'all or nothing approach' also allowed claimants to avoid having damages reduced because of contributory negligence, provided they could show that the defendant had the last chance to avoid the accident completely.

---

12   (1809) 103 ER 926, 926–7.
13   (1809) 103 ER 926, 927.
14   (1842) 10 M & W 546.

As a result of the growing discontent with the state of the common law, the Law Revision Committee was given the task of considering 'whether, and if so, in what respect the doctrine of Contributory Negligence requires modification'.[15] After reviewing the relevant case law, the Committee recommended 'that in cases where damage has been caused by the fault of two or more persons the tribunal trying the case (whether that tribunal be a judge or jury) shall apportion the liability in the degree in which each party is found to be in fault'.[16] This resulted in the enactment of the Law Reform (Contributory Negligence) Act 1945 Act (the '1945 Act').

KEY LEGISLATION

Law Reform (Contributory Negligence) Act 1945

1   Apportionment of liability in case of contributory negligence

(1)   Where any person suffers damage as the result partly of his own fault and partly of the fault of any other person or persons, a claim in respect of that damage shall not be defeated by reason of the fault of the person suffering the damage, but the damages recoverable in respect thereof shall be reduced to such extent as the court thinks just and equitable having regard to the claimant's share in the responsibility for the damage:

Provided that—

    (a) this subsection shall not operate to defeat any defence arising under a contract;

    (b) where any contract or enactment providing for the limitation of liability is applicable to the claim, the amount of damages recoverable by the claimant by virtue of this subsection shall not exceed the maximum limit so applicable.

(2)   Where damages are recoverable by any person by virtue of the foregoing subsection subject to such reduction as is therein mentioned, the court shall find and record the total damages which would have been recoverable if the claimant had not been at fault.

...

(5)   Where, in any case to which subsection (1) of this section applies, one of the persons at fault avoids liability to any other such person or his personal representative by pleading the Limitation Act 1939, or any other enactment limiting the time within which proceedings may be taken, he shall not be entitled to recover any damages ... from that other person or representative by virtue of the said subsection.

(6)   Where any case to which subsection (1) of this section applies is tried with a jury, the jury shall determine the total damages which would have been recoverable if the claimant had not been at fault and the extent to which those damages are to be reduced ...

4   Interpretation

The following expressions have the meanings hereby respectively assigned to them, that is to say—

'court' means, in relation to any claim, the court or arbitrator by or before whom the claim falls to be determined;

'damage' includes loss of life and personal injury;

...

15   Law Revision Committee, *Eighth Report (Contributory Negligence)* (Cmd 6032), 3.
16   Law Revision Committee, *Eighth Report (Contributory Negligence)* (Cmd 6032), 19. For an analysis of the Committee's recommendation, including some of the difficulties, see J. Steele, 'Law Reform (Contributory Negligence) Act 1945: Collisions of a Different Sort' in T. Arvind and J. Steele (eds), *Tort Law and the Legislature: Common Law, Statute and the Dynamics of Legal Change* (Hart Publishing, 2013), 167–76.

> 'fault' means negligence, breach of statutory duty or other act or omission which gives rise to a liability in tort or would, apart from this Act, give rise to the defence of contributory negligence.

The 1945 Act removes the common law's 'all or nothing' approach, and instead allows the court to reduce the damages recoverable 'to such extent as the court thinks just and equitable having regard to the claimant's share in the responsibility for the damage'.

Contributory negligence under the 1945 Act does not apply to intentional torts. The impact of the 1945 Act and some of the difficulties have already been briefly discussed in terms of trespass to the person in Chapter 11. The Act is based on the parties' 'fault' which is defined as 'negligence, breach of statutory duty or other act or omission which gives rise to a liability in tort or would, apart from this Act, give rise to the defence of contributory negligence'.[17] Contributory negligence is therefore defined under the Act as the test for contributory negligence that existed at common law prior to 1945. The impact of the Act was to change the outcome of a finding of contributory negligence (from a complete defence to apportionment), and not the test for what constitutes contributory negligence.[18] Prior to 1945, contributory negligence did not apply to intentional torts. This was because it was considered inappropriate to have a complete defence against someone who had committed a deliberate wrong.[19]

16.3.2 Elements of contributory negligence

The application of the 1945 Act resulted in an apportionment approach to contributory negligence. There are therefore now three distinct elements to the contributory negligence defence:
(1)   Was the claimant contributorily negligent?
(2)   Did the contributory negligence contribute to the damage suffered?
(3)   By how much should the damages be reduced as a consequence of the claimant's actions?

16.3.2.1 WAS THE CLAIMANT CONTRIBUTORILY NEGLIGENT?

The first question requires a consideration of whether the claimant has acted with a lack of reasonable care for their own safety. Just as people have a duty of care to look out for others, they are expected to show a reasonable degree of self-regard.[20] The claimant's damages will therefore be reduced if the defendant can show that they could have reasonably foreseen injury to themselves, but did not act as a reasonable person would have to prevent the injury from arising.

The concept of 'fault' under the 1945 Act has generally been given a broad interpretation. It is clear that the defendant does not have to show that the claimant owed a specific 'duty' to themselves, or that the claimant has acted 'negligently' in an orthodox sense of the word. An example of this is provided by *Reeves v Commissioner of Metropolitan Police* [2000],[21] where the House of Lords held that both the intentional act of the deceased and the negligent actions of the police contributed to the suicide. The damages awarded were reduced by 50% on the basis that the deceased's suicide was contributory negligence under the 1945 Act. The majority of

---

17   Law Reform (Contributory Negligence) Act 1945, s 4.
18   *Co-operative Group (CWS) Ltd v Pritchard* [2012] 1 All ER 205, 214–15 per Aikens LJ.
19   See G. Williams, *Joint Torts and Contributory Negligence* (London, 1951), 198 and Murphy's criticism of this analysis in J. Murphy, 'Misleading Appearances in the Tort of Deceit' (2016) 75(1) *Cambridge Law Journal* 301, 326–9.
20   *Jones v Livox Quarries Ltd* [1952] 2 QB 608.
21   The facts of this case were discussed earlier at 2.4.2.

the House of Lords applied a 'common sense' test to determining fault, as opposed to requiring evidence of a specific negligent act.

16.3.2.2 DID THE CONTRIBUTORY NEGLIGENCE CONTRIBUTE TO THE DAMAGE SUFFERED?

The second question is based on the defendant's actions contributing to the cause of the *damage* and not the cause of the *accident*. This was effectively highlighted in the case of *Froom v Butcher* [1976], where the claimant was injured in a car accident that was solely the fault of the defendant. The claimant, however, suffered more serious injuries because he was not wearing a seatbelt. Even though the car accident would have happened regardless of whether the seatbelt was worn, the lack of a seatbelt contributed to the damage that was suffered. There was therefore a successful plea of contributory negligence, and damages were reduced accordingly.[22]

The courts look beyond a simple 'but for' test when determining whether the claimant's actions contributed to the damage suffered. When considering this issue in *Jones v Livox Quarries* [1952], Denning LJ commented that:

> There is no clear guidance to be found in the books about causation. All that can be said is that causes are different from the circumstances in which, or on which, they operate. The line between the two depends on the facts of each case. It is a matter of common sense more than anything else.[23]

The extent of the second test was more recently examined by the Court of Appeal in *St George v Home Office* [2008].

KEY CASE

St George v Home Office [2008] EWCA Civ 1068

The claimant was 29 years old and was serving a four-month sentence at Brixton prison. He had been addicted to alcohol and drugs since he was 16 years old and, when he entered the prison, was using heroin, drinking heavily and had previously experienced withdrawal seizures. Even though the claimant had declined to see a doctor, his health screen confirmed his drug use and that he had epileptic fits. Despite this, the claimant was assigned to a top bunk in his prison ward, and prisoners were not allowed to switch beds. He had a seizure that caused him to fall from the top bunk, suffering a head wound and recurrent seizures. The claimant was rushed to hospital, but suffered severe brain damage and was left seriously and permanently disabled.

The trial judge found that the Home Office was negligent in its treatment of the claimant. This included assigning him a top bunk when it was aware of his previous epileptic fits and not responding appropriately during his seizure. The judge also held that the claimant's lifestyle decisions resulted in a finding of contributory negligence and a 15% reduction in the damages awarded.

The Court of Appeal found that the claimant was not contributorily negligent as his lifestyle choices were not adequately connected to the injuries suffered. The 'but for' test was clearly met; if he had not been using drugs and alcohol, he would not have gone into withdrawal and therefore would not have fallen off the bunk bed. When considering this issue, Dyson LJ, however, commented that:

> [56] In my judgment, the Claimant's fault in becoming addicted to drugs and alcohol in his mid-teens was not a potent cause of the status and the consequent brain injury which were

---

22 *Froom v Butcher* [1976] 1 QB 286, 292.
23 [1952] 2 QB 608, 616; see also Lord Reid in *Stapley v Gypsum Mines Ltd* [1953] 2 All ER 478, 485–6.

triggered by his fall on 3 November 1997. It was too remote in time, place and circumstance and was not sufficiently connected with the negligence of the prison staff or, ... was not sufficiently 'mixed up with the state of things brought about' by the prison staff on 3 November to be properly regarded as a cause of the injury. To use the language of Denning LJ, the Claimant's addiction was no more than part of the history which had led to his being a person whose medical and psychological conditions were as they were when he was admitted to Brixton prison on 29 October 1997.

This case highlights how the second element ('Did the contributory negligence contribute to the damage suffered?') goes beyond a simple 'but for' test, and instead looks holistically at the claimant's actions to see if there is an adequate link with the damage suffered.

16.3.2.3 BY HOW MUCH SHOULD THE DAMAGES BE REDUCED AS A CONSEQUENCE OF THE CLAIMANT'S ACTIONS?

The third question is often the most difficult for students, especially when answering a problem question. The relationship between the second and third test was highlighted by Lord Denning in *Davies v Swan Motor Co (Swansea) Ltd* [1949], where his Lordship stated:

> While causation is the decisive factor in determining whether there should be a reduced amount payable to the plaintiff, nevertheless the amount of the reduction does not depend solely on the degree of causation. The amount of the reduction is such an amount as may be found by the court to be 'just and equitable' having regard to the claimant's 'share in the responsibility' for the damage. This involves a consideration, not only of the causative potency of a particular factor, but also of its blameworthiness.[24]

An example of the way in which both causative potency and moral blameworthiness play a role was supplied in *Froom v Butcher* [1976].

KEY CASE

Froom v Butcher [1976] 1 QB 286

The claimant was injured in a car accident with the defendant, which was a result of the defendant's negligent driving. The defendant admitted liability but argued that the injuries were largely the result of the claimant's failure to wear a seatbelt and damages should be reduced accordingly. The trial judge rejected this argument and held that a failure to wear a seatbelt is not sufficient for a finding of contributory negligence and the reduction of damages. The defendant appealed to the Court of Appeal.

Lord Denning MR allowed the appeal, stating that:

The question is not what was the cause of the accident. It is rather what was the cause of the damage. In most accidents on the road the bad driving, which causes the accident, also causes the ensuing damage. But in seat belt cases the cause of the accident is one thing. The cause of the damage is another. The accident is caused by the bad driving. The damage is caused in part by the bad driving of the defendant, and in part by the failure of the plaintiff to wear a seat belt. If the plaintiff was to blame in not wearing a seat belt, the damage is in part the result of his own fault.

24   *Davies v Swan Motor Co (Swansea) Ltd* [1949] 1 All ER 620, 632.

He must bear some share in the responsibility for the damage: and his damages fall to be reduced to such extent as the court thinks just and equitable.[25]

The Court of Appeal held that if the claimant had been wearing a seatbelt, he would have suffered the minor injury of a broken finger. The absence of a seatbelt meant that he also suffered head and chest injuries. However, instead of apportioning liability on the basis of the cause of the damage (which would have seen a significant reduction), the Court of Appeal reduced damages by 20% on the basis of contributory negligence as that was determined to be 'just and equitable' in the circumstances.[26]

Whilst the apportionment is clearly a matter of the individual judge's discretion, the Court of Appeal indicated some general standards for the apportionment of contributory negligence for failure to wear seatbelts:
(1) the seatbelt would have completely prevented injury – 25% reduction;
(2) the seatbelt would have resulted in less severe injuries – 15% reduction; and
(3) the seatbelt would not have made any difference in the injuries suffered – 0% reduction.

These guidelines have also been applied to similar scenarios, including failure to wear a helmet while cycling[27] or while riding a motorcycle.[28]

The courts generally do not engage in a detailed empirical or evidence-based review of the matter, and apportion largely on a 'gut' reaction to the situation.[29] This is reflected in the rough and ready apportionment results commonly seen in contributory negligence cases. Goudkamp and Nolan reviewed 368 first instance decisions of contributory negligence between 2000 and 2014, finding that the most popular apportionments were 50%, followed by 33.3% and then 25%.[30]

The requirement that the reduction be 'just and equitable' clearly leaves significant discretion for the judge. This is evident in the case of *Jackson v Murray* [2015], where three courts had three different opinions on apportionment on the grounds of contributory negligence. In this case, two children got off a minibus, one of whom stepped out from behind the vehicle and into the path of the defendant's car. The driver was going too quickly and was not keeping an adequate look-out for the possibility that children may attempt to cross. He therefore did not see the child and ran into her, causing serious injuries. At first instance, the trial judge held that the driver was negligent, but that the child was also contributorily negligent. Contributory negligence was assessed at 90% and the award of damages was reduced accordingly. On appeal, the court disagreed with the apportionment and instead reduced the amount to 70%. This was further reduced by the Supreme Court to 50%, on the basis that the 'parties are equally responsible for the damage suffered'.[31] This case also reaffirms that the focus of the courts is on the different parties' *contribution to damage*, as opposed to questioning whether the accident would have occurred in the first place.

---

25 *Froom v Butcher* [1976] 1 QB 286, 292.
26 *Froom v Butcher* [1976] 1 QB 286, 296.
27 In obiter in *Smith v Finch* [2009] EWHC 53 (QB). It should, however, be noted that it is not a legal requirement in the UK to wear a helmet when cycling, but it is to wear a seatbelt when in a car and a helmet when on a motorcycle.
28 *Capps v Miller* [1989] 2 All ER 333, 341 (as per Croom-Johnson LJ).
29 This is not always the case and in *Badger v Ministry of Defence* [2006] 3 All ER 173, Stanley Burnton J utilised expert medical opinion to assist with the apportionment for negligent exposure to asbestos, where smoking also contributed to the deceased's lung cancer.
30 J. Goudkamp and D. Nolan, 'Contributory Negligence in the Twenty-First Century: An Empirical Study of First Instance Decisions' (2016) 79 MLR 575, 599.
31 [2015] UKSC 5 at [44].

■ VIEWPOINT

Should the courts engage with more empirical evidence when making determinations on contributory negligence? Would this provide more consistency in decision-making?

PROBLEM QUESTION TECHNIQUE

Anja's brother Bruno has just called her from hospital after being involved in a serious car accident. He was riding his bike along High Street and was hit by a drunk driver, who was also speeding and not paying attention to the road. Bruno was riding his bike responsibly but was not wearing a helmet. This was because he had just spent £85 on an expensive haircut, and he did not want to 'ruin the look' before going on a big date that night. He has suffered significant head injuries, which would have been completely avoided had he been wearing a helmet.

▸ Would Bruno be held contributorily negligent for the accident? Specifically, is the failure to wear a helmet (particularly for such a trivial reason) not taking reasonable care for his own safety? Think about whether the fact that there is no legal requirement to wear a helmet while riding a bike would make an impact.

▸ Did the failure to wear a helmet clearly contribute to the damage suffered? Think about whether Bruno would have avoided head injuries if he had used a helmet.

▸ What is a just and equitable apportionment of the damages? Is it likely to result in a small or large reduction in damages? Think about the fact that even though the majority of the damage suffered was a result of the failure to wear a helmet, this will not be the basis of the apportionment. Instead, focus on the relatively minor failure by Bruno compared with the significant wrongful behaviour of the driver to determine what a 'just and equitable' reduction is likely to look like.

▸ Also consider the impact of *Froom v Butcher* and the 'standard' reduction of 15% – however, the court may reduce this considering the serious negligence of the driver.

16.3.3 Contributory negligence: concluding remarks

A final issue to (briefly) consider is whether contributory negligence is actually a tort law defence. Whilst we frequently refer to the defence of contributory negligence, there is an ongoing debate about whether it can correctly be described as a 'defence'.

DIFFERENT PERSPECTIVES on contributory negligence

J. Goudkamp, 'Rethinking Contributory Negligence' in S. Pitel, J. Neyers and E. Chamberlain (eds), Tort Law: Challenging Orthodoxy (Hart Publishing, 2013)

Goudkamp contends that contributory negligence 'is a remedial rule' and therefore not a defence in the true sense of the word. This argument is premised on a number of observations about how contributory negligence works in practice. First, contributory negligence does not impact recovery of costs of the parties. Provided the verdict is entered in their favour, the claimant is entitled to a costs order – even if the majority of the award of damages is reduced by contributory negligence. Second, contributory negligence is excluded from default and summary judgments, which are only determinative in relation to liability. The fact that a default or summary judgment has been entered against the defendant does not prevent them from subsequently invoking contributory negligence in order to reduce the size of the remedy to which the claimant is entitled, when the quantum of damages is decided. Third, if the defendant admits liability, they do not waive the right to plead contributory negligence. The combination of these factors means Goudkamp is of the opinion that contributory negligence is better seen as a remedial rule than a defence.

R. Bagshaw, 'Balancing Defences' in A. Dyson, J. Goudkamp and F. Wilmot-Smith (eds), Defences in Tort (Hart Publishing, 2015)

Bagshaw disagrees with Goudkamp's classification of contributory negligence as a remedial rule as opposed to a defence. Instead he contends that defences should be seen as doctrines that allow a defendant to resist in whole, or in part, a tort claim against them other than through denying one of the elements (i.e. that there was no duty of care owed). Bagshaw argues that this approach 'has the advantage of collecting together claim-resisting rules that reflect similar substantive values weighing against allowing a claim to succeed, thus highlighting the similarity between' different defences.[32] Contributory negligence involves 'balancing', and therefore allows a defendant to raise issues of co-responsibility for the wrongs concerned to resist the tort law entirely or in part. It should therefore be seen as a defence.

B. McDonald, 'Privacy Claims: Transformation, Fault, and the Public Interest Defence' in A. Dyson, J. Goudkamp and F. Wilmot-Smith (eds), Defences in Tort (Hart Publishing, 2015)

McDonald in contrast argues that contributory negligence is a 'key defence to a negligence action'. This is on a different basis to Bagshaw. She argues that if negligence is focused on the defendant's failure to take reasonable precautions against foreseeable risks of injury to the claimant, it is clearly appropriate to also consider the claimant's behaviour in relation to that risk. It is also relevant that the negligent actions of neither the claimant nor the defendant need to be 'culpable behaviour from a moral standpoint' as negligence liability is not concerned with degrees of conduct.[33] Therefore, a small degree of negligence will be sufficient for both negligence and contributory negligence.

Irrespective of this debate, the principle of contributory negligence is clearly very important to the operation of tort law in the UK.

Contributory negligence is the most common and arguably most important defence in tort law. There are three steps involved in contributory negligence:

(1) Was the claimant contributorily negligent?
(2) Did the contributory negligence contribute to the damage suffered?
(3) By how much should the damages be reduced as a consequence of the claimant's actions?

When utilising this defence, the defendant does not justify or deny their negligent behaviour; instead they claim that the claimant has also been negligent. The impact of this is that the damages that need to be paid are apportioned between the parties. Whilst historically contributory negligence worked as a complete defence, the enactment of the 1945 Act resulted in a 'just and equitable' apportionment.

16.4 Volenti non fit injuria

Volenti non fit injuria, which translates as 'to a willing person, no injury is done', provides a complete defence to tort claims. The defence was described by Lord Shaw in *Letang v Ottawa Electric Railway*

32 R. Bagshaw, 'Balancing Defences' in A. Dyson, J. Goudkamp and F. Wilmot-Smith (eds), *Defences in Tort* (Hart Publishing, 2015) 92–3.
33 B. McDonald, 'Privacy Claims: Transformation, Fault, and the Public Interest Defence' in A. Dyson, J. Goudkamp and F. Wilmot-Smith (eds), *Defences in Tort* (Hart Publishing, 2015) 298.

Co [1926] as 'if the defendants desire to succeed on the ground that the maxim *volenti non fit injuria* is applicable, they must obtain a finding that the claimant freely and voluntarily, with full knowledge of the nature and extent of the risk he ran, impliedly agreed to incur it'.[34]

16.4.1 *Volenti* and consent

Volenti is clearly linked with consent. Whilst there are a number of similarities, and *volenti* is often referred to as the 'defence of consent', there are some important differences. The presence of consent is often utilised to defeat an alleged tort, and it is based on the fact that the claim cannot succeed if the claimant consented to the action in question. For example, there is no battery if there was consent to the complained-of touch. Consent therefore is based on the certainty that a state of affairs will arise. In contrast, *volenti* is about accepting the *risk* that something will happen. It must be shown that the claimant voluntarily agreed to take the risk, knowing the full nature and extent of the specific risk. It is based on the probability that a state of affairs may arise. There is clearly an overlap with consent, in that by agreeing to take the risk, the claimant has consented to the risk; but they still cover distinctly different scenarios. Whilst there has been some judicial confusion between and conflation of the two principles, as early as 1887 in *Thomas v Quartermaine,* it was emphasised that the maxim was *volenti non fit injuria* and not *scienti non fit injuria*, indicating the difference between being aware of a risk and knowing a specific outcome.

The application of consent as a defence has already been raised in the chapter on intentional torts, particularly trespass to the person torts.[35] The statutory restrictions on consenting to personal injury and death under the Unfair Contract Terms Act 1977 and the Consumer Rights Act 2015 have also been discussed in the chapter on occupiers' liability.[36] These issues therefore do not need repeating and the rest of this section will focus only on *volenti*.

16.4.2 Elements of *volenti*

There are two elements of the *volenti* defence, namely did the claimant (1) voluntarily agree to take the risk, and (2) know the full nature and extent of the risk involved?[37]

16.4.2.1 DID THE CLAIMANT VOLUNTARILY AGREE TO THE RISK?

The claimant must voluntarily agree to accept the risk in question. This was outlined by Lord Denning in *Nettleship v Weston* [1971], when he stated:

> nothing will suffice short of an agreement to waive any claim for negligence. The plaintiff must agree, expressly or impliedly, to waive any claim for any injury that may befall him due to the lack of reasonable care by the defendant: or, more accurately, due to the failure of the defendant to measure up to the standard of care that the law requires of him.[38]

The scope of what is meant by 'voluntary' is controversial; as outlined by Gordon, 'few branches of English case law are as confused and inconsistent as the decisions on a man's right to complain of

---

34 [1926] AC 725, 731.
35 See 12.6.1.
36 See 8.3.4.2.
37 *Morris v Murray* [1991] 2 QB 7, 15: 'the *volenti* doctrine can apply to the tort of negligence, though it must depend upon the extent of the risk, the [claimant's] … knowledge of it and what can be inferred as to his acceptance of it … [He] cannot be volens … in respect of acts of negligence which he had no reason to anticipate'.
38 *Nettleship v Weston* [1971] 2 QB 691, 701.

physical injury after he has knowingly incurred danger'.[39] For example, in *Thomas v Quartermaine* [1887],[40] it was held that employees who acted in the course of dangerous employment conditions (such as factories, mining and building railways) with full knowledge of the risk and danger of their work environment had voluntarily agreed to these risks. The approach in *Thomas v Quartermaine* was highly criticised, especially in light of the fact that at the time many people did not have any option but to accept employment in dangerous workplaces, and in doing so, their employers were able to escape liability for negligence. The difficulty in assuming that agreeing to be employed in dangerous circumstances was akin to voluntary acceptance was effectively summarised by Hawkins J in *Thrussell v Handyside* [1888], as 'his poverty, not his will, consented to incur the danger'.[41]

Thomas v Quartermaine was questioned in *Smith v Baker* [1891],[42] where the House of Lords took a different approach to the application of *volenti* in dangerous work environments. In this case, the claimant was injured while operating a drill on a railway cutting. A crane was lifting stones and hoisting them over the workmen without their being warned of this fact. The claimant was hit by one of these stones, as he was too busy to see that the crane was being used. The majority of the House of Lords held that mere knowledge of the danger did not constitute voluntary acceptance. Three of the Law Lords (Halsbury, Watson and Morris) based their decision preponderantly on the fact that the claimant had been injured solely by the actions of the employer, as opposed to injuring himself. Lord Halsbury stated that there was no actual knowledge of the specific danger, only of the general possibility of danger. Lord Bramwell dissented and held that the claimant had knowledge of the danger and undertook his work, which was enough for *volenti* to apply.[43] The case did not, however, remove the possibility of the defence applying to workplace environments, but emphasised that a balance needs to be struck when considering these issues. As outlined by Lord Herschell:

> The maxim is founded on good sense and justice. One who has invited or assented to an act being done towards him cannot, when he suffers from it, complain of it as a wrong. The maxim has no special application to the case of employer and employed, though its application may well be invoked in such a case.[44]

The application of *volenti,* particularly in a workplace setting, therefore requires a 'balancing' of the specific situation and an analysis of what, if any, pressure has been placed on the claimant to accept the risk involved. An example of this balancing occurred in *ICI Ltd v Shatwell* [1965].

KEY CASE

ICI Ltd v Shatwell [1965] AC 656

In this case, two brothers were injured as a result of an accidental explosion at a quarry where they worked. The brothers needed to test the circuit they were working on by connecting long wires, as this ensured that they could be 80 yards away and in a shelter. There was insufficient wire to run the test that way, but the brothers decided to run the test with short wires. The process they used to test with short wires had occurred regularly without accident until the previous year. After research showing that

---

39 D.M. Gordon, 'Wrong Turns in the *Volens* Cases' (1945) 61 LQ Rev 140, 140.
40 (1887) 18 QBD 685.
41 (1888) 20 QBD 359, 364. For an application of this, see *Bowater v Rowley Regis BC* [1944] KB 476, 479 (as per Scott LJ).
42 [1891] AC 325.
43 For further analysis of this case, see D.M. Gordon, 'Wrong Turns in the *Volens* Cases' (1945) 61 *LQ Rev* 140, Part III.
44 [1891] AC 325, 360.

this method was dangerous, the employer issued specific rules to the employees (including the Shatwell brothers) that testing needed to occur from a shelter.

Lord Hodson recognised that 'economic pressures are usually present which make it unjust to allow an employer where a servant has been injured to say in defence that the servant ran the risk with his eyes open, being fully aware of the danger he incurred'.[45] Similar comments were made by Lord Pearce, stating:

> the plea is in fact very rarely applicable to master and servant cases. It does not apply to consent obtained by any pressures whether social, economic, or simply habit. The master has an important duty of care for his servant; in general he has more skill in organisation, a wider foresight and more opportunity for innovation. So the assent of the servant to the master's failure very seldom in fact amounts to a real case of *volenti non fit injuria*.[46]

This was, however, one of the rare cases. When applying the principle to the facts of the case, it was held that there had been voluntary acceptance by the Shatwell brothers.

> As between these two brothers there can be no doubt that each agreed with the other to accept the risk of an explosion taking place at a time when neither had taken cover. Their employers, the appellants, had done everything they could to see that orders were complied with in an endeavour to ensure that no testing should

be done in the open. They had done so before the Regulations of 1959 came into force. On February 10, 1960, they produced a set of rules which were brought to the attention of the men who knew that they were acting in defiance of them. The men knew also that in May, 1960, a shot firer who broke the rules was suspended from work and had his shot firing certificate revoked. Rates of pay were geared so as to offer no inducement to save time by omitting safety precautions.

It was argued ... that the risk of a detonator being exploded by the galvanometer, the testing instrument used, was so small that no one believed in the possibility of an explosion, so that it cannot be said that the brothers Shatwell or either of them appreciated the risk. If they did not appreciate the risk, of course the doctrine of 'volens' would have no application, but I cannot accept that the risk was not truly appreciated. They were handling explosives in defiance of regulations designed to ensure the safety of the men working in the quarry by insistence on the taking of cover. Moreover, they were qualified shot firers who knew that they were dealing with a dangerous quantity of explosive when they entered on the foolhardy course which resulted in the accident.[47]

This case highlights the balancing approach taken by the courts when considering the application of *volenti* to negligence in the workplace and how they will look carefully at what, if any, pressure has been placed on the claimant to consent to the danger in question.

The application of the *volenti* defence has also been specifically considered in relation to volunteers, participation in sports, the consumption of alcohol and/or drugs and suicide. Each of these matters will be briefly discussed.

First, voluntarily accepting the risk associated with rescuing another will not suffice for a successful claim in *volenti*. If a brave woman runs into the ocean to save a drowning child, it could be argued that she has voluntarily assumed the risk of injury or drowning. There are, however, public policy concerns about *volenti* applying in this manner, as it would allow negligent parties to

---

45   [1965] AC 656, 681.
46   [1965] AC 656, 686.
47   [1965] AC 656, 681–2 (Lord Hotson).

avoid liability for harm suffered by the brave actions of rescuers. These issues were considered in *Haynes v Harwood* [1935], where a police officer sustained injuries as a consequence of stopping the defendant's runaway horses. Roche LJ in the Court of Appeal commented that the defence did not apply in the circumstances, as

> all the plaintiff knew was that two heavy cart-horses attached to a large van were running away in a crowded street, and that at any rate one woman and a number of children were in great peril; moved, as I think, by a duty both legal and moral … moved by such a duty, and not from any choice involving a consent to take any risk upon himself, the plaintiff acted and sustained his injuries. He knew nothing of what had been done or by whom, and there was no material choice or consent such as is contemplated and required by the maxim in question.[48]

The defence of *volenti* will therefore not apply to rescuers as the 'moral duty' forming the basis of the claimant's actions will not be considered as voluntarily assuming the risk of the specific danger. The defence may, however, apply if it is shown that the rescuer acted with 'wanton disregard' for their own safety.[49]

Secondly, and on a similar basis, people engaging in inherently dangerous sporting activities will not voluntarily consent to injuries arising from actions 'which fell far below the standards which might reasonably be expected in anyone pursuing the game'.[50] In *Condon v Basi* [1985], the defendant tackled the claimant in a manner that resulted in the claimant breaking his leg. It was held that the defendant had acted negligently in the tackle, but it was argued that the claimant had voluntarily assumed the risk of such injuries. As the injury was caused by a tackle conducted outside the standard rules of the game, the *volenti* defence did not apply.

Thirdly, voluntariness will also not be found if the claimant had consumed so much alcohol and/or drugs[51] or was suffering from any sort of mental incapacity[52] that meant that they were unable to understand (and therefore accept) the nature of the risk. As emphasised in *Morris v Murray* [1991],[53] there is a very high level required, and the claimant must show that they were exceptionally impacted to the point that they were unaware of the risk being taken.

Finally, can *volenti* apply to cases where the claimant committed suicide due to the negligence of the defendant? There is an argument that, in these circumstances, the claimant voluntarily assumed the risk by their own suicidal actions. This has, however, been rejected by the court. The matter was considered in *Reeves v Commissioner of Metropolitan Police* [2000] in relation to a suicide whilst in police custody. The House of Lords held that the application of the *volenti* defence would be inconsistent with the police officer's obligations when they know (or should reasonably know) that someone may be suicidal. This applies whether or not the claimant was considered to be of a 'sound mind' at the time of the suicide.[54] In *Corr v IBC* [2008], Lord Bingham again rejected the application of the defence, stating that the claimant's suicide 'was not something to which [he] consented voluntarily and with his eyes open but an act performed because of the psychological condition which the … breach of duty had induced'.[55]

---

48   [1935] 1 KB 146, 166–7.
49   *Baker v TE Hopkins & Son Ltd* [1959] 1 WLR 966.
50   *Condon v Basi* [1985] 2 All ER 453, 455; *Wooldridge v Sumner* [1963] 2 QB 43.
51   *Morris v Murray* [1991] 2 QB 6.
52   *Kirkham v Chief Constable of Greater Manchester* [1990] 2 QB 283; *Corr v IBC Vehicles* [2008] 1 AC 884.
53   [1991] 2 QB 6.
54   A more detailed discussion of the facts of this case occurs earlier at 2.4.2.
55   [2008] UKHL 13; [2008] 1 AC 884.

16.4.2.2 DID THE CLAIMANT KNOW THE FULL NATURE AND EXTENT OF THE RISK INVOLVED?

The defendant must also show that the claimant had knowledge of the full nature and extent of the risk involved. This is a strict test as the claimant needs to be aware of *the specific risks* associated with the action, not merely that there is generally *a risk*. We take risks every day; each time you cross a road, there is *a risk* that you will be hit by a driver who does not stop at the pedestrian crossing. If you are hit by a dangerous driver, the *volenti* defence will not apply because you lacked knowledge of the full nature and extent of the risk of that particular driver. This strict test was applied in *Dann v Hamilton* [1939].

KEY CASE

Dann v Hamilton [1939] 1 KB 509

The claimant knowingly got into the car with a driver who had consumed significant amounts of alcohol. There was another passenger in the car who refused to go any further with the driver and warned the claimant that she should also get out of the car, but the claimant continued the journey. The driver then had an accident in which he was killed, and the claimant was injured. The court had to consider whether the *volenti* defence applied to the claimant's actions, especially as she had specifically been warned of the risk of continuing the journey with the driver.

Asquith J held that, whilst the claimant had knowledge that this had a higher risk of negligent driving and a car accident, this was not sufficient knowledge of the full nature and extent of the

risk involved for a successful *volenti* defence. His Honour, however, went on and stated that this did not apply in all circumstances and that

> there may be cases in which the drunkenness of the driver at the material time is so extreme and so glaring that to accept a lift from him is like engaging in an intrinsically and obviously dangerous occupation, intermeddling with an unexploded bomb or walking on the edge of an unfenced cliff.[56]

This case therefore confirms the strict approach to *volenti* and the need to show that the claimant had accepted the specific nature of the risk in question.

The defence of *volenti* is no longer relevant in the context of road traffic accidents. Section 149 of the Road Traffic Act 1988 prevents the defence of *volenti* applying to passengers of motor vehicles on public roads. It is still, however, applicable to other vehicles, and the defence was successfully pleaded in *Morris v Murray*. In this case, the claimant accepted a flight in a friend's light aircraft even though he was aware that the friend had consumed a considerable amount of alcohol that day. The plane crashed, killing the pilot and seriously injuring the claimant. The autopsy revealed that the pilot had consumed the equivalent of 17 whiskies before flying. Fox LJ referred to Asquith's comments about extreme and glaring cases, stating that 'the question before us [is] whether this present case is one of them'.[57] After considering the facts of the case, he held that

> in embarking upon the flight the plaintiff had implicitly waived his rights in the event of injury consequent on Mr. Murray's failure to fly with reasonable care. The facts go far beyond *Dann v Hamilton* … It is much nearer to the dangerous experimenting with the detonators in *Imperial Chemical Industries Ltd. v Shatwell* …. I would conclude, therefore, that the plaintiff accepted the

---

56 [1939] 1 KB 509, 518. This was also discussed in *Pitts v Hunt* [1991] 1 QB 24.
57 *Morris v Murray* [1991] 2 QB 6, 13.

risks and implicitly discharged Mr. Murray from liability for injury in relation to the flying of the plane. The result, in my view, is that the maxim *volenti non fit injuria* does apply in this case.[58]

The requisite knowledge of the risks must be *subjectively* held by the claimant. The defendant will therefore not be able to fulfil the requirements of the defence by showing that a reasonable person in the claimant's position should have been aware of the nature and extent of the risks involved.[59] The defendant will have to show that the claimant was *actually* aware of the risks, not that they *should* have been aware of them.

PROBLEM QUESTION TECHNIQUE

Anja's sister Darya is currently working at Carpenters-R-Us, the local joinery. Carpenters-R-Us has specific rules and regulations in place for the safety of the employees, including that two employees are needed to lift any items over 25kg. Failure to abide by these rules results in disciplinary action. Carpenters-R-Us pays the employees relatively high wages because of the dangerous nature of the work; however, it reduces employees' pay if they do not complete the required number of furniture pieces per day. Last week, Darya injured herself lifting a 26kg piece of furniture and is now unable to work for at least six weeks. Carpenters-R-Us is refusing to pay compensation and has threatened Darya with termination for breaching the health and safety rules. On the day that Darya injured herself, there was no other employee available to assist her, and the workshop scales were broken.

▸ Is Carpenters-R-Us able to establish a defence of *volenti*?

▸ It should be acknowledged that there are some similarities to *ICI v Shatwell*, in that Darya was working in breach of the employer's rules.

▸ Consider the differences between this situation and *ICI v Shatwell*. Will the employers be able to show that Darya voluntarily agreed to the risk, especially considering that there was economic pressure on her to complete the work as quickly as possible (i.e. threatened wage deductions)?

▸ Would Darya would be able to fulfil Carpenters-R-Us's rules? Think about the fact that there was no employee available to assist Darya, the workshop scales were broken and that the item was only slightly above the 25kg limit.

16.4.3 *Volenti*: concluding remarks

For a successful *volenti* defence, the defendant will need to show that the claimant (1) voluntarily agreed to take the risk in question, (2) knowing the full nature and extent of the risk. If successful, the *volenti* is a complete defence. The defence has some similarities with consent; however, it applies to situations where the claimant has voluntarily accepted the risk of something happening and not where they have consented to a specific outcome or action. Whilst *volenti* is still very much part of the English common law of torts, it does have limited practical value. First, due to statutory intervention, the defence of *volenti* no longer applies in relation to road traffic accidents.[60] Secondly, it rarely succeeds when raised before the courts.[61] Finally, the prohibition on consenting to personal injury and death under the Unfair Contract Terms Act 1977 and the Consumer Rights Act 2015

---

58 *Morris v Murray* [1991] 2 QB 6, 17.
59 See comments by Fox LJ in *Morris v Murray* [1991] 2 QB 6, 14.
60 Road Traffic Act 1988, s 149(3).
61 R. Kidner, 'The Variable Standard of Care, Contributory Negligence and *Volenti*' (1991) 11 *Legal Studies* 1, 12.

raises significant philosophical questions on if and how the common law can justify a defence based on an individual's consent, particularly in cases of physical injury.

■ VIEWPOINT

What role does *volenti* play in modern day society? Do you think people should be able to voluntarily accept the risk of another person's negligent actions?

16.5 Illegality

The final defence to consider is illegality, which – like *volenti* – operates as a complete defence and defeats any potential claim. The defence of illegality is based on the maxim of *ex turpi causa non oritur actio*, and translates as 'no cause of action may be founded on an illegal act'. For a successful illegality defence, the claimant must show that: (1) the claimant has engaged in illegal or immoral behaviour, (2) there was a sufficient link between the illegal behaviour and tort, and (3) when considering all the relevant factors, the claim should be defeated.

16.5.1 Rationale of illegality

The rationale for illegality is to prevent a claimant from benefiting from illegal or immoral activities. This was highlighted by Lord Mansfield CJ in *Holman v Johnson* [1775] as 'no court will lend its aid to a man who founds his cause of action upon an immoral or an illegal act'.[62] For instance, a criminal who is injured escaping from police when fleeing the scene of a burglary will not have a claim in tort law.[63] In *Vellino v Chief Constable of Greater Manchester* [2002],[64] the Court of Appeal held that illegality prevented a cause of action arising from a claim of negligence against the police. The claimant argued that the police were negligent in their arrest, as they allowed him to escape out a second-storey window causing him to be seriously injured. The claim was dismissed on the grounds that there was no duty of care on the police to ensure the claimant was not injured in a foreseeable attempt to escape from lawful custody. The Court of Appeal commented, however, that the illegality defence is not limited to tort law, and applies to a range of other private law causes of actions, including contract and unjust enrichment.

The exact rationale behind the illegality defence and if/when it should apply has been subject to ongoing debate. There has been significant academic and judicial commentary about the role of illegality,[65] and the Law Commission published the *Consultative Report on the Illegality Defence* in 2009.[66] The key rationale is consistency and integrity within the legal system,[67] and ensuring that the legal system does not 'give with one hand what it takes away with another, nor condone when facing right what it condemns when facing left'.[68] Whilst this seems like a clear and obvious goal, how that actually works in practice is highly contested.

---

62 (1775) 1 Cowp 341, 343.

63 *Ashton v Turner* [1981] QB 137.

64 [2002] 1 WLR 218.

65 See, for example, S. Green and A. Bogg (eds), *Illegality After Patel v Mirza* (Hart Publishing, 2018) and J. Goudkamp, 'The End of an Era? Illegality in Private Law in the Supreme Court' (2017) 133 LQR 14. As discussed below, there were also four Supreme Court decisions on the issue in three years.

66 LCCP 189, 2009.

67 Law Commission, Consultative Report on the Illegality Defence (LCCP 189, 2009 at [2.5]; *Patel v Mirza* [2016] UKSC 42 at [120] (per Lord Toulson); [2017] AC 467.

68 *Hounga v Allen* [2014] UKSC 47 at [55]; [2014] 1 WLR 2889 (per Lord Hughes).

16.5.2 Elements of illegality

There are three elements to the illegality defence:

(1)   the claimant has engaged in illegal or immoral behaviour;

(2)   there was a sufficient link between the illegal behaviour and tort; and

(3)   when considering all the relevant factors, the claim should be defeated.

16.5.2.1 ILLEGAL OR IMMORAL BEHAVIOUR

The claimant must have engaged in illegal or immoral conduct. This requirement is linked with the rationale of the defence discussed above, as highlighted by McLachlin J of the Supreme Court of Canada in *Hall v Herbert* [1993]:

> [There] is a need in the law of tort for a principle which permits judges to deny recovery to a plaintiff on the ground that to do so would undermine the integrity of the justice system. The power is a limited one. Its use is justified where allowing the plaintiff's claim would introduce inconsistency into the fabric of the law, either by permitting the plaintiff to profit from an illegal or wrongful act, or to evade a penalty prescribed by criminal law. Its use is not justified where the plaintiff's claim is merely for compensation for personal injuries sustained as a consequence of the negligence of the defendant.[69]

Stuart-Smith LJ highlighted in *Vellino v Chief Constable of Greater Manchester* [2002] that criminal activities must be sufficiently serious for the defence to be applicable. When determining what would be 'sufficiently serious', his Lordship highlighted that 'generally speaking a crime punishable with imprisonment could be expected to qualify'.[70] It is therefore important to first identify if the claimant has engaged in any illegal or seriously immoral conduct, before proceeding to see if this conduct is sufficiently linked to their tort claim.

16.5.2.2 SUFFICIENT LINK

The next issue to consider is whether there is a sufficient link between illegal behaviour and the tort. The courts have had an ongoing issue determining the extent of the illegality and the specific consequences of successfully pleading the defence. As outlined by Bingham LJ:

> Where issues of illegality are raised, the courts have (as it seems to me) to steer a middle course between two unacceptable positions. On the one hand it is unacceptable that any court of law should aid or lend its authority to a party seeking to pursue or enforce an object or agreement which the law prohibits. On the other hand, it is unacceptable that the court should, on the first indication of unlawfulness affecting any aspect of a transaction, draw up its skirts and refuse all assistance to the plaintiff, no matter how serious his loss nor how disproportionate his loss to the unlawfulness of his conduct.[71]

There are many instances where the illegal actions of the claimant can, and should, have no bearing on the liability of the defendant. For example, if a minor were subject to a severe battery while they were (illegally) drinking alcohol, the defendant ought not to be able to use their actions of under-age drinking as a way to avoid liability for a tort claim against them.

---

69   [1993] 2 SCR 159, 179–80.

70   [2002] 3 All ER 78 at [70].

71   *Saunders v Edwards* [1987] 1 WLR 1116, 1133.

There are, however, much more serious cases where the illegal actions of the claimant are held to justify a complete defence to any tort claim. For example, in *Clunis v Camden and Islington Health Authority* [1998],[72] the claimant had a schizoaffective disorder that caused him to stab and kill a third party. The claimant was convicted of manslaughter on the grounds of diminished responsibility and detained in hospital. The stabbing would not have occurred had the defendant provided the claimant with adequate care. The claimant therefore brought an action on the grounds that he had suffered injury, loss and damage as a result of the defendant's breach of a common law duty to treat him with reasonable professional care and skill. It was further argued that the illegality defence does not apply to causes of action founded in tort law. The Court of Appeal dismissed this argument, stating that 'the plaintiff has been convicted of a serious criminal offence. In such a case public policy would in our judgment preclude the court from entertaining the plaintiff's claim.'[73] The defence of illegality can therefore clearly apply to tort causes of action.

The extent of the principle in *Clunis* was not clearly identified. Do the illegal actions of the claimant prevent recovery of all damages, or only those that are 'inextricably bound up with or linked with the criminal conduct'.[74] The link between illegality and causation was highlighted by Lord Asquith in *National Coal Board v England* [1954]:

> It seems to me in principle that the plaintiff cannot be precluded from suing simply because the wrongful act is committed after the illegal agreement is made and during the period involved in its execution … If two burglars, A and B, agree to open a safe by means of explosives, and A so negligently handles the explosive charge as to injure B, B might find some difficulty in maintaining an action for negligence against A. But if A and B are proceeding to the premises which they intend burglariously to enter, and before they enter them, B picks A's pocket and steals his watch, I cannot prevail on myself to believe that A could not sue in tort. … The theft is totally unconnected with the burglary.[75]

An example of the second scenario is *Delaney v Pickett* [2011],[76] where the claimant and defendant were transporting a relatively small amount of cannabis to sell it illegally. The defendant negligently drove into the path of an oncoming vehicle, injuring the claimant. The claimant sued for personal injury. The claim was upheld as the accident arose from the negligent driving of the defendant and not as a result of the illegal activity of selling cannabis. This can be contrasted with *Pitts v Hunt* [1991], where the claimant and defendant had been consuming alcohol together before driving on the defendant's motorcycle (with the claimant as a passenger). The claimant knew that the defendant did not have a licence or insurance, and yet he encouraged him to drive recklessly. The two parties were involved in an accident, with the defendant dying and the claimant suffering serious injuries. The claimant sued the defendant in negligence, but the claim failed. The Court of Appeal held that the claimant

> was playing a full and active part in encouraging the young rider to commit offences which, if a death other than that of the young rider himself had occurred, would have amounted to manslaughter … Thus on the findings made by the judge in this case I would hold that the plaintiff is precluded on grounds of public policy from recovering compensation for the injuries which he sustained in the course of the very serious offences in which he was participating.[77]

72 [1998] QB 978.
73 [1998] QB 978, 989.
74 [2009] 1 AC 1339, 1354.
75 [1954] AC 403, 429.
76 [2011] EWCA Civ 1532.
77 [1991] 1 QB 24, 46. See J. Goudkamp, 'The Defence of Illegality in Tort Law: Wither the Rule in *Pitts v Hunt*?' [2012] CLJ 481 for analysis and criticisms of this decision.

PART 5

There are two 'forms' (also referred to as 'rules' or 'claims'[78]) of the illegality defence. The narrower form prevents the claimant from obtaining damages for losses that flow from the *criminal punishment imposed*. The justification for this prohibition is the avoidance of inconsistency between the criminal law and tort law. In contrast, the wider form prohibits the claimant from recovering compensation for losses that they have suffered as a *consequence of their criminal actions* and is based on policy grounds and public notions of the fair distribution of resources. The difference between the two forms of the illegality defence was discussed by the House of Lords in *Gray v Thames Trains*.

KEY CASE

Gray v Thames Trains Ltd [2009] 1 AC 1339

Gray was a passenger on a train involved in a negligent rail crash. He sustained minor physical injuries and also developed Post-Traumatic Stress Disorder (PTSD). Whilst Gray received treatment for the condition, he killed someone. Due to the PTSD, he pleaded guilty to manslaughter on the grounds of diminished capacity and was detained in hospital. Gray commenced an action in negligence against Thames Trains. He claimed the following: general damages for his conviction, detention and feelings of guilt and remorse, damages to his reputation, special damages for loss of earnings due to imprisonment, and an indemnity against any claims that may be brought against Gray by dependents of his victim.

When approaching illegality in tort law, the House of Lords had to decide between a broad test (preventing a person from recovering compensation for losses suffered in consequence of their criminal act) or a narrower test (preventing a person from recovering damage that was a consequence of a sentence imposed for a criminal law). The majority held that the losses arising in that case fell within the narrower test. Lord Hoffmann stated,

> Mr Gray's claims for loss of earnings after his arrest and for general damages for his detention, conviction and damage to reputation are all claims for damage caused by the lawful sentence imposed upon him for manslaughter and therefore fall within the narrower version of the rule... But there are some additional claims which may be more difficult to bring within this rule, such as the claim for an indemnity against any claims which might be brought by dependants of the dead pedestrian and the claim for general damages for feelings of guilt and remorse consequent upon the killing. Neither of these was a consequence of the sentence of the criminal court.[79]

When addressing the wider test, his Lordship states that,

> It differs from the narrower version in at least two respects: first, it cannot, as it seems to me, be justified on the grounds of inconsistency in the same way as the narrower rule. Instead, the wider rule has to be justified on the ground that it is offensive to public notions of the fair distribution of resources that a claimant should be compensated (usually out of public funds) for the consequences of his own criminal conduct. Secondly, the wider rule may raise problems of causation which cannot arise in connection with the narrower rule.[80]

When determining whether the wider form should be used, the courts undertake a balancing test based on the specific facts and the causative relationship between the wrongdoing and the damages claimed.[81]

---

78 See, for instance, discussion in *Gray v Thames Trains* [2009] 1 AC 1339 and *Henderson v Dorset Healthcare University NHS Foundation Trust* [2020] UKSC 43.

79 [2009] 1 AC 1339, 1376.

80 [2009] 1 AC 1339, 1376. This has however been questioned and the 'consistency principle' has been held to apply to both the narrow and wide forms; see for example Lord Sumption in his dissenting judgment in *Patel v Mirza* [2017] AC 467.

81 See, for example, discussion by Lord Sumption in *Les Laboratoires Servier v Apotex Inc* [2015] AC 430, 445.

16.5.2.3 BALANCING THE RANGE OF FACTORS

The final element of illegality is a more vague and more general one; when considering all the relevant factors, should the claim be defeated? This element has had a difficult and highly litigated history. In addition to the difference between the wide and narrow approach to illegality in tort law, there was also a debate on the illegality defence more generally between a rule-based test or a range of factors approach (also referred to as the policy-based approach). The former states that the illegality defence will apply where the claimant must rely on the unlawful conduct to make out their claim. The latter instead requires the court to balance a range of policy arguments when considering whether the claimant should be prevented from making a claim.

English law's approach to the illegality defence was unsettled for a period of time, and resulted in an unusual situation where the matter was considered by four Supreme Court cases in three years: *Hounga v Allen* [2014],[82] *Les Laboratoires Servier v Apotex Inc* [2015],[83] *Bilta (UK) Ltd v Nazir (No 2)* [2016][84] and *Patel v Mirza* [2017].[85] These cases – and the different judgments in the cases – went back and forth between the rule-based approach and the range of factors approach. The final case of *Patel v Mirza*, which was heard with a bench of nine, provided some much-needed clarity on the situation. The Supreme Court was unanimous in relation to the result in the case, and six judges came down strongly in favour of the range of factors approach.

KEY CASE

Patel v Mirza [2017] AC 467

Mr Patel transferred £620,000 to Mr Mirza for the purposes of insider dealing under s 52 of the Criminal Justice Act 1993. This did not end up occurring and Mr Mirza failed to repay the money despite promising to do so. Mr Patel therefore brought a claim to recover the sums paid. Lord Toulson JSC (with whom Baroness Hale, Lord Kerr, Lord Wilson and Lord Hodge agreed) held that the range of factors approach should be applied to the illegality defence. Whilst not wanting to provide a prescriptive list of issues to consider, some guidance was supplied by the court:

In considering whether it would be disproportionate to refuse relief to which the claimant would otherwise be entitled, as a matter of public policy, various factors may be relevant. ... I would not attempt to lay down a prescriptive or definitive list because of the infinite possible variety of cases. Potentially relevant factors include the seriousness of the

conduct, its centrality to the contract, whether it was intentional and whether there was marked disparity in the parties' respective culpability.

The integrity and harmony of the law permit – and I would say require – such flexibility. Part of the harmony of the law is its division of responsibility between the criminal and civil courts and tribunals. Punishment for wrongdoing is the responsibility of the criminal courts and, in some instances, statutory regulators. It should also be noted that under the Proceeds of Crime Act 2002 the state has wide powers to confiscate proceeds of crime, whether on a conviction or without a conviction. Punishment is not generally the function of the civil courts, which are concerned with determining private rights and obligations. The broad principle is not in doubt that the public interest requires that the civil courts should not undermine the effectiveness of the criminal law; but nor should they impose what would amount in substance

82 [2014] 1 WLR 2889.
83 [2015] AC 430.
84 [2016] AC 1.
85 [2017] AC 467.

to an additional penalty disproportionate to the nature and seriousness of any wrongdoing.[86]

The Supreme Court therefore found, by a majority, in favour of the range of factors approach. This provides the defence with significant flexibility and allows courts to consider the relevant public policy issues. It must, however, be recognised that the range of factors approach makes the law and its application more uncertain and unpredictable.

Whilst *Patel v Mirza* focused on an illegality defence for a contract claim, the Supreme Court emphasised that the same approach should be taken for other private law causes of action. An example of the 'range of factors' approach in a tort law context is the Supreme Court case of *Hounga v Allen*.

KEY CASE

Hounga v Allen [2014] 1 WLR 2889

The claimant in this case was a young Nigerian girl who assumed a false identity to gain entry into the United Kingdom to work as an au pair for the defendant. During her 'employment', the claimant was subject to 'serious physical abuse', harassment and discrimination by the defendants. She sued the defendants in tort, and they raised the illegality defence. The question before the Supreme Court was whether the illegality of the claimant's entry into the country, and subsequent employment, barred her claim in tort.

The Supreme Court affirmed that the defence of illegality 'rests on the foundation of public policy', and this should be central to the question of whether the defence is successful.[87] The court weighed up a number of factors, including:

- the claimant did not profit from her tortious claim, as it was compensation for damage she had suffered;

- there had been no penalty imposed by the criminal law for the claimant's entry into the country;
- a successful tortious claim would not compromise the integrity of the legal system; and
- application of the defence could give tortious immunity to employers of people with illegal contracts or worse to people who engage in human trafficking, thus encouraging these actions.[88]

The Supreme Court emphasised that the 'considerations of public policy which militate in favour of applying the defence so as to defeat [the] complaint scarcely exist'. The defence was therefore not successful.[89] The Court was particularly aware of the legal obligations and protections in place for victims of human trafficking and the public policy considerations relevant to the application of the illegality defence.[90]

The approach in *Patel v Mirza* raises the question of the relationship between the House of Lords approach in *Gray v Thames Trains Ltd* and the Supreme Court's range of factors approach. This situation was clarified (to a certain extent) in *Henderson v Dorset Healthcare University NHS Foundation Trust* [2018].

86 [2017] AC 467, 477.
87 [2014] 1 WLR 2889, 2903.
88 [2014] 1 WLR 2889, 2904 (Lord Wilson), 2910–11 (Lord Hughes).
89 [2014] 1 WLR 2889, 2904.
90 [2014] 1 WLR 2889, 2910–11 (Lord Hughes).

KEY CASE

Henderson v Dorset Healthcare University NHS Foundation Trust [2020] UKSC 43

The claimant was suffering from paranoid schizophrenia and had a long history of mental health difficulties. From 2003 she had various formal and informal hospital admissions. In 2010 her condition worsened, and while experiencing a particularly severe psychotic episode she stabbed her mother to death. During the episode, the claimant was under the care of the defendant and there were a number of failings in the care and treatment that was provided. It was admitted by the defendant that the killing of the claimant's mother was preventable, and if it had provided adequate treatment, the incident probably would not have occurred.

The claimant was charged with the murder of her mother, and the prosecution accepted a plea of manslaughter by reason of diminished responsibility. She was detained under a hospital order and will not be released for a significant period of time. The defendant admitted liability and consented to judgment being entered, with damages to be assessed. The damages claimed were under six heads:

1) General damages for personal injury (a depressive disorder and PTSD);
2) General damages for loss of liberty caused by her compulsory detention;
3) General damages for loss of amenity arising from the consequences of having killed her mother;
4) The sum of £61,944, being the share of her mother's estate;
5) The cost of psychotherapy; and
6) The cost of a care manager /support worker.

The defendant submitted that the entirety of the claim should be defeated on illegality or public policy grounds. The claimant argued that, despite the factual similarities with *Clunis*, this case did not survive the Supreme Court's discretionary approach laid down in *Patel v Mirza*. Jay J dismissed the claim entirely on the basis that he was bound by the decisions in *Gray and Clunis*.

The claimant appealed to the Court of Appeal, which stated that 'the *Clunis* and the *Gray* cases are binding authority that [the] claim for damages is barred on the ground of public policy unless the *Clunis* case has been overruled and the Supreme Court [in *Patel v Mirza*] decided to depart from its previous decision in the *Gray* case in a material respect'.[91] The question before the Court of Appeal was whether the *Gray* and *Clunis* cases survived the judgment of the Supreme Court in *Patel v Mirza*. After considering all three cases, it was held that both cases remain binding and the entirety of the claim was dismissed on the grounds of illegality.

The case was then appealed to the Supreme Court. There were three principal issues considered in the appeal: (1) whether *Gray* could be distinguished, (2) whether *Gray* should be departed from and *Clunis* overruled, and (3) whether all heads of loss claimed were irrevocable.

On the first point, the appellant argued that there was a lower degree of personal responsibility in the current case when compared with that of *Gray*. This was unsuccessful and the Supreme Court held that *Gray* could not be distinguished as it 'involved the same offence, the same sentence and the reasoning ... applies regardless of the degree of personal responsibility for the offending'.[92]

On the second point, the Supreme Court considered three separate arguments: (a) that the reasoning in *Gray* could not stand with the approach to illegality adopted in *Patel*, (b) that *Gray* should be held not to apply where the claimant has no significant personal responsibility for the criminal act and/or there was no penal sentence imposed, and (c) the application of the 'trio of considerations' approach in *Patel* leads to a different outcome. The Supreme Court rejected these three approaches, again emphasising the similarities of the current case with *Gray* and the fact that the appellant was convicted of the serious offence of culpable homicide. The Supreme Court emphasised that

91 [2018] 3 WLR 1651, 1670.
92 *Henderson v Dorset Healthcare University NHS Foundation Trust* [2020] UKSC 43 at [86].

the wrongdoing by the appellant was 'heightened' due to the fact that NHS funding is of significant public interest and importance. Taking funds from the NHS budget to compensate someone for the consequences of her criminal conviction for unlawful killing would go strongly against the public confidence. The Court also confirmed that there was no conflict between *Gray* and *Patel*, and the public policy based rules in the former case are '*Patel* compliant' thus should be applied and followed in comparable cases.

On the final point, the Supreme Court held that all heads of loss claimed are irrevocable. The damages for loss of liberty and loss of amenity during the appellant's detention were barred by the narrower rule. The other heads of loss were barred by the wider rule as they were expressly consequences of the appellant killing her mother.

PROBLEM QUESTION TECHNIQUE

Anja's niece Eliska is 17 years old. She is trying to save money for a trip to Australia. She lied about her age and used a fake ID to get a job working in a bar, as that paid her more than her current work filling supermarket shelves. During her employment, the owner of the bar subjects Eliska to sustained sexual harassment and then fires her when she will not return his advances. When Eliska threatens the employer with a claim for sexual harassment and unlawful dismissal, he states that it 'was all her own fault for lying about her age'.

▸ Does Eliska's employer have a defence of illegality? Consider specifically that the facts of this case are similar to *Hounga v Allen*, although the illegal actions of both Eliska and her employer are arguably less serious.

▸ In your answer, use the 'range of factors' approach to show how the courts will weigh up various matters to determine the relevant public policy considerations:

  – Is the claimant looking to profit from her tortious claim (i.e. sexual harassment and unlawful termination claims seek to compensate for harm committed)?

  – Is working in a bar whilst under age a minor offence compared with sexual harassment and unlawful termination?

  – Will a successful tortious claim compromise the integrity of the legal system? Specifically, if the defence was successful, would it encourage the abuse of minors working illegally?

DIFFERENT PERSPECTIVES on illegality

S. Green, 'Illegality and Zero Sum Torts' in S. Green and A. Bogg (eds), Illegality After Patel v Mirza (Hart Publishing, 2018), 187–212

Green here advocates that illegality should have a narrow role to play, particularly in tort law defences, stating that 'the defence of illegality is a conceptual misfit within the law of torts'. She argues that the defence should not apply to 'zero sum torts', which are defined as torts where neither party is better off (and may even be worse off) after the commission of the tort. This can be compared with contract law, where the parties are aiming to improve their own position. One of the key purposes of tort law is to compensate people for damage sustained, and it therefore protects the most basic, immediate and universal rights of individuals. Green's argument is premised on two basic principles:

(1) Individuals have a right not to be deprived of what they have.

(2) Individuals' illegal actions do not justify private violations of this right.

Green then provides a threefold taxonomy for classifying the illegality case law (causal story cases, external event cases, and internal event cases). It is argued that for each category, the illegality defence does more harm than good, and the issues related to any criminal offences committed should be dealt with by the existing elements and concepts in tort law. When considering the relationship between the criminal law and tort law, Green comments that

> given the rich and complex nature of the criminal law, those whose actions result in the most serious of consequences are not necessarily the most morally deficient members of society. For anyone, the denial of a tort claim in addition to a criminal penalty is in effect a double penalty. For those already treated in a heavy-handed way by the criminal law, the result is even more disproportionate. That is not to suggest that those whose actions seriously impinge on, or destroy, the lives of others do not deserve a measure of punishment and censure, whatever their moral standing, but that the complexities of that question are amplified, rather than reduced, by bringing the law of tort to bear on it.[93]

N. McBride, 'Not a Principle of Justice?' in S. Green and A. Bogg (eds), Illegality After Patel v Mirza (Hart Publishing, 2018), 85–106

McBride's chapter questions Lord Goff's observation that 'the principle [of *ex turpi causa non oritur actio*] is not a principle of justice; it is a principle of policy, whose application is indiscriminate and so can lead to unfair consequences as between the parties to litigation'.[94] In contrast, McBride argues forcefully that there is nothing unjust about the defence of illegality and, in fact, justice sometimes requires that the courts give effect to the defence. Unlike Green, he argues that illegality should play an expanded role in private law, including the law of torts.

The author utilises three different views of 'justice': moralistic, allocative and political. A claimant will have difficulties relying on the moralistic view of justice when arguing against the application of the illegality defence, as there is no right against the courts to a remedy. The allocative view of justice is more complicated, particularly for tort law, as McBride notes that awarding the claimant nothing may be a violation of the their primary right. The question therefore depends on whether it would be unjust in the political sense; the concepts of allocation and politics are essentially linked – 'the question of whether that allocation is just in the allocative sense will depend on whether that allocation is just in the political sense'.[95]

McBride argues that there are two key principles relevant to a consideration of political justice and the illegality defence – (1) the law should not contradict itself, and (2) crime must not pay. It is also important that people cannot benefit from living in a political order without shouldering the burdens of that order, the need to respect the law and legal institutions, and finally the political order must be prepared to defend itself. It is argued that all these concepts justify the application of the illegality defence, and highlight that utilisation of this defence by the court does not automatically involve 'injustice' to the claimant.

■ VIEWPOINT

Does the defence of illegality involve injustice to the claimant, or are these concepts separate to the application of tort law?

---

93 S. Green, 'Illegality and Zero Sum Torts' in S. Green and A. Bogg (eds), *Illegality After Patel v Mirza* (Hart Publishing 2018), 208-9.

94 *Tinsley v Milligan* [1994] 1 AC 340, 355.

95 N. McBride, 'Not a Principle of Justice?' in S. Green and A. Bogg (eds), *Illegality After Patel v Mirza* (Hart Publishing 2018), 99.

16.5.3 Illegality: concluding remarks

Illegality is an interesting, but exceptionally complex, tort law defence. Its controversial and difficult nature has attracted significant case law and academic literature over a relatively short period of time. The defence is strongly grounded in public policy, with the maxim *ex turpi causa non oritur actio* translating as 'no cause of action may be founded on an illegal act'. Like *volenti*, it is a complete defence, and the claimant must show that: (1) the claimant has engaged in illegal or immoral behaviour, (2) there was a sufficient link between the illegal behaviour and tort, and (3) when considering all the relevant factors, the claim should be defeated. Illegality applies more generally to the law of obligations, a recent Supreme Court case, which confirmed the flexible 'range of factors' approach, was based on contract law. Whilst the court made it clear that the range of factors approach also applied to the illegality defence in tort law, future case law will be necessary to determine how this will occur in practice.

16.6 CHAPTER SUMMARY

Once a tort claim has been established, it is important to consider whether there are any potential defences that can be raised. Unlike tort causes of action, the burden of proof for defences is on the defendant and not the claimant. While other chapters have considered a range of defences applicable to specific torts, this chapter covers defences that can be applied generally to tort law causes of actions. It has focused on the three that are most commonly covered in tort law courses: contributory negligence, *volenti* and illegality.

The three defences considered have different outcomes and rationales. Contributory negligence was traditionally a complete bar to a tort claim; however, the Law Reform (Contributory Negligence) Act 1945 created a system of apportionment between the claimant and the defendant. The current approach to contributory negligence is justified on the basis that the claimant also acted in a negligent manner, and therefore results in the apportionment of damages between the claimant and defendant. In contrast, *volenti* and illegality are complete defences which bar the tort law claim in its entirety. The former is based on the fact that the claimant voluntarily accepted the risk in question, and the latter prevents people from basing a cause of action on their own illegal or immoral behaviour.

Each of these defences has its own elements. For contributory negligence, the defendant must show that (1) the claimant was contributorily negligent, (2) this contributed to the damage suffered, and (3) by how much the damages should be reduced as a consequence of the claimant's actions. For a successful *volenti* defence, it must be shown that the claimant (1) voluntarily agreed to take the risk, and (2) knew the full nature and extent of the risk involved. Finally, for the illegality defence, (1) the claimant must have engaged in illegal or immoral behaviour, (2) there was a sufficient link between the illegal behaviour and tort, and (3) when considering all the relevant factors, the court holds that the claim should be defeated.

Finally, each of the defences raises different theoretical and philosophical challenges. Whilst the rationale behind contributory negligence is clear and non-contentious, there are challenges with how apportionment should occur and whether the courts should focus on moral blameworthiness and/or direct contribution to the damages suffered. *Volenti* is related to consent, but instead of the claimant consenting to the action in question, they have voluntarily accepted the risk of the defendant's negligence. Whilst *volenti* is still a valid defence, it is rarely successful. Furthermore, common law and statutory developments have significantly reduced its application. The application of the defence also raises some important and difficult questions on whether people should be able to consent to another's negligence. Finally, illegality has a strong connection with public policy, but the courts have struggled to develop a test that adequately balances fairness (i.e. having the flexibility to look at the entirety of the circumstances) with certainty (i.e. having a clear principle that can be applied consistently across a wide range of cases). The scope and application of the illegality defence has been subject to frequent judicial consideration, with a recent Supreme Court case confirming the discretionary 'range of factors' approach. It is clear, however, that further case law is necessary to further refine this approach and determine how it applies to tort law cases.

FURTHER READING

A. Dyson, J. Goudkamp and F. Wilmot-Smith, *Defences in Tort* (Hart, 2015)

R.E. Goodwin, '*Volenti* Goes to Market' (2006) 10 *The Journal of Ethics* 53

J. Goudkamp, *Tort Law Defences* (Hart, 2013)

J. Goudkamp and D. Nolan, *Contributory Negligence in the Twenty-First Century* (OUP, 2019)

S. Green and A. Bogg (eds), *Illegality After* Patel v Mirza (Hart, 2018)

A.J.E. Jaffey, '*Volenti Non Fit Injuria*' (1985) 4(1) *Cambridge Law Journal* 87

R. Kidner, 'The Variable Standard of Care, Contributory Negligence and Volenti' (1991) 11 *Legal Studies* 1

B. McDonald, 'Reforming a Reform: Why Has It Been So Hard to Reform Proportionate Liability Reforms?' in K. Barker and R. Grantham (eds), *Apportionment in Private Law* (Hart Publishing, 2018)

J. Steele, 'Law Reform (Contributory Negligence) Act 1945: Collisions of a Different Sort' in T. Arvind and J. Steele (eds), *Tort Law and the Legislature: Common Law, Statute and the Dynamics of Legal Change* (Hart, 2013) 159.

Roadmap: Defences

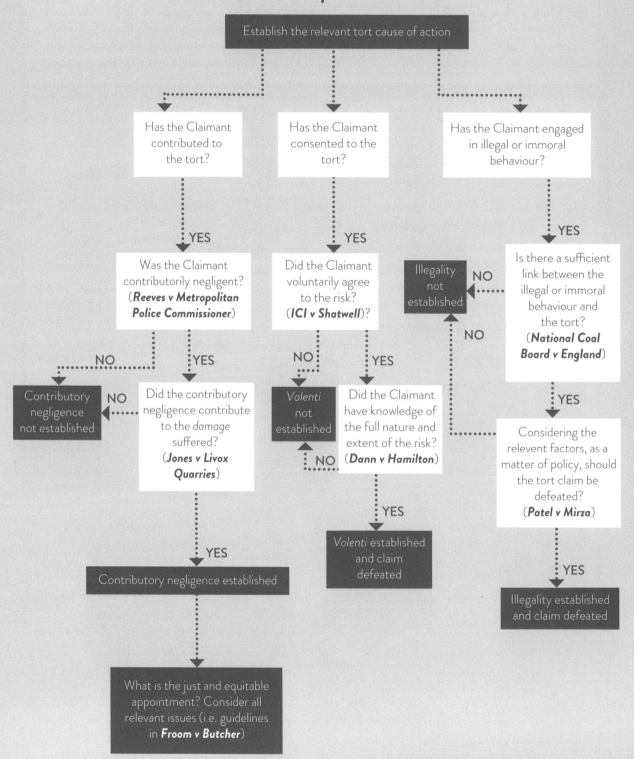

Establish the relevant tort cause of action

Has the Claimant contributed to the tort?

Has the Claimant consented to the tort?

Has the Claimant engaged in illegal or immoral behaviour?

YES

Was the Claimant contributorily negligent? (**_Reeves v Metropolitan Police Commissioner_**)

YES

Did the Claimant voluntarily agree to the risk? (**_ICI v Shatwell_**)?

YES

Is there a sufficient link between the illegal or immoral behaviour and the tort? (**_National Coal Board v England_**)

Illegality not established

NO

NO

NO

YES

Contributory negligence not established

NO

Did the contributory negligence contribute to the *damage* suffered? (**_Jones v Livox Quarries_**)

NO

Volenti not established

NO

Did the Claimant have knowledge of the full nature and extent of the risk? (**_Dann v Hamilton_**)

YES

Considering the relevent factors, as a matter of policy, should the tort claim be defeated? (**_Patel v Mirza_**)

YES

Contributory negligence established

YES

Volenti established and claim defeated

YES

Illegality established and claim defeated

What is the just and equitable appointment? Consider all relevant issues (i.e. guidelines in **_Froom v Butcher_**)

17 DAMAGES

LEARNING OBJECTIVES

By the end of this chapter, you should be able to:

- Describe the purpose of damages in tort law
- Distinguish between compensatory, nominal, aggravated and exemplary/punitive damages
- Outline the differences between pecuniary and non-pecuniary losses
- Identify the different pecuniary and non-pecuniary losses for personal injury and the rules associated with accessing each type of loss
- Recognise the complexities of compensating benefits in tort law damages and apply the general principles developed by the courts
- Apply the different legislative regimes associated with tort actions that result in wrongful death
- Apply the different time limitations under the Limitation Act 1980
- Consider how courts can make different damages orders (i.e. interim payments, periodical payments etc.)
- Recognise the different situations where multiple parties can be held liable under a single tort claim

CHAPTER CONTENTS

17.1	Introduction	422
17.2	Purpose of damages in tort law	423
17.3	Property damage	426
17.4	Personal injury	427
	17.4.1 Pecuniary losses	427
	17.4.2 Non-pecuniary losses	430
17.5	Compensating benefits	430
17.6	Actions after death	432
	17.6.1 Law Reform (Miscellaneous Provisions) Act 1934	432
	17.6.2 Fatal Accidents Act 1976	433
17.7	Time limitations on tort law claims	435
17.8	How damages can be awarded	439
17.9	Contribution and apportionment	442
17.10	Chapter summary	443
Further reading		444

PROBLEM QUESTION

Deepa, Khalid and Deepa's 8-year-old daughter, Nira, were taking a drive one Sunday afternoon. Deepa and Khalid had been dating for a number of years, but had only been living together for 18 months. Their car was hit by a negligent delivery driver, who was employed by Kwik Kourier Pty Ltd. Deepa and Nira were seriously injured and, after 90 minutes of excruciating pain, Khalid died from his injuries. In his will, Khalid left all of his (limited) estate to Save the Children Fund.

The car was significantly damaged but, if repaired properly, would still be safe to drive. The car was only worth £2,000, but it would cost nearly £4,000 to repair it to a standard that was safe on the road. Deepa was insistent that the car be repaired, as it was a present from Khalid before he died and 'she wants to keep part of him with her'.

Deepa and Nira were rushed to the local NHS hospital. They received most of their medical services under the NHS, but Deepa decided to have one of her operations under private care as there was an exceptionally long waiting list at the local hospital. In addition to the NHS services, both Deepa and Nira received a range of private health services that were not provided under the NHS, including specialised rehabilitation, hydrotherapy and physiotherapy. Deepa has also been seeing a private counsellor to work through the trauma of the accident and loss of Khalid.

Deepa was a very successful stockbroker and worked long hours, so Khalid was the primary caregiver and provided her with significant support, including almost all the childcare and house duties. Since the accident, Deepa has returned to work but is earning significantly less due to her physical impairments. Her mother has been providing considerable assistance with housework and childcare, but sometimes Deepa has to hire professional paid support. Aware of Deepa's limited cooking skills, people from her work and Nira's school have organised a roster to provide the family with cooked meals for the next year. One of Deepa's friends also organised a crowdfunding venture to send Deepa and Nira on an international holiday.

Deepa and Nira previously had very energetic lifestyles, and particularly enjoyed family hikes and bike rides. Unfortunately, since the accident, they have not been able to engage in these activities.

Nira has ongoing physical difficulties from the accident and is very likely to have a reduced life expectancy. The driver has admitted liability, but both parties have agreed to determine the quantum of damages at a later stage when the long-term consequences of Nira's injuries are more certain. The house that Deepa and Nira are living in currently is adequate for their needs, provided they have access to significant care. Deepa, however, wants to move to a £1.1 million luxury bungalow that has been renovated to make it disability friendly. It also has a range of additional benefits, such as a jacuzzi, movie room and swimming pool, which will provide her and Nira with a higher standard of living. She would like to access an interim payment of this amount to purchase the bungalow.

Advise Deepa of her rights.

17.1 Introduction

Once it has been established that there is a claim available in tort and there is no defence completely barring the claim, the court must decide on an appropriate remedy (or potentially remedies) for the wronged party. In the great majority of cases, this remedy will be in the form of damages, which is the focus of this chapter. It must, however, be recognised that there is the potential for other remedies, such as an injunction or potentially specific performance (i.e. requiring the defendant to perform a specific action), for particular torts. This is particularly relevant for trespass to land, under the Protection from Harassment Act 1997, defamation and privacy.[1]

This chapter focuses on the key issues associated with damages in tort law. It starts by considering the different purposes of damages, linking in with the discussion in the Introductory Chapter. The different principles associated with compensating property damage are then outlined, focusing on when the courts will award cost of cure damages as opposed to diminution of value. The most controversial aspect of tort law damages is how to compensate for personal injuries, and the difficulties arising in both pecuniary and non-pecuniary losses will be analysed. The area is further complicated by how the courts should deal with compensating advantages, particularly what impact the generosity of others should have on the damages the defendant is required to pay. There are a number of statutes relevant to the award of damages in tort law, and the chapter addresses three of these – the Limitation Act 1980, the Fatal Accidents Act 1976 and the Law Reform (Miscellaneous Provisions) Act 1934. The different ways damages can be awarded are considered, namely provisional

---

1   See, for example, 2.4.1, 10.3, 12.7.2, 13.6.2 and 14.3.4.

damages, interim awards and periodical payments orders. The situations where multiple parties can be held liable under a single tort claim are also discussed.

It must be recognised that awarding damages in tort law is exceptionally complicated, and the process connects with a range of other topics. Multiple books have been written focused solely on tort law damages. This area is inherently linked with complex civil procedure rules, which can only be briefly discussed in this chapter. It is both unnecessary and beyond the scope of this chapter to go into detail about how damages are calculated, and therefore only the general principles will be outlined.

MAKING CONNECTIONS

A number of torts are also criminal offences, particularly trespass to the person torts. Therefore, the defendant may also have a finding of criminal liability and be subject to criminal sanctions. When this occurs, the victim can access damages through the Criminal Injuries Compensation Scheme, which is paid for by the government, or a tort law claim. The latter is likely to result in higher damages, but the defendant must have sufficient means to pay the amount awarded (or be insured).

17.2 Purpose of damages in tort law

The majority of this chapter will focus on 'compensatory damages', although other types of damages will be briefly discussed. The aim of *compensatory* damages in tort law is to, as far as monetary compensation can, put the victim in the same position they would have been in had the tort not been committed against them.[2] This is often not a straightforward exercise, as shown by *Whittington Hospital Trust v XX*.

KEY CASE

Whittington Hospital NHS Trust v XX [2020] UKSC 14

The claimant became infertile due to the defendant's negligence. The NHS Trust had not detected signs of cancer from the claimant's cervical screening tests in 2008 and 2012. When the cancer was detected in 2013, it was so advanced that the treatment made the claimant, who was 29 at the time, infertile. She was able to collect and freeze some eggs prior to her treatment, and it was probable – with the use of surrogacy – that she would be able to have two children with her own eggs. Commercial surrogacy is illegal in the UK, but occurs in a number of other jurisdictions, including California. The claimant and her partner always wanted four children, so she claimed damages for the cost of two further children through commercial surrogacy in California with donor

eggs. The NHS argued that this cost should not be awarded as it was against public policy.

The Supreme Court held that the claimant was entitled to damages for physical injury of surgery and chemotherapy, long-term disabilities and psychiatric injury, as well as the complete loss of fertility. The claimant was also entitled to damages for the cost of surrogacy arrangements using her own eggs and the cost of using donor eggs. The majority of the Supreme Court held that the claimant was also entitled to the cost of international commercial surrogacy.

Lady Hale started her judgment by stating that:

The object of damages in tort is to put the claimant, as far as possible, back in the position in which she would have been had the tort not

---

2   See discussion in 1.3.

been committed. Money has to compensate, as far as it can, for those injuries that cannot be cured. For some women, the ability to bear and to rear children is a vital part of their identity. What then should be the measure of damages for a woman who has been wrongfully deprived of the ability to bear children herself? Along with general damages for pain, suffering and loss of amenity, should it include the cost of making surrogacy arrangements with another woman to bear a child for her to bring up? In particular, should it include the cost of making commercial surrogacy arrangements abroad?[3]

After considering the relevant legal issues, her Ladyship commented that 'attitudes to commercial surrogacy had changed ... perceptions of the family had also changed and using donor eggs could now be regarded as restorative'?[4] and 'the courts have bent over backwards to recognise the relationships created by surrogacy, including foreign commercial surrogacy. The government now supports surrogacy as a valid way of creating family relationships.'[5]

This case is a useful example of how complicated the assessment of tort law damages can become. The aim of tort law is to put the person into the position they would have been in had the tort not been committed against them. The court was therefore required to find a monetary equivalent to the claimant's infertility and inability to have her own family, which raised complicated issues of public policy, family relationships and restorative justice.

Tort law damages can be contrasted with contractual damages, which are forward looking and aim to put the claimant in the position they would have been in had the contract been performed. The focus of tort law compensatory damages is outlined by Lord Blackburn in *Livingstone v Rawyards Coal Co* [1880], with the court ordering the defendant to pay 'that sum of money which will put the party who has been injured, or who has suffered, in the same position as he would have been in if he had not sustained the wrong for which he is now getting his compensation or reparation'.[6]

Whilst it is clear that compensation is the key principle behind tort law, there are a range of other objectives and purposes that have been put forward as playing a role in the development of tort law, including deterrence and personal or institutional accountability. The focus on compensation and compensatory damages can be contrasted with other types of possible damages, including nominal damages, aggravated damages, and exemplary (or punitive) damages.

Table 17.1: Summary of damages

Type of Damage	Explanation	When Awarded	Relevant Cases
Nominal Damages	Tokenistic damages designed to highlight that a legal wrong has been committed, but that no substantive harm has been suffered by the claimant.	These are most often awarded in trespass to the person cases which are actionable *per se* (i.e. without the need to prove that damage has actually been suffered).	*R (Lumba) v Secretary of State for the Home Department* [2012] 1 AC 245 (false imprisonment)

---

3   [2020] UKSC 14 at [1].
4   [2020] UKSC 14 at [7].
5   [2020] UKSC 14 at [52].
6   (1880) 5 App Cas 25, 39.

Type of Damage	Explanation	When Awarded	Relevant Cases
Aggravated damages	Damages which are still compensatory in nature, but are awarded at a higher level to compensate for the manner in which the tort was committed. These damages are awarded because the court finds that the actions of the defendant have aggravated the injury to the claimant (generally to their feelings, person autonomy and/or dignity).	Aggravated damages are not applicable to all torts and will be limited to causes of actions in which the claimant's feelings are closely linked with the tortious actions, for example trespass to the person, breach of confidence and defamation.	*Appleton v Garrett* [1996] PIQR P1 (trespass to the person) *Campbell v MGN Ltd* [2004] 2 WLR 1232 (breach of confidence) *Rowlands v Chief Constable of Merseyside Police* [2006] EWCA Civ 1773 (malicious prosecution)
Exemplary (or punitive) damages	Damages which are not focused on compensation, but instead are intended to punish specifically harmful conduct by the defendant. Unlike compensatory damages, exemplary damages focus on the actions of the defendant as opposed to the harm suffered by the claimant. The application of these damages in tort law is controversial.	Three situations that have justified the award of exemplary damages: (1) oppressive, arbitrary or unconstitutional actions by government services, (2) conduct calculated to make a profit exceeding the compensable payment under the tort, (3) where these types of damages have been expressly authorised by statute.	*Rookes v Barnard* [1964] AC 1129 (economic torts) *Cassell v Broome* [1972] AC 1027 (defamation) *Kuddus v Chief Constable of Leicestershire* [2001] UKHL 29 (malicious prosecution)

DIFFERENT PERSPECTIVES on damages in tort law

J. Morgan, 'Abolishing Personal Injuries Law? A Reply to Lord Sumption' (2018) 34 Professional Negligence 122–42

Morgan contends that in addition to the key aim of compensation, tort law has other purposes – specifically discussing the role of deterrence and accountability. He argues that 'tort liability has a significant effect on those subject to it ... Its influence on behaviour persists notwithstanding insurance and vicarious liability. It cannot be assumed that government regulation would be a perfect replacement for tort's deterrent effect.' Morgan further states that liability in tort law provides the ability for victims to hold tortfeasors accountable for the harm that they cause. Both of these purposes therefore require consideration when determining an appropriate way to deal with tortious actions.

R. Stevens, Torts and Rights (OUP, 2007)

In his book, Stevens argues that the purpose of damages in tort law is not to compensate the harm that has been caused by the defendant, but instead to respond to the damage to the underlying rights of the claimant. He contends that tort liability should occur through a 'rights-based analysis' where damages are awarded as the next best thing to the claimant's primary right that has been infringed by the defendant. Under this model, Stevens argues that tort is a species of wrong and breaching a duty is an infringement of a right. Secondary rights arise from obligations generated by the infringement of primary rights and are remedial in nature. This means that the only rights in tort law are secondary remedial rights. It therefore follows that the law of torts does not give rise to a normative or social agenda in and of itself, but instead it is merely a way of vindicating primary rights.

J. Conaghan, 'Civil Liability: addressing failures in the context of rape, domestic and sexual abuse', Inaugural Lecture, University of Bristol, 19 February 2015
In her inaugural lecture, Conaghan addresses the role of civil liability specifically in the context of rape, domestic violence and sexual abuse. She considers a range of real-life cases where people, particularly women and children, have been injured or killed by people they know as a result of institutional failures. Conaghan highlights how, in these situations, it is difficult for victims to obtain redress from the institution that has failed them, generally the police. She further contends that this has a range of negative impacts and that 'a fairer, more proportionate solution' is needed. She highlights the potential for tort liability to go beyond merely compensating the victim for the harm that has been committed against them. Drawing on the work of the American scholar Charles Epp, Conaghan argues that holding these parties liable can be used to bring about 'institutional accountability' and potentially wide-scale change, in this case providing additional protection for vulnerable people in our society.

■ VIEWPOINT

What do you think should be the main purpose (or purposes) of damages in tort law?

17.3 Property damage

When property has been damaged during the commission of a tort, the claimant can recover the cost of this property damage from the defendant. There is, however, a question about how the cost should be determined, and whether it is fairer to award the diminution in value or the cost of cure. These can be significantly different. Imagine if someone runs into the back of my 15-year-old Alfa Romeo worth £700. There are significant dents and damage, but the car is still safe to drive. Due to the age and model of the car, it may cost £1,000 to fix. The accident has, however, only resulted in the car's value reducing to £500. Should I be able to claim the £1,000 to fix the car, or only the £200 reduction in its value?

In *Dodd Properties v Canterbury City Council* [1980],[7] the Court of Appeal held that there was no hard and fast rule, and instead the specific facts of each case should be considered – particularly the claimant's future intentions with the property and what was reasonable in the circumstances. This was applied in *Southampton Container Terminals Ltd v Hansa Schiffahrtsgesellscaft mbH (MV 'Maersk Colombo')* [1999][8] where a crane was negligently damaged and could no longer be used. The claimants sought damages of £2.35 million for the cost of replacing the crane, whereas the defendants argued that it should only have to pay £665,000 as this was the approximate market value of the damaged crane. David Steel J awarded the lower amount on the basis that, prior to the accident, the claimant had already ordered a new larger crane.

Sometimes, replacing an item will result in the claimant being in a 'better' position than they were before the tort was committed. In that case, the court has discretion to reduce damages for the additional advantage received by the claimant. This occurred in *Voaden v Champion* [2002], where a negligently moored ship resulted in the loss of the claimant's pontoon. The pontoon that was lost had an estimated 8-year life expectancy remaining, and was replaced with a new pontoon that cost £60,000 and had a life expectancy of 30 years. On the basis that the claimant had been put in a 'better' position than before the tort was committed against her, the claimant was only awarded 8/30ths of the cost of the pontoon, being £16,000. In this case, the new pontoon provided the

---

7   [1980] 1 WLR 433.
8   [1999] All ER (D) 960.

claimant with a real benefit; however, Rix LJ held that this would not apply if 'the betterment has conferred no corresponding advantage on the claimant'.[9] As an example of this scenario, his Lordship referred to *Harbutt's 'Plasticine' Ltd v Wayne Tank and Pump Co Ltd* [1970][10] where the replacement of an old factory with a new one provided no benefit to the claimant as the building was not improved in any way.

PROBLEM QUESTION TECHNIQUE

The car was significantly damaged in the accident but, if repaired properly, would still be safe to drive. The car was only worth £2,000 but would cost nearly £4,000 to repair it to a standard that was safe on the road. Deepa was insistent that the car be repaired, as it was a present from Khalid before he died and 'she wants to keep part of him with her'.

▸ Would Deepa receive the cost of cure (£4,000) as opposed to diminution of value (£2,000)?

▸ Consider the test in *Dodd Properties v Canterbury City Council*, where the Court of Appeal stated that the court will consider both the claimant's future intentions and 'reasonableness'.

▸ Despite the fact that there was a significant difference in cost, does the fact that Deepa has an intention to repair the car justify cost of cure damages?

17.4 Personal injury

Damages for personal injuries are often divided into 'pecuniary' and 'non-pecuniary' losses. Pecuniary losses refer to financial losses that can be measured in quantifiable monetary terms, for example lost wages, out-of-pocket medical costs, costs of future care etc. In contrast, non-pecuniary losses are non-financial losses that cannot be easily quantified in monetary terms, for example, pain and suffering, emotional distress and loss of amenities.

17.4.1 Pecuniary losses

The pecuniary losses recoverable for personal injuries include medical and related expenses, loss of earnings, care needs and reduced life expectancy. The award of damages covers both costs already incurred, which are generally quite simple to calculate, and costs that will be incurred in the future, which are considerably more complicated and uncertain. Claims for future costs are calculated according to current principles and supported by detailed evidence from the claimant and relevant experts. These are highly contested aspects of claims for pecuniary losses, and therefore need to be supported by proper evidence in order to succeed.

17.4.1.1 MEDICAL AND RELATED EXPENSES

Whilst the majority of medical costs in the UK are likely to be covered by the National Heath Service (NHS), some claimants seek private medical care. The Law Reform (Personal Injuries) Act 1948, s 2(4) states that in the event that private medical care is utilised by the claimant, these costs can be claimed as damages – even though the claimant could have prevented the costs from arising

---

9   [2002] EWCA Civ 89 at [85].
10   [1970] 1 QB 447.

PART 5

by seeking treatment from the NHS. If the claimant received their treatment from the NHS, they will not, however, be able to recover damages for the cost of the equivalent private treatment.[11]

■ VIEWPOINT

In light of the access to the NHS, how should tort law deal with a claimant who elects to use private health services?

There are also a significant number of other medical expenses that may not be provided under the NHS that the claimant will be able to claim from the defendant, for example dental, physiotherapy, specialist services and speech therapy.

17.4.1.2 LOSS OF EARNINGS

The claimant will be able to recover the loss of net earnings (i.e. income after National Insurance and income tax) as a result of the harm suffered.[12] This includes past losses (i.e. work unable to be performed before the trial) and future losses (i.e. work unable to be performed after the trial). The courts will use the 'multiplier method' to determine the amount awarded, multiplying the annual amount by the number of years they expected to work until retirement. The final award will then be reduced on the assumption that the lump sum will be invested and because of the 'vicissitudes of life'.[13] The claimant will also be able to claim damages if they have difficulty finding another job, or their position in the labour market was weakened because of the injuries suffered.[14]

17.4.1.3 PAST AND FUTURE CARE NEEDS

In the event of serious physical injuries, the claimant is likely to need significant ongoing assistance, and the cost of this care is recoverable. If the care is provided by a professional, this will clearly be covered by the damages award. It is, however, more complicated when family or friends provide the assistance. In *Donnelly v Joyce* [1974],[15] the Court of Appeal emphasised that this sacrifice should not go unrewarded, and it awarded the victim the cost of the care provided to her by her mother. The approach to this assistance was changed by the House of Lords in *Hunt v Severs* [1994].[16] In this case, the court held that if care is provided for by a third party (i.e. spouse, family member or friend), the damages are awarded to the claimant but held on trust for the third party.[17] The Law Commission in 1999 recommended that the *Hunt v Severs* rule be overturned and that the damages should be payable to the claimant without needing it to be held on trust for the third party.[18] This

---

11   *Lim Poh Choo v Camden and Islington Area Health Authority* [1980] AC 174.

12   *British Transport Commission v Gourley* [1956] AC 185.

13   This occurs through the 'Ogden Tables', entitled '*Actuarial tables for use in personal injury and fatal accident case*'. These are described as the following: 'These tables, complete with explanatory notes, are an aid for actuaries, lawyers and others when calculating the lump sum to be paid in compensation for financial losses or expenses (such as care costs) directly caused by personal injury or death. Widely known as the Ogden tables, they are prepared by an inter-disciplinary working party of actuaries, lawyers, accountants and insurers.' For further details see: https://www.gov.uk/government/publications/ogden-tables-actuarial-compensation-tables-for-injury-and-death.

14   *Smith v Manchester City Council* (1974) 17 KIR 1.

15   [1974] QB 454.

16   [1994] 2 AC 350.

17   *Hunt v Severs* [1994] 2 AC 350.

18   Law Commission's Report No 262 (1999) *Damages for Personal Injury: Medical, Nursing and Other Expenses; Collateral Benefits*.

recommendation has not been implemented, and so the *Hunt v Severs* rule remains part of tort law damages.

17.4.1.4 REDUCED LIFE EXPECTANCY

The claimant can also claim for their 'lost years'. These are damages recovered for the period which the claimant's life expectancy is reduced. This occurred in *Pickett v British Rail Engineering Ltd* [1980], where the claimant was awarded damages for the years lost due to contracting mesothelioma from his employment.[19] The justification of this damage is that the claimant has objectively suffered a loss, even though there is no subjective loss.[20] In *Pickett*, the House of Lords was also concerned about the impact of the lost years on the dependants of the deceased.[21]

PROBLEM QUESTION TECHNIQUE

Deepa and Nira were rushed to the local NHS hospital. They received most of their medical services under the NHS, but Deepa decided to have one of her operations under private care as there was an exceptionally long waiting list at the local hospital. In addition to the NHS services, both Deepa and Nira received a range of private health services that were not provided under the NHS, including specialised rehabilitation, hydrotherapy and physiotherapy. Deepa has also been seeing a private counsellor to work through the trauma of the accident and loss of Khalid.

Deepa was a very successful stockbroker and worked long hours, so Khalid was the primary caregiver and provided her with significant support, including almost all the childcare and house duties. Since the accident, Deepa has returned to work but is earning significantly less due to her physical impairments. Her mother has been providing considerable assistance with housework and childcare, but sometimes Deepa has to hire professional paid support.

▶ Will Deepa will be able to claim the cost of all private health services utilised, including the operation, the specialised health services and the counselling? Does the fact that she could have accessed some of these under the NHS impact her claim?

▶ What rights does Deepa have regarding her reduced income? How will the courts determine what should be paid (specifically remember to consider the difference between her pre- and post-accident earnings, and multiply this by the number of years until retirement, and a reduction of the appropriate amount as per the Odgen tables)?

▶ Will the care provided by Deepa's mother be claimable? What impact does the rule in *Hunt v Severs* have on the claim?

▶ Consider also whether Nira would be entitled to claim damages for her reduced life expectancy.

---

19 [1980] AC 136.

20 For further discussion, see *Wise v Kaye* [1962] 2 WLR 96. The objective sum for 'loss of expectation of life' was abolished by s 1(1)(a) of the Administration of Justice Act 1982, and it is now awarded on a subjective basis under s 1(1)(b). For the interaction between reduced life expectancy and compensation for loss of future earnings, see *Whipps Cross University NHS Trust v Iqbal (by his mother & litigation friend Iqbal)* [2007] EWCA Civ 1190.

21 [1980] AC 136.

17.4.2 Non-pecuniary losses

The claimant is able to claim for non-pecuniary losses associated with the harm they have suffered. The main types of non-pecuniary loss are damages for pain and suffering and loss of amenities. For pain and suffering, the courts will award an amount based on the specific characteristics of the claimant. In contrast, loss of amenities damages are determined on an objective basis. However, in *Lim Poh Coo v Camden and Islington Area Health Authority* [1979], the House of Lords held that the fact the claimant was unconscious did not remove the deprivation of the ordinary experiences and amenities of life.[22]

The starting point for these awards is the Judicial College *Guidelines for the Assessment of Damages in Personal Injury Cases*. The 15th edition of these Guidelines was published in November 2019.[23] This is just a starting point, and the exact level of damages awarded will depend on a range of other factors including the severity of the injury suffered, the impact the injury has had on the claimant's day-to-day living, and age and life expectancy.

Despite the importance of the Judicial College Guidelines, the courts have the final discretion to award damages that they believe are just. In *Heil v Rankin* [2001], a specially constituted five-judge Court of Appeal increased the base amount awarded for serious injuries on the basis that it had fallen below that which was 'fair, just and reasonable'. In doing so, Lord Woolf MR commented that 'in considering whether the level of the awards of damages for non-pecuniary loss is too low, there is no change in the law involved even if we come to the conclusion that a change in the level is required. The court is doing no more than considering the adequacy of the level of current awards by applying existing principles and, in so far as they are inadequate, bringing them up to date.'[24]

PROBLEM QUESTION TECHNIQUE

Deepa and Nira were seriously injured [in the accident]. They previously had very energetic lifestyles, and particularly enjoyed family hikes and bike rides. Unfortunately, since the accident, they have not been able to engage in these activities.

▸ Consider whether both Deepa and Nira will be able to obtain damages for their injuries? How will the amount be calculated?

▸ Will Deepa and Nira be able to claim damages for loss of amenities and their lack of ability to enjoy activities previously engaged in? What impact does the fact that Nira is not aware of the deprivation have on this claim?

▸ Remember to refer to the Judicial College Guidelines for the Assessment of Damages in Personal Injury Cases.

17.5 Compensating benefits

How should tort law respond when the claimant has received a *benefit* from being the victim of a tort? It is human nature that often when an individual is injured, family, friends and sometimes even the community at large will come together and provide assistance during their time of need. This raises the question of whether any benefits received by the claimant (known as 'compensating benefits')

---

22 [1979] 3 WLR 44, 53–4.
23 The Hon. Mrs Justice Lambert, Peter Carson, Stuart McKechnie, Steven Snowden and Richard Wilkinson, *Guidelines for the Assessment of General Damages in Personal Injury Cases*, 15th edn (Oxford University Press, 2019).
24 [2001] QB 272, 300.

should be taken into account when awarding damages? If so, this will result in a reduction in the amount of damages the defendant is required to pay. The answer is often far from straightforward. If compensating benefits are taken into account, it can seem unfair that the government, friends and family or charities are subsidising the defendant. However, if they are not taken into account, it can result in the claimant being overcompensated.

This is a complicated question, and the courts have highlighted the need to balance 'justice, reasonableness and public policy' when making their determination.[25] There is often no clear answer. As outlined by Lord Bridge in *Hussain v New Taplow Paper Mills Ltd* [1988]:

> where there is no statute applicable the common law must solve the problem unaided and the possibility of a compromise solution is not available. Many eminent common law judges, I think it is fair to say, have been baffled by the problem of how to articulate a single guiding rule to distinguish receipts by a plaintiff which are to be taken into account in mitigation of damage from those which are not.[26]

The general approach is to consider *who* has provided the compensating advantage – the claimant's own foresight, a third party or the defendant?

Table 17.2: Compensating benefits

Who Provided the Benefit	Examples	Outcome	Case(s)
The claimant's own foresight	Payments from pensions[27] or personal insurance policies	The compensating benefit will generally not result in a reduction of damages	*Bradburn v Great Western Rail Co* (1874) LR 10 Ex 1 *Parry v Cleaver* [1970] AC 1
Generosity of others	General assistance in the form of housekeeping, providing meals, childcare etc. or charitable donations	The compensating benefit will generally not result in a reduction of damages	*Jones v Stroud District Council* [1988] 1 All ER 5
Actions of defendant	A negligent employer who gives an injured employee a lump sum of money or paid time off work	The compensating benefit is normally deducted from the final quantum awarded to the claimant	*Hussain v New Taplow Paper Mills Ltd* [1988] AC 514 *Williams v BOC Gases Ltd* [2000] ICR 1181

One particularly complex area is the impact of social security benefits on payments made by the government. This is an area largely covered by a number of complicated pieces of legislation.[28] In

---

25 *Parry v Cleaver* [1970] AC 1, 13 (Lord Reid).
26 [1988] AC 514, 528.
27 *Parry v Cleaver* [1970] AC 1. If the claimant did not contribute to the pension payments, then this will be a compensating benefit akin to sick pay and it will result in a reduction of the amount paid by the defendant: see *Hussain v New Taplow Paper Mills Ltd* [1988] AC 514.
28 For example, Law Reform (Personal Injuries) Act 1948; Social Security (Recovery of Benefits) Act 1997; Social Security (Recovery of Benefits) Regulations 1997.

general, the government has the power to recover benefits paid by both court judgments and out-of-court settlements, and these are processed by the Department for Work and Pension's Compensation Recovery Unit.[29]

PROBLEM QUESTION TECHNIQUE

[Deepa's] mother has been providing considerable assistance with housework and childcare, but sometimes Deepa has to hire professional paid support. Aware of Deepa's limited cooking skills, people from her work and Nira's school have organised a roster to provide the family with cooked meals for the next year. One of Deepa's friends also organised a crowdfunding venture to send Deepa and Nira on an international holiday.

▸ Will the compensating benefits of assistance with housework, childcare, cooking and the international holiday be taken into account when determining damages to be paid by the defendant?

▸ Remember to consider who is providing these benefits and the impact it has on an award of damages.

17.6 Actions after death

If the victim of the tort is killed because of the tortious actions of the defendant, there are many difficult questions concerning the rights of the victim's family and estate. The majority of this area is now covered by statutory provisions, specifically the Law Reform (Miscellaneous Provisions) Act 1934 and the Fatal Accidents Act 1976.

17.6.1 Law Reform (Miscellaneous Provisions) Act 1934

This Act gives the deceased's estate the right to any surviving or existing causes of actions in tort.

KEY LEGISLATION

Law Reform (Miscellaneous Provisions) Act 1934

1   Effect of death on certain causes of action

(1)   Subject to the provisions of this section, on the death of any person after the commencement of this Act all causes of action subsisting against or vested in him shall survive against, or, as the case may be, for the benefit of, his estate. Provided that this subsection shall not apply to causes of action for defamation …

(1A) The right of a person to claim under section 1A of the Fatal Accidents Act 1976 (bereavement) shall not survive for the benefit of his estate on his death;

(2)   Where a cause of action survives as aforesaid for the benefit of the estate of a deceased person, the damages recoverable for the benefit of the estate of that person—

　　　(a) shall not include—

　　　　　(i)   any exemplary damages;

　　　　　(ii) any damages for loss of income in respect of any period after that person's death;

　　　(b) …

---

29   This is, however, a considerably complicated area and has been subject to a number of Law Commission recommendations: see Law Commission, *Damages for Personal Injury: Medical, Nursing and Other Expenses* (No 262, 1999).

(c) Where the death of that person has been caused by the act or omission which gives rise to the cause of action, shall be calculated without reference to any loss or gain to his estate consequent on his death, except that a sum in respect of funeral expenses may be included.

Under s 1(1), on death, all causes of action vested in the deceased (except defamation and the right to bereavement damages) survive for the benefit of their estate. Loss of income for any period after the deceased's death is not recoverable under s 1(2)(a)(i); however, funeral costs (if incurred by the estate) may be recoverable (s 1(2)(c)). Pain and suffering incurred before death may also be recovered, but must have been more than momentary.[30]

PROBLEM QUESTION TECHNIQUE

After 90 minutes of excruciating pain, Khalid died from his injuries. In his will, Khalid left all of his (limited) estate to Save the Children Fund.

▸ What rights are there under the Law Reform (Miscellaneous Provisions) Act 1934? Who can enforce these rights?

▸ Remember that the 1934 Act specifically covers any existing causes of action from Khalid (except for defamation and the right to bereavement damages) and the cost of organising a funeral.

▸ Would there be any claim for Khalid's pain and suffering? Was this more than 'momentary' under *Hicks v Chief Constable of South Yorkshire Police*?

17.6.2 Fatal Accidents Act 1976

The second relevant piece of legislation is the Fatal Accidents Act 1976, which provides dependants of someone who has been killed by 'any wrongful act, neglect or default' with independent causes of action for their own losses.[31] Access to the rights under this Act are, however, dependent on the claimant (1) falling within the definition of a 'dependant' of the deceased under s 1(3) of the Act, and (2) showing that they were, in fact, financially dependent on the deceased.

KEY LEGISLATION

Fatal Accidents Act 1976

1   Right of action for wrongful act causing death

(1)   If death is caused by any wrongful act, neglect or default which is such as would (if death had not ensued) have entitled the person injured to maintain an action and recover damages in respect thereof, the person who would have been liable if death had not ensued shall be liable to an action for damages, notwithstanding the death of the person injured.

(2)   Subject to section 1A(2) below, every such action shall be for the benefit of the dependants of the person ('the deceased') whose death has been so caused.

(3)   In this Act 'dependant' means—

(a) the wife or husband or former wife or husband of the deceased;

(aa) the civil partner or former civil partner of the deceased;

---

30   *Hicks v Chief Constable of South Yorkshire Police* [1992] 2 All ER 65.
31   Fatal Accidents Act 1976, s 1(1).

(b) any person who—
  (i) was living with the deceased in the same household immediately before the date of the death; and
  (ii) had been living with the deceased in the same household for at least two years before that date; and
  (iii) was living during the whole of that period as the husband or wife or civil partner of the deceased;
(c) any parent or other ascendant of the deceased;
(d) any person who was treated by the deceased as his parent;
(e) any child or other descendant of the deceased;
(f) any person (not being a child of the deceased) who, in the case of any marriage to which the deceased was at any time a party, was treated by the deceased as a child of the family in relation to that marriage;
(fa) any person (not being a child of the deceased) who, in the case of any civil partnership in which the deceased was at any time a civil partner, was treated by the deceased as a child of the family in relation to that civil partnership;
(g) any person who is, or is the issue of, a brother, sister, uncle or aunt of the deceased.

The Act has very specific and strict requirements. In *Kotke v Saffarini* [2005],[32] a claim under the Fatal Accidents Act 1976 was rejected by the courts even though the claimant and the deceased had been in a relationship for a number of years, the deceased provided the claimant with financial support, they had a child together and had talked about marriage. The Court of Appeal agreed with the trial judge's decision that the claimant was not a 'dependant' under the Act as they each lived in their own property, and therefore the claimant had not been 'living with the deceased in the same household for at least two years' as required by s 1(3)(b)(ii) of the Fatal Accidents Act 1976. This strict approach of the Act has been criticised by academic literature,[33] courts[34] and the Law Commission, which 'took the view that the present fixed list should be replaced by a generally worded test', specifically whether there was a 'relationship of dependency'.[35]

If an individual fulfils the definition of a 'dependant' of the deceased, and shows that they were financially dependent on the deceased, they will be entitled to claim all pecuniary losses suffered by them due to the death. This includes the financial or non-financial contributions made by the deceased to the dependent (i.e. lost wages and/or domestic assistance provided). The Act specifically states that when assessing damages, any compensating benefits that have accrued or may accrue as a result of the death shall be disregarded.[36] There is also a rather peculiar section that expressly excludes a *female's* remarriage or the prospect of remarriage as a relevant consideration in determining awards for damages[37] (but a male's prospect of remarriage is strangely not mentioned!).[38]

---

32 [2005] EWCA Civ 221.
33 R. Kidner, 'A History of the Fatal Accidents Acts' (1999) 50 *NILQ* 318; S. Waddams, 'Damages for wrongful death: has Lord Campbell's Act outlived its usefulness?' (1984) 47 *MLR* 437.
34 *Shepherd v Post Office* [1995] 6 WLUK 107.
35 Law Commission, *Claims for Wrongful Death* (No 263, 1999) at [1.5].
36 Fatal Accidents Act 1976, s 4.
37 Fatal Accidents Act 1976, s 3(3). For discussion of ss 3(3) and 4 of the Act, see Lord Sumption's decision in *Cox v Ergo Versicherung AG (formerly known as Victoria)* [2014] UKSC 22; [2014] AC 1379.
38 For a discussion on the historical basis of the Fatal Accidents Act 1846 (which preceded the Fatal Accidents Act 1976), see J. Murphy, 'Contemporary Tort Theory and Tort Law's Evolution' (2019) 32(3) *Canadian Journal of Law & Jurisprudence* 413, 427–78.

In addition to damages for loss of dependency, bereavement payments are available for an even smaller number of claimants, namely the deceased's wife, husband or civil partner (or parents if the deceased is a minor).[39] The bereavement payment amount is a fixed amount, currently set at £12,980,[40] which is not connected to the extent of the claimant's grief or their relationship with the deceased. This payment has also been heavily criticised,[41] with the Law Commission recommending in 1999 that it be uplifted from £10,000 (at the time) to £30,000[42] and extended to a larger range of beneficiaries.[43]

The Fatal Accidents Act 1976 clearly has a number of limitations. The Law Commission undertook a detailed review of the Act in 1999 and made a number of recommendations. Ten years later, the Law Commission again considered the Act as part of the *Civil Law Reform Bill Consultation Paper*,[44] and further recommendations were made. No recommendations from either review have yet been implemented.

■ VIEWPOINT

How should the Fatal Accidents Act 1976 be updated to make it more accurately reflect modern-day families?

PROBLEM QUESTION TECHNIQUE

Deepa, Khalid and Deepa's 8-year-old daughter, Nira, were taking a drive one Sunday afternoon. Deepa and Khalid had been dating for a number of years, but had only been living together for 18 months.

▸ Will Deepa or Nira have any rights under the Fatal Accidents Act 1976 to bereavement payments or loss of dependency?

▸ Consider how long Deepa and Khalid have been living together and whether she fulfils the definition of 'dependant' under s 1(3)(b) (i.e. has she been 'living with the deceased in the same household for at least two years' before he was killed). Remember that this test applies despite the fact that parties may have been dating for a number of years and/or have a strong relationship of dependency.

▸ Consider also whether Nira fulfils the definition of a dependant under the Act.

▸ Will Deepa be entitled to the bereavement payment? Remember the limited categories of spouse or civil partner.

17.7 Time limitations on tort law claims

The Limitation Act 1980 provides strict statutory deadlines for when certain claims must be brought before the court. If these timelines are not met, the claim will be statute-barred and the claimant will not be able to sue, unless they can show one of the limited exceptions. Under s 2 of the Act, the

---

39 Fatal Accidents Act 1976, s 1A.
40 It can, however, be increased from time to time by statutory instrument: Fatal Accidents Act 1976, s 1A(3).
41 P. Cane, Atiyah's Accidents, Compensation and the Law, 7th edn (Cambridge University Press, 2006), 90.
42 Law Commission, Claims for Wrongful Death (No 263, 1999) at [6.51].
43 P. Cane, *Atiyah's Accidents, Compensation and the Law*, 7th edn (Cambridge University Press, 2006), 90; Law Commission, *Claims for Wrongful Death* (No 263, 1999) at [6.31].
44 Law Commissioner, *Civil Law Reform Bill Consultation Paper* (CP53/09, 2009).

time limit for general tort law claims is six years from the date on which the action accrued. There is a stricter one-year time limit in place for actions based on defamation and malicious falsehoods.[45]

KEY LEGISLATION

Limitation Act 1980

2   Time limit for actions founded on tort

An action founded on tort shall not be brought after the expiration of six years from the date on which the cause of action accrued.

4A   Time limit for actions for defamation or malicious falsehood

The time limit under section 2 of this Act shall not apply to an action for—

(a)   libel or slander, or

(b)   slander of title, slander of goods or other malicious falsehood,

but no such action shall be brought after the expiration of one year from the date on which the cause of action accrued.

11   Special time limit for actions in respect of personal injuries

(1)   This section applies to any action for damages for negligence, nuisance or breach of duty (whether the duty exists by virtue of a contract or of provision made by or under a statute or independently of any contract or any such provision) where the damages claimed by the plaintiff for the negligence, nuisance or breach of duty consist of or include damages in respect of personal injuries to the plaintiff or any other person.

(1A)   This section does not apply to any action brought for damages under section 3 of the Protection from Harassment Act 1997.

(2)   None of the time limits given in the preceding provisions of this Act shall apply to an action to which this section applies.

(3)   An action to which this section applies shall not be brought after the expiration of the period applicable in accordance with subsection (4) or (5) below.

(4)   Except where subsection (5) below applies, the period applicable is three years from—

(a)   the date on which the cause of action accrued; or

(b)   the date of knowledge (if later) of the person injured.

Actions for damages for 'negligence, nuisance or breach of duty' are provided with more complex time limits. The starting point is three years from either the date the action accrues or the date of knowledge of the person injured.[46] There are, however, a range of exceptions provided by the Act. The time limit is extended in cases of disability, which is defined to include infancy.[47] Under s 33, the courts also have general powers to 'disapply' the specified time limits if 'it would be equitable to allow an action to proceed'.[48] When determining whether it would be equitable, the court is to have regard to all the circumstances of the case, including the length of and reasons for the delay, the impact of the delay on the evidence adduced by the claimant, the conduct of the defendant, whether

---

45   Limitation Act 1980, s 4A (one year from the date the action accrued).
46   Limitation Act 1980, s 11(4).
47   Limitation Act 1980, s 28, defined in s 38(2).
48   Limitation Act 1980, s 33(1).

the claimant acted promptly and reasonably, and any steps taken by the claimant to obtain medical, legal or other expert advice.[49]

More flexible time limits are available for actions in 'negligence, nuisance or breach of duty'. In *Stubbings v Webb* [1993], the House of Lords held that trespass to the person claims did not come under this definition and therefore did not benefit from these provisions.

KEY CASE

Stubbings v Webb [1993] AC 498

The claimant was a 36-year-old woman who claimed that she was sexually abused by her adoptive father and raped by her stepbrother when she was a minor. She wished to commence claims against both the alleged perpetrators for trespass to the person, but they contended that any potential claim was statute-barred by the Limitation Act 1980. The claimant argued that the claim was not statute-barred due to s 11(4), as it had been less than three years since she was aware that she had a potential claim. She argued that whilst she was aware that she had been sexually abused by both defendants, she was unaware that she had suffered sufficiently serious injuries that would justify starting proceedings for damages until she became aware of the potential link between her ongoing psychiatric problems and the abuse she had experienced as a child.

The House of Lords unanimously held that the question of whether the claimant's situation met the requirements of s 11(4) was irrelevant, as her claim was not under s 11 but instead under the general tort time limit in s 2. Lord Griffiths commented that:

> I should not myself have construed breach of duty as including a deliberate assault. The

phrase lying in juxtaposition with negligence and nuisance carries with it the implication of a breach of duty of care not to cause personal injury, rather than an obligation not to infringe any legal right of another person. If I invite a lady to my house one would naturally think of a duty to take care that the house is safe but would one really be thinking of a duty not to rape her? .... It thus follows that the plaintiff's causes of action against both defendants were subject to a six-year limitation period. This period was suspended during her infancy but commenced to run when she attained her majority: see section 28 of the Act of 1980. This period expired many years before she issued her writ in these proceedings. There are no provisions for extending this period and her actions are therefore statute-barred and cannot proceed.[50]

The impact of this case was that victims of trespass to the person torts (often cases of serious sexual and physical abuse) were generally in a worse-off position when compared with victims of negligence or nuisance torts. This is particularly concerning as many victims of serious sexual abuse understandably do not have the strength or ability to commence actions until a significant period of time has passed.

The rule in *Stubbings v Webb* also created procedural complexities. Claimants utilised a range of mechanisms to avoid the inflexibility created, for example claiming that their abuse resulted from individual or institutional negligence, therefore giving themselves access to the more generous limitation periods for negligence actions. In *S v W (Child abuse: damages)* [1995],[51] the rule in *Stubbings v Webb* meant that the victim could sue her mother for negligently failing to protect her from sexual and physical abuse by her father, but not sue her father for the abuse itself. Whilst the

---

49 Limitation Act 1980, s 33(2).
50 [1993] AC 498, 508.
51 [1995] 1 FLR 862.

Court of Appeal was bound to make this outcome, Lord Ralph Gibson commented that 'the result of the judge's ruling was, as he rightly said, illogical and surprising. That fact, in my view, is a good reason for inviting the attention of the Law Commission to the interrelation of these provisions and to the absence of any longstop limitation period of this and any other parts of the Act.'[52]

The outcome of *Stubbings v Webb*, and the complexities the case created, was criticised by the Law Commission in 2001, which described the case as being 'anomalous' with the rest of tort law.[53] The Law Commission recommended legislation to address the situation,[54] but it was not implemented. Fortunately, the situation was rectified by the House of Lords in *A v Hoare* [2008].

KEY CASE

A v Hoare; X and another v Wandsworth London Borough Council; C v Middlesbrough Council; H v Suffolk County Council; Young v Catholic Care (Diocese of Leeds) and others [2008] 1 AC 844

This case involved six conjoined appeals on the interpretation of the Limitation Act 1980. It involved one claim against an individual, with the remaining claims against public authorities and a Catholic Church care organisation. The claimants all alleged that they were subject to sexual abuse and that the institutional negligence of the different defendants allowed the abuse to occur. The claimants had started proceedings after the six-year limitation period under s 2 had expired. Their claims were denied in the lower courts due to the application of the principle in *Stubbings v Webb*. The claimants then appealed to the House of Lords on the basis that *Stubbings* was wrong and should be overturned, thus allowing them to request the court to exercise its discretion under s 33 to 'disapply' the specified time limits on the grounds that it would be equitable to allow an action to proceed.

Lord Hoffmann highlighted the complexities that had been created by the decision in *Stubbings v Webb*:

> Lord Reid's observation in *Ex p Hudson* [1972] AC 944, 966 that unsatisfactory decisions of the highest court can cause uncertainty because lower courts tend to distinguish them on inadequate grounds is also pertinent to the consequences of *Stubbings*. Claimants who have

suffered sexual abuse but need to seek the discretion of the court under section 33 are driven to alleging that the abuse was the result of, or accompanied by, some other breach of duty which can be brought within the language of section 11. Thus, in addition to having to decide whether the claimant was sexually abused, the courts must decide whether this was the result of 'systemic negligence' on the part of the abuser's employer or the negligence of some other person for whom the employer is responsible. In the appeals before the House, the appellants put forward at least four alternative theories of liability on which they wish to rely if the rule in *Stubbings* is upheld. These are, in increasing degree of artificiality (1) breach of a direct duty of care owed by the employer to the claimant; (2) breach of a duty of care by other employees; (3) breach of a duty of care by the abuser himself and (4) breach of a duty by the abuser to notify the employer of his own wrongful acts. In *KR v Bryn Alyn Community (Holdings) Ltd* [2003] QB 1441, para 100 Auld LJ said that the need to frame a claim in one or other of these ways when the real cause of complaint was sexual abuse for which the employer was vicariously liable was causing 'arid and highly wasteful litigation turning on a distinction of no apparent principle or other

---

52   [1995] 1 FLR 862, 867.
53   Law Commission, *Limitation of Actions* (Law Com No 270, 2001) at [1.5].
54   Law Commission, *Limitation of Actions* (Law Com No 270, 2001) at [1.14].

merit'. I therefore think that it would be right to depart from *Stubbings*.[55]

The judges unanimously agreed that the decision in *Stubbings v Webb* was unjust and/or contrary to public policy. This was most clearly outlined in Baroness Hale's comments:

> [U]ntil the 1970s many people were reluctant to believe that child sexual abuse took place at all. Now we know only too well that it does. But it remains hard to protect children from it. This is because the perpetrators are so often people in authority over the victims, sometimes people whom the victims love and trust. These perpetrators have many ways, some subtle and some not so subtle, of making their victims keep quiet about what they have suffered. The abuse itself is the reason why so many victims do not come forward until years after the event. This presents a challenge to a legal system which

resists stale claims. Six years, let alone three, from reaching the age of majority is not long enough, especially since the age of majority was reduced from 21 to 18.

> Fortunately, by the time the problem was recognised, some flexibility had been introduced in personal injury cases, albeit to meet the rather different problem of the insidious and unremarked onset of industrial disease. Then along came *Stubbings v Webb* [1993] AC 498, holding that this flexibility did not apply to cases of deliberate assault. For the reasons given by my noble and learned friend, Lord Hoffmann, I agree that *Stubbings* was wrongly decided and have nothing to add on that point.[56]

This case addressed the concerns raised by the Law Commission, and meant that victims of trespass to person torts could utilise the more flexible time limits available for actions in negligence, nuisance and breaches of duty.

17.8 How damages can be awarded

Damages in tort law will in the majority of cases be compensated by the payment of a 'lump sum', meaning that the entire amount awarded by the court is given in one payment.[57] This allows the claimant and defendant to part ways after the court has made the decision on liability and quantum of damages. This approach can be overly simplistic, particularly for complex personal injury cases where the full impact of the damage may not be totally clear until a later stage. In a slightly tongue-in-cheek view of tort law damages, Lord Scarman highlighted that when awarding damages in these situations, 'there is really only one certainty: the future will prove the award to be either too high or too low'.[58] If liability is admitted or found by the courts, the parties may agree to delay the determination of quantum until a future date as this will allow a more accurate calculation of the harm suffered by the claimant.

If a claimant needs access to initial funds before a full hearing, it is possible for the court to approve an interim payment of an appropriate amount.[59] The courts also have a discretionary power to award the claimant provisional damages where there is 'a chance that at some definite or indefinite time in the future the injured person will, as a result of the act or omission which gave rise to the cause of action, develop some serious disease or suffer some serious deterioration in his physical or mental condition'.[60] These orders first allow damages to be awarded to the claimant on the assumption that they will not develop the disease or suffer the deterioration. If the claimant develops the disease or

---

55 [2008] 1 AC 844, 857.
56 [2008] 1 AC 844, 864.
57 *Fetter v Beale* (1701) 1 Ld Ray 339.
58 *Lim Poh Choo v Camden and Islington Area Health Authority* [1980] AC 174, 183.
59 *Stringman (A Minor) v McArdle* [1994] 1 WLR 1653.
60 County Courts Act 1984, s 51 and Senior Courts Act 1981, s 32A and s 34A.

suffers the deterioration, the court will then make a further award of damages. The effect of this is to make a more accurate and realistic determination of the needs of the claimant in situations where the ongoing nature of the harm is difficult to determine.

In situations where the claimant has a long-term condition that will require ongoing access to money, a substantial one-off payment may not be appropriate as the claimant could struggle to manage a large single sum of money. In these instances, it could be more beneficial to receive ongoing smaller amounts, and the courts can make alternative payment arrangements including structured settlements to allow for an ongoing 'stream' of income to the claimant. Courts can now also make reviewable periodical payments under s 100 of the Courts Act 2003, which amends the Damages Act 1996, s 2.

KEY LEGISLATION

Courts Act 2003

100   Periodical payments

(1)   For section 2 of the Damages Act 1996 (c. 48) (periodical payments by consent) substitute—
'Periodical payments

(1)   A court awarding damages for future pecuniary loss in respect of personal injury—

(a) may order that the damages are wholly or partly to take the form of periodical payments, and

(b) shall consider whether to make that order.

(2)   A court awarding other damages in respect of personal injury may, if the parties consent, order that the damages are wholly or partly to take the form of periodical payments.

(3)   A court may not make an order for periodical payments unless satisfied that the continuity of payment under the order is reasonably secure.'

This section allows a court to award damages for future pecuniary losses in respect of personal injury in the form of periodical payments *if* it is satisfied that the continuity of payment under the order is reasonably secure. The case of *Eeles v Cobham Hire Services* [2010] highlights how issues of interim awards and periodical payments work in the context of large personal injury claims.

KEY CASE

Eeles v Cobham Hire Services Ltd [2010] 1 WLR 409

The claimant in this case, Benjamin Eeles, suffered a serious head injury in a car accident when he was nine months old. At the time of the hearing, he was 11 and had made a good physical recovery, but had ongoing difficulties including fine motor skills, cognition and intellect. Benjamin will need ongoing assistance including physiotherapy, occupational therapy and speech therapy, and he will never have the capacity to manage his own affairs. The defendants did not dispute liability, but the parties agreed that it would not be able to adequately quantify the claim until Benjamin was older and the extent of the injury was more accurately determined. Before a final hearing on damages, Benjamin's parents requested an interim payment of £1.2 million for the purchase and refurbishment of a large house to assist with Benjamin's therapy and development. The trial judge awarded this amount of money, but the defendant appealed on the basis that this large award was not a reasonable proportion of the likely final sum, especially as it was appropriate to award a periodical payment order for Benjamin's long-term care.

Smith LJ handed down the judgment of the court. His Lordship emphasised that the court must not order an interim payment that is more than a reasonable proportion of the likely amount of the final judgment. This involved considering a 'broad assessment' of the merits of both sides to make a preliminary estimate and allowing a 'comfortable margin' in case this estimate was too generous. The correct approach to making an interim payment in a personal injury claim was then explained:

4. Before making an order, the court would not necessarily need to inquire as to what the claimant intended to do with the interim payment: *Stringman (A Minor) v McArdle* [1994] 1 WLR 1653. If of full age and capacity, the claimant would be entitled to do with it as he wished. If he was a minor or patient, control of the money would be exercised by the Court of Protection. None the less, claimants often wished to explain why they wanted a particular sum at the time. Typically, a claimant might want to demonstrate the need to buy or adapt accommodation or to provide a care regime. He might wish to demonstrate the need for such a facility in order to show that the final award would be of sufficient size to warrant the making of an interim payment of the amount sought. Judges were warned against making an interim award which would have the effect of creating a status quo in the claimant's way of life which might have the effect of inhibiting the trial judge's freedom of decision ...

5. With the rise in the value of claims for severe injuries, it has become quite common for very substantial interim payments to be made, based upon a reasonable proportion of the likely amount of the final capital award. However, under the amended Damages Act 1996 it became possible for a judge to make a periodical payments order ('PPO') in respect of some or all of the heads of future loss, index-linked to reflect future changes in the value of money and continuing for the whole of the claimant's actual life. Since this court in *Thompstone v*

Tameside and Glossop Acute Services NHS Trust [2008] 1 WLR 2207 affirmed that, when making a PPO, the court had the power to apply whatever index was most appropriate to the head of loss concerned, the benefits of a PPO have been generally recognised and such orders are now routinely made.

6. When considering how to allocate the various heads of future loss between a capital award and one or more PPOs, the trial judge has to consider what allocation will best meet the claimant's needs .... The trial judge's task is to weigh the various aspects of the claimant's needs, in the light of the sums which are to be awarded under each head of loss and in the light of the available financial advice.[61]

After reviewing the facts of the case and the arguments from both sides, Smith LJ gave judgment of the court, holding that in light of the fact that the likely amount of the capital award was only £590,000, there would be very little room for a further interim payment, and therefore the application for a £1.2 million interim payment was refused. His Lordship also provided a helpful summary of the approach that should be taken when determining whether to make an interim payment where a trial judge may also wish to make a PPO:

43. The judge's first task is to assess the likely amount of the final judgment, leaving out of account the heads of future loss which the trial judge might wish to deal with by PPO. Strictly speaking, the assessment should comprise only special damages to date and damages for pain, suffering and loss of amenity, with interest on both. However, we consider that the practice of awarding accommodation costs (including future running costs) as a lump sum is sufficiently well established that it will usually be appropriate to include accommodation costs in the expected capital award. The assessment should be carried out on a conservative basis. Save in the circumstances discussed below, the

interim payment will be a reasonable proportion of that assessment. A reasonable proportion may well be a high proportion, provided that the assessment has been conservative. The objective is not to keep the claimant out of his money but to avoid any risk of overpayment.[62]

This case highlights the need for judges to carefully balance current and future needs of claimants when determining how damages should be paid, and how this can be particularly difficult when dealing with young claimants who will need to have long-term assistance.

PROBLEM QUESTION TECHNIQUE

Nira has ongoing physical difficulties from the accident and is very likely to have a reduced life expectancy. The driver has admitted liability, but both parties have agreed to determine the quantum of damages at a later stage when the long-term consequences of Nira's injuries are more certain. The house that Deepa and Nira are living in currently is adequate for their needs, provided they have access to significant care. Deepa, however, wants to move to a £1.1 million luxury bungalow that has been renovated to make it disability friendly. It also has a range of additional benefits, such as a jacuzzi, movie room and swimming pool, which will provide her and Nira with a higher standard of living. She would like to access an interim payment of this amount to purchase the bungalow.

▸ The court has the power to award an interim payment to Deepa, but is it likely to do so in this situation? Think specifically about the similarity with of *Eeles v Cobham Hire Services*.

▸ Is the bungalow absolutely necessary for Deepa and Nira's needs, or is it providing a number of additional benefits?

▸ Think about whether the amount of compensation due to the claimants is clear, and whether providing such a large interim award would mean that they do not have adequate funds left for periodical payments for Nira's long-term care.

17.9 Contribution and apportionment

A further damages issue arises in situations where multiple parties can be held liable under a single tort claim. This must be distinguished from situations of contributory negligence where the damages are apportioned between the defendant and the claimant. When there are multiple *defendants*, it must be determined whether the situation is joint liability, independent liability or several concurrent liability, as they all have different outcomes.

Table 17.3: Types of liability

Type of liability	Example	Explanation
Joint liability	During his employment at the Cheesecake Factory, Raj is sexually harassed by his boss, Bernadette.	In this case, two parties caused the same damage by acting with the same common goal. The standard example of this is vicarious liability, where the employee is directly liable under tort law and the employer is vicariously liability under tort law.[63] In this scenario, Raj can sue either the Cheesecake Factory or Bernadette, or both parties together, for the whole amount of damage suffered.

62   [2010] 1 WLR 409, 417–418.
63   For further analysis, see Chapter 15 (Vicarious Liability).

Type of liability	Example	Explanation
Independent liability	Leonard gets into a fight with Sheldon and Penny. Penny punches Leonard in the face, giving him a black eye, and Sheldon kicks Leonard in the leg, causing a fracture.	This is a case where two (or potentially more) parties cause different and divisible harms to the claimant.[64] In this scenario, Leonard could commence one action for trespass to the person against both defendants, but each would only be required to pay for the actual harm they had caused (i.e. Penny would pay for the damages for the black eye and Sheldon would pay for the damages for the fractured leg).
Several concurrent liability	Amy is learning to drive and stalls her car in the middle of the road. Howard and Stuart are both driving negligently and run into Amy's car at the same time, causing her personal injuries.	This is a case where the actions of two (or potentially more) separate defendants happened completely independently but contributed to the claimant suffering the same harm. Both parties are liable for the entire amount, and can claim a proportion of the damages paid from the other party under the Civil Liability (Contribution) Act 1978. In this scenario, Amy could sue either Howard or Stuart for the entirety of her personal injuries, or could sue them both together. If Amy chooses to sue only Howard or Stuart, they would then be able to take a separate action against the other driver for the appropriate portion of the damages.[65]

PROBLEM QUESTION TECHNIQUE

[Deepa and Khalid's car] was hit by a negligent delivery driver, who was employed by Kwik Kourier Pty Ltd.

▶ Is this joint liability, independent liability or several concurrent liability?

▶ What impact does this have on whom Deepa could sue (i.e. the delivery driver for negligence, or Kwik Kourier Pty Ltd under vicarious liability, and/or both parties together)?

17.10 CHAPTER SUMMARY

The awarding of damages for tort law is an incredibly difficult and procedurally complex topic. How, why and in what manner tort law damages are awarded has often received significant media attention, and has given rise to controversy and discussion in political, academic and regulatory circles. This concern is frequently focused on the perception of the situation, as opposed to engaging with the reality of tort law damages.

Whilst a detailed coverage of all aspects of damages is beyond the scope of this chapter, a number of different topics were covered. The focus of the chapter was *how* damages are awarded after a successful tort claim, as opposed to the specific calculation of these damages. Damages come in the form of

---

64   See, for example, *Holtby v Brigham Cowan (Hull) Ltd* [2000] 3 All ER 421.
65   The court would determine what was 'justice and equitable': Civil Liability (Contribution) Act 1978, s 2(1). For an example of this, see *Prendergast v Sam and Dee Ltd* [1989] 1 Med LR 36.

pecuniary and non-pecuniary losses, and can be awarded for property damage and personal injuries, as well as specific statutory damages if the tortious action results in death. The award of damages can, however, be statute-barred by the Limitation Action 1980 – although there are a number of discretionary exceptions to these limitations.

In certain instances, multiple defendants can be held liable under a single tort action. If this occurs, it must be determined whether the situation is joint liability, independent liability or several concurrent liability, as they all have different outcomes. Whilst most tort law damages are paid out in a single lump sum, this can often be overly simplistic, particularly for complex personal injury cases where the full impact of the damage may not be certain until a later stage. The law has therefore developed a range of different ways in which the award of damages can be considered, namely provisional damages, interim awards and periodical payments orders.

The chapter also engaged with some of the theoretical aspects of tort law damages, including the different purposes of tort law damages. The awarding of damages in tort law is inherently linked to some of the philosophical challenges discussed in the Introductory Chapter. There has been an increased concern that a harmful 'compensation culture' has developed in the UK; however – as also discussed in Chapter 1 – it is more an issue of perception than reality. The limits of damages awards under traditional tort law mechanisms can make alternative compensation schemes look attractive, but these all have their own limitations and remove the link between moral blameworthiness and liability. An enhanced discussion of these and other challenges can be found in Chapter 1, as well as in the Further Reading outlined below. We encourage students to engage with these debates to get a wider perspective on the challenges associated with tort law damages.

FURTHER READING

P. Atiyah, *The Damages Lottery* (Hart, 1997)

N. Bevan and H. Gregory, 'Periodical Payments' (2005) 155 *NLJ* 565, 907, 980 (a series of three articles)

C. Brown, 'Deterrence in Tort and No-Fault: The New Zealand Experience' (1985) *Calif L Review* 976

P. Cane and J. Goudkamp, *Atiyah's Accidents, Compensation and the Law*, 9th edn (CUP, 2018)

J. Conaghan, 'Tort Litigation in the Context of Intra-familial Abuse' (1998) 61 *MLR* 132

The Hon Mr Justice James Edelman, Dr Jason Varuhas and Simon Colton, *McGregor on Damages*, 20th edn (Sweet & Maxwell, 2019)

R. Lewis, A. Morris and K. Oliphant 'Tort Personal Injury Claims Statistics: Is There a Compensation Culture in the United Kingdom?' (2006) 14(2) *Torts Law Journal* 158

J. Morgan, 'Tort, Insurance and Incoherence' (2004) 67 *MLR* 384

A. Morris, 'Spiralling or Stabilising? The Compensation Culture and our Propensity to Claim Damages for Personal Injury' (2007) 70 *MLR* 349

J. Murphy, 'Contemporary Tort Theory and Tort Law's Evolution' (2019) 32(3) *Canadian Journal of Law & Jurisprudence* 413

J. Stapleton, 'Tort, Insurance and Ideology' (1995) 58 *MLR* 820

Lord Sumption, 'Abolishing Personal Injuries Law – A project', a speech at the Personal Injuries Bar Association Annual Lecture, London, 16 November 2017

Lord Young, *Common Sense, Common Safety* (Cabinet Office, 2010)

INDEX

A

Abandoning the search
for a principle, 63
Abatement, 229
Absolute privilege in
defamation, 323, 337
Actions after death, 432
Fatal Accidents Act
1976, 433–435
Law Reform (Miscellaneous
Provisions) Act
1934, 432–433
Act of God, 236
Adverse physical outcome,
loss of a chance of
avoiding, 118–123
Aggravated damages, 349,
361, 424, 425
Aims of tort law, 3
Alternative systems, 8–9
Ambulance services, 21,
38–40, 76, 273
calls, duty to respond
to, 38–40
duty of care, 38, 39
fire service, 38
policy, 37
private law claims, 36–38
Analogy, reasoning by,
18–20, 51, 89, 290
Apportionment of damages, 73,
126, 128, 130, 373, 393,
396–402, 418, 442
Asbestos/mesothelioma, 9,
70, 71, 110, 127–133,
135–138, 170, 429
Assault, 2, 9, 16, 34, 242,
261–267, 272, 275, 278,
281, 283, 285, 294,
318, 332, 347, 348,
356, 367, 369, 379,
382, 384, 437, 439
immediate and direct
violence, 262, 265–267
intentional threat,
262, 265–267

Assumption of responsibility/
risk, 28, 34, 39–40,
43, 47, 49–54
economic loss, 43,
47, 49–54
negligence, 28, 34, 39–40,
43, 47, 49–54
negligent misstatements, 49
police, 28, 39–40
policy, 28
public bodies, 28, 34, 40
third parties, 37
See also Volenti non fit injuria
Autonomy, 1, 4, 10, 24, 101,
103, 139, 220, 242,
261–262, 272, 281, 292,
342, 363, 371, 376, 425
Awareness of false
imprisonment, 274

B

Battery, 4, 242, 261–264, 268–
272, 275, 278, 281–283,
294, 342, 367, 403, 410
consent, 270–273
definition, 262, 268
direct and immediate
force, 268–270
hostility, 270–272
intention, 268
recklessness, 263
touching, 262, 264, 268,
270–272, 342
without consent, 268,
270–272
Bereavement damages,
33, 432–433, 435
Blood products, infection with
contaminated, 205–211
Bodily integrity, 83, 100,
114, 236, 268
Bolam test, 19, 96–104, 122
Breach of confidence, 4, 296,
339–352, 357–363,
368–371, 383, 425
celebrities/public figures,

246, 334, 346, 351,
353–355, 369, 371
Human Rights Act 1998,
339–345, 357, 363,
366, 370–371
Injunctions, 357–360, 364
misuse of private
information, 296, 339,
350–351, 368, 370
photographs, 342, 350,
356, 360–361,
367, 369–370
public interest, 300–301,
308, 320, 322–327,
330, 347, 352–354,
358, 366–370
reasonable expectation
of privacy, 339, 343,
347–352, 356, 360,
362, 369–371
children, privacy rights
of, 355–360
remedies, 329–330
unauthorised use, 357–360
Breach of contract,
inducing, 247–257
economic torts, 247–251
causing loss by unlawful
means, 249–251
industrial action, 248
intimidation, 251–252
Breach of duty, 11, 72–73,
75, 86–87, 90, 94, 100,
108–109, 113–114, 118,
120, 126–127, 129–130,
133–134, 145, 147–148,
155–157, 180, 194,
198, 406, 436–438
breached, whether the duty
had been, 12, 30–31,
39, 45, 87, 88, 90,
93, 95–96, 100, 103,
133, 138–139, 156,
161, 166, 170–173,
183, 194, 197–198
children, standard of care for,
93–96, 172–174, 183–
184, 186, 188–189, 207

duties owed to claimants, whether, 4, 8, 16–21, 30–34, 46, 51–52, 55, 78–79, 87, 151, 153, 161, 166, 169, 171–172, 182, 183, 185, 187–188, 190, 197
employers' liability, 52, 70–72, 92, 110, 112, 126–127, 131, 138, 170, 376, 379–381, 388, 404–405, 408, 414
failure to warn patients of risks, 100, 107, 138–140
insurance, 7–9, 45, 50–51, 79, 107, 167, 182–183, 411, 425, 428, 431
objective standard of care, 87–93
risk, relevance of, 91–93
specific circumstances, 89–91
professionals, standard of care for, 96–99
reasonable care, 92, 100
res ipsa loquitur, 102–103
scope of duty, 143, 149–154
Social Action, Responsibility and Heroism Act 2015, 101–102
Burden of proof, 102–103, 108–109, 120, 126, 278, 373, 418
but for test, 108–109
false imprisonment, 278
But for causation, 108–118, 123–127, 132, 139, 150–151, 155, 398–399
adverse physical outcome, loss of a chance of avoiding, 118–123, 125
apportionment of damages, 126, 128, 130
basic, 108–110
burden of proof, 108–109
standard of proof in civil law vs criminal law, 108
clinical negligence, 120
informed consent, 100
divisible injuries, 110–111
employers' liability, 110, 112, 126–127, 131, 138
factual causation, 106
Fairchild exception, 126–131, 133

indivisible injuries, 110–112, 131
inform, failure to, 100–101
intervening acts, 113
joint and several liability, 129, 132, 203
loss of a chance, 118, 123
material contribution to injury, 115–118, 133
material increase in risk, 128
overdetermination, 125–126
successive factors, 112–115
two hunters problem, 125–126

C

Capacity, 26, 87, 93–94, 280–281
Caparo test, 13, 16–22, 28, 34, 59
Carelessness, 102–103, 113, 261–262, 300
but for test, 113
defamation, 300
intentional torts against the person, 261–262
Causal inquiry, significance of, 107–108
Causation, 75, 78, 87, 94, 100, 105–142, 151, 155–157, 170, 195, 383, 398–399, 411–412
but for causation, 108–118, 123–127, 132, 139, 150–151, 155, 398–399
adverse physical outcome, loss of a chance of avoiding, 118–123, 125
basic, 108–110
divisible injuries, 110–111
indivisible injuries, 110–112, 131
material contribution to injury, 115–118, 133
successive factors, 112–115
causal inquiry, significance of, 107–108
corrective justice, 107–108
employers' liability, 110, 112, 126–127, 131, 138
exceptions to the but for test, 123

better financial outcome, loss of a chance of achieving, 123–125
failure to warn, 138–139
material contribution to risk, 126–132
overdetermination, 125–126
single agent, 132–138
factual causation, 106
foreseeability, 145, 154, 161
legal causation, 106
product liability, 195
psychiatric harm, 64, 66, 70, 72, 78, 82–83
real or operative causes, 114, 155
remoteness, 143–161
role of, 107–108
See also But for test; Intervening acts
Celebrities/public figures, 246, 334, 346, 351, 353–355, 369, 371
Injunctions, 330
privacy, 334, 346, 351, 353–355, 369, 371
social media, 332–333
Children, 31–32, 34, 45, 68, 75, 87, 93–94, 146–147, 168, 172–174, 183–184, 186, 188–189, 207, 279, 322, 334, 339, 347–348, 354–356, 360–361, 381, 386, 400, 406, 423–424, 426, 433, 439
allurements, 172, 184, 188
contributory negligence, 400, 406
foster children, 68, 378
occupiers' liability, 168, 172–174, 183–184, 186, 188–189
privacy, 347–348, 354–356, 360–361
product liability, 207
psychiatric harm, 68, 75
remoteness, 146–147
standard of care, 93–95
owed by an occupier, 172–174
Civil law, 108, 279, 435
but for causation, standard of proof, 108

Claimant, 156–158, 221, 225–226, 232, 267–268, 394–408
  act, *novus actus interveniens*, 156–158
  contributory negligence, 394–402
  hypersensitivity, 221, 225–226, 232
  knowledge about nature and extent of risk, 402–408
  reasonable expectation by, 267–268
  See also Volenti Non Fit Injuria
Clapham omnibus, man on the, 96, 98
Compensating benefits, 430–434
Compensation, 1–10, 14, 23–24, 33, 36, 64–65, 80, 101, 107–108, 112, 128–129, 131–133, 137, 214, 229, 231, 262, 264, 290, 307, 329, 347, 349, 361–362, 379, 381, 392, 394, 408, 410–414, 423–429, 432, 435, 442, 444
  aims of tort law, 1–10
  alternative systems, 8–9
  Compensation Act 2006, 129, 131, 133, 142
  culture, 5–6, 10, 101, 444
Confidentiality, 246, 348–352, 359, 366, 368
  See also Breach of confidence
Confinement, 272–277, 282
Consent, 90, 100, 156, 234, 236, 239, 262, 268, 270–271, 278–281, 292, 312–313, 320, 328, 347–348, 360, 367, 392–393, 403, 405–409, 418, 440
  battery without, 262, 268, 270–271
  defences, 278–281, 328
  defences to the rule in *Rylands v Fletcher*, 234
  informed consent, 101
  volenti non fit injuria, 403
Conspiracy, 252–255
  lawful means (simple), 252
  unlawful means, 253
Consumer protection, *see* Product liability

Consumer Protection Act (CPA) 1987, 194, 196, 198–215
  common law negligence, 197–198
  contractual remedies, 195–197
  damage, 200–202
  defect, 203–209
  defences, 209–212
  producer, 202–203
  product, 199
Contract, 15, 20, 35–36, 38, 43, 47–54, 71, 78, 106, 115, 124–129, 134, 138, 144, 148–149, 153–161, 163, 165, 170, 175–183, 194–205, 213, 242–256, 273, 275, 279, 304, 345, 351–353, 375–381, 385–387, 396, 403, 408–409, 413–414, 416, 418, 424, 429, 436
  causation, 106, 115, 124–129, 134, 148–149, 153–161
  damages, 424, 429, 436
  defamation, 304
  defences, 396, 403, 408–409, 413–414, 416, 418
  duty of care, 15, 20, 35–3, 38
  economic loss, 43, 47–54
  economic torts, 242–256
  intentional torts against the person, 273, 275, 279
  occupiers' liability, 170, 175–183
  privacy, 345, 351–353,
  product liability, 194–205, 213
  vicarious liability, 375–381, 385–387
Contribution, 106, 114–118, 126, 128–129, 133, 134, 136–137, 157, 176, 203, 381, 400, 418, 434, 442–443
Contributory negligence, 88, 94, 156–157, 278, 282, 392, 394–402, 406
  causation, 156–157
  children, 400, 406
  damage reduction as a consequence of claimant's actions, 442
  defences, 392, 394–402
    elements of, 397–402

historical approach, 394–397
intentional torts against the person, 278, 282
reasonable care, exercise of, 88, 94
Corrective justice, 8, 36, 88, 107–108, 231, 388
  causation, 107–108
  duty of care, 36
  insurance, 8
  standard of care, 88
  vicarious liability, 388
CPA, 194, 196, 198–215
  See also Consumer Protection Act (CPA) 1987
Criminal law, 1–2, 27, 106, 108, 144, 264, 267–268, 279, 281, 315–316, 410, 412–414, 417
  but for causation, standard of proof, 108
  intentional torts against the person, 264

D

Damages, 2–10, 23, 43, 49, 64–65, 73, 79, 88, 94, 108, 111, 113–114, 118–130, 135, 137, 149–150, 153–160, 177, 195–196, 200, 203, 212, 218, 223, 226–229, 237–240, 262–265, 274–275, 284–288, 296–309, 318–319, 329–335, 347, 349–354, 360–402, 411–418, 422–443
  actions after death, 432
    Fatal Accidents Act 1976, 433–435
    Law Reform (Miscellaneous Provisions) Act 1934, 432–433
  aggravated damages, 349, 361, 424, 425
  alternative systems, 8–9
  apportionment, 73, 126, 128, 130, 373, 393, 396–402, 418, 442
  award of, 5, 130, 227, 329, 361, 378, 400–401, 422, 427, 432, 440, 444

bereavement damages, 33, 432–433, 435

calculation of damages, 423, 427–428, 430, 433, 439, 443

compensating benefits, 430–434

concurrent liability, 51, 160, 442–444

Consumer Protection Act 1987, 200–202

contributory negligence, 442

death, 432–433

defamation, 298–309, 318–319, 329–335

dependents, claims by, 432

exemplary damages, 23, 276, 362, 425, 432

fatal accidents, 80, 147, 282, 422, 432–435

future losses, 46, 428

injunctions, 23, 228, 357, 360, 364

joint and several liability, 129, 132, 203

Judicial College guidelines, 430

loss of a chance, 118–125, 139

loss of amenity, 227, 415–416, 424, 441

loss of earnings, 43, 112, 412, 427–428

nominal damages, 274, 276, 424

non-pecuniary losses, 4, 347, 422, 427, 430, 444

pain and suffering, 3, 76, 427, 430, 433

pecuniary losses, 421–422, 427, 430, 434, 440, 444

privacy, 347, 349–350, 354, 360–370

product liability, 195–196, 200, 203, 212

property, 46, 55, 57–58, 147, 154, 158, 187, 190, 213, 422, 426, 444

proportionality, 281, 358

purpose of damages, 421, 423, 425

remedies, 4, 24, 38, 163, 193, 195–196, 205,

218, 221, 226, 231, 240, 261, 329–330, 341, 360–364, 368, 422

time limitations on tort law claims. 435

Danger, creation of a source of, 231

Death, 3, 9, 16–17, 64, 68–69, 78, 83, 110, 125, 177, 179–180, 194, 200–201, 204, 211, 281–282, 305, 346, 359, 369, 371, 392, 403, 408, 411, 415, 428, 432–435, 444

dependents, claims by, 432

fatal accidents, 433–435

Defamation, 4, 52, 296–335, 392, 422, 425, 432–436

absolute privilege, 323, 337

challenges, 330–335

human rights, 331–332

social media, 332–333

society's views, 333–334

communication, 317

companies, 305–306

damages, 298–309, 318–319, 329–335

Defamation Act 2013, 299, 301–306, 310, 313–314, 320–328, 330, 335, 364

defamation tourism, 301, 304

defences, 319–328

consent, 328

honest opinion, 321

operators of websites, 327

privilege, 323

publication on matters of public interest, 323

truth, 320

deterrence, 306

distributors, 327

elements of, 309–319

defamatory publication, 309

statement published to a third party, 317

statement referred to the claimant, 316

harassment, 332

honest opinion defence, 300–301,

320–322, 392

Human Rights Act 1998, 331

initial issues, 300–309

legislative reform, 301

libel and slander, 302–303

who can sue, 304–309

innuendo, 299, 324–325, 333

jurisdiction, 301, 304–305, 328

libel and slander, distinction between, 302–303

malice, 300, 302, 305, 319, 322–324, 328, 330

photographs, 316, 319, 334

political parties, 309

privilege, 300–301, 307, 320, 323–325, 330

absolute, 323–324

qualified, 301, 323–325, 330

Reynolds defence, 301, 324, 326–327, 330

public authorities, 304, 306–309, 331

public interest defence, 300–301, 308, 320, 322–331

publication, 323

reasonableness, 300, 315–316

refers to claimant, whether statement, 316

remedies, 298–309, 318–319, 329–335

reputation, 299–301, 304–305, 307, 309–314, 319–320, 323, 328–335

Reynolds test, 301, 324, 326–327, 330

serious harm requirement, 301–303, 310, 313–314, 319, 332, 335

social media, 332–333

strict liability, 300

structure, 299–300

award of damages, 300

defamatory publication, 300

defensible publication, 300

truth, 320

websites/internet, 327
whether statements are
    defamatory, 300
who can sue, 304
Defamatory publication, 300
    Innuendo, 299,
        314–315, 334
    Statement, 300–301, 304,
        307–308, 310–334
Defective premises, 42, 54–58
Defective Premises Act
    1972, 56, 58
Defective products, 196, 198,
    202, 205, 212, 213, 215
    See also Product liability
Defences, 3, 26, 88, 156–157,
    177, 198, 209–210, 221,
    229, 234–236, 240,
    256, 264, 270, 274, 280,
    299–301, 307, 319–320,
    325, 328–329, 331,
    335, 373, 391–419
    Consent, 90, 100, 156, 234,
        236, 239, 262, 268,
        270–271, 278–281,
        292, 312–313, 320,
        328, 347–348, 360,
        367, 392–393, 403,
        405–409, 418, 440
    contributory negligence,
        392, 394–402
        elements of, 397–402
        historical approach,
            394–397
    defamation, 319–328
        consent, 328
        honest opinion, 321
        operators of
            websites, 327
        privilege, 323
        publication on matters of
            public interest, 323
        truth, 320
    definition of, 393
    detention/legal
        authority, 282
    illegality, 409–418
        elements of, 410
        rationale of, 409
    lawful arrest, 282
    necessity, 279
    in private nuisance, 229–231
        prescription, 229
        statutory authority, 230

stranger act, 230
to the rule in Rylands
    v Fletcher, 234
    act of God, 236
    claimant, 235
    consent, 234
    stranger act, 235
    statutory authority, 235
self-defence, 264,
    278, 281, 392
volenti non fit injuria,
    156, 177, 373, 393,
    402–403, 408
    and consent, 403
    elements of, 403–408
Dependents, claims by, 432
Detention/lawful authority, 282
Deterrence, 3, 8–10, 91, 94,
    264, 306, 424–425
Discharge of duty, 53–54, 83,
    163, 170, 172, 181, 189
    exclusions, 178, 180,
        187, 190
        Occupiers' Liability Act
            1957, 178, 180
        Occupiers' Liability Act
            1984, 187, 190
    warnings, 176, 178,
        186, 189–190
        Occupiers' Liability
            Act 1957, 176
        Occupiers' Liability Act
            1984, 189–190
Disclaimers, 47, 49–50
Distributive justice, 36,
    79–80, 107
Divisible injuries, 110–111
Duty of care, 2, 4, 8, 11–40,
    45–49, 51–56, 59, 62,
    66–68, 72–73, 78–79, 87,
    89–97, 103, 109, 119, 122,
    127, 133, 138, 140, 145,
    150–151, 153, 156, 161, 163,
    166, 171–173, 176–177, 180–
    182, 185, 189, 194, 197–198,
    203, 385–386, 393, 397,
    402, 405, 409, 438
    acts vs omissions, 24–25
        general rule, 24
        liability, 25
    ambulance services, 38, 39
    analogy, reasoning
        by, 18–20, 51
    Anns, retreat from, 55–57

control mechanism,
    as, 14, 67, 79
Donoghue v Stevenson,
    14–16, 196–197
economic loss, 45–47,
    49, 51–56
establishment of, 16–19
    from Caparo to
        Robinson, 16
    legally significant
        features, 19
fire services, 38
floodgates argument, 57, 79
foreseeability, 16–17, 19,
    22, 25, 30, 64, 66,
    70, 72, 78, 82, 83
incremental approach, 22,
    28, 35, 47, 79–80
liability of public
    bodies, 28–37
    general principles, 28
    Human Rights Act
        1998, 30
    police and emergency
        services,
        application of, 37
misfeasance vs
    nonfeasance, 24–28
    general rule, 24
    liability, 25
modern tort of negligence,
    foundations of, 14–16
neighbour principle, 15
non-delegable duty of care,
    373–375, 385–388
novel situations, 18, 20, 54
omissions, 24–25
product liability, 194,
    197–198, 203
psychiatric harm, 62,
    66–68, 72–73, 78–79
public bodies, 28–40
third parties, 25, 33, 37,
    39, 44, 54, 69
type of loss, 43, 48, 57, 63

E

Economic loss, 42–59, 83,
    146–147, 151–152, 154,
    157–159, 183, 196,
    242, 244–245, 253
    analogy, reasoning by, 51
    assumption of responsibility/
        risk, 43, 47, 49–54

consequential economic loss, 43–44
contract, 43, 47–54
damages, 49
defective buildings, 54–59
duty of care, 45–47, 49, 51–56, 59
fiduciary relationships, 47–48, 53–54
Hedley Byrne principle, 46–54, 58
  Disclaimers, 47, 49–50
  extension of *Hedley Byrne* principle, 50
  references, 47–48, 52, 57
incremental principle, 47
insurance, 43, 45, 50–51, 58
material physical damage, 43, 55–57
negligent misstatements, 49
proximity, 43, 47, 50, 59
pure economic loss, 42–60
  definition, 44
  development, 50
  Murphy, before, 55–58
references, 47–48, 52, 57
relational economic loss, 44–46
reliance, 51–52
special relationships, 47, 50, 54
Economic torts, 4, 62, 242–257, 361, 425
  distinction made by the House of Lords in *OBG*, 245–251
  causing loss by unlawful means, 249
  inducing breach of contract, 247
Eggshell skull rule, 148
Emergence services, liability of public bodies, 37
  ambulance services, 21, 38–40, 76, 273
  fire services, 38
  police, 28, 39–40
Employers' liability, 52, 70–72, 92, 110, 112, 126–127, 131, 138, 170, 376, 379–381, 388, 404–405, 408, 414

asbestos/mesothelioma, 126–127, 131, 138
causation, 110, 112, 126–127, 131, 138
course of employment, 381–385
non-delegable duty of care, 373–375, 385–388
proper system of work, 83, 92, 176, 183
psychiatric harm, 70, 72–73, 78, 83
references, 47–48, 52, 57
stress at work, 71–73
supervision, effective, 380
trade unions, 248, 252, 307
vicarious liability, 2–3, 9, 21, 373, 375–388, 425, 442–443
Employment relationships, vicarious liability and, 375–379
Escapes, 232–237
  See also Rylands v Fletcher, rule in
Exceptions to the but for test 123
  better financial outcome, loss of a chance of achieving, 123–125
  failure to warn, 138–139
  material contribution to risk, 126–132
  overdetermination, 125–126
  single agent, 132
Exclusion clauses, 167, 178–180
Excuse, 235, 271–272, 285
Exemplary damages, 23, 276, 362, 425, 432
Expert opinions, differences in, 96–103
Ex turpi causa rule, 409–418
  See also Illegality

F

Facebook, 62–63, 77, 288, 299, 313, 327, 333
Failure to warn, 100, 107, 138
  exceptions to the but for test, 138–139
  patients of risks, 100
Fair, just and reasonable test, 8, 17–18, 20, 22–23, 377

False imprisonment, 4, 242, 260–278, 282–283, 292, 424
  authorisation, without legal awareness, 274
  battery, 270
  burden of proof, 278
  confinement, 272
  damages, 274–276
  definition, 272
  freedom of movement, restrictions on, 272, 277
  intention, 273
  necessity, 279
  prisoners, 275
  recklessness, 262
Fatal Accidents Act 1976, 80, 147, 282, 422, 432–435
  actions after death, 433–435
Fault, 2, 5, 7, 9, 11, 23, 37, 62, 69, 87, 95–96, 112, 116, 134, 156, 194, 199, 205–206, 214, 232, 235–236, 240, 282, 319, 365, 392, 395–399, 402, 416
Fiduciary relationships, 47–48, 53–54
Financial loss, 3–4, 48, 287–288, 301, 305–306, 336
  See also Economic loss
Floodgates argument, 57, 79
Foreseeability, 11, 16–17, 19, 22, 25, 30, 64, 66, 70, 72, 78, 82–83, 94, 145, 154, 161, 225–226, 232–233,
  Causation, 145, 154, 161
  duty of care, 11, 16–17, 19, 22, 25, 30
  nuisance, 225–226
  omissions, 25
  psychiatric harm, 64, 66, 70, 72, 78, 82–83
  public bodies, 30
  Rylands v Fletcher, actions under, 232–233, 240
  standard of care, 94
Future losses, 46, 428

G

Government regulation of privacy rights, 344, 425

H

Harassment, 4, 34, 242,
260–266, 284, 287–295,
332, 341–342, 344,
347, 368–371, 392,
414, 416, 422, 436
amounts to harassment
of another, 290
assault, 266
course of conduct, 263,
288–292, 342
definition, 263, 287
knows or ought to know
amounts to harassment,
263, 288–290
Protection from Harassment
Act 1997, 4, 242, 260–
264, 284, 287–288,
290–295, 341–342,
344, 422, 436
stalking, 242, 287–288,
342, 368
telephone calls, 266,
288, 342
Wilkinson v Downton,
tort in, 287
Health and safety at work, 101
See also Employers' liability
Hedley Byrne liability,
development of,
46–54, 58, 152, 159
disclaimers, 47, 49–50
extension of *Hedley Byrne*
principle, 50
references, 47–48, 52, 57
Hillsborough disaster, 63,
73–78, 261, 270
Historical approach to
contributory negligence,
394–397
Hostility, in battery,
268, 270–272
HRA, see Human Rights
Act (HRA)
Human Rights Act (HRA)
1998, 30, 32–36, 227,
288, 345, 356, 362
defamation, 296, 331
liability of public
bodies, 30–37
privacy, 345, 356, 362
Rylands v Fletcher, the
rule in, 227

I

Illegality, 373, 391, 393–
394, 409–420
elements of, 410–418
illegal or immoral
behaviour, 410
range of factors,
balancing, 413–419
sufficient link, 410–412
ex turpi causa rule, 409–418
rationale of, 409–410
See also ex turpi causa
Immediate and direct
violence, 266–267
Imprisonment, 4, 242,
261–264, 272–278,
282–283, 292, 294, 303,
307, 410, 412, 424
See also False imprisonment
Incremental principle, 22,
28, 35, 47, 79–80,
132, 364, 387–388
Independent contractors, 182,
376, 379, 386–387
Indivisible injuries, 110–112, 131
Injunction, remedies, 24, 218,
220, 222–223, 226–229,
241, 286–289, 299,
307, 329–331, 343,
351–353, 356, 360–364,
367, 369, 370, 422
Injuries, 5–6, 9, 21, 64, 66, 76,
80, 86, 88–89, 93, 100,
106, 109–111, 114, 122, 126,
131, 147, 156–157, 171, 173,
176, 184–185, 189–190,
206, 212–213, 219, 238,
263, 268, 271, 279, 284,
329, 384–365, 398–401,
406, 410–412, 422–424,
427–428, 430–433,
436–437, 441–443
divisible, 110–111
indivisible, 110–112, 131
material contribution
to, 115–118
Innuendo, 299, 324–325, 333
Insurance, tort law and, 7–9,
45, 50–51, 79, 107, 167,
182–183, 411, 425, 428, 431
Intention, 9, 14, 25, 27, 49–50,
65, 144–146, 158–162,
180, 194, 201, 224–225,
239, 242–295, 300, 310,

316, 319, 365, 381, 392,
397, 403, 413, 426–427
See also Intentional torts
against the person
Intentional threat, 265–267
Intentional torts against the
person, 261–294
assault, 264–268
immediate and direct
violence, 266–267
intentional threat,
265–267
reasonable expectation by
claimant, 267–268
battery, 268–272
direct and immediate
force, 268–270
hostility, 270
intention, 268
without consent, 270
criminal offences
defences, 278–282
consent, 278–279
contributory
negligence, 282
detention/lawful
authority, 282–283
lawful arrest, 282–283
necessity, 279–281
self-defence, 281–282
false imprisonment, 272–278
awareness, 274–275
confinement, 272–274
within prison system,
275–278
malicious prosecution,
292–294
Protection from Harassment
Act 1997, 287–292
amounts to harassment
of another, 290
course of conduct, 289
harassment in 21st
century, 291
knows or ought to
know amounts to
harassment, 290
reasonable expectation by
claimant, 267–268
Wilkinson v Downton,
tort in, 284–287
Interests, 2–4, 10, 14, 20–21, 53,
65, 72, 88, 100–102, 112,

146–147, 163, 201, 213–215, 218–231, 236–240, 242, 252, 254, 256, 279–281, 292, 300, 320, 324, 340, 343–344, 350, 357–358. 363, 365, 368, 377–378
protected by tort law, 3–5
Internet, 63, 76–77, 143, 151, 212, 289, 296, 299, 301, 303, 317, 327–328, 356, 383
Intervening acts, 26, 75–77, 152, 155–157, 162
acts of the claimant, 156–158
third party, 155–156
See also Novus Actus Interveniens
Invasion of privacy, 220, 286, 340–345, 349, 364, 366–368, 370
See also Privacy

J

Joint and several liability, 129, 132, 203

L

Law Commission, 54, 79, 82, 185, 365, 409, 428, 432, 434, 435, 438–439
damages, 428, 432, 434–435, 438–439
illegality, 409
occupiers' liability 185
privacy, 365
psychiatric harm, 79, 82
pure economic loss, 54
Lawful arrest, 282
Lawful means conspiracy (or simple conspiracy), 252
Law Reform (Miscellaneous Provisions) Act 1934, 422, 432–433
actions after death, 432–433
Learned Hand test, 93
Legislative reform, defamation, 300–301
Liability, 1–17, 21, 24–40, 43, 47–59, 62, 63, 65–66, 72–80, 82, 91, 93–94, 101, 107, 111–118, 120, 122, 126,

128–129, 132–133, 135, 137–140, 144–145, 149, 151, 153, 155–156, 160–161, 163–167, 169–215, 226–237, 246–251, 256–257, 262, 264, 275, 287, 292, 300–301, 317–318, 328, 330, 341–342, 364–365, 373, 375–388, 393, 396–397, 399–410, 415, 422–425, 438–444
Hedley Byrne liability, development of, 50–54
of omissions, 25
product, 193–216
common law negligence, 197
Consumer Protection Act 1987, 198–209
contractual remedies, 195–197
limitation of, 212–215
See also Consumer Protection Act (CPA) 1987
of public bodies, 28–40
general principles, 28–30
Human Rights Act 1998, 30–37
police and emergency services, application of, 37–40
vicarious, 374–390
development of, 375
non-delegable duties, 385–388
relationships of employment, 377–381
Libel, 2, 111, 288, 298–308, 329–331, 367, 436
Limitation periods, 56, 213, 215, 318, 437–438
damages, 437–438
defamation, 318
economic loss, 56
product liability, 213, 215
Local authorities, 30, 308, 378
Loss of a chance, 118–125, 139
Loss of amenity, 227, 415–416, 424, 441
Loss of earnings, 43, 112, 412, 427–428

M

Malice, 52, 254, 263–264, 293, 300, 302, 305, 319, 322–324, 328, 330
defamation, 300, 302, 305, 319, 322–324, 328, 330
Material contribution, 106, 115–118, 126, 133–134, 136–137
to injury, 115–118, 133
to risk, 126–132
Medical expenses, 284, 428
Mental harm, 4
See also Psychiatric harm
Mesothelioma/asbestos, 9, 70, 71, 110, 127–133, 135–138, 170, 429
Minors, 31, 416
See also Children
Misuse of private information, 296, 339, 350–351, 363, 368, 370, 383

N

Necessity, 100–111, 198, 240, 274, 278–281, 392
best interests of patients, 100
causation, 111
defences, 392
intentional torts against the person, 274, 278–281
medical treatment, capacity to content to
product liability, 198
trespass to land, 240
Negligence, tort of, 2, 4, 7–8, 11–59, 62–82, 87–102, 106–140, 144–161, 163, 165, 171, 175, 179–180, 182–183, 185, 194–198, 201, 205, 213–215, 218, 232–240, 261–262, 278, 282, 287, 373, 378, 380, 386, 392–418, 423, 425, 436–439, 442–443
assumption of responsibility, 28, 34, 39–40, 43, 47, 49–54
contributory negligence, 88, 94, 156–157, 278, 282, 392, 394–402, 406
corrective justice, 8, 36, 88, 107–108, 231, 388

damages, 423, 425, 436–439, 442–443
defences, 392–418
definition, 11–12
Donoghue v Stevenson, 14–16, 196–197
fair, just and reasonable test, 8, 17–18, 20, 22–23, 377
floodgates argument, 57, 79
foreseeability, 11, 16–17, 19, 22, 25, 30, 64, 66, 70, 72, 78, 82–83, 94, 145, 154, 161
historical development, 14–16
Human Rights Act 1998, 30–37
Insurance, 7–9, 45, 50–51, 79, 107, 167, 182–183
joint and several liability, 129, 132, 203
neighbour principle, 15
proximity, 11, 17, 19, 22, 30, 43, 47, 49–50, 63, 74–75, 82–83, 90
reasonableness, 11, 18–19, 22, 91, 97
remoteness, 23, 26, 46, 49, 106, 143–161
strict liability, 95
See also Contributory negligence; Standard of care
Negligent misstatements, 49
Negligent services, 46
Neighbour principle, 15
Nervous shock, 62, 64, 284
No-fault accident compensation scheme, 9
benefits and detriments of instituting, 9
Nominal damages, 274, 276, 424
Non-delegable duties, vicarious liability and, 373–375, 385–388
Non-pecuniary losses, 4, 347, 422, 427, 430, 444
Non-visitors, 165, 167, 169, 183–185, 187–191
Novel situations, 18, 20, 54
Novus actus interveniens, 75–77, 152, 155–157

claimant act, 156–157
third party act, 155–156
Nuisance, 4, 145, 163, 217–221, 223–240, 292, 308, 341–345, 368, 392, 436–437, 439
private, 219–230
public, 237–239
See also Private nuisance
See also Public nuisance

O

Objective standard of care, 7, 86–89, 95
specific circumstances, 89–91
Occupier, definition of, 165–167
Occupiers' liability, 4, 27, 163–192, 194, 205, 214, 403
allurements, 172, 184, 188
children, 168, 172–174, 183–184, 186, 188–189
contract, 178–180, 182
control of premises, 165–166
danger, in vicinity of, 172, 176, 180–181, 184, 186–190
Defective Premises Act 1972, 56, 58
duty of care, 163, 166, 171–173, 176–177, 180–182, 185, 189
exclude liability, notices which, 178–180
faulty execution of work, 174–176
independent contractors, 181
insurance, 167. 182–183
invitees, 166–167, 169
knowledge, 167, 185–186
licensees, 166–167, 169
occupier, definition of, 165–167
reasonable care, 166, 182
risks willingly accepted by non-visitors, 176–177
standard of care, 172
trespassers, 183–187, 190
visitors, 164–172, 174, 176, 178, 181–190
definition, 167–169
lawful, 184–186

skilled visitors, 174–176
volenti non fit injuria, 177
warnings, 168, 175–176, 178, 186, 189–190
Occupiers' Liability Act 1957, 165, 167–170, 172, 174–176, 181, 187–190
content of duty, 170–176
children, standard of care of, 170–174
exercise of calling, 174–176
discharge of duty, 176
engaging contractors, 181–183
exclusions, 178–179
warnings, 176–178
premises, 169–170
visitor, definition of, 167–169
Occupiers' Liability Act 1984, 165, 167–170, 183–185, 187–190
content of duty, 188–189
obvious dangers, 188
discharge of duty, 189–191
exclusions, 190
warnings, 189
non-visitors, 186–187
owed a duty by non-visitors, circumstances of, 187–188
Omissions, 26–27, 130, 133, 238, 276, 326, 385, 397, 433, 439
Operators of websites, 301, 327–328
Overdetermination, 105, 107, 125–126
exceptions to the but for test, 125–126

P

Pain and suffering, damages for, 3, 427, 430, 433
Past and future care needs, 428–429
Pecuniary losses, 421–422, 427, 430, 434, 440, 444
loss of earnings, 43, 112, 412, 427–428
medical and related expenses, 427

past and future care
needs, 428–429
reduced life expectancy,
427, 429, 442
Personal injury, 6–7, 9, 66,
79, 108, 111, 114, 122–123,
147–148, 154, 158, 163,
179–180, 197, 200–201,
204, 218, 221, 236,
238–240, 396, 403, 408,
411, 415, 427–430, 432,
437, 439–441, 444
damages, 427–430, 432,
437, 439–441
loss of a chance,
118–125, 139
loss of amenity, 227,
415–416, 424, 441
loss of earnings, 43, 112,
412, 427–428
non-pecuniary losses,
4, 347, 422, 427,
430, 444
pecuniary losses, 421–
422, 427, 430,
434, 440, 444
loss of earnings, 428
medical and related
expenses, 427
past and future care
needs, 428
reduced life
expectancy, 429
product liability, 197,
200–201, 204
psychiatric harm, 66, 79
Rylands v Fletcher, actions
under, 236, 238–240
PHA, 287–292
See also Protection
from Harassment
Act (PHA) 1997
Police, 9, 14, 16–23, 25–26,
28, 30–31, 33, 36–40,
46, 63, 67, 73, 77–78,
80, 81, 83, 155–156, 186,
239, 262–263, 267–268,
274–275, 278–279,
281–283, 292–293,
311–312, 314–315, 318, 333,
340, 346, 348, 352, 361,
365–366, 397, 406, 409
duty of care, 16–23, 25–26,
28, 30–31, 33, 36–40

Human Rights Act
1998, 30–31, 33
intentional torts against
the person, 262–263,
267–268, 274–275,
278–279, 282–283,
292–293
liability of public
bodies, 28–40
Osman case, 31–33
psychiatric harm, 63,
67, 73, 77–81, 83
Policy, 7–8, 18, 20, 27–28,
31–32, 37, 45, 52, 63–67,
127–128, 138, 167, 171, 182,
185, 219, 255, 274, 276,
279, 352, 370, 375, 379,
383, 388, 393, 405, 411–
418, 423–424, 431, 439
Prescription, 69, 81,
227–230, 236, 392
defences in private
nuisance, 229–230
Primary victims, 66,
68–71, 74, 78, 83
psychiatric injury, 66,
68–71, 74, 78, 83
Prison system, false
imprisonment
within, 275, 278
Privacy, 1, 4, 10, 220,
286, 339–371
breach of confidence,
348–363
misuse of private
information,
350–351
reasonable expectation
of privacy, 351–357
remedies, 360–362
unauthorised use,
357–360
celebrities/public figures,
246, 334, 346, 351,
353–355, 369, 371
children, 347–348,
354–356, 360–361
copyright, 340, 345
freestanding tort, 363–369
harassment, 341–342,
344, 347, 368–371
injunctions, 343, 352–353,
356, 360–364,
367, 369–370

malicious falsehood, 341,
345, 367–368
misuse of private
information, 339, 350–
351, 363, 368, 370
privacy, definition of,
339–344
protection in 21st century,
369–370
protection of, 340–348
common law, 340–344
government regulation
of privacy rights,
344–348
Private nuisance, 4, 145,
163, 217–237, 292,
308, 341–345, 368,
392, 436–437, 439
amenity interests,
interference with, 227
balancing of interests,
219–220, 224, 240
character of locality,
change in, 228, 231
defences in, 229–231
prescription, 229–230
statutory authority, 230
stranger act, 230–231
definition, 219
Human Rights Act 1998,
219–220, 227
indirect interferences,
225, 239–240
injunctions, 218, 220,
222, 226–229
intention, 224
interests in land, 218–221,
223, 237–240
locality rule, 221–224,
228, 231
nature of damage
suffered, 219–221
noise, 223–224,
227–228, 239
prescription, 227–230, 236
public interest, 227–228
public nuisance, 237–240
remedies, 226–229
abatement, 229
damages, 226
injunctions, 226
Rylands v Fletcher, actions
under, 231–237

sensitivity of the claimant, 225–226, 232
statutory authority, 230
television reception, interference with, 219
title to sue, 219–221
trespass distinguished, 239–240
unreasonable interference, 221–226
  claimant's hypersensitivity, 225
  duration and extent, 222
  interference with a right, 225
  locality, 223
  motivation, 224
  time of day, 222
Privilege defence in defamation, 323–327
  absolute privilege, 323–324
  qualified privilege, 323–325, 330
Producer, 194, 198–206, 210–215
  Consumer Protection Act 1987, 202–203
Product, 199–200
  Consumer Protection Act 1987, 199–200
Product liability, 2, 4, 163, 193–215
  blood products, infection with contaminated, 205–206, 208–209, 211
  children, 207
  common law negligence, 197–198, 201
  Consumer Protection Act 1987, 198–212
    damage, 200
    defect, 203
    defences, 209
    producer, 202
    product, 199
  contractual remedies, 195–196
  defences, 209–212
  Donoghue v Stevenson, 195, 197
  instructions, 199, 204–205, 210

knowledge, 200, 205, 207, 210–215
limitation of, 212–215
manufacturers, 198, 203, 205–207
non-standard products, 206, 208–209, 215
Product Liability Directive, 198, 213
property damage, 213
replacements, 207
retailers, 196
strict liability, 194, 214
suppliers, 203
toxic shock syndrome, 205
warnings, 204–205, 208
Professionals, standard of care for, 96–99
Property damage, 46, 55, 57–58, 147, 154, 158, 187, 190, 213, 422, 426, 444
Protection from Harassment Act (PHA) 1997, 4, 242, 261–264, 284, 287–288, 290, 292, 294, 341–342, 344, 422, 436
  intentional torts against the person, 261–264, 284, 287–288, 290, 292, 294
    amounts to harassment of another, 290
    course of conduct, 289
    knows or ought to know amounts to harassment, 290
Provisional damages, 439, 444
Proximity, 11, 17, 19, 22, 30, 43, 47, 49–50, 59, 63, 74–75, 82–83, 90, 197, 221
  economic loss, 43, 47, 49, 50, 59
  police, 17, 19, 30
Psychiatric harm, 63, 74–75, 82–83
Psychiatric injury, 3–4, 11, 43, 61–83, 138, 148, 263, 266, 277, 285–287, 294, 423, 437
  abandoning the search for a principle, 63
  Alcock control mechanisms, 67, 73–83
  Bystanders, 78–79

close ties of love and affection, 74, 77, 82
control mechanisms, 67, 79
floodgates argument, 79
foreseeability, 64, 66, 70, 72, 78, 82–83
Hillsborough Stadium disaster, 63, 73–78
immediate aftermath, 69, 74–76
Law Commission, 79, 82
post-traumatic stress disorder (PTSD), 62, 68
primary victims, 66, 68–71, 74, 78, 83
recognised psychiatric illnesses, 70, 77, 82
rescuers, 69, 77–81
secondary victims, 66–69, 73–79, 83
stress at work, 71–73
sudden shocking events, 73, 75–77
witnesses, 64, 67
Publication, 16, 211, 246, 286, 288–289, 296–301, 305–306, 309–311, 315–320, 324–335, 339, 342–370
Public bodies, liability of, 28–40, 186
  general principles, 28–30
  Human Rights Act 1998, 30–37
  police and emergency services, application of, 37–40
Public figures, 246, 334, 346, 351, 353–355, 369, 371
  See also Celebrities/ public figures
Public interest, 28, 30, 171, 227–228, 231, 237, 240, 279–280, 300–301, 308, 320, 322–327, 330–331, 335, 347, 352–354, 358, 366–367, 370, 392, 402, 413, 416
Public nuisance, 237–239
Pure economic loss, 4, 16, 43–59, 83, 146, 151–152, 154, 157–159
  defective premises, 54–58
  definition of, 44
  negligent services, 46–50

Hedley Byrne liability, development of, 50–54
relational economic loss, 44–46

Q

Qualified privilege in defamation, 323–325, 330

R

Reasonableness, 11, 18–19, 22, 91, 97, 103, 179–180, 212, 224, 226, 300, 315–316, 427, 431
Recklessness, 262–265, 269, 286–287
Reduced life expectancy, 427, 429, 442
References, 47–48, 52, 57
Relational economic loss, 44–46
Relationships, 19, 30, 47, 74, 252, 359, 375–379, 381, 386–388, 424
Reliance, 37–38, 51–52
Remedies, 4, 24, 38, 163, 195–196, 205, 218, 221, 226, 231, 240, 261, 297, 329–330, 341, 360–368, 422
  Abatement, 229
  breach of confidence, 360–362
  contractual, 195–197
  damages, 422–443
  injunction v damages, 226–229
Remoteness, 23, 26, 46, 49, 106, 143–161, 195
  basic form of, 145–148
  children, 146–147
  contributory negligence, 156–157
  eggshell skull rule, 148–149
  foreseeability, 145, 154, 161
  intentional torts, 158–161
  novus actus interveniens, 155–158
    claimant act, 156
    third party act, 155
  product liability, 195
  scope of duty, 149–155
Republication, 317–310,
327, 336
Reputation, 1–4, 10, 50, 52, 152, 292, 296, 298–301, 304–305, 307, 309–314, 319–320, 323, 328–336, 357, 412
Rescuers, 69, 77–81, 279, 406
Res ipsa loquitur, 102–103
Right to sue for defamation, 304–308
  companies, 305–306
  geographical limitations, 304
  public authorities, 306–309
Risk, 3, 5, 7–9, 19, 26–28, 30, 33–36, 45, 52, 58, 66, 68, 70–72, 77, 81–83, 85, 88, 90–95, 97, 99–101, 103, 106–107, 114–115, 119, 121, 123, 126–130, 133–140, 144, 150, 153–154, 156, 163, 172, 175, 177, 179–180, 184, 186–192, 206, 208–209, 211, 214–215, 229, 231, 233–234, 236, 271, 305, 319, 356, 359, 376–378, 382, 387–388, 393, 402–409, 418, 442
  material contribution to, 126–132, 134, 137
  objective standard of care, 87–89
  patients of, failure to warn, 100–101
Rylands v *Fletcher*, rule in, 2, 4, 145, 163, 231–237, 240
  Act of God, 235
  Cambridge Water case, 232–234
  danger, 231
  defences to, 234–235
    act of God, 235
    claimant's own fault, 235
    consent, 234
    statutory authority, 235
    stranger act, 235
  fault, 232, 235–236, 240
  fire, 234–235
  foreseeability, 232–233, 240
  mischief, 232
  non-natural use of land, 232
  statutory authority, 235
  strangers, acts of, 235
strict liability, 232–237
Transco v Stockport MBC, 232, 234–235, 237

S

SAAMCO principle, 146, 149–154
SARAH, 101–102
  See also Social Action, Responsibility and Heroism (SARAH) Act 2015
Scope of duty, 143, 149, 151, 154
Secondary victims, 66–69, 73–79, 83
Self-defence, 264, 278, 281, 392
Single agent, 132–133, 137, 142
Skill, 51, 87–90, 96, 98–99, 197–198, 376, 405, 411, 440
Slander, 2, 288, 298–304, 436
Social Action, Responsibility and Heroism (SARAH) Act 2015, 101–102
Social media, 297, 299, 327, 331–335, 338, 354–356, 361, 369, 371
  Facebook, 63, 77, 288, 299, 313, 327, 333
  Twitter, 327, 333
Society's views, and defamation, 333–335
Stalking, 242, 287–288, 342, 368
Standard of care, 7, 87–97, 102, 172, 403, 408
  Bolam test, 19, 96–104, 122
  carelessness, 102–103, 113, 261–262, 300
  children, 93–96, 172–174, 183–184, 186, 188–189, 207
  expert opinions, differences in, 96–103
  Learned Hand test, 93
  learner drivers, 7, 11, 88, 95
  objective standard, 7, 87–89, 91, 93–96, 103, 185
  occupiers' liability, 172
  professional standards, 96–99
  reasonableness, 91, 97, 103

res ipsa loquitur, 102–103
special skills, 87–89,
    96, 98–99
Statutory authority, 230,
    235–236, 239, 392
    defences in private
        nuisance, 230
    defences to the rule in
        Rylands v Fletcher, 235
Stranger act, 230,
    235–237, 392
    defences in private
        nuisance, 230
    defences to the rule in
        Rylands v Fletcher, 235
Stress at work, 71–73
Strict liability, 95, 163, 194, 214,
    232–234, 237, 300, 365

T

Television reception,
    interference with, 219
Third parties, 7–8, 24–28, 33–
    34, 37, 39, 44, 54, 69, 111,
    124–125, 149, 155–160, 170,
    196, 230, 235, 246, 249–
    252, 257, 268, 292–293,
    299–300, 310, 317–319,
    336, 354, 373, 375, 383,
    385–386, 411, 428, 431
Threat, intentional, 265–267
Time limitations on tort
    law claims, 435
Title to sue, 219–221
    private nuisance, 219
Tort law, 1–10, 63–64, 67,
    77, 94, 107–108, 120,
    263–264, 278–279, 287,
    292, 296, 344–345, 361,
    363–366, 370, 373, 375,
    392–396, 401–402,
    409, 411–414, 416–419,
    421–430, 435–436,
    439, 442–444
    aims of, 3
    claims, time limitations
        on, 435
    damages, purpose of,
        423–426
    history of, 1–2
    interests protected by, 3–5

limitations of, 5
Trade unions, 248, 252, 307
Trespass to land, 2, 4, 218, 225,
    239, 342, 345, 422
    actionable *per se*, 239
    boundaries, crossing, 239
    direct interference, 239
    intention, 239
    objects on someone's land,
        putting or placing, 239
    permission, lack of, 239

U

Unauthorised use, 339, 343,
    349, 357, 362, 370
Unfair contract terms, 49,
    178–179, 403, 408
Unlawful means conspiracy,
    250, 252–255, 258
Unreasonable interference,
    private nuisance, 2,
    219, 221, 224, 342
    claimant's hypersensitivity,
        221, 225–226, 232
    duration and extent, 221, 222
    interference with a
        right, 221, 225
    locality, 221, 223
    motivation, 221, 224
    time of day, 221, 222

V

Vicarious liability, 2–3, 9, 21,
    373–387, 425, 442–443
    akin to employment test,
        377, 379, 383
    close connection test,
        377, 381–385
    control test, 379–381, 386
    development of, 375–376
    employment relationships,
        375, 378–379
    independent contractors,
        376, 379, 386–387
    justifications, 382, 387–388
    non-delegable duties,
        373–375, 385–387
    wrongful and unauthorised
        mode of doing acts, 381

Violence, immediate and
    direct, 262, 265–267
Visitor(s), 165–191, 220, 344
    definition of, 167–169
    occupiers' liability
        to, 167–183
Volenti non fit injuria, 156,
    177, 373, 391–394,
    402–4–9, 418
    consent, 403
    elements of, 403–407
        claimant knowledge
            about nature and
            extent of risk, 407
        claimant volunteer
            acceptance to
            risk, 403
    knowledge, 403–404,
        407–408
    occupiers' liability, 156, 177
    sport, 405–406

W

Warnings, 29–30, 72, 109,
    146, 157, 168, 171, 174–
    178, 181, 186, 189–190,
    204–205, 208
    occupiers' liability, 146,
        157, 168, 171, 174–178,
        181, 186, 189–190
    product liability,
        204–205, 208
Websites/internet, 63, 76–77,
    151, 212, 289, 296, 299,
    301, 303, 317, 327–328,
    356, 383, 392
    defamation, 296, 299, 301,
        303, 317, 327–328
    See also Social media
Wilkinson v Downton,
    intentional tort in, 4, 242,
    261–264, 284–287,
    291–292, 294, 340
    harassment, 291
    intention, 284–287
Words, assault by, 266
Wrongs, 2, 5, 24, 26, 35–36,
    124, 144, 250, 256,
    373, 375, 379, 381,
    384, 388, 402